POVERTY IN AMERICA:
The Forgotten Millions

POVERTY IN AMERICA:
The Forgotten Millions

AN EDITORIALS ON FILE BOOK

Editor: Oliver Trager

·Facts On File
New York • Oxford

362.5

POVERTY IN AMERICA:
The Forgotten Millions

Published by Facts On File, Inc.
460 Park Ave. South, New York, N.Y. 10016
© Copyright 1989 by Facts On File, Inc.

Library of Congress Cataloging-in-Publication Data
Main entry under title:

Poverty in America: the forgotten millions
p. cm (An Editorials On File book)
Includes Index
1. Economic assistance, Domestic—United States.
2. Poor—United States. 3. Homeless persons—United States
4. Public welfare—United States. I. Trager, Oliver
HC110.P63P68 1989 362.5'0973 88-33399
ISBN: 0-8160-1984-3
CIP
AC

Printed in the United States of America

9 8 7 6 5 4 3 2 1

Contents

POVERTY IN AMERICA:
The Forgotten Millions

Preface

More than 20 years after President Lyndon B. Johnson declared an "unconditional" war on poverty the poor are still with us. Poverty not only persists in the United States, but there are new structures of misery that are proving even more tenacious than the old.

Despite an unprecedented six straight years of peacetime prosperity, more than 32 million Americans live below the poverty line. In 1987, the median income of the American family reached a new high, yet one in every five children lives in poverty. The U.S. Conference of Mayors estimates that three million Americans, one million of them children, are homeless.

Amid America's relative affluence, the poor remain almost unnoticed—invisible to the majority who have little or no contact with urban or suburban slums or with the seemingly isolated pockets of rural poverty.

To be sure, the issues of poverty and welfare continue to public attention but consensus on how best to address the national scourge of 32 million poor is totally lacking. The Reagan administration worked for eight years to restructure welfare and other programs that it says do harm to the very people they are supposed to help. Critics assert, however, that the administration simply abandoned the poor.

Poverty in America: The Forgotten Millions explores the questions and issues that lie behind the statistics and personal tragedies. How has the shelter system for the homeless failed and how can it be improved? Will a raise in the minimum wage improve the plight of the poor? Do the poor have the necessary access to health care? Will welfare reform be effective? Has the transition from a manufacturing economy to a service-oriented one increased poverty? Have budget cuts in social services contributed to the desperation of the poor? Are illiteracy and poverty linked?

In *Poverty in America: The Forgotten Millions*, America's leading editorial writers and cartoonists examine the issues relating to the poor that promise to be with us into the 21st century.

January, 1989   Oliver Trager

Part I:
Poverty & Hunger

It is disturbing that in a nation as affluent as the United States, large numbers of poor people exist. The spectre of poverty raises profound questions about the distribution of economic rewards and challenges our very faith in the American Dream—that those who work hard will advance. It becomes difficult to believe in this most basic of American values when millions who do work remain impoverished—the working poor who are unable to take advantage of opportunities to a better life.

America's poor perhaps symbolize the country's greatest contradiction. To understand their deprivation, imagine what it would be like to live on an income equal to that of the poverty threshold. In 1987 the poverty line for a family of four was $11,611. Assuming that one-third of this amount is spent on food, this fraction is equivalent to 88 cents per meal per person. Many working poor families have incomes well below the poverty line and they often find it tough to meet even their basic food, shelter and medical needs. That many families earning an income two to three times that of the poverty line experience financial difficulties is further testimony to the plight of the poor.

Though no official "hunger count" exists in the United States, the Physician's Task Force on Hunger in America estimated in 1985 that some 20 million citizens suffer from hunger. They found that the majority of this number, over 15 million, are people who live below the poverty line but who receive no food stamp assistance.

The working poor are not an isolated few. In 1987, two million adults—50 percent more than in 1978—worked full time throughout the year, yet they and their families remained in poverty. Another 7.1 million poor worked either in full-time jobs for part of the year or in part-time jobs. Because of limited job opportunities, inadequate skills and the low wages prevailing in some occupations or geographic areas, they continue to have low earnings. The vast majority of the impoverished who do not work are children, the disabled or elderly persons who can do little to enhance their income.

The federal government implemented policies that provided substantial assistance to the working poor throughout most of the 1960s and 1970s. Economic policies sought to minimize unemployment. Job-training and job-creation efforts were expanded. The minimum wage increased, providing a reasonable wage floor and Congress enacted new initiatives, including equal opportunity laws. Welfare and social insurance programs were generally strengthened. All of these factors contributed to progress in the provision of economic security.

Federal policy changes in many of these areas have recently resulted in less assistance for the working poor. Though the political climate may be more favorable to antipoverty programs than it was at the beginning of the decade, opposition to these programs remains strong. In addition, ongoing budget deficits make it unlikely that the federal government will commit substantial additional funds to alleviate the hardships faced by the poor. Current economic trends do not bode well for this group. Few signs are evident that the unemployment rate will drop significantly or that wage rates will rise sharply in that the U.S. trade deficit dampens wage growth and causes job losses.

The outlook for the poor is not completely dismal. Despite retrenchments, the policy framework for assisting the working poor has remained essentilly intact. The direction and benefits of federal policies for the poor depend on the political will to design and adopt federal policies that provide assistance. Efforts that help individuals work their way out of poverty and off of welfare offer promise as an attempt to balance the goals of economic self-sufficiency while supporting the underlying premise and promise of the work ethic. The 1986 election results were an additional signal of the continued public support for the notion that the federal government should play an active role in helping the poor, indicating that policies designed to help the working poor may again become a national priority.

Panel Fails to Find Widespread Hunger in U.S.

After three months of study and hearings, the 13-member Task Force on Food Assistance Jan. 10, 1984 presented President Reagan with a series of recommendations for alleviating the problem of hunger in the United States. The federal advisory committee concluded that although "there is hunger in America...there is no evidence that widespread undernutrition is a major health problem in the U.S." Following the release of a summary of the panel's report, 42 national religious and antipoverty groups issued a joint statement condemning the group's recommendations, saying that the proposed program "would make this tragic problem worse."

The most controversial of the panel's proposals was that states should have the option of participating in the food stamp program, while dropping out of other food assistance programs, or should be able to establish their own programs, for which they have attained eligibility criteria and uniform national benefit levels. Another of the panel's recommendations was to increase the ceiling on assets for a household seeking food stamps to $2,250 from $1,500 for nonelderly households, and to $3,500 from $3,000 for elderly households. The panel also encouraged establishing tax incentives for corporations donating food and for farmers permitting charities to take unharvested crops from their fields.

The Washington Times
Washington, DC, January 11, 1984

When the Reagan administration dared to restructure social spending programs, anecdotes of the dipossessed and starving were as common in newspapers and television news shows as the weather reports. When Ed Meese said that there was no solid evidence of hunger in America, only anecdotal evidence, he was boiled in his own oil. Now the president's task force on hunger has released its final draft report, and even it isn't sure what the story is.

"While we have found evidence of hunger in the sense that some people have difficulties with access to food, we have also found that it is at present impossible to estimate the extent of that hunger," the report states. This tells us that perhaps there is some trouble with the delivery system, but not that the source of hunger in America is the cold heart of Ronald Reagan.

What is hunger? According to the report, "To many people hunger means not just symptoms that can be diagnosed by a physician; rather it implies the existence of a social, not a medical problem. To most Americans hunger means a situation where some people — even occasionally — cannot obtain an adequate amount of food, even if the shortage is not prolonged enough to cause health problems." This is the sense in which witnesses before the task force and many of the reports and studies it considered spoke of hunger. Objectivity has been better demonstrated.

Why the hungry people? Has there been a reduced commitment to the poor since Reaganism came on line? Federal expenditures and resources made available for domestic food assistance grew from $16.4 billion in 1981 to $19.3 billion in the fiscal year just ended. This does not represent a cancelling of the social contract.

Government programs don't reach everyone. Some of that discrepency is made up by private initiatives. But there are going to be some deserving people who either don't know the aid is there, or are incapable of applying for it. Some children might go to bed hungry some nights, but that is due more to parental neglect than policy.

Nobody likes to see a ragged figure seeking his dinner in a trashcan — and street people are among this nation's hungry. Yet they suffer behavioral deficiencies as well as deficiencies of income. Their hunger has sources beyond the control of the Department of Agriculture.

Also beyond the balm of the government healers are the underlying reasons why some single-parent households come up short at the end of the month. And why some people who have never had the need for food assistance find themselves out of work and missing a meal. Until the entire population becomes a ward of the state, these shortcomings will persist (and when the entire population becomes a ward of the state, these shortcomings will grow into societywide disaster. Nobody eats well when all consume and none produce wealth). Until then, mismanagement of personal finances will clear cupboards, as will the refusal to take jobs below one's 'dignity.'

The task force offers several recommendations, including making states pay for errors in payments — they usually go to the benefit of beneficiaries — and letting states decide whether they might be better off administering their own nutrition programs.

The report has the great chefs of centralized largesse and Reagan dismemberment sharpening their knives, which could be what led task force chairman J. Clayburn LaForce to state yesterday that hunger is "a real and significant problem throughout the nation." We check our facts, and wonder what he means.

THE SACRAMENTO BEE
Sacramento, CA, January 11, 1984

If the President's Task Force on Food Assistance was really supposed to determine how much hunger there is in America — ostensibly its prime objective — then, by its own admission, it failed. At present, it said, it is "impossible to estimate the extent of that hunger with any reasonable degree of objectivity." If its purpose, however, was to justify the administration's parsimony and insensitivity and to obfuscate a serious problem beyond recognition, then this panel, composed largely of conservatives, succeeded admirably.

Twenty years ago, study after study dramatized and verified the existence of something that many Americans then believed had disappeared from this country: an endemic poverty and the malnutrition that went with it. If this task force has any impact at all — and one has to hope it doesn't — it is to render the problem invisible once more — to cover it with so much bureaucratic gibberish that it is abstracted out of the national conscience.

Hunger does persist, said the panel, "but allegations of rampant hunger simply cannot be documented." Forget the loaded word "allegations" which subtly impugns the integrity and patriotism of those who make such "allegations." The reason the panel was unable to document anything was because it and its staff never made any serious atttempt to find out. It never met to determine how it would operate until most of the staff work, such as it is, was done, had no voice in choosing that staff — which the administration chose for it — and was not even allowed to meet informally to discuss the issues until a report had already been drafted.

Various subpanels did hold hearings here and there, but in a manner that even some of its own members regarded as inadequate. If the task force ever really heard the voices of the hungry or, indeed, just the voices of the church groups who, with desperately limited resources, are trying to feed them, there is no evidence of it in this report.

There will be a lot of controversy about some of the task force's recommendations, particularly its proposal for combining federal food assistance programs in optional block grants to the states. Very likely that proposal, if adopted, would lead to a new round of discrimination against the very poor — women and children most of all — in those areas of the country where standards of worthiness are still more related to color and personal relationships than they are to abstract standards of humanity and acceptable levels of nutrition. But that controversy, too, is a diversion serving the central function of the report, which is to bury the reality of the lengthening soup lines under an avalanche of rhetoric large enough that no one will ever notice them again.

Arkansas Gazette.
Little Rock, AR, January 11, 1984

For some reason, the denial that there is significant hunger in America — after all, isn't this "the bread basket of the world"? — has become something of an article of faith in some recent national administrations. For example, in the early days of its tenure, the Lyndon Johnson administration recognized the needs of America's hungry and malnourished, but later, as food programs vested the administration, it was common for the Agriculture Department to argue that all was well, not to worry.

The difference with the Reagan administration is that it has refused to recognize the existence of significant hunger from the outset. Some hunger, yes, but not enough to worry much about. As if to underscore the point, President Reagan last September named a task force to examine the problem, saying he was perplexed by reports of hunger "in this great and wealthy country." In December, Edwin Meese III, the White House counselor, observed that there were no "authoritative figures" to document hunger but "only anecdotal stuff," and that people go to soup kitchens "because the food is free." Later, in something of a defense of Meese, Mr. Reagan said simply that "we are doing more to feed the hungry in this country today than has ever been done by any administration."

Well, the task force came in with its report this week and it certainly is not out of line with the view of its creator. The group said it had "not been able to substantiate allegations of rampant hunger," and contended that "for the vast majority of low-income people," public and private food programs are "sufficient for those who take advantage of them."

The "hunger problem" thus taken care of, the task force recommended lumping existing federal nutrition programs into block grants for the states to spend more or less the way they see fit. This means, in translation, says one critic, "you would see a transfer of school lunch money to middle class school districts and away from pregnant mothers." Middle class school districts have more political clout than pregnant women with low incomes.

Senator Ted Kennedy, as might be expected, calls the report "a transparent coverup of the serious and worsening problem of hunger in America," adding: "In effect, this commission says to the hungry. 'Let them eat block grants.' " Appropriately wary, the National Governors Association says it opposes a block grant plan because it "serves to place a cap on the federal share of the program so that federal funds will no longer change readily as the number of eligible needy persons increases or decreases in an individual state." Senator Robert Dole says that Congress "is not likely to favor it," but Senator Jesse Helms just loves it: "I'm sure that the task force finding will disappoint those who wish to use the hunger issue as a pretext for pouring more of the taxpayers' money into these programs without regards to whether programs are being operated in a prudent manner."

So there you have it. On the one side are those such as Senator Kennedy whose primary concern is for the plight of the hungry — yes, they exist in droves — and on the other are those such as Jesse Helms, Edwin Meese III and Ronald Reagan whose primary concern is for the bureaucratic administration of nutrition programs.

The Reagan administration has been in office long enough now that it has acquired a vested interest in the subject, and like some administrations before it, believes that it has done such a super job that there's nothing, really, to worry about. Hunger, unfortunately, cannot be so easily wished away.

The Boston Globe
Boston, MA, January 10, 1984

After all the cautious analysis and the political evenhandedness is stripped away from the report of President Reagan's task force on the extent of hunger in this country, one clear — and troubling — fact remains: every day, children, elderly people and whole families wake up hungry and go to bed hungry.

They may be families like the one in New Hampshire where the parents, a jobless father and a pregnant mother, eat but four days a week in order to stretch their food stamps to provide adequate meals for their three young children. They may be the even more desperate families like the one in Boston which turned down an offer of a week's supply of macaroni and cheese from a community food pantry because they had no cooking facilities in the car in which they were forced to live.

There may indeed be no "rampant hunger" in America. Yet the commission has concluded, when viewed in the light of the nation's "communal commitment to ensure that everyone has adequate access to food," then indeed "there is hunger in America."

This task force — appointed by President Reagan, dominated by Republicans, and numbering among its members former Gov. Edward J. King — has come to a conclusion that should resolve, once and for all, any doubt that as a first and essential step, existing food assistance programs should be expanded and improved.

It may well be, as Reagan and his anecdotal counselor Edwin Meese assert, that more is being spent now on food assistance programs than ever before. That "more" is clearly not quite enough, and there also seems some question whether the slight increases in these programs which the task force has proposed will also be quite enough.

The major specific proposal in the task force's draft report — to lump all federal nutrition programs, including food stamps, into a single block grant to states — does not seem particularly helpful either. Even if food needs vary somewhat from state to state, that does not mean that some locally administered program (as yet undesigned) is going to improve on the success of the food stamp program.

As the National Governors Assn. notes, the existing food stamp program — even if it is chronically underfunded — is still more likely to respond quickly to relative increases or decreases in the number of needy people from state to state than will autonomous programs funded through annual block grants.

The task force is now beginning a section-by-section review of the draft report prepared by its staff. As a first step, it should heed its own conclusions — that "there is hunger in America" — and fashion a clear set of proposals for action to address that troubling fact.

Detroit Free Press
Detroit, MI, January 11, 1984

THE PRESIDENT'S hunger panel says the "sad truth" is that there is hunger in America, but that it can't be measured with precision. Both in the tone of the report and in the angry response to it, the administration and its Democratic critics are in danger of falling into the trap of debating the statistics of hunger while letting slip the reality: Hunger and malnutrition are social and public health problems that federal policies are making it harder to deal with.

The 13-member Task Force on Food Assistance, in its final report, declared that it couldn't document the claims of widespread distress. The report also asserted that cutbacks in federal spending for feeding programs have not harmed the poor.

Nobody seemed to notice that the panel's two major findings contradicted each other. If it is true that widespread hunger is no longer a major American problem, it can only be because of the spread of federal feeding and nutrition programs — the very programs that have suffered cutbacks. There is no way reductions in federal aid for such programs could avoid leaving some people hungry again or increasing the pressure on privately financed feeding programs.

But where is the documentation? The harsh numbers? Statistical evidence of hunger in America is difficult to produce. But the statistics for other social phenomena indicate the problem. Record numbers of men, women and children aren't pouring into soup kitchens because they like the menu. Cities aren't struggling to build more shelters for homeless people because folks enjoy their homey atmosphere. Alarming numbers of black babies in Detroit and Michigan aren't dying at birth because their mothers are eating too well.

To its credit, the panel did not dismiss the problem totally. It called for a slight expansion of federal food assistance programs and the conversion of food stamps to cash benefits for the elderly and disabled. The food stamp program now provides benefits averaging 47 cents a meal, and the proposed expansion would increase monthly benefits for each food stamp recipient by an average of 80 to 90 cents or a penny a meal. If there are any hungry Americans out there, that should take care of them.

The panel also called for replacing the present stable, uniform system of federal nutrition programs with a patchwork of state programs financed by block grants, a system that did not work efficiently or equitably 15 years ago, and would not work today. Neither the call for the dismantling of the federal food programs or the underlying tone of the panel's conclusions suggests anyone in the administration understands the hunger issue yet.

One panel member, Dr. George Gordon Graham, has declared that "The biggest problem among the poor is obesity — not hunger." Anyone so insensitive as not to recognize that many poor people are both obese and malnourished because of their low quality, starchy diets should never sit on a panel charged with documenting hunger. It only fuels the suspicion that the task force on hunger found no more evidence of hunger than it wanted to unearth.

The Providence Journal

Providence, RI, January 11, 1984

Hunger is unlike some other afflictions in that it can't be measured precisely. You can't get a count of the hungry, the way you can, say, for hospital patients or victims of auto accidents. And even if you could, how do you measure the degree of hunger?

This is the sort of problem that perplexed President Reagan before he appointed his Task Force on Food Assistance last August. And the measurement of deprivation has bedeviled the panel through all its deliberations.

Now the task force is getting ready to issue its final report, and it has concluded that while hunger persists in this country, "rampant hunger" cannot be documented. Therefore, it sees no need for major new spending programs to feed people at or near the poverty level. In consequence, it seems reasonable to question whether the recent hunger controversy hasn't been overdone.

Major food assistance is available from federal programs, despite the cutbacks that have been made in budgeted funds, the panel has decided. The amounts available to various groups might be changed by some of the group's recommendations; the form of the assistance certainly would be changed, if Congress adopted its proposal to make participation in the food assistance programs optional for the states.

At any rate, the task force hasn't used the provocative terminology that got Edwin Meese, presidential adviser, into hot water just before Christmas. And it doesn't quarrel openly with the president of the U.S. Conference of Mayors, who declared at that time that a study by his group found "more hunger. . .than at any period of time since the late 1930's."

In fact, the task force has found a need for a slight expansion of food assistance programs and the conversion of food stamps to cash payments for the needy aged, blind and disabled. (Many in the latter groups may have to buy prepared meals because they are not able to cook for themselves.) This would be offset by reduced benefits for some families.

The most controversial recommendation may well be the one that would let the states create "autonomous" food assistance programs. This would let individual states vary the programs in accordance with age, income and cost of living differences. But the National Governors Association has objected. Appropriation of a lump sum to each state would place a cap on the federal share and impede changes as the number of needy persons rose or fell, it argued. Moreover, that smacks of a move to turn the federal responsibility back to the states, it said, whereas the NGA seeks "an increased federal role in income security and a minimum national standard of assistance."

For one category of the needy, Aid to Families of Dependent Children, the task force urged simpler application procedures for food stamps. This would not meet criticisms that food stamps often are used for expensive foods and unwise purchases. Welfare officials have struggled with this problem for years; but even those most concerned about cheating have not been able to agree on what foods should be banned or how the ban could be policed.

Controversy over feeding the hungry may die down, in any event, as the economic recovery gains strength. The latest federal figures show that unemployment is lower; as personal income rises, the ranks of the poor may decline. Thus, a new federal budget that contains no increases for food programs could very well prove adequate and escape the criticism that was leveled at the budget in 1983.

THE MILWAUKEE JOURNAL

Milwaukee, WI, January 11, 1984

President Reagan's Task Force on Food Assistance has contributed pathetically little in terms of either new information or recommendations for eradicating hunger in America.

The task force concluded the obvious: "There is hunger in America." As for remedies, the commission mainly recycled old Reagan proposals — such as the idea of returning food programs to the states in the form of block grants.

The task force focused excessively on trying to quantify hunger according to a scientific standard, a goal bound to thwart the commission's mission, which was "to examine the extent of America's hunger problem." In the absence of a national hunger standard, the task force should have been content to draw reasonable conclusions based on facts presented.

We assume that evidence of starvation is rare. However, we think it is not rare for public health nurses and social workers to find children in homes where there is inadequate food.

The national task force should have relied heavily on information provided by such organizations as the Hunger Task Force of Milwaukee. It testified at a hearing in Peoria (Ill.) that the Wisconsin Information Service (WIS) reported a 500% increase in requests for emergency food supplies between the winter of 1981 and 1983. When requests for food aid increases so sharply, it is logical to assume that some people are in the grip of hunger.

The hunger task force also reported that emergency meal programs in Milwaukee were now serving 29,000 meals a month. St. Benedict the Moor's meal program reported an increase from 150 meals a day in 1981 to 500 in 1983.

The task force testified further that limits on federal funding forced the nutrition program for women, infants and children to confine its aid to only 32.5% of the estimated eligible population of 40,000 women and children in the Milwaukee area. Thus, 27,000 eligible Milwaukee area women and children went without basic nutritional instruction and vouchers for nutritious foods such as fortified cereals, milk, cheese, eggs and juices. That is perhaps the saddest of all indicators of need, because chances are that some of the low-birthweight and impoverished infants denied food under this program will suffer serious developmental problems that could inhibit their abilities to function in later life.

All told, the task force's preliminary report and recommendations have strengthened the belief that it was created to validate Reagan policies, not to ease the plight of the poor.

'I'M HUNGRY, BUT I SUPPOSE THAT'S MERELY ANECDOTAL.'

OKLAHOMA CITY TIMES

Oklahoma City, OK, January 12, 1984

CRITICAL reaction to the report of President Reagan's Task Force on Food Assistance — dealing with hunger in America — follows a predictable philosophical line.

The welfare-state camp takes issue with one of the main recommendations of the report: that optional block grants be made available to states that wish to take over the federal food program. The critics say this would be a disaster for the nation's poor and a "retreat from the commitment to end hunger in America."

What really appalls them is that the task force dared to suggest veering away from the centrist approach to solving problems. Thus, they have yet another beef against the Reagan administration's effort to de-emphasize the federal government role in American life.

The task force report also disappoints critics because it takes a low-key, non-hysterical look at the hunger problem. It recognizes shortcomings exist and need to be dealt with, but it refuses to accept the proposition that the United States is afflicted with widespread hunger.

Criticism from 42 national religious, senior citizens' and civil rights groups contends the task force recommendations would make a "tragic problem" worse. That's hard to buy in view of one recommendation the task force says actually could bring a $500 million increase in food stamp benefits. This would result from proposals to allow food stamp recipients to own more assets and to raise their maximum food stamp allotments.

The extra cost would be offset partially, the panel proposes, by requiring states to bear the expense of errors in food stamp overpayments above 5 percent.

An interesting analysis in The Wall Street Journal by two economics professors of the history of the federal food program provides clues to the enigma of why hunger should still exist despite the billions spent to eliminate it. J. Fred Giertz of the University of Illinos and Dennis H. Sullivan of Miami University (Ohio) say the explanation revolves around a structural change in the program in 1977.

Previously, participating households received monthly food stamp allotments sufficient to buy a minimally adequate diet. The required payment varied from nothing for the poorest recipients to about 85 percent of the face value of the stamps for the least-poor eligible families.

After the change, food stamps were made free to all recipients based on a formula tied to their previous allotments. This freed up cash formerly used to buy stamps to spend on other items the family considered important. Thus, in a sense, the authors observe, these people are hungry "by choice" in that they have opted for better housing, warmer homes and so on, rather than fully adequate diets. The "hunger problem," then, is really a relative matter.

Roanoke Times & World-News

Roanoke, VA, January 10, 1984

THE FINDINGS of presidential study commissions often rouse more controversy than they settle. That's likely with the report of President Reagan's Task Force on Food Assistance. It won't end the debate over the extent of hunger in America. And at least one of its proposals — to shift responsibility for food-aid programs to the states — should be strongly resisted.

On one point, there may be consensus. The report says that precisely measuring the degree of hunger in the United States is impossible. A 13-member commission certainly can't make that determination in five months of part-time work. A few federal studies have been done. But collecting sufficient data takes, at least, several months, and evaluation can take years. By the time a report's issued, the picture is out of date.

As the independent reporting service Congressional Quarterly noted last spring, the gap in data is filled by "personal impressions, anecdotal reports and conflicting claims from partisan sources." One of the anecdotal reports came from a member of the president's own commission, who noticed there are a lot of black athletes and concluded that black children may be the best-nourished in the country.

If that kind of remark makes you wonder about the judgment and objectivity of the commission, you're not alone. From the first, there were complaints that it was top-heavy with conservative Republicans likely to be myopic about social problems. Some of the panel's findings and recommendations do seem to reflect a certain unfriendliness toward federal participation in food assistance. The report says that the Reagan administration's budget cuts in this category haven't hurt the poor, which contradicts just about all the available evidence. And while conceding that hunger persists in America, it offers an array of proposals that, on balance, could quickly make matters worse.

Key to this is a recommendation that Congress make it optional for states to take part in existing federal food assistance programs. This is a terrible idea. It would be an invitation to states to return to those days when less enlightened and socially conscious governments — many of them in the Deep South — scrimped on welfare as a way of encouraging the poor to move out.

Both in justice and as a practical matter, states shouldn't be known either as persecutors of the needy or as welfare havens. In the past two decades, federal programs have done much to make public assistance more uniform. Prominent among those is the food-stamp program, one that the commission wants not to reform, but to make expendable.

It is apparent that very few Americans starve. For a variety of reasons, a lot of them seem to go hungry at least some of the time. Malnourishment — lack of a balanced diet — is surely a significant problem. Unquestionably, many of the poor contribute to their own difficulties through ignorance, a preference for liquor over solid food, a squandering of resources.

It also is evident that the billions Uncle Sam spends on food assistance could be much better managed. That's true for many private organizations as well. Getting available aid to the right people in the right places at the right time is a logistical obstacle that cries out for attention. There are many facets to the entire situation. As the panel says, major new spending initiatives or programs probably aren't called for.

But neither is an attempt by the federal government to rid itself of responsibility by chopping the hunger problem into 50 pieces and turning it over to the states. That's not improved management. That's copping out.

The Kansas City Times

Kansas City, MO, January 2, 1984

The worst expectations from the president's task force on hunger apparently have been fulfilled.

Haven't we heard this somewhere before? Last summer, President Reagan was incredulous that people might be hungry, vocalizing numerous administration actions before forming the commission to produce facts. More recently, Edwin Meese said he hadn't seen any hungry kids.

Critics worried the much-touted task force would echo official positions, that it would be manipulated to reinforce conservative efforts to cripple public nutrition foundations. Thoughtful social leaders cautioned against using a flashy and phony "investigation" to vindicate controversial policies already in place. But if you take an extremely sensitive issue, add election-year political appointees and lack of professional expertise, and modest scrutiny of a group's objectivity is rational.

Preliminary snippets from the draft report refer to the absence of a "massive hunger problem" and the fact that there are "categories" of malnourished (a considerably more severe condition than hunger) people. Neither are of enough consequence, in the report writers' frame of reference, to worry the nation.

What do they want: bodies littering the sidewalks? Photographs of pot-bellied children? A national starvation rate like the ghoulish traffic death count?

A ray of hope exists. The final report could be more realistic if enough task force members show the courage to resist. Mayor Richard L. Berkley, a member, has said that hunger is a problem. He and other knowledgeable members need all the support they can get to ensure that the task force's work is not worse than irrelevant.

Poverty Rate Rises in 1983

The nation's poverty rate rose in 1983 to its highest level in 18 years—15.2% of all Americans, according to the Census Bureau report Aug. 2, 1984. The rate, up from 15% in 1982, was the highest since the start of President Lyndon B. Johnson's antipoverty campaign in 1965, when the rate was 17.3%.

The number of poor people grew by 868,000 from the year before to a total of 35.3 million in 1983, the bureau reported. The poverty line was drawn at a cash income of less than $10,178 for a family of four. The median family income increased 1.6% in 1983 to $24,580, after adjustment for inflation. It was the first gain in four years.

The poverty rate for blacks was 35.7% in 1983, for Hispanics 28.4% and for whites 12.1% The poverty rate for children under the age of six was 25% in 1983; for people over 65 and older it was 14.1%. On a regional basis, the Northeast had the lowest poverty rate, 13.4%, in 1983; the South had the highest, 17.2%.

Political reaction to the report was immediate. "Today, we have the smoking gun of Reagan unfairness," House Speaker Thomas P. O'Neill, Jr. (D, Mass.) said. "Under Reagan, the poor are getting poorer."

The White House blamed the Carter administration for stalling economic growth and leading the country into recession, which, it said, raised the poverty rate to the recent highs. It saw a leveling off in 1983 and predicted a drop in the rate next year.

A report on "The Reagan Record" by the Urban Institute Aug. 15 concluded that President Reagan's economic policies had "helped the affluent" and been "detrimental to the poor and the middle class. The institute, a nonpartisan think tank, took a similarly pessimistic view of the future. It assumed that taxes would have to be raised and federal spending cut to cope with budget deficits, and it said this would result in a slowing of the nation's rise in standard of living. Only the most affluent families, it said, were likely to make major income gains in the rest of the decade.

The Boston Globe
Boston, MA, August 4, 1984

We had to go through, unfortunately, a recession. That did drive up the poverty rate in 1982, but I would be happy to take an invitation to come back here and testify next spring, because I am absolutely confident that the poverty rate is going to decline dramatically for 1983 . . . . – Reagan Administration Budget Director David Stockman, before a House Ways and Means subcommittee, October 1983.

The desired invitation will surely be proferred.

Statistics released by the US Census Bureau Thursday show that, despite the economic rebound, both the number and percentage of Americans in poverty increased between 1982 and 1983.

Children under six bore the heaviest burden; 900,000 additional people fell into poverty, bringing the total to 35.3 million, or 15.2 percent of the population. Of the newly poor, 325,000 of them were under six.

For this apparent anomaly, rising poverty at a time of economic growth, David Stockman and his boss, President Reagan, need to be called to account.

Surely part of the problem is that, contrary to the simple-minded supply-side view that economic growth automatically benefits all, a rising tide does not lift all boats. For those without skills or without day care, economic growth does not mean economic opportunity.

From that perspective there can be no justification for the wholesale cuts in job-training programs and day-care funding advocated by the Administration, especially when those reductions were made concurrently with a toughening of welfare eligibility standards,

which reduced the income of thousands of the poorest Americans.

What to say to the children? There can be no doubting that the road to opportunity is very narrow for the children of poverty. A series of policies that increases the numbers of poor children mortgages their future and threatens the social fabric of the nation.

Most of the affected children live in single-parent households headed by a woman. What do the statistics say about Reagan's claim that his Administration has been antiwomen? It says those claims are hollow.

And what about the stock Republican reaction to New York Gov. Mario Cuomo's assertion in his keynote address to the Democratic convention that there were "two cities" in America, one riding on the economic recovery, the other left untouched. The Republicans said it was a divisive lie. The statistics suggest it was the hard truth.

Stockman, Reagan, et al have complained in the past that "poverty counts" are wrong because they exclude the value of such things as food stamps. So, the Census Bureau counted poverty nine different ways, using various theories. Under every one, poverty increased between 1982 and 1983; under six of the alternative measurements, it increased more than under the official definition.

The line out of the Administration, following the Census Bureau report, was that, well, whatever we promised in the past things *really* are getting better for the poor now, in 1984. Their record as prognosticators is not good; and even if they are right this time, the new data suggest just how deep the suffering induced by Administration policy has been.

THE COMMERCIAL APPEAL
Memphis, TN, August 7, 1984

WALTER MONDALE'S campaign has just got a boost and President Reagan's a jolt from two government announcements: The Census Bureau said the poverty rate rose to 15.2 percent last year and the Labor Department reported that unemployment climbed to 7.5 percent in July.

House Speaker Tip O'Neill was unable to contain his glee at the news. "Today," he roared, "we have the smoking gun of Reagan unfairness. Under Reagan, the poor are getting poorer."

At the risk of diminishing O'Neill's partisan joy, the figures call for a careful look. It will show that while they are worrisome, they do not reflect the economic disaster the speaker alleges.

First, the Census Bureau noted that the poverty rate had inched up for the past five years. It would be difficult even for O'Neill, the President's sharpest critic in the Democratic hierarchy, to blame him for conditions in 1979 and 1980.

Second, the bureau said the change in the number of poor, to 15.2 percent last year from 15 percent in 1982, was not "statistically significant" and could have resulted from an error in its survey of 62,000 households.

Third, the survey was made in March. The administration is quick to assert that 5 million jobs have been created since then and predict that poverty will fall to 13 percent this year.

Fourth, the bureau counts only cash income when it determines who is and isn't poor. If non-cash benefits were counted — such as food stamps, housing subsidies and Medicare and Medicaid — last year's poverty rate could have been as low as 10.2 percent.

The main reason there was more poverty in 1983 was a growth in two sectors of the population that tend to be poor: persons living alone and families headed by females. It will be interesting to see how O'Neill and other Reagan detractors manage to blame him for more men leaving their families, a decades-long sociological trend.

WHAT ABOUT the 0.4 percent jump in unemployment in July, the first increase in 20 months? Jobless statistics are notoriously unreliable in early summer. June's reported huge gain in jobs was too large, as was the July loss. The month's real rate probably was 7.3 percent.

Reagan, however, can take no comfort from statistical explanations of what appears to be bad news. Voters are moved by headlines, not fine print. Unless the economy resumes creating jobs this fall, the President himself risks joining the unemployed.

St. Louis ✤ Review

St. Louis, MO, August 10, 1984

We were jolted back to reality last week with the news that the unemployment rate had jumped four-tenths of a percentage point to 7.5 percent. This was the largest one-month rise in two years and the first increase since November 1982. Translated into human lives that brought the total number out of work to 8.5 million people.

Unemployment increased sharply among adult women, rising to 6.9 percent. Black workers experienced a statistical increase to 16.9 percentage points. Among black teenagers unemployment figures jumped to 42.4 percent.

Some economists saw this as good news, interpreting it as a healthy slowing in the rapid rate of economic recovery. Indeed the stock market saw it as very good news, a herald of controlled inflation rates.

As the economy has improved in recent months many people have found employment. In truth recent calculations show that more people are employed now than at any time in our history. That is somewhat to be expected as our population rate and the number of two-earner families are both at all-time highs.

We are happy with this good news, but in real terms of people out of work, and the resultant impact on the lives of the workers and their families, higher unemployment numbers are never good news. For the unemployed these are perilous times and unhappy ones. The soup kitchens and food distribution agencies which sprang up during the recent recession are still in business.

Whether this single month's returns are an isolated blip in the overall improving trend or the beginning of an upward trend we are concerned. We are sure the politicians of both major parties are also watching it closely. It will affect the political campaigns and certainly our votes. As Christians our concern for the welfare of others should be evident in all that we do.

In a very real sense a genuine concern for the unemployed and their prospects for new jobs is a facet of our concern for life itself. Higher executive pay and a booming stock market affect relatively few people. The welfare of the unemployed and the unemployable is a continuing concern, especially if their numbers are continuing to grow.

The Star-Ledger

Newark, NJ, August 10, 1984

The concept goes back at least to biblical times and the Gospel According to St. Matthew—"For ye have the poor always with you"—and probably before. The problem of poverty is among the oldest of the problems of mankind.

With the enormous gains experienced in the United States and other Western democracies this century, substantial progress against poverty has been made. But the problem not only persists, it is forcing us to revise some of our earlier thinking.

For example, it is a widely held concept that the numbers of poor move up and down as the economy moves. This has been generally true in the past, but some disturbing new statistics cause some questions about its present relevancy.

Last year was a year marked by one of the strongest economic recoveries in recent history. Economic growth was up; unemployment was down and prices were steady. Despite this, the number of those Americans officially in poverty increased.

The Census Bureau reported that the number of those classified as living in poverty increased 900,000 last year, breaking the 35-million mark. Its definition of poverty is a family of four with an annual income below $10,178. The percentage of Americans living in poverty is now 15.2 percent, up from 15 percent.

Since the statistics were released in an election year, they immediately became part of the campaign debate. House Speaker Thomas O'Neill saw them as proof of the "unfairness" of the Reagan Administration while a White House spokesman saw them as evidence of a leveling off of a trend that was worse under the Democrats.

Such political statements are as inevitable as they are unhelpful. What the statistics do seem to indicate is that we may be developing a new class of poor today, people who are unable to participate fully in the economy and who will not gain from its benefits.

If the same sort of indications continue in future statistical reports, there may be a national need to develop new policies. Regardless of the outcome of the election, the next president may find planning new strategies to combat poverty a major priority.

The Virginian-Pilot

Norfolk, VA, August 7, 1984

Measuring the numbers of people living in poverty has never been a tidy exercise.

A 1959 study by the Joint Economic Committee of Congress reported that the proportion of the U.S. population in low-income status was 19 percent in 1957. But the Conference on Economic Progress, whose national committee included labor leaders and industrialists, argued in 1962 that 77 million Americans — 43 percent of the population — had incomes providing them with a less than acceptable standard of living.

In 1964, however, as the anti-poverty war was getting under way, the President's Council of Economic Advisers reported that between 33 million and 35 million Americans were "living at or below the boundaries of poverty in 1962." Other commentators had put the number at 50 million, or nearly one-fourth of the nation. Yet others had concluded that but one-tenth of Americans were poor.

The latest poverty statistics from the Census Bureau are no less controversial than previous years' figures. The Democrats are already using them as ammunition in the presidential campaign. Rep. Thomas P. "Tip" O'Neill Jr., Democrat of Massachusetts, points to the unexpected rise in the numbers (from 34.4 million in 1982 to 35.2 million in 1983) and proportion (from 15 percent in 1982 to 15.2 percent in 1983) of impoverished Americans as proof positive that President Reagan's restraints on spending for selected social-welfare programs have hurt the weakest members of society.

But of all the statistics about the poor in America in the last quarter-century, one fact stands out: Assuming a consistency of federal poverty measurements (adjusted for inflation, of course), it seems to be clear that the poor, as an identifiable group, constitute a smaller portion of the populace today than was the case at the beginning of the anti-poverty war. Thus it is arguable that the anti-poverty programs, together with increases in Social Security, have made a difference. They have made a difference, moreover, despite the rising percentage of elderly in the population, as well as the rising percentage of single-parent (generally, female) households.

Manifestly, even under the Reagan administration, more help for the poor is available today than there was two decades ago. Need an education? If you missed out in school, a slew of adult-education and job-training programs are offered for little or no cost by public schools and community colleges. Ill? Medicaid will help. Worried about the children getting enough to eat? There are free school lunches and food stamps. Day care for small fry? It often may be had at little or no cost while mother trains to make a living. Need special training and counseling to get a job? Look around — there are agencies dedicated to those tasks. Can't get a job? Employers can get a tax credit for putting young, unskilled workers on the payroll at minimum wage. And so on.

Yet the poor are still with us, in the millions. Many of these poor are temporarily poor; they will escape poverty with work and luck. Many will be poor all their lives — they suffer severe mental, emotional and physical handicaps that limit their prospects. Finally — and most distressingly — there is another group: There are many who are poor because they fail to discipline themselves to become valuable members of the labor force. Increasingly, they are teenage girls who become pregnant out of wedlock, thus crippling their life's chances early on. According to the Census Bureau, the poverty rate for households headed by women last year was 500 percent — *500 percent* — higher than the rate for households headed by married couples.

The challenge presented by the lamentable rise in teen-age pregnancies is being addressed more and more by non-governmental groups. Civic groups, city governments, black and Hispanic leaders and non-profit family-planning organizations are setting out to persuade young people to postpone parenthood until they become self-supporting members of society.

This movement is gathering momentum. How effective it will be cannot be foretold. But it offers the best hope• of breaking the dismal cycle of poverty in welfare families headed by females.

The Burlington Free Press

Burlington, VT, August 6, 1984

Democrats and Republicans already are engaged in a heated debate over the validity of Census Bureau figures which show that the number of Americans living in poverty rose by nearly 900,000 last year to reach 35 million.

According to the figures, 15.2 percent of the nation's population fell below the annual income of $10,178 for a family of four which was set as the upper edge of poverty in 1983. The rate was up slightly from 15 percent in 1982.

Reacting to the figures, House Speaker Thomas P. O'Neill, D-Mass, said, "Today we have the smoking gun of Reagan unfairness." But the White House claimed credit for leveling off the rate of increase which had jumped under President Reagan's Democratic predecessor.

Democrats, of course, are planning to attack Reagan on the issue of his unfairness to the poor and his bias toward the wealthy. "In 1982, when Reagan policies sent the poverty rate to 15 percent, the administration said that the trend would be 'dramatically' reversed in 1983," O'Neill said. "Today, we learned just the opposite has happened ... Making the rich richer and the poor poorer has not helped the average American family."

Meanwhile, the White House said there are a lot fewer poor people than it seems --- if a different yardstick is used to measure them. Gordon Green, the Census Bureau's assistant population division chief for socioeconomic statistics, said the poverty rate would drop to between 10.2 percent and 13.9 percent if such benefits as food stamps, public housing, school lunches and Medicaid counted as income. But poverty organizations charge that use of such figures is an effort to hide the poor.

Using the poverty stricken as a political football in an election year may strike many people as a callous strategy on the part of both parties.

The only way to help the poor is to provide the means for them to climb out of the maw of poverty through a variety of training programs.

That can best be done when Congress and the White House dampen their rhetoric and take concerted action to deal with the problem.

The Dispatch

Columbus, OH, August 6, 1984

Any level of poverty in this country is disturbing, and the recent Census Bureau report that poverty afflicted 15.2 percent of the population in 1983 should certainly prompt analysis and action to lower the rate.

The bureau figures must be viewed in the proper context. They include within the poverty category a family of four with a total income of less than $10,178. This does not take into account, however, the value of non-cash benefits that the family may be receiving, such as food stamps, public housing, school lunches and Medicare. If these were included, the percentage of the population living in poverty could fall to 10.2 percent.

Americans' inclination to help the poor will also prompt calls for greater public assistance for those living in poverty. While immediate aid might be called for, the best solution is to enable the poor to find employment so that they can become independent of government handouts. Increasing federal spending — thereby expanding the size of the deficit — saps the vitality of the private sector and its ability to create jobs for the presently unemployed.

In short, the response to the poverty problem must be a reasoned one that seeks the long-term independence of the poor while helping them meet their immediate needs. The Reagan administration has adopted just such an approach, and it is this approach that should be pursued. It is the only one that holds out the promise that the poverty problem can eventually be solved.

THE TENNESSEAN

Nashville, TN, August 9, 1984

IF President Reagan still wants the evidence to back up charges that his budget cuts have hurt the poor, it has been mounting recently with the latest report of the Census Bureau saying the national poverty rate is increasing.

In its annual report on poverty, the bureau said the number of poor people grew 868,000, from 34.4 million in 1982 to 35.3 million in 1983. The new figure, it said, was "unexpectedly high." In fact, the bureau noted that the number of poor people has increased by 6 million since 1980.

The poverty data were based on 62,000 households, which is statistically a large sampling. Opinion polls during a campaign, for example, usually are based on interviews with 900 to 1,600 people.

At a congressional hearing last November, Mr. David A. Stockman, director of the Office of Management and Budget, said, "I am absolutely confident that the poverty rate is going to decline dramatically for 1983." Mr. Stockman apparently based that on an improving economy.

Examining the extent of poverty in 1982-83, the Census Bureau said, "There was no improvement among groups that usually benefit from economic growth." As an example it said that, "Married-couple families have had substantial declines in poverty in previous post-recession years, but showed no significant change between 1982 and 1983."

Although the Census Bureau didn't examine the effect of budget cuts, a recent study by the Congressional Research Service said the President's 1981 budget cuts threw more than 587,000 persons into poverty. The study found that the combination of the recession and budget cuts threw nearly 2.2 million into poverty, but that 587,000 could be directly attributable to the effects of the budget cuts alone. And this would have been worse if Congress hadn't resisted many of the deeper cuts.

Still another study by the General Accounting Office, said that 493,000 families and more than one million children lost Aid to Families with Dependent Children funds because of budget cuts.

At his recent televised news conference, President Reagan dismissed as "demagoguery" charges that his policies have been unfair to the poor. Well, it is difficult to think of the Census Bureau, the Congressional Research Service and the General Accounting Office all engaging in "demagoguery," particularly the Census Bureau which is part of the executive branch.

Mr. Reagan pretends not to understand the fairness issue — that his policies have helped those on the top, but forgotten those on the bottom whose plight has steadily grown worse. He spoke of the country saying it "is a shining city on a hill." In response to that New York Gov. Mario Cuomo reminded the President that the nation is more a "Tale of Two Cities," and one has never been seen by Mr. Reagan.

"In this part of the city," said Governor Cuomo, "there are more poor than ever, more families in trouble, more and more people who need help and can't find it...that there are people who sleep in the city streets, in the gutter where the glitter doesn't show..."

There are cold figures about poverty in the land, among the young, the elderly, and those who have watched middle class aspirations slip from their grasp as they went over the poverty line. If Mr. Reagan has not seen a single fact or figure to support facts about his policies, they are easily and quickly available.

Roanoke Times & World-News

Roanoke, VA, August 6, 1984

THE NUMBER and proportion of Americans in poverty continue to increase, and the Reagan administration keeps saying, "Who, me?" Logically and reasonably, it cannot claim credit for economic gains without also accepting responsibility for the losses -- especially those that its policies directly caused.

The Census Bureau compilation says that 868,000 more people fell below the official poverty line last year ($10,178 annual income for a family of four), bringing the national total to 35.2 million: one out of seven Americans. The poverty rate for 1983 was 15.2 percent, compared with 15 percent the year before and 14 percent in 1981.

A White House spokesman again conjured up the ghost of Jimmy Carter, saying that the former president's policies started an upsurge in poverty that only now is leveling off. The administration also dragged out other figures that attempted to redefine poverty and show that it's not really as extensive as claimed.

Earlier efforts by the administration to change the terms of the argument have backfired. When it included in family income the value of food stamps and other public assistance, the result was a drop in the absolute numbers of poor — but a rise in the rate at which people were becoming poor.

It's apparent that trickle-down economics isn't helping the people at the bottom. Another aspect of the fairness issue is how those people have been directly affected by the administration's spending priorities. After Democratic vice presidential candidate Geraldine Ferraro declared that budget cuts had hurt the poor and disadvantaged, President Reagan responded that "there is not one single fact or figure to substantiate that charge."

The president has made an art of the wounded denial, not to mention the juggling of statistics. But despite his claims that outlays for means-tested programs have increased under his administration, there are ample facts and figures to substantiate the charges he tries to dismiss. A few of them:

● A study by the non-partisan Congressional Research Service (aided by private economic consultants) estimates that 1981 budget restrictions in social programs pushed at least 560,-000 people into poverty. Of that number, 331,900 were children. The number of people in poor families headed by women rose by 283,000.

● The General Accounting Office, an investigative arm of Congress, said last spring that reductions in the Aid to Families with Dependent Children program had hurt half a million poor families.

● A study by the Congressional Budget Office says that as a result of President Reagan's policies, families with incomes below $10,000 lost $23 billion in after-tax income and benefits over a three-year period. (Meantime, families with incomes over $80,000 gained $35 billion from those policies.)

● The recession — greatest poverty-maker of all — put more Americans than ever in need of help. Not all are getting help, even if some program outlays have risen. If that added demand is factored in, says the Center on Budget and Policy Priorities, programs for the needy have been reduced by about $16 billion during Reagan's tenure.

Political analyst Richard Scammon reminded his fellow Democrats three presidential campaigns ago that social and peace issues would not play well with the electorate because a majority was unyoung, unpoor and unblack. For similar reasons, the Democrats may founder with the "fairness issue," especially if they try to convince members of the middle class that they are actually poor and don't know it.

Nonetheless, it's legitimate to call any administration, and all political parties, to account for how the less fortunate are faring. Aside from questions of justice, a society — especially a democratic one — is weakened if there is a stratum of people not just poor but also downtrodden and forgotten.

THE SACRAMENTO BEE

Sacramento, CA, August 10, 1984

The impact of Reaganomics on the poor is again in the news. Last week, the Census Bureau reported that the national poverty rate rose in 1983, as it has in each year of this administration, to reach its highest level in almost two decades. The White House, which just last fall was confidently predicting a "dramatic" decline in poverty, is trying to minimize the significance of these figures.

No such luck. Despite the president's claim, at his last news conference, that "there is not one single fact or figure to substantiate (the charge) that our budget practices have victimized the poor and the needy," there is in fact not one single fact or figure that *doesn't* prove the point. Report after report issued in recent months shows the administration's budget-cutting has made more people poor, and has made the poor poorer.

The Congressional Research Service has just demonstrated, for instance, that the 1981 budget reductions pushed 560,000 people, the majority of them children, below the poverty line — and that figure doesn't even take into account the impact of cuts in unemployment insurance, reductions in non-cash benefits like food stamps, or any cuts enacted since 1981. A study by the General Accounting Office shows 493,000 single-parent families removed from the welfare rolls by the 1981 budget cuts, most of them pushed — or pushed further — into poverty. And the Congressional Budget Office finds that, because of the budget and tax changes of the past three years, households earning less than $10,000 will lose $23 billion in income and benefits between 1983 and 1985.

This story, bad enough for the country generally, is worse for particular groups. One Hispanic in four, one black person in three — and one black youngster in two — now lives in poverty. President Reagan can campaign on the argument that the poor have to suffer in order to make the rest of us better off, or he can claim that, eventually, the poor will be better off as well, although there's no evidence for that speculation. What the president cannot assert — because it isn't true — is that the poorest Americans have reason to be grateful to his administration.

Rockford Register Star

Rockford, IL, November 14, 1984

Already, the bounty of this land awaits tapping for the annual Thanksgiving Day feast. And store windows are filling up with toys and other delights for Christmas. So it's business as usual?

Hardly, as dramatically demonstrated in a study by Catholic bishops. They condemn "the fact that more than 15 per cent of our nation's population live below the official poverty level" and they say that those who regard 6 per cent joblessness as "full employment" embrace a position that is "morally unjustified."

The study probably will come under attack from some as an intrusion of religion into politics, but it shouldn't. The study states no positions on church parochial issues. And the only politicians who might be affronted are those willing to campaign on a platform supporting poverty and unemployment.

But, mindful that their criticisms incorporate many of Walter Mondale's campaign charges against the Reagan White House, the bishops released their finding after the national elections. Said Archbishop Rembert Weakland, Milwaukee, who headed the drafting committee, "We knew that there were those political ramifications" but said bishops had not tried to weigh whether "these are Democratic or Republican views."

That may be one way of trying to broaden the study's appeal. But such discretion leaves to fate or some other force the responsibility for this nation's economic conditions during the last four Reagan years, the period under study.

While praising capitalism's "virtue" in the market place and avoiding what some feared would be a turn to socialism, Catholic bishops decried as a "scandal" and "disgrace" the "glaring disparities" between rich and poor.

Specifically, the report said it was "a disgrace that 35 million Americans live below the poverty level and millions more hover just above it."

Its most telling sentence: "In our judgment, the distribution of income and wealth in the United States is so inequitable that it violates this minimum standard of distributive justice."

Yet to come are fine-tuning of the bishops' report and response to its charges, either to affirm or rebut. But those of us who are employed cannot wait while the nation tries to right its economic wrongs. Thanksgiving is too near. Christmas is too near.

We commend every thoughtful, giving person in the Rockford community to those agencies who staff the emergency lines against hunger and deprivation — the pantries, church soup kitchens, Salvation Army and welfare agencies of all religious sects. The need is now. The time to act is now — as generously as circumstances permit.

The Register

Santa Ana, CA, October 3, 1984

The Census Bureau has recently analyzed some numbers in new ways, coming up with an estimate that during 1983 nearly 30 percent of Americans — 29.6 percent, actually — received direct payments from the government. The figure did not include farmers or farm workers (if it had, it would probably have been higher).

The figure may be taken as a barometer of how thoroughly the United States is being transformed into what economists Terry Anderson and P.J. Hill call, in a 1980 book published by the Hoover Institution at Stanford, a "transfer society."

Anderson and Hill suggest that there are essentially two different kinds of economic activities: productive activities and transfer activities. "Productive activity adds not only to the personal wealth of individuals but also to the total wealth of society," they say. To be productive in an economy based on voluntary exchange, a producer must satisfy consumer desires — produce something that leads a consumer to believe he or she is better off for having acquired the product or service.

By contrast, "transfer activities add to the wealth of specific individuals or groups of individuals but reduce the wealth of other individuals or groups in the society. Because transfers consume resources, such activities decrease the total product of society."

A government-enacted transfer is not a costless activity. It is accompanied by legislation, lobbying, and attempts on the part of those from whom wealth is being seized to defend their resources — in short, the valuable time of talented people, the one resource that can never be recovered.

"Another way of viewing these activities," say Anderson and Hill, "is to measure the net change in social output. In this context, productive activity is a positive-sum game, or social interaction, that enlarges the pie. Transfer activity, on the other hand, is a negative-sum game — a series of social interactions that decreases the size of the pie. There is less after the social interaction than before."

According to census director John Keane, this new report is designed to help analyze the economic well-being of the U.S. population. The analysis should be rather simple. Almost a third of us are on the receiving end of an activity whose impact is to reduce the wealth — that is to say, one measurable aspect of personal and social well-being — of society as a whole. Such activities consume about a third of domestic income.

In other words, about a third of what people produce is seized by government for activities whose result is to make society as a whole poorer.

From a broad perspective, the solution should be simple. Reduce government-mandated transfer activities to a minimum — approaching zero — to permit society as a whole to become more prosperous. Using a third of our resources for negative-sum games that decrease the size of the pie is, in the long run, a prescription for pauperism.

There's a political problem, however. That 30 percent on the receiving end constitutes a powerful bloc in a democratic society, with a short-term vested interest in continuing the game. Don't bore me with talk about "society as a whole." I'm "entitled."

So the game goes on.

ST. LOUIS POST-DISPATCH

St. Louis, MO, October 4, 1984

Having already exhibited a notable lack of interest in vigorous enforcement of federal laws to protect minorities, the Reagan administration is now planning to remove the federal government even further from civil rights enforcement. In a plan that is billed as a pilot project to reduce federal regulation and strengthen the role of state governments, the administration is setting out to delegate to selected states the responsibility for investigating complaints of discrimination in the use of federal block grants distributed to states by the Health and Human Services Department for various social programs. The project seems more like buck-passing of a dubious kind.

Apparently HHS did not check with its own assistant general counsel for civil rights, Albert Hamlin, who says the department's own regulations limit its authority to delegate enforcement responsibility, adding that only the department or other federal officials are authorized to investigate complaints. Spokesmen for civil rights groups are even more blunt, saying such delegation would be illegal and that some states lack the capacity and the inclination to enforce federal civil rights laws. Raul Yzaguirre, president of a Hispanic organization, made the pertinent point that a state accused of discrimination would be in the position of investigating itself.

The HHS project, referred to as President Reagan's "new federalism" approach, appears to be one more case in which the administration is using the slogan of reduced federal regulation as camouflage for reducing protection for citizens. Reduced regulation has so far meant relaxed environmental law enforcement. More relaxed enforcement of civil rights laws seems to be next.

The Birmingham News

Birmingham, AL, November 25, 1984

A triad of interlocking issues President Reagan and Congress will have to confront come January is composed of federal spending, welfare and taxes. Social Security and assistance for the elderly and handicapped are *not* at issue. The left, led by Walter Mondale, has, of course, already called for raising taxes by some $80-plus billion to move toward controlling deficit spending by increasing revenues.

And leaks and statements by White House officials indicate that the administration foresees another spending deficit of at least $170 billion, even allowing for growth in the economy and shrinking unemployment. The same people are suggesting significant cuts cannot be made without sharply reducing spending for welfare and social programs, given the fact that they are indexed to the cost of living and make no allowances for population growth.

So it is high time that the public, Congress and the administration judge the results of some 20 years of Great Society programs, admit they have failed to accomplish the goals Congress assumed they would and seek a less socially destructive way to reduce the poverty level across the board.

In that wise, Charles Murray, a senior research fellow for the Manhattan Institute for Policy Research, has gathered massive data that demonstrate the counterproductive results of the Great Society programs. He has published the data and his conclusions in a new book titled *Losing Ground* (Basic Books).

Murray argues that the poor have been damaged by the good intentions of government instead of being helped, as many people assume on the basis of dollars spent. He points out that the rapid progress made by the poor and minorities during the 1950s and early 1960s and since was first slowed, then stopped and finally reversed because of federal welfare policies.

For instance, the data show that in 1950, about 50 million Americans, more than one-third of the population, lived below the poverty line. But by 1968 poverty had fallen to 13 percent of the population. It reached a low of 11 percent by 1973. But by 1980, poverty grew to 13 percent and today, official data put it at about 15 percent.

Murray contends that the fall in the poverty rate — from 1950 to 1973 — cannot be explained by welfare spending during the Kennedy and Johnson administrations. In 1950, for instance, federal public assistance was less than $4 billion in 1980 dollars. It never exceeded $10 billion until the 1970s. But during the Eisenhower, Kennedy and (the first) Johnson administrations, the poverty level fell at its fastest rate. In the late 1960s and since, welfare expenditures grew faster and faster, while progress in reducing poverty slowed and ultimately reversed.

In finding an explanation for the rapid fall in the poverty rate, Murray turns for clues to the economy as a whole. He found that the economic growth rate averaged 2.7 percent from 1953 to 1959. The economy grew at a much faster rate — 32 percent — during the early '70s. But the data show that many poor people had become so dependent on federal assistance, they would not voluntarily leave the safety net.

Murray says the data of the late '60s and '70s clearly mark the beginning of government-created dependency.

One may recall that those were the years when welfare aid was liberalized and benefits increased. Disability criteria for Social Security were liberalized and increased. More people were brought under unemployment insurance and benefits were increased and the time period covered was extended.

The war on poverty also had other undesirable effects. In 1950, illegitimate births among whites were 2 percent; today, despite all manner of contraceptive devices, they stand at 11 percent. For blacks in 1950, illegitimate births were 17 percent; today they are more than 50 percent. Even conceding that illegitimate births are not a moral issue, one cannot ignore the fact that they are a social and economic problem of great proportions, since poverty is far greater among households headed by women than for any other group.

As Congress and the Department of Health and Human Services clearly know by now, babies born to young, unskilled and unmarried women almost guarantee another generation sentenced to poverty. According to Murray, Census Bureau figures show that 86 percent of white households and 77 percent of black households were two-parent families in 1940. The rate for two-parent families among whites had fallen marginally, but for blacks the percentage had dropped to 69 percent in 1968 and to 59 percent in 1980.

In the meantime, the poor as well as the middle class have demonstrated rising expectations as to what the economy can deliver in the way of living standards. In many cases, the poor have organized themselves, appointed spokesmen and joined the many groups lobbying Congress for more assistance. In the meantime, crime and drug abuse increased by huge percentages; only recently have they begun to decline. Unemployment has outstripped population growth, and education, the way out of poverty, has deteriorated.

The country has been living beyond its means in the government area alone to the tune of nearly $2 trillion dollars. It is questionable whether the economy can much longer marshal the investment dollars necessary for growth, in the face of increasing spending by government at all levels.

Of course, Murray's interpretation of the data is not the only one. Other respected scholars have reached similar conclusions. Others will surely disagree, arguing that more federal assistance is required to attack a 15 percent poverty level.

But surely it is beginning to dawn on official Washington that 17 years of social experiments have proved that good intentions that do not reckon with historic patterns of human behavior are insufficient to deal with poverty. Jobs, of course, are the quickest way out of poverty. An expanding economy is the best place to look for job formation. But an economy cannot grow, if government policies result in draining the vitality from the economic sphere and starving it for capital.

THE DAILY OKLAHOMAN

Oklahoma City, OK, August 18, 1984

THE opening of the Republican convention Monday in Dallas will coincide with the 20th anniversary of the launching of President Johnson's "war on poverty" when he signed the Economic Opportunity Act into law.

The coincidence is ironic because the conservative-oriented GOP and its incumbent president, Ronald Reagan, were roundly chastized at the Democratic convention a few weeks ago for their purported mistreatment of the poor. Speakers claimed millions of Americans are living in poverty because of Reagan-induced federal budget cuts.

Last week the Urban Institute asserted the income gap between the poor and the wealthy has widened during Reagan's term, at least partly because of spending restraints in social programs benefiting the poor and tax-rate cuts favoring the rich.

But the pertinent question is why, after 20 years and the expenditure of billions of federal dollars in the war on poverty, 35.3 million Americans, or 15.2 percent of the population, are still said to be living below the poverty line.

Actually, the Reagan administration — or, more accurately, Congress — has not cut entitlements. These are the benefits to which the poor are entitled by law and which are indexed for inflation. Indeed, some critics say the nation won't get a handle on federal spending, and thus the deficit, until the entitlements are curbed. Of course, this would be politically difficult although not impossible to do.

The point is that, despite the rhetoric, many of the "welfare poor" may be better off because their income, such as it is, stretches further as a result of the decline in inflation attributable to the administration's economic policies.

The Star-Ledger

Newark, NJ, March 10, 1984

This is a nation that takes pride in its commitment to care for its poor and its elderly. It is a redeeming legacy that was given impetus in the mid-1930s, the genesis of the liberal body of massive social legislation spawned by the economic misery of the Great Depression.

The New Deal of President Franklin D. Roosevelt laid the sturdy cornerstone that was built on by succeeding Democratic presidents—Harry Truman, John Kennedy, and in its most expansive scope by Lyndon Johnson's Great Society. A number of their socially oriented programs were notable successes; others were egregious failures, marred by spending excesses, bureaucratic ineptness, wasteful practices, and, to a lesser degree, fraud.

Fifty years later, the failings are distressingly more visible than the accomplishments. Poverty remains inexorably resistant to massive federal spending. Worse still, it grew rapidly between 1979 and 1982 despite the infusion of a costly array of entitlement programs like food stamps, public housing, Medicare and Medicaid.

In 1982, the latest available statistics, the Census Bureau estimated that 15 percent of the population subsisted in poverty, perceptibly higher than the 11.7 percent in 1979—an increase of 47.1 percent. In the same period, there was a 10 percent decline in the real value of non-cash government benefits for the poor. The cutting and leveling off of domestic spending by the Reagan Administration was a further complicating factor.

The nation's older population fared better in that time period. The incidence of poverty among the elderly declined, a positive social trend that could be directly attributed to the liberal assistance they received from the government medical insurance programs—Medicare and Medicaid.

It may well be that poverty, even in a nation that is the most affluent in the world, will always be with us. But the accelerated rise in the number of America's severely deprived citizens is a harrowing reminder that we have yet to deal with this enormous social problem in a more effective and efficient manner to ease the burdensome existence afflicting millions of Americans in this land of plenty.

BUFFALO EVENING NEWS

Buffalo, NY, March 7. 1984

WASHINGTON HAS begun to refine and improve the standards used in defining poverty in the United States. But the sobering conclusion of a recent Census Bureau study is that, by both old and revised definitions, the proportion of Americans living in poverty climbed steeply in the four years from 1979 through 1982.

Under the more standard definition, the number of Americans below the poverty line jumped from 11.7 percent to 15 percent of the total population.

This calculation counts only cash payments, such as welfare checks, in computing income for families and individuals. The broader and more complete calculation adds to cash benefits non-cash assistance, such as food stamps, public housing, Medicaid and Medicare, in determining whether individuals or families fall below or rise above the official poverty level. That appears the more meaningful standard, since government assistance, whether cash or non-cash, helps low-income people combat poverty and its problems.

Yet even when non-cash benefits were added in, the study showed those living in poverty rose from 6.8 to 10 percent.

The Census Bureau does not attribute the expanded numbers of Americans in poverty to cutbacks in federal social programs. Rather, it cites the broader problems of the recent recession and the inflation that drove up retail prices 33 percent during the four years studied. The recession, of course, caused heavy unemployment while inflation cheapened the purchasing power of every dollar earned or received in government cash benefits.

Thus, the study highlights one grim aspect of the cold shower the economy underwent in these years, especially 1981 and 1982, and the extent to which it victimized low-income persons. Presumably, the rapid expansion of the national economy that began in late 1982 and early 1983, combined with the continued low level of inflation, has by now lifted millions of Americans out of poverty.

All this underscores the importance of sustaining the recovery, which means in part that Washington must shrink those awesome federal deficits.

In looking for spending cuts, however, Washington should avoid significant further reductions in the very social programs that helped sustain the increasing numbers of low-income persons documented in the Census Bureau report.

AKRON BEACON JOURNAL

Akron, OH, March 3, 1984

THE EQUATIONS may differ, but the results are the same: The number of poor people in the United States is growing at a distressing rate.

Last week's news from the Census Bureau was discouraging indeed, even when the Reagan administration's own formula for tallying poverty was followed to the letter.

The nation registered a marked increase in poverty from 1979 to 1982, regardless of whether the value of food stamps, government health programs and public housing were plugged into the equation.

Standard practice is to exclude these non-cash benefits when the Census Bureau totals the number of people with incomes falling below the poverty level. Based solely on cash income, 15 percent of all Americans were considered poor in 1982, more than a 3 percent rise from 1979.

Reagan officials have long challenged the Census Bureau's method of ignoring non-cash benefits, arguing that it just makes U.S. poverty figures look a whole lot worse.

But in fact, the picture didn't look much prettier when, at the request of Congress, the Census Bureau played by the Reagan rules.

When food stamps, Medicaid, subsidized housing, etc., were plugged into the poverty equation, the percentage of poor people in the United States totaled 10 percent, again more than a 3 percent increase from 1979.

Yet there was another disturbing finding. The three-year growth rate of poverty under this alternate definition was actually much higher than under the standard definition — a startling 47 percent increase.

In either equation, the bottom line is that a one-two combination of inflation and recession packed a tragic punch for millions of people. The statistics represent not a mere sum of numbers, but human hardship in the starkest of terms.

And they are frightening, especially since they don't yet reflect the Reagan administration's cutbacks in social programs. Most of those reductions occurred in 1982. When the next round of statistics is compiled, the report may contain even gloomier news.

There is already enough reason for Congress to deal forcefully with the disturbing trend that these statistics have uncovered. Alternate equations for poverty don't mean much to people who are poor.

The Des Moines Register

Des Moines, IA, March 21, 1984

Federal money pays more than half of Iowa's welfare bill, and Iowa's welfare program is not in compliance with federal regulations, the U.S. Department of Health and Human Services says. The state could lose some federal funds if the discrepancy is not resolved. It will be, but the best solution will entail some nonsensical figure-juggling.

The state's Aid to Dependent Children grants are based on a "standard of need" developed by Iowa State University eight years ago and updated for inflation.

In arriving at payment rates, the Iowa Department of Human Services deducted the value of food stamps. Since food-stamp allowances correspond to family sizes, ADC payments provide different-sized families different percentages of the standard of need.

This is inequitable, the feds said. It strikes us as more equitable than ignoring food-stamp benefits — but the regulations specify percentages, not fairness.

Evening up the percentages could deny benefits to some needy families and overpay others. The alternative is to juggle the standard-of-need formula — solving the problem on paper without significantly changing the size of the grants or total state cost.

The standard of need purports to assign exact monthly costs to every basic household necessity for an average family of a certain size, although no two families' needs are alike. Hence, juggling the figures to conform with the present payment schedule in the interest of fairness is defensible. But it's a sad commentary on bureaucratic inflexibility that such phoniness is necessary.

OKLAHOMA CITY TIMES

Oklahoma City, OK, February 27, 1984

UTILIZING the old football maxim that a good offense is the best defense, several Democratic congressmen have proposed legislation to increase benefits for the poor. They are acting despite conflicting statistics on how much poverty exists in the United States.

For some time various analysts have questioned official government figures on the "poverty line" because they include only cash benefits in calculations of family income. Critics have pointed out consistently that if non-cash benefits were figured in income, the poverty rate would be much lower.

Non-cash benefits include such items as food stamps, Medicaid, free school lunches, housing subsidies and health programs.

Last summer the U.S. Census Bureau reported 34.4 million Americans, or 15 percent of the population, fell below the poverty level in 1982. That level was pegged at $9,862 a year for a family of four.

Now the Census Bureau has acknowledged that a lot fewer Americans are below the poverty line if non-cash benefits are counted in the income calculations. That would reduce the poverty rate by as much as 33 percent, depending on how the benefits were calculated and the values assigned them, the bureau said.

Notwithstanding the implica-tion of its name, the Census Bureau apparently does not actually count the families under the poverty level but determines the total through a formula that takes inflation into account. Thus, the more inflation, the higher the poverty line goes and the more families fall under it.

With the slowing of the inflation rate in the past year or so, presumably the poverty level will remain relatively stable — unless the 0.6 percent rise in the Consumer Price Index for January, announced Friday, is an omen of what is to come.

Another complication is the increasing number of women and children in fatherless families who constitute an "under-class" the expanding economy will not reach.

This calls for specific action to correct the problem. Yet three House Democrats — Charles Rangel of New York, Harold Ford of Tennessee and Henry Waxman of California — propose using the blunderbuss approach. They have a bill to reduce recent budget cuts and set minimum benefits for welfare, *enlarge eligibility* for many of the benefit programs, mandate health insurance for the unemployed and boost job programs.

The growth in entitlement programs, where eligibility is set by law, is one of the chief causes of the massive deficits plaguing the government today. Some congressmen never learn.

THE INDIANAPOLIS STAR

Indianapolis, IN, November 15, 1984

"Pushing poverty" is what Ben Wattenberg calls the "awfulizing" of news about poverty in America even when much of the news is good.

Are the poor really getting poorer, has the Reagan administration really ripped apart the "Safety Net," is less and less being spent on poverty today than under Democratic presidents?

The answer to all three questions is "No."

As Wattenberg points out in his series running in *The Star*, the U.S. Bureau of the Census reported in 1959 that 22.4 percent of the people lived below the poverty level. In 1979, 11.6 percent lived below the poverty level.

In 1970 a total of $1,354 per beneficiary was spent on social and welfare spending. In 1980 it was $2,140, after discounting for inflation.

During the Reagan years the amount being spent on social and welfare spending, as measured by the key of annual transfer payments, has not fallen but risen. In 1980 transfer payments totaled $251.4 billion. By 1983 they had risen to $345.7 billion.

If all funds spent upon a poor family of four in one year were averaged the total would be $34,000. That is how much the family would get if "poverty money" went directly to the family as cash, economist Walter Williams estimates.

Actually, the family averages only about $8,000 in cash and in-kind benefits. The remaining $26,000 is "overhead" siphoned off by the welfare bureaucracy.

The Catholic bishops, liberals, reformers, politicians, social critics and others are factually right when they say that poverty still exists in America and morally right when they say that those who have the strength and funds should help the poor.

Helping the impoverished elderly, disabled and sick requires doctors, nurses and other health care personnel, hospitals, nursing homes and of course funds to pay for these necessities.

But helping the great bulk of poverty victims escape from poverty is another matter. Since 1964 more than $1.6 trillion has been spent fighting poverty in America. Yet some 34.4 million Americans still live in poverty by federal government estimates.

At the prevailing rate of the cost of elevating Americans above the poverty level since 1964, estimates Rep. Philip M. Crane, R-Ill., it will cost the taxpayers approximately $330 trillion to elevate the 34.4 million Americans who are still in poverty.

Clearly, there is much that is wrong, to put it mildly, with the U.S. way of fighting poverty.

A substantial part of what is wrong, there can be little doubt, is the vested interest of the multibillion-dollar poverty bureaucracy and the politicians, "leaders" and organizations that feather their own nests with federal grant money while pushing for bigger, richer outlay programs.

There has got to be a better way. We hope that the younger generation of Americans can find it.

Poverty Rate Declined, Median Income Gained in '84

The U.S. poverty rate declined in 1984 for the first time since 1978, while median family income increased the most since 1972, according to a Census Bureau report issued Aug. 27, 1985. The decline in poverty was the first after five straight years of increases. Median family income in 1984 was $26,430, up 3.3% from 1983 after adjustment for inflation. The poverty rate was 14.4% in 1984, a drop of nine-tenths of a percentage point from the year before.

The total number of poor people in 1984 was 33.7 million, a fall of 1.8 million from 1983. A family of four was considered in poverty if its cash income was $10,609 or below. Poverty among whites fell by seven-tenths of a percentage point to 11.5%. For white children, the poverty rate was 16.5%, a decline of one percentage point. White median income rose 3.3% to $27,690.

Among blacks, the poverty rate declined by 1.9 percentage points, to 33.8%. There were 9.5 million poor blacks in 1984; that was 398,000 fewer than in 1983. The poverty rate for blacks younger than 18 was 46.5%, unchanged. For black children under six, however, the percentage in poverty rose to 51.1% from 49.4% in 1983. Black median family income rose 1.9%, to $15,430.

The Hispanic poverty rate rose by three-tenths of a percentage point, to 28.4%. For Hispanic children younger than 18, it rose by 1.1 percentage points, to 39%. For Hispanic children younger than six, the poverty rate fell by 1.2 percentage points, to 40.6%. Hispanic median family income rose 6.8%, to 18,830.

For children of all races younger than six, the poverty rate dropped by one percentage point, to 24%. Of all age groups, people older than 64 experienced the greatest drop in the poverty rate. It fell by 1.8 percentage points, to 12.4%—2% below that of the general population. Families headed by women also saw a drop in poverty, their rate falling to 34.5% from the 1983 figure of 36.1%. The total number of members of such families also fell, dropping by 408,000 to 16.4 million. Families headed by women accounted for 16% of all families and for 48% of poor families.

President Reagan Aug. 17 issued a statement hailing the census findings as evidence that the "greatest enemy of poverty is the free enterprise system" and that the U.S., "after a difficult decade, is once again headed in the right direction," toward the elimination of poverty. White House Communications Director Patrick J. Buchanan hailed the figures as a "triumph" for President Reagan's economic policies.

Critics, however, stressed that the poverty rate was still higher than at any time during the 15 years before Reagan took office. They expressed doubt as to whether the improvement would survive the economy's slowed performance. One think tank, the Center on Budget and Policy Priorities, said the figures showed that the gap between rich and poor was growing and was now "wider than at any time in the last 40 years." The group pointed to census figures comparing the percentage of national income received by families in the lower two-fifths and upper two-fifths of the income scale. In 1983, the lowest two-fifths had received 15.8% of all income, while the highest two-fifths had received 67.1%. In 1984, those figures had changed, respectively, to 15.7% and 67.3%.

THE KANSAS CITY STAR

Kansas City, MO,

September 3, 1985

The Census Bureau reports that the poverty rate has dropped to 14.4 percent, nearly a percentage point less than in 1983. Thus 1.8 million people are no longer officially poor.

It's positive change. The nation must be glad the trend now is down rather than up as it has been for years. This is the first decline statisticians consider significant since 1976.

Notice the inclination when a new set of statistics come out to cheer or boo for the "winning" side. Thus the tail wags the dog.

What must not be passed over is the simple fact that nearly 34 million Americans do live in poverty. And if you want to draw fine lines and say some of them are not really in such bad poverty because they get free medical care or subsidized school lunches, that would be accurate. It does not lessen the hardships of those trapped by others' flaws, like the more than 13 million poor children. Or the desperation of nearly 4 million elderly. Or those situations when people fall between cracks. We hear their stories during a United Way campaign or a drive for utility assistance and wonder how clever reporters find families it's so easy to be sympathetic about. Ask state workers or social agencies. Such needy are the norm. Profiles and statistics are mainly for the convenience of bureaucrats and record keepers. Real people defy such pigeonholes.

With the new Census figures, administration friends credit the Reagan revolution with success, while advocates of the poor suggest it's better only because conditions were so bad a few years ago. They warn that improvement will not continue. No one knows, of course.

But public and private resources make life bearable for people caught in need, though they won't make them well-to-do. Government programs are the reason poverty is so much less among the aged than it was a quarter century ago. Medicaid and Aid to Families with Dependent Children acknowledge the value this society puts on children, whether or not their parents are successful.

It's crucial to remember the 34 million individuals still struggling. And not to discredit for them programs that keep American poverty from being terminal, as it is in less fortunate countries.

The Dallas Morning News

Dallas, TX, September 3, 1985

NO doubt Ronald Reagan's critics, who are surely not hidebound in their hostility, will now come forth and announce they were wrong after all.

They'd thought Reaganomics not only enriched the rich but impoverished the poor. Yet now the Census Bureau says that in 1984 the poverty rate *fell* by more than it had fallen in a decade. "More Reagan, less poverty!" will doubtless become the new chant.

Fat chance. Critics will point out that the poverty rate is still higher than when Reagan took office. And that the rate for black children under six rose even in 1984, a statistic highly correlated with huge increases in the pregnancy rate among unwed black teen-agers.

The "poverty line" is now $10,169 for a family of four, and is adjusted each year for inflation. It includes only *cash* income — or, cash income reported for tax-filing purposes. It does not include the many "in-kind" benefits available, e.g., medical, housing and day-care assistance as well as food stamps. All told, such benefits make it possible to do far better on government assistance than by working for the minimum wage.

Indeed, government studies have found that if in-kind benefits were counted, the "poverty rate," now at 14.4 percent, would be cut by a third to a half. No wonder: From 1965-83, cash assistance for the poor rose in constant dollars by about $10 billion annually, but for in-kind benefits, $50 billion.

It becomes clear that one reason the poverty rate has actually increased despite these massive expenditures is that in-kind benefits aren't counted. The other reason is that unless you're defined as poor, you're ineligible for these benefits, which, as Charles Murray and others have documented, makes those working low-paying jobs feel like "chumps."

Because there *are* tragically poor people in America, it is all the greater tragedy that too few of the welfare state's benefits get to them. The system actually ensures that the more money it spends, the worse poverty becomes — and this is then cited as a reason to spend even more!

Birmingham Post-Herald

Birmingham, AL, August 30, 1985

It has been a while in coming, but there is good news in the latest Census Bureau report on poverty. For the first time since 1978, the nation's poverty rate declined in 1984. The drop from 15.3 percent in 1983 to 14.4 percent is the largest one-year decline since 1968.

The Reagan administration was quick to claim the decline as vindication for its policies. Critics were just as quick to note that the poverty rate remained higher than in any year between 1970 and 1980 — and to blame the administration.

Actually, both probably overstate the impact of governmental policies. The poverty rate is closely tied to economic activity. When private enterprise is booming, the number of people in poverty declines. When businesses run into hard times, the poor increase in number as jobs disappear. Government policies do affect the economy, but not necessarily to the degree politicians would like to believe.

Last year was a good year for the economy. With more jobs generated by a stronger than expected recovery, median family income climbed by 3.3 percent, pulling 1.8 million individuals above the official poverty line of $10,609 annual income for a family of four.

The poverty line figure does not take into account such non-cash benefits as food stamps, Medicaid and housing subsidies, which means the official poverty rate is probably overstated.

But wherever the line is drawn, the important fact is that there were fewer poor people in this country at the end of 1984 than at the beginning. Of equal importance, the decline in poverty occurred in most classifications. Whites, blacks, Hispanics, the elderly and families headed by women were all better off. Two exceptions are found among black children under the age of 6 and Hispanic children under 18, both of which had higher poverty rates in 1984.

One year's decline does not constitute a trend. And the poverty rate remains higher than it should be in an affluent country. But the latest poverty report does provide hope that we are moving in the right direction.

THE INDIANAPOLIS STAR

Indianapolis, IN,
September 13, 1985

Not everyone rejoiced when the Census Bureau reported a startling decline in the poverty level in 1984.

The bureau reported that 1.8 million less people were poor than in 1983 and that only 14.4 percent of Americans had cash income under $10,609, the inflation-adjusted poverty threshhold for a family of four. That was a drop of eight-tenths of a percentage point and the first decline since 1978.

That news was heartening in itself. But when the bureau added in such non-cash income as housing subsidies, food stamps, Medicaid and school lunches, the poverty level fell to 9.7 percent.

It was that last figure that made Rep. Robert Garcia, D-N.Y., uncomfortable. Garcia represents one of the poorest districts in the country — the South Bronx — and he is understandably interested in keeping federal welfare programs generously funded and keeping himself elected by delivering to his constituency.

If the Census Bureau goes around reporting that less than 10 percent of the people are poor, Garcia is afraid Congress will reduce spending. Though he can't do anything about the census statistics, he wants to tell the bureau how to report them.

He has sponsored an amendment to an appropriations bill that would limit the bureau to reporting only the official poverty figure, that is the one that counts only cash income, not rent subsidies, health care and the like.

This despite the fact that such in-kind benefits last year totaled roughly $113 billion, or four times the cash assistance given to the needy. And despite the fact that for years the poverty level figures have been deliberately skewed by not counting non-cash benefits as income.

Now that those benefits are included in a separate breakdown of figures, poverty levels are not just representative, they are factual. The trouble is that some people, Garcia included, would rather not confuse Congress and the public with the facts.

Herald American

Syracuse, NY,
September 4, 1985

Last year the national poverty rate dropped nine-tenths of a percent, the largest one-year decline in more than a decade.

Predictably, the Reagan administration was overjoyed with the figures, which were made public last week. Pat Buchanan, the White House communications director, called them a "triumph" for President Reagan's policies.

The news, indeed, is good. The decline means 1.8 million fewer people were officially classified as poor in 1984 than in 1983. That is a major improvement — the product of 1983's robust economy.

However, the poverty figures don't bear out Buchanan's unrestrained glee.

The fact is more than 33 million Americans continue to be officially classified as poor. (For 1984, a family of four with cash income of $10,609 or less was considered poor.) That means 14.4 percent of all inhabitants of the "land of opportunity" are squeezing out a minimal existence — at least in financial terms.

In only two years since 1966 has the poverty percentage been higher — 1982 and 1983. A decline was due, but the poverty rate remains significantly above the last year of Jimmy Carter's presidency (14.4 percent now, 13 percent in 1980).

Worst of all, the overall decline in the poverty rate last year was not reflected in family types where poverty is at its highest levels. The rate for black children under age 6 continued to rise — to an incredible 51.1 percent last year. The poverty rate for Hispanic children under age 18 rose (to 39 percent) and the rate for black children under 18 was unchanged at 46.5 percent.

There was a slight decline in poverty among families headed by women, but the figure remains appallingly high; more than one such family in three lives below the government's poverty line.

Still, nearly 2 million people out of poverty is a reason to rejoice — and to build on the effort. Unfortunately, there is fear the 1984 trend will falter in 1985 because the national economy has turned sluggish.

However, it is no reason to declare a "triumph." The nation can't afford to "level off" with 33 million poor.

The Honolulu Advertiser

Honolulu, HI, August 29, 1985

Well, yes, the dramatic 5.1 percent decrease in the poverty rate in 1984 is good news. That 1.8 million Americans were no longer classified as poor is a welcome development, though it is a fair bet most are not jumping for joy.

The reason they and others at the bottom of the economic ladder are likely not celebrating is that the news is really not so much "good" as "less bad." That is because the poverty rate had risen steadily for the previous five years, adding 11 million to its ranks.

FURTHER, 1984 was a year of economic "recovery." This year, however, economic expansion has slowed and unemployment, which reached record heights, has stopped falling.

So it's likely that many of those 1.8 million people now find themselves back among the "official poor" even as they learn they were out last year. It is likely, in short, that figures for this year will reflect a resumed growth in the rate of poverty.

The main reason cited for the drop in the rate last year was the welcome decline in inflation. But that scourge of rich and poor alike, it must be remembered, was lowered at the cost of the high unemployment rate.

The Reagan administration is, of course, hailing this development as evidence of the correctness of its policies and its view that private enterprise and not government programs do more to help the poor. But the reality is that government programs also have a role. The biggest drop in poverty, for example, was among the elderly who have received increased Social Security payments.

FINALLY, there is a very troubling sign within the Census Bureau report which brought this "good" news. That is the growing disparity in the distribution of income that has become a hallmark of the Reagan economic policy.

As Newsday's Robert Reno notes, "The poorest 40 percent of American families received 15.7 percent of the national income in 1984 while the richest 40 percent received 67.3 percent. . . . For the poorest group, it is the lowest percentage they have received in 37 years of record-keeping. For the richest group, it is a 37-year high."

Many people in this country are doing quite well, and visibly so. That makes it all the easier to forget those not prospering. And that polarity between the rich and the poor is a dangerous trend for our social harmony and well-being that portends far more than a welcome but minor one-year drop in the poverty rate.

Rocky Mountain News

Denver, CO, September 1, 1985

IT has been a while in coming, but there is good news in the latest Census Bureau report on poverty. For the first time since 1978, the nation's poverty rate declined in 1984. The drop from 15.3 percent in 1983 to 14.4 percent is the largest one-year decline since 1968.

The Reagan administration quickly claimed the decline vindicated its policies. Critics were just as quick to note that the poverty rate remained higher than in any year between 1970 and 1980 — and blamed the administration.

Actually, both probably overstate the impact of governmental policies. The poverty rate is closely tied to economic activity. When private enterprise is booming, the number of people in poverty declines. When businesses run into hard times, the poor increase in number as jobs disappear. Government policies do affect the economy, but not necessarily to the degree politicians would like to believe.

Last year was good for the economy. With more jobs generated by a stronger than expected recovery, median family income climbed by 3.3 percent, pulling 1.8 million individuals above the official poverty line of $10,609 annual income for a family of four.

The poverty line figure does not take into account such non-cash benefits as food stamps, Medicaid and housing subsidies, which means the official poverty rate is overstated.

But wherever the line is drawn, the important fact is that there were fewer poor people in this country at the end of 1984. than at the beginning. Of equal importance, the decline in poverty occurred in most classifications. Whites, blacks, Hispanics, the elderly and families headed by women were all better off. Two exceptions are found: black children under the age of 6 and Hispanic children under 18 both had higher poverty rates in 1984.

One year's decline does not constitute a trend. And the poverty rate remains higher than it should be in an affluent country. But the latest poverty report does provide hope that we are moving in the right direction.

Ronnie's comet

Wisconsin ▲ State Journal
Madison, WI, August 29, 1985

The U.S. Census Bureau has reported that the number of Americans living in poverty dropped last year to 33.7 million, a decrease of 1.8 million, or 5.1 percent, from 1983.

Good news, right? Yes, with important qualifications.

The drop in the national poverty rate, from 15.3 percent to 14.4 percent, was spread among almost all large groups, including the elderly, female heads of households and blacks.

But there was no change in the severe poverty rates of black and Hispanic children. About 46.6 percent of all black children and 39 percent of children of Spanish origin are poor.

For blacks of all ages, the poverty rate dropped from 35.7 percent to 33.8 percent, but that's still nearly three times the rate (11.5 percent) among whites.

The new poverty rate is the first drop in the national index since 1976, but it still is the third-highest since 1966.

There was no significant drop in poverty in either the Midwest or Northeast; only the "Sun Belt states" of the South and West showed improvement in income.

President Reagan hailed the new figures as "further proof that the greatest enemy of poverty is the free enterprise system." He's correct. The best welfare program is always a good job.

The administration should not rest on its laurels, however, nor use the figures as an excuse to cut job-training efforts aimed at permanently breaking the poverty cycle. Much more work remains.

ST. LOUIS POST-DISPATCH
St. Louis, MO, August 29, 1985

The U.S. Census Bureau had some good news and some bad news the other day. The number of people living in poverty declined last year in the first major improvement since 1976, but the status of minorities showed little improvement over the previous year.

The government's annual report on poverty showed that last year, 14.4 percent of the population — 33.7 million people — had incomes below the official poverty line, which was $10,609 for a family of four. That was a drop of 1.8 million people from the 15.3 percent in poverty in 1983. The report drew immediate comment from President Reagan, who praised his administration and called the report "news for which every American can be thankful." But can we really be thankful?

The data showed that the number of blacks in poverty declined to 33.8 percent from 35.7 percent, the number of whites in poverty declined to 11.2 percent from 12.2 percent, and the rate remained virtually unchanged for Hispanics — 28.4 percent compared to 28.1 percent in 1983. Despite the slight overall improvement, the figures showed that the number of blacks in poverty remained three times the number of whites below the poverty level. And the number of Hispanics below that level was more than twice the number of whites.

Mr. Reagan says the good news is that we can all be thankful. But the bad news is that there still is a major problem for which we cannot be thankful. When one out of every three blacks in this prosperous nation is living below the poverty line, when one out of every four Hispanics is living in poverty, there hardly is cause for celebration. The American public would be better served if the president would focus more of his efforts on winning the war on poverty and less on patting his administration on the back.

The Hartford Courant
Hartford, CT, September 9, 1985

Last year's nine-tenths of a percentage point drop in the national poverty rate represents a a triumph for Reaganomics, said White House communications director Patrick J. Buchanan. The fact that the poverty rate declined to 14.4 percent of Americans is "further proof that the greatest enemy of poverty is the free-enterprise system," President Reagan said.

Indeed it's welcome news that poverty rates — which have risen steadily since 1978 — have finally dipped. Not only that, but the reduction in 1984 was the largest since 1968. The Census Bureau reported a decline in poverty among almost all the groups at highest risk: black adults, households headed by women and the elderly. For the first two groups, the cause for the decline is almost certainly higher employment. Poverty among the elderly has diminished because Social Security benefits were adjusted to keep up with the cost of living.

Still, the jubilation should not be overdone. Even 1984's lowered rate is higher than the poverty rate was when Mr. Reagan first took office. It's the third-highest poverty rate since 1966 — exceeded only by rates of 15.3 percent in 1983 and 15 percent in 1982. The Census Bureau's report also revealed a widening gap in income levels between the poorest and the richest Americans — another troubling trend.

Moreover, although the total number of poor people declined last year by 1.8 million, a staggering 33.7 million people were poor. Nearly one-fourth of children under 6 still live in households whose income is below the poverty income level of $10,609 per family of four. Among black children, the poverty rate actually rose to 51.1 percent.

Such statistics are no doubt depressing to a nation hungry for good news about poverty, but the other America must not be ignored.

Mr. Reagan deserves his share of credit for an economy that's far stronger today than it was in the waning days of the Carter presidency. What's perplexing, however, is that the poverty rate has not declined even further. After all, 1984 was a boom year.

In the richest nation on Earth, 14.4 percent of the population is poor — and that's much more than it should be.

Harvard Study Calls Hunger 'Epidemic' in U.S.

A private panel of 22 doctors and public health officials Feb. 26, 1985 charged that hunger had reached "epidemic proportions" in the U.S. It found that more than 20 million Americans went hungry at least two days a month, and that the problem was "getting worse, not better" because of cuts in federal programs. The charges were contained in a report by the Physician Task Force on Hunger in America, sponsored by the Harvard School of Public Health. Researchers for the year-long study said they had traveled back roads, opened refrigerators and searched out "the human face of hunger." They said their statistics had come from the Census Bureau and the U.S. Department of Agriculture.

The study's findings differed markedly from those published in January 1984 by a special presidential advisory committee. That panel had found that "undernutrition" was not "a major health problem in the U.S."

Among the findings of the study:

■ From 1982 to 1985, $12.2 billion was cut from federal food stamp and child nutrition programs. "The recent and swift return of hunger to America can be traced in substantial measure to clear and conscious policies of the federal government," the study said.

■ Second Harvest, and organization of food banks, had noted a 700% increase in food distribution since 1980.

■ Clinics in poor regions of the nation had reported cases of kwashiorkor and marasmus, two "Third World diseases of advanced malnutrition," along with vitamin deficiencies, diabetes, "stunting," "wasting" and other ailments related to hunger.

The task force's chairman, J. Larry Brown of the Harvard School of Public Health, said an increase of $5 billion to $7 billion in new food aid would largely solve the problem.

A report by the private panel issued Jan. 14, 1986 said that in 1984 the federal food stamp program had served just 55% of those eligible. In 1980, that figure had been 65%, the report said.

"Not only is hunger increasing as a problem, but federal food programs designed to feed the hungry have been weakened," the report charged.

WORCESTER TELEGRAM.

Worcester, MA, January 20, 1986

Harvard University doesn't have a homeless problem — it has a classic public relations problem.

Students were loudly indignant because Harvard put up some barriers to prevent street people from hovering over heat grates next to a dormitory. The grates over the grates were a reaction to complaints of voyeurism and other intimidation from the wanderers.

Harvard higher-ups are now being battered from pillar to post for denying the warm spots to the street people in the coldest week of the year.

But as is the case with many issues surrounding people who come under that big catchall term "the homeless," there is another side to the story.

Cambridge, like Worcester, Springfield and Boston, has places where street people can get warmth, and maybe a bed if they show up early. They can at least get inside the door to a shelter and be much more comfortable than they would if they spent the night over a steam grate.

For reasons best left to psychiatrists and social workers, some street people avoid shelters or institutions. If there is danger to them and they don't seek help and it appears they can't make a choice, then they should be carted away by the police and cared for in a proper place.

For what they did, some Harvard administrators look colder than the statue of old John Harvard on his chair in the Yard, but maybe what they did was get some people off steam grates and headed toward shelters where they belong.

FORT WORTH STAR-TELEGRAM

Fort Worth, TX, January 30, 1986

Now the whole world knows what we suspected all along: That much-ballyhooed survey of the nation's "hungriest counties," which included 29 counties in Texas, was not as accurate as it was cracked up to be.

Surely you remember the survey. It was conducted by the Harvard University School of Public Health and the Physicians Task Force on Hunger in America and pinpointed 150 counties the survey takers alleged to be the worst "hunger counties" in America. It was released among much fanfare a couple of weeks ago.

The survey listed Brazos County — home of Bryan, College Station and Texas A&M, among other things — as the hungriest county in Texas and the 46th hungriest in the nation, which stirred up a lot of criticism from Brazos County officials, who knew better.

The researchers took Census Bureau data and identified counties in which 20 percent of the population falls below the federal poverty level. Then, from Department of Agriculture statistics, they identified the counties on the list in which fewer than one-third of the eligible residents actually receive food stamps. From that study, they compiled their list of "most hungry counties."

After it was made public, we said in an editorial that the study "suffers from a lack of common sense and is more concerned with statistics and politics than it is with hunger." Most of the Texas counties listed, for example, are sparsely populated rural counties, where people are much less likely to rely on food stamps than are their counterparts in urban areas. Surprisingly, none of the counties was in far South Texas, where hunger is more prevalent than it is in other areas of the state.

Well, the researchers themselves now admit that "flawed statistics" led them to erroneously conclude that Brazos County is the state's hungriest. The study did not adjust the data to allow for Brazos County's sizable college student population, most of whom fall below the federal poverty level because they go to school instead of work.

Three other Texas counties on the list have sizable college populations — Walker County, home of Sam Houston State; Hays County, site of Southwest Texas State, and Brewster County, home of Sul Ross State. Their college student population wasn't considered, either.

What it all means, of course, is that the survey was basically meaningless, which a number of us said at the time it was released. The real shame, of course, is that hunger *does* exist in this country and flawed surveys such as this one do those who suffer from it more harm than good.

FORT WORTH STAR-TELEGRAM

Fort Worth, TX, January 16, 1986

It is undoubtedly true that there are too many hungry people in Texas and in the nation as a whole.

No sensible person can quibble with that.

And the situation might be helped if the underfed were better identified, because part of the problem is getting help to those who need it most.

What does *not* help is the study released this week by the Harvard University School of Public Health and the Physicians Task Force on Hunger in America.

The study suffers from a lack of common sense and is more concerned with statistics and politics than it is with hunger.

Harvard researchers took Census Bureau data and identified U.S. counties in which 20 percent of the population falls below the federal poverty line (currently $10,609 for a family of four). Then, from Department of Agriculture statistics, they identified the counties on that list in which fewer than one-third of the eligible residents actually receive food stamps. Then they made their list of the 150 "worst" counties.

In other words, the study (as does the task force) assumes that food stamps, not a family's ability or determination to feed itself, are the only remedy for hunger, having first assumed that no family can eat on $10,609 a year — which is more true in some places than in other places. It is more true, for instance, in urban areas than in rural areas.

One result of this misguided faith in statistics is that the 29 Texas counties listed among the 150 worst "hunger counties" in the nation are in some cases unlikely candidates for such an honor.

With the exception of Brazos County (Bryan-College Station), these Texas counties are all basically rural and generally sparsely populated.

So are the other U.S. counties that top the list —

most of them are small enough in population that researchers could have interviewed every resident. Eureka County, Nev., first on the list of "hunger counties," has fewer than 1,200 residents. Petroleum County, Mont., No. 2 on the list, has fewer than 700.

Notably missing from the Harvard list are the poorest and probably hungriest counties in Texas (most of them concentrated in South Texas and the Rio Grande Valley), the urban counties in Texas (recent studies have indicated an embarrassing number of poor and hungry residents in Tarrant County and have spurred efforts to improve delivery of services to them) and *any* counties at all in 26 states, including the entire Northeast.

The focus, going back to the study's basic assumptions, is on the issuance of food stamps, not the number of hungry people. It makes sense that Bronx County, N.Y., (pop. 1.5 million) has a lot more hungry residents than does Mason County, Texas, (pop. 4,000), whatever the national poverty level or the food stamp quotient.

In short, their own findings should have set off alarm bells and raised some serious questions for the researchers.

Last year, the Physicians Task Force performed a service (and differed greatly from a Reagan administration report) when it estimated that 20 million Americans are underfed. In that case, task force researchers went beyond statistics to actually, in their words, "come face to face with hunger" by traveling the nation talking to citizens and surveying clinics and food banks. That report drew the nation's attention to the problem of hunger and blamed it — with some justification — on government policies.

This week's follow-up study, statistically impressive but unrealistic in its reasoning, serves little purpose other than to confuse the issue and gain publicity for the group doing the studying.

THE INDIANAPOLIS STAR

Indianapolis, IN, January 24, 1986

From his desk at Harvard University, a professor of hunger apparently didn't realize that Americans don't have to live by food stamps alone.

Prof. Larry Brown, who heads a task force on hunger, has taken some criticism for his assumption that Americans are starving all over the country and therefore need lots more food stamps.

His Physicians Task Force on Hunger in America criticized the food stamp program for not helping enough people, using some dubious methods of research and statistics to come to its conclusions.

"It couldn't be considered a scientific report," noted Robert Leard, administrator of the U.S. Agriculture Department's Food and Nutrition Service.

The task force report identified 150 "hunger counties," where fewer than one-third of the eligible residents actually receive food stamps.

Researchers picked the 150 counties by first finding 716 counties where 20 percent of the residents live below the poverty line.

Then they selected those counties where at least 33 percent of those who are eligible don't actually get food stamps.

What the study failed to consider is the fact that other agencies also are available to people in need. Rescue missions are scattered all over the United States, providing various kinds of help for poor people.

Churches throughout the country have various kinds of food programs, including low-cost or free meals.

Some states have township trustees or other local officials who help out people on a short-term basis.

Investigators for the task force may discover this other side of the story when they visit Oklahoma, Texas, Georgia, Florida, Arkansas, Missouri, South Dakota and Idaho next month for some on-the-spot research.

Until then Missouri Social Services Director Joseph O'Hara has summed up the results quite well: "The findings from the study are meaningless."

Richmond Times-Dispatch

Richmond, VA, January 19, 1986

Yet another of those hunger-in-America reports is in the media spotlight, its PR campaign operating in high gear in the quest for headlines. And just as with previous reports that sought to identify "hunger counties" in America, officials in areas targeted by this latest report say they are mystified as to why their counties were chosen. The real mystery, however, is how the report's pseudo-scientific findings could be taken seriously.

Released by the Harvard University School of Health and the Physicians Task Force on Hunger in America, the report listed 150 "hunger counties," including Charles City and Mecklenburg counties in Virginia. To compile such an alarming list, the group used a remarkably simple methodology: If only a small percentage of those eligible for food stamps in a particular county actually took them, then the area was considered "hungry." Thus Charles City was 49th on the list because only 13.7 percent of those eligible for food stamps took them. Mecklenburg ranked 100th because just 25 percent of those eligible used them. A spokesman for the group added that it was disturbing to see the nationwide figure fall from 65 percent to 55 percent in the last 10 years.

We ourselves are more disturbed about the not-so-hidden presumption of this report: Hunger isn't necessarily being hungry. It's being low-income without taking government handouts. The group evidently reasons that the poor are incapable of feeding themselves: Only if they do it at taxpayer expense can they get enough to eat.

Despite the best efforts of groups like this to recruit people for the government dole, many of the poor resist. Local officials had a variety of explanations for their reluctance: Some take pride in refusing aid, some value their independence, some grow and can their own food, some rely on family or friends. Many are perfectly capable of providing for themselves. "In Charles City, a family of four can live pretty well on $10,000," said one official, because of the low cost of living there.

That seems reasonable enough, but a spokesman for the physicians' group said it would continue to study the problem. We don't like the sound of that. Next thing you know the group will report a high incidence of insanity in "hunger counties" — as manifested by poor inhabitants' refusal to take handouts.

"YOU CAN'T FIGHT ATTACK HELICOPTERS PILOTED BY CUBANS WITH BAND-AIDS AND MOSQUITO NETS." – PRES. REAGAN

ST. LOUIS POST-DISPATCH

St. Louis, MO,
January 16, 1986

A national study that says hunger persists in 17 Missouri counties is being challenged as misleading by state and local officials, most of whom doubt that the problem is as pervasive as the study indicates. The study, done by Harvard University's School of Public Health and the Physicians Task Force on Hunger in America, says the Missouri counties are among 150 "hunger counties" in the nation.

State officials say the study's conclusions are based on questionable research methods. The researchers used census data to identify 716 counties in the nation where at least 20 percent of the population fell below the federal poverty guideline. They then used federal statistics to determine the number of people who were potentially eligible for food stamps and the number who actually got the stamps. The difference between those two numbers was used to determine the extent of hunger.

State officials say the researchers failed to take into account factors that preclude some families from participating in the food stamp program. For example, some farmers may be dirt poor, but they may be denied food stamps because their assets — including land and farm machinery — push them above the federal poverty level.

But this and other arguments against the study's findings do not answer the real question of whether hunger is in fact a pervasive problem in some Missouri counties. State officials need to find out conclusively; and if it is, they and local officials ought to devote their attention to finding ways to feed the underfed.

FORT WORTH STAR-TELEGRAM

Fort Worth, TX, January 16, 1986

The Harvard University School of Public Health and the Physicians Task Force on Hunger in America have committed the cardinal error of leaping before looking in releasing their latest findings on national undernourishment.

The hunger finders used census data to identify 716 counties in the United States in which 20 percent of the population survives on incomes below the federal poverty level of $10,609 per year for a family four. Then they extracted the numbers of families eligible for food stamps and compared that figure to the numbers actually getting them.

Eureka! They found 150 counties with very low participation in the food stamp program and labeled them "hunger counties." They found 29 so-called hunger counties in Texas, the largest number in the nation.

That finding would be a serious blemish on the image of the Lone Star State if the hunger county concept had much validity. Fortunately it doesn't. It amounts to another instance of putting garbage into a computer and extracting rubbish.

Granted, there is considerable hunger in Texas. Too much for comfort. The Texas Legislature took note of that and took some significant steps during its last session to address the problem. More needs to be done.

But reports such as the one that propelled the "hunger counties" statistical monstrosity into the public domain could undermine efforts to address the hunger problem in Texas and around the nation seriously. Such reports undermine the credibility of valid information needed to focus attention on the hunger problem.

The number of persons receiving food stamps cannot be considered a valid yardstick for finding where the problem of hunger is most prevalent. There are, after all, wide variances in the cost of living and lifestyles and demographics throughout the nation. And there are a number of other factors that skew statistical comparisons.

A spokesman for the researchers says the findings will be used later this year as a guide to field investigation into why food stamp participation varies so widely.

It would have been far better for the researchers to have completed that investigation before prematurely releasing any findings on "hunger counties." It is quite possible they will find less real hunger in many of those counties than they will in those counties where the majority of those eligible for food stamps get them.

The Evening Gazette

Worcester, MA, January 18, 1986

The stories of the homeless in our streets ebb and flow with the thermometer. When the mercury drops and most folks scurry home to well-insulated houses, someone takes note of the homeless and there's a headline.

This past week it's been a story of how homeless men, trying to hover over heat-expelling grates near a Harvard University dormitory, were harassing students. The dean had the grates fenced off. Whereupon another group of students protested at cutting the helpless off from this source of comfort and threatened to take them into the dormitory.

When the temperatures climb again, the plight of these homeless persons fades from consciousness as they return to their hidden haunts.

There has been considerable effort to find and maintain shelters for those who seem to have no place to go. Some do find a warm bed and a warm meal. But the public in general fails to understand that even the homeless, however disoriented they may be, have the right to spurn shelter. For any and all reasons, some quite far-fetched, those who prefer the cold streets have a right to their preference.

In Cambridge, it may have been that the nearby shelter would have confiscated someone's wine bottle or pint of cheap whiskey for the individual's own protection. Or the shelter may have insisted that those who enter take showers and be examined for respiratory infections. Or it may be as simple as fear of numbers of people that send these individuals to an alley or back yard where heat exhaust keeps them from freezing to death.

The problems of the homeless/the deinstitutionalized/the untreated/the addicted/the mentally impaired have always been with us.

More than 150 years ago when the first state asylum was opened in Worcester, those who operated it faced the same issues — who would be treated, how soon could they be discharged, should alcoholics and drug addicts be included with the obviously mentally ill, who would pay the costs for the people who could not help themselves.

The problems continued without real solutions during and after the Civil War, when veterans returned with problems. During the early years of this century, drug addiction and alcoholism cases were considered nuisances and removed from poor farms and hospitals, which solved neither the problems of drunks/addicts, the indigent or the mentally ill.

In the 1930s and later, the state hospitals were loaded with thousands of patients who got little treatment; meanwhile, the skid rows of our cities were populated with the homeless and wandering.

Then came the "enlightenment" of deinstitutionalization — and the skid rows spread as the homeless and helpless increased. The gulf between those who can't cope and become homeless and the rest of the population is widening. In an affluent society, the bag lady rummaging through a garbage can, the ragged man trying to keep from freezing, all unfortunates are more evident.

The problem of the homeless has been with us for a long time and it's not going to go away easily. But we have to keep trying to find that balance between individual freedom and individual survival.

Roanoke Times & World-News

Roanoke, VA, January 19, 1986

GIVE A big, fat 'F' to the Physicians Task Force at the Harvard School of Public Health for its recent report naming America's 150 worst "hunger counties," including two in Virginia.

The presumed aim of the task force — to see whether and where government anti-hunger programs are failing to work — is admirable. But the report's research is shoddy; its conclusions unsupported by the evidence it cites. The study is next to worthless.

By their own admission, none of the researchers actually visited any of the counties on the list. Instead, they massaged a few government statistics, and in a way that raises more questions than it answers.

First, the task force identified all the counties in the United States where more than 20 percent of the residents earn under the federally defined poverty level, which is currently a household income of $10,609 for a family of four. Next, the task force identified the counties in that high-poverty group where fewer than one-third of the eligible residents receive food stamps. The computer spewed out a list of 150 such counties; they are — voila! — the nation's "hunger counties."

Or are they?

The concept of a federal poverty level, established in the 1960s, was an important breakthrough in helping to understand the nature and extent of the problem. Define poverty simply as being at the bottom of the economic heap and the poor will be with us always; inevitably, some households will have lower incomes than others. But define poverty as lack of enough income to maintain a minimally decent standard of living, and it becomes possible to speak of eliminating povery and to measure progress toward that goal.

But despite its virtues, the yardstick is at best a rough measure. It should be used with more caution than the task force displayed. For example, the fact that $10,609 goes a lot farther in Southside Virginia than in the South Bronx may help explain the inclusion of Mecklenburg and Charles City counties on the task-force list, yet not a single county in New York. Without taking variations in the cost of living into account, how can such county-by-county comparisons be made with anything approaching precision?

Moreover, many of the "hunger counties" are small, which can skew statistical analyses, and many are in the nation's Farm Belt, a discovery about which the researchers professed surprise.

Yet how surprising should that be? After all, it is too much food production — not too little — that lies at the heart of the economic woes of the agricultural Midwest. Perhaps poor people in the Farm Belt, including bankrupt farmers and workers laid off from farm-related industries, don't use food stamps because it's not food they need. Perhaps not, of course: The point is that the possibility was simply not checked out.

Other potential sources of error have been raised by state and local officials defending themselves in the wake of the report. The population of Madison County, Idaho, purportedly the fifth hungriest in the country, turns out to be 93 percent. Mormons tend to turn to the church rather than to the government for assistance in hard times. In Brazos County, Texas, rated the worst in that state, about a third of the population consists of Texas A&M students, many of whom may be poor officially but not in fact. A bit of leg-work might have discovered whether such places indeed possess special characteristics that render the official poverty and food-stamp figures misleading.

Legwork is needed for more than just potentially special cases. The task force's methodology rests on this key assumption: Low participation in food-stamp program by the poor people of a given county is evidence of widespread hunger in that county. Perhaps that's true, but it is not self-evidently true. There's no less logic in assuming the exact opposite: that counties where poor people tend not to get food stamps are places where poor people tend not to apply for food stamps because they see no need for them. Only on-the-spot field work can determine which assumption is correct, and to what degree.

Though close to useless, the task force's work is not entirely so. Juxtaposing the rates of poverty and food-stamp use in each county in America is an interesting idea that eventually could lead to important findings. But the immediate results of such a juxtaposition are no more than clues pointing to areas for further examination. In a rigorous study, such a juxtaposition would be a rough first step, and not the final step, in determining whether and where hunger is a serious problem.

By leaping to conclusions so far in advance of its evidence, the task force has brought no credit to itself — and has unwittingly provided ammunition for those who wish to dismiss out of hand the notion that hunger still exists in America.

Reagan Stirs Controversy by Saying Hungry are Uninformed

President Reagan May 21, 1986 remarked that lack of information, and not government policy, was to blame for any hunger in America. Poverty activists and experts on hunger assailed his remarks.

"I don't believe that there is anyone going hungry in America simply by reason of denial or lack of ability to feed them," Reagan said. "It is by people not knowing where or how to get help." The president made the remark in a White House question-and-answer session with high school students.

A Harvard University report issued that day blamed Reagan administration polices for spreading hunger. The report charged that the administration used federal rules to build "barriers which knock people off the rolls" of federal nutrition assistance programs. According to the report, the number of America's poor had grown by four million from 1980 to 1985, but the number of food stamp recipients had stayed steady at 19.8 million. It estimated that 15 million people in need did not receive federal nutrition assistance.

The study had been prepared by the Physican Task Force on Hunger in America, a panel of 22 medical experts and religious leaders affiliated with the Harvard School of Public Health.

Chicago Defender

Chicago, IL, May 29, 1986

President Reagan's statements on the problems of America's hungry have raised a furor of pro and con response. One of the key things he said was, "I don't think there is anyone going hungry in America simply by reason of denial, or lack of ability to feed them. It is by people not knowing where or how to get this help."

That's an interesting thought. But for all of its interest, it doesn't really help to put one crumb of bread in the mouths of America's hungry.

This is more unfortunate since America doesn't have a food-producing problem. In many ways, we have been the breadbasket of the world. In fact, we yield so much produce that our government sometimes pays farmers *not* to plant their crops since the hugh surpluses would hurt the national market.

This may help farmers but it doesn't do much to help the hungry. In fact, one of the real purposes of government, other than to rule people, is to provide for their welfare. This latter responsibility is neither new to the world nor unique to our country.

Even in biblical times, governments protected their people from attack and gathered grain in general storage areas to be used for feeding them during periods of sickness, drought, flooding or any other life-threatening castastrophes.

Classical times permitted individuals to assess a person's wealth by the fashions worn. Aristocrats, slaves, businessmen, warriors, etc., dressed differently from each other. In fact, sometimes, slaves were noticably marked for easy recognition.

We have no such markings to distinguish the rich from the poor in America. And our hungry people are not as easy to identify as in olden days because the United States, in a large part, is a nation of distant neighbors. Many of us don't even know the members of the family who live in our same apartment building, condo complex or block. As a result, we don't even begin to know their economic levels or whether they are having trouble putting food on their tables. This problem is made worse when one considers America's homeless people, many of whom ravage garbage cans and dumpsters for food.

So even if one supposes that the president was correct in his statement, we nonetheless must admit that his actions are some of the biggest reasons why the food distribution information has been so clouded.

As Robert Greenstein, director of the Center on the Budget and Policy Priorities said about Reagan, "...it was his administration that abolished the food stamp outreach program, in 1981." The plan provided information to people on how to get food aid.

Therefore, even if the president was not talking solely about that program, his administration's cuts in nutrition programs is symptomatic of a general, combative attitude against such government subsidies and their recipients.

The Washington Post

Washington, DC, May 25, 1986

PRESIDENT REAGAN has made another of those remarks about the poor that put the let's-have-a-flap industry into high gear all over town. At a question-and-answer session for high school students, Mr. Reagan said "our programs of social aid to our own people are such that where there is hunger . . . you have to determine that that is probably because of a lack of knowledge on the part of the people as to what things are available. Not only is the government doing much in that line, but there has been about a three times increase in private charity. . . . And between those two sectors, I don't believe that there is anyone that is going hungry in America simply by reason of denial or lack of ability to feed them. It is by people not knowing where or how to get this help."

The outcry was swift and predictably overstated. If the president distorted the full nature of the hunger problem, the critics distorted the distortion. "The president announced today that hunger in this country is caused by ignorance," Sen. Edward Kennedy said, and suggested that administration policies were the greater cause. Try it this way:

1. The president is right in saying that part of the hunger or poverty problem is that people don't know "what things are available." The purest of federal welfare programs and largest other than Medicaid is food stamps. For other forms of aid you have to be old or blind or disabled or have dependent children; for stamps all you have to be is poor. Only about two-thirds of the people eligible for stamps are in the program. Millions don't sign up—particularly elderly eligibles and members of the working poor. A survey some years ago showed that ignorance of the rules was a major cause. (And yes, as part of the budget cuts of 1981 the administration killed an "outreach" program meant to help dispel that ignorance.)

2. The president is wrong in suggesting that ignorance of the rules is all there is to it. Far from it. More than three years into the recovery from the last recession, the unemployment rate is still over 7 percent, the percentage of the unemployed who lack unemployment insurance is at a record high, a seventh of the population lives below the poverty line, the poverty rate for children is 21 percent, the share of all income going to the richest fifth is up, the share to the poorest fifth is down. A lot of people are hurting. The president glides by that.

3. Although this administration's budget cuts and economic policies have exacerbated these problems, the causes are deeper and predate the Reagan years. For instance, basic welfare benefits through Aid to Families with Dependent Children have lost a third of their purchasing power to inflation over the past 15 years (even as female-headed families have come to account for a greater share of the poor). In fact, it was only last year that the value of these benefits finally ticked up again—because inflation declined. Increasingly, economists who deal in such matters have also begun to worry about a fundamental wage erosion in the lower and middle reaches of the economy, the result in part of foreign competition but, they suspect, of much else as well. There are other such broad trends—the extent to which housing costs have outstripped incomes in recent years, for example—against which existing government programs are only palliatives. President Reagan isn't thinking about these issues. Neither are most other current political figures, in either party. That is what the debate should be about, and not the president's unfortunate off-the-cuff remark.

THE ATLANTA CONSTITUTION
Atlanta, GA, May 27, 1986

Secure in his conviction that he presides over a healthy, well-fed country, Ronald Reagan told a group of schoolchildren Wednesday that if Americans are going hungry, it must be because they don't know where the soup lines are. Hunger *still* does not concern the president, who cited a three-fold increase in private philanthropy as proof of the nation's abundance.

Reagan is nothing if not consistent, but things have changed since he began whittling away in '81 at social-service programs, such as food stamps, which he charged were being wasted on people who were neither hungry nor "truly" poor.

The charges were never borne out by anything but echoes from yes-men such as Edwin Meese, who in Reagan's first term caused a furor by declaring there was no "authoritative" evidence that children were going hungry. So the administration tightened food stamp eligibility requirements, scrapped outreach and information programs and dropped hundreds of thousands of people, improperly, from the welfare and disability rolls.

Unsurprisingly, the ranks of the poor and hungry grew right along with the implementation of those see-no-evil policies, as the latest findings make clear. From the House Select Committee on Hunger: One in seven people is still living below the poverty line. And a *minimum of 20 million* Americans go hungry at least two days a month, according to the Harvard-based Physicians Task Force on Hunger in America, which faulted the administration for erecting "barriers" to broad participation in help programs.

"As hunger and poverty have increased, an adequate response to it has not," the group said, particularly with regard to food stamps. Only 59 percent of the people living in poverty got them last year, compared with 68 percent in 1980 — a decline attributable not just to dollar cutbacks, but to a "lack of coordinated government efforts" to inform people about them, according to the Children's Defense Fund, an advocacy group.

Reagan is right to observe that many Americans don't know where to go for help, but he is a bit late with the observation. It was he who eliminated the program to inform them about food-stamp benefits. Perhaps if he could begin to grasp that he is not an innocent bystander to the spectacle of hunger and malnutrition and their cruel erosion of health, but a key player, he would stop pooh-poohing such programs and move instead to restore them.

The Pittsburgh PRESS
Pittsburg, PA, May 24, 1986

President Reagan, who tends to downplay the problems of the poor and the homeless, came up this week with another understated view about hunger in this country.

The president said no one was going hungry because of a lack of free or low-cost food or outside help. It was simply a "lack of knowledge ... as to what things are available."

To some extent, the president could be right. But as critics were quick to point out, his administration in 1981 abolished a five-year, $21.4 million program aimed at informing the poor of government aid available to them.

And if there are difficulties for the hungry in learning about food and other help, does not much of the blame belong with the government bureaucracies which deal with and deliver that assistance?

In any event, Mr. Reagan's remarks in a question and answer session with a group of high school students in the White House suggest, at the least, an insensitivity to the problems of the most troubled among us.

And they follow a pattern of dubious statements on the subject from the White House, as exemplified by Edwin Meese in 1983, when he was a presidential counselor. At that time, Mr. Meese referred to "allegations" of hunger as "purely political" and went on to say that some people in soup lines didn't belong there, that they were mooching a free meal.

The next year, Mr. Reagan came up with the observation that some people sleeping on outdoor heating vents were homeless by choice.

Again, there may have been grains of truth in what was said. The turning out of mental patients from institutions in recent years has provided a new subgroup of rootless and disabled persons — and added to the problems of hunger and homelessness. No doubt some abuses in food distribution have occurred.

Yet the hungry and the poverty-stricken remain more than a figment of imagination in the minds of Mr. Reagan's critics. They are, in fact, a sizable presence despite the economic recovery this country has been enjoying.

An estimated 33.5 million Americans live in poverty now, up by more than 4 million since 1980. According to a study released this week by the Physicians Task Force on Hunger in America, 10 million to 15 million of these are eligible for food stamps but are not receiving them — perhaps half because, as Mr. Reagan observed, they don't know how to go about applying for them.

If so, the burden of finding out should not be put entirely on their shoulders.

The poor and the hungry didn't get that way because they are smart and resourceful, as Mr. Reagan expects them to be. They need not only information about possible assistance but direction and support in obtaining it.

That can come from sympathetic elected officials, government and private agencies. They shouldn't be standing on the sidelines, waiting for the poor and needy to overcome their "lack of knowledge" all by themselves.

THE TENNESSEAN
Nashville, TN, May 28, 1986

ALTHOUGH one of President Ronald Reagan's more endearing qualities is his cheerful outlook, the President should realize the tremendous difference between optimism and naivete.

Take his recent explanation of America's hungry and homeless problem. Mr. Reagan was asked last week why he was not going to participate in the historic Hands Across America fund-raising event. After expressing doubt that this nation truly has homeless and hungry people, he went on to say that the problem of hunger in America was due to "people not knowing where and how to get this help."

The President's initial refusal to participate in Hands Across America was somewhat curious. The event seemed to have been scripted for Mr. Reagan. It was emotional. It was patriotic. It had hundreds of celebrity participants. It was bound to receive tremendous media coverage on an otherwise uneventful, long, holiday weekend.

Moreover, Hands Across America precisely subscribed to Mr. Reagan's notion of how America should help its people who are hungry, homeless, or destitute. It was a privately initiated fund-raising event that called on individuals, not government, to give to help others. It was pure charity.

At the last minute, Mr. Reagan changed his mind, and last Sunday the President and some members of his family joined with almost five million other Americans in forming a human chain across the nation to aid America's needy people.

The First Family's participation in the event was welcomed. Yet it is hard to be enthusiastic about Mr. Reagan's show of humanity while he clings to the embarrassing fantasy that there really is a chicken in every American pot.

And that flawed theory becomes a real problem because the President is obviously basing crucial decisions on it. In his last budget battle with Capitol Hill, the President requested less social service money and more arms money than either of the budget proposals of the House or the Senate.

The President should take off his rose-colored glasses, and look past the White House lawn at the thousands of Americans who have no food, no beds, no roofs, and no hope. To deny their existence is not optimistic — it is naive. And coming from the leader of a nation, it is frighteningly dangerous.

The Philadelphia Inquirer

Philadelphia, PA, May 27, 1986

An America that enthusiastically embraced Ronald Reagan's guns-not-butter agenda for a second term joined hands the other day to raise money to replace some of the funding the administration has cut from programs for the hungry and homeless.

Smiling, front and center, on the north portico of the White House, was Mr. Reagan himself, not one to be left behind. Does anyone remember that days before — fielding questions from high school students — the President said it was simply "lack of knowledge" of food programs that was causing this so-called hunger problem?

A Harvard public health professor, J. Larry Brown, noted after the talk: "For the President to lead the way in eliminating the federal outreach funding [for food stamp benefits] and then turn around and say people don't know about the program, is correct but a bit puzzling."

Does anyone remember that in 1983, it was his counselor Edwin Meese 3d, now attorney general, who contended it was, perhaps, too much knowledge that was filling up soup kitchens where "the food is free"?

The East Harlem Interfaith Welfare Committee recently reported that family food emergencies were on the upswing: "They go to soup kitchens, to their family; they are borrowing and begging and stealing."

Does anyone remember that while the House and Senate have been laboring to restore funds for human services, the White House has been fighting tooth-and-nail to boost the military budget?

President Reagan: "We have found that when bureaucracy gets going with a program of this kind, there comes into being a looseness, and you find that people who should be responsible for themselves are benefiting at the cost of their fellow citizens, the taxpayers."

He was talking — again to the students — not about Pentagon waste and fraud, but about the freeloaders he loves to hate, always with a smile, people who are poor and, yes, hungry and homeless.

They are not government's — not society's — problem, in Mr. Reagan's world. And in a strange way, the Hands Across America response buys into that philosophy; a painless, one-shot, extra-governmental expression of concern and good will that papers over — and thus makes more palatable — the Reagan guns-not-butter agenda.

Charity is booming, the President observes, as federal social spending diminishes. And so it is. Social Darwinism wears a smile button these days. And the war on poverty has taken on a perverse new meaning.

Los Angeles, CA, May 23, 1986

The only reason some Americans are going hungry, President Reagan said this week, is that they aren't aware of the help available to them. That's not the case. And to the extent that people *are* going hungry because of a lack of knowledge about benefits, Reagan administration policies have played  an important role in keeping them uninformed.

More importantly, hunger is a consequence of poverty. And between 1980 and 1984, nearly 3 million Americans slipped below the poverty line. Logically, the food stamp rolls should have grown during that period, but just the opposite happened. Because of new procedures ordered by the Reagan administration, 3 million fewer people received food stamps in 1984 as in 1980.

The administration claims those who were cut from the rolls didn't deserve benefits anyway. But the reduction in the number of food stamp recipients was the result of a range of bureaucratic impediments that had a lot more to do with cutting federal spending than cutting fraud.

For instance, an administration explicitly committed to reducing red tape sharply increased the amount of paperwork required to qualify for food stamps. Moreover, the Reagan administration in 1981 eliminated the Food Stamps Outreach program, established to inform the poor and hungry about food stamp benefits.

The result is that in this land of plenty, there are more hungry people now than there have been since the 1960s. Americans, of course, don't suffer Ethiopian-style starvation. But many struggle with inadequate diets that hinder their physical and intellectual capacities. According to a 1985 study by Harvard's Physicians Task Force on Hunger, 20 million Americans go hungry for at least several days every month.

The president may like to think that's just because the poor don't know what's available. The sad truth is, there's just not enough help for those who need it.

St. Petersburg Times

St. Petersburg, FL, May 26, 1986

A Harvard University study of hunger in America charges that the Reagan administration's red tape is keeping as many as 15-million poor people from receiving food stamps.

President Reagan can't quite believe it — but if some people are hungry, he says, it's because they are ignorant about federal benefits. In tone and words, Mr. Reagan's hard-line policies against the poor have changed little in five years.

Based on a five-month national survey, the Harvard researchers accused the Reagan administration of using food stamp regulations to build "barriers which knock people off the rolls." The report by the Physician Task Force on Hunger in America said that complex regulations and frequent rule changes have kept many families from obtaining help and discouraged others from even applying.

"Presently, the federal food stamp program constitutes a litany of hopelessness for many of the most economically vulnerable families in America," the study said.

The panel of 22 medical experts and religious leaders affiliated with the Harvard School of Public Health called for Congress to change the system and feed the hungry.

Congress passed the Family Nutrition Assistance Program in 1964 to give the poor a way to buy a minimally adequate diet. In 1967, a Harvard physicians' task force found widespread hunger in urban slums and rural areas. In 1974, Congress required every state to carry out the program.

The food stamp and child nutrition programs worked human miracles. In 1979, the physicians took another tour and found that severe hunger in America had been virtually eliminated.

The Reagan administration soon reversed that great humane victory. While the nation spends $31-million an hour on weapons for Mr. Reagan's massive military buildup, more than $12.2-billion has been slashed from food stamps and child nutrition programs.

One of the first cuts was a program that provided food stamp offices with specialists who helped attract eligible families to the programs. Although some of the hungry may not know how or where to get food stamps, millions are turned away by red tape, intimidation and embarrassment.

That is no accident. It is the clear and conscious policy of a mean-spirited administration. It is not only callous, but a false economy. Nutrition programs for the poor are by far the best health dollars the government spends. Infants and children served by emergency food programs are much less likely to need costly, taxpayer-financed hospital care.

But the worst part is that millions are hungry in this bountiful nation — and Mr. Reagan ignores their misery.

HUNGER?
WHAT
HUNGER?

AVTH
5/25/86, The Philadelphia Inquirer.
UNIVERSAL PRESS SYNDICATE.

SYRACUSE HERALD-JOURNAL

Syracuse, NY, May 23, 1986

President Reagan — aka the Great Communicator — had a really tough message for those people who go to bed hungry every night in American.

Basically, what the president told a group of high school students who tossed a question at him about why we give aid to other countries when there are hungry people in the United States, was that people who don't get enough to eat — and who are not intentionally dieting — are just plain dumb.

How do you like that for a double whammy? If you're hungry in the U.S., you're also stupid. The president told the students there's plenty of food in this bountiful nation, but the reason for hunger is "people not knowing where or how to get this help."

And that is the truth, sure enough. But it's not really what we'd call "the truth, the whole truth and nothing but the truth." It is the truth of convenience for President Reagan, who basically views domestic programs — like food stamps, school-lunch programs for poor children and aid to women who have too many kids, too little education and perhaps no husband, or to people who are old and having a hard time making ends meet on Social Security — as money that could be better spent on new weapons systems.

Some of those who disagree with the president's social policies agree with Mr. Reagan that ignorance is part of the hunger problem in the United States. But they add, the president's administration has gone out of its way to make it more difficult for the poor, the homeless, the have-nots of our nation to become educated to those agencies that can help them.

The Reagan adminstration succeeded in killing a federal outreach program that informed needy people on how to obtain food stamps. And it's helped reduce food stamp applicants, according to the Childrens Defense Fund, which studied the issue. In 1985, 59 of every 100 persons below the poverty level received food stamps, compared to 68 of every 100 in 1980. There are as many poor people, but fewer applicants because of eligibility restrictions and because the federal government no longer makes an effort to inform poor people what benefits are available.

So the president is being honest in his appraisal of hunger in America, but he fails to take enough credit for helping to make poverty what it is today.

Michael Meyers, executive director of the Research and Advocacy Center for Equality in New York City, speaking in Syracuse Wednesday, said the tendency today is to blame the poor for being poor. It is, Meyers said, the "in philosophy." Why not? The nation is merely following its leader.

And the leader says that if you're hungry, it's your fault because you're ignorant — and many Americans agree. It follows that if you're homeless, it's because you're too dumb to find a home; if you're out of work, illiterate, surrounded by urban crime, hooked on drugs or alcohol, it's because you're too stupid to help yourself.

"Ignorance" is an easy out for people like President Reagan — and his Central New York cheerleader, Rep. George Wortley, for that matter — who don't want to face up to or spend money on a myriad of social problems.

We hope the high school students President Reagan was trying to impress are smart enough to recognize half-truth reasoning. After all, if the president was right about ignorance and hungry people, we'd have to believe some of our elected officials often re-elected without right...

Rockford Register Star

Rockford, IL, May 28, 1986

If to err is human, President Ronald Reagan can be monumentally human and his fellow Americans are equally divine in their forgiveness. Witness the president's continued strength in popularity polls despite an amazing capacity for stuffing his feet in his mouth.

There he went again last week, just when several million Americans were queuing up to hold hands all the way across American to relieve hunger in the United States. He told high school students visiting the White House:

"I don't think there is anyone going hungry in America simply by reason of denial or lack of ability to feed them. Where there is hunger, you have to determine that that is probably because of a lack of knowledge on the part of the people as to what is available."

Some who oppose the administration's budget preference for guns over butter, might — with clear malice — choose to paraphrase the president's remark as, "There are no hungry people, just dumb people."

Whatever, after President Reagan had time to reflect, he and and Nancy decided they should do something about the hungry, and joined hand-holders on Sunday. The hand-holding line against hunger in the U.S. was thoughtfully rerouted through the White House gate.

There he goes again, winning the hearts of his fellow Americans.

Poverty Rate Dropped in '85 But Remains Higher than in '70s

The Census Bureau reported Aug. 26, 1986 that the U.S. poverty rate had declined in 1985 to 14%, from 14.4% in 1984. The decrease in 1985 was the second consecutive annual decline in the rate. However, the percentage of households with incomes below the poverty line remained significantly higher than at any point during the 1971-80 period, when it averaged 12.6%. For a family of four, poverty was defined in 1985 as an annual cash income of less than $10,989. In 1984, the poverty line for a family of four had been $10,609. For a family of three, the 1985 poverty line was $8,573. The number of people living below the poverty line was placed at 33.1 million in 1985, 600,000 fewer than in 1984. The Census Bureau said that it did not consider the decline statistically significant.

Analysts presented three scenerios to explain the persistence of high poverty rates in 1985 despite economic recovery. Isabel Sawhill, an economist for the Urban Institute, cited the Reagan administration's reduced spending on antipoverty programs. Sawhill said that if Congress restored funds that had been cut from social programs, the poverty rate would drop by one or two percentage points.

Robert Greenstein, director of the Center on Budget and Policy Priorities, a research and advocacy group, said that the income gains from economic recovery had been unevenly distributed. He pointed out that between 1980 and 1985, the annual income of the average family in the poorest 40% of the population had declined by more than $200 after adjusting for inflation. The annual income of a typical family in the richest 40% had increased by $2,915, he said.

Gordon Green, a Census Bureau official, attributed the persistence of high poverty rates to the increased role of noncash benefits, such as food stamps and housing assistance, in government aid. Noncash benefits were not counted as income in measuring the poverty rate.

The poverty rate among blacks declined in 1985 to 31.3% from 33.8% in 1984. The number of blacks living below the poverty line in 1985—8.9 million—was the lowest since 1980. Among whites, the poverty rate dropped to 11.4% in 1985 from 11.5% the previous year. The poverty rate for Hispanics rose to 29% from 28.4%. For people 65 and older, the poverty rate rose to 12.6% from 12.4% in 1984. For children under 18 living in families, the poverty rate dropped to 15.9% from 16.5% among whites and to 43.4% from 46.5% among blacks. Poverty among Hispanic children rose to 39.9% in 1985 from 39% a year earlier. The poverty rate for female-headed households in 1985 was 34%, a slight drop from 34.5% in 1984. Nearly half of the families living below the poverty line in 1985 were headed by women. Regionally, the poverty rate dropped most sharply in the Northeast, falling to 11.6% in 1985 from 13.2% the previous year. Poverty rates in other regions were largely unchanged.

THE ⚓ SUN

Baltimore, MD, August 29, 1986

A single, misleading expression can have devastating social consequences if it finds its way into policy-making. One such expression that may play this costly trick is the announcement by the U.S. Census Bureau that the poverty rate fell in 1985.

True, the number of poor people in American decreased. But it dropped less than one-half of one percent — to a still-bloated 14 percent of the population. In real terms, the decline represents only 600,000 people. Out of a total population of 237 million, the drop is insignificant.

The newest poverty figures mean that one out of every seven Americans is poor. While that represents some progress for the Reagan administration, remember that this administration has presided over the highest annual poverty levels since 1966 — two years after Lyndon Johnson declared war on poverty.

More distressing are the social realities behind the statistics. The majority of America's poor are non-whites. Twenty-nine percent of the Hispanic population lives below the poverty line; nearly one-third of blacks are poverty-stricken. By contrast, only 11 percent of the whites are poor.

Further, the Census Bureau study is riddled with evidence of the increasingly sharper contrasts between the haves and have-nots. It shows that while the annual income of a family in the poorest 40 percent of the population dropped by more than $230 last year, the annual income of a family in the top 40 percent skyrocketed by nearly $3,000. And despite a much-heralded 5-percent rise in median annual income among black families in 1985, they still lag more than $10,000 behind median family income nationally.

Most startling is that the poverty rate for 1985 remains precisely what it was in 1981, when recession officially hit America. After three years of economic recovery, it is clear that Reaganomics has had a vastly inequitable impact. The inescapable conclusion is that the exclusively pro-business bent of the Reagan administration and the reduction in spending on anti-poverty programs has taken a decisive social toll.

The smug "America is back" rhetoric that dominates the national dialogue ignores the fact that we seem to be building a class-ridden society of two Americas — and only one is back.

The Charlotte Observer

Charlotte, NC, September 2, 1986

Poverty in America declined sharply through the 1960s, leveled out in the 1970s, and then rose again in the early 1980s. Census Bureau figures released last week show that it is heading down again, declining in 1985 for the second straight year.

That is good news, but not much. In dropping to 14% in 1985, the poverty rate is only back to where it was in 1981 — and that was the highest since 1966, in the early years of the War on Poverty. In the South, which remains the nation's poorest region, the poverty rate is 16% — significantly above the national average, if not dramatically so.

Such numbers are deceptively bloodless. There are some 33 million poor people in America today, including almost 9 million blacks. Among blacks, the poverty rate continues to be discouragingly high, over 30%.

The poverty rate among all children under 18 is just over 20%. That means one American child in five is growing up poor. And because poverty is considerably higher among children than among the elderly, there is little hope that the mere passage of time will reduce the overall figure.

Such numbers are at best crude measures. Because the official figures measure only cash income — excluding such noncash benefits as food stamps and Medicaid — it is arguable that the poverty rate overstates the number of people in official poverty. But with the official poverty level for a family of four set at less than $11,000, the people just above it are hardly living in luxury.

It is also arguable that because the Census figures include cash assistance — such as welfare payments — dependency is more widespread than the official poverty rate would suggest. That is, the poverty rate understates the proportion of the population dependent on assistance for a minimal standard of living. If society's goal is to end dependency, not just ameliorate poverty, then the problem is worse than the poverty rate suggests.

Either way, what the numbers continue to show is that despite the considerable success in reducing poverty in the 1960s, little progress has been made in that effort since. In 1985, the United States had 33 million people living in poverty — roughly the same number of poor people it had two decades before. Whatever the arguments over how to change that, the numbers underscore a chilling and long-standing failure of American economic and social policy.

THE WALL STREET JOURNAL.

New York City, NY, August 28, 1986

Poverty statistics released by the Census Bureau Tuesday revealed that the percentage of American families classified as poor fell again in 1985, although nowhere near as dramatically as in 1984. The most heartening news was that the median income of black families rose 5% in real terms, nearly four times the gain of all families, although the median remains well below that for white families.

We hesitate to make too much of this because poverty statistics, while based on a survey of nearly 60,000 households by the Census Bureau, are in other ways about the most squishy of all federal numbers. The government arbitrarily says a family is "poor" if it has cash income below a certain level, which happened to be $10,989 for a family of four in 1985. The number is adjusted annually for inflation, but leads and lags can still create statistical anomalies depending on whether inflation is high or low.

Cash income makes no allowance for in-kind aid, such as food stamps or Medicaid, which are substantial additions to income for some poor families. Some Census Bureau researchers suspect that the "free answer" method of interviewing household heads, which relies on their memories and honesty, understates income. Then there are the constant changes in family makeup—such as the trend toward more single heads of household—which probably have more to do with whether or not families are poor than anything the government does to help them.

Still, the recent dip in the numbers need not be surprising. It corresponds to other economic data, such as measurements of real incomes, the percentage of the work force employed and household assets. They all support the notion that American families, for all their problems, have been doing better financially in the past few years.

Yet the latest poverty figures will not be greeted happily by those of the nation's politicians who would prefer to see poverty more, rather than less of an issue. The issue is normally phrased in the very simplest of terms: Is the government doing enough for the poor? We hear complaints this week that the 14% of the population classified as poor, though down in 1985 from 1984, remains higher than the percentage of the 1970s.

Columnist Warren T. Brookes noted last year that the decline in the number of families living in poverty in 1984 was the sharpest since 1967. But 1984 also happened to be the first year in 15 when federal social spending *declined*. Now, this correlation could be circumstantial. As it happens, until the 1984 reversal, both social spending and the percentage of families living in poverty climbed right through the late 1970s and early 1980s, irrespective of whether a Democrat or Republican was in the White House.

At least the 1985 numbers, whatever their worth, make it difficult to argue that the country is moving in the wrong direction. We ourselves think the elimination of poverty should indeed be a political issue, which is why we support tax reforms and other policies that we think will cause the national economy to function more efficiently. The biggest thing the government can do to help the poor is provide the opportunities that come with a vigorous economy.

Birmingham Post-Herald

Birmingham, AL, September 3, 1986

The Census Bureau has reported that the nation's poverty rate dipped slightly to 14 percent last year from 14.4 percent in 1984. Not surprisingly, Democrats on Capitol Hill charged that the relatively high figure highlighted a failure of Reaganomics.

Release of poverty statistics and criticism by the out-of-power party is an annual event, about which two things can be said.

One, an unacceptably large number of Americans are poor in a rich country. And, two, the Census Bureau's methods for calculating poverty are flawed and misleading. They considerably overstate the problem, which nevertheless is serious.

The bureau calls a family of four poor if its cash income was less than $10,989 in 1985. It makes no adjustment for geographic variations in the cost of living. Thus a family earning $10,000 in New York City and rural Alabama would both be listed poverty-stricken, although the latter's money would go much further.

Also, the bureau ignores the value of non-cash benefits, such as food stamps, Medicare and housing subsidies, all of which have played an increased role in recent years. If those values were calculated as income, the poverty rate would be substantially lower.

In studying people's incomes, the bureau does not examine payroll data or income tax returns. It interviews 60,000 households said to be representative of the nation. However, when a clipboard-bearing man from the government quizzes the head of a poorish household, he or she will sensibly understate family income so as not to jeopardize benefits.

The bureau's methodology partly explains why the poverty rate in the 1980s has been higher than in the previous decade, when it ranged from 11.1 percent to 12.6 percent. The back-to-back recessions in 1980 and 1981-82 offer another explanation.

None of this means that the poverty figures are valueless or should be disregarded. On the contrary, they pinpoint a major cause of economic suffering in America: broken families.

The bureau found that one-third of all families headed by a female lives in poverty. By contrast, 93 percent of two-parent families are not poor. And since more than 40 percent of black families are headed by women, the black poverty rate is high: 31.3 percent.

The figures indicate that the most effective action government can take to lessen poverty is to encourage husbands and wives to stay together. Success on that front would rapidly cut the poverty rate, no matter how it is measured, in half.

the Charleston Gazette

Charleston, WVA, September 1, 1986

DISTURBINGLY, the gap between haves and have-nots is widening in America, and the society's leaders respond with a shrug.

New York Gov. Mario Cuomo protested recently that affluent Americans scarcely notice that 33 million live in poverty and that joblessness has become a larger fixture in U.S. life.

"Millions of Americans are celebrating life as never before," Cuomo told the American Newspaper Publishers Association in San Francisco. " ... Inflation is down. Real estate is booming. The stock market has gone through the roof. There is prosperity." Many people focus on "where to find the best sparkling water, 10-speed bicycles, the latest in designer cowboy boots and imported pasta machines."

But in the "other city," he said, people are left out.

"There are millions of homeless and hungry, more than at any time since the Great Depression. In *this* America, more than one child in every five is growing up in poverty — among black children, more than one in two. ... .

"There are 8½ million people out of work in this America. There are 5½ million more settling for part-time work because they can't find a full-time job."

Cuomo said the Reagan era has magnified the gulf between classes.

"It is becoming clearer, gradually, that the budget and tax changes of the last five years have brought by far the greatest benefit to the wealthiest among us — in effect, taking money away from moderate-income households and the poor. ... .

"Since 1980 the median income of those Americans who, every day, are learning more and more about doing without, has fallen by some $500 a year, while the incomes of the top 10 percent have risen by more than $5,000 annually. And today, the top one-fifth of Americans are receiving a greater share of the nation's income than at any time since 1948."

During the 1980s, he said, "the denial of compassion has been made both respectable and comfortable." When Catholic bishops warned of growing despair among the poor, "the president himself said not a word. ... If the president was silent, though, some of his champions were not. They went on television and called the bishops 'whiny,' 'sniveling' and 'unrealistic.' "

Cuomo said America must realize that poverty, even when suppressed from view, hurts the whole society.

"We cannot afford unemployment when each percentage point costs us $40 billion in lost revenues and increased social spending.

"We can't survive the competitions of an international economy when one-seventh of our potential work force is lost to drugs, when we fall to 14th in average life expectancy and 14th in keeping infants alive in their first year of life, when the federal budget grows by more than 20 percent while spending for education is cut by almost one-third."

Ironically, many of the newspaper publishers in San Francisco griped that Cuomo's speech was too negative.

The response by these well-heeled societal leaders proved Cuomo's point.

Poverty Rate Declined to 13.6% in '86

The nation's poverty rate declined to 13.6% in 1986 from 14%, the Census Bureau reported July 30, 1987. The decline marked the third straight year in which the percentage of Americans living below the poverty line had shrunk. According to the bureau, 32.4 million Americans had incomes below the poverty level in 1986, a statistically insignificant change from 33.1 million in 1985. The poverty line for a family of four in 1986 was established as $11,203, an increase of about 1.9% (to adjust for inflation) from the previous year's $10,939 level. The poverty rate for children under 18 remained virtually unchanged in 1986 as 19.8%.

The same report indicated that median family income in 1986 was $29,460, 4.2% higher than the 1985 figure even after the 1.9% adjustment for inflation. Median income, which meant that equal numbers of families had incomes above and below that level, had now increased for four straight years.

The upper one-fifth of income levels received 46.1% of all family income in 1986, thought to be the highest level ever recorded for that category of the population. The middle three-fifths received 50.2% of all income, and the poorest fifth of the population got just 3.8% of total income. In 1980, by contrast, the top fifth had received 44.2% of income, while the poorest fifth got 4.1% of the total.

Gordon Greene, an official in the bureau's population division, said that in addition to the widening disparity between the rich and poor in income, statistics showed an increasing gap between whites and blacks in family income and the poverty rate. The statistics were based on a survey of 60,000 households nationwide.

The Virginian-Pilot

Norfolk, VA, August 7, 1987

The latest check on the United States' economic pulse provides a good-news/bad-news prognosis. The good news is that the economy continues its recovery from the terrible 1982 recession; the bad news is that the gap between the nation's economic "haves" and "have-nots" appears to be widening.

This information comes from the U.S. Census Bureau's annual analysis of the economy, and is based on interviews with 60,500 households chosen to be representative of the national population. In 1986, the bureau reports, median family income increased by 4.2 percent *after* adjusting for inflation. That indicates a major boost in income for most Americans, and it marks the fourth consecutive year that real income has grown. (Median family income means the midpoint, not the average, of all families: half of all families had more income than the median; half had less.)

The growth in the economy has benefitted a cross-section of Americans: In the past four years, median family income rose 8.5 percent for Hispanics, 10.2 for whites and 14 percent for blacks. The percentage of Americans who are below the poverty line (set this year at $11,203 for a family a four) fell last year to 13.6, down from 14.0 in 1985.

But two negatives dampen the report's otherwise rosy outlook. First, despite the major gains in the past four years, Americans have not advanced beyond where they were in 1973 — before oil embargoes and recessions took their toll. In 1973, the median family income was $29,734 (adjusted to 1986 dollars); today, even with last year's growth, it's slightly lower: $29,458.

Second, and most important, despite all the recent gains in income, the distance between the poorest and the richest Americans has grown since the recession. In 1980, the poorest one-fifth of U.S. households received 4.1 percent of all household income. Today, they get 3.8 percent. Meanwhile, the richest one-fifth of Americans today receive 46.1 percent of all income, up from 44.1 percent in 1980.

Officials of the Census Bureau say the "increase in income inequality" is largely due to two changes in the nation's demographic makeup: The growth of two-income families has boosted the number of families in the high-income brackets. The growth of single-parent families (usually headed by women) has increased the number of families at the low end of the scale.

Government can help ease the disparity between the haves and the have-nots through tax policy (last year's reforms eliminated taxes for most low-income Americans and wiped out some tax shelters for the rich), welfare reform, job training, education (including sex education) and — in the case of many one-parent families — more rigorous enforcement of child support. But the lesson in the poverty statistics is that, even in good economic times, single-parent households are at a great disadvantage, and what society and government can do to alleviate the problem remains a challenge of baffling complexity.

Detroit Free Press

Detroit, MI, August 3, 1987

"MICRO-ENTERPRISE", is a new name for an old approach to foreign aid: helping the world's poor help themselves. A bill to provide $125 million in loans to tiny businesses run by the poor deserves its already broad support of 39 Senate sponsors who range from Sen. Orrin Hatch, R-Utah, to Sen. Edward Kennedy, D-Mass., but it may need even more help.

An oft-cited model for this type of program is the Grameen Bank of Bangladesh. Its founder, Dr. Muhammad Yunus, believes "every human being has a tremendous capacity to do things for himself or herself, but we have created a society where (he or she is) not able to."

His bank opens its doors to the poor, not as a charitable proposition, but as "a business proposition," complete with interest rates, a 98-percent repayment rate and modest profits. The bank's success is based on the simple principle of self-help, which the Reagan administration now oddly ends up opposing. This opposition makes little sense. The micro-enterprise legislation would provide for private-public co-operation, opportunity to work — and at minimal cost to U.S. taxpayers.

The program is not, of course, the panacea for the world's hunger and poverty problems. The Agency for International Development (AID) objects to micro-enterprises on the grounds that they have only limited impact. This does not, however, take into account several larger co-operative ventures started with loans from the Grameen Bank. Other problems, not unique to this program, include relatively high administrative costs and possible abuse of the system. AID also argues that the micro-enterprise bill places too many restrictions on whom it can help.

Those concerns should be addressed, but then self-help deserves a try.

The Honolulu Advertiser
Honolulu, HI, August 6, 1987

Poverty has declined for the third year, down to 13.6 percent of the nation's people, the lowest rate since 1980. And the median family income — the point with half of all families making more and half less — rose 4.2 percent, to $29,458.

This is good news. It's attributable to recovery from the recession of the early 1980s and control of inflation during the Reagan years.

Still, with the poverty threshhold for a family of four at a low $11,203, poverty is still shockingly high, especially after four years of economic recovery. The poverty rate was lower throughout the 1970s and median family income was higher in several years.

The income distribution gap is also widening. The share of income received by the richest one-fifth of the population has increased, mostly due at the expense of the "middle classes," though the poorest one-fifth's share dropped slightly.

Most troubling though is that 22 percent of all children under 6 live in poverty (for black children the rate is 45.6 percent; for Hispanics it is 40.7). Just over half of all the families living in poverty are headed by women.

Against this background there is much needed discussion in Washington of reforming welfare and expanding government benefits and protections after six years of Reagan administration cuts in social spending.

When the value of non-cash benefits such as food stamps, subsidized housing and medicare are factored in, the nation's poverty rate drops to about 9 percent. That's still high for the richest nation on earth, but closer to an acceptable level.

The Washington Post
Washington, DC, August 3, 1987

THE POVERTY RATE is back about where it was when President Reagan came to office, but with this enormous difference. Then it was headed sharply up, mainly by virtue of the roaring inflation rates of the latter Carter years; incomes were overmatched by prices. Now it is drifting down, partly because so much of that inflation was wrung out of the economy by the Federal Reserve Board in the first Reagan term.

That major accomplishment is the important good news in the poverty figures just published for last year. It competes for the headlines with what continues to be pretty sobering news as well. On the one hand, the poverty measure is well below the high of 15.2 percent it touched in 1983. On the other hand, at 13.6 percent after four years of recovery, it remains well above the comforting lows of 11.1, 11.2 and 11.4 percent attained at various points in the 1970s. Forget the usual tinny games of credit and blame; the economy seems to have lost important ground.

The overall rate is not the only basis for believing this; there are chronic problems with the distribution of poverty no less than its extent. Too many groups are being left too far behind. The poverty rate for children continues to be a disheartening 20 percent (as against only about 12 percent for the elderly). For blacks it is 31 percent, for black children nearly 43 percent, for Hispanics 27 percent. The richest fifth of all families had 43.7 percent of family income last year, the highest ever, while the poorest two-fifths had 15.4 percent, an all-time low. The gap has been growing for a number of years. It has been calculated that the richest fifth of families had about $40 billion more in income last year than they would have had if their share of family income had stayed the same as in 1980. There are all kinds of reasons; wage deterioration in the lower reaches of the economy, where the minimum wage has not been raised since 1981, seems to be one. The government reports that 41 percent of all poor people 15 years old and older worked last year, the highest percentage in almost 20 years, and about 2 million worked full-time year-round.

The Census figures reflect only cash income, not the in-kind benefits to which the government has increasingly turned in recent years. Counting these—there are problems with how to value them—the poverty rates are lower, but the pattern is the same. There's also a gap in this society between profession and performance. It's not as fair an economy as we like to believe.

THE HAVES AND THE HAVE-NOTS

POVERTY RATE FALLS IN U.S. ———— NEWS ITEM

©1987 THE ORANGE COUNTY REGISTER

UNWANTED!

RATTLESNAKE RON ROBS THE POOR & GIVES TO THE RICH!!

ST. LOUIS POST-DISPATCH

St. Louis, MO, July 11, 1987

Anticipating hard financial times, the mayors of America's largest cities say they hope the next president will come to their rescue with a commitment to reverse the decline in federal aid to cities. In response, some GOP candidates say cities must do more to help themselves.

Most already have. They have slashed their work forces and reduced services to a minimum in order to balance their budgets, and they are raising taxes and charging fees for some services that formerly were free. Belt-tightening alone, however, won't make cities healthier. Federal assistance to local governments has fallen by $56 billion since 1980. Putting cities on fiscal diets won't compensate for this shortfall.

Nor do all urban problems stem from reductions in federal aid. Some result from the general shift of the urban work place from manufacturing to a largely white-collar and service-oriented economy. The latter absorbs fewer unskilled workers and offers less opportunity for advancement for those on the lower end of the economic ladder. Some mayors say this shift is once again turning cities into sites of much wealth and far too much poverty.

All this is worth considering in the context of urban leaders' hope for a president perceptive enough to see that the cities need help. But instead of looking to Washington for all the answers, cities must also look to their own private sectors. That means putting some of the onus on major companies to help train the unskilled for meaningful work. No better solution to poverty and other urban ills has ever been invented.

Omaha World-Herald

Omaha, NE, August 5, 1987

Time was when the Census Bureau's annual report on poverty in America could be counted on to touch off a midsummer round of Reagan-bashing. It hasn't happened this year, however. Why not? Perhaps it is because the situation for low-income people, as reflected in the most recent report, got better again last year — for the third straight year.

In the summer of 1984, the bureau's report indicated that 15.2 percent of the U.S. population the previous year lived in households with an income below the poverty line. That was up from 15 percent in 1982. It was the highest the poverty figure had climbed since 1969.

The bureau said the increase, which came on the heels of the worst economic recession since the 1930s, was statistically insignificant.

But it was an election year. Democrats seized on the figure to dramatize their charges that the Reagan administration lacked a commitment to help the poor. Then-House Speaker Tip O'Neill led a chorus of criticism, referring to the 15.2 percent poverty figure as "the smoking gun of Reagan unfairness."

Never mind that increases in the poverty rate weren't invented by the Reagan administration. Substantial increases also occurred in the last three years affected by the policies of the Carter administration, with the poverty rate rising from 11.7 percent in 1979 to 13 percent in 1980 and 14 percent in 1981.

This year's report, which covers 1986, put the 1986 poverty figure at 13.6 percent. If non-cash benefits such as food stamps and federally subsidized housing and health care are included in the computations, Census Bureau officials said, the proportion of Americans below the poverty line would be about 9 percent.

Poverty-line estimates, to be sure, don't tell everything about the problem of poverty in America. They shed relatively little light on the wrenching problems of homelessness and inadequate nutrition. For some people, particularly in single-parent households, the situation got worse instead of better, the report indicated.

Moreover, how "poor" a household actually is depends not only on its income but also on its non-income resources, its expenses and the help it receives from relatives and friends.

At the same time, the figures indicate that the situation got generally better instead of worse last year. The number of people below the poverty line dropped to 32.4 million in 1986 from 33.1 million the year before. Median family income rose 10.7 percent in real dollars from 1982 to 1986. The Census Bureau said it was the longest period of sustained income growth since the 1960s.

The White House, consequently, is entitled to a measure of satisfaction — even if its critics, who have been searching elsewhere for smoking guns, cannot bring themselves to give credit where it is due.

The Evening Gazette

Wichita, KS, August 5, 1987

That almost three-quarters of a million people moved across the poverty line to a better economic status last year is good news, whatever the causes. President Reagan attributes the progress to keeping inflation in check. Others cite socio-economic reasons.

Median family income increased 4.2 percent after adjustment for inflation, one of the largest jumps in 15 years and the fourth consecutive annual advance. Median family income was $29,458 in 1986, meaning that half of all American families had more income, half had less.

The Census Bureau, which compiled the figures, says there were a number of social and economic factors behind the gain. Because of divorces, separations and children living with single parents, families are smaller and income is spread over fewer members. In addition, the country has been recovering from the recession of the early 1980s.

In the prosperous Northeast, family incomes are highest, with the median at $32,160. Median family income rose the most in the South in 1986, but at $26,708 is still the lowest in the country.

A close analysis of the various income groups warrants some concern, however. Families in the bottom fifth of the income range stayed about the same, folks in the middle lost slightly, and those at the top of the income ladder gained somewhat. This indicates that the differences between wealth and poverty is widening. The poverty threshold for a family of four is just over $11,000.

Still, the fact that the country as a whole is gaining instead of sliding backward speaks well for current economic policies and means better lives for more families.

The Arizona Republic

Phoenix, AZ, March 7, 1987

AS the decade of the '80s begins to wind down, a dramatic shift in American living patterns is beginning to develop.

Reversing nearly a generation-long demographic trend, the idyllic appeal of rural and small-town life in America is being replaced by the economic lure of urban life. In the process, not only are non-urban areas losing population, but more people living there are unemployed and living in poverty.

According to a recent report in *The New York Times*, nearly half of the 2,400 or so rural counties in the United States now are losing population, compared with only 460 experiencing losses in the 1970s. Meanwhile, nearly half of those 2,400 counties had jobless rates of more than 9 percent in 1985, as opposed to only 300 counties with a rate over 9 percent in 1979.

Those looking for the obvious might point to the economic decline of the nation's farming industry as the primary contributor to the increasing rural-urban gap. According to the findings of many economists, however, the phenomenon can be best explained in the context of a nationwide "industrial revolution."

While the fortunes of farming operations — supplying 9 percent of non-urban employment — no doubt have declined recently, the economic underpinnings of rural America, as in urban areas, have been traditionally based on manufacturing and related operations. As more of these industries are replaced by high-tech operations, new job openings are created, mainly in the ever-growing service sectors which tend to locate in urban settings.

Since many rural areas are poorly equipped to handle the transportation, communications and technical-skill levels required to entice high-tech operations and their service-related spinoffs, the economic future of non-urban America remains, at best, uncertain. Other factors contributing to the rural downturn involve international and regulatory constraints, such as the impact of foreign competition on the domestic mining industry.

The report paints a not-so-pretty picture of rural life in America today. It should serve as a reminder to the artisans of public policy — on national and local levels — that economic misfortune is more than just a big-city issue.

Honolulu Star-Bulletin

Honolulu, HI, August 4, 1987

U.S. family income increased last year and the number of Americans living below the poverty level dropped.

The Census Bureau reported an increase in median family income of 4.2 percent between 1985 and 1986. According to the bureau's annual study of income and poverty, median family income was $29,458 last year, up from $29,269 a year earlier. It was the fourth consecutive year that family income increased.

The number of people living in poverty dropped about 700,000, from 33.1 million to 32.4 million. That represents a decline in the national poverty rate from 14 percent to 13.6 percent, the third consecutive annual decline. The poverty threshold for a family of four in 1986 was $11,203.

Those encouraging trends reflect the current national economic recovery, one of the longest on record. If the recovery continues through next year, Republican presidential candidates may have a more helpful legacy from the Reagan administration than the Iran-Contra fiasco would suggest.

St. Petersburg Times

St. Petersburg, FL,
August 8, 1987

President Reagan hailed the Census Bureau's report that the poverty rate has dipped slightly as the median family income has risen. But there is an ominous trend in the American economy: The difference between the rich and the poor is widening, economic inequality is increasing, the rich are getting richer and the poor are poorer.

Mr. Reagan welcomed the report that the proportion of Americans living in poverty last year was 13.6 percent, the lowest level since he took office. He said the figures demonstrate that "sustained, noninflationary growth is the government's single best tool for fighting poverty and building a better life for our nation's families."

Although the number of poor people has declined slightly, the 32.4-million Americans in poverty are poorer than ever before and from 2-million to 3-million of them are homeless. In the world's richest nation, that is a disgrace.

The nation's tax laws are still rigged to protect the rich, pinch the middle class and penalize the poor. The share of total income received by the most affluent fifth of all households rose to 46.1 percent in 1986, from 43.3 percent in 1970. For the poorest fifth, the share of total income dropped to 3.8 percent from 4.1 percent.

The "middle class" share for the middle three-fifths of the population declined to 50.2 percent in 1986 from 52.7 percent in 1980.

Even though dry statistics cannot tell the human despair and pain of poverty, Americans need to know that 22 percent of all children under 6 years old were living in poverty last year. For black children under 6, the poverty rate was 45.6 percent. The comparable figures for Hispanic children was 40.7 percent. For whites, 17.7 percent of children under 6 were living in poverty.

The effects of poor nutrition, inadequate health care and cultural deprivation will burden many of them for life — and the next generation of American taxpayers will pay for the neglect of the young in increased crime and welfare costs.

Poverty Rate Was Unchanged in 1987; Incomes Rose

Real U.S. family income rose 1% in 1987 to a record high while the poverty rate remained nearly flat at 13.5%, the Census Bureau reported Aug. 31, 1988. The bureau said that inflation-adjusted median family income grew for the fifth straight year in 1987, to $30,850, surpassing the record $30,820 set in 1973. The median income among white families in 1987 rose 1.1% to $32,274. But among black families, median income fell 0.8% to $18,098, and among Hispanics, income slid 2% to $20,306. The black and Hispanic declines fell within the margin of sampling error, the bureau said. Per capita income in 1987 rose 1.6% to a record $12,287, reflecting higher incomes of singles and the elderly.

In 1987, the richest 20% of all families (those with incomes above $52,910) earned 43.7 of all income, while the poorest 20% (those with incomes below $14,450) earned only 4.6%. In 1967, the richest 20% had only 40.4% of income.

The bureau reported that 32.5 million Americans lived below the poverty line in 1987. The change, from 13.6%, or 32.4 million, in 1986 was regarded as statistically insignificant. Although the poverty rate had peaked in 1983 at 15.2%, it remained higher in 1987 than it had been during the entire decade of the 1970s, with more Americans living in poverty than in 1967.

Not surprisingly, reaction to the report differed.

"The growing economy has indeed lifted the standards for everyone," said White House spokesman, Marlin Fitzwater. While calling the poverty increase among blacks "disappointing," Fitzwater saw the study as "a good report" that "documents a decrease in poverty [and] a continuing rising income."

Rep. Thomas J. Downey (D, N.Y.), the chairman of the House Ways and Means subcommittee on welfare, said: "The statistics hide the grim reality that, after five years of the Reagan recovery and despite the fact that the unemployment rate dropped almost a full percentage point over the same period, the poverty rate declined only one-tenth of one percent. The Reagan boom has been a bust for many American families."

The Washington Post

Washington, D.C., Sept. 1, 1988

THE POVERTY figures released yesterday are not good news. The famous rising tide no longer lifts all boats. The economy continued to do well last year; the poor did not. The unemployment rate was down, real median family and per-capita income both were up—yet the poverty rate remained essentially unchanged at 13.5 percent. The current expansion is more than five years old, and 32.5 million people continue to live below the poverty line—more than a seventh of the population. You wouldn't know it from the presidential campaign, but not even trickle-down is working.

Both parties have hyped the poverty figures in recent years. When the rate was rising in early 1980s, the Democrats blamed the Reagan budget cuts; they made it part of the fairness issue. When it started down in 1984, the Republicans used it to prove the contrary proposition—that poverty didn't depend on social spending but on economic growth, which they claimed the same budget cuts had fostered. The Democrats overstated the importance of social programs; the rate started up (from a recent low of 11.4 percent in 1978 to a high of 15.2 in 1983) with the high inflation and recession of the Carter years. The Republicans likewise overstated the efficacy of benign neglect; that is what these latest figures show. The society has always been less equitable than most Americans believe. Now it also seems to be less equitable than it used to be.

The richest two-fifths of families now have the highest share of total income (67.8 percent) and

the poorest two-fifths the lowest (15.4) in the 40 years the Census Bureau has compiled such statistics. The poverty rate is not merely high for this point in the business cycle; it masks important differences between groups. The rate last year went down for whites (to 10.5 percent) but up for blacks (to 33.1). For the elderly it was lower than for the society as a whole; for children, much higher. A fifth of all children are now poor, and two-fifths of the poor are children. The rate for younger children is higher than for older ones. Of black children under 6 years of age, 49 percent lived in poverty last year; of white children under 6, just under 17 percent did so.

The causes, or some of them, are familiar. Wages in parts of the economy are weak. Among other things, they have been bid down by the baby boomers, many of whom are also still at early and lower-paid points in their careers. A sixth of all families and more than 40 percent of all black families are headed by women. A third of these female-headed families are poor. Some benefits have also lagged; the government lifts relatively fewer people out of poverty than it used to.

Is that the way it ought to be, or not? We don't ask idly. There is, we remind again, an election going on. Presumably the distribution of income in the society is one of the things the election is, or ought to be, about. Where, on these issues, are Michael Dukakis and George Bush? The poverty of discourse is as lamentable as the poverty of income that it ignores.

WORCESTER TELEGRAM

Worcester, MA, Sept. 12, 1988

The U.S. poverty rate fell in 1987 for the fourth consecutive year — a sign that even people with low incomes have benefited from the long period of economic growth in the mid-1980s.

The Census Bureau has also announced that the inflation-adjusted median income of American families rose during 1987 for the fifth year in a row and that many families have improved their income status from middle-class to wealthy.

All this is clearly good news, even though Michael Dukakis and the Democrats will quickly find ways to make it seem that the news is bad.

It is already being pointed out, for instance that the number of people in poverty was slightly higher last year, that only the rate declined — because the population grew faster than the number of poor. Even so, it's good that the rate continues to decline. Both the rate and the number of poor did nothing but rise during the previous administration.

It is also being charged that the steady rise in income of middle-class Americans, to the point where some have grown wealthy, is a bad thing, that it means the rich are getting richer while the poor get poorer.

But how can it possibly be bad that the great majority of Americans — the productive ones with the skills and the good jobs — are doing a little better each year? Isn't this what the American dream is all about?

Moreover, if these many millions of middle-class people are earning more, they are paying more taxes. And it is tax revenue that funds Social Security and welfare, both of which have disbursed more dollars every year. Taxes also pay for the government programs that give welfare recipients the training to hold good jobs and get off welfare.

Those Census Bureau figures are encouraging. It is only through prosperity that the nation can hope to do better by its poor — and to help the poor do better for themselves.

THE SACRAMENTO BEE
Sacramento, CA, Sept. 13, 1988

The Census Bureau's new report on Americans' incomes in 1987 traces the pattern of a society going two directions. Although unemployment fell sharply in 1987 and the median income of U.S. families rose by 1 percent in constant dollars, the poverty rate held steady and the number of Americans living in poverty rose. Work and economic growth are the traditional American antidotes to poverty; troublingly, poverty is not responding to the medicine.

The pattern of stubborn poverty resisting economic growth is even more striking when looked at over the period of a decade. Although the unemployment rate in 1987 (6.2 percent) was nearly identical to that in 1978 (6.1 percent), the 1987 poverty rate, 13.5 percent, was more than one-fifth higher than a decade earlier. This was true even though a much higher proportion of Americans was in the labor force than ever before and even though poverty among the elderly, most of whom do not work, has fallen below the rate for the population as a whole. In past economic recoveries, steady economic growth and an expanding work force have pulled workers out of poverty. In this one, it hasn't happened.

According to the census statistics, the burden of this persistent poverty falls, to an unprecedented extent, on young families and children. In 1978, households with a family head aged 25 to 34 were less likely to live in poverty than the population as a whole. But by 1987, the poverty rate of such families had increased 40 percent, and they were more likely to be poor than other households. And because it is into such families that most children are born, there has been a steadily higher rate of poverty for the young. In 1987, one American child in five was poor.

It's no secret why low-income workers, including many more young families and their children, are worse off than their counterparts a generation ago. Even as the U.S. economy has created millions of new jobs over the last decade, lagging productivity and tougher foreign competition have restricted wages and good job opportunities for young and less-educated workers. At the same time, those families have been hit with higher tax burdens and, in the early 1980s, declining government benefits. The difficulties faced by young families are probably nowhere worse than here in California, where national trends are compounded by soaring housing costs, property-tax inequities and post-Proposition 13 fees that load more of the cost of government on the young.

In the 1960s and 1970s, dismayed by the spectacle of rampant poverty among elderly people who had given their nation a lifetime of work and service, Americans successfully met the challenge by improving Social Security and enacting Medicare. As a result, the proportion of poor older citizens has been cut by two-thirds, to the lowest level in U.S. history in 1987.

Today, it should be equally dismaying to see more and more young working families rewarded for their efforts by an existence below the poverty line. Economic misery among children and young parents breeds poor health, diminished educational achievement and child abuse, conditions that recreate poverty and foster all forms of social pathology in future generations. The difficult policy challenge of the 1990s is to ensure that hard work and a rising economy once more guarantee young families an opportunity for a decent start in life.

the Charleston Gazette
Charleston, WVA, Sept. 7, 1988

IF YOU'RE an adult, white male with an elite career, the news is good.

But for women, children, blacks and Hispanics, a new Census Bureau report tells them something they know already: the rich are getting richer, the poor are getting poorer, and that great backbone of American society — the middle class — is getting smaller.

The bureau's report, released last week, says median family income for whites has risen slightly, while Hispanic and black families suffered a decline.

Most important, the bureau confirms the charge that, as the rich increased their wealth in the Reagan years, they did so at the expense of not only the poor but especially of the middle class.

In 1987, the richest 20 percent of Americans got 43.7 percent of all income, while only 4.6 percent went to the poorest one-fifth of the nation. The middle 60 percent of Americans earned 51.7 percent of national income.

That's a disturbing change since 1967. Twenty years ago, the wealthiest 20 percent of Americans took 40.4 percent of national income, the poorest 20 percent earned 5.5 percent of America's income, and the middle 60 percent received a 54.1 percent share of national income.

Thus the gap between haves and have-nots is spreading, mostly at the expense of the middle class.

Worse, the bureau says 20 percent of all of America's children live in poverty. They constitute 40 percent of the U.S. poor. "When poverty rates for children continue to rise this far into an economic recovery, one has to wonder who is recovering," commented Robert Fersh of the Food Research and Action Center. "The entire society will pay the price down the road for children in poverty."

Americans have lived by two axioms: First, a large middle class is the foundation of a democratic society. Second, the hope of all parents is that their children will reach a higher standard of living than they achieved — namely, that they will become a part of the American middle class. Condemning children to poverty and shrinking the middle class has thrown those expectations into question.

Is this what Republicans call progress?

THE INDIANAPOLIS NEWS
Indianapolis, IN, Sept. 13, 1988

No doubt both Democrats and Republicans found something to crow about in last week's 1987 Census Bureau statistics.

The current administration can point to a slight dip in the percentage of Americans living below the poverty line — about $11,612 for a family of four — and to a 1 percent rise in the median family income after adjusting for the rise in consumer prices.

The Democratic challengers can counter that while the nation's poverty rate for whites dropped by one-half percent in 1987, the rate for blacks rose 2 percentage points. In 1987, 10.5 percent of white Americans lived in poverty; the poverty rate for blacks was 33.1.

But leaders from both parties need to re-examine these statistics in light of the current unemployment rate. As The New York Times pointed out recently, the jobless rate for the same period dropped from 7 percent to 6.2 percent. If jobs are all that's needed to end poverty, then the overall poverty rate should have dropped correspondingly.

Part of the problem is that minimum-wage jobs do not lift a family out of poverty. If one parent works full time at minimum wage and another half time, their combined income still falls below the poverty cutoff for a family of four.

The answer, however, is not a federally mandated higher minimum wage. About two-thirds of the nation's minimum-wage workers are under 25, and 40 percent are teen-agers. A higher minimum wage likely would reduce the number of jobs and deprive young men and women of valuable experience.

Nor is the answer larger welfare checks for poor families. In many cases, these handouts do little more than perpetuate the welfare cycle.

Better alternatives are expanded tax credits for the working poor and improved job-training programs at the local level. These programs not only help people get minimum-wage jobs, but teach them the skills to move into better-paying jobs.

Likewise, better education at all levels prepares children for better jobs later in life.

Both Democrats and Republicans need to take a hard look at these most recent census figures. For those who believe jobs alone will interrupt the cycle of poverty in the United States, the figures just don't add up.

THE INDIANAPOLIS STAR
Indianapolis, IN, Sept. 6, 1988

Not surprisingly, the good news about median family income is being overshadowed by charges that the gap between the rich and poor is wider than at any time in the last 40 years.

Median family income for 1987 was $30,850, up from $30,534. That good news appears in the same Census Bureau report that said nearly one-third of black Americans live in poverty.

The bureau's annual study of income and poverty said that poverty among blacks climbed 2 percentage points to 33.1 percent last year, which means that there were 9,632,000 poor blacks in 1987 — 700,000 more than a year earlier.

This prompted Robert Greenstein, head of the Center on Budget and Policy Priorities, a private anti-poverty group, to make his remark about widening gap between rich and poor and say that the nation's economic recovery is "very uneven" and "the people at the bottom, many of them, are being left farther behind."

There is some truth in that, but it is not the whole truth.

The figures on poverty are nothing to cheer about. They show the number of persons in poverty was 32.5 million in 1987, up from 32.4 million in 1986. The poverty level for a family of four was $11,611.

The bureau's figures were challenged by Stuart Butler of the conservative Heritage Foundation, who said if such benefits as food stamps and subsidized housing were added, "you'll find that the poverty level among blacks is almost half of what the published data suggest." Moreover, the figures do not include earnings in the underground economy.

Butler also said the reported expansion of poverty among blacks is largely attributable to the breakup of families. He said about half the families are headed by women, and that the number of families with one earner or no earners "heavily pulls down the average for the whole community."

Poverty figures make good ammunition for the "outs" during an election campaign. Yet it is only fair to point out that the figures show that there are 211.7 million Americans above the poverty level and, as the record median family income indicates, the number of Americans sharing in the recovery is considerably larger than the populations of most countries.

That is not good news. It is very good news.

Poverty remains, and a compassionate society should work to eliminate it. Honest people differ on how to go about it. But one thing is certain. It should be done in a way that pulls the poor up out of poverty, not a way that drags everyone else down.

The Philadelphia Inquirer
Philadelphia, PA, Sept. 6, 1988

Anyone who's starry-eyed about the 17 million new jobs created by the long economic expansion can return to Earth by reading the new numbers on U.S. poverty for last year. The rising tide of the economy has touched people very unevenly, reducing the number of Americans below the poverty line by 2.8 million, to a current total of 32.5 million. The percentage of people living in poverty last year, however, was 2.1 percent higher than the percentage achieved a decade ago — the last time unemployment was so low.

Just as dismaying, this spotty success against poverty had a racial bias. During the economic recovery, the number of blacks living in poverty has dipped by just 200,000. Poverty remains a fact of life for one in every three black Americans and for one in every four Hispanic-Americans.

Poverty's persistence alongside prosperity, and its prevalence among minorities, should shame the nation into a renewed commitment to change. Yet when the new figures came out last week, the Reagan administration expressed contentment that the poverty rate had dipped and murmured regret that blacks didn't share in the progress. The message tucked between the lines: Little is trickling down to the poor, but so what? The War on Poverty in the 1960s didn't work and even mucked things up. Obviously, if you subscribe to the latest cant — *nothing works* — then it's no big deal that the recovery isn't exactly mowing down poverty.

But the trendy notion that anti-poverty policies are bound to fail is a lie. There *are* government programs that help disadvantaged people to succeed. Head Start works for preschoolers. (The fact that the gains erode as such youngsters advance toward high school suggests the need for stronger support throughout their school years, not abandonment of the concept.) The success of programs to keep children from having children — such as the high school health clinics in Baltimore and St. Paul — shows that such efforts need not be as ineffectual as they are in Philadelphia. Year in and year out, the federal Job Corps, the California Conservation Corps and other efforts to build youths' discipline and self-esteem have proven their value.

These success stories have something in common: They attack a component of poverty early or even pre-emptively. That comports with a principle on which almost everyone can agree: It's infinitely harder to put failed, alienated persons back into a positive, self-sustaining pattern than to keep them from hitting bottom in the first place.

The "nothing works" line is a simplistic distillation of the high-explosive broadsides fired against social programs in recent years, such as Charles Murray's book *Losing Ground.* Mr. Murray and other critics of these programs make some valid points. These include the difficulty of foreseeing all the consequences of a program — positive and negative — as well as the degree to which anti-social decisions by disadvantaged individuals are actually rational reactions to the unintended negative effects of such programs. This latter point, for example, is the premise behind Congress' current attempt to rewrite the welfare equation so that AFDC mothers will have better incentives for undertaking training and going to work.

Twenty-six years have passed since Michael Harrington's book *The Other America* put poverty on the public agenda. Now, out of every 15 people, two are poor instead of three. That's not good enough. It's now clear that economic expansion alone can't do it all. With all respect toward poverty's staying power, it's high time for this nation to get talking, and striving, and — yes — *experimenting* to find ways to do better.

THE TENNESSEAN
Nashville, TN, Sept. 4, 1988

THE U.S. Census Bureau's annual poverty figures are out and they don't hold much cheer for the nation.

There were 32.5 million Americans living in poverty in 1987, or 13.5% of the population.

This was not much different from 1986, when 32.4 million, or 13.6% of the population, were below the poverty line.

But those figures don't exactly reflect the true nature of the situation. While the overall rate was about the same, there was wide variation between population groups.

The poverty rate for white people went down slightly to 10.5%. But the poverty rate for blacks was 33.1% last year, up two percentage points from the year before. The number of blacks living in poverty rose from 8.9 million to 9.7 million from 1986 to 1987. The poverty rate for Hispanics also increased from 27.3% to 28.2%.

This is due in large part to the higher unemployment rate among minority groups and the failure of programs designed to bring more members of these groups into the mainstream of the economy.

The Census Bureau's figures are not cause for much rejoicing. Perhaps there should be some satisfaction that the overall rate didn't register a sizable increase. But this may not mean much among the groups that did see an increase. ∎

THE LINCOLN STAR

Lincoln, NE, Sept 9, 1988

On the surface, life in the United States appears to be basically satisfying for the vast majority of citizens. But an unending array of concerns are brought into public discussion, unmasking what many believe is a growing anxiety among the electorate.

In November, the victory in the presidential race and perhaps in some congressional contests may go to the candidates who manage to more effectively deal with that anxiety. While the economy is said to be in good shape, millions of Americans are "underemployed," working fewer hours than they want or at lower pay than their qualifications should earn for them.

While median family income is up, there is a widening gap between rich and poor. In 1987, the richest 20 percent of Americans earned 43.7 percent of all family income, compared to 40.4 percent in 1967 and 42.7 percent in 1982.

And a substantial part of the higher median income is the result of the large number of two-income families. Yet, many two-income families are still struggling to stay afloat. Home ownership is becoming more difficult for young families as prices soar into the six-figure range and wage increases are minimal.

An Associated Press story Thursday said "the belief that America's economic standing in the world will be rescued by emerging high technology industries was questioned Wednesday by a prestigious study group which said the country is fast losing its dominance in many of these fields."

Having lost the heavy industrial war, we now may be losing the high technology war.

Another Thursday news story reported the nation's public health system to be in disarray, a serious blow to such threats as AIDS, environmental safeguards and services for the poor. The private health care delivery system, in many ways, is provoking growing alarm.

In total, many citizens are uncomfortable about the future and are likely to vote in November on the basis of who they see as most likely to bring a new era of confidence. That doesn't mean slogans such as "time for a change" will determine the general election, but that the door is open for the candidate who can speak effectively to the growing economic and sociological challenges of the day.

ST. LOUIS POST-DISPATCH

St. Louis, MO, Sept. 8, 1988

Based on the findings of a new Census Bureau study, one can safely assume it is not yet morning in a large part of America. The census study says blacks (and Hispanics) are worse off, while whites in general are doing just fine under this administration's economic policy.

Vice President George Bush isn't anxious to concede as much. When his Democratic presidential opponent, Gov. Michael Dukakis, mentioned the other day that the poor had become poorer and the rich richer under the Reagan administration, Mr. Bush refused to respond. And why should he? Admitting that times aren't good for many Americans would call into question his stock campaign praise of an economic policy that he claims has added 17 million new jobs.

But the census report offers oblique comment on that policy and on the quality of jobs it produced by noting that the number of poor Americans remains higher than at any time during the 1970s in spite of the fact that unemployment is down. It says over 32 million Americans were poor last year, and that the income of nearly 40 percent of these Americans did not even reach the halfway mark of the poverty line of $11,612 for a family of four.

In a way, there's no contradiction between these shameful numbers and the Bush rhetoric about prosperity. Many of the new jobs he mentions simply pay too little to lift people out of poverty. Yet the Reagan-Bush administration remains opposed to raising the minimum wage.

Because blacks and Hispanics hold a disproportionate share of the bottom-rung jobs, they have lost ground during the administration's uneven economic recovery. According to the census study, the proportion of whites who are poor dropped last year to 10.5 percent, from 11 percent in 1986. Yet the proportion of poor blacks actually rose to 33.1 percent last year, compared to 31.1 percent in 1986. Among Hispanics, the poverty rate rose to 28.2 percent last year, compared to 27.3 percent the year before.

The report also notes that the median income of white American families rose to $32,274 last year, compared to $31,935 in 1986. For black American families, the median fell to $18,098 last year from $18,247 in 1986. The median income for Hispanics was $20,306 last year, down from $20,726 a year earlier.

Some supporters of the administration have defended the worsening condition of the poor by blaming the victims. They argue, for example, that the rise in poverty among blacks can be explained by the fact that a majority of black families are now headed by females. But that doesn't excuse the administration's failure to adopt policies that help families enter the economic mainstream whether they are headed by two parents or by one.

Apparently Mr. Bush is untroubled by the numbers, and so is not moved to act. For his part, Mr. Dukakis has got to do more than deplore his opponent's indifference. He has got to tell the American public what he would do to improve the lot of the millions of Americans whose boats are being swamped by the very tide of prosperity that is lifting only the yachts.

The Idaho STATESMAN

Boise, ID, Sept. 6, 1988

The trickle down theory is all wet.

That's the inescapable conclusion to be reached from the government's latest poverty figures. The Census Bureau's annual study of income and poverty is rich in numbers. But you needn't be a statistician to figure the bottom line: The rich got richer and poor got poorer last year. Especially the black poor and the young poor.

Poverty among blacks climbed 2 percentage points in 1987 to 33.1 percent, meaning that nearly a third of America's blacks — 9.7 million — live below the poverty line. Black children are even worse off. Nearly half of blacks under age 3 live in poverty. For black children through age 18, the poverty rate is 45.6 percent, up 2.6 percent from 1986.

These figures compare starkly with overall poverty figures. For Americans as a whole in 1987, the poverty rate remained about the same as the year before, 13.5 percent. Although the total number of poor increased in 1987, the population overall increased faster than the number of poor.

The poverty level varies by family size. For a family of four, it was $11,611 in 1987.

These numbers are disturbing, especially because America, as Republican politicians are quick to point out, is doing well. We are in the fifth full year of economic expansion. Unemployment is down. Real median family and per-capita incomes are up. And yet one in every seven Americans live below the poverty line.

The truth is that the divergence between rich and poor in this country is bigger than ever and growing rapidly. The richest two-fifths of families now account for 67.8 percent of total income while the poorest two-fifths have 15.4 percent.

Equality of wealth is not possible, perhaps not even desirable in a free society. And yet the emergence of two cultures, one white and relatively well off, the other poor and black, bodes ill for the nation's future.

The next president and the next Congress — who, by the way, we are in the midst of choosing — must address this dichotomy. Providing wealth to all Americans is not the goal. Increasing opportunity for all Americans to improve their lot is.

Richmond Times-Dispatch

Richmond, VA, Sept. 2, 1988

A rising tide, President Reagan likes to say in arguing that a prosperous economy benefits all segments of society, lifts all boats. As statistical confirmation of that, the Census Bureau has just released figures showing that the nation's per capita income is now at an all-time high of $12,290 and that its poverty rate declined for the fourth consecutive year in 1987, dropping to 13.5 percent. That is down from a high of 15.2 percent in 1983 and is the lowest level since Mr. Reagan took office in 1981.

The rate might actually be lower than the bureau's figures. In calculating income, it did not include non-cash benefits that many families receive, such as Medicaid, food stamps and housing subsidies. Had they been added, the bureau estimates the poverty rate might have dropped to as low as 8.5 percent. The poverty line was drawn at a cash income of $11,611 for a family of four.

Including non-cash benefits in income calculations would have significantly changed the black poverty rate, which increased 2 percentage points over 1986 to 33.1 percent. Even considering non-cash items, however, poverty among blacks is distressingly high. And distressingly difficult to combat. Many liberal politicians will blame the policies of Ronald Reagan, especially his attempts to de-emphasize government social programs. But the problem is far more intractable than such criticism implies.

Douglas Besharov of the American Enterprise Institute has described most of the poverty afflicting poor blacks as "the poverty of divorce and illegitimacy. And no one has come up with any remotely feasible plan to deal with this."

Stuart Butler of the Heritage Foundation referred to statistics showing that "poverty among black Americans is more than three times as common as among whites, mainly because an alarming number of black families — more than half — are now headed by unmarried women, many of them barely old enough to have children."

Clearly, the "rising tide" of a prospering economy will not always lift a teen-age mother who has neither the skills nor the time to hold a full-time job that offers growing opportunities. And it would be extremely difficult if not impossible to create government socio-economic programs to solve the problems that put, and keep, such people in poverty. Does anyone seriously believe that the federal government could prevent unwed teen-agers from bearing children they cannot support, force the parents of such children to get married and prohibit divorces that might plunge a mother and her children into poverty? While trying to force fathers to support their children is a proper function of government that ought to be more vigorously performed, finding errant fathers and extracting money from them can be formidable tasks.

Poverty obviously is not a problem for the government alone to solve. For some people, the causes are more moral than economic. They must be dealt with accordingly.

THE ASHEVILLE CITIZEN

Asheville, NC, Sept. 6, 1988

A rising tide lifts the yachts — but not all of the boats.

That disturbing conclusion can be drawn from the recently released figures showing that poverty has increased among America's blacks.

The U.S. Census Bureau reported that the poverty rate for blacks increased from 31 percent in 1986 to 33 percent in 1987. Overall, the poverty rate fell from 13.6 percent two years ago to 13.5 percent last year.

The cold percentages translate into millions of black people. There were nearly 9.7 million poor blacks as of 1987, 700,000 more than a year earlier.

"It seems that this is a very uneven economic recovery. The gains are not being evenly shared ... the gap between rich families and poor families is now wider in this country than at any point in the past 40 years," said Robert Greenstein, head of the Center on Budget and Policy Priorities, in response to the report.

For citizens of the wealthiest nation in the world, these numbers and conclusions should bring deep concern. For the past eight years well-off people have basked in the morning-in-America glow of President Reagan and his policies.

But at the same time those policies have pulled away the safety net for many of our less fortunate neighbors.

Perhaps the greatest social catastrophe we have ignored during the Me Decade is the plight of black young people.

The poverty rate for black children 18 and younger was 45.6 percent last year, up from 43 percent in 1986.

Nearly 50 percent of blacks younger than 3 lived below the poverty level in 1987. That means every other black child in this country went to bed each evening living with the threat of hunger and homelessness.

The Reagan administration has justified its policies by the theory of trickle-down — the idea that everyone benefits when the well-off become more prosperous.

But the Census Bureau report shows that the process has not worked as it's often described, that not everyone has shared the wealth of the 1980s.

In his acceptance speech at the Republican convention, George Bush acknowledged that economic growth has passed many Americans by, and he promised a stronger effort to close such gaps. Making the "American dream" accessible to everyone is a traditional theme of the Democratic Party, of course, and it figures prominently in the campaign of Michael Dukakis.

Twenty years ago the Kerner Commission issued a report in response to the urban riots, saying that America was drifting toward two separate nations, one black and one white.

We appear again to be on that course. A task of the next president, whether Bush or Dukakis, should be to reverse the trend and see to it that opportunity becomes available to all.

THE DAILY OKLAHOMAN

Oklahoma City, OK, Sept. 2, 1988

THE periodic debate over how many Americans are living in poverty has been stirred up again by release of an annual report on family income.

The Census Bureau reported median income rose by 1 percent to $30,850 last year, but the number at the poverty level was slightly higher.

Like most statistical studies, the bureau's figures are subject to challenge as well as widely varying interpretation.

Liberals are pointing with glee to a finding in the report that the number of poor black Americans reached 9,683,000 last year, an increase of 700,000 over 1986.

Government statisticians arrived at this figure by defining the poverty level as $11,611 in cash income for a family of four. But that doesn't take into account government supplements like food stamps, subsidized housing and medical benefits. According to a Heritage Foundation study, 70 percent of the poor receive such in-kind income.

Conservatives note that the incidence of poverty is highest in households headed by a female with no husband present, which suggests that the breakup of families may be as big a factor as anything.

The current welfare system weakens families and encourages a general dependency on government. Rather than forced redistribution of income, as some liberals advocate, an overhaul of welfare programs offers one of the best opportunities to reduce poverty.

The Miami Herald

Miami, FL, Sept. 5, 1988

THE RICH got richer, the poor got poorer, and ethnicity continued to define who was which in America in 1987. That's the troubling news from the latest Census Bureau report on the nation's poverty rate, and Republicans and Democrats both immediately seized it as vindication of their differing prescriptions for the economy.

The report showed that the much-vaunted Reagan economic recovery has helped many: Last year saw the lowest proportion of Americans living in poverty since President Reagan took office. The poor now number 32.5 million, or 13.5 percent of the population.

Despite the good news, however, the rising tide of a more-robust economy didn't lift all boats, as the Democrats gleefully remind that the President had promised. The percentage of whites living below the poverty line, defined by the Government last year as a total income of $11,611 for a family of four, fell to 10.5 percent from 11 percent in 1986. But the percentages of poor blacks and Hispanics grew. Blacks' poverty rate rose 2 percentage points, to 33.1 percent. Among Hispanics, the rate rose nine-tenths of a percentage point, to 28.2 percent.

Thus the achievements of Reaganomics are increasingly leaving the poor and minorities behind. This is particularly disturbing given another Administration "success" story: the decline in the unemployment rate to 5.4 percent in 1987 from 7 percent in 1986.

Census Bureau officials refused to speculate on the reasons for the disparities, but the make-up of poor families is a good place to look. An alarming number of black families are headed by women who, if they work, earn far less than men.

This suggests that even though the number of jobs has increased markedly, many who hold those jobs aren't earning a living wage. Expanding community and government programs that train people for jobs that can sustain them could help. It's equally imperative to reduce the incidence of teen-age pregnancies among both whites and blacks. Teen mothers tend overwhelmingly to be poor, and their babies are likely to grow up poor. Many will in turn become teen mothers themselves.

Fortunately, both parties have discovered day care as an issue that has risen to the top of Americans' list of concerns. George Bush and Michael Dukakis approach the day-care issue from different perspectives, but it's heartening that they are approaching it. Day care could help employable-but-unemployed single parents get onto payrolls and off welfare rolls.

The challenge of the next Administration, no matter which party wins the Oval Office, is to dislodge those little ships from the economy's murky bottom. It can be done if there's a serious commitment to doing it.

The Wichita Eagle-Beacon

Wichita, KS, Sept. 10, 1988

WHEN the Reagan administration's supply-side ideologues said that a rising economic tide would lift all boats, they may not have known that the yachts would swamp the poor folks' rafts. As seen in the latest Census Department figures, at no time in the past 40 years has there been such a disparity between the rich and poor in America.

The new data show that the wealthiest 40 percent of Americans received an unprecedented 67.8 percent of the nation's income in 1987. The poorest 40 percent of the population earned only 15.4 percent of the national income, the lowest share ever recorded. The differential is even greater when it is noted that the top one-half of 1 percent of the U.S. population controls 35 percent of the country's wealth. The super-rich now own more than the bottom 90 percent of the U.S. people combined.

What's surprising is that there is so little outcry that the gaps between rich and poor in the United States resemble those of some Latin American countries. Indeed, neither Michael Dukakis nor George Bush has made the income figures a focal point of his presidential campaign.

But the numbers are social dynamite, especially when they are examined by race. In 1987, 13.5 percent of Americans — or 32.5 million people — lived below the official poverty line of an $11,611 annual income for a family of four. About 10 percent of white Americans were poor, but 33.1 percent of blacks and 28.2 percent of Hispanics lived in poverty.

Overall, 20.6 percent of American children were poor, but 49 percent of black and 39.8 percent of Hispanic youngsters were in poverty.

That means the underprivileged in America are increasingly racial minorities and children. Those people are being left out of the American dream, most of them condemned to live without hope of a better future.

There needs to be a new commitment to fighting poverty in America. Welfare reform with strong work incentive and job training provisions is crucial. Urban schools need to be improved because education is the surest way out of poverty. More money must be spent on child nutrition and programs combating teenage pregnancy.

But, most importantly, political candidates must confront the dangers of a nation permanently divided between haves and have-nots. If America is to be a country of justice, it must give its poorest members a chance to succeed.

The New York Times

New York, NY, Sept. 3, 1988

A new Census Bureau report offers discouraging news: the poverty rate among minorities increased and the already high rate among children did not improve. That far overshadows the slight decline in the number of whites living in poverty.

For fairly large pockets of poverty to persist — and even worsen — at a time of decreasing unemployment suggests a sobering point: Job growth alone is not enough. Government needs to play an active role in helping the poor.

The Census report shows that the overall proportion of poor Americans remained essentially the same, 13.5 percent in 1987, compared to 13.6 percent in 1986. But disturbing trends continue.

Whites who were poor in 1987 constituted 10.5 percent of the population, down from 11 percent in 1986. But among blacks, the number who were poor last year increased to 33.1 percent, up from 31.1 percent in 1986. Similarly, the proportion of Hispanic people who were poor rose from 27.3 percent to 28.2.

The new data also show that the rich get richer and the poor get poorer. In 1987, the wealthiest 40 percent of the population received a record 67.8 percent of the income. Meanwhile, for the second straight year, the poorest 40 percent of the population continued to receive only 15.4 percent of the national income, the lowest percentage ever recorded.

Poverty weighs heavily on the young, with profound consequences for the future. The overall poverty rate for children remained about the same, 20.6 percent in 1987 compared with 20.5 percent in 1986. But the number of black children under 6 who were poor in 1987 rose to 49 percent from 45.6 percent. And 39.8 percent of Hispanic children under 18 were poor, up from 37.7 percent.

The Reagan Administration has clung to the notion that a rising economic tide would lift all boats. The unemployment rate dropped from 7 percent in 1986 to 6.2 percent in 1987. Why didn't the poverty rate drop accordingly? Apparently many of those new jobs don't pay enough to keep a household above the poverty level, now defined as $11,600 for a family of four.

All Americans have a stake in reversing the trend to a wider gap between rich and poor. Remedies are clear. Expanding the earned income tax credit would help working poor families. Pending welfare reform legislation would help move more recipients into jobs. Increased welfare benefits would especially help poor, single mothers. And increased health and education services would help give poor children a fair chance to succeed.

St. Louis Review

St. Louis, MO,
Sept. 9, 1988

Last week the Census Bureau published its statistics on poverty in the United States. There is some good news and a lot of bad news.

The good news is that the percentage of Americans living in poverty did not increase from 1986 to 1987 In fact there was a decrease of one-tenth of a percentage point. In 1986, 13.6 percent of the total population were living in poverty. In 1987 that figure dropped to 13.5 percent. The Census Bureau said that the change was "not statistically significant." The total number of Americans living in poverty actually increased from 32.4 million to 32.5 million due to the growth in overall population during that period. That's just part of the bad news.

A further breakdown of the statistics shows a significant decline in the proportion of white Americans living in poverty. However, the proportion of black and Hispanic Americans living in poverty rose significantly. From 1986 to 1987 the percentage of poor blacks increased two points, and the percentage of poor Hispanics increased almost one point.

The meaning and implications of these statistics will surely be the topic of discussion and debate, especially in an election year. The role of government in dealing with poverty is indispensable. But we ought not to be too quick in assuming that the elimination of poverty in our country is a task solely of government bureaucracy. That is particularly true when faced with the disparity between white Americans and ethnic Americans. Why are white Americans becoming richer and minority Americans becoming poorer?

There may be no simple answer to that question, but let's look at ourselves at least as much as we look at the system. The roots of racial prejudice are deep in our culture. Although great advances have been made during the past 25 years toward equity of employment and opportunity for all, the statistics suggest that we have a way to go. New structures supported by government are necessary, but self-examination by individuals regarding hiring policies is also called for.

It is indeed a national disgrace for 32.5 million people to be living in poverty. Add to that racial prejudice which could affect the rights of minorities to earn a living and escape from their poverty and we have a national sin.

THE DENVER POST

Denver, CO, Sept. 1, 1988

THE NATIONAL debate over homeless people has failed to produce a consensus even as to how many unfortunates fall into that category. Now the U.S. Census Bureau is planning an extraordinary effort to find out.

Estimates of the number of people without shelter range from 250,000 to 3 million. On March 20, 1990, special teams of census takers will try to get a more exact count. In a novel twist, homeless people will be hired to count the homeless — on the logical theory that homeless persons are more likely to know where to find persons without homes. While most Americans will be counted on the official census day of April 1, the homeless will be tallied earlier because they are easier to find in cooler weather — when many of them take refuge in shelters.

Officials also will try to advertise the census through the potent communications "grapevine" of people living on the streets.

The special effort is doubly laudable. An accurate count of all citizens is critical for the fair distribution of funds in a host of federal programs. But additionally, gathering facts about the true numbers and condition of homeless people may help solve a problem that now is often relegated to the status of a partisan football.

The News and Observer

Raleigh, NC, Sept. 4, 1988

Facts, as President Reagan has said, are stubborn things. And stubborn facts keep rubbing the luster off the five-year economic recovery that Republicans hope will propel their ticket to victory in November. The Census Bureau has just published a fresh batch of statistics showing that the recovery has left millions of Americans behind.

Perhaps the most telling of the Census statistics are those pointing to a widened gap between the rich and the poor — and between the rich and the middle class as well. The top 20 percent of American families accounted for 43.7 percent of total national income last year, up from 40.4 percent in 1967. But while the richest one-fifth of Americans gained over the past 20 years, the lowest one-fifth saw their share of total income drop from 5.5 percent in 1967 to 4.6 percent in 1987. Meanwhile, the income share of the middle 60 percent fell from 54.1 percent in 1967 to 51.7 percent in 1987.

It's true, as Republicans may protest, that these figures have to do with long term social and economic trends, not just Reagan administration policies. Still Republicans held the executive branch for all but six of these years, and the Reagan tax-and-budget policies clearly tilted toward the well-to-do.

Vice President Bush celebrates the fact that the United States has created 17.5 million new jobs during the current recovery. And between 1986 and 1987, the Census Bureau reports, median family income rose 1 percent — to $30,853 — and the poverty rate fell slightly.

But the existence of gaps in the recovery is unmistakable.

Even as the unemployment rate dropped significantly, the number of people living below the official poverty line — $11,600 for a family of four — hardly changed, dropping from 32.5 million to 32.4 million. Plainly, millions of people aren't "recovering."

Among white Americans, the poverty rate declined from 11 percent to 10.5 percent. But among black Americans, the poverty rate rose from 31.1 percent to 33.1 percent. Children under 18 years old accounted for 40 percent of the people in poverty.

For the problems highlighted by the Census Bureau statistics, government isn't a cure-all. For example, the growth of families headed by black females is a challenge to churches and other institutions in black communities. Economic growth, too, must play a role in pulling people out of poverty and in bolstering middle-class families.

Yet, the government of a nation whose Constitution requires it to "promote the general welfare" cannot in good conscience ignore the Census Bureau's facts. It cannot ignore the facts — stubborn facts — that show the rich having gotten richer and not only the poor but also much of the middle class having gotten poorer.

Lincoln Journal

Lincoln, NE, Sept. 2, 1988

The Census Bureau's annual family income report is one of those classic the-glass-is-half-full, no, the-glass-is-half-empty propositions. Advocates of both contentions are absolutely correct.

Projected median family income in the United States did rise by 1 percent last year. Half of the theorized families in the country were listed with before-federal-tax income of $30,853. Half had less. Of the more favored half, nearly half of them had family income of at least $50,000 annually.

This state of affairs is rich material for the Reagan administration and the Bush-Quayle ticket to cite as evidence of national economic gain under Republican occupancy of the White House.

It is also a statistical truth that from 1986 to 1987, the gap between America's rich and poor continued to widen. Black American poverty today is greater than it was a year ago — by some 700,000 men, women and children. For them, the claims of great economic improvement ring cynically.

That circumstance should be material the Dukakis-Bentsen combination is likely to work.

Right-wing organization spokesmen instantly were critical of a national poverty rate calculated at 13.5 percent. And they have a fair point. If non-cash benefits of federal human services programs are figured into the theoretical mix, the Census

Bureau says the poverty rate might be as low as 8.5 percent.

But there also is touch of disingenuousness here. Conservatives cite breakup of families — not the economy — as a primary cause of 32.5 million Americans now living at or below the poverty level. In the absolutely worst fix are black children. The poverty rate among blacks 18 or less was 45.6 percent. For black children under three years, 49.1 percent — almost one of two — lived in poverty last year.

The potential social dynamite in that statistic has been expanding year after year.

Stuart Butler of the politically conservative Heritage Foundation may be accurate saying the cost of living for a rural family in Gum Tree, Va., is less than for a family in Manhattan — as if many single-parent black families can afford a Manhattan address. But that line still does little to address the widening division countrywide between rich and poor.

National data indicating 43.7 percent of all family income went to the top 20 percent last year (up from 42.7 percent in 1982) while the share for the lowest 20 percent dropped to 4.6 percent should be worrisome, wherever one lodges on the political spectrum. When the top 20 percent eats nearly 10 times more of the income pie than is available to the bottom 20 percent, trouble is in the wings.

Arkansas Gazette

Little Rock, AR, Sept. 13, 1988

It is a strange sort of "prosperity" when millions of people are slipping farther behind, but that is what the country has experienced these last few years.

Noneconomists — ordinary people, that is — had already noticed the phenomenon. Now its existence has been confirmed by the Economic Policy Institute. Using Census Bureau data, the institute has determined that real wages (adjusted for inflation) dropped 7 per cent between 1979 and 1987. Only relatively well paid salaried workers have prospered during that period. Their income went up three percent.

The gap between rich and poor widened between 1979 and 1987, the institute found. The 40 percent of American families on the low end of the scale lost income. The gains the administration boasts of were confined to the upper end. The inequality between the income of whites and blacks grew larger also. And even the "typical" American family had to have more members working more hours just to stay even with where it was in 1979. Those that couldn't do this actually lost ground.

One reason for this is that so many of the new jobs created under the present administration are low-paying, parttime positions, lacking the benefits that sometimes mean the difference in keeping one's head above water. About 17 percent of all the workers added during the great business expansion of the '80s had no health insurance; 40 per cent had no pension plans.

In 1987, the fifth year of economic recovery, the poverty rate was 13.5 percent — higher than any year in the 1970s. If this be prosperity, we are making the least of it.

DESERET NEWS

Salt Lake City, UT, Sept. 4, 1988

A report on poverty in the U.S., released this week by the U.S. Census Bureau, is sure to provide ammunition for the presidential campaign. But voters may be confused as both parties use the same Census data as proof for opposing arguments.

The Reagan administration and George Bush will point to the good news, and there is plenty. For example, the study shows:

— Median family income grew 1 percent in 1987 to $30,850. It was the fifth consecutive year there has been an increase.

— Per capita income grew 1.6 percent to $12,290, an all-time high when adjusted for inflation.

— Median income for families headed by single mothers was reported at $14,620, a significant 3.4 percent increase.

— The number of people below the poverty line remained at 13.5 percent, essentially unchanged from the previous year, while it declined by 7 percent for people living on farms. The study used the federal definition of poverty, namely $11,611 for a family of four. There is no adjustment for regional differences, say between rural Utah and Manhattan.

— The poverty rate for people over 65 stands at 12.2 percent and has been cut in half since 1970.

Yet Michael Dukakis is sure to seize on the negatives of the same report to bolster his campaign. For example:

— While the median income of white families was up, it did not substantially change last year for blacks or Hispanics.

— The poverty rate for whites dropped to 10.5 percent, but it grew 2 percent for blacks to 33.1 percent and stayed at 28.2 percent for Hispanics.

— Forty percent of those living under the poverty level were children under age 18.

— The richest 20 percent of the population earned 43.7 percent of all family income last year, compared to 40.4 percent 20 years ago, and 42.7 percent five years ago. The poorest one-fifth of the population earned 4.6 of all family income, down from 4.7 five years ago.

Politicians will probably use the Census report this fall like some people use the Bible, citing their favorite references to prove a point — and ignoring the rest.

THE INDIANAPOLIS STAR

Indianapolis, IN, Sept. 9, 1988

Fewer than 5 million Americans lived on farms in the United States last year, according to the Census Bureau. That is barely 2 percent of the population, and the lowest U.S. farm population since before the Civil War.

Even those figures, though, do not register fully the phenomenal growth of productivity on American farms. A more startling fact does: 20 percent of U.S. farmers raise 80 percent of the food grown domestically. Put another way, a farm population of about one million, and hired help, provides the bulk of the food needs for four-fifths of our 243 million people.

Farm population continues to decline. Mechanization and marketing changes have made the small acreage farm difficult to operate efficiently. The resultant sellout or merger may be a social and cultural loss, but it is prompted by economic reality. Americans historically go where opportunity calls.

Even so, a surprising fact was reported by Ernest Wilkinson, *The Star* farm writer. During the 1970s, a time of relatively few agricultural problems, farm population declined at a yearly rate of 2.9 percent nationally. During the 1980s, a decade that has meant hard times to many farmers, population has fallen by an annual rate of only 2.5 percent.

Those numbers seem to indicate that the exodus is leveling off. If that is the case, it is good news. Barely one American in 50 now lives on a farm. That is few enough.

Minimum Wage Bill Dropped

Senate Democratic Leader Robert C. Byrd (W. Va.) withdrew a minimum wage bill from consideration Sept. 26, 1988 in concession to a Republican filibuster. In five days of debate, Democratic efforts to break the filibuster fell short by seven votes Sept. 22 (53-43) and by four votes Sept. 23 (56-35). It required 60 votes to end debate under the Senate's cloture rule.

The bill, a main priority for organized labor, would have raised the federally mandated minimum wage to $4.55 an hour over three years, from its current level of $3.35 an hour. The legislation was adamantly opposed by the U.S. Chamber of Commerce and the National Federation of Independent Business. Senate Republicans insisted that a higher wage floor would have to be accompanied by a "training wage" at 80% of the minimum, for a 90-day period for new people entering the work force.

Unions opposed the lower wage for trainees as creating a two-tier system that would permit companies to hire young workers for three months then fire them and hire others at the subminimum wage. Sen. Edward M. Kennedy (D, Mass.), chairman of the Senate Labor and Human Resources Committee, made a counterproposal to broaden an existing labor law provision by letting an employer hire more full-time students at 85% of the minimum wage compared with the GOP proposal.

But neither the debate, nor the bill, moved further toward resolution.

The Boston Herald
Boston, MA, July 6, 1988

THE SENATE is preparing to take up Sen. Ted Kennedy's proposal to increase the minimum wage to $4.55 an hour, and we earnestly hope its members will look beyond the mythology and easy rhetoric of "economic justice" to the hard reality of how jobs are created ... and destroyed.

If Congress could truly legislate high salaries for all Americans, why not a minimum wage increase to $10 an hour? Or $100? Why not a law abolishing poverty once and for all?

The answer, of course, is that it is the market — the economic engine of supply and demand, buyers and sellers — that creates wealth, not government. As the distinguished economist Thomas Sowell warned on our Op-Ed page recently, an increase in the minimum wage would destroy hundreds of thousands of jobs, hurting disadvantaged and marginal workers — which, more often than not, means black teenage workers — the most.

When Congress decrees, "You *must* pay every worker $4.55 an hour," it imposes a terrible dilemma on the struggling employer wishing to hire a marginal worker whose labor is only worth, say, $3.75 an hour. Does he hire him and promptly start losing on the deal? Or does he decline to hire, and leave him unemployed? "Minimum-wage legislation hurts the *least* employable," writes scholar Matthew Kibbe of the Center for the Study of Market Processes, "by making them *un*employable."

We suppose Kennedy's motives are noble. But his grasp of economic realities is as tenuous as ever, and his bill would be disastrous for America's poorest and shakiest working men and women. When the minimum-wage increase is considered, we hope senators will vote No.

THE SACRAMENTO BEE
Sacramento, CA, July 11, 1988

Congress is moving toward an increase in the minimum wage, but without much enthusiasm. A higher minimum wage, while justified in moral terms, no longer works very well to raise the incomes of poor working families, most of whom are already above the minimum. If Congress wants its bill to have some effect, it should combine a higher minimum wage with an increase in the earned-income tax credit, as Rep. Thomas Petri is proposing.

Because inflation has eaten away 22 percent of the real value of the current $3.35-an-hour minimum wage since it was enacted in 1981, there is little question that a higher minimum wage is justified as an act of solidarity with Americans who work at the bottom of the wage scale. But many legislators, Democratic and Republican, who've supported past minimum-wage increases now recognize that poorly designed minimum-wage legislation can hurt low-wage workers as much as it helps them. Thus, how far to raise the minimum has become a touchy issue.

According to estimates by the Congressional Budget Office, raising the hourly minimum to $5.05 by 1992, as proposed in the bill passed by the House Education and Labor Committee, could cost 500,000 jobs. (Unhappy with this news, Rep. Augustus F. Hawkins, author of the bill, simply had the estimates deleted from the CBO report). The job loss would fall heavily on low-skill teenagers, who comprise a third of the minimum-wage work force and already have unemployment rates triple that of other workers. Worried about the potential for job loss, lawmakers in the House and Senate are looking to hold any increase to around $4.25, the figure California has already instituted.

While that would send the right symbolic message without wiping out too many jobs, it would not do much to help low-wage families. That's why Petri, a Wisconsin Republican, is pushing the House to also increase the earned-income tax credit.

Under current law, low-income working parents receive a sliding refundable tax credit on wages up to $15,320. The credit raises the threshold at which parents begin to pay income tax, and because it is refundable, it rebates a portion of their Social Security payroll tax. The effect is to increase the take-home pay of low-wage workers whose paychecks support a family. Unfortunately, the current earned-income tax credit, passed in 1975, is so low that it provides no income supplement to parents working full time at the minimum wage.

To remedy that, Petri is suggesting that the amount of wage income subject to the credit be raised, that the credit be indexed to inflation and that the size of the credit be adjusted for family size. That reform would directly, and permanently, increase the incomes of the families that the minimum-wage law is meant to help, but without the risk of pricing them out of their jobs. Hawkins and other Democratic supporters of the higher minimum-wage legislation have resisted a higher earned-income credit as an inappropriate addition to their bill. But if the minimum-wage bill is to be true to its heritage as an anti-poverty measure, it should include Petri's compassionate and well-conceived proposal.

The Atlanta Journal
THE ATLANTA CONSTITUTION
Atlanta, GA, May 23, 1988

Opponents of a higher minimum wage have proved one point: The idea is wildly inflationary.

Scarcely a year ago, the U.S. Chamber of Commerce was warning that an increase would cost the nation 300,000 jobs. Today, the White House claims that the smallest boost under consideration (from $3.35 per hour to $4.65 by 1992) would cost 600,000 jobs. An increase to $5.05 by 1992 would cancel 850,000 jobs, insist the Reaganites.

Conclusion: When it comes to bashing the minimum wage, fears are being inflated at triple-digit rates.

True, any increase will prompt some employers to trim their payrolls. And yes, higher wages could boost prices for some products, which might shrink markets and result in smaller work forces.

But these liabilities are not nearly as severe as opponents claim. The minimum wage has gone up several times since its New Deal inception, and the sky has not fallen. What *has* fallen in recent years is the purchasing power of minimum wage workers. Since 1981, they have grossed $6,968 a year. That sum was a pittance then — but the cost of living today is more than 27 percent higher.

Have most employers raised their prices since 1981? Sure. Have they given themselves and their skilled workers raises since then? You can count on it. Were there some adverse effects to these actions? Yes, but on balance they were seen — correctly — as necessary costs of doing business.

Yet whenever Congress tries to insist on a (barely) decent wage for the working poor, conservatives suddenly start to worry about an economic Armageddon. They insist that their opposition is in the best interests of minimum-wage workers. For all the hot air behind that argument, it still won't fly.

The Washington Post
Washington, DC, July 18, 1988

THE MINIMUM wage was last increased in January 1981. In the 7½ years since, it has lost a fourth of its purchasing power. At $3.35 an hour—about $7,000 a year for a person who works full-time year-round—it is not enough to keep even a family of three above the poverty line, and efforts are under way in Congress to move it up again. No issue is more controversial—pay is the slicing of the pie—and as always, there has been resistance. But the critics, even the well-disposed among them, are wrong.

The minimum has been increased 15 times since its enactment at 25 cents an hour in 1938. The basic argument against increasing it is every time the same. The cost will be passed along in both higher prices and fewer jobs. No lunch is free; in helping some people, the government is hurting others, and it should leave these trade-offs to the market, which will make them most efficiently.

In recent years a newer argument has been added. It questions the benefits of the policy as well. A column by Robert Samuelson is the best recent example. It makes the point that most of the people and most of the jobs in the minimum-wage economy are neither the kinds you think they are nor the kinds you want to build a policy around. On the contrary, as Mr. Samuelson rightly observes, most of the people are young (a third are teen-agers), most don't stay in these jobs very long, and most aren't poor; their family incomes are well above the poverty line. Most of the jobs are also part-time—a third are in restaurants—and they make up a declining share of all jobs in the economy—only about 4 percent today.

That figure can be read two ways: as reassuring evidence that there aren't that many minimum-wage jobs left to worry about because the market has gradually moved wages up on its own, or as proof of how much the minimum has been allowed to erode (and 4 percent of the jobs in the economy is still about 5 million jobs). But that is not the main problem with this minimizing argument. The main problem is that it looks through the wrong end of the telescope. It's true that most people on the minimum wage aren't poor.

It's also true that an awful lot of poor people are at or near the minimum wage.

In 1986 there were 5.5 million families with children living in what the federal government defined as poverty. About 3 million of these were headed by people who worked at least part of the year part-time; more than 900,000 were headed by full-time year-round workers. In some of the latter families, there were other workers as well. Not all these people were in jobs that are covered by the minimum. But most were, and the minimum has an influence on all wages in the lower regions.

We live in a society that claims to value work—and does—but work hasn't done it for these people. The wage structure has failed them. It fails children as well. More than a third of all poor people are children. The poverty rate among children is 20 percent—half again the rate for the population as a whole—and a fourth of the 12 million poor children in the country live in two-parent families in which one of the parents works full-time year round.

No device now in contemplation would move more people out of poverty than a restoration of the minimum wage. Opponents say an increase in the earned-income tax credit would be a more efficient alternative. It would; this refundable credit, a form of negative income tax, puts money directly in the pockets of the working poor with children and of no others. It is a rifle; the minimum wage is a shotgun.

But the tax credit now costs the Treasury about $6 billion a year. Congressional and other experts say it would take more than a doubling of this amount to shift as much money to poor people as the minimum-wage increases that have been proposed—and no such increase in the tax credit is in sight. There is neither the money (an increase in the tax credit, unlike an increase in the minimum wage, shows up in the budget) nor the will. The tax credit and minimum wage should both be increased—but as a matter of simple justice the minimum wage can and should be increased now.

THE DAILY OKLAHOMAN
Oklahoma City, OK, May 24, 1988

EARLIER this year, the Congressional Budget Office produced a report which showed that increasing the minimum wage from the current $3.35 an hour to $5.05 over four years could cause a loss of nearly 500,000 jobs.

Majority Democrats suppressed the report and ordered a substitute which eliminated any reference to the economic impact of the proposed hike.

This brazen manipulation of an agency that is supposed to be nonpartisan and nonpolitical so disturbed Rep. Thomas Petri, R-Wis., that he asked the White House to provide an assessment of the minimum wage legislation.

Beryl W. Sprinkel, chairman of the president's Council of Economic Advisers, responded with figures projecting a loss of more than 850,000 jobs by 1992. He also said the increase would cost consumers $21.3 billion a year, would raise the federal deficit by as much as $9 billion a year and would cause the gross national product to decline by up to $31.6 billion a year.

"Increasing the federal minimum wage would do little to help the working poor," Sprinkel said. "Under 20 percent of minimum wage workers are poor and many would lose employment."

Liberals in the House and Senate are using every trick in the book to cloud the issue and push through one of organized labor's pet bills, even to the point of denying lawmakers information compiled by their own budget office.

Thanks to Rep. Petri, they didn't get away with it.

AKRON BEACON JOURNAL
Akron, OH, July 15, 1988

DEMOCRATS have become sheepish about raising the minimum wage. They're not ready to drop the idea. But they're moving in that direction. They should go all the way.

A compromise is in the works that would increase the minimum wage from $3.35 an hour to $4.25 or $4.55 over three years. That closely resembles legislation recently approved by the Senate Labor Committee. It's a vast improvement over a House bill that would set the minimum wage at $5.05 by 1991.

What Democrats are seeking is a bill that President Reagan and Republicans would find too politically embarrassing to oppose. They're playing to the notion that something must be done. After all, they argue, the minimum wage hasn't been increased in seven years, losing 20 percent of its purchasing power. Democrats insist it's a matter of fairness.

The economics of the minimum wage, however, argue not for a slight increase but for no increase at all. Indeed, the decision to back away from the House bill suggests that studies showing an increase in the minimum wage would boost inflation and unemployment are beginning to make an impression.

A Congressional Budget Office study, which House Democratic leaders initially tried to suppress, predicted that a $5.05 minimum wage would cost 250,000 to 500,000 jobs. Respected economists concur, pointing out that even a less dramatic increase would have an adverse effect on the economy. Inflation would not skyrocket, but why push up prices to gain so little?

Most minimum-wage jobs are not held by adults over 25 or heads of households. The typical minimum-wage earner is young, single and from a family with an income far above the poverty line. Roughly a third are teen-agers; indeed, according to the Bureau of Labor Statistics, only 2.2 percent of the adult work force is employed at $3.35 an hour.

An increase in the minimum wage would reduce opportunities for young people looking to gain experience and get a start in the job market. That seems especially wrongheaded in view of double-digit unemployment rates among teen-agers. Black teens face a horrendous jobless rate, reaching as high as 40 percent. They won't be helped by legislation that makes it more difficult to find work.

Much more fair and beneficial are various proposals to improve the earned-income tax credit. Available to working poor people with children, the credit could be increased to ease tax burdens further without adding to business costs, inflation or unemployment.

A larger earned-income tax credit would add slightly to the deficit, requiring tough choices about spending and revenues, hardly popular ideas on Capitol Hill. But if helping working parents with low incomes is the goal — and it should be — an improved tax credit is the better approach. A boost in the minimum wage would do little for poor families and close doors on young people.

The Washington Post
Washington, DC, June 8, 1988

THE MINIMUM wage has been stuck at $3.35 an hour for more than seven years, during which it has lost a fourth of its purchasing power. An increase in the minimum would do more than any other bill before the Democratic Congress to reduce the poverty rate and narrow the ominous income gap between rich and poor, which in recent years has widened. So if not the creaky Senate surely at least the House, where the Democrats hold a 3-to-2 majority, will raise the minimum easily, right? Wrong, sad to say.

The Democrats purport to be the party of social conscience, to be moved by the cause of poor children especially. The children's poverty rate is near 20 percent. But Harvard economist and welfare expert David Ellwood says in a new book that half of all poor children live in two-parent families as opposed to the single-parent model around which so much debate revolves—and that in almost half of the two-parent families, one adult works full-time year-round. The wage structure is too weak to lift those families above the poverty line. The faded minimum wage is part of that. When increased to its current level on Jan. 1, 1981, it was about half the average hourly wage in the economy. Now it is a third. Then, a person who worked full-time year-round at the minimum could earn 96 percent of the official poverty line for a family of three. Now the same effort yields 74 percent of that threshold amount.

The House Education and Labor Committee has reported out a bill that would restore the minimum's purchasing power by lifting it to $5.05 over four years. The last increment was added as a bargaining chip in place of an indexing provision lost in committee; a better measure of the bill is the goal of $4.65 over three years. Five million people now work at the minimum or below (some jobs are exempt), and another 9 million work in the zone the bill would directly affect; these are a seventh of the work force altogether.

Critics are right to say that a higher minimum would mean the loss of some jobs, as employers struggled to absorb the cost. But many more people would gain from an increase than would lose. Most opponents aren't trying to maximize employment; they're trying to hold down wage rates. Too many Democrats are reluctant to offend.

The party leadership needs to crack the whip on this issue. We don't just mean Jim Wright and Tom Foley in the House, but Jesse Jackson, Michael Dukakis, the people who would restore the party to national leadership. We don't just mean lip service, either; they should actively lean on the balking Democrats. What better measure exists of what the party still stands for, of whether it makes a dime's worth of difference who wins in November, than this bill to restore a few dimes' worth of decency to the work place?

The Miami Herald
Miami, FL, May 22, 1988

THE Davis-Bacon Act of 1931 was passed during hard times and with the best of intentions: to ensure that construction workers on Federally funded public-works projects were paid a living wage.

Where Davis-Bacon applies, all bidders — union or nonunion — must pay the "prevailing wage." For years, the U.S. Labor Department has interpreted "prevailing wage" to mean "union scale," regardless of whether such wages actually "prevail" in an area.

As a result, the Feds often pay more than the market price. Contractors put the extra costs at about 30 percent, depending on the city. The costs include not only union-scale wages but also extra paperwork.

The Depression-era law has outlived its usefulness and ought to be repealed. Instead of moving in that direction, however, some congressmen actually want to expand Davis-Bacon's effect on projects funded by Community Development Block Grants (CDBG) and Urban Development Action Grants (UDAG).

Davis-Bacon already applies to construction wages on such projects. Now, under a bill sponsored by Rep. Bruce Vento, a Minnesota Democrat, Davis-Bacon would apply to any construction remotely connected with a CDBG or UDAG project, even if funded by local taxpayers or private groups. If CDBG funds were used to clear a blighted area for redevelopment, for instance, then Davis-Bacon would apply to whatever was built there.

The National Association of Counties (NACo) vigorously opposes this change, and for good reason. NACo officials foresee a devastating impact on economic development and public housing. The bill could raise costs by as much as 35 percent and render many projects economically unfeasible.

Ironically, then, the result would be that the poorest Americans would suffer in order to subsidize the wages of workers who are already among the nation's best paid — a result far different from the original intent of Davis-Bacon. That's why the expansion bill ought to be rejected.

THE KANSAS CITY STAR

Kansas City, MO, April 7, 1988

The effort to raise the $3.35 an hour minimum wage, unchanged since 1981, has gained ground in Congress in recent days. The House Education and Labor Committee approved a bill that would boost the minimum to $5.05 an hour over the next four years. It awaits floor debate. A similar bill is pending in the Senate Labor and Human Resources Committee. Even though a presidential veto is threatened, this legislation should move forward.

To hear opponents tell it, the boost would bring the economy crashing down about us. Their line is that the higher wages would bring unemployment and cause inflation to soar.

Experience over the half century of the minimum wage law shows these fears are unfounded. Increases in 1974 and 1977 represented a fraction of 1 percent of the national payroll. Of a work force of more than 115 million, about 6 percent is paid at or below the minimum wage. After most minimum wage hikes, unemployment has fallen.

The unemployment factor also negates the contention that employers will lay off great hordes of minimum wagers or not hire new workers. Contrary to their claims the typical minimum wage earner is not a fry cook at a fast food place. The Federal Minimum Wage Study Commission found that 69 percent of these earners are adults, 20 or older. Less than a third of them, 31 percent, are 16 to 19. The average is female, white and middle-aged.

In addition to the wage rise, the House bill would exempt businesses with revenues of less than $500,000 a year, up from the current $362,500. Missouri and Kansas legislatures also have introduced minimum wage legislation.

What other category of American workers has not received a pay raise since 1981? This group has suffered a 27 percent loss of purchasing power, which is reason enough to raise the minimum wage. The other is fairness, which is lost on a lot of the opponents who think they can't operate without cheap labor.

BUFFALO EVENING NEWS

Buffalo, NY, July 11, 1988

ALL YEAR LONG Congress has dithered over enacting an increase in the nation's $3.35-an-hour minimum wage. What started out as a brave march has slowed to a legislative crawl.

Now, there are reports of a consensus among House and Senate leaders for a gradual, modest increase, and Congress should get on with the task before it.

Some are concerned that an increase in the minimum wage will rebuild inflationary pressures, because employers will try to pass along higher costs to customers who buy their products, or that a higher wage floor will raise unemployment levels as employers try to contain costs by cutting back on the number of workers. There may be something to those arguments, but they are not so convincing as to block the first raise in the minimum wage in seven years.

If anything about the future is predictable, it is that demographic trends promise a scarcity of labor in the years ahead. That represents a social sea change from the immediate past when millions of "baby-boomers" surged into the labor market, creating surpluses.

One consequence of this sea change will be that many employers will have to raise wages to attract and hold the relatively fewer numbers of young workers. Inflation might edge upward because of that. But surely little of it would be caused by a higher wage floor that merely restored the after-inflation purchasing power of the current minimum when it was enacted in 1981.

Furthermore, if a higher minimum risks eliminating some jobs, it will also create others by expanding the purchasing power of many low-income workers.

Beyond such concerns lie important considerations of human equity and decent wages that reward and encourage work. These touch fundamental social values entirely apart from estimates of future jobless and inflation rates that may prove inaccurate.

Inflation has withered the original buying power of the $3.35 minimum wage when it took effect to $2.61, a very real 22 percent loss for workers purchasing bread, milk and meat for their families. If $3.35 an hour was a just wage minimum in 1981, in real after-inflation terms, then it certainly is today.

Critics also contend that a higher minimum wage will benefit only a relatively few American workers — something under 5 million. But these are the very workers who depend the most on the protection derived from a decent floor under their pay.

The Senate Labor Committee has approved a proposal to increase the minimum wage by $1.20 an hour in three 40-cent jumps over three years, beginning Jan. 1. That would raise the minimum to $4.55 in 1991. House leaders are reported ready to go along with that program.

This would do no more than keep the minimum current with inflation, and even less than that immediately. It's a barely adequate response. But if that is all Congress can do, it should do it without succumbing to additional indecision and delay.

Telegraph Herald

Dubuque, IA, June 12, 1988

In the debate over a proposed increase in the federal minimum wage, each side makes some valid points. Reality and reason are somewhere in the middle.

Proponents of an increase in the minimum wage, which has been $3.35 an hour since 1981, point to the eroded purchasing power of earners. As U.S. Rep. Augustus Hawkins, D-Calif., wrote last year, lost purchasing power was cited by President Reagan when he called for higher salaries for the vice president, senior cabinet members, federal judges and members of Congress. There is some inconsistency when the president calls for pay increases for high-level government officials because inflation has eroded purchasing power but resists hikes in the minimum wage. However, it cannot be overlooked that the salaries must remain competitive to attract and retain quality public servants. The hard truth is that this is less of a problem at the lower end of the wage scale.

In making their case for an increase, proponents usually explain it in the context of a full-time employee with a family. That is far from a typical case. The National Federation of Independent Businesses reports that of 114 million people in the workforce, about a half-million are actually attempting to support a family on a minimum wage job. Of the 114 million, less than 5 percent work for minimum wage. Of those, two out of three are part-time, two of three are under age 25 and six of 10 are single.

Opponents say jobs will be lost if the minimum wage is increased. Even the Congressional Budget Office — its bosses include the Democratic majority, which supports the hike — estimated that 250,000 to 500,000 jobs would be eliminated with a wage increase to $4.65 an hour. Surveys of employers found that the last increase in the minimum wage resulted in reduced hours for employees, layoffs, more labor-saving equipment and higher prices for consumers. As Mark A. DeBernardo of the U.S. Chamber of Commerce concluded, "Given the experience of past minimum-wage increases, the choice may not be between a job at $4.50 per hour or a job at $3.35 per hour — the choice may be a $3.35-per-hour job or no job."

Both sides have valid points. A middle ground seems fair and reasonable. The minimum wage has not changed in eight years, but the cost of virtually everything has increased greatly during that time. U.S. workers — whether they are trying to support a family, save for college or just earn some spending money — should receive an increase.

However, the amount of increase proponents seek is so aggressive that too few workers might benefit by it. A hike into the $4.50-$4.65 range is likely to result in a repeat of what occurred earlier this decade — including fewer hours and fewer employees. A more modest increase would minimize the negative impact on employment levels and businesses' expense (which contribute to consumers' costs). But people should not be surprised when there are cuts in hours and employment; they are inevitable.

The minimum wage should be increased moderately, to help workers while still keeping as many employed as possible.

Chicago Tribune

Chicago, IL, June 17, 1988

The chances that economists will agree on something are only slightly better than the odds that you will win the next $50 million Illinois lottery. When they do agree, it's even less likely that politicians will accept their advice.

We are now witnessing that extremely rare occurrence, a consensus among economists. Conservative, radical, neo-whatever, they agree that raising the minimum wage will boost consumer prices and kill jobs. It may be billed as a move to lift the lot of America's poorest workers but what it actually will do is shove those workers out of the labor force and onto unemployment rolls.

And for once, the economists' unusual agreement and the solid reasoning behind it has made an impression on lawmakers. A tiny one, to be sure, but at least it is a beginning. The U.S. House is scheduled to begin floor debate next week on a bill that would increase the minimum wage by 50 percent, lifting it to $5.05 an hour over four years. What's astonishing is that the Democratic-sponsored legislation, introduced 15 months ago, has taken so long to gain support in an election season, when foolish political promises are as prevalent as tree pollen. Even some Democrats are wavering in their support.

The bill's sponsors, Sen. Edward M. Kennedy of Massachusetts and Rep. Augustus Hawkins of California, had underestimated the intelligence of their colleagues. They thought they would have it on the President's desk early last fall. Democratic staff members of the House Education and Labor Committee tried to round up votes by persuading the supposedly impartial Congressional Budget Office to censor some material critical of the bill. The office reported earlier this year that raising the minimum wage to $5 05 an hour would cost as many as 500,000 jobs; that was omitted from its final report.

Government can order employers to raise wages but it can't force them to hire at that rate. Some marginal businesses and ones that can't be profitable at the new wage will cut workers' hours to compensate. Others will cut their work forces, reduce benefits or curtail services. Employees most likely to be laid off will be young and minority, with few skills and scant work experience, and senior citizens working part time.

In a competitive, unregulated labor market, workers earn more by being more productive or valuable. Giving minimum-wage workers a 50 percent raise increases the price of their labor but does not necessarily increase their productivity. It encourages unions to bargain for higher pay, lifting the entire wage scale. And that makes it still more difficult for struggling U.S. manufacturers to compete with foreign producers both in this country and in world markets, further reducing the number of U.S. jobs.

If Congress votes to raise the minimum wage, it is also voting to raise prices and unemployment rolls.

THE DAILY HERALD

Biloxi, MS, March 8, 1988

Since a House subcommittee stripped a controversial indexing provision from a bill proposing to boost the federal minimum wage from $3.35 an hour to $4.65 over the next three years, congressional approval this year is enhanced.

Organized labor has targeted the minimum wage, last raised in 1981, as its major goal in the 100th Congress and election year politics guarantees top billing for an issue that affects about 5.1 million hourly wage workers.

The strongest argument for an increase is the fact that the earnings level of minimum-wage workers has steadily declined below the government's official poverty line since 1980 and has been stagnant while average earnings of other hourly wage workers have increased.

Congress is faced with the risky task of restoring a proper equity without deleterious effects on a shaky economy. Too sharp an increase could be counter-productive, boosting inflation and reducing employment opportunities in traditional low-wage states such as Mississippi.

It's a package labeled "Handle With Care."

Portland Press Herald

Portland, ME, March 12, 1988

For years, Maine and virtually every other state had minimum wage laws that mirrored the prevailing federal law. Whenever Congress raised the minimum wage, the Maine Legislature promptly followed suit. The uniform system, so far as anyone could tell, worked well.

Then a few years ago the Legislature decided Maine should go it alone. Today, the state minimum wage is $3.65 an hour, 30 cents higher than the federal minimum. And it may go higher still under a measure that would boost the Maine minimum to $4.05 by 1990, 70 cents more than federal law.

But maybe not. Congress is now studying legislation to put the federal minimum wage, in stages, to as high as $5.05 by the end of 1991. If so, Maine's minimum would be $1 below the federal minimum. It's likely that lawmakers would then increase the state minimum to the new federal level, or maybe higher still.

Is there any sense in all this leapfrogging? To us, not much. Far better to return to the system of a uniform minimum wage. Fiddling with the state minimum can create unnecessary problems.

No one argues that anyone with a family who is toiling for either the federal or state minimum is earning a living wage. That's below the poverty level. But the state should make certain that, in proposing to raise the state wage higher still this year, it doesn't injure the very people it is trying to help.

Further increasing the state minimum wage will provide a pay increase for the poorest workers — providing they have jobs. But others will be pushed out of the job market because of the elimination or non-creation of new jobs. Additionally, some of the lowest-paid workers may find themselves on the tax rolls and will wind up even worse off than before.

True enough, raising the minimum wage sounds noble. But there are problems involved. Maine can eliminate some by returning to the system of keeping our wage laws in conformity with those of the federal government.

St. Paul Pioneer Press & Dispatch

St. Paul, MN, March 29, 1988

Congress appears ready to pass legislation to raise the federal minimum wage from the current $3.35 an hour to $5.05 an hour in several steps over four years.

Proponents claim the hikes would boost the standard of living for the 4.7 million Americans who earn it without causing a harmful ripple in the economy. Opponents, including President Reagan, contend boosting the minimum wage would force employers to reduce minimum-wage jobs, thereby hurting the very folks the law was intended to help.

While the issues are clouded in statistics, raising the minimum wage clearly would help some and hurt others. If Congress is determined to legislate prosperity — a questionable power at best — it should at least soften the potential negative impact on teenage workers by adopting a two-tiered system that allows employers to initially pay young job-seekers a lower minimum wage.

The Houston Post

Houston, TX, April 4, 1988

Congress is finding pressure to raise the minimum wage hard to resist in this election year. But for the sake of the U.S. economy, lawmakers should summon up the political will to reject the idea.

Unions and other backers of bills to boost the minimum wage point out that it has been seven years since the current $3.35-an-hour rate was set. They argue that an increase would stimulate the economy and help the working poor without having to raise taxes.

But before Congress votes on the bills, one of which would push the wage rate to $5.05 an hour over four years, it should examine economists' warning about long-term adverse consequences.

Raising the wage rate would aggravate already high unemployment among youth, especially minority youth. Many employers can't afford to pay the current $3.35 an hour to the unskilled young.

Instead of helping the working poor while avoiding new taxes, a boost in the minimum wage could reignite inflation by forcing some businesses to raise their prices. It could also cause some employers to eliminate jobs or refrain from creating new ones.

Furthermore, raising the rate would send the wrong signal to our competitors in world commerce just as we are beginning to make a little headway against our massive $170 billion trade deficit.

A minimum wage raise would be a Pandora's box, not a panacea.

CHARLESTON EVENING POST

Charleston, SC, July 11, 1988

When they expound on the benefits of increasing the federal minimum wage, advocates seem always to tell one side of the story. Take Sen. Edward M. Kennedy, D-Mass., for example. Sen. Kennedy's bill, recently approved (with compromises) by the Senate Labor Committee, would raise the current $3.35 hourly minimum to $4.55 over the next three years. "Five million men and women in America will get the benefit of that increase — and they deserve it," Sen. Kennedy said. "They're the working poor. They'd rather work than live on welfare ..."

The working poor — like anyone else — deserve a fair day's wage for a fair day's work. But sight should not be lost of the other side of the minimum wage story, the side Sen. Kennedy conveniently ignores. He doesn't mention the young and inexperienced — many of them blacks and Hispanics — who would be denied jobs because of a higher minimum wage. How many employers will be willing to pay more for inexperienced, unskilled help? Not many, and that's why a higher minimum wage works to the disadvantage of the young unless the authorizing legislation expressly exempts teen-agers

The Chattanooga Times

Chattanooga, TN, March 25, 1988

Ever notice that the loudest arguments against raising the minimum wage are usually raised by those whose pay is many times that figure — and who probably never worked at the minimum wage level? The arguments are being raised again now because Congress is preparing to vote next month on legislation to raise the minimum wage to $5.05 an hour over five years. The increase is long overdue and deserves passage.

The federal minimum has been set at $3.35 since 1981, which works out to slightly less than $7,000. But that figure is deceptive. Since 1981, inflation has reduced its purchasing power by $1 an hour. The proposed increase would not match that inflation, although it would ease matters somewhat. Nevertheless, while the Reagan administration continues to oppose any increase, its attempts to justify that position fail to persuade.

A fact sheet distributed by the Labor Department argues that a single person who works full-time at a minimum wage job earns enough to stay above the poverty line. It goes on to say that nearly half the heads of households who are below the poverty line are unemployed. It follows then, says Labor, that merely increasing the minimum wage will not have a "significant impact in reducing poverty."

Of course, the department's emphasis on reducing poverty is not the point. Workers deserve more than the opportunity to subsist just above the poverty line, and anyway the salary of an employee who earns $3.35 an hour and who works a minimum 40 hours a week for the year would be well below the poverty line for a three-member family. According to the AFL-CIO, most minimum-wage workers are adults, two-thirds are women and most provide the only income for their families.

A familiar argument against an increase in the minimum wage is that it would cost jobs. That is, employers faced with paying workers another 50 cents an hour next year, with subsequent raises, would fire employees to offset costs. There are differences of opinion on this matter, but it's worth noting that many businesses that employ so-called minimum wage workers — fast-food outlets, for example — are actually advertising jobs with starting salaries *above* the minimum wage. Is it likely, then, that a pizza delivery company offering starting workers $3.80 an hour is going to lay off workers if the minimum wage next year is pegged at $3.85? Hardly.

In fact, many states already require a minimum wage higher than the federal minimum; California, for example, will mandate $4.25 an hour in July. Most states, Tennessee included, adhere to the $3.35 minimum wage. But now Congress is moving to help those who traditionally have been able to exert little influence on Capitol Hill. It's time to raise the minimum wage, especially one that forces poverty upon even the smallest families.

THE LINCOLN STAR

Lincoln, NE,
March 14, 1988

A George Washington University study has reported that part-time work has grown nearly 50 percent faster than full-time employment in the 1980s. Last month, it was said, the number of Americans at work rose by 280,000 but 200,000 of those were people working part-time who want but can't find full-time jobs.

While recognizing the values associated with part-time work opportunities, a study spokesman said that "the vast majority of America's 19.5 million part-time workers hold low-wage, dead-end jobs which offer few, if any, benefits or promotional opportunities."

A report on the study contained the views of interested parties on differing sides of this issue. Business interests spoke of the need for their companies to be as competitive as possible and that included such labor cost efficiencies as part-time jobs.

On the other side are those who examine the consequences of such a low-cost labor policy. The issue is one that is just below the surface of the current national campaigns being waged for presidential nominations by the Republican and Democratic parties.

It puts somewhat in perspective the bottom line of the faltering protectionist campaign that has been a part of Rep. Richard Gephardt's presidential bid. At the end of Gephardt's line are jobs that pay a living wage.

A living wage is not the $100 or so per week that a breadwinner might make working a part-time job. Such jobs are often without any fringe benefits, not even health insurance, and offer little opportunity for advancement.

Many of these jobs are hidden by the high employment figures so frequently cited by the Reagan administration.

While the economics of the matter are understandable from a business point of view, the humanitarian aspect of the situation is equally important. The nation can hardly afford to be satisfied with conditions that reduce millions and milions of people to a poverty level. We cannot be satisfied with a system in which millions and millions find no opportunity to attain a decent standard of living.

Gephardt and other protectionists do not have the answer, but the answer must ultimately be provided through education, job training and whatever other approaches that offer promise. If this growth of part-time jobs continues, as is expected, it will become more and more of a political issue and less under the control of the private job market.

The Atlanta Journal
THE ATLANTA CONSTITUTION

Atlanta, GA, May 23, 1988

Opponents of a higher minimum wage have proved one point: The idea is wildly inflationary.

Scarcely a year ago, the U.S. Chamber of Commerce was warning that an increase would cost the nation 300,000 jobs. Today, the White House claims that the smallest boost under consideration (from $3.35 per hour to $4.65 by 1992) would cost 600,000 jobs. An increase to $5.05 by 1992 would cancel 850,000 jobs, insist the Reaganites.

Conclusion: When it comes to bashing the minimum wage, fears are being inflated at triple-digit rates.

True, any increase will prompt some employers to trim their payrolls. And yes, higher wages could boost prices for some products, which might shrink markets and result in smaller work forces.

But these liabilities are not nearly as severe as opponents claim. The minimum wage has gone up several times since its New Deal inception, and the sky has not fallen. What *has* fallen in recent years is the purchasing power of minimum wage workers. Since 1981, they have grossed $6,968 a year. That sum was a pittance then — but the cost of living today is more than 27 percent higher.

Have most employers raised their prices since 1981? Sure. Have they given themselves and their skilled workers raises since then? You can count on it. Were there some adverse effects to these actions? Yes, but on balance they were seen — correctly — as necessary costs of doing business.

Yet whenever Congress tries to insist on a (barely) decent wage for the working poor, conservatives suddenly start to worry about an economic Armageddon. They insist that their opposition is in the best interests of minimum-wage workers. For all the hot air behind that argument, it still won't fly.

Arkansas Gazette.

Little Rock, AR, July 11, 1988

There was a time when institutional investors, like children in an earlier era, were "seen and not heard." Using other people's savings stashed in pension funds and similar packages, the money managers accumulated portfolios of stocks and bonds, watched the market, and rolled their holdings when they thought they saw an opportunity for profit. In threats of corporate raids or proxy fights, they usually voted with management.

Two developments are changing the money managing business:

★ The emphasis of corporate management has shifted from the production of goods and services to empire building. Mergers and acquisitions seem to have replaced technology and efficiency as the top priority of many companies.

★ Fund managers, who control an enormous volume of assets, are awakening to the potential power their proxies command at the stockholders' meetings.

Professional asset management is an ancient trade that may have predated banks. Joseph, for example, reportedly was in charge of the pharaoh's fiscal affairs. In modern times, the development of pension systems and other forms of deferred compensation created a demand for people who could make wise investments and (presumably) earn money for their clients. The relentless growth of pension and mutual funds and assorted other accumulations of assets loaded the "institutions" with tremendous resources. Fund managers control an estimated $2 trillion in stock and bond holdings.

Portfolios of this size rule out the old option of selling the stocks of a company that did not measure up to the expectations of the investment adviser. Institutions reportedly own 53 per cent of Ford Motor Company ($12.1 billion), 46.1 percent of IBM ($29.6 billion and 57.8 percent of Philip Morris ($12.2 billion). Pensions own almost half the stock of companies that make up Standard and Poor's 500 Index. Holdings of this size leave the fund managers with no place to go if they want to unload equities of a disfavored company.

A corporate management team that decides to sell off assets, elect directors unacceptable to a key fund manager, or create a "poison pill" to discourage a hostile takeover may need more than a full-page advertisement in *The Wall Street Journal* to execute the maneuver.

Managers generally have been content with a passive role but the situation could change quickly when they realize the power inherent in the proxies they hold. They could decide to put a person (or persons) of their choosing on the board, or they might team up with Carl C. Ichan or T. Boone Pickens and take over IBM. Nothing short of a major ruling by the Securities and Exchange Commission or even a new body of laws could stall such a deal.

Those who wonder what would be wrong with having the California Public Employees Retirement System (assets $46 billion) and a couple of other like-minded funds in control of a major corporation obviously have not examined the possibilities. The potential for insider trading — with board members of the company dealing stock for the benefit of their clients and themselves — would create a no-win game for the outside investor.

When a pension fund manager takes a seat on the board of Texaco or Ford, the SEC and Congress should be prepared to shift into high gear and deal with a "new" threat to individual initiative and even to the private enterprise system.

Omaha World-Herald
Omaha, NE, March 9, 1988

The desire of some members of Congress to increase the federal minimum wage is understandable. It's easy to sympathize with workers who can earn barely enough to support themselves, let alone a family. Even so, a proposal to raise the minimum wage from the current $3.35 to $4.65 over the next three years might hurt some of the very people it is designed to help.

The plan, proposed by Sen. Edward Kennedy, D-Mass., and Rep. Augustus Hawkins, D-Calif., was approved Thursday by the House labor standards subcommittee. It would raise the minimum wage 50 cents an hour beginning Jan. 1 and 40 cents an hour in each of the next two years.

Minimum wage workers, including those who need their minimum-wage job as a second source of family income, could be put out of work by the increase. Some employers simply won't be able to afford the extra payroll costs, particularly since the added wages won't necessarily translate into increased productivity.

People who work for small businesses, where stretching budgets to cover increases is often difficult, stand to be especially hard hit if the Kennedy-Hawkins bill became law. It isn't only the increased mimimum wages that cost more. When workers at the bottom wage level receive a raise, workers at the next pay level sometimes also expect pay increases.

When labor costs rise, employers look for ways to stay within their budget. They reduce overtime, put full-time workers on part-time hours or lay people off and try to get along with a smaller work force.

Raising the minimum wage, in other words, is not the way to make things better for the working poor.

The Providence Journal
Providence, RI, March 11, 1988

Members of both Congress and the Rhode Island General Assembly are in the process of considering bills that would raise the legally mandated minimum wage. One measure, which recently emerged from the U.S. House of Representatives' labor standards subcommittee, would boost the national minimum from $3.35 to $4.65 an hour over the next three years. And locally, the Senate recently approved a bill that would immediately hike the state rate from $3.65 to $4.00 an hour.

The emotional temptation, as well as the political pressures, to pass these measures will be great. After all, what could be more personally satisfying, and more politically rewarding, than to be able to "give" people more money by raising their wages?

Yet if such proposals are enacted, they will end up having damaging consequences for many of the people they are designed to help.

Measures raising the minimum wage are incapable of accomplishing their supposed goal — namely, raising the incomes of the working poor. In fact, if legislators actually believe the government can, by simple legal fiat, increase people's occupational value, they should not limit themselves to proposals like those currently before Congress and the General Assembly. Why be so modest — requiring, for example, that Rhode Island workers be paid at least $4.00 an hour (or $8,320 a year)? Why not be truly progressive and humanitarian and raise the minimum wage to, say, $15 an hour? Then everybody could make at least $30,000 a year and be comfortably middle class.

The fallacy behind such a move is obvious. Employers could not afford to pay such rates for all positions, but would not be legally allowed to offer jobs to potential workers at lower rates. As a result, the vast majority of jobs — and most of the businesses themselves — would simply evaporate. Instead of everybody becoming middle class, nearly everybody would end up unemployed — and broke.

Well, the same process, albeit on a more limited scale, occurs when the minimum wage gets a relatively modest boost — such as the hike of 35 cents an hour currently proposed for this state. Some of the working poor — those who are lucky enough to keep their jobs — will earn somewhat more ($728 over the course of a year) if the minimum rate is raised. But what will happen to the rest of the working poor? They will become unemployed — with no income at all — because businesses will cut back on their work force to cope with the increased labor costs brought on by the rise in the minimum wage.

The only effective way to increase real wages is to boost economic productivity. Management can do its part through greater capital investments and more efficient administrative and operational techniques. And workers can help by improving their occupational training and gaining greater experience on the job (in this regard, since young people are the ones most likely to be holding relatively low-skilled minimum wage positions, they are also the ones most likely to lose opportunities for gaining beneficial work experience when such entry-level jobs are cut back due to increases in the minimum wage).

All this may seem to be a hard and slow process, and in many respects it is. But the good thing is that it works. And that is a lot more than can be said for hiking the minimum wage, which is a generous-sounding, but counterproductive. attempt to find a quick fix.

Los Angeles Times
Los Angeles, CA, July 27, 1988

Millions of hard-working Americans are losing the battle against inflation. They have scraped by for seven years on the federal minimum wage, $3.35 an hour. At that stagnant rate, full-time workers earn less than $7,000 a year—a salary below the poverty level for a family of three. No matter how hard they work, no matter how high prices rise, the workers cannot count on a yearly pay raise. They get a raise not when they deserve one but only when politics allows it.

It is up to Congress to increase the minimum wage, but politics complicates that task. The Reagan Administration and most Republicans oppose any increase for fear that an increase will cost jobs, raise prices and hurt the very people whom Congress wants to help. Looking back on the historical record, the theory does not wash in practice.

Most Democrats argue for an increase. Legislation sponsored by Edward M. Kennedy (D-Mass.) in the Senate and Augustus F. Hawkins (D-Los Angeles) in the House would raise the minimum wage to $4.55 an hour. The increase, based on raises of 40 cents an hour over the next three years, is a reasonable proposition.

After seven years, any increase will be of some help to workers trying to catch up with inflation, but Congress must not wait another seven years to act again. A compromise that would have indexed the minimum wage at 50% of the average private wage failed to pass. Congress can make up for that lapse only by raising minimum wages annually.

Although no date has been scheduled for floor action on the measures in the House and Senate, most Democrats are anxious to bring the bills to a full vote by Labor Day. If they succeed, they will force President Reagan to think carefully about vetoing a pay raise for nearly 5 million Americans during an election year.

Workers who earn the minimum wage include teen-agers, young adults on their first jobs and spouses who work part time just to help out. But nearly 1 million heads of households support families on the minimum wage. They have lost nearly one-third of their buying power since Congress last raised the rate in January, 1981, although workers have been luckier in six states—including California, where the minimum wage rose to $4.25 on July 1.

Most Americans believe that hard work pays off. It is hard to go on believing when a welfare check is worth more than a pay check, or a pay check stands still while the cost of rent, groceries and just about everything else keeps going up and up.

Congress has raised the minimum wage only 15 times since 1938, when the Fair Labor Standards Act guaranteed that a working man could support his family with dignity. A pay increase that allows hard-working Americans to keep pace with inflation is long overdue. That is not too much to ask for the men, women and teen-agers who are no strangers to hard work.

Part II:
Homelessness & Housing

The shortage of permanent housing for the poor is high on the list of America's seemingly entrenched problems. Social historians have condemned the dire housing conditions in the worst neighborhoods of our cities since the beginning of the industrial revolution. After a century of irregular but steadily advancing national affluence coupled with increased government intervention, there is a persistant perception among both scholars and lay people that a significant number of the country's poor are inadequately housed.

The continued existence of substandard housing is not the result of lack of interest in the problem by national opinion or federal leadership. Dating back to the turn of the century there has been periodic reform in public housing and since 1949 the promise of decent housing for all citizens has been a high national priority. The Housing Act of 1949 specifically seeks to achieve "a decent home and a suitable living environment for every American family."

But today, after 40 years of endeavor, billions of dollars spent and a general improvement from the days of severe dillapidation, national housing policy is in a state of flux. Since 1965 successive administrations have experimented with a series of housing programs. Each new program has been launched with high hopes and fanfare, only to be scaled back or canceled a few years later. Beginning with Lyndon Johnson's Great Society, each administration has had a different theory concerning the nature of the country's housing woes and different formulas to cure them. The merry-go-round of housing policy has currently halted, prompting housing advocates to accuse the Reagan administration of indifference to both ends and means of a coherent or sympathetic housing program.

Housing advocates, the traditional champions of housing subsidies and housing reform, admit that they have grown weary of the battle and have displayed little unity against what they claim is the government's tendency to withdraw from the housing arena. But they argue that we have reached a point where we must take stock of what can and should be done about housing policy. They argue that past approaches to improving housing must be reappraised, that new approaches be designed, and, above all, that the goals of a national housing program be clearly articulated.

Crystallizing a new American housing vision raises many conceptual questions. Why has housing for the poor been such an apparently intractable problem? How effective have past housing programs been and how well have they met contemporary goals? What has been the role of the private sector in improving conditions? Who, among the poor, are in the greatest need of housing assistance and why? Where, in our urban areas, should housing for the poor be located?

One factor that is often pointed to as linking housing issues with the emergence of homelessness is that the homes of the poor often stand in the way of progress. As cities have grown and their economic bases have changed, the configuration of land uses have become increasingly modified by redevelopment. Urban slums, strategically located by accidents of urban history and cheaper to acquire and redevelop than better-off neighborhoods, are usually the target of real estate developers. Less dramatically, low-income neighborhoods may be "gentrified" by venturesome private purchasers and rehabilitation. Both practices can displace poorer residents in favor of prosperous ones. Many of the displaced end up on the streets or on the doorsteps of local shelters.

Many homeless advocates argue that the problem is more profound than a lack of physical shelter. Some of the homeless have roofs over their heads: adult homes, single-room occupancy hotels (SROs), city shelters or psychiatric emergency rooms and wards.

"Who are the homeless?" is an often asked question with no simple answer because there are distinct, quite different groups of homeless citizens: the "bag ladies" who huddle in the entranceways to stores; young workers, particularly, from the minorities, who cannot find an affordable place in the economy of the eighties; runaways and abused women who leave their homes as an act of self-preservation; AIDS victims who are impoverished by the high cost of treating the disease and evicted by ignorant or homophobic landlords; ex-mental patients who have been theoretically "deinstitutionalized," but in fact have been simply dumped onto the streets of our cities. The homeless are mothers, fathers, children, veterans, the aging, the sick, laid-off workers and—a rapidly increasing segment—the employed. Families in which both parents work live in tents or cars because they cannot afford basic housing. What they all have in common is that they have been uprooted and sent out, totally unprepared, into a world of bewildering transition and danger.

Confusing matters is the discrepancy in counting the homeless ranks. With all its computers and wealth of resources and research, our society has been unable to even come close to agreeing to how many U.S. citizens are without homes. Do they number 300,000, as recent Reagan administration figures bare, or three million as claimed by homeless advocates?

Many of the homeless choose the streets over the shelter system in their city. In New York City, where the homeless situation is most acute, the shelter system is bureaucratically organized, often in the worst sense of the word. In addition, shelters can also be fearful places, a consequence of the young homeless people, mentally disturbed men and women, and racial and ethnic tensions. The availability of narcotics, particularly "crack" cocaine, at the shelters and the emergence of AIDS have compounded the dilemma of those ensnared in the web of homelessness.

Homeless Americans Increase as Studies Are Released

A report issued by the Housing and Urban Development Department (HUD) May 1, 1984 estimated the number of homeless people in the U.S. to be between 250,000 and 350,000. The number was far below estimates by many national organizations that the number of homeless was in the range of two to three million. In releasing the report, HUD Secretary Samuel Pierce Jr. called it "the first national profile of the homeless population, based on systematically collected data."

The report estimated that about half the homeless suffered from alcoholism, drug abuse or mental illness. It said that about two-thirds were single men, 13% were single women, 21% were families, and 44% were minorities. The median age was reported to be late 20s to mid-30s. The largest numbers of homeless were found in Los Angeles (31,300 to 33,800), New York (28,000 to 30,000) and Chicago (19,400 to 20,300). The study was said to be based on interviews with 500 observers in 60 metropolitan areas, site visits to 10 cities and national surveys of shelters and state programs. HUD Acting Assistant Secretary Benjamin F. Bobo said the survey showed that homelessness "is not as widespread a problem as previously had been thought."

There were numerous critics of the report, however, who disputed the findings. "I would say 250,000 to 350,000 is a very conservative estimate," J. Thomas Cochran, deputy executive director of the U.S. Conference of Mayors, commented May 1. "I'd be shocked if it was that low," Rep. Barney Frank (D, Mass.) said. "They're trying to define the homeless out of existence, he continued, "because they don't want to have to spend money on the problem." Mitch Snyder, director of Community for Creative Non-Violence (CCNV), called HUD's estimate "an absolute absurdity." CCNV's estimate, based on a survey of at least 75 cities, according to Snyder, was that there were at least two million homeless in the U.S. Philadelphia Mayor Wilson Goode told a congressional hearing May 2, on behalf of the U.S. Conference of Mayors, that, "Anyone who doesn't believe that homelessness is a real problem is not walking the streets of our cities."

The American Psychiatric Association Sept. 12, 1984 said that the policy of discharging mentally ill patients from institutions into local communities had failed, and that the resulting plight of homelessness was "a major societal tragedy." The association presented its views in a bluntly worded, 312-page report released at a Washington, D.C. news conference. It was called the first major attempt to study the homeless mentally ill and consider plans to help them. The report cited studies estimating that a total of 250,000 to three million Americans might be homeless, with 25% to 50% of them suffering from such serious mental illnesses as manic depression and schizophrenia.

"Hardly a section of the country, urban or rural, has escaped the ubiquitous presence of ragged, ill and hallucinating human beings wandering through our city streets, huddled in alleyways or sleeping over vents," the report said. The study said that the main cause of the problem was the failure of the deinstitutionalization policy that had been in effect for the previous 30 years. Under that policy, large numbers of the chronically mentally ill were to have been shifted from state hospitals to community treatment centers. The process had been spurred by the availability of new mood-altering drugs, the legal and legislative push for patients' rights, and budget-cutting pressures.

The report noted that although the policy had cut the number of patients in large public mental housing by more than three-fourths (from about 560,000 in 1955 to 130,000 in 1980), the hoped-for community services never materialized, leaving many former patients to walk the streets. This "disastrous" failure to provide the mentally ill with health care, or even with food or shelter, left many of them "cast adrift under conditions that most persons think can no longer exist in this country," the report said.

The report also called for a loosening of strict involuntary-commitment laws and regulations. In most states, the law limited involuntary hospitalization to individuals who were deemed a menace to themselves or others. The study suggested that for some of the chronically mentally ill who could not cope with community life, institutions were still the best answer.

A report issued Dec. 16, 1987 by the U.S. Conference on Mayors said that the demand for emergency shelter in 26 major cities had risen 21% in 1987 and that the demand for food assistance had risen by 18% despite economic improvements in most of those cities. According to the study, families with children now constituted one-third of the homeless population in the cities surveyed. About one-quarter of the homeless were individuals deemed severely mentally ill. More than 70% of the cities surveyed said that families were the one group for which emergency shelter and other services were most often in short supply.

Another of the study's findings was that 22% of the homeless held full- or part-time jobs but that there was just not enough affordable housing available for low-wage earners. The average wait for subsidized housing in the cities surveyed was estimated to have reached 22 months.

Nearly all of the cities surveyed believed that the plight of the homeless would worsen in 1988, largely because of a lack of federal and state funds to ease the chronic low-income housing shortage.

THE DENVER POST

Denver, CO, November 17, 1984

IN A PERFECT world, we wouldn't have hundreds of homeless people in downtown Denver seeking shelter, food, jobs and care for their children. There would be no debate over the Catholic Archdiocese's plan for a $6.5 million shelter at 23rd Street and Broadway near downtown Denver.

But, of course, the world isn't perfect. And now neighbors plan to voice objections about the shelter during the Denver City Council meeting Monday night. Their complaints go like this:

We shouldn't institutionalize the poor and the homeless in one location, encouraging the riffraff to locate downtown. We shouldn't threaten adjoining businesses and the future of the Curtis Park residential neighborhood. Besides, why not spread out the shelters geographically? Make them smaller. Why concentrate the burden here?

The facts:

Of the 2,000 to 5,000 Denver area homeless, a considerable number are being cared for in the suburbs, usually by church-related groups. But the downtown area has a strong appeal, for reasons which may be fraught with human frailty but which still are quite real.

Transportation is a major factor. Many of the homeless come into Denver by bus and train, and those lines empty into downtown. Downtown also offers chances for manual labor and odd jobs, attracting the hopeful homeless.

Alcoholics will not be accepted at the new center, just as they are not accepted at the Samaritan Shelter at 1836 Logan St., which the new center will replace.

The archdiocese knows that an important component of the homeless is the growing number of needy families. Having arrived here, they cannot find work and are unable to pay $400 a month for housing. Timely help is a sound social investment, forestalling heavier welfare burdens later on.

Some critics seek oversimplified solutions. But the archdiocese must provide a realistic answer, tempered by a humanitarian response. The solution proposed isn't perfect, but neither are the circumstances that brought the homeless to our door. An open-hearted response is the best one — in fact, it's the only one that will work. The archdiocese's plan should go forward.

THE PLAIN DEALER

Cleveland, OH, May 3, 1984

How many homeless are there in the United States? The usual estimate was in the millions until Tuesday, when the federal Department of Housing and Urban Development (HUD) released a study saying that the number is much lower, perhaps 250,000 to 350,000. Some public interest groups have expressed dismay over the small number; but at least one group has said that although the estimate probably is low, it nevertheless provides a serviceable starting line for administrative action

Accepting the low-end figures from HUD does not mitigate the crisis. If there are, say, 300,000 homeless rather than 3 million, there still are only 91,000 shelter beds, meaning that at least two-thirds of those without homes virtually are shelterless. In Cleveland, the ratio is better: some 500 homeless to 350 beds. Yet the need still is painfully clear. Federal benefit cuts, increases in poverty-level expenses, rising long-term unemployment, the delay and resulting shortage of low-cost housing ... all are conditions that contribute to a worsening and inexcusable national dilemma.

It may be, as some Washington observers suggest, that HUD played with the statistics; that it managed to deflate the figures in the face of public pressure to recognize the problem and political pressure to minimize it. But if so, then the scheme was only marginally successful. The estimates may be low, but there is no longer any opportunity for the administration to deny the problem, as it tried to do with the related hunger crisis. Some $60 million earmarked for food and shelter by Congress last fall has yet to be appropriated, and other federal funds have lapsed. As a result, there are currently no federal funds available to aid the homeless. In trying to quantify the problem, the Reagan administration now must provide the money; reluctant federal agencies now must manage it.

It is not surprising that the administration has failed to support legislation designed to aid the homeless. Federal spending cuts in social programs and entitlements doubtless have aggravated the problem. But the administration's own estimates now show that hundreds of thousands of Americans are outcast. It cannot still ignore them without being callous and cruel.

Los Angeles Times

Los Angeles, CA, December 25, 1984

A small tent city at the Civic Center shelters some of the homeless of Los Angeles this Christmas. The tents, filled with rows of cots and donated blankets, are cold, but not as cold and damp as the doorways and alleys in which many of the homeless have been sleeping. Unless it rains hard, workers will strike the tents this week. But while the tents are there, perched fittingly between the Los Angeles City Hall and the Los Angeles County Hall of Administration, they are both a shelter and a challenge to officials in both buildings to do more for the homeless once the tents are gone.

We would settle for an answer along the following lines: The city's Mayor Tom Bradley and the county's Board of Supervisors would announce that each is designating a high-level official to take responsibility for identifying abandoned buildings or vacant land that could be used for shelter when the tents are gone. Officials such as Maureen Kindel, president of the city Board of Public Works, and county Supervisor Deane Dana would be good choices.

That selection made, the officials would expedite work needed to bring the buildings into compliance with health and safety codes. The last step would be working with nonprofit organizations already involved in housing, such as Volunteers of America and Skid Row Development Corp., to arrange for managing the shelters and providing services. It is crucial to maintain job counseling and other services for the homeless so that the poor are not simply swept off the streets and forgotten.

So far the bulk of work to help the homeless and other people on the edge of existence has come from the nonprofit groups. Los Familias del Pueblo is trying to set up a 100-bed shelter mainly for families. The San Fernando Valley Interfaith Council seeks to convert a North Hollywood motel into a 77-room shelter because at present there is only one small shelter in the San Fernando Valley to supplement county housing vouchers to help the homeless. The Downtown Women's Center has raised $1.3 million, but still needs $500,000 more toward renovation of a residential hotel to house 50 women. And the Single Room Occupancy Corp. is moving to renovate existing Skid Row hotels to provide safer housing. These and other efforts must be duplicated 10 and 20 times to accommodate the need.

Two procedural moves by the county would also help. At present, people must work 68½ hours a month to receive a $228 general relief grant, and must prove that they have applied for at least 20 jobs. Should they miss any work, they are suspended from relief payments for 60 days. This often means that they are out on the street because they lack reserves. It would be far more humane, and in the long run more cost-effective, simply to dock a relief recipient for time missed rather than to impose a full suspension.

The county also needs to pay providers of housing more quickly. Under its current voucher system it pays hotels and shelters $8 a night for each indigent person housed, but the payment takes three months. Groups operating shelters or seeking to open them operate on tight budgets and need the money faster than that.

The tent city was the work of the Homeless Organizing Team, backed by the Catholic Worker organization and the Interfaith Hunger Coalition. They did more than provide crude shelter from pouring rain for the needy—in the truest spirit of the season. Their tents also called attention to the broader problem of the homeless. Many people in Los Angeles have worked in their own small but effective ways to help the homeless for several years. It is time for government to make a major commitment to shelter the needy, and not just at holiday time.

LOS ANGELES HERALD

Los Angeles, CA, August 24, 1984

The package of assistance for the homeless that the Board of Supervisors passed last week is both legally and morally necessary. But in fulfilling the county's obligation to provide better facilities for its homeless, Supervisor Ed Edelman's program may create problems as well as solve them.

Certainly, one problem that will be solved is legal. A Superior Court judge has ruled that the county cannot fulfill its legal obligation to the homeless by simply handing out vouch-

ers for $8 rooms in sleazy Skid Row hotels. The package allows the distribution of vouchers for more expensive, non-private shelter.

That's fine, if all the county is worried about are the estimated 300-500 homeless who, according to the most conservative estimates, are currently without shelter on Skid Row. But what if there are 30,000-50,000 homeless in the county, as studies have contended? And what if the county follows through on the package's pledge to simplify the complicated application procedures that deny many shelter? That's likely to sharply increase county responsibilities. And if we really want to aid these people, we should provide the training that will help them get back on their feet. Who will pay for it all?

Edelman's package calls for turning to nonprofit, nongovernmental agencies which are already sheltering many homeless. But to do so, those agencies must find financing for new shelters. And while there are a number of possible sources — mostly federal — none are sure things.

Moreover, if these agencies do come up with the facilities, someone will still have to pay the boarding expenses of the homeless. County general relief funds are the most obvious candidate. But if the new package ends up generating requests for shelter from only 10,000 of the estimated 30,000-50,000 remaining homeless, the county general relief budget will increase by nearly 40 percent over its current $87 million.

That doesn't mean Edelman's plan is unwise. It contains worthy reforms. But if we want to make life better for our homeless, it will likely cost a lot more than we're currently prepared to spend. There is, after all, no such thing as a free roof. ■

The Dispatch

Columbus, OH, December 27, 1984

Various agencies in the large United Nations organization have worked hard to ease the suffering of the world's poor. But a recent decision by the General Assembly is sickening.

The assembly voted to spend $73.5 million to build a conference center in Ethiopia where, at this very minute, hundreds of thousands of persons are starving to death. The United States voted against the center. It was joined by a handful of other nations. These votes were not enough to stop the expenditure, however.

How can such a project be justified in the face of the human suffering that overwhelms Ethiopia and many surrounding nations? It can't be justified, of course. That $73.5 million could be used to inoculate a million children from all major communicable diseases, or to dig 25,000 wells and install pumps to provide water for 12.5 million people. Instead, the funds will be used for plush offices for U.N. dignataries and for pleasant accommodations for visiting officials.

The center will undoubtedly have window coverings so the bigwigs can be insulated from the reality of life in Africa. That reality is millions of people in more than a score of African nations suffering from disease and malnutrition.

Here is a glimpse of what life is like there. This is an excerpt from an Associated Press story on refugees from Ethiopia who are seeking relief in neighboring Sudan:

"The new refugees — weak, diseased and emaciated after walking up to 300 miles at night over stony mountains and parched river beds — often arrive with nothing but thin, ragged clothing on their backs. Relief workers tell of throngs of the sick and dying standing for hours on the stark, windswept plain before the Tokalbad camp near Kassla while a medical staff of one doctor and a nurse from the private French charity Medicin Sans Frontieres try to identify those most critically in need of help. At night, when temperatures plunge near freezing, refugees at the Tokalbad camp huddle together for warmth and protection from the wind. There are no tents."

But there will be a $73.5 million conference center, thanks to the misguided largess of the U.N. General Assembly.

The TENNESSEAN

Nashville, TN, September 25, 1984

THE problems of homeless people are not single-fold. Most "street people" have no money for any necessity, including food and clothing. And although poor health is common for the homeless, they have no money for medical care.

Nashville's Council of Community Services has written an ambitious proposal to give medical aid to the city's homeless people. It has applied for a $1.3 million grant from the Robert Wood Johnson Foundation and the Pew Memorial Trust to open a downtown clinic for transients. Nashville is among the 24 cities in contention for one of 14 four-year grants to be awarded in December.

The Council of Community Services has built a strong case for the clinic programs. The Council counted 820 homeless people in a two-hour period last December, and 689 last June. Figures from the Salvation Army, the Union Rescue Mission and other agencies indicate that 10,000 homeless people were in Nashville in 1983.

If Nashville is awarded the grant, the clinic for transients, accommodating 150 people per month, could open next March. Plans call for the clinic to offer mental health counseling and alcohol and drug treatment referral, in addition to basic medical care. The clinic would be housed in a building on Demonbreun Street that has been donated by the Salvation Army.

A grant review committee was recently in Nashville to talk with community leaders and assess the tentative plans for the clinic. Although the committee chairman, Dr. Philip Brickner, acknowledged Nashville's problem, he emphasized that other cities have similar homeless populations. The committee has asked for additional details concerning the clinic, including staff specifications, and an assessment of available funds to renovate the Demonbreun Street building. The committee also wants letters from other medical institutions, specifically the Metro Health Department, and Meharry and Vanderbilt Medical Schools, on the possibility of their working with the clinic.

The grant application has already been an eye-opener for Nashville. It has stimulated a productive dialogue within the city about possible ways that Nashville can alleviate the plight of its most desperate inhabitants. The Council of Community Services is commended for an impressive, ambitious proposal. It deserves the support of the city during the final days of the grant procedure.

ST. LOUIS POST-DISPATCH

St. Louis, MO, September 21, 1984

Hardly a section of the country, urban or rural, has escaped the ubiquitous presence of ragged, ill and hallucinating human beings wandering through our city streets, huddled in alleyways or sleeping over vents.

That is the shocking but accurate picture of many thousands of America's homeless mentally ill. It was drawn in a report by the American Psychiatric Association, which has not been known for the kind of blunt language now used to describe "a major tragedy."

Nobody knows how many of these homeless persons, often young, frequently suffering from schizophrenia or forms of depression, have been "cast adrift under conditions," the APA says, "that most persons think can no longer exist in this country." Some estimates place the homeless mentally ill as high as 3 million.

But it is a fact that most of them are incapable of taking care of themselves, or even of following a consistent treatment for their illnesses. It is also a fact that those homeless young people sleeping on grates do not do so by choice, contrary to President Reagan's suggestion last January.

How did this national tragedy come to pass? The blame is widely shared. The APA says a major factor was the policy of "deinstitutionalization" developed 30 years ago. The concept was that by removing the mentally ill from overcrowded mental institutions, better care could be provided in smaller community treatment facilities. Health officials and many psychiatrists welcomed the idea then, and so did state governments that hoped to save money by shrinking their hospital systems.

The trouble is that community treatment facilities were not developed adequately, nor were such basic necessities as shelter and food. States saved money; many of the mentally ill were cast adrift.

Another factor has been the development of laws intended to protect the mentally ill from unjustified commitment to institutions. In Missouri and many states, for example, commitment requires proof that an adult is a danger to himself or others. Even when commitment is obtained, the patient may be released when drug treatment makes him, temporarily at least, no longer a danger to anyone. Hence the mentally ill can be denied needed treatment, or subjected to a revolving door policy that amounts to the same thing.

These well-intentioned laws ought to be revised so as to protect the patient's right to treatment along with his legal rights. The equally hopeful movement away from large mental institutions needs rethinking: Good hospitals retain an important place in the consistent treatment of the chronically mentally ill, and good community care facilities are required for outpatient care. Above all, the APA says, food and shelter have to be provided in some form before health care can succeed.

None of this can happen unless there is "markedly increased funding" from government and private sources. Adequate mental health care in this country requires, first of all, a caring public that recognizes the scope of the tragedy.

THE SACRAMENTO BEE
Sacramento, CA, September 23, 1984

There's little question about the obligation or the readiness on Sacramento's part to shelter homeless people who have nowhere else to turn. Since the 1930s this community has tried to see to their needs one way or another. The question that arises in the 1980s is whether this or any other major California city has the resources alone to deal effectively with the complex economic, social and medical problems that homelessness presents today.

Today's homeless are mostly single, transient, chronically jobless, often alcoholic or drug dependent and — a large new category of relatively recent years — those with mental illness or retardation who once found asylum in state institutions but now largely are left to the mercies of the street. All of those numbers increase with recession and unemployment; they also reflect the local and nationwide dearth of affordable low-cost housing.

A city-county task force last year found that on a given night as many as 275 single persons are homeless in Sacramento. In a makeshift effort to deal with the problem, shelters on Front Street last winter provided emergency housing. But those are temporary facilities, and the Sacramento Housing and Redevelopment Agency now is considering various options for more permanent care — including providing for the homeless who want it access to the variety of social services that might help stabilize their lives.

The options under consideration point up the difficulties facing the community in dealing with the problem. While one or two large shelters, with a single or combined capacity of 160 beds, would centralize management and social program access, such concentration presents the political hurdle of neighborhood acceptance. Dispersing smaller shelters, on the other hand, while it might ease the impact on a given neighborhood, would nonetheless increase the number of such neighborhood problems and make management more difficult. Vouchers to pay for shelter in local hotels and motels would be prohibitively expensive — an ongoing $2 million a year, far more than the operating costs of any of the permanent shelter options. Thus although concentration in one or two shelters may prove the practical course, it's clear that no cheap or easy solutions are available.

As the community looks at its options, a larger point becomes ever more evident: Sacramento, like other cities, is wrestling with a problem that transcends local boundaries. It's also one that arises in considerable measure from larger government failures — insufficient low-cost housing, the "dumping" of the mentally ill — that are properly state and federal concerns.

Although some federal and state money recently has become available ($70 million in Federal Emergency Management Act funds to be spread nationwide, and $5 million in state Emergency Shelter Program funds), it is hardly adequate when it comes to a problem of this magnitude.

Even if some of that money eventually comes this way, for now Sacramento will have to dig deep locally to provide as best it can for the homeless. Humane concern for those least able to cope makes it imperative. At the same time, however, the message needs to go to Washington and the state Legislature loud and clear. Even the larger cities cannot on their own deal effectively with the size and kind of problem homelessness has become.

THE SUN
Baltimore, MD, December 29, 1984

Help is on its way for 2,500 of Baltimore city's homeless. Thanks to the Robert Wood Johnson Foundation and the Pew Memorial Trust, two national foundations, $1.4 million is expected to be spent in Baltimore over the next four years. The two foundations, with co-sponsoring support from the U.S. Conference of Mayors, are distributing nearly $25 million to health and social service organizations in 18 U.S. cities.

The Health Care for the Homeless Coalition, a group of 32 public and private agencies that assist the city's needy, applied for the foundation grants. The money will be used to provide health care services for homeless men at Christopher Place through Johns Hopkins Hospital and medical services for women at My Sister's Place through Mercy Hospital. Both hospitals will provide in-patient services. In addition, there will be dental services through the city's health department and mental health services through Johns Hopkins. Further plans call for adding a podiatry center.

This project, which is expected to begin next week, deserves public attention and encouragement for at least two reasons. First, any attempt at reducing the human suffering and personal trauma associated with the growing homeless population in large cities is commendable. "The Health Care for the Homeless Program is intended to meet many of their most acute needs — especially their medical problems — head on," said Dr. David E. Rogers, president of the Robert Wood Johnson Foundation. "This program seeks to retrieve those lives that otherwise might be lost."

Second, the program combines both public and private cooperation in addressing and helping solve the plight of homeless men and women. Often government programs labor without cooperation or input from private programs, and vice versa. Robert I. Smith, president of the Glenmede Trust Company, which is the trustee of the Pew Memorial Trust, said, "Government has an important responsibility . . . but government alone can't solve all our problems."

Not only do we agree, we applaud all groups involved in this effort toward making life healthier for Baltimore's homeless residents.

THE DENVER POST
Denver, CO, December 8, 1984

THE AGREEMENT under which the Denver Archdiocese will proceed in providing a shelter for the homeless at 23rd Street and Broadway represents virtually no change in the situation.

The church will build the shelter essentially as planned; the neighbors are still unhappy. The Peña administration, despite its predictable concern for neighborhood feelings, really resolved little with its intervention.

There have been some cosmetic changes, to be sure. Transients will be allowed to stay at the new Samaritan House up to 90 days; if the maximum stay had been 60 days — or less, as originally planned — the shelter would have required a special city permit. There also will be room in the building for what the archdiocese hopes will be "fancy shops." And it's to be called Samaritan "House" instead of "shelter."

To no one's surprise, these adjustments haven't mollified the neighborhood groups that don't want another shelter in their area. They feel their neighborhood is becoming an indigent zone. They're worried about running a gauntlet of street people every time they want to walk between downtown and their homes and businesses. They complain that the church never consulted them or tried to accommodate the neighborhood's anxieties.

The church, though, is committed to providing a temporary base for rootless families and emergency shelter for the homeless. It will try to find jobs and more-permanent arrangements for those trying to re-establish themselves; it will save others from freezing to death.

If nothing else, these events have demonstrated the need for more attention to the problem. Peña aide Sandy Drew asserts that the city is now convinced it needs to put together a policy for the homeless, including zoning to spread out the burden and careful review of two or three other shelter-permit applications now pending.

For its part, the church says it's willing to work with neighbors. But it hasn't detoured from its mission to help the hopeless. Nor should it. If churches are discouraged from fighting for the helpless, who will?

THE TENNESSEAN

Nashville, TN,
December 26, 1984

VOTERS of the District of Columbia voted by a 5-2 majority last month to require the local government to provide "adequate overnight shelter" for its homeless people.

It was the first such ballot initiative in the nation, but it may not be the last if the nation's homeless — many of them mentally ill and unable to hold jobs — keep crowding the streets and federal and local governments continue ignoring their responsibilities to these people.

The city of Washington opposes the voters' decision as being too costly and has gone to court to block it. The mandate could eventually be thrown out, but eventually society is going to have to deal realistically with this problem.

Every city has its homeless tramping the streets and living in misery. Washington estimates that between 5,000 and 15,000 of its 623,000 people are on the street. Surveys in the downtown area of Nashville indicate there may be as many as 1,500 homeless people here. The U.S. Department of Housing and Urban Development estimated last April that there are 250,000 to 350,000 homeless people in the country. But a number of mayors, members of Congress and social service groups denounced the estimates as being too small.

Whatever the true figure, it is likely to get larger. The policy of turning mental patients out of hospitals to fend for themselves has tremendously increased the street population. The continuing unemployment problem, particularly for the unskilled, has also contributed greatly to the number of homeless people. The permanent displacement of many types of workers with skills no longer in great demand is also a factor.

The federal government and some cities seem to think the problem of the homeless will go away if ignored. That is not likely. This seems to be a lasting problem which has become firmly embedded in the modern computer society. It will not go away until the public demands action from its elected officials. Perhaps the people of the District of Columbia raised a standard of leadership last month.

The News American

Baltimore, MD, September 27, 1984

A disturbing article by *The News American's* Vesta Kimble deserves the close and immediate attention of Gov. Hughes, the members of his child abuse task force and the leadership of the General Assembly — all of whom, thank heaven, are in a mood to seek laws to protect children and everybody else in institutional settings from maltreatment by (a) crazies and (b) the unqualified.

As reporter Kimble detailed in a Wednesday story, the state government, with the help of federal funding and under federal policy, has been moving mentally retarded people from hospitals such as Rosewood to shelter homes run by various private organizations, the idea being that such homes are more salubrious for the retarded than large, impersonal institutions. The idea, too, is that the patients will receive care comparable to that in a hospital.

But comparable it is not — at least in the case of poor Rubben Briggs, a 12-year-old, paraplegic, retarded, blind cerebral palsy victim who suffered a seizure in a Randallstown shelter last week and in the process got his head caught between the mattress and the bedrail. He died. Theoretically, the child was under the 24-hour supervision of a counselor living in the house. In actual fact, that counselor was not required to keep a round-the-clock watch. And didn't.

And how qualified is the personnel of these shelters? With the transfer of 230 patients to shelters so far, and another 600 to follow, this is one of two key questions — the other being whether people in Rubben's condition should be moved out of hospitals where hourly checks of patients is the policy.

In January the state is putting in new standards for shelter workers — but they are not good enough. A house counselor will be required to have a two-year college degree but no experience, or some education and a year of experience, or a high school diploma and three years of experience. Tougher standards, you will not be surprised to learn, are required of mental hospital workers — even though the responsibilities of the shelter personnel are similar. But worse is the standard for shelter-home assistants, the people who take over in a house counselor's absence: The only requirement they have to meet is an ability to read and write — and have an interest in working with the mentally retarded.

Not good enough by a long chalk. The state this fiscal year is spending $48 million, half of it federal money, for the shelter home program. We have no argument with the concept.

But the prospect that the patients in the homes stand to be subjected to care of a lesser quality than in the hospitals, indeed subjected to unqualified workers, is frightening to us, and should be to the families of those patients. And to Gov. Hughes and the people who make this state's laws.

The Kansas City Times

Kansas City, MO, September 27, 1984

Two major elements aid community mental health care's success. One is money. Another is making sure the right patients use that level of treatment. The extent of failure recently documented by the American Psychiatric Association is not acceptable.

Therein is painted a grisly sketch of victims in the gap: sick, adrift, hungry, homeless. They truly are victims — of internal disorders and society's broken commitment. Moreover, the estimated million people who fit that extreme mold do not include another layer, those who should be getting treatment. They limp but not badly enough. Yet.

Certainly not all of America's homeless people are the fault of the mental health system. Blame the economy. And blame changes in welfare thresholds. Blame public hardheartedness.

Nor can the concept be faulted. Reducing state hospital populations in favor of less restrictive and timely therapy is an excellent policy. But it's a fact that although community treatment is less expensive than intensive institutional care, it costs. A lot. In the campaign to take the sick out of institutions, professionals never meant folks inside were malingerers or not really sick. But the massive reduction of state hospital loads since the mid-1950s has been too tempting as a way of cutting mental health budgets. Money saved should have been shifted to local facilities. Too often, it was not.

At the same time, the idea of comprehensive care near home has appeared so compassionate and ideal that some deny the existence of severely and chronically ill who need hospitals. Between the battle over money and misdirected kindness, the bewildered live as badly on the street and in substandard "homes" as they ever did in state hospitals. Some worse.

In so many cases, workers inside mental health systems have juggled resources to patch the inadequacies. In Missouri, for example, efforts have been made to put the fruits of meticulous searches for institutional economies into regional care. But the current year's allocation for community placement is 15 new patients a month. *For the entire state.* It's a starting point for reflection when legislators — and the currently shocked taxpayers they represent — appropriate mental health money for next year.

The TENNESSEAN
Nashville, TN, October 12, 1988

CONGRESS gave the Pentagon $264 billion to spend in 1984. In a budget that size, $8 million hardly amounts to spare change.

But most of the $8 million that Congress had intended to go to shelter the homeless has been spent instead on fixing-up Army Reserve operations.

In establishing the Defense Department's 1984 budget, Congress allocated $8 million to convert some military installations into shelters for homeless people. At the time, there were about 600 Army facilities considered to be good prospects for conversion.

But it didn't work out that way. Pentagon officials found that many military installations were just too remote to be used successfully as shelters for the homeless. Officials also discovered that many base commanders had strict regulations about the number of people and the use of buildings on their bases.

The Pentagon was only able to spend about $1 million of the funds. The remaining $7 million was slipped, with congressional approval, into the Army Reserve's operating budget, and eventually went to repair "defense facilities for defense purposes."

Pentagon officials still believe this is a worthy program, and say they will keep trying to make it work.

The amount of money involved may not be much to the Pentagon. But $8 million certainly could have gone a long way to provide shelter for some homeless people.

The Atlanta Journal
THE ATLANTA CONSTITUTION
Atlanta, GA, October 16, 1984

It should not have been necessary for a federal judge in New York to reaffirm the constitutional right of homeless people to vote, but it was.

Peter Dyer, a 32-year-old man who contends that he lost his job because of Reagan administration budget cuts, filed a class-action suit in federal district court after he was denied the right to register and to vote because registrars were skeptical when he listed a New York City park as his legal residence since 1981.

Judge Mary Johnson Lowe agreed with Dyer's assertion that the homeless are still full-fledged citizens with the same constitutional rights as everyone else, regardless of their dire, if often temporary, financial straits.

The ruling may — as some officials had argued — make the jobs of voter registrars more difficult and increase the likelihood of abuses such as multiple registrations. Those are merely inconveniences, though, that can be overcome by a little more diligence and careful checking on the part of registars.

While it directly affects about 150,000 people in the state of New York, 60,000 of them in New York City, the ruling also should be instructive for cities and counties across the country, many of which have had to deal with sizable homeless populations in the wake of high unemployment and a national recession.

If it flies in the face of the American sense of fairness to imprison poor people solely because of their debts, then it would be equally heartless to deprive the destitute and unfortunate of their basic rights solely because of their impoverished state.

FORT WORTH STAR-TELEGRAM
Fort Worth, TX, December 24, 1984

How many homeless are there in America?

It is a haunting question, especially coming during this holiday season.

Is the total, as the Department of Housing and Urban Development estimates, about 250,000 to 300,000 — a number larger than the population of Arlington?

Or, is the total, as some advocates of the homeless estimate, about 2 million to 3 million — about the population of this region?

Either total is significant.

Either total is haunting.

And, while those at every level of government debate about who should look out for them, two charitable foundations are moving full speed ahead to assist them.

The Pew Memorial Trust and the Robert Wood Johnson Foundation have committed $25 million to provide free health care to the homeless in 18 major cities.

The money will start going out in a few weeks.

As Johnson Foundation Vice President Drew Altman put it:

"We don't want to get into political questions of who is responsible for the plight of the homeless. All we know is that people are suffering and we have an obligation to help them."

Well put.

He added that doctors and nurses at the free clinics to be funded by foundation money will treat illnesses and injuries and refer advanced cases to hospitals. Mental health services and treatment for drug and alcohol abusers also will be provided. They also will be referred to the proper agencies for housing, job and welfare assistance.

The action of these two foundations will have several positive effects.

First, it will assist the homeless and do it immediately.

Second, it should cause others to join in and help them.

Third, it will make private citizens and public officials more aware of the needs of the homeless and more determined to ease their plight.

Finally, it is hoped the action eventually will lead to fewer of the homeless.

For only when that happens will the question of their numbers be less haunting.

The Philadelphia Inquirer
Philadelphia, PA, December 25, 1984

Two foundations — the Pew Memorial Trust in Philadelphia and the Robert Wood Johnson Foundation in Princeton, N.J. — have put timely focus on an urgent need by making grants totaling $25 million to 18 U.S. cities to provide health care for the homeless. Philadelphia is one of the recipients, with a $1.4 million grant to be administered by the Philadelphia Health Management Corp., a private, nonprofit organization. Supplemental city services, including use of medical care centers, will be provided by the Department of Health.

Shelter and food quite properly have been perceived as priority requirements of the homeless. Commendable public and private efforts have been made to provide both. However, many of the homeless are presumed to be in dire need of medical attention. Some suffer from mental illness, but a far greater number, in all probability, are victims of chronic disabilities, debilitating diseases or sporadic physical ills including those resulting from long exposure to cold and dampness. The need for dental work may be pervasive.

Very little is known about the health of the homeless in specific terms, but it is visibly apparent that many of them need medical care and are not getting it. One result of the foundation-supported project should be greater knowledge of the physical and mental conditions of the homeless and to what extent poor health has contributed to their destitution.

It will be essentially an outreach program with medical teams going to the homeless — on the streets, in shelters, at centers where meals are provided, wherever they can be found. Attempts will be made to persuade but not coerce them to visit clinics and hospitals. Transportation will be provided.

There undoubtedly will be resistance. The right to be stubborn and independent, common traits among the homeless, must be respected. So must their distrust and fear, perhaps well justified, of governmental and institutional bureaucracies. Much improvising may be required as the medical teams gain experience. Patience should be their credo.

The homeless must be helped but they also need understanding. It will take a heavy dose of the latter to deliver health care to those who need it most.

PORTLAND EVENING EXPRESS

Portland, ME,
January 10, 1985

Along with other large cities, Portland is a magnet for the homeless and the derelict. Admittedly, that causes a drain on the city's resources. But the solution to the problem is not the one recommended by the mayor of Elizabeth, N.J.—ship the unfortunate back to their last known address.

Elizabeth Mayor Thomas Dunn defends the proposal by saying it would assure that city residents who lack shelter would receive the social services while making sure that other communities carry their share of the burden.

Maybe so, but trucking the homeless out of town has a cruel note to it that harkens back to the long-abandoned practice of driving vagrants out of town.

Make no mistake, Portland's resources are strained. Social service agencies have a total of less than 45 beds for the homeless, nowhere near enough to go around. Some nights the beds are filled and the homeless are forced to fend for themselves in alleys, doorways or under bridges.

An Emergency Shelter Task Force studying the needs of the homeless in Portland has concluded that more beds are needed and has encouraged the YMCA to expand its emergency shelter program. Whether that alone would fill the need is uncertain since nobody really knows how many persons live on Portland streets. Most of them suffer from mental illness, are addicted to drugs or alcohol or have been released from institutions.

But it's clear that need exceeds supply. The YMCA, the 24-Hour Club and The Bible Speaks report that their overnight shelters are usually filled and turning away the destitute.

Portland may never be able to provide all the emergency aid that's needed. But the community's commitment to providing care to those unable to help themselves is a far better approach than simply shipping them elsewhere.

THE MILWAUKEE JOURNAL

Milwaukee, WI, January 5, 1985

They are the nation's urban vagabonds — men and women for whom the word "home" has come to mean temporary shelters or even heating grates on downtown streets. Their grim lives are not the romantic hobo fantasies spun in an earlier era by folk singers Woody Guthrie, Pete Seeger and others.

By one estimate, the number of homeless in the Milwaukee area increased from 6,000 in 1982 to 7,500 in 1983. But the number is difficult to pin down because only those who use the city's nine temporary shelters can be counted. Many others — the poorest of the poor — sleep on or near the heating grates or even in parks and doorways.

Two recent developments give reason for hope for the genuinely needy among the homeless.

One is the receipt of a private grant of up to $1.4 million to help meet the health care needs of such hapless citizens. The funds were awarded to Milwaukee's Coalition for Community Services by the Robert Wood Johnson Foundation of Princeton, N.J., and the Pew Memorial Trust of Philadelphia.

Because the homeless are so preoccupied with their most basic survival needs, they often neglect their health. The grant will be used to put social and health workers in the shelters, from which referrals will be made — not just to health institutions, but to any other agencies that can help the homeless.

The other development — a lawsuit that seeks welfare benefits for three homeless Milwaukeeans — may also turn into a plus. Legal Action of Wisconsin is suing Milwaukee County for denying general assistance (welfare) benefits to the three people *because* they are homeless.

Wisconsin law does not require a welfare applicant to have a permanent address. But the county does have such a requirement, as insurance against abuse by anyone who might travel from state to state in search of ever-larger grants.

That's a legitimate concern. But, ironically, in seeking to address it the county is denying aid to the very people who need it most — those who have no homes. Without money, how can these people afford apartment or room rent? Many who might be employable really have tried repeatedly, and unsuccessfully, to find a job — the ticket off the welfare rolls.

Surely a verification system could be worked out to improve safeguards against abuse while also providing help for the legitimately needy homeless. It's in no one's interest — government's or society's in general — to perpetuate the cycle of poverty by imposing a residency rule that ensures that the homeless will remain homeless.

THE SACRAMENTO BEE

Sacramento, CA, January 29, 1985

Mayor Anne Rudin is right: It is "inhumane and inappropriate" to dump homeless persons with mental problems into the county's shelters on Front Street. But as county Mental Health Director Ronald Usher says, "If we can't (send them there), someone better tell us where we can send them."

Such problems arise usually after a person with mental problems has been treated at the county's mental health center on Stockton Boulevard and upon release has nowhere to go. Very often this is a person with long-term chronic mental illness who has suffered a temporary acute episode. The Stockton Boulevard facility, however, only handles acute, short-term cases. It is not equipped to deal with the chronic, long-term disabilities that afflict many of the homeless persons wandering city streets and forced to take refuge where they can.

What may be even worse than the issue the mayor raises is what happens to those released from the mental health center who say they have family or friends but in fact do not. Many then seek shelter under bridges or in riverside hobo camps where they are often preyed upon. That's also true of countless others who receive no treatment at all.

All of this goes back to the late 1960s and early '70s, when then-Gov. Ronald Reagan and the Legislature moved to empty California's mental hospitals with the thought that most such patients would find better treatment in their own communities. Encouraged by the federal government and the medical community, most other states did the same. It was thought that the new psychotropic drugs then emerging would make it possible to create community mental health facilities able to treat both acute and chronic cases.

That has proved to be an exaggerated and unrealized hope. When the mental hospitals began emptying, the state and federal governments assured communities they would receive financial assistance in developing comprehensive local mental health facilities and programs. The scandal of the nation is that neither Washington nor the states came through with the promised aid. Most communities, Sacramento among them, used what scant subventions they did receive to establish facilities to deal mainly with emergency-level, acutely ill mental patients. That's still the case today, and the county can hardly be blamed for releasing some patients from the Stockton Boulevard facility to the shelters.

Some improvement of the situation is in the offing. Legislation signed last year promises more state financial assistance to the counties for developing longer-term community care facilities. The governor has added more money to those funds in his 1985 budget. Even so, the amount Sacramento is likely to receive will make possible only a start on the kind of long-term facilities and treatment programs that are desperately needed. It's a start, but hardly more than that. The state and federal governments need to do a great deal more to meet their obligations.

The Pittsburgh Press

Pittsburgh, PA, April 15, 1985

Most people agree on two things about emergency shelters, those homes for the homeless:

They are needed and they should be located somewhere else.

It is that "not in my backyard" reticence that stirs people to rail against group homes which cater to the down-and-out. The Alcoholic Recovery Center on the North Side is the latest to fall victim to a community's aversion to playing host to society's misfits.

Thus, it is encouraging that a plan is being drawn by the ACTION Advisory Committee on Housing for the Homeless to deal with the problem.

Although he did not reveal any specifics on just what is being planned, Jonathan Zimmer, executive director of ACTION-Housing, said he hoped it would respond to some of the needs of the homeless in this area.

The sooner the plan is developed, the better. In the meantime, the mere knowledge that attention is being paid to the long-neglected problem of group homes and halfway houses is cause for cheer.

But the presentation of an idea that, on the surface, looks like it may be the heretofore elusive solution, is downright heartwarming.

And just such a promising idea has sprung from David Hughes, a candidate for City Council, who has called for the city to require that a section of future industrial park developments be reserved for "social service neighborhoods."

Mr. Hughes sees these special sections as an "alternative to locating social services agencies like ARC House in residential neighborhoods."

It's a star-spangled idea, one that should be given careful consideration.

It just might be the key to the answer that everyone was looking for.

Los Angeles Times

Los Angeles, CA, January 8, 1985

The tents are down. The homeless are back on the streets. And Los Angeles city and county governments have taken little new action to alleviate their plight.

City and county governments traditionally have been wary of crossing jurisdictional lines, but this problem begs for the attention of both. The county has responsibility for welfare questions, and the city oversees many building and safety aspects involved in sheltering the homeless. It is time for leadership from both the mayor's office and the county Board of Supervisors to pull all the players together in one room and lock the door until they have assigned tasks to start finding land and money for shelters, with set deadlines for doing so.

For at least the rest of this fiscal year there will be $3 million available through the Federal Emergency Management Agency for shelter, food, mortgage and rent assistance for the homeless. That money will be administered by United Way in partnership with seven other local and state groups. United Way, which is trying to establish a shelter-development corporation, might also be a good mechanism through which businesses concerned about the future of the downtown area could be enlisted to provide construction and technical assistance.

There should be two objectives in any action: First, safe temporary housing must be provided to those unable to provide it for themselves through accident of disability or joblessness; to date, few new beds have been created for the homeless. Second, psychological and medical services as well as job counseling and aid with other problems must be provided, on a paid or volunteer basis, to avoid simply warehousing the poor.

So far the county has done only what the courts have ordered it to do. The city has been equally reluctant to take the lead. The homeless don't really care who helps, but someone must. Next Christmas there need be no tent city if both governments act now.

The Washington Post

Washington, DC, August 23, 1986

FOR NEARLY a year the goal of finding adequate shelter for the District's homeless people has been sidetracked by an escalating war of wills between Mitch Snyder's Community for Creative Non-Violence and the Reagan administration. Now a federal court decision and a series of informal meetings between federal and District officials may have finally broken the logjam.

It began two years ago when Mr. Snyder got permission to use a vacant building at Second and D streets NW as a shelter. Even then the structure was in poor condition. Mr. Snyder asked the government to renovate it last year, then went on a hunger strike when the government refused.

On the weekend before Election Day, federal officials said that President Reagan agreed to make the building "a model physical shelter," and Mr. Snyder ended his 50-day fast. But it was a flimsy agreement at best. Disputes arose over what constituted a "model" facility as living conditions at the shelter went from marginal to deplorable. Mr. Snyder wanted a $10 million facility that, among other things, would have given homeless people their own private rooms. Federal officials stuck with an offer of $2.7 million, an amount that was probably too small to make the building safe, much less a model. Citing Mr. Snyder's "intransigence," federal officials said they would close the shelter and offered the $2.7 million to the District government to help it find accommodations for the 600 homeless people at the shelter. Mr. Snyder sued in federal court, arguing that the government had a legal and constitutional obligation to do things his way.

U.S. District Judge Charles Richey has justifiably thrown out the suit, but he softened his ruling with the rather grandiose stipulation that the federal government cannot reclaim its building without developing "interim and long-range plans to eliminate homelessness in the Nation's Capital." Going further, Judge Richey rightfully implored the District government, which had simply sat on the sidelines during this fracas, to take up its moral responsibility in finding shelter for those homeless people with the $2.7 million offered by federal officials. That is the right thing to do. This is not a federal issue, nor is it a situation that Mr. Snyder should control.

Currently, District officials are meeting with their federal counterparts and have the help of the D.C. Coalition for the Homeless. They are studying other sites for smaller, more manageable facilities and finding available space in existing shelters. That is the sensible course. Mr. Snyder will appeal the court's ruling, and Mayor Barry says he will try to stay out of the dispute, but those are not the issues of consequence. Winter is approaching. Adequate shelter must be found. Those are the issues.

THE WALL STREET JOURNAL.

New York, NY,
August 7, 1985

The tragic proportion of New York City's housing crisis is borne out by daily reports of evictions of vulnerable tenants, particularly the poor and the elderly, from the most miserable of that city's domiciles, known in city parlance as SROs. That stands for single-room-occupancy hotels. For many of the city's most beleaguered residents, they are the last stop before the street. Owners of SROs, buildings that often sit on prime Manhattan land, try to evict residents so they can upgrade their properties—to luxury condominiums, for example.

The sad anomaly of the weak facing eviction because they are in the way of the wealthy is but another chapter in New York's long-running housing scandal. Such things are wholly attributable to a long history of bad housing policy, primarily rent control and rent "stabilization." The South Bronx, with its gutted, abandoned buildings, looks like a war zone. A decade ago, the city almost went bust—you might say it was busted—trying to make up in public housing what was being destroyed by rent controls.

City and state politicians are forever fighting battles against property owners, who themselves begin to react in strange and sometimes antisocial ways. One New York SRO landlord plotted to demolish two of his buildings in the middle of the night last winter but the city thwarted his plan.

Mayor Edward Koch has just signed a new ordinance that puts a moratorium on conversion, alteration or demolition of SRO buildings for the next year. The act at least has humanitarian merit. John Cardinal O'Connor hailed it as a "monumental step" toward ameliorating the shortage of housing for the city's disadvantaged residents.

The cardinal and the mayor are both caring men and we wish they could be right. But, of course, they aren't. The economic pressure simply is too great. SRO owners have even gone so far as to offer the city $30,000 for each vacated unit in their buildings. The politicians chose to use their police powers instead.

The city's proscription of SRO conversion only temporarily postpones further shrinkage of its low-end housing market. It certainly does nothing to encourage growth of the city's housing stock (which is the long-run answer to the problem of providing adequate housing for the poor and elderly).

The only way New York's housing crisis will be abated is by abolishing rent controls and other restrictions that destroy property's value, thus allowing all rents to find their proper level. It makes no sense for nearly destitute people to be living next door to gleaming skyscrapers in mid-Manhattan. New York's housing crisis never needed to happen and the tragedy will continue so long as politicians ignore the real causes and continue to patch, patch, patch.

Buffalo Evening News
Buffalo, NY,
April 14, 1987

THE SENATE has now authorized a cluster of health, shelter and food programs all focused on assisting the homeless, one of the human tragedies found on too many of America's streets. The House adopted a similar but more expensive bill last month, and the differing versions of the aid packages must now be compromised.

Both the proposed legislation and an emergency $50 million appropriation enacted in February attempt to cope with a problem that is increasingly visible but still not well understood. Estimates of the number of homeless persons in America range all the way from 250,000 to three million. A Harvard University study last year put the number at roughly 350,000. Some two-thirds or more are single men, although experts believe that single women with children constitute the fastest-growing segment of the homeless population.

If the numbers are disputed, the causes of the problem are even more so. Some critics blame it on Reagan-era cuts in housing and poverty programs. Others blame the loss of middle-class jobs. Still others see the "deinstitutionalization" of mental patients, begun in the 1970s, as a major cause, along with ongoing demolition of low-income housing units resulting from local redevelopment programs.

Whatever the cause and whatever the precise number of homeless, recent studies estimate that the number of homeless increased by 25 percent last year.

The new legislation approved separately by the Senate and House would address both mental and physical problems found among the homeless. It would authorize funds for emergency and subsidized housing, with one effort involving the homeless in the building and renovating of shelter. There would be funds for a study of homeless children and educational assistance for them, as well as expanded federal money for food stamps.

Providing realistic assistance that effectively eases the plight of the homeless will not be an easy task. Their problems are numerous and varied, and too little is known about enduring solutions.

Yet a study by the U.S. Conference of Mayors last year found that the growing numbers of homeless on America's streets were beginning to overwhelm local public and private resources. Thus, we hope the more than $400 million likely to be authorized in a House-Senate compromise will be followed up by specific federal appropriations that will expand Washington's ability to help.

Simply throwing money at the problem won't solve it, of course. But the plight of the homeless must be addressed, and Congress is moving compassionately toward that end.

Portland Press Herald
Portland, ME, April 15, 1987

Take a figure, any figure. Now divide it by half. Then divide it in half again.

On a smaller and less flamboyant scale, you have just accomplished what the Hands Across America promoters did. You finished your arithmetic with a number that makes up one-fourth of the number you selected at the outset.

Specifically, what the Hands Across America drive did was:

Set out to collect from $50 million to $100 million to combat hunger but fell far short. Only $31.8 million was raised last May as millions of people formed a hand-to-hand chain across the country. Then, more than half the money went to administrative and policing expenses, leaving only about $15 million to be distributed throughout the country.

Allegheny County's share, it was announced the other day, is $48,672. But half of that amount will be used for salaries at food banks, leaving less than $25,000 for the purchase of food.

The result — at least locally — is that one of every four dollars donated actually will buy food for the hungry.

The Hands Across America chain was an inspiring few hours in America's history. The tableau of a nation united hand-to-hand from Atlantic to Pacific is one that will not easily be forgotten. In that respect, it was an unqualified success.

But the money that finally is to be spent on food is strictly from hunger.

THE ☀ SUN
Baltimore, MD, April 19, 1987

The Senate's passage of a $423 million homeless aid bill signals a new awareness on the part of lawmakers that the federal government does, indeed, bear some of the responsibility for alleviating the plight of the homeless.

That's a start. Still, the Senate bill, like that passed by the House, is a short-term emergency measure to help states and cities bolster the capability to provide basic resources — food, shelter and medical care. These are essential, certainly. Yet the enormity of the homeless population indicates a long-term federal commitment is needed. Not simply to funnel more money to the states. But to find out what the homeless require and to fashion comprehensive policy changes to get at the causes of the underlying problems.

Thus, we view the bills passed by Congress with guarded optimism on two fronts. First, the biggest hurdle is yet to come. While Congress has made a theoretical commitment, the final homeless aid bill — to be hammered out by a conference committee — will be a legislative charade if it is not funded. While there is a good chance money will be incorporated into a supplemental appropriations bill, the federal deficit cloud looms over the entire appropriations process.

Second, the homeless aid measures in both houses were drafted hastily, in the spotlight of burgeoning public concern and pre-election politicking. There is the very real danger that homeless aid will become another drug bill — the political fad of the moment that fades when the next social issue captures the interest of the electorate and its representatives in Washington.

Still, while a continuing federal commitment is critical to tackling homelessness, Washington clearly cannot, and should not, set up structures and run programs for the homeless.

Major initiatives are sorely needed at state and local levels. Especially in Maryland. Although the General Assembly recently endorsed a plan for community-based assistance to keep individuals discharged from mental health facilities from ending up on the streets, the state does not yet have an organized plan for dealing with the homeless.

Capitol Hill has generated a promising momentum. Now it is up to lawmakers at every governmental level to direct and sustain that impulse.

The Boston Globe
Boston, MA, April 6, 1987

It seems that the purveyors of the cute and cuddly – known as toy manufacturers – always come up with something new to entice a consumer-oriented society. The "Bag Lady" doll, however, is the ultimate in vulgarity and poor taste.

Homelessness can be taken lightly only by those who have never carried all they possess – often castoffs salvaged from other people's trash – in paper bags. For those consigned by mental illness or poverty to sleep on the streets regardless of the weather, homelessness is a bitter reality. These persons do not deserve to be exploited for gain by the smug and the comfortable.

The dolls, which are being sold in Copley Place, are part of the Sher-Stuff line of dolls manufactured in California. They sell for $50 to $400 each. The manufacturer says the dolls are "really cute" and "enhance the image of the bag lady." Albert J. Gardetto, owner of Noah's toy store, calls the dolls "a slice of Americana" and an "objet d'art."

Kip Tiernan, founder of Rosie's Place, a South End shelter, returned to Gardetto a $100 donation, which was part of his profit on sales of the doll. Tiernan assesses the dolls more accurately: "They are not cute, nor are [the bag ladies'] lives enhanced by such outrageous disregard for their privacy. It is true that the doll represents a slice of Americana. In fact, it represents the worst of what we have become. It seems we are willing to do anything to make a buck."

If consumers abet the exploitation by purchasing these obscene dolls, there is no telling which group will be the next to be degraded in the name of Americana. Will it be cancer sufferers, AIDS victims, disabled veterans, the retarded, the addicted or suicides? The misery of others, it is obvious from the "Bag Lady" dolls, will not be allowed to stand in the way of profit-making ideas.

The poor and troubled are entitled to privacy and justice. The Bag Lady doll is a striking demonstration of how they more often are subjected to ugliness and injustice. As Tiernan notes, there are no Ivan Boesky dolls.

Rockford Register Star

Rockford, IL, May 27, 1987

At least six million Americans will never forget Sunday, May 25, 1986. On that day, their hands were part of a 4,152-mile chain spanning the nation from Los Angeles to New York City.

As a spectacular, patriotic feat, it was a monument to American organizational know-how. As a means of raising funds for the hungry and homeless — the purpose of Hands Across America — it has been disappointing.

The disappointment has been heard on the local and state level, where the dollars from the proceeds have been slow to appear. That shouldn't be surprising. Last year, in the face of the vast undertaking and its goal of $100 million, disappointments seemed likely.

Nevertheless, hundreds of Rockford area residents paid $10 each to join Illinois hands spanning 301 miles of our state. Illinois was the second-largest fund raiser. But the final U.S. total came up only $15 million, and the Hands people's formula figured Illinois — with all its hungry and homeless — will get only $700,000. At last report, little or none had reached those Illinois agencies who are fighting hunger on the front lines.

One problem inherent in Hands' massive scope is its limitations in communicating all the rules on divvying-up. Perhaps such matters lacked proper attention in the first place. Whatever, a year after Hands Across America, grass-roots agencies dealing with hunger know they can only get help through a statewide coalition. And that coalition is having trouble getting its money from Hands.

Eventually, there will be some help for the hungry and homeless of Illinois. But it won't be the kind of help local agencies visualized. And it certainly won't solve any urgent problems of the hungry and homeless today, or a week from today.

Those problems are best solved right here in our own community. That may be the best lesson of all to be derived from Hands Across America.

FORT WORTH STAR-TELEGRAM

Fort Worth, TX, May 23, 1987

Remember all the drama and passion various members of Congress displayed last winter on behalf of the nation's homeless?

Recall the urgency some members attached in January to legislation designed "to provide urgently needed assistance to protect and improve the lives of the homeless?"

If you close your eyes, you can probably still picture those televised news reports of congressmen, joined by a host of fellow travelers along compassion's highway, spending the night with the pitiful homeless, huddled for warmth atop steam grates on Washington sidewalks.

You might be surprised, then, to learn that legislation designed to provide "emergency" assistance to the homeless still has not met with final approval in Congress.

It seems that when the TV cameras were turned off and the reporters all turned their attention to other matters, those members of Congress who had been so devastated by the plight of the homeless sort of lost interest in the whole thing.

As a matter of fact, it wasn't until last week — a good four months after all the hoopla caused by congressmen sleeping on the sidewalk — that the Senate and the House got around to appointing conferees to work out the differences in the two chambers' "emergency" bills.

Maybe they will come up with something before next winter, when those icy gales return

Then again, maybe not.

The Wichita
Eagle-Beacon

Wichita, KS, May 17, 1987

TODAY, there are somewhere between 2 and 3 million Americans whose poverty denies them a place of residence. There always have been homeless people in America, but now their ranks are swelling at an astonishing rate. Unemployment, lack of adequate low-income housing, deinstitutiona- lization of mental patients, and cutbacks in social services — all have contributed to the irony of homelessness in the wealthiest na- tion on earth.

Low-rent housing units increasingly are being demolished, abandoned, sold and con- verted. At the same time, most low-rent housing construction and rehabilitation pro- grams have ended since the Reagan admin- stration took office in 1981. As the demand or low-income housing soars, therefore, the supply of available units is disappearing.

People who can't find work generally can't pay rent. While 10 years ago most of the nation's homeless may have been alcoholic men, the homeless of today include young people, single mothers, children and the el- derly — people from all kinds of situations whose common bond is poverty. Entire fam- lies often are harbored at homeless shelters. Many of these homeless are displaced work- rs or the discouraged unemployed who ave given up the search. There simply eem not to be enough jobs to go around.

Almost one-fourth of the homeless are for- mer mental patients. With the advent of community-based care for the mentally ill, many institutionalized patients were forced to leave mental hospitals and join the search for low-income housing. What resulted is an asylum without walls, where the homeless mentally ill seek out parks, subways and bus stations for shelter.

Since 1981, more than $12 billion has been cut from food stamp and child nutrition pro- grams. Regulations at that time also changed the eligibility requirements for Aid to Fam- ilies with Dependent Children. Half of the working families receiving assistance at that time were cut from the program, and an- other 40 percent suffered reduced benefits under the program. A parent in these diffi- cult situations often is forced to choose be- tween paying the rent or feeding the kids.

The administration must take a large share of the blame for the inadequate supply of low-income housing, as well as for the holes in the safety net of programs designed to help the poor, the unemployed and the mentally ill. It's unacceptable that economic considerations so often should take prece- dence over those who need help the most. In the issue of the homeless, particularly, it's time to change that kind of thinking.

The Evening Gazette

Worcester, MA, May 29, 1987

Several proposals in Congress are aimed at fixing up and expanding the supply of public housing. Unhappily, most of these ideas are based on the tired theory that spending billions of dollars is a solution to social or economic problems. History teaches that this isn't so.

In the decades after World War II, Washington channeled vast sums into public housing construction, creating in many cities huge new ghettos, with all the attendant social problems.

The federal government then shifted to funding of mixed subsidized and non-subsidized housing. More recently, under President Reagan's "new federalism," it has retreated from the housing business, presumably turning over the problem to state governments. But Washington is still being blamed for the high cost of housing and the resulting homeless problem.

U.S. Sen. John Kerry's proposal to spend $3 billion a year for six years on public housing rehabilitation would simply return us to the old days of massive federal spending, with no guarantee that society would benefit in the long run.

Yes, some of the existing public housing projects are worth saving. Worcester's Great Brook Valley and its tenants have benefited from a recent multi-million-dollar facelift of the property. But many projects nationwide will never be any more than depressing slums, no matter how much money is poured into them. Why go on with these repair and decay cycles?

The federal role in housing should be limited. Greater emphasis needs to be put on the states and localities coming up with their own creative solutions for housing shortages. Reopening wide the money pipeline from Washington would be a mistake, especially at a time when huge federal deficits already threaten to tip the economy into recession.

Wisconsin ▲ State Journal

Madison, WI, May 14, 1987

Everywhere, it seems, well- meaning people are overreacting to the "plight of the homeless." As a result, people who once thought of themselves as drifters or hobos have become the *cause celebre* of the 1980s.

Congress is proposing to spend $725 million to help the homeless — yet no one really has any idea about how many homeless Americans there really are, nor is it clear how this "throw-money-at-the-problem" solution fits into the federalist scheme of things.

Some advocates for the home- less claim there are 2 million or more people sleeping on the streets at any given night, but the federal Department of Housing and Urban Development estimated just three years ago that the actual number was closer to 300,000. Some critics say even the HUD estimates are overblown.

Wouldn't it be nice if Congress got a firmer grip on the reality of the homeless problem before tax- ing and spending the rest of us out of our homes? Local governments and private agencies have valiantly increased their efforts to deal with homelessness. Why can't Congress try to build on existing state, local and private programs by providing federal aid to be spent according to local discretion?

How about stopping the use of federal money to tear down exist- ing low-income housing, or taking a hard look at the effects of kicking people out of institutions before they are ready to cope?

Overreaction to the homeless problem is not confined to Con- gress. In Dane County, Legal Ac- tion of Wisconsin filed suit challeng- ing the county's practice of denying general-relief benefits to people who lack a permanent residence.

That prompted a ruling by Dane County Circuit Judge James Boll, who said state welfare policy takes precedence over county rules, and that in this instance, state policy is less stringent than county rules.

In issuing a temporary injunc- tion granting relief benefits, Boll said "(the homeless) may well suc- ceed in establishing that the county does not have the authority to add preconditions to eligibility, and that it has done so, regardless of its lack of authority."

Dane County Executive Jona- than Barry has properly decided to appeal Boll's ruling, explaining that it will encourage general-relief fraud while removing an incentive for homeless people to be placed in the Dane County Men's Shelter.

". . . The real issue is are we going to perpetuate relief for the poor or are we going to use relief as a lever to help people get off (re- lief?)" Barry asked.

Indeed, that is the question. Whether this ruling is correct on its legal points is for a higher court to decide, but it doesn't make sense to "help the homeless" by encouraging them not to look for homes.

The Washington Post

Washington, DC, June 28, 1987

SOME 12 MILLION American households are poor enough to be eligible for federally subsidized housing. By one estimate, that figure will rise by 5 million in the next 20 years. But the same study says that the nation's low-income housing stock—now about 12.9 million units—will shrink to 9.4 million during the same period. For years the basic argument about federally subsidized housing was over the rate of increase in the number of new units. But the country now faces the problem of how to prevent a dramatic *decrease.*

Since 1976, thousands of low-income Americans have been housed through 15-year federal rent supplement contracts that will begin to expire in 1991. But another 700,000 low-income tenants have been living in housing that was subsidized by previous federal programs, and they could be displaced as early as 1989. Those 700,000 people were beneficiaries of federal programs that gave private owners an "up front" subsidy or monthly payments to reduce their mortgage interest rates. The owners then agreed to house lower-income families in their units. Although the mortgages were generally subsidized for 40 years, several owners—with as many as 334,000 of the units—will be able to prepay their mortgages after only 20 years. When that happens, the owners will no longer be obligated to rent to lower-income tenants.

Federal officials say that only 10 percent of the owners involved in the mortgage subsidy programs have sought higher-income families. Their recommendation has been to give the poor housing vouchers that are good for five years. But that will not be adequate with so many federal housing programs due to expire at the same time. Congress and the administration have been evading an important question—what to do about people at the bottom end of the income range who will not be able to afford a rental of an apartment or a house of their own. Housing was one of the major federal programs for the poor that suffered deep budget cuts. The cuts went too far. It will be costly, but the next administration is going to have to answer the question currently being ignored: Where will the poor live?

The Christian Science Monitor

Boston, MA, September 9, 1987

STORIES about the homelessness in the United States have mostly melted off the front pages like old snow.

An exception recently has been the coverage of the off-again, on-again plan to clear homeless men off the streets of Los Angeles by arresting them.

But the homeless still need help, and so it is heartening that legislation providing them with emergency aid is working its way through Congress.

A conference committee has reconciled House and Senate versions of the bill; the compromise must go back to the respective houses for a vote, likely later this week or next. Actual appropriation of the aid is part of a bill that has also gone to conference.

Perhaps more important, this year may yet see the passage of a comprehensive housing bill.

There is supposed to be such a bill every year; in fact, during the Reagan years, such a bill has been passed only once, in 1983 – when a housing bill was attached to legislation the administration wanted. In the other years there has been a holding-pattern level of funding, but no policy legislation.

Homelessness is such a sticky problem because it is several issues at once, each needing a solution. Homelessness is an affordable-housing issue; it is also an employment issue, a mental-health care issue, an aspect of the domestic-violence issue, a veterans'-rights issue. It is sometimes even a street-beautification issue. Unfortunately each view has its own constituents, who tend to dismiss other aspects of the problem.

Still, housing is, to risk restating the obvious, pretty basic. The need for an innovative comprehensive national housing policy is as great today as in the immediate postwar period, when the GI Bill helped make homeowners of US veterans.

If any of the many presidential contenders want to attract attention and perform a public service as well, they could do worse than to come up with creative proposals for a national housing policy.

The Boston Globe

Boston, MA, June 24, 1987

This country is in its 55th month of continuous economic expansion since the severe recession of 1981-82 ended. The expansion has sometimes been rapid and sometimes been sluggish, but with low inflation the economic gains have been real.

Massachusetts, which in earlier decades went through the pain of losing most of its basic manufacturing industries such as shoes, textiles and steel products, has made the transition to computers, electronics and software services. It now enjoys virtually full employment for the first time since World War II.

In the midst of this prosperity, there is hidden suffering. More persons are actually living in poverty now than when Jimmy Carter was in the White House. Nor are these impoverished persons, welfare drones. The "working poor" have jobs but earn less than the federal government calculates is needed to provide food, clothing and rent. For a man or woman with two children, the government estimates that an annual income of $9,044 is required to meet those basic needs. The number of working poor earning less than that figure is 40 percent higher now than it was in 1979.

Why? One reason is that in the nearly seven years of the Reagan administration, there has been no increase in the minimum wage. It is still at the level of $3.35 an hour set under Carter. Yet during these seven years, consumer prices have risen by 30 percent.

Reagan has obscured this grim fact with the diversionary argument that an increase in the minimum wage would cause small businessmen to hire fewer workers, and that what is needed is a new sub-minimum wage to encourage employers to hire unemployed teenagers. These arguments rest on the myth that most workers receiving the minimum wage are youngsters working on their first jobs. The reality is that of the nearly seven million workers who earned the minimum wage last year, one-half of them were adults 25 years or older; one-fifth were 20 to 24.

Nor is this poverty primarily a minority problem. The overwhelming majority (83 percent) are white, and they are predominantly young adult women. These women cannot work their way out of poverty by earning the current minimum wage. There should be a substantial increase in the minimum wage. Sen. Edward Kennedy has introduced such a bill. It deserves prompt enactment.

There would remain, however, those women who cannot work because they cannot find satisfactory day care for their children. Sen. Christopher Dodd (D-Conn.), chairman of the Senate Subcommittee on Children and Families, has begun a series of public hearings on this problem. Everyone agrees that children are the nation's most precious resource, but more businesses provide parking places for their employees' cars than provide care for their employees' children.

Day-care workers are notoriously ill-paid and undertrained. Seventy percent of them earn less than the minimum wage. Forty percent change jobs every year, more than twice the turnover in other occupations. The only word to describe these conditions is scandalous.

The public mood on this problem is changing significantly. One clue is the statement at the first hearing by Sen. Orrin Hatch (R-Utah), a staunch conservative, who declared: "It is time for conservatives to wake up. If they are pro-family, then, by gosh, they have to do something about this enormous problem."

There is much to be done, and the time is late if an entire generation of impoverished children is not to be lost.

Bel-Air Home purchased by friends for President and Mrs. Reagan

CARING FOR THE HOMELESS IN LOS ANGELES

ST. LOUIS POST-DISPATCH

*St. Louis, MO,
August 22, 1987*

When the Reagan administration says the Defense Department is hard up for money, thousands of the nation's homeless have to believe it. In 1984, Congress appropriated $8 million to turn hundreds of surplus military barracks and other buildings in or near urban areas into shelters for the homeless. Not only has the department converted no more than eight of these into facilities for the nation's homeless, it has spent most of the money on weapons and equipment.

Needless to say, a federal district judge in Washington has assailed the Defense Department's behavior. The judge made his comments when ruling in favor of a lawsuit, which accused the Pentagon of thwarting Congress' mandate by refusing to issue regulations. The judge has ordered Defense Secretary Caspar W. Weinberger and the Pentagon to issue by Nov. 18 the necessary regulations for converting all the barracks.

Secretary Weinberger seemed to have had good intentions when he first responded to the law by ordering the armed forces to identify the hundreds of surplus military facilities that could be used by local governments and volunteer agencies to shelter the homeless. At that time, Mr. Weinberger said the Pentagon wanted to "play a part" in solving this problem. It isn't the military's job to take care of the nation's social problems, but a law is a law. And this one ought to be obeyed. It makes no sense for unneeded government property to remain vacant when it could be used for a humanitarian purpose.

Los Angeles Times

Los Angeles, CA, June 16, 1987

Emergency responses are no substitute for a coherent, consistent policy. That is why keen interest is focused on Los Angeles City Hall as a so-called Comprehensive Homeless Policy, the emergency Skid Row encampment and Central City rezoning all come up for action this month.

Public confidence has understandably been eroded by the way in which matters have been handled until now. The police sweeps of Skid Row, on again and off again, were ill planned and uncoordinated with broader city policy. They were a measure in themselves of the importance of Mayor Tom Bradley's getting more deeply and seriously involved in this and the allied issues.

The 60-day emergency encampment may create more problems than it solves. Clearly there was need for an alternative to the sidewalk encampments that had become centers for crime and threats to public health. But tents in a vacant lot are not an acceptable substitute for permanent facilities. Yet there do not appear to be plans for more appropriate facilities that will be all the more necessary when the tent encampment closes just as the rainy season approaches. The short-term emergency facilities now authorized by the City Council for periods of severe weather are the clearest evidence of all of the shelter shortage.

There will always be some confusion about the various issues on Skid Row. There are several populations. Most are permanent residents, some are short-term homeless, some are mentally ill and critically in need of special services. About 8,000 live in single-room-occupancy hotels, 2,000 more use missions, and about 1,000 are without shelter.

The city has had no choice but to address the crisis created by the burgeoning sidewalk population. But that concern must not be allowed to divert attention from the long-term need for housing. The Community Redevelopment Agency reports than an additional 1,731 beds will be available in the next 18 months, including 996 in the Skid Row area. It is not clear how many of those will be allocated to relieve long-term Skid Row housing needs. The slowness of the rehabilitation of additional hotels in the Skid Row area has drawn sharp criticism. Hopes for a more significant increase in housing have been dimmed by new zoning proposed by the City Planning Department that would target all housing for the area between Main and San Pedro, south of 3rd and north of 7th, maintaining as a light-manufacturing zone the larger area that runs from San Pedro east to Alameda. It would be a grave error to place any obstacles in the way of maintaining and developing Skid Row housing all the way east to Alameda.

There are two encouraging notes. The City Council this week will consider the mayor's proposal for a six-month freeze on the demolition of single-room-occupancy hotels and on rents in these hotels. Both are important. Pressure is building on Skid Row to replace the hotels with commercial buildings. Some housing already has been lost.

Bradley has a special role to play in this. He needs to be heard, stating clearly his goals for the long-term development of Skid Row and the provision of adequate, appropriate shelter for the population—both permanent and itinerant, residential and temporarily homeless. His commitment to suspend sidewalk sweeps and arrests of the homeless when alternative housing is not available is reassuring. But the plans for those alternative accommodations are not clear.

St. Petersburg Times

St. Petersburg, December 21, 1987

Winter is beginning to grip this country, and all across it, in the cities, the signs of strain are in the streets. American people are without homes — confused people, problem people, ordinary people.

In downtown Los Angeles, a 12-acre camp is established, with provisions for 600 to live; when it opened in June, protesters called it a "concentration camp." In Tallahassee, a man who calls himself a poet was found under a bridge, his home carved into the clay hillside, with steps, platforms and ashtrays. "I needed low-income housing," he explained. In St. Petersburg, the wind chill factor dropped into the 20s, but emergency shelters didn't open because the temperature stayed above 40 degrees; in some of the year-round shelters, people were huddled on the floors.

Mike Lyles, who helps people in Pinellas County find low-cost housing, gets depressed about this time of the year. "There's a tremendous sense of frustration that you can't do more," says Lyles, who works for the Community Service Foundation. "It's very discouraging, especially to watch the children. These are the kids that grow into a cycle of poverty."

In the shelters across America, more than a third of the occupants are now families, and their numbers are on the rise. One of every five of the country's homeless has a job, but still can't afford shelter. Only one out of three is mentally ill. No one is certain just how many people are without a home — 750,000, maybe 1-million, maybe 2-million. What is certain is that the numbers are increasing. Everyone who works with the homeless has seen it. A new U.S. Conference of Mayors survey of 26 major cities found that the demand for shelter space increased 21 percent in the past year.

"If the record number of people on America's streets and soup kitchens had been driven there by a natural catastrophe, many parts of our country would be declared disaster areas," says Boston Mayor Raymond L. Flynn, who helped produce the mayors' conference report. ". . . What is most tragic is that all this suffering is unnecessary in a nation as wealthy as ours."

In the past seven years, as the rich have hit prosperity, the poor have hit the streets. With its skewed economic and social agenda, the Reagan administration has created new classes of homeless. Their ranks have been bolstered by the working poor, those who have seen the purchasing power of their minimum wage slip 27 percent since it last increased. More than 33-million people have been pushed into poverty, including 9-million who work. At the same time, as the number of poor has increased 10 percent since 1981, President Reagan has cut federal housing assistance by 75 percent.

For those clinging to the bottom rungs of this nation's economic ladder, Mr. Reagan has pried loose their fingers. His new era of federalism has left cities and their homeless behind. Even those in his own party realize it. Addressing the National League of Cities last week, Frank Fahrenkopf Jr., Republican National Committee chairman, said: "Let us recognize that the traditional Republican approach, to improve opportunities by improving the economy, and the traditional Democratic approach, to rely on government services, have both failed to crack that hard and resilient barrier which seems to deflect all our best efforts to help the hard-core urban poor."

The solution lies not only in improving the social-service structure that Reagan has gutted, and in providing real wages for real work, but it also begins with a renewed national awareness and compassion for those in need. Most insidious about the borrow-and-spend years of President Reagan, perhaps, has been their effect on the national conscience. For seven years, the message of this administration has been one of self.

In Irvine, Calif. two months ago, the City Council decided to convert kennels at the city's animal shelter into shelter for homeless people, a move that triggered great controversy in that community. Residents said they were concerned the shelter would hurt their neighborhood, that is, when the animals were replaced by people. Another group of residents worried about the animals and whether there was adequate new shelter space for them once the people took their place.

In America, it is growing so cold.

THE TAMPA TRIBUNE

Tampa, FL, December 28, 1987

Justice, reinforced with a substantial dose of common sense, has prevailed in New York City's program to relocate some of its homeless street people. An appellate division of the State Supreme Court has overruled a lower court by upholding the city's right to hospitalize mentally ill individuals who pose a threat to themselves and to others.

The case involved Joyce Brown, a 40-year-old woman who had established a sidewalk residence near a warm air vent on Manhattan's upper east side. She had exhibited psychotic behavior, shouting obscenities at passers-by, urinating on money given to her by strangers and darting into lanes of passing traffic.

She was one of a number of street people picked up as part of a program initiated by Mayor Koch to treat homeless persons who are incapable of caring for themselves. Her objection to being removed from the street was championed by the American Civil Liberties Union, which argued the city had failed to show that the woman posed a real and present threat.

A lower court agreed, saying that while Miss Brown's behavior did not conform to conventional standards, it was not sufficient evidence of mental illness or a danger to society. The appellate body, in a 3-to-2 ruling, found that the original trial judge had placed too much emphasis on the woman's testimony, and not enough on the psychiatrists who had treated her. The ACLU says it will appeal.

That would be a proper and productive course of action. A firm precedent needs to be established that will determine the extent of a community's jurisdiction in policing its streets and in dealing with rootless individuals whose aberrant conduct represents a risk to themselves and to others.

Mayor Koch had only the best intentions in dealing effectively with Joyce Brown and others in similar circumstances. In addition to providing "loving care and a safe environment," the mayor has said the city will now go to court seeking an order that Miss Brown be treated for her psychotic problems.

"I want this woman to get well as soon as possible," he said.

Urban centers with large numbers of street people (Tampa included) have been placed in a difficult position as a result of the philosophy of "deinstitutionalization." The mental hospitals have discharged their ambulatory patients, but the communities to which they returned have inadequate facilities to manage them or deal with their psychoses on the basis of voluntary commitments. At what point may municipal authorities intervene and subject such people to involuntary therapy and custodial care?

Let's hope the Joyce Brown case will finally answer that question. Life on the streets is not the benign existence portrayed in sterotypes of "Bobo, the happy hobo." It is a raw, cruel struggle for survival in an atmosphere of filth, brutality, rape, thievery and murder. It is tragically abnormal.

New York's Mayor Koch deserves credit for his attempt to manage what has largely proved unmanageable. We would like to see him win this one and establish an example for other cities. But we dread the consequences of a loss, with the surrender of all the Joyce Browns — and the streets — to madness and anarchy.

SYRACUSE
HERALD·JOURNAL
Syracuse, NY, May 22, 1988

Who would pay $1,230 a month for a 9 by 12 living space? Not many people.

Who would pay $1,230 a month for a place without a bathroom, where garbage bags function as closets and there are no tables or chairs? Who would pay this extraordinary sum for living conditions that mirror the destitution of some impoverished nations?

You would. You do.

The state is spending, in some cases, $1,230 for one-room hovels for homeless families in the infamous Martinique Hotel in New York City, according to Legal Aid attorneys. Calling it a "hotel," however, is to defame the label. The Martinique is a subsidized slum, paid for by the taxpayers of New York state.

"I will not pay for rooms that do not meet minimum standards," said state Social Services Commissioner Cesar Perales, after the state ordered an inspection of the hotel on Thursday.

The state is not "paying" for anything; it is being robbed by profiteers, who capitalize on the hopeless. How else could anyone with even a shred of conscience condemn 455 families to such appalling conditions, and bill the government as though these tenants were occupying suites in upper Manhattan?

Although the state officials decided to inspect the Martinique earlier this week, it is hard to believe they didn't know or hadn't heard about the welfare hotel. Its pathetic conditions have been depicted in the media — the children who share living space with drug addicts, for example.

More surprising is the ignorance of the officials who sign the checks for the Martinique, the people who think it makes sense to pay more than $1,000 for rooms without bathrooms and closets.

Maybe it's easier to just pay and look the other way. Maybe officials, particularly in New York City, don't know what to do with the homeless, and allowing them to live in a shell of building is as good a solution as any.

The problem of providing shelter for the homeless, of providing affordable housing shouldn't be minimized. But, neither should New York state underwrite slumlords who have no regard for humanity other than as a vehicle to increase their riches. Surely there are better ways to spend money to aid the helpless.

ON THE ROAD AGAIN

THE ARIZONA REPUBLIC
Phoenix, AZ, May 31, 1988

THE common wisdom, set forth by well-meaning politicians and sympathetic media gurus, is that the homeless in America are just like everyone else, only less fortunate.

Unfortunately, this is untrue. Moreover, by perpetuating this myth, the cause of the street people is impeded, workable solutions to their formidable problems made more difficult.

As pointed out in recent reports by both *The New Republic* and the Heritage Foundation, the so-called homeless crisis is much more than merely a fallout from "Reagan budget cuts" and much less than a national problem requiring a comprehensive federal solution.

The first myth in need of demolition is that old favorite, the homeless family. In reality, families make up a small proportion of street people. Study after study has shown that the typical homeless situation involves single men and women suffering from chronic alcoholism, drug abuse or mental illness.

Comprising as much as two-thirds of all the homeless, these individuals do not require housing and handouts as much as they require treatment and, in many cases, institutionalization in medical and psychiatric facilities.

As for the makeup of homeless families, the majority are not suddenly jobless factory workers or farmers who have lost their land. Comprehensive studies of the urban homeless show that the typical family living in a shelter is headed by a single, minority woman, usually on welfare, who never held a job or worked only sporadically and often was deeply troubled, financially and socially.

Affordable housing or free shelter, along with social assistance, can alleviate the situation temporarily. However, long-term solutions for homeless families entail breaking the vicious poverty cycle perpetuated by government welfare programs — programs that, however well-intended, are anti-family and anti-work.

Perhaps the biggest myth about the homeless, a particular favorite of the politicians, is that their difficulties require a massive commitment to public housing. That the homeless need housing is undeniable. That more public projects will effectively serve that need is not.

Since an adequate supply of decent housing already exists in nearly every city in the nation, the problem for the poor and the homeless is not finding adequate shelter, but affording it. Just as important, such housing should be located near employment, education and social services.

Instead of pouring more money into building housing projects that typically imprison the poor amid criminal elements and far away from opportunities for advancement, Washington's policy-makers should offer low-income families a discount ticket to economic freedom. Such a program, providing rental vouchers to poor families, already exists, but it is woefully underfunded by the same politicians who decry the lack of housing.

The first step toward solving the homeless problem can be accomplished only when the myths about the crisis are no longer believed. Perhaps then we can begin emptying the shelters for good.

The Atlanta Journal
THE ATLANTA CONSTITUTION
Atlanta, GA, May 13, 1988

A generation ago, most poor people needed better housing. Today, many would be grateful for any housing at all. What's more, a national shortage of cheap lodging is likely to worsen in coming years.

Reaganomics didn't create this problem, but it has done little to find solutions — and now time is running out. Congress can only vamp a few bars until a more astute administration takes center stage. Even so, much can be accomplished.

Task No. 1: Congress needs to fashion a strategy for retaining 500,000 subsidized housing units that might be lost within the next 15 years. Federal subsidies that created the units are set to expire in many instances, freeing owners to hunt for more lucrative tenants. In other instances, changes in the tax laws or lapsed subsidy programs may cause owners to default.

A sharp drop in affordable housing is the last thing the working poor need. The lodging market has already evaporated for them. In 1974, when 8.9 million families needed low-income housing, 10.8 million units were available, according to one study. By 1983, when 11.9 million families sought cheap quarters, 8.8 million units were available. In 2003, by this trend, 17.2 million families will scramble for 6.9 million units.

If government doesn't act fast, today's homeless throng will become tomorrow's homeless multitude. There's no mystery about a remedy: The homeless need homes.

What happened to the ones that poor folks used to have? Many were converted into more fashionable residences as urban neighborhoods experienced a renaissance. Others were bulldozed for urban renewal or private business developments. Others just decayed to the point they were unlivable. Nobody replaced the loss: High construction costs force landlords to concentrate on the top end of the market.

That's why government must help. The estimate on lost subsidized units showed up in a recent study done by the National Low Income Housing Commission at the request of Congress. Preserving the 500,000 units would cost $17.7 billion over the next 15 years, the report calculated.

It's a bargain. New construction costs run astronomically higher than preservation costs for existing units. Direct subsidies to renters ultimately cost more, too, because as the supply of low-end housing shrinks, rents go up. And if homelessness is allowed to increase, governments will pay out vast sums for emergency services.

The commission believes Congress should set up an agency in the Department of Housing and Urban Development that — with help from local governments — would keep an eye on housing needs and costs. And while the commission didn't say so, it is obvious that government must continue to sweeten the kitty for some landlords.

The thousands of homeless Americans on our streets already add up to a national disgrace. We mustn't let it get worse.

The Cincinnati Post
Cincinnati, OH, July 2, 1988

Despite pressure from activists concerned about the homeless, it appears the single-room apartments being renovated downtown with a $2 million public subsidy will remain just out of reach for the very poor. That means the city must renew its search for housing affordable to people on General Relief.

The YMCA of Greater Cincinnati and developer Winston Folkers are intent on charging between $140 and $215 a month for the 220 units at the YMCA building on Central Parkway. Cincinnati City Council is considering whether a further subsidy would bring rents lower. But city administrators warn that the YMCA might back out of the deal.

That should not be risked. The YMCA rooms will find plenty of needy takers at their present rents. But the problem of housing for those on General Relief remains unaddressed.

These people receive as little as $138 a month. Most rent is too high for them, and there are long waiting lists for federal housing subsidies. Even rooms in boarding hotels like the Dennison and Fort Washington rent for around $160 a month.

The problem is that the number of people on relief has risen in the 1980s — just when the inexpensive old hotels were disappearing. The result is too many people forced to live on the streets or sleep at flophouses. Without a permanent residence, those capable of working have trouble finding jobs.

The Anna Louise Inn, at Lytle and Third streets downtown, testifies to the need for single-room housing. For 79 years, women in transition — because of unemployment or divorce or illness — have found refuge at the Inn until they were able to get on their feet. The 238 residents pay just $30 a week for rent and another $10 a week for hot meals, making it affordable for those on welfare.

City administrators should diligently search out a site for another such facility. The city should be prepared to underwrite the cost of the development — sufficiently to make it affordable to the poorest Cincinnatians.

THE BLADE
Toledo, OH, March 23, 1988

HOMELESSNESS in America is a pictorial and emotional issue which has defied solution. Now a study of housing in this country has spelled out just how pervasive a problem obtaining a place to live has become for some people.

"America is increasingly becoming a nation of housing haves and have-nots," says a report prepared by the Harvard Joint Center for Housing Studies. For Americans who have prospered in recent years — the "haves" — there are ample opportunities to find decent places to live at an affordable price.

For a growing number of persons living on modest incomes, however, there has been a triple whammy: lagging income growth, relatively high interest rates, and high inflation in the late 1970s. This is reflected in the fact that two million households that would have been able to afford homes in 1980 cannot do so now, the report stated.

For these younger or less affluent Americans, this has meant a rush for rental housing. Meanwhile, rents have risen since 1981 at a rate 14 per cent higher than prices generally.

In suburban areas in the Northeast and in southern California the human dilemma that rising housing costs have produced is especially stark. In well-off suburbs in Connecticut, even modest houses routinely begin at $200,000. That puts those areas out of bounds for most families of modest income; many such persons either are forced to live far away from where they work or try to meet enormous mortgage payments.

For increasing numbers of low-income persons, soaring housing costs simply means that no housing whatsoever is affordable. That adds up to sleeping outside, finding a center for the homeless in which to live, or living with friends or relatives.

Government is being prodded to intervene on behalf of homeless persons. But the toughest nut to crack will be to find ways to increase the amount of available housing for both middle and low-income persons.

Recently a housing bill was passed by Congress to provide $15 billion over the next two years, but that by itself will not solve the problem. The legislation raises more questions than it answers, such as: Is more subsidized housing the answer? Is creation of some kind of new federally insured government-mortgage program a solution? Or is the answer is to let the system operate as it has and rely on market incentives to get builders to provide the housing that is needed.

As long as well-heeled Americans can find decent places to live, this issue will not be high on the national agenda. But that does not mean that candidates should not begin addressing it this election year.

Budget Cuts Affect Poor

President Reagan Feb. 4, 1985 sent to Congress a $973.7 billion federal budget for fiscal 1986 that proposed to offset a continuing buildup of U.S. military strength with drastic cuts in domestic spending—including, for the first time, many programs primarily affecting the middle class.

Two major programs of the Department of Housing and Urban Development would be eliminated under the President's budget—the no-strings-attached revenue sharing program for states and localities, and urban-development action grants, which cities used to spur private investment in distressed areas. Because of spending lags, however, $1.16 billion in revenue sharing would be spent in fiscal 1986 and $522 million in action grants would be spent.

The budget would cut by 10%, to $3.5 billion, community-development block grants. The budget also proposed a freeze on increasing housing assistance, which currently reached 3.9 million families. Subsidies for construction of housing for the elderly and handicapped, such as a project in Buffalo, N.Y. praised by President Reagan during a 1984 campaign stop, would be ended. Operating subsidies for existing public housing would be cut 10% to $1.1 billion.

The House of Representatives June 12, 1986 passed a comprehensive public housing bill that would require more federal money to be spent on rehabilitation of existing housing than on new construction. The bill, which passed by 340 to 36, would allot between $15.2 billion and $18.9 billion for housing assistance, according to *Congressional Quarterly* June 14. Precise figures were not available because Congress had not set overall spending levels for 1987. The bill was a compromise on an initiative sponsored by House Democrats that would have provided an estimated $23.3 billion for housing.

The Senate was considering a similar bill. President Reagan had vowed to veto any housing bill that did not cut spending. The House bill would continue most programs at current levels. Under an amendment to the bill, $860 million in funds earmarked for construction of new public housing in the fiscal year 1986 would be used instead to rehabilitate existing projects. The bill's Democratic sponsors had opposed the amendment, defending the need for new construction by pointing to the long waiting lists for public housing in cities such as New York.

The bill would renew two programs that President Reagan had tried to eliminate, Urban Development Action Grants (UDAG) and Community Development Block Grants. Southern and Western representatives had opposed the UDAG program but were induced to support it after the legislation was modified to expand the program to more distressed areas around the country. Previously, the grants had gone mostly to cities in the Northeast and Midwest.

BUFFALO EVENING NEWS
Buffalo, NY, July 20, 1985

THE U.S. DEPARTMENT of Housing and Urban Development has raised legitimate questions about potential conflicts of interest concerning three members of the Buffalo Common Council. These involve allocations of more than $200,000 in federal block grant funds to three private community organizations with which the Council members or members of their families have been associated.

Two of the Council members have acted to sever their ties to the affected groups. Council Member at Large Herbert L. Bellamy, however, refuses to resign as board chairman of 1490 Senior Citizens and threatens to sue HUD if it denies that organization the $114,200 it has been receiving annually in block grant money. While Bellamy has every right to take court action, he would be better advised to accommodate HUD's requirements.

Bellamy contends his role does not involve any conflict because, as an at large Council member, he does not have detailed authority over how block grant money is distributed. But all members of the Council vote on City Hall plans for allocating this money, and it is reasonable to urge that they not be in the position of approving funds for community organizations in which they have an interest, however unselfish and civic-minded.

This is in no way to reflect on the integrity of the Council members or the sincerity of their commitments to these worthy community organizations. It is simply to recognize that government officials must avoid the appearance of conflicts in exercising their public functions. Objectivity is best assured when Council members do not have a particular interest in the organizations to which they allocate public funds.

The HUD guidelines are sound, and for the good of the organizations involved, the Council should abide by them.

The Philadelphia Inquirer
Philadelphia, PA, November 31, 1985

Two real estate company officials who took easy advantage of an incredibly sloppy — if well-intentioned — Reagan administration effort to sell off abandoned housing in Camden have been convicted, and thanks for that. True, the bumbling U.S. Department of Housing and Urban Development (HUD) may well have been begging to be swindled, but blaming the victim doesn't excuse the crime.

In the end, actually, it was more than a government agency that was victimized by pervasive housing fraud in Camden. The homeless welfare recipients who bought into the scam have lost their homes. Taxpayers are out millions of dollars.

The way the crooked officials of Bonafide Investment Co. worked their operation was outlined by Inquirer staff writer Tim Weiner in a series of articles a year ago: The company bought houses dirt cheap from HUD, did some cosmetic touching up and then resold them at profits of $15,000 or more apiece. To make the scam work, the company filed hundreds of fake documents to obtain federally insured mortgages for poor, unqualified buyers.

When the buyers couldn't keep up payments, they lost the houses and the government was stuck paying off the mortgages — lining the pockets of speculators and leaving the buyers out in the cold. Government accountants later would discover similar frauds in New York and Memphis, costing taxpayers more than $2 million in those cities alone.

That's an expensive record for an ill-managed Reagan administration program to get the federal government out of the housing business by pushing bulk sales of vacant urban properties to private investors.

It would be pleasant to speculate that, as further indictments are handed down in the Camden case (as is expected) and if the U.S. attorney's office in New Jersey continues its successful prosecutions, the word might go forth that HUD is no longer the patsy it was once.

It would be pleasant to muse that a lesson may have been learned that "privatizing" willy-nilly without tightly supervising the transfer of federal property is all but issuing a license to steal.

It would be pleasant and, unfortunately, profoundly optimistic.

THE ARIZONA REPUBLIC
Phoenix, AZ, May 29, 1985

LOCAL governments nationwide are redefining their role by paying private industry to provide an increasing range of public services.

There is still much to be learned about this growing trend, but the Department of Housing and Urban Development has underwritten the first comprehensive survey on the movement.

The Reagan administration is pushing the trend as its transfers more federal programs to local and state governments. In many cases, it transfers relatively little or no federal funds, which pressures local governments to seek ways to cut service costs.

The move to reduce government work in the private sector — from garbage pickup to street repair — is long overdue.

A government's primary role is to make and carry out public policy — not perform such work as building trades, sewer cleaning and street paving. Where economically feasible, the private sector should be given a chance to perform.

The survey shows that localities are paying private firms to operate mass-transit systems, hospitals, jails, custodial services, trash collection, landscaping and other services.

However, it is one thing to readjust government's intrusion into the private sector over the past 30 years and quite another to dump federal costs on cities and towns.

There is a limit to the number of federal programs the administration can continue to transfer to local governments in its bid to cut huge U.S. deficits.

Yet, local and state governments have, for far too long, invaded private industry by creating their own bureaucracies for many services. Indeed, official power brokers have built up large patronage systems this way to keep themselves in office.

These bureaucracies have grown with salaries and benefits often above those for comparable workers in private industries.

That is one reason why the city of Phoenix requires city departments to bid against private contractors for many publicly financed services — from trash collection to custodial services.

Competitive contracting by local governments not only increases their accountability, but makes them look at many more options in conducting public business.

It is true, in some cities, that private contractors have replaced some old-time power brokers by donating large sums to political campaigns. However, that has been and is being much better controlled than during the old days of big-city bosses.

The bottom line is whether state and local governments can do public work more efficiently and at less cost by outside competitive contracting than in mushrooming bureaucracies whose primary goal is self-perpetuation.

Chicago Tribune
Chicago, IL, July 16, 1985

Joseph Cardinal Bernardin was right when he said the only way to correct the problems of Chicago's high-rise public housing projects is to replace them with "a new concept." After three decades of patchwork remedies for the problems of giant complexes like the 20,000-resident Robert Taylor Homes and the 14,000-resident Cabrini-Green Homes, the social and psychological decay continues. The cardinal is hardly the first outside observer to reach this conclusion. The challenge for political, business and other civic leaders is to do something about it without repeating the mistakes of the past.

When construction began here in the 1950s with two of the nation's largest public housing complexes, high-rise projects promised new hope to its newly relocated residents. High-rise designs continue to work well as housing for senior citizens. But for families with small children and teenagers they soon turned into congested havens for crime, a bottomless pit for federal dollars and a social reservation that isolated residents from conventional notions of neighborhood and community. Social critics correctly called them "warehouses for the poor."

Of course, most residents of subsidized housing are law-abiding citizens who only want a decent place to live. Those fortunate enough to live in low-rise, townhouse and scattered-site housing show crime and maintenance rates that are not significantly worse than in any other low-income neighborhood. But in the dark, narrow corridors and stairwells of high-

rise projects, the law-abiding majority finds itself endlessly terrorized by hoodlums and vandals. The best tenants tend to move out as soon as they are able, depriving the young people who remain of valuable role models who could offset the demoralizing influences of gang leaders, drug peddlers and pimps.

The city's Roman Catholic archbishop visited several of the city's public housing units, consulted with priests and nuns who work with residents and arrived at a dismal but obvious conclusion: Chicago's public housing is a "dead-end street" for most of its 140,000 residents and it is time for government and business leaders to "start all over again."

The alternative adopted years ago by St. Louis when it demolished its high-rise Pruitt-Igoe projects with explosives looks more appealing by the day. But the demand for low-cost housing in St. Louis was nowhere near as severe as it is in Chicago. Even if public housing residents here are given vouchers to move into conventional apartments, as those who want to get the government out of this line of property management have suggested, where is new housing to be found? Pruitt-Igoe's 2,088 units are dwarfed by Chicago's mammoth projects. And the very mention of scattered-site public housing raises the tempers of those who support public housing only as long as it is not in their neighborhood.

But the problems must not be shoved aside while another generation is lost. The challenge today is the same as it was three decades ago: to house today's poor without creating new ghettoes in the future.

THE BLADE
Toledo, OH, May 6, 1985

FEDERAL housing assistance to low-income renters has tended to concentrate poverty in squalid housing projects. This fact is reason enough for one to be encouraged by the Reagan administration's experimental program designed to give poorer recipients greater freedom in deciding how much they spend on rent and where they live.

During the next five years the U.S. Department of Housing and Urban Development plans to provide housing vouchers to about 4,500 families in 20 locations across the country. To qualify for the vouchers, recipients must be making less than half the median income in the area where they live.

A federal voucher is worth the difference between 30 per cent of the recipient's monthly income and HUD's estimate of moderately priced housing in the market area.

Heretofore, HUD required aid recipients to contribute 30 per cent of their monthly income toward the rental payments. The government made up the difference, providing the total did not exceed the designated rent ceiling.

The new program retains the same formula with one significant exception. If a subsequent rent increase exceeds HUD's ceiling, tenants will be allowed to pay the difference without fear of losing their federal assistance.

The experimental system is preferable to the current program because tenants will have the option to spend a few dollars more for apartments closer to their jobs or schools. Those tenants who can find housing for less than the voucher's value will be permitted to pocket the difference. In either event, recipients will have the freedom of choice that is denied to them under HUD's more restrictive current regulations.

The new program also is cost-effective because it encourages recipients to find private rentals instead of being confined to traditional public-housing facilities that have proved to be enormously expensive to build and maintain.

This is not to suggest that the voucher system is a panacea for low-income housing problems. But as an alternative to failed public housing projects, this rental voucher experiment is certainly worth the try the Administration is giving it.

THE LOUISVILLE TIMES
Louisville, KY, April 25, 1985

There is no room in the inn for thousands, perhaps millions of Americans if the estimates of the number of homeless people in the United States are believable. They vary widely — from 300,000 to 3 million — but the consensus is that the ranks are growing.

The U. S. Department of Housing and Urban Development conservatively estimates the increase between 1980 and 1983 at 10 per cent per year. The U. S. Conference of Mayors says the number of homeless people swelled by 38 per cent in 1983 alone. And the National Board Emergency Food and Shelter Program, a coalition of charities, estimates that 22 per cent more people sought space in public shelters in the past year than in 1983, despite improvements in the economy.

Last week the House Government Operations Committee urged the federal government to declare a state of emergency, saying President Reagan should direct the appropriate federal agencies to make services to the homeless a priority. Rep. Ted Weiss, D-N. Y., whose subcommittee held eight months of hearings, described the problem as a "great unrecognized crisis" that requires federal efforts.

Yet, there is no emerging plan for addressing the problem. The Reagan administration hasn't asked Congress to continue the $210 million appropriation in the current budget to provide emergency services through charitable organizations. In fact, the federal government apparently with no hesitation is

Speaking of child pornography . . .

continuing to back away from the role it assumed in the Roosevelt era of seeking to ensure for all Americans housing that is safe, clean and fit for raising a family.

As a result, public housing authorities around the nation — the "landlords of last resort" — are bracing for cuts in the federal operating subsidies that keep them afloat and for massive reduction — possibly even the elimination — of funding for badly needed capital improvements.

Sharp cuts in Community Development Block Grant funds, which most cities have used, in part, for housing

rehabilitation, have been proposed. Funds for new public housing have virtually dried up and private, low-income housing construction is now jeopardized by proposed revisions of the tax code.

A recent HUD study concludes "the reform proprosals would reduce or eliminate current tax breaks available for rental housing . . . and the supply would decline over time because of reduced maintenance of the existing stock" and condominium conversions. In addition, the elimination of tax incentives is expected to drive rents up by more than 25 per cent.

The usually low-key HUD Secretary Samuel R. Pierce Jr. — who President Reagan reportedly once addressed as "Mr. Mayor" when he didn't recognize Mr. Pierce as a member of his Cabinet — is doing what he should have all along: emerging as an advocate for his department and those it is supposed to serve.

The alternatives he suggests — rent subsidies for poor tenants and tax credits to owners who rehabilitate low-rent apartment units — are worth exploring as possible long-term solutions to the low-income housing crunch. In the meantime, the demonstrated need for emergency housing and other services for the homeless must be met. Whatever the numbers, the ranks of homeless and ill-housed are too large now. To sit idly by while they increase is contrary to everything for which this nation stands.

THE TENNESSEAN
Nashville, TN, March 25, 1985

THE U.S. Department of Housing and Urban Development has set up a system of "luxury fees" to be charged public housing unit residents for the power used to run their air conditioners, freezers, clothes driers and extra refrigerators.

The fees, which are due to go into effect April 1, could run as high as $65. Paying this amount would be out of the question for many living in the public housing units.

The residents of the units are upset over the fees, mostly about those affecting their air conditioning. This is understandable. There aren't many luxuries in the housing projects, and certainly air conditoning is not one. Few people do without air conditioning in these times, either at home or at work.

The Metropolitan Development and Housing Agency is trying to get a 90-day extension past the April 1 deadline and hopes eventually to obtain some permanent waivers for elderly and handicapped residents. HUD's regulations imposing the fee include guidelines for requesting a delay.

The Reagan administration doesn't ordinarily show much sympathy for the poor in its rush to trim government spending by gutting social programs. But there is hope the administration will relent in this case and make some changes in its regulations.

Life in the closely-packed housing projects, some of them crime ridden and infested with drug peddlers, is difficult enough already. It would be a nightmare to some residents without air conditioning.

DESERET NEWS
Salt Lake City, UT, July 23, 1984

One of the problems with government programs is that all too often they seem to produce the opposite effect of their stated goals.

For example, the federal government has a program with the tongue-twisting title of Department of Housing and Urban Development Section 8 Moderate Rehabilitation Program. Its aim is to provide subsidized rental housing for low-income tenants.

The HUD program is supposed to finance renovation of old apartments through rent subsidies. The needy tenant will pay 30 percent of his gross income and taxpayers will guarantee the difference.

But some developers have quickly learned they can make a lot more money if the subsidized rent on an apartment is $400 a month instead of $200. Something like that already has happened on one Salt Lake project

The program was meant to keep costs low and work up to the maximum subsidy, which is 120 percent of regional market in rents, something to be granted only in rare cases.

What happens is that some developers push rehabilitation costs up to justify the higher rents — and higher subsidies. Instead of starting low and working up as costs dictate, they tend to try for the maxiumum and work backwards. A HUD economist admitted this week that "lately, most get the upper range."

Another HUD official said the program was never meant to encourage maximum rent charges. But it's happening and the taxpayer is getting stuck with the difference, to say nothing or adding more red ink to the federal budget deficit.

If the goal is low-cost housing for the needy, why build in incentives for developers to make it more expensive? That doesn't make sense.

It's just another example of why government social programs tend to cost so much — and produce so little.

ST. LOUIS POST-DISPATCH
St. Louis, June 10, 1985

Without thinking much about it — or without caring much about it — the Reagan administration has been moving the federal government away from using its powers to help provide shelter for low-income Americans.

In recent years, several housing assistance and construction subsidy programs have been cut back or marked for elimination by the administration. Meanwhile, the president's tax reform proposals, if approved, would also make it harder for the private sector to provide shelter at prices that low-income families can afford.

True, aspects of the tax package might dampen the price of some single-family homes, but that effect will most likely be seen in higher-priced housing, not in the price of homes that would fit into the budgets of working class families. For them, housing choices are likely to remain limited. For many, renting will be the only possibility — and an increasingly costly one at that.

A recent study by the General Accounting Office has come up with some interesting evidence in that regard. On the positive side it found that households with very low incomes (those with gross incomes of 50 percent or less of the median family income in their area) are somewhat better housed today than they were a decade ago. In 1975, 22 percent lived in inadequate units that lacked plumbing, kitchens or other features. By 1981, only 18 percent lived in such housing.

However, the burden of paying for better surroundings has increased dramatically, making it significantly harder for millions of struggling households to keep a roof over their heads. In 1975, 9.3 million low-income households paid 50 percent or more of their gross income for rent, the GAO found. By 1983 the number of households facing that burden had grown to over 12 million. More telling still, the low-income households where rent consumed 70 percent or more of their income shot up from less than 2 million to 3.6 million, from 21 percent to 30 percent of that income category.

Only 22 percent of the households in that income category were fortunate enough to pay 30 percent or less of their income for rent — yet that figure is the benchmark the federal Department of Housing and Urban Development uses as a definition of a "reasonable and affordable rent burden."

There is no secret about what is going on here. The lesson this country — and most other industrialized nations — learned long ago is that housing is something that the private market does not supply very well without a helpful hand from government. Of late, that hand has been removed in favor of the invisible hand of the marketplace. And the poor are paying the ever-rising price.

This is not to say that every federal housing program is sacred. Some have been social and economic disasters. But the fact remains that the magic of the marketplace is not magic enough to provide decent shelter for the poor. Letting the market take care of such things represents an easy — and superficially cost-effective — way for the administration to address a complex and difficult public policy challenge.

The numbers in the GAO report testify to the failure of that approach and to the need for the nation to come up with a better one.

The Atlanta Journal
and
THE ATLANTA CONSTITUTION
Atlanta, GA, August 23, 1985

The Reagan administration is about to put the wrecking ball to a structure that only needs remodeling. It wants to abolish the federal standards that are imposed on homes bought with government-guaranteed loans. Buyers could find themselves at the mercy of builders, and the feds could wind up underwriting some inferior homes.

Marked for extinction are the Minimum Property Standards, used by such agencies as the Federal Housing Administration, the Veterans Administration and the Farmers Home Administration. The Reaganites would rather rely on state and local building codes. In areas with strict codes that would be fine. The problem is, laws vary widely from jurisdiction to jurisdiction.

Rather than abolition, the standards need more flexibility. Some rules governing marketability and livability could even be lifted. For example, it is now *verboten* to locate bedrooms and bathrooms directly off living rooms. Closet and cabinet space must conform to federal standards.

There is a good case to be made for cheaper homes with less cabinet and closet space and less-than-ideal floor plans. There is a case, too, for regs that allow such things as wooden porches in the Sun Belt and deep windows on flood-proof sites.

But the case for scrapping *all* federal rules is shaky. The regulations on safety and quality have helped home-buyers and the government alike. Why remove them?

For home-buyers, they have ensured adequate ventilation, tight roofs, solid foundations and overall durability. The standards have been widely adopted because builders often don't know in advance what financial arragements will be made for purchase of their properties.

For the feds, the standards serve to minimize financial risk. They represent not so much runaway government as wise business practices. When borrowers default on guaranteed mortgages, the government ultimately must resell the property. Shoddy work may encourage defaults and make resale more difficult.

Flexible federal rules would encourage housing that is cheaper and more varied in design, but no rules could leave home-buyers and government out in the cold.

The Washington Post
Washington, DC, August 26, 1985

THE DEBATE over national housing policy for the poor is about to change dramatically. The theme for the past 10 years has been expansion; the question has been how large an increase to have in the number of subsidized units each year. Beginning in 1991 the issue may instead be whether to acquiesce in a decline.

The reason lies in the mechanism through which most subsidized housing is now provided, the so-called Section 8 program. It operates through contracts with landlords. The landlords agree to build or otherwise provide the housing units. The government provides tenants who will pay 30 percent of their incomes toward agreed-upon rents; the government then pays the rest. The contracts are typically for 15 years.

The problem is that, in the early 1990s, the contracts signed when the program began in the mid-1970s will start expiring, and units will begin to fall out of the program. Some 200,000 units will be lost in 1991, and from 1991 through the year 2001 about 1.2 million, if Congress takes no offsetting action. That is more than a quarter of all the subsidized units the government now maintains—and those existing units already fail to meet the national need, as measured by income levels. Estimates ordered up by Sen. Donald Riegle Jr., ranking minority member of the Senate housing subcommittee, indicate Congress would have to appropriate $73 billion in the 1990s just to keep the program whole.

The outlook is exacerbated by the administration's announced intention to shift from Section 8 commitments to a new voucher system beginning in fiscal 1988 (for the next two years its position is that for budgetary reasons there should be a moratorium on new units of any kind.) The problem is that voucher commitments as now envisioned would be for only five years. Thus voucher appropriations would also start expiring in the early 1990s, and have to be renewed.

There is a certain amount of irony surrounding the Section 8 program. It was started in the Nixon-Ford administrations as an alternative to public housing and other construction subsidies, a way of getting the government "out of the housing business." In some ways it has had the effect instead of involving the government more deeply, as the long-term Section 8 commitments have mounted. Now the Reagan administration again wants to get the government out of the housing business; that is part of the purpose of vouchers. The administration has fought subsidized housing proponents in Congress pretty much to a draw over the past few years; the expansion rate of the programs has been markedly slow. But there is no consensus on what policy ought to be.

What Sen. Riegle's useful compilation shows is that the problem will shortly be much more complex. Congress should take advantage of this timely warning and try for once to legislate thoughtfully and in advance, before the problem is upon it.

Millions Join 'Hands Across America' To Aid Poverty and Homelessness

More than five million Americans held hands May 25, 1986 in a human chain that stretched across virtually all of the U.S. Known as Hands Across America, the event had been organized to shine a national spotlight upon the problems of poverty and homelessness. The chain reached some 4,150 miles through 16 states and 550 cities and towns from Battery Park in New York City to the wharf of the *Queen Mary* in Long Beach, Calif. Arid desert stretches and occasional shortages of volunteers caused a few holes along its length.

The event's organizers May 29 said that 5,442,960 people had taken part, slightly short of their target of 5.5 million. Another 1.5 million were said to have joined similar events staged in area's distant from the line's path. No one was initially sure how much money the chain had raised, but the goal had been $50 million-$100 million. Participants had been expected to contribute $10-$35 each, to be turned over to poverty groups after expenses had been paid.

The mood along the chain was said to be festive. Weeks of publicity had led up to the event: a Hands Across America pop song and music video had been released, and the event's official logo had appeared on T-shirts, signs and billboards. Major corporations had signed up as sponsors and the chain featured such celebrities as singer Frank Sinatra, film director Steven Spielberg and baseball star Pete Rose.

Another participant was President Reagan, who joined hands in a segment of the line that stretched over the White House grounds. His wife, Nancy, and his daughter Maureen Reagan also took part. Maureen Reagan reportedly had urged her father to join the event after he caused a small furor earlier in the week with some remarks about the poor.

Many advocates for the homeless were angered by the participation of a president whose policies they blamed for worsening poverty. "It's not fair for him to stand there and act as if he's a caring person for America," said Mitch Snyder, director of the Washington, D.C.-based Community for Creative Non-Violence. For the most part, the activists were said to reserve judgment on how much good the event itself would do their cause.

the Charleston Gazette

Charleston, WVA, May 28, 1968

THIS PAST weekend an incredible number of Americans joined hands to protest hunger among fellow citizens. The chain didn't extend from coast to coast unbroken as had been hoped by sponsors.

Even so, the event was an unqualified success: Americans, it is clear, don't want members of their society going to bed hungry.

But how many Americans are suffering daily hunger pangs? That's the sticky question, and answers are as far apart as were East Coast handholders from West Coast participants.

Organizers of Hands Across America have said that "there is widespread hunger and famine in America." Some put the total at 20 million.

S. Anna Kondratas, an analyst for The Heritage Foundation, a conservative think tank based in Washington, D.C., challenges that statement and statistic. She insists that the incidence of hunger is small and that chronic hunger is grounded more in dietary ignorance than in federal frugality.

In the late 1970s hunger and malnutrition, she says, "because of lack of income were not a problem. ... Since then, federal spending on food programs has gone up, not down. A greater proportion of the poverty population is receiving food stamps today than ever before. Indeed, one in 10 Americans is a food stamp recipient. Supplementary private-sector food assistance also is expanding rapidly. And food costs comprise a smaller proportion of personal income than five years ago, while per capita caloric consumption is up."

What concrete evidence exists to explain rising hunger rates?

Nothing, says Kondratas. "The perception of widespread hunger is rooted in subjective, anecdotal impression, based on isolated and unrepre-

sentative cases." (Here we apparently have the reverse side of the perception coin as often pronounced by President Ronald Reagan from the speaker's podium in his little asides about rampant welfare chiseling.)

"The methodologies of the much-publicized studies that purported to 'find' 20 million hungry Americans and to identify 150 'Hunger Counties' have been soundly discredited. Other studies, also given significant publicity, are based on equally questionable assumptions and shaky methodologies. One claim that the plight of the rural poor is worsening, for example, was based on 1976-1980 nutritional data."

Perhaps the worst criticism to be aimed at the problem of the plight of America's hungry is that it has forever been a political soccer ball ideological partisans can propel hither and yon with wild abandon. Who cares whether the hungry are fed so long as the ideological opposition can be hurt with a telling kick.

Intractable pockets of poverty undoubtedly remain, Kondratas admits. Likewise true for millions of families is the problem of providing daily adequate nutrition. Policymakers mustn't forget, she says, "the poor, the hungry, the homeless, or any less-fortunate American." Annual health and nutrition surveys should be funded to produce accurate, current estimates of the nutritional status of all Americans. "This would help identify the scope of the problem and at-risk groups, as well as changes over time."

Hands Across America participants, we're confident, want the truth about American hunger no less than do Kondratas and any concerned citizen. Also manifest is it that Americans, no matter party and ideology, expect the distress of the hungry in their midst to be removed.

ARGUS-LEADER
Sioux Falls, SD, May 25, 1986

The hype is finally over.

Today, Hands Across America, the most ambitious of recent fund-raising spectaculars, will succeed or flop.

If all goes according to plan, about 6 million Americans will join

Editorial hands this afternoon for 15 minutes, forming a human chain 4,000 miles long.

The purpose is noble: to raise money for hungry and homeless people. But some critics say that the biggest beneficiaries will be celebrities' and other participants' egos, and that Hands Across America is little more than moral exhibitionism on a grand scale.

It is a showy affair. And compared to the billions of dollars that America already spends on poverty programs, it won't raise much money. Nonetheless, organizations, sponsors, participants and contributors deserve a big hand.

Organizers hope — perhaps too optimistically — to raise up to $100 million to help hungry and homeless people. Even participants are expected to contribute at least $10 each. (If you'd like to contribute, call 1-800-USA-9000.)

Those not impressed enough to give should be impressed by the logistics of the effort. The human chain will cross 16 states and the District of Columbia on its wandering, 4,000-mile route from coast to coast.

Keeping gaps in the line to a minimum of miles will be especially difficult in rural Arizona. Organizers have given up entirely on one 94-mile stretch of desert highway in that state.

But even with gaps, it will be hard to call Hands Across America a failure.

Even if it doesn't raise a lot of cash, Hands Across America will bring attention to the problems of hungry and homeless people. It already has.

The mega-fund-raiser also has enhanced America's sense of unity.

There might be more efficient and less spectacular ways to raise money. But there's nothing wrong with letting participants in a worthy cause have a little fun. There's nothing wrong with letting people who do something good feel good.

USA for Africa, the sponsor of Hands Across America, and Citicorp and Coca-Cola Co., the main corporate sponsors, deserve the nation's appreciation. So do all the other organizers, participants and contributors who made Hands Across America work.

The Evening Gazette
Worcester, MA, May 24, 1986

There was a time when charity fund-raising was the role of the social elite. They had the money and knew how to get more.

Today, it's often a mass-participation activity, an amalgamation of show business and big business. The causes vary, but the organizers tend to be luminaries of film, television, rock music or sports.

There are fund-raisers, and there are mega-fund-raisers. Clearly, Hands Across America is in the latter category. About 5.5-million people are said to be ready to join hands for 15 minutes tomorrow afternoon, forming a human chain 4,000 miles long. Participants are asked to contribute at least $10; those who give $25, $35 or more will receive — what else? — commemorative souvenirs.

The California-to-New York chain is expected to span 17 states and the District of Columbia. Its organizers hope to raise $50 million to as much as $100 million to combat hunger and homelessness in America. Bill Cosby, Kenny Rogers, Lily Tomlin and Pete Rose are co-chairmen. Celebrities who have said they will take part run the gamut from President and Nancy Reagan to Bo Derek

The concept is symbolic since completing an unbroken chain would be next to impossible, particularly along some lightly populated stretches in the Southwest. It has been calculated that 1.1 million people would be needed to string themselves across Arizona and New Mexico — that's two of every three people living anywhere near the route.

But nobody is expected to check the actual number of participants or how many times the chain is broken. Organizers are talking about success before the first pair of hands are joined.

While Hands Across America may be the largest contact fund-raiser thus far, it is not the first of its kind. An Olympic torch relay in 1984 covered 9,300 miles and produced $12 million for the Boys Club, Girls Club, YMCA and the Special Olympics. More recently, Live Aid, an all-star rock concert held in London and Philadelphia last year raised $70 million in pledges for African famine relief. Band-Aid followed to help midwestern farmers.

But this one is different because its focus is on what is purported to be widespread hunger and homelessness in the world's most affluent nation. Taken out of context, such a claim might be misinterpreted by people in other countries who are unaware of the generous and compassionate nature of our society. Certain conditions accepted as normal in other parts of the world are viewed as unacceptable in the United States.

Hands Across America is an expression of caring, an event that gives millions of people food for thought, as well as something beneficial to do on a Sunday afternoon. But the worldwide concern over hunger and homelessness must last longer than 15 minutes. Invisible hands across this country should always be extended to those in need.

The Salt Lake Tribune
Salt Lake City, UT, May 27, 1986

The whole thing was typically and extravagantly American; hokey, but for a good cause, a grand party with a mission and, most important, successful. It was America's first cross-country charity event.

"It" was Sunday's Hands Across America fund-raiser. Some five million Americans, including President and Mrs. Reagan and a sizeable portion of the White House staff, joined hands for a few minutes along a circuitous route from California to New York, through 14 other states and the District of Columbia.

Participants weren't limited to residents of those states. There were several thousand Americans, like the 300-plus Utahns who went to Arizona to join the chain, who made an extra effort to join in.

Although there were some gaps in the chain, despite frantic, last-minute work to close them, the event was a dramatic demonstration of the sense of charity that is quintessentially American.

Hands Across America was a frank acknowledgment by several million citizens that even in the wealthiest and most powerful land on Earth, there exists poverty and hunger and they want to do something about it.

Sponsors anticipate that the effort will net about $50 million or more for the hungry and homeless.

The event was not without its detractors, principally critics of President Reagan's domestic policies who used the occasion to chide him because of cuts in federal welfare programs. And the Soviets had to get their licks in, too.

Radio Moscow asserted that Mr. Reagan has proposed nothing to deal with "the now-disastrous problems of hunger and poverty in the country."

Nevertheless, Hands Across America was a heartening sign that a lot of Americans feel obligated to help the all too many of their fellow citizens who are hungry and downtrodden.

The Rev. Billy Graham, who participated in the extravaganza on the Mall in Washington, D.C., sounded an appropriate note of reservation. "I trust as people give of themselves and their time and money to build a human wall of compassion . . . that their outpouring of brotherly concern will maintain momentum not only today, but for many years to come."

Given the historical record of ongoing and unstinted American support for charitable works, Mr. Graham's concerns are, to a large extent, probably unwarranted.

Richmond Times-Dispatch
Richmond, VA, May 29, 1986

Yet another star-studded, mega-media care-a-thon has come and gone, but Hands Across America promoter Ken Kragen says he hopes the generosity exhibited during the event won't stop with the tax-deductible $10 check participants wrote to stand in line with the likes of Bill Cosby, Kenny Rogers and Shamu the Killer Whale. He's urging individuals to get involved with community groups working to ease the plight of the hungry in America, of whom he believes there are some 20 million.

Similar figures are also being tossed about by people who — unlike Mr. Kragen — see the Hands project as an excuse for some good old-fashioned Reagan-bashing. "Six million people would not be holding hands this weekend if there were not 20 million Americans without food — the public is saying that government has failed," said liberal Massachusetts Sen. Edward Kennedy. Another critic said there was something "obscene" about the president's participation in Hands Across America.

When Mr. Reagan dared to suggest that part of the poverty problem in the United States results because some poor people aren't aware of the government benefits available to them, he was roundly denounced by many who insisted the real problem is that he has cut federal spending on the poor. A new report from the Harvard-based Physicians Task Force charges that the federal response to hunger in this country has not been "adequate."

In response to this claim, two things may be said. First, documentation for the 20 million estimate is less than reliable. The physicians group arrived at it in a 1985 report entitled "Hunger in America" based partly on the false assumption that anyone under the poverty line who is not receiving food stamps must be hungry. There was no field investigation to substantiate it or the estimate. That same assumption was also behind the Task Force's January report, "Hunger Counties 1986," which purported to show where American hunger is most prevalent. But when reporters sought out the counties listed in the report, they found no evidence of widespread hunger. A General Accounting Office review of the report concluded that "the study's overall methodological limitations are such as to cast general doubt on the study's results . . ."

Second, spending on food programs during the Reagan years is up, not down. In fiscal 1981, the last budget year of the Carter administration, food programs' spending totaled $15.6 billion. By 1984, it was up to $18.6 billion, and this year it will top $19 billion. Participation in the food stamp program is also higher.

To be sure, the United States is not free of hunger. That's why we welcome Mr. Kragen's appeal for individual volunteerism on behalf of established community organizations, such as the United Way or the Central Virginia Food Bank. The food bank, for instance, helps to feed more than 100,000 needy people each month through its member charities, according to food bank Executive Director Jean P. Machenberg

The work of groups such as this one may not end hunger, but it contributes far more to the effort than those who content themselves with mere Reagan-bashing.

The Burlington Free Press
Burlington, VT, May 29, 1986

Joining hands across the United States to demonstrate sympathy for the nation's hungry was a gesture that probably did more to make middle-class Americans (and well-fed, too) feel good about themselves.

But in today's society the feel-good experience draws high ratings with the populace. After all, isn't the White House the seat of that attitude? And didn't President Reagan make an eleventh-hour decision to add his presence to the event even though he believes the hungry can get food if they know where to turn for help?

Inject a substantial amount of Hollywood hype into the proceedings and you have the ingredients for a good show, if nothing else. It may do little to put food into the mouths of the hungry but it certainly makes for good television.

That the hungry may have been somewhat cynical about the much-publicized event might be taken to mean that they yearned for a more concrete demonstration of concern for their plight. Gestures don't put food in the hungry mouths of men, women and children; genuine steps to solve the problem are much more effective. In the line that stretched across the country Sunday, there probably were many people who applauded the Reagan administration when it cut the food stamp program, school lunch money and other needed items from the budget. They probably share Reagan's view that the poor must lift themselves by the bootstraps in order to join their affluent compatriots in sharing the American Dream. Hypocrisy is alive and well and living in the United States.

It perhaps was the supreme irony that Reagan stood in that line after making so many disparaging remarks about the poor and their ignorance of ways and means of helping themselves. Yet he is the one who cut funds for the very programs that would provide the hungry and the homeless with such information.

From a practical standpoint, Hands Across America was supposed to raise $50 million to feed the hungry. But the promoters now say they started with a $12 million deficit. Whatever the amount raised, they claim that 60 percent will be used to provide food for the hungry and 40 percent will pay for yet more studies of poverty in the nation. How many studies must be conducted before reaching the conclusion that there are homeless and hungry people in the country who genuinely need help?

What is troublesome about the proliferation of these media events is that they create an impression that hunger in Africa, foreclosures in the Farm Belt, the plight of AIDS victims and poverty in America can be remedied on a one-shot basis. Would that it were so. But it simply isn't. Only if the public sustains its interest in those problems will they be solved on a long-term basis.

So many Americans who linked hands Sunday for 15 minutes and sang "We Are the World," "America the Beautiful" and "Hands Across America" may have felt good about themselves for a brief moment.

But the homeless and the hungry probably felt as miserable as they always do while wondering where they could find sustenance for the day and shelter for the night.

The Detroit News
Detroit, MI, May 21, 1986

The Hands-Across-America extravaganza scheduled for this Sunday is having a few problems. It's doubtful that the six million or so individuals needed to form a human chain clear across the continent can be persuaded to turn out on Memorial Day weekend. Medical authorities in the Southwest are warning against the effects of standing in the hot sun all day. A promoter who tried — and failed — to organize a human chain during the 1976 Bicentennial is suing for "copyright" infringement.

But the biggest problem for Hands Across America may be to convince fellow Americans that the event is a legitimate charity drive, not a hype for a political agenda that most ordinary folks probably don't share. Americans' charitable instincts are generous and easily aroused. But if it turns out that Hands Across America is really just more guerrilla theater on behalf of left-wing ideology, then people are justifiably more likely to put their hands across their wallets than join hands across the country.

Singer Harry Belafonte, one of the chief promoters, has been making a pretty good case that politics is the real aim of Hands Across America. On the *CBS Morning News* yesterday, he gave an astonishing rationale for his support.

"Most Americans," he announced loftily, "don't even want to believe that the problem of hunger and homelessness exists. . . . Politics has done much to obscure the issues. . . . There's an absence of political will." As if that weren't enough of an insult to his countrymen, whom he accuses of being ignorant and heartless in the same breath, he went on to speak admiringly of how such paragons of human rights as the Soviet Union and Cuba handle hunger and homelessness.

"When you go to the Soviet Union, when you go to Cuba, when you go to so many countries with which this democracy of ours must compete, it is in the constitution of those countries that nobody goes hungry, that nobody goes homeless. It should be a fundamental part of the rights of the people of this nation that no American goes hungry or homeless. I would love to see some legislation. . . ."

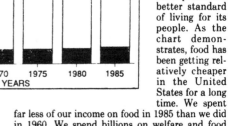

FOOD AS A SHARE OF INCOME

☐ Per capita income 1982
▨ Per capita food exp. 1982

Constant 1982 dollars

10000

5000

0

1960 1965 1970 1975 1980 1985

YEARS

Source: U.S. Department of Commerce

His interviewer, evidently dumbstruck at the profundity of all this, failed to ask Mr. Belafonte whether he felt the constitutions of Russia and Cuba are worth the paper they're written on. The interviewer also failed to ask just what kind of "legislation" he and his colleagues have in mind. Farmer collectives, perhaps?

The pity is that so many good people — and so many guilt ridden corporate sponsors — are anointing such drivel with their time and money. No country on earth provides a better standard of living for its people. As the chart demonstrates, food has been getting relatively cheaper in the United States for a long time. We spent far less of our income on food in 1985 than we did in 1960. We spend billions on welfare and food stamps for the needy. Charitable giving has been rising, not falling — despite the alleged uncompassion of the Reagan years.

If Hands Across America had limited itself to a simple expression of compassion and charity for the less fortunate, it might command our support and attention. But instead it is exploiting people's sense of compassion on behalf of a radical agenda. If Mr. Belafonte thinks socialism feeds people, he's seriously out of touch with reality.

The Russian and Cuban constitutions may sound fine to a naive entertainer, but those constitutions are nothing but paper covers for systems that don't work well enough to feed their own people. Despite that constitution, it's a well-known fact that the Soviet regime deliberately used mass famine in the 1930s as a device to force farmers to collectivize. The Soviet puppet regime in Ethiopia has been following a similar policy with ghastly consequences.

So our suggestions for this weekend is to stay home Sunday, give to your favorite charity, and save your energies for celebrating Memorial Day. The soldiers who have kept our nation free and who have protected the most productive society on earth deserve far more attention than the heavily politicized crew promoting Hands Across America.

Washington, DC, May 23, 1986

Helping hands are reaching across the USA and around the globe this weekend.

On this continent, millions of us are paying up to $35 for the privilege of joining hands Sunday in a 4,100-mile line stretching, with some gaps, from sea to shining sea. Hands Across America impresario Ken Kragen — ordinarily a manager for Hollywood superstars — hopes to raise $50 million for hungry and homeless people in the USA.

On the same day, millions of runners in 232 cities from Adelaide, Australia to London, England, to Juneau, Alaska will compete in a 10-kilometer "Race Against Time." Sport Aid impresario Bob Geldof — ordinarily an Irish rock star — hopes to raise millions to aid starving people in Africa.

Picture Hands Across America: People from New York to California linked hand-to-hand as far as the eye can see, with one common goal — helping the USA's neediest.

Picture Sport Aid: Millions of runners pounding the pavements of Europe, Africa, Asia, North and South America, with one common goal — helping Africa's neediest.

It's splendid that two stars from the entertainment business persuaded millions of people to get off their sofas and actually do something for the needy. But it is imperative that the money and good will generated around the globe not be misused.

Both impresarios have good track records for raising and distributing funds — Geldof from Band Aid; Kragen from USA for Africa. But whenever millions are raised, there's a risk of waste or fraud. In the USA, Kragen must not let the high cost of Hands Across America eat up the receipts. He must insist that the money go to legitimate organizations that actually serve the hungry and homeless.

And don't forget, private aid is no substitute for the government safety net. Just this week, Harvard physicians reported that hunger is growing across the USA, in part because of federal aid cuts. One-time charity events, no matter how splendid, cannot replace the day-by-day flow of government aid. There must be no gaps there.

Some critics claim that hunger is not a serious problem in this country, that the poor have access to plenty of food but choose to eat non-nutritiously. Tell that to folks in line at the soup kitchens. That's unfair and insulting to the hungry.

Others argue that benefits like Hands Across America are just middle-class fads — they make donors feel good while distracting them from the gritty truths about poverty. That's unfair to the donors, and it ignores the substantial good that $50 million could do for the hungry and homeless.

These events give ordinary people a rare chance to share the *experience* of helping. Most of us are neither wealthy enough to practice philanthropy nor selfless enough to run skid row missions. But we all have hands to clasp and feet to run. Our sweat will be sweet and blisters painless if they help ease pangs of hunger and the pain of homelessness.

If Hands Across America and Sport Aid are even partially successful today, tomorrow's world will be a far more caring place.

The Seattle Times

Seattle, WA, May 25, 1986

TODAY at noon millions of people will be joining hands across America, across counties, and across parks — including Seward and Myrtle Edwards in Seattle. It's a giant well-hyped gesture that promises to raise money for the hungry homeless and leave the participants feeling good.

Hands Across America is an inevitable outgrowth of an extended period of mega-benefits. Pockets have been emptied in support of USA for Africa, Live Aid, Comic Aid, Farm Aid and Fashion Aid. Elizabeth Taylor and friends even staged a similar benefit to raise money for AIDS research — sort of an AIDS Aid.

The gimmick, if it can be called that, should be wearing a bit thin. Yet it isn't. Millions of people paid at least $10 apiece to clasp hands in a human (and maybe a few cows) chain snaking across the United States from New York to Los Angeles. Cut off from the main event, many cities and counties are staging mini versions of the massive handholding.

Apparently most of these people don't accept President Reagan's insensitive and inaccurate perception: There's help for the hungry and homeless; they just don't know where to look. Some will be in the chain because $10 is a small price to pay for a good party. Others, the true believers, will be there because they think they can make a difference in the monumental problems of hunger and homelessness in America.

But mostly they'll be there to share newly awakened feelings of community — united against poverty and deprivation. And because they've passed the food banks and seen the long lines of people huddled together waiting for a box of rations to see them through another week.

San Francisco Chronicle

San Francisco, CA, May 28, 1986

THE MONETARY TARGET of $50 million for the nation's poor may never be realized, but the Hands Across America effort has achieved a measure of success by renewing concern with the problems of hunger and homelessness.

More than 5 million people stood Sunday on a line that stretched 4152 miles through 16 states and Washington, D. C., from Manhattan to Long Beach. Organizing the project cost from $12 million to $14 million, most of it donated by corporate sponsors. Each person who stood on line was asked to give at least $10.

An estimated 2.5 million people are homeless in the country now, and the goal of $50 million is admittedly only a fraction of what is needed for assistance each year. But the mind-staggering event, despite its megahoopla, raised a real consciousness that could maintain the true spirit of Hands Across America for months to come.

THE ABIDING ISSUES of hunger and homelessness have been raised by the millions of Americans who stood on line and the millions of others who helped fulfill the promise of the occasion. Their continued commitment and involvement in the fight against poverty will determine whether Sunday was just another nice day for hand-holding and group singing.

AUGUSTA HERALD

Augusta, GA, May 28, 1986

Mitch Snyder, a "Hands Across America" organizer, sure knows how to welcome a guy to a party. Here's what he said about President Reagan's participation in the event Sunday:

"We are not impressed that Reagan is going to come out and clasp hands with someone ... because this administration's involvement in housing the homeless and feeding the hungry has been absolutely nil."

At first, "Hands" organizers were angry with the president for not participating; then when he announced he would, one of their chief spokesmen slammed him. The president is to be excused if he feels there's no pleasing that crowd. The rest of us are left wondering about the "compassion" of people who invite someone to a party and then insult him when he gets there.

Snyder has made a career, not to mention worldwide fame, protesting the Reagan administration's "inhuman" treatment of the hungry and homeless in the District of Columbia. He seems to be oblivious to the fact that a greater proportion of federal dollars is being spent on feeding hungry Americans than ever before.

One in every 10 Americans is receiving federal food stamps today, and this does not even count private sector assistance programs which were expanding rapidly even before Sunday's coast-to-coast snake dance. In all, the U.S. government under President Reagan is spending $18.6 billion a year on various food assistance programs.

Perhaps, as a Heritage Foundation study reports, the problem is not as widespread as the Mitch Snyders of this world would have you believe. There does remain, however, some very tough pockets of poverty that are not getting the relief to which they're entitled.

Heritage recommends that to get at those pockets the government use some of its poverty money to fund annual health and nutrition surveys "to produce reliable and current estimates of the nutritional status" of poor people and other Americans. Then target the dollars to those areas.

In any event, if hunger and malnutrition constituted a problem that could be solved by throwing money at it, it would have been solved by now. The problem would seem to be in how and where the dollars are spent, i.e., distribution. And in a lack of nutritional information on the part of many recipients.

Food assistance programs should be supplemented with education programs accompanied by a shakeup in the bureaucracies that are administering them. The nation needs a bigger bang for its nutritional buck.

Receipts Tallied from 'Hands Across America'

The Hands Across America poverty benefit had raised $32 million to date, according to a report, the event's organizer Sept. 24, 1986 with the city of Los Angeles. The report, filed by the group USA for Africa, said that after expenses some $15 million would be left to help the poor. The spectacular national benefit had been staged in May with the announced goal of raising from $50 million to $100 million.

The event's organizers groups Nov. 20, 1986 disbursed $576,655 in grants, the first money to be paid out from the receipts.

THE ARIZONA REPUBLIC
Phoenix, AZ, August 26, 1986

THE broken line of Americans snaking across purple mountain majesties and fruited plains last May might have accomplished more than its promoters ever imagined: It may have dealt an overdue deathblow to the fad of charity chic celebrity fundraisers.

Hands Across America — the quixotic dream of an unbroken line of hand-holding Americans stretching from sea to shining sea — was conceived for the purpose of raising $100 million for the nation's hungry and homeless.

The effort was something less than a smashing success. The image of singer Robert Goulet being helicoptered out to a lonely vigil in the western Arizona desert to symbolically link a 100-mile-wide gap in the line was as ludicrous as pictures of TV anchorwomen singing and weeping in contrived emotions were embarrassing.

As recently as early August the event's organizers were claiming to have raised $38 million. In fact, Hands Across America raised enough money to cover its $16 million in expenses, thanks to corporate underwriting, with another $16 million left over for the poor.

So far, not one red cent has gone to the needy, although the promoters are promising to begin allocations sometime this fall. Meanwhile, the mean-spirited organizers have nothing but bad things to say about those who stood in line without making a monetary contribution or who have failed to fulfill a pledge.

Americans, through both private charities and tax-supported government programs, generously contribute tens of billions of dollars annually to the poor, the hungry and the homeless. Faddish celebrity events accomplish nothing permanent, make no lasting contribution to entrenched social problems and misdirect energy and resources away from established charities.

Perhaps the abysmal failure of Hands Across America will spell the end, at least for a while, of celebrity chic charity ends-in-themselves.

THE PLAIN DEALER
Cleveland, OH, August 28, 1986

Hands Across America is faced with the embarrassing fact that expenses about matched what will be given away. The Memorial Day weekend extravaganza sought to raise both money and public consciousness to combat hunger and homelessness in this country. It was a spinoff of efforts to combat famine in Africa.

It was an exciting, never-done-before event. To some extent the organizers succeeded. Millions of dollars were raised. For a moment at least, the nation focused on deprivation in a land of plenty.

But The Plain Dealer's disclosure of high costs associated with the project has prompted organizers to try to clarify their figures. Instead of nearly $33 million in receipts, Hands now says the public gave $24.5 million. Of that, some $8.5 million went for expenses. Another $8 million given up front by corporate contributors also went for expenses. The $16 million net has been invested in U.S. Treasury bills while decisions are reached for spending it on the hungry and homeless.

That's a tidy sum, but far from the $50 million or more that the Hands' leaders had talked about raising. The percentage actually going for charitable purposes is far less than what the public had understood to be the case with the parent project, USA for Africa. The fact that only about half the money donated will go to the needy is more than a disappointment. It is shameful.

Granted, some people participated and did not pay, or pledged money and reneged. Granted, such an ambitious project had not been tried before. Expenses for a simultaneous, coast-to-coast event were bound to exceed those of established charities. But single-event costs normally do not surpass 30% of the gross. Hands officials lately said expenses were only 34% of public donations, a statement that ignores the expenses covered by corporate gifts. When Hands gives a more detailed breakdown of expenses next month, the public should be watching to see what happened to so much money given in the name of the hungry and the homeless.

The Hutchinson News
Hutchinson, KS, September 1, 1986

Further reports are in on the glitzy Hands Across America gimmick.

The latest report is no better than the earlier ones.

The well-hyped gimmick was supposed to do great things for the poor. It turns out that it did great things mainly for someone else. More than half the money raised went to pay expenses for the raising of the money.

About $16 million is "in the bank" and available to help the poor, spokesman Joyce Deep reported in Los Angeles. Expenses so far have eaten up $16.5 million, she said.

If the local United Way campaign (or any other local charitable fundraising organization) admitted that its administrative expenses were greater than the money it used for charity, the local folks would chase the directors out of town.

They should, because the admission of such high administrative expenses reveals abundantly the inefficiencies of such a project. Inefficiency is too nice a word, however.

The good people who put up money for the poor by way of Hands Across America were taken. All they have is a lesson, which may be somewhat valuable for the future.

The lesson is that glitzy, one-day public relations gimmicks will never solve a complex problem like poverty. Indeed, such gimmicks make solutions even more difficult, since the gimmicks create the illusion that something has happened when it has not.

The Philadelphia Inquirer

Philadelphia, PA, August 28, 1986

The word this week was that Hands Across America was coming up short, that about half the money collected has gone to cover expenses, insurance, promotion, etc. That says a few things about charity and bureaucracy and about good-hearted, one-shot campaigns to ease chronic and complex social problems.

No one is knocking the consciousness-raising of Hands, but in pure dollars and cents, its $16 million kitty is going to be a drop in the bucket. And, though it was a private affair (no "Big Government" allowed), it has left a lot of unfinished business.

In spending fully as much to stage the event as was collected, one pundit noted, Hands outdid the Pentagon in the overhead department. Was it perhaps, a summer, feel-good frolic? Was it, perhaps, the easy way out?

The homeless, of course, are still with us — four out of 10 the victims of eviction, according to one survey. Meanwhile, the real value of the minimum wage declines, the proportion of renters spending more than a quarter of their income on rent has risen from 31 to 53 percent, and government subsidies for low-income housing have plummeted.

And those fewer federal dollars — as has been demonstrated in Philadelphia recently — are as likely to be squandered and mismanaged as when the largesse was rolling in.

Cities belatedly — and the states even more belatedly — have set up shelters to take up the slack in the safety net. There is the usual struggle between civil libertarians and mental-health advocates over institutionalizing street people who appear unable to fend for themselves.

Still the homeless stack up, surviving, begging, scraping. They cannot be swept up like the confetti after the corporate Olympics, like the ribbons from an unveiled Miss Liberty. They are not a photo opportunity, not scrapbook material.

Who is left to provide — to continue, not simply to care, but to house and feed the homeless? Hands Across America was here yesterday, but it is gone today. It touched a nerve of compassion in America, but its momentum will have been lost if it does not stimulate intelligent policy, sacrifice and, yes, budgetary commitment — long-term government commitment — that goes beyond sympathy and charity.

Hands, in the end, may have succeeded most in demonstrating what it could not do.

THE TAMPA TRIBUNE

Tampa, FL, August 23, 1986

Hands Across America was supposed to be a massive fund-raising effort and the symbolic uniting of people against hunger by forming a human chain from coast to coast.

The chain was somewhat less than complete but hosts of Americans, including President and Mrs. Reagan, did join hands on the appointed day and came away with a feeling of satisfaction that something positive was being done to help the helpless.

After all, some $41.6 million was raised and, even at today's prices, that will buy a lot of groceries. In fund raising, however, the gross amount is not necessarily the figure that is translated into aid. It costs money to raise money and Hands Across America was no exception.

Dave Fulton, press secretary for the charity, has said that administrative costs reached $12 million and that as much as $5 million was spent on such things as toll-free telephone numbers.

A recent article in the Cleveland Plain Dealer speculated that only about half of the $41.6 million will be cleared for assistance to people in need. That hardly squares with guidelines established by the Los Angeles Social Service Department. This is the agency that regulates fund-raising operations based in California, and it says that at least 70 percent of the money generated by a not-for-profit foundation must go to a charitable cause. Hands Across America has its headquarters in Los Angeles.

The final results are not yet available. Marty Rogol, Hands Across America executive director, says that about $8 million in pledges remain unpaid, but money continues to come in, he adds.

Rogol admits that administrative costs have been high but offers the excuse that no one had ever before done an event on such a grand scale and there was nothing to measure it against.

There is now. The split of funds between administrative costs and aid recipients puts one in mind of the story about the toll collector who separated the dollars as they came in, counting, "One for me and one for the bridge."

Future grand events on the Hands Across America scale, if there are any, should be examined carefully in advance to see if there aren't more efficient ways to raise money for charity.

The Evening Gazette

Worcester, MA, September 8, 1986

Those highly visible charity drives, drawing dozens of celebrities and massive media coverage, are much less visible when it comes to accounting for the distribution of funds.

Hands Across America officials are still trying to explain what happened to the money raised last May to benefit the country's homeless. USA for Africa is attempting to justify what was done with funds from "We Are the World" donations, concerts and albums. Actually, Hands Across America failed to raise the amount of money it had expected following USA for Africa's success. But both projects seem to have gone down the garden path in allocating the funds. Using the organizers' own figures, less than half the $78 million the two events raised has been sent to the hungry in Africa or will aid the homeless in the United States.

USA for Africa concerts, album royalties and donations totaled $44.5 million through January 1986. Of that amount, $19 million has been spent for relief. More money is to be allocated for development projects, but there has been criticism because $5 million was pledged to the wealthy African Development Bank to disburse in $150,000 grants. Although famine-stricken Ethiopia's suffering was used as the centerpiece of publicity to solicit donations, that country has received only $3 million of the USA for Africa funds.

The more recent Hands Across America has yet to sort out its finances fully. The organizers say many pledges are still outstanding, one reason why the ratio of expenses is so high, compared to income. The $33 million collected so far, including $8.5 million from Coca-Cola that went directly to organizing the effort, is expected to be augmented by in $8 million uncollected pledges. Total expenses are between $16 million and $17 million. The money not used for expenses, an estimated $16.5 million, has been put into U.S. Treasury bills to be distributed to projects that work with the hungry and homeless.

These celebrity fund-raisers were heralded as impromptu affairs, even though they use full-time organizers, professional managers and promoters. Many Americans responded to the pleas by performers, thinking that their donations were going to help the hungry at home and abroad. It is disappointing that the scope of the effort and the cost of administration have eroded a good deal of the money collected for the needy.

It seems evident that professional agencies that have been in the relief business for a long time — United Way, International Red Cross, Catholic Relief Services and others — are far more capable of disbursing aid and getting more for the money than star-studded one-time spectaculars. They do it quietly but efficiently.

It's a virtue to be generous and help those in need. Americans tend to respond positively to charity appeals. But most donors want to make certain that the aid gets to where they intended it to go.

'Grate American Sleepout' Dramatizes Homeless Issue

In March of 1987, several politicians and notables from the entertainment industry joined homeless activists and homeless people in a demonstration dubbed "The Grate American Sleepout" in Washington, D.C. The demonstration was organized to dramatize the plight of homeless Americans and to protest Reagan administration policies regarding the issue of homelessness in the U.S. For three nights, several hundred people, including actor Martin Sheen and Sen. John Kerry (D, Mass.), slept out in Lafayette Park near the White House.

The Oregonian

Portland, OR, March 3, 1987

Congressmen, actors and activists — even the real homeless who could find leftover space — camped out on the heat grates of Washington the other night to focus attention on the plight of the homeless, as the House moved toward a vote on a $500 million assistance package.

Despite some talk of limousine liberalism, the "Grate American Sleep-Out," was, by its own standards, a stunning success in terms of nationwide press coverage.

Yet the real plight of the homeless was brought into sharper focus by one who did not spend the night at this media-oriented slumber party. Rep. Ron Wyden, D-Ore., dropped by for the festivities, but said he would not be able to stay, because he was recovering from the flu.

Wyden unwittingly highlighted the real point with regard to the nation's homeless people. Sick or well, they don't have the option of a warm, dry bed.

The Washington Post

Washington, DC, March 4, 1987

SEVERAL MEMBERS of Congress, the mayor and a few movie stars were scheduled to spend last night on a grate to demonstrate their concern for the homeless. The gesture continues the strange glamorization of this issue that no one fully understands yet so many want to use.

The problem of the homeless has arrived in our midst with what has to be called unnatural speed. Five years ago, if headlines are the measure, it hardly existed. Now it pervades the society. To what extent has reality changed, to what extent is this a genuine public discovery of wretchedness previously ignored, to what extent is it a media artifact? No one quite knows, and at a certain level it does not matter. The people are there, and plainly wretched. The issue has been seized on by such as several members of Congress and the mayor who were to sleep last night on the grates, seized on as proof of neglect by the society at large, the government and this administration, as proof of their own caring and as a lever to pass an easy bill and set the stage for passing others.

A bill is fine, and some of the funds for emergency measures are needed. But the issue is more complex than this hasty solution suggests. Who are the homeless? Why are they suddenly in evidence when they were not before? What are their problems and what are the solutions? Are they mainly deinstitutionalized mental patients? Or are they victims of the weak economy of recent years?

It isn't a tidy world, but no program can be meaningful for long without a better sense than anyone seems to have of what its purposes and dimensions are. The bill in Congress would create an Interagency Office on Homelessness. Do the homeless really need a separate agency to champion their cause within the government? Or do they not need stronger support from agencies along the way to becoming homeless, better help in their lives before they end up on the grates and in the makeshift shelters?

The limited amount the bill would provide cannot solve the problem of the homeless, whatever that is; it is a token amount. The bill would give an additional $70 million to the Federal Emergency Management Agency to distribute food; $100 million to cities, states or other intercessors to renovate buildings for use as shelters; $30 million for transitional housing; extra funds for outpatient mental health care. Calling a halt to the emptying of mental hospitals until the necessary community mental health programs are in place is a better idea. The bill skips on the surface.

The homeless, we say again, are wretched people who need help. If the government can help them with some emergency funds, it should. But there is a side to this stampede toward the TV cameras that does no one credit and will *not* help the homeless. It is much more help for the helpers, at best an impulse without clear content, aid of the kind we should all have learned long ago to distrust.

The Burlington Free Press

Burlington, VT, March 11, 1987

Sleeping on a heating grate during frigid winter nights is an ordeal that most people would not want to face.

To the nation's homeless, however, it makes the difference between life and death. Lacking shelter, they must make do with what is available. So their bleak existence is governed by their ability to find food and shelter. Soup kitchens provide sustenance. Heating grates offer warmth to carry them through cold nights.

Those who wish to demonstrate their sympathy for the homeless can best help by supporting community efforts to do something to alleviate their plight. Donating time and money will do more to help than anything else.

Last week's Washington sleep-out by members of Congress and stage and screen stars who supported a $500 million emergency bill for the homeless drew considerable media attention. Yet it had a hollow ring. Sleeping on heating grates for one night in no way approximated the day-to-day ordeal of the homeless. Even they expressed little respect for the celebrities who spent the night with them. The homeless people knew that it was a one-night stand for their sympathizers. When it was over, chances are, many of the celebrities were whisked away in their warm limousines to homes where warm beds were awaiting them.

Meanwhile, the homeless continued their grim struggle for survival on the streets of the nation's capital.

The deprivation of the homeless is not a media event; it is rather a cause for deep concern that unfortunate citizens of one of the world's richest countries must live and die on the streets of its cities.

And symbolic gestures cannot lessen the depth of their suffering.

The Register

Santa Ana, March 5, 1987

Actor Martin Sheen, a handful of other actors, and a half-dozen congressmen, including the young Joe Kennedy, bundled up in sweaters and sleeping bags and spent Wednesday night on two steam grates outside the Library of Congress. It was all to dramatize the plight of the homeless and stir up support for a bill virtually assured of passage: another $500 million for the federal government to fritter away in yet another symbolic display of phony compassion.

Even advocates of this legislation admit it will do little to alleviate homelessness. It will allocate $100 million for emergency shelter programs, $100 million to house homeless families through rent subsidies, $100 million for medical and mental health care, $100 million to rehabilitate surplus government property into shelters and $70 million for emergency food and shelter.

If the Salvation Army and various skid-row ministries were coming into a $500 million windfall, help would get to homeless people quickly. But we're talking about the federal government, which has spent billions over the years only to make poverty more hopeless. Rent subsidies are expected to help only 1,300 people nationwide. Surplus government properties are mostly military installations in the boonies, far from where most homeless people are. The vast bulk of this money will go to upper-middle class bureaucrats to administer programs to badger the poor.

We've never thought of Martin Sheen as a rigorous philosophical thinker, but those who make assertions about rights should think first. Sheen, speaking on behalf of the homeless (by whose authority is unclear) claimed: "They demand that here and now ... that basic shelter be recognized as an absolute and basic human right."

Never mind that "basic shelter" is not defined, making the statement incoherent. Presuming it could be defined, is it a human right?

Shelter does not fit into this category. Except in a few tropical climates, shelter requires conscious effort and manipulation of the environment. It is not free. It is coherent to say one has the right to work and strive for shelter and other necessities. But one doesn't have the right to *have* them without working or trading.

Sheen and many others seem to have confused "right" with "privilege bestowed by government." But government is not some magical institution that can conjure benefits and privileges out of the ether. It is a human institution that has nothing except what it takes by force or the threat of force from others who have worked for what they have — that is, by violating their real rights.

We'll credit the compassion of self-styled advocates for the homeless when they concentrate more on setting an example (opening their own homes to poor people?) and inspiring individual effort than using the issue to expand the power and scope of government. If they really want to help further, they would seek to dismantle government programs and policies that drive up the cost and reduce the variety of housing.

Sleeping on a grate to urge passage of a symbolic boondoggle is an empty gesture, not a serious statement.

The Oregonian

Portland, OR, March 4, 1987

Statistics tend to be just as cold as the conditions in which the homeless sleep in the nation's cities this winter. But behind the impersonal numbers are desperate human beings increasingly finding nowhere to turn.

In a survey of 25 of their cities, mayors report that the demand for emergency shelter by the end of 1986 was up 20 percent over the previous year. Yet a fourth of those seeking shelter were turned away for lack of facilities.

While the cities' burden has been growing, federal support has been shrinking. Since 1981, federal funds for housing alone are estimated to have dropped from $30 billion to $8 billion.

When measured against the need while the federal government has been turning its back on the nation's homeless, a $500 million bill pushed by House Majority Leader Tom Foley, D-Wash., looks anything but excessive. It would expand emergency shelter, housing for the needy, health care and food supplies. Indeed, it would seem to be about the minimum commitment that an affluent nation can make to those whose resources are slimmest and whose needs are greatest.

While spending a winter in Washington, D.C., to dramatize untenable conditions, Portland's champion of the homeless, Michael Stoops, promoted a demonstration involving others joining him in a night on the heating grates of the nation's capital.

Oregon has gone through its "Oregon's Night Inn," intended both to give all homeless people a warm place to sleep for one night and also to get a reasonably accurate count of their numbers.

While these events make a potent point, they nonetheless constitute gestures to emphasize the problem rather than a solution. But the symbols mesh with the statistics in a powerful combination that ought to suggest to Congress to keep the bill moving along.

THE INDIANAPOLIS STAR

Indianapolis, IN, March 10, 1987

It would be wrong to conclude that the dozen congressmen and the handful of Hollywood celebrities who spent a night on a heating grate in Washington, D.C., last week engaged in nothing more than a publicity stunt that trivialized the plight of the homeless. Their motivations were sincere, their discomfort was real and they will speak with greater understanding when they discuss the problems of the two million to three million Americans who live on the nation's streets.

But participants in the event — dubbed the "Grate American Sleep-Out" — must admit that they gained only a distant glimpse of homelessness and did not experience the real thing. The congressmen could ward off the chill of the 20-degree night with thoughts of the warm beds that awaited them after they were through demonstrating their concern.

Real homeless people live without the certain knowledge that their condition is temporary and voluntary. The prospect of spending not one night on the streets, but also the next night and the night after that, with no end in sight, is the true source of homeless people's despair.

The sleep-out brings to mind the time former Agriculture Secretary John Block fed his family for a week on a food-stamp budget. At the end of the week, Block announced that government food-stamp allotments are sufficient to provide a nutritious, well-rounded diet. Maybe so. But after seven days of beans and cheese sandwiches, the Block family could look forward to a steak dinner. Block might not have been so smug about the adequacy of federal food programs if he had found himself forced to stick to his experiment indefinitely.

A night on the streets (protected by bodyguards and with the option of quitting any time) or a week on food-stamp rations (no doubt prepared in a modern kitchen and served in a comfortable dining room) teaches few lessons about poverty. When the congressmen and celebrities see a homeless person — ragged, unclean, quite possibly mentally disturbed — they should not imagine that they can truly identify with him. When the former Cabinet member sees a food stamp recipient in a grocery store contemplating whether to buy a treat for her children, he should not pretend that he knows what it's like.

The most they can have gained is an appreciation of the width of the gulf that separates rich from poor in this country. Compassion can grow from such an appreciation, and in that sense a voluntary stint of poverty might serve a valuable function. But the veterans of such experiences cannot claim to have had a true taste of misery. The real misery of poverty is not being able to escape it.

Richmond Times-Dispatch

Richmond, VA, March 9, 1987

One would think that life is difficult enough for Washington's street people without subjecting them to the congressional slumber party that took place around heating grates in the nation's capital last week. So large did the crowd of liberal lawmakers, spouses and assorted glitterati become, in fact, that some street people had to pack up and find another grate. Else they might have been trampled by the many television crews seeking interviews and by the congressmen elbowing their way into the limelight.

This publicity stunt — which The Wall Street Journal reported was "rather extreme even by the press-hungry standards of Congress" — may seem a curious way to demonstrate compassion for the homeless. Said Rep. Dick Armey, R-Texas, "They'd do the homeless a lot more good if they took a homeless person home with them." But the participating lawmakers were not so much interested in drawing attention to the poor themselves as they were in drawing attention to a bill approved by the House that would provide hundreds of millions of dollars in additional aid to the nation's homeless. The sleep-in, they hope, will improve the bill's chances of passing the Senate and being signed into law by President Reagan.

Thus does moral exhibitionism replace thoughtful debate in setting the legislative agenda. Unfortunately there is no assurance that this sort of feel-good politics will in any way help the poor. The House bill proposes, for example, the creation of an independent Inter-Agency Task Force on Homelessness to coordinate federal activities. Will another layer of federal bureaucracy really help the poor? Or will it turn out to be just another federal office that lobbies for ever higher and higher funding to hire more and more bureaucrats?

There is little evidence that the sleep-in participants, or Congress for that matter, have carefully thought out the homeless issue. Not so long ago, people used words like "bums" and "vagrants" to describe the homeless. Their sorry condition was, generally considered to be their own fault, though of course that was not always the case. Now their existence allegedly proves neglect on the part of the Reagan administration.

Although few would suggest that the homeless aren't deserving of some help, exactly what form that help should take remains unclear. Before deciding that matter, Congress needs to be able to answer questions such as: Where did these people come from? Are they all without means of support? To what extent has the deinstitutionalization of mental patients during the last decade exacerbated homelessness in this country? Congressional sleep-ins can't answer these questions. Such grandstanding suggests that the participants are more interested in gaining publicity than in helping the homeless.

LAS VEGAS REVIEW-JOURNAL

Las Vegas, NV, September 20, 1987

A couple of months ago we were treated to the spectacle of a batch of celebrities, including our own Martin Sheen (at least we're beginning to think of him as "our own" Martin Sheen, because he spends so much time hanging around the test site and getting popped for trespass and whatnot) bedding down for the night on a Washington, D.C., steam grate.

Sheen, along with young Joe Kennedy and other upper-class do-gooders sacked out on the street to demonstrate compassion for the homeless. As several perceptive columnists pointed out at the time, Sheen and Kennedy and their fellow demonstrators could have made a more convincing point by inviting some of the homeless to their own posh residences for the night

Be that as it may, we do have a problem with the homeless in this country. If you don't believe it, just cruise past the Las Vegas Rescue Mission some morning or evening and take a look at the dozens of homeless people who seek food and shelter there each day.

Young Kennedy and others of like mind will tell you that the blame for the homeless problem lies squarely at the feet of Ronald Reagan and his administration's heartless economic policies.

Blaming Reagan economic policies for the homeless problem meshes neatly with the wider agenda of the left. But the real root of the problem might be traceable to failed, though well-intentioned ideas of the past. These ideas, by the way, are exactly the kind that young Kennedy could have been expected to advocate, had he been in the political arena at the time.

What we are talking about is the policy, adopted almost universally by the mental health community a generation ago, which opened the doors of state mental hospitals nationwide.

As U.S. Sen Pete Domenici, R-New Mexico, put it in a recent article: "With giant strides in the development of medicines, a new philosophy of community treatment and later court decisions that clarified the civil rights of mentally ill persons, hundreds of thousands of patients were released from state hospitals. The number of patients in state hospitals has dropped from 559,000 to 126,000 in three decades."

For some, Domenici says, the newly found freedom outside the walls worked out well, especially for those former patients whose family and friends were supportive, who had homes to return to, who took their medication regularly.

But many hundreds of thousands of others ended up on the street, and there many are today. Domenici said that perhaps as many as 50 percent of the homeless on the streets today suffer from serious, debilitating mental diseases.

Domenici has introduced a bill in the Senate that seems to us a welcome approach to the homeless problem. Carrying a price tag of about $200 million a year for five years, the Domenici bill would set up a program to identify those among the homeless who are mentally ill, and provide transitional residential centers where these people would be cared for until they are deemed able to make it on their own.

The Domenici bill makes sense. It is about time that the ideological trappings be stripped from the homeless debate and the root causes of the problem identified and dealt with.

The Houston Post

Houston, TX, March 6, 1987

Far be it from us to say that some of the dozen congressmen were more concerned with attracting attention to themselves than to the plight of the homeless. But while some who spent a night on a Washington, D.C., street probably were sincere, one does wonder.

There were sleeping bags, bodyguards and other non-streetperson accouterments. And they did attract attention, which led to the one certain negative of the whole episode. The hoopla caused by congressmen, celebrities and camera crews displaced the regulars from a few heating grates, leaving them more homeless than ever.

THE ☁ SUN

Baltimore, MD, March 8, 1987

From its inception, the "Grate American Celebrity Sleepout" was a splashy public relations stunt. Mitch Snyder, advocate for the homeless, recruited about a dozen members of Congress and a handful of Hollywood celebrities to spend Tuesday night sleeping in the streets of the nation's capital.

There was an edge of unbelievability in trying to imagine that Congressman Joseph Kennedy, who left the kids home with a sitter in Boston; or D.C. Mayor Marion Barry, who rides in the back of a chauffeur-driven Chrysler; or actress Terry Moore, widow of millionaire Howard Hughes, or any of the others could *really* experience the pain and desperation of homelessness. In fact, after an evening in the 20 degree bone-chilling D.C. cold, Rep. Tony Coelho, who spent the night away from his four-bedroom home in Alexandria, Va. bluntly admitted: "I don't want to do this again."

But the short-lived discomfort apparently paid off. The politicos and movie stars hovered together and humbly drank hot coffee and soup provided from the Salvation Army and the House of Ruth. They passed around the free ham sandwiches. All the while, television cameras and journalists hovered around the ersatz homeless. By some accounts, the dominant theme of the event was business as usual, with the Capitol Hill legislators vying for attention in the media limelight; this kind of stuff plays well back home.

The hypocrisy of the whole ordeal was most evident in the willowy images of a few street people wandering in the night because their usual spots on the grates were crammed with so many cameras and reporters and stars that there was no room for them. With the event timed to conclude just hours before the House took up a $750 million emergency aid bill, the sleepout smacked of grate-grandstanding.

San Francisco Chronicle

San Francisco, CA, March 5, 1987

A DOZEN MEMBERS of the House of Representatives and a handful of Hollywood stars sought to raise the nation's awareness of the plight of America's homeless, estimated to number up to 3 million people, but strong congressional support is needed to secure emergency shelter and medical help.

The celebrities, bundled up in a rag-tag assortment of heavy coats and nondescript headgear, spent a cold night huddled around heating grates near the Capitol. The temperature was down to 34 degrees, with winds at 10 miles per hour. "If we can just get this country to start doing something about the homeless," said Rep. Tony Coelho, D-Merced, the House Democratic leader. "It's step by step."

THE "GRATE AMERICAN Sleep-Out" was organized to give impetus to House action today on legislation that would authorize $100 million for renovation of underused public buildings, $70 million for charitable organizations and local food and shelter programs, $30 million for transitional housing such as group homes, $100 million for emergency shelters, $100 million for rental subsidies and $100 million for emergency outpatient health care.

The congressmen who slept in the streets hope to start a momentum that will swing the votes of their colleagues toward urgent aid for the homeless. It is a national problem, growing every year, and has to be dealt with now.

The Miami Herald

Miami, FL, March 9, 1987

HOW MANY homeless are there in America? Between one million and 10 million. The number's fluidity reflects the problem's complexity.

There are the temporarily homeless, seeking help after loss of a job or a streak of bad luck; the helpless, mental patients released from state-run institutions but dependent upon Government benefits. Chronic homeless are the destitute, skid-row alcoholics and drug addicts, and the few free spirits who choose to wander endlessly.

The House of Representatives last week approved a bill appropriating $725 million to aid them all. The vote, 264 to 121, split mostly along party lines, with some Republicans raising legitimate budgetary objections.

The bill's appropriations, though hefty, reflect an understanding of the multiple needs. The bulk of the money, $400 million, goes to housing and shelter. The Federal Emergency Management Agency (FEMA) gets $20 million to continue a successful temporary emergency-shelter program begun five years ago. The Department of Housing and Urban Development (HUD) gets the rest of the $400 million for everything from rehabilitating permanent housing for families to converting unused Government buildings to shelters. Some $75 million would go to Health and Human Services for health care, mostly in outpatient services. And $225 million would increase the amount of food stamps for qualifying families. The balance expands Federal job training and adult-education programs.

The House wisely included funding for some solutions to the problem as well as temporary measures, but the Senate should look hard at the bill's largesse. FEMA, whose program is staffed by three people, recently pointed out to HUD folks an overlooked idle $10 million for housing.

The homeless need help. But it must be aimed at their specific circumstances and within the nation's budget.

THE CHRISTIAN SCIENCE MONITOR
Boston, MA, March 10, 1987

AS the United States moves along through the fifth year of an economic expansion, it has become apparent that homelessness is not just a temporary symptom of recession.

The homeless are not just going to "go away." Although their numbers are the subject of contention, there are unquestionably enough of them to be a national disgrace. Their presence on the streets, under the bridges, on the margins of society, is a daily rebuke to Americans' sense of their country as a land of opportunity.

And so the passage by the US House last week of a $500 million package of aid to the homeless is a heartening indication that national attention is now being focused on the homeless and their needs.

This action, moreover, comes at a time when attention in Washington is shifting to domestic social issues – witness the passage of the drug bill last summer and the current discussions on insurance against catastrophic illness.

Of course the homeless-aid bill has some distance to go. And separate appropriation legislation would be necessary before the money is actually spent. Moreover, the House bill – sponsored by Reps. Mike Lowry (D) of Washington and Stewart McKinney (R) of Connecticut – has no Senate companion yet. Senate majority leader Robert Byrd, however, has instructed his committee chairmen to move expeditiously to put together a bill, and bipartisan legislation, expected soon, will be "fast tracked" once it is introduced, observers say.

The $500 million figure in the House bill derives more from its sponsors' sense of what is politically feasible at this time than from what the homeless actually need. The half billion would go to fiscal 1987 funding for some eight or nine programs; roughly half of the aid would go for immediate services (shelters, food, and health care) for the homeless.

An additional $100 million would be for more intermediate, "transition" services, and $125 million would go for permanent housing for the chronically mentally ill and for rent subsidies to homeless families. (The total amount authorized by the bill comes to $750 if aid authorized for spending through 1990 is counted.)

These two groups – the chronically mentally ill, and homeless families – are the particular targets of this House bill. These two groups were thus singled out because of their specific needs, and because they represent growing sectors of the homeless population. The fact of homeless mothers and children is especially jarring.

This is not to say that other groups of homeless do not have their needs – an article on the opposite page today discusses the needs of homeless veterans, for instance. But the sponsors of the House bill have had to choose their battles.

Still, it is heartening to see Congress work together in bipartisan fashion on an issue like this. There are even hopeful signs that the Lowry-McKinney bill may get some low-key support, or at least not a veto, from the administration. Politics, as Bismarck said, is the art of the possible. Surely the Reagan administration should welcome aid for the homeless as an issue it can "get out front" on; surely, too, a President who has so often spoken of his country as a land of opportunity will want to support measures to extend that opportunity to all citizens.

'PARDON ME, BUT ARE YOU A CELEBRITY DEMONSTRATING THE PLIGHT OF THE HOMELESS, OR ARE YOU JUST ANOTHER BUM ON A STEAM GRATE?'

The Birmingham News

Birmingham, AL, March 5, 1987

The presence of about a dozen members of Congress and several actors on heating grates near the Capitol did not make the night any warmer for the thousands of homeless people around the nation.

It may even have crowded some of those unfortunate people off the only warm place some of them have to sleep.

The "Grate American Sleepout" was yet another example of the disturbing trend toward government by media event, which threatens to replace reasoned debate in the conduct of vital national affairs.

The demonstration was timed just hours before the House of Representatives was to take up a $500 million, one-year emergency bill to aid the homeless. We sympathize with the plight of those who have nowhere to sleep, but we think the best solutions for their problem can come from careful study and responsible discussion in the Congress, not from grandstanding before the television cameras outside.

At the risk of sounding petty, we point out that these same members of Congress who participated in this demonstration of solidarity with the needy are pocketing a hefty pay raise this year. And members of the motion picture industry have spent enough money lobbying Congress just on the issue of royalties on videotapes to put a lot of homeless people into decent housing.

The point is, all policy-making involves ranking priorities and trying to match goals to resources. It is a complicated process. Media events such as the celebrity pajama party in Washington oversimplify the problem and obscure the difficult choices that have to be made.

This is not the way to find rational solutions.

THE RICHMOND NEWS LEADER

Richmond, VA, March 6, 1987

Thank Heaven for the homeless. What *would* Congress do without them?

On Wednesday night, Washington's weather turned brisk, and a handful of Congresspersons bedded down on a Capitol Hill grating to sleep with the homeless. Photographers showed up, so Joe Kennedy and others obligingly posed.

Perhaps the "demonstration" or show of "solidarity" accomplished something. At least the stars made it into the papers. When it comes actually to helping the homeless, they don't have any real answers either.

As one caller asked us: If it had snowed while the compassionists slept on the streets, how would Mayor Marion Barry's plows have known the difference between snow flakes and congressional flakes?

THE TENNESSEAN

Nashville, TN, March 5, 1987

THE Appalachian Regional Commission, an integral part of the Lyndon Johnson administration's War on Poverty, has waged a constant war with the Reagan administration in order to stay alive.

The commission was established in 1965 to help the poorest people in the 13-state Appalachian region from New York to Mississippi. It has provided funds for water supply projects and sewers, for child development projects and health care centers, for highway construction and industrial parks.

But the ARC has been near the top of the administration's hit list since Mr. Ronald Reagan was first elected. Each year, he has tried to cut the agency's budget to the nub, and each year Congress has restored most of the funds.

The 13 governors of ARC states got together in Washington recently to brace themselves for another battle against the White House. West Virginia Gov. Arch Moore, current ARC co-chair, declared that the ARC had to get "back on the front burner," and reported that the agency is requesting a $300 million appropriation for 1988. Its 1987 appropriation was $100 million.

The commission is coupling that budget request with a resolve to monitor its budget so that the funds are properly targeted and spent. It has adopted guidelines to limit spending in economically competitive counties, and concentrating on depressed counties, so that counties with good employment and low poverty will only be eligible for 30% funding for an approved project. Counties where poverty and unempoyment are high will be able to get up to 80% of an approved project's funding.

As all government agencies, the ARC needs to be constantly monitored and assessed so that it can directly address the needs of the people. It may need to concentrate on some geographic areas, or some areas of concern, such as illiteracy or job training. It might decide that some of the 397 counties in the ARC are economically able to be dropped from ARC assistance.

But it is shortsighted to think of the ARC only in terms of a geographic region or a fiscal budget item. The ARC exists to help 20 million of this nation's poorest and most helpless people. But as long as poverty, disease, and unemployment tie the hands of the people of Appalachia, those people need to be bound together by the united help of the ARC. ∎

DAYTON DAILY NEWS

Dayton, OH, March 9, 1987

Democrats have pushed through the U.S. House a bill designed to provide some relief for the homeless. The effort would cost a half billion dollars. House Republicans generally hold that if such a program is to be passed — given the deficit problem — the money should be taken from existing programs. What they really mean is that the money should come from existing urban-aid programs, a category that has been sharply cut in the last few years.

A case can be made that, these days, anyone who proposes a new spending program should show where the money will come from. However, last year, when Congress was authorizing new billions for drug programs, few Republicans were saying the money shouldn't be spent unless Congress could find a place to cut elsewhere.

Homelessness is a problem of the '80s. Whether the reason is the de-institutionalization of large numbers of people who are only marginally equipped to function on their own, or cuts in federal programs, or the gradual disappearance of certain kinds of jobs, or the breakdown of the family, or the alignment of the stars, the problem is real. Mayors, social service agencies and police know it is real. Dayton's St. Vincent DePaul facility for the homeless is full every night, and still there is demand for more space.

Is the problem unsolvable? There is little reason to think so. Other countries — even democracies — manage to keep the problem under greater control. Homelessness is not unheard of in Europe, but travelers notice a clear difference between major American cities and European ones on this score.

There seems, however, to be no simple solution for this society. Do you simply build huge warehouses for lost souls and force them in, knowing full well that they have problems ranging from mental illness to drugs to alcohol to physical ill health to stupidity to bad luck? How long do you let them stay — or force them to? If you house such a mixture of people, in whose neighborhood do you put it?

Perhaps the closest thing to an answer is that society in general must recognize the problem, and that enough resources must be allocated so that homeless people can be dealt with as individuals. The government, charities, churches and citizens must cooperate.

The bill that passed the House last week 264-121 would authorize $100 million for the renovation of unused public buildings, another $100 million for new emergency shelters, another $100 million to help individuals pay for housing, another $100 million for related emergency medical care and another $100 million divided among charities and various transition efforts, such as group homes.

The money is tiny by federal standards, but at least the bill represents an understanding that existing efforts are not solving the problem. At least the bill would have the federal government doing something.

Homeless Aid Bill Enacted

A bill authorizing more than $1 billion in emergency aid for the nation's homeless over the next two years was cleared by Congress June 30, 1987 and signed into law by President Reagan July 22. A White House official said July 23 that the president had signed the bill in the evening without fanfare to demonstrate a "lack of enthusiasm" for the measure. While he favored helping the homeless, in general, the official said, "we were concerned about too much money being thrown at programs that have a mixed record."

The legislation, which was assigned top priority for the first session of the 100th Congress by the speaker of the House, Rep. Jim Wright (D, Texas), authorized $443 million in aid to the homeless in fiscal 1987 and $616 million in fiscal 1988, which would begin Oct. 1, 1987. The money would be distributed to states and cities, hospitals and clinics, and local public and private nonprofit organizations for a variety of programs including food and shelter, job training, teaching of basic skills, education of children, treatment of mental illnesses, alcohol and drug abuse, and other health care.

An Interagency Council on the Homeless was to be created to coordinate federal programs for the homeless and to assess the scope of the homeless problem in America.

Congress, in a reversal of the usual procedure, already had appropriated $355 million for aid to the homeless in a $9.4 billion fiscal 1987 supplemental appropriations bill signed by President Reagan July 11. In signing the bill, Reagan had indicated his displeasure with the homeless-aid program, as well as other programs funded by the measure. (Usually, Congress first authorized a program and then appropriated the money to fund it.)

The TENNESSEAN
Nashville, TN, August 3, 1987

WITH studied reluctance, President Reagan has signed a bill authorizing the federal government to provide slightly more than $1 billion in emergency assistance to the homeless.

The new law provides emergency shelter and some permanent housing for the homeless individuals and families, as well as a range of services including health care, education and job training.

It is the first comprehensive effort on the part of the Congress to address the growing problem of homelessness in America. While the President has been generally in favor of helping the homeless, the administration felt it provided too much money for homeless activities. Nevertheless Mr. Reagan approved it.

Nobody is quite sure how many homeless people there are in the U.S. The Department of Housing and Urban Development put the total at 250,000 to 350,000 back in early 1984. That was probably an underestimate at that time. Advocates for the homeless say that the current number is probably two million or more.

The cities, aided in small part by the private charities and organizations have borne the brunt of the burden. But the cities, most of them under fiscal strains, have found it difficult to cope with providing emergency food and shelter. Job and skills training have been even more difficult to accomplish.

The larger cities, as would be expected, have the biggest homeless populations. Under the formula for distributing aid, such cities as New York and Los Angeles will get bigger shares. But nearly all the cities with a homeless problem will get some federal help, at least enough to aid them in dealing with their own local problem, providing they can put together a comprehensive homeless assistance plan.

Under the new law, the money provided would enable cities and states to purchase or renovate buildings for shelters. The law also provides for emergency assistance to people with chronic mental illness. It also provides money for job training and teaching homeless adults reading, writing and other basic skills.

The roots of the homeless problem are many, ranging from people who have been "deinstitutionalized," to displaced workers lacking in job skills as the economy shifts. Nobody knows of any instant cures for all the homeless problem. But a compassionate society ought to do as much as it can to help them. The Congress has made a good start. ∎

The Atlanta Journal and THE ATLANTA CONSTITUTION
Atlanta, GA, July 28, 1987

Very quietly last Wednesday evening, President Reagan signed a bill allocating more than $1 billion for aid to the homeless over the next two years. White House aides said the ritual was understated because the president is not enthusiastic about the costs of the program.

Give the president credit for ratifying the measure despite his qualms. But really, the undeniable need for this program points to some embarrassing shortcomings of this administration. For all the president's talk about shrinking the government, the fact is, we need to spend more, not less, on social programs. His reluctant signature on this bill acknowledges as much.

No, no. The Reaganites did not invent homelessness. Our transitional economy laid the groundwork. Displacement of the poor from remodeled central cities played a part. Negligent state and federal policies toward the mentally ill exacerbated the problem.

Then came Reagan's budget-whackers. They put the brakes on housing programs. They knocked thousands of mental patients off federal assistance rolls. Their urban agenda amounted to little more than empty talk about enterprise zones. Suddenly, the nation is faced with a large population of homeless people — a problem that mocks our belief in ourselves as a people of plenty.

Congress did the right thing. Not only does the bill ante up millions for emergency food and shelter, it seeks permanent housing for mental patients, families with children and the handicapped. It provides money for rehabilitation of single-room occupancy buildings. It authorizes block grants to states for emergency aid to the homeless mentally ill. It allocates cash for community-based drug and alcohol treatment programs. It eases federal rules for homeless food-stamp applicants. And so on. The programs are an obvious necessity.

No wonder the president waited until evening shadows fell before signing this package into law. The program seeks to mitigate damage inflicted by short-sighted administration policies. In a small way, it corrects a mistaken course.

The Dispatch

Columbus, OH, August 4, 1987

It was good news, indeed, to learn from the Census Bureau last week that the proportion of Americans living in poverty last year dropped to the lowest level since 1980.

Even better was the news that median family income after adjustment for inflation took one of its biggest jumps in the past 15 years.

The bureau said the number of people below the government's official poverty line ($11,203 for a family of four in 1986) fell from 33,064,000 in 1985 to 32,370,000 in 1986 — from 14 percent to 13.6 percent of the population. Median family income rose to $29,458, a 4.2 percent increase from 1985.

Gordon Green, assistant chief of the Census Bureau's population division, said the figures are the result of "no economic downturn, four years of sustained economic growth, more people working, low inflation, lower unemployment, and job creation" in recent years. President Reagan properly pointed out that the figures showed that "sustained non-inflationary growth is the government's single best tool for fighting poverty."

This week, the Census Bureau's Green further added to the good news by noting that the actual share of Americans living in poverty may be even lower than the 13.6 percent indicated.

The reason: The official statistics are based on family income. But many government programs provide assistance that isn't in the form of cash, and therefore isn't counted when poverty is calculated.

If benefits such as food stamps, Medicare and subsidized housing were included, the national poverty rate could drop as low as 9 percent, according to alternative, "experimental" calculations by the Census Bureau.

"We are now in a position where almost two-thirds of all means-tested benefits are in non-cash form, and yet they are not included in the official estimates of poverty," Green said.

These means-tested benefits, which are distributed to people based on their income, totaled just over $59 billion last year, based on what it would have cost to purchase those goods and services in the marketplace.

By comparison, government cash benefits for individuals and families totaled about $32 billion. These included Aid to Families with Dependent Children, general assistance, Supplemental Security Income and some veterans programs.

The means-tested, non-cash benefits include food stamps, free and reduced-price school lunches, public and subsidized housing programs and Medicaid. In addition, Medicare contributed nearly $76 billion, although it is not means-tested.

As good as all this sounds, we can and should strive to do better. In 1973, for example, an all-time low 11.1 percent of the population, compared with today's figure of 13.6 percent, was living in poverty. Then came those oil embargoes, a general economic slowdown and three recessions, which pushed up the figure. The most recent high was 15.2 percent in 1983.

Another concern is that the figures also reflected a greater concentration of wealth among higher-income groups — "an increase in income inequality," as Green described it. In 1970 the lowest fifth of households got 4.1 percent of total income, the middle three-fifths got 52.7 percent and the top fifth 43.3 percent. By 1986, the figures show, the bottom fifth had dropped to 3.8 percent, the middle three-fifths to 50.2 percent and top fifth had risen to 46.1 percent.

Among the possible reasons for the change, Green said, are the greater growth in high-paying and low-paying jobs than in middle-paying ones, a huge increase in population due to the baby boom, which has made the economy struggle to find enough jobs, and the increase in female-headed families that tend to have low incomes.

These are concerns that can and must be addressed on several fronts, of which continued economic prosperity is only one of them. But if the economy remains sound and steps now under consideration to reform our welfare system and reduce teenage pregnancy are finally taken, chances are they will be.

THE CHRISTIAN SCIENCE MONITOR

Boston, MA, August 18, 1987

IT is really tough to be homeless in America today. Even for those sheltered in the (relative) comfort afforded by motels out in the suburbs, homelessless can lead to loss of civil rights.

Those caught in "short-term housing emergencies" that grow longer term by the day face such challenges as unwillingness of local school districts to accept their children, lack of any of the tenants' rights they would be accorded in traditional public housing, and even, as our reporter discovered while researching yesterday's story on homelessness in the suburbs, deprivation of rights of free speech: One family was threatened with eviction when the management of the motel where they were staying discovered they were talking with a reporter.

All right, you may say, these people should be grateful for what they've got. The motels are a much pleasanter alternative to the sorts of shelters that are set up in armories and the like.

Point well taken. It's also true that some of the procedures that seem like an assault on civil liberties – searches of those entering shelters, for instance – are also a protection for many.

But policies for helping the homeless, particularly families whose plight is the result mainly of the very tight squeeze on inexpensive housing, should be geared toward keeping them "in the system," to the extent possible: in the housing market, and not just warehoused; in the employment market, and not just resigned to idleness; in the school system, and not dropping out.

The Pittsburgh
PRESS

Pittsburgh, PA, July 31, 1987

President Reagan keeps asking for more powers, such as the line-item veto, to trim excess fat from spending bills. That might be helpful, but why does he keep failing to use the veto authority he already has?

The latest example is a typical congressional effort to solve a genuine problem — in this case, the plight of homeless Americans — by flinging money at any program that seems remotely plausible. The $1 billion measure creates a federal Interagency Council on the Homeless, which will probably become another permanent paperwork machine while Congress seeks other social ills to "solve."

Instead of vetoing the bill, Mr. Reagan signed it in the evening. A White House staffer said this unusual timing was intended to signal "lack of enthusiasm." Decisiveness, not meaningless signals, is what stops unjustified legislation. Mr. Reagan should show some.

Far-Reaching Fair-Housing Bill Passed by Senate

The Senate Aug. 2, 1988 passed fair housing legislation that would expand protection against housing discrimination and expedite review of complaints. The measure was approved by a 94-3 vote, eight years after a filibuster had killed similar legislation. Adding tough enforcement provisions to the Fair Housing Act of 1968, the bill would require the Department of Housing and Urban Development to investigate discrimination complaints and to act on behalf of victims of discrimination by bringing suit against landlords. It also would ban discrimination in public and private housing against the disabled and forbid limitations on renting to families with children, except in clearly defined retirement communities.

Civil-rights organizations hailed the passage of the long-stalled bill after a 20-year-battle. "This bipartisan bill is the most dramatic improvement in civil rights legislation since 1965," said Ralph G. Neas, executive director of the Leadership Conference on Civil Rights, referring to the year in which the Voting Acts had been passed.

Sen. Edward M. Kennedy (D, Mass.), with Sens. Arlen Specter (R, Pa.) and Orrin Hatch (R, Utah) a chief sponsor of the bill, said it would correct a two-decade oversight and provide a "meaningful remedy" to housing discrimination.

The Senate bill would now go back to the House, which had passed a housing bill that varied slightly from the Senate measure. President Reagan had gone on public record in favor of the legislation and was thought certain to sign it into law.

Pittsburgh Post-Gazette

Pittsburg, PA, August 9, 1988

Who would have expected 20 years ago that in 1988 conservatives as well as liberals, realtors as well as civil-rights activists, would be supporting a measure to provide tougher enforcement of federal laws prohibiting housing discrimination?

That is what happened last week as the U.S. Senate 94-3 approved a fair-housing measure little different from one passed 376-23 by the House on June 29. HB 1158 tightens a 1968 law that has made it illegal to discriminate in the sale or rental of public or private housing on the basis of race, color, sex, religion or national origin.

It also extends the law's protection to people with disabilities and to families with young children. For instance, all new multi-family housing, public or private, built for occupancy 30 months from now must "be reasonably accessed and adaptable to handicapped persons," such as having light switches low enough for people in wheelchairs and bathrooms wide enough for a wheelchair. HB 1158 would not affect present buildings.

Because of compromises necessary to obtain passage of the 1968 law, the federal role has largely been limited to mediation. Enforcement of the anti-bias laws depends on private lawsuits or the U.S. Justice Department, which can sue when officials believe they see a significant pattern of housing discrimination.

Apparently one reason HB 1158 got wide congressional approval is that there has come to be a general recognition that that process simply wasn't sufficient. The federal Department of Housing and Urban Development (HUD) estimates that 2 million cases of housing discrimination on racial grounds alone occur each year.

HB 1158 sets up a procedure if conciliation efforts fail. HUD would make an investigation.

If it then issued a "charge" of discrimination, the aggrieved person could go one of two ways — either to a full-blown trial in federal court with Justice Department lawyers representing him or through a new HUD administrative-law-judge procedure. If the administrative law judge found there had been discrimination, he would have the authority to award compensatory damages, issue an injunction and impose civil fines of $10,000 to $50,000. Either party could obtain a judicial review of a decision in the federal courts.

The inclusion of that procedure for judicial review is a second reason why HB 1158 received support from conservatives and realtors. For some reason, civil-rights groups had included in the original bill only the administrative law judge procedure. Realtors argued, rightly in our opinion, that that constituted a denial of their constitutional right to a trial.

Once a compromise was struck in June that included judicial review, the logjam was broken and all sides began pushing the bill, including the Reagan White House. Conservatives and realtors, and especially those who are Republican, realized this would help broaden the appeal of the potential GOP presidential nominee, Vice President George Bush. Therefore, not just liberals such as Sen. Edward Kennedy, but also conservatives such as Sen. Orrin G. Hatch hailed the passage of HB 1158. The Utah Republican said, "This is a historic day. This is a historic bill."

In a time when cynicism is easy, there is something heartwarming about the ability of people from so many ideological persuasions to come together over such a touchy issue as a stronger law against housing discrimination. Even during a period when many have worried that public concern about discrimination has slackened, it is obvious that the consciousness of many leaders of our society has been raised.

Birmingham Post-Herald

Birmingham, AL, August 10, 1988

Twenty years ago, Congress passed a law banning discrimination in the rental and sale of housing, but it left out effective enforcement provisions. It is about to correct the oversight, a move being hailed by civil rights groups and politicians of nearly every stripe.

Up to now, individuals who felt they were discriminated against because of race, sex, religion or national origin had to take their complaints to court at their own expense. The Justice Department also could file suit if it detected a "pattern or practice" of discrimination. Neither remedy was widely used.

Congress is putting finishing touches on legislation that will give the Department of Housing and Urban Development authority to investigate complaints and, if it can't settle the problems through mediation, take the cases to an administrative law judge who could impose heavy fines against landlords or real estate agents guilty of discrimination.

While it was at it, Congress added provisions barring discrimination against handicapped persons and families with children. Exceptions to the latter are allowed in housing specifically designated for the elderly.

Election year politics played a significant role in passage of the new law. Democrats wanted to appear as a champion of civil rights, and Republicans were eager not to be seen as against equality for all. President Reagan, who has taken many lumps from civil rights groups, has called it a "landmark" bill and claims credit for pushing it. Vice President George Bush has eagerly endorsed it.

The measure is being hailed as the most significant civil rights legislation in 20 years, and rightly so. It will put the federal government on the offensive against widespread discrimination in housing. It will put teeth in the largely toothless 1968 Fair Housing tiger.

The Atlanta Journal
THE ATLANTA AND CONSTITUTION
Atlanta, GA, August 12, 1988

When it was passed 20 years ago, the Fair Housing Act of 1968 — prohibiting bias based on race, religion or ethnicity — was considered by many a radical government intrusion into free enterprise. To blacks and other minorities, however, it was a godsend, even though it was flawed.

While it prohibited discrimination, it left the victims of discrimination to their own devices if they wanted to seek redress of their wrongs. It authorized the government to serve only as a mediator between harmed individuals and landlords accused of bias. It could not prosecute offending landlords. The difficulty of proving such a case and a lack of resources discouraged many aggrieved parties from pursuing legal action.

But now, Congress has fixed the flaw. In the process, it has broadened the act to provide protection to the handicapped and to families with children — both long overdue for coverage.

After a near-unanimous vote in the Senate, all that is needed to make the new bill law is an agreement on minor differences between Senate and House versions and President Ronald Reagan's signature, which won't be a problem, for a change. The president has said he is anxious to sign the legislation.

Sen. Edward M. Kennedy (D Mass.) called the bill the most important expansion of civil rights since the 1960s. He is right. It closes a gaping hole in the nation's fair-housing laws. It was a bit disingenuous, in the first place, to leave enforcement of the act to private individuals. That is clearly government's responsibility. The bill gives the feds the power to back up the nation's rhetoric about justice and fairness.

It will require all multifamily housing of four or more units to be accessible to the handicapped, and mandates that handicapped tenants be permitted to make necessary modifications to their premises as long as they return them to their original condition when they move out.

Another provision should be of particular benefit to single-parent families, many headed by financially strapped working mothers who cannot afford to buy their own homes. With the exception of specified retirement communities, which are exempt for obvious reasons, landlords will not be able to turn away families with children under 18. Adults-only apartment complexes have sprung up like mushrooms in recent years, further depleting an already limited supply of affordable housing.

Credit Congress for finally completing the job it started in 1968. With the president's signature, the country will have a fair-housing bill that lives up to the nation's ideals and does not give short shrift to some Americans simply because they are handicapped or have young children.

The Dallas Morning News
Dallas, TX, August 4, 1988

No American should be denied housing because of discrimination. Yet the federal law that was enacted 20 years ago to prevent such injustice clearly has not been working well enough. A recent study by the Housing and Urban Development Department estimated that as many as 2 million instances of housing discrimination occur each year.

For that reason, the fair housing legislation that was overwhelmingly approved by the Senate this week has to be regarded as one of the most welcome expansions of civil rights in recent decades. The measure puts teeth in the 1968 law by empowering the federal government for the first time to prosecute violators if mediation fails to resolve a housing dispute.

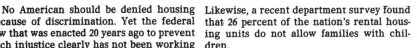

At present, the government generally can do little more than try to arbitrate between landlords and aggrieved parties.

In addition, the legislation extends the protections of the Fair Housing Act (which now mostly covers racial minorities and women) to handicapped people and to families with children. The need for such an expansion has become eminently clear. Disabled people, of whom there are approximately 36 million, continue to be excluded from large segments of the housing market.

Likewise, a recent department survey found that 26 percent of the nation's rental housing units do not allow families with children.

The legislation's 94-3 victory owes itself to months of negotiations among lawmakers of both parties, as well as civil rights groups and Realtors. One stumbling block was overcome, for example, when the bill's sponsors agreed to exempt certain senior housing from the prohibition against families with children. What resulted from all that hard bargaining was a well-balanced measure that will protect all Americans against housing discrimination without expanding federal authority beyond what is reasonable.

The legislation now goes back to the House, where a similar measure was approved in June, for the small differences between the two versions to be worked out. House members may want to consider simply accepting the Senate amendments, thus avoiding the need to convene a conference committee and allowing the president to sign the bill before Congress takes its summer recess next week. The sooner that lawmakers can end the 2 million housing injustices that occur each year, the better.

News-Tribune & Herald
Duluth, MN,
August 10, 1988

Kids are people too . . .

That might sound corny, or maybe like the title of a children's show on PBS, but in a very literal sense, kids — that is to say minors — and their parents are about to gain some rights that they have long been denied. And it is long overdue.

The U.S. Senate Tuesday passed a bill calling for fair housing rights for families with children and for the handicapped, seconding a similar bill already enacted by the House. After ironing out some differences, the bill will go to President Reagan, who is expected to sign it. He should.

It will mean goodbye to housing discrimination against families with children, and good riddance. The right to choose where one wants to live without fear of discrimination has been extended to almost every segment of our society in the past 25 years, except to children.

Since children don't seek places to dwell without parents, or other adults responsible for them, rules excluding children from apartment buildings or other adults-only developments also end up excluding adults. That is wrong.

We recognize some adults do not like living among children. But what is more important — protecting the rights of families to choose where they want to live or protecting the rights of someone to be shielded from children? No one is denying the latter group anything except, they imagine, peace and quiet.

We applaud this legislation and believe it will be even more beneficial than its supporters might imagine. People live best together when there's a cross-section of ages — older folks, people with children, young adults — all sharing the same "neighborhood." We suspect Mr. Wilson doesn't really mind having Dennis the Menace next door at all.

Minneapolis Star and Tribune

Minneapolis, MN, July 25, 1988

Two million prospective home-buyers and renters are still discriminated against each year on the basis of race, color, religion, national origin or sex. That may seem incredible 20 years after Congress passed the Fair Housing Act of 1968. But coming from the Department of Housing and Urban Development (HUD), the figure may well be a conservative estimate. And it's helped push the U.S. House of Representatives — with President Reagan's support — to vote 376-23 in favor of adding long-missing teeth to the act's good intentions. The Senate is expected to go along, and the president to sign the new measure into law. It will be about time.

Nothing is more basic to the integration of American society than the freedom to choose where one will live, according to one's means. Yet in 1968, at the supposed height of the civil-rights movement, Congress dared pay no more than lip service to that ideal. It banned housing discrimination, but said little about enforcing the ban. HUD's authority was limited mainly to mediating disputes. The Justice Department could prosecute only if it found a "pattern or practice" of discrimination. Otherwise, it was up to the victims to file a civil suit. Little wonder that of HUD's estimated 2 million victims each year only about 5,000 bothered to file complaints under the 1968 law.

That should change under the proposed legislation. The bill would allow HUD to take individual cases before an administrative judge who could levy fines up to $10,000 for first offenders. Or either party could take the case directly to federal court — an option whose late addition caused the National Association of Realtors to drop its long-standing opposition to giving HUD a direct enforcement role. The bill is therefore called a compromise, but civil-rights lobbyists say it's tough enough.

The bill would also extend protection to two new classes: the handicapped and families with children. Newly built apartments would have to have ramps, wide doorways and other features to make them accessible to the handicapped. And only certain retirement communities would be permitted to bar children. The latter provision is perhaps the most controversial part of the bill. But it addresses one of the most prevalent forms of residential discrimination, involving 26 percent of all rental housing. And if a Fair Housing Law is to live up to its name, it must be fair to all.

DESERET NEWS

Salt Lake City, UT, August 3/4, 1988

By overwhelmingly passing a tough fair housing bill, the Senate this week put teeth in federal laws forbidding discrimination against renters and home buyers. Some of it was badly needed, but there is reason to wonder if the law doesn't go too far in some respects.

Fair housing laws already apply in cases of race or gender. The new measure extends protection to the handicapped and families with children. It also provides for government prosecution instead of civil lawsuits, and stiff fines that start at $10,000 for a first conviction.

The Senate measure is similar to a House bill passed earlier. The two versions must be ironed out and the Senate bill is expected to prevail. It will then go to President Reagan, who has already praised the legislation.

Major impacts will be immediate. For example:

— Families with children cannot be denied rental housing, except in senior citizen communities. So-called adult complexes will not be able to turn away families with children under age 18. Landlords fearful that children will be too noisy or will tear the apartment to shreds will have to rent to families anyway.

— Handicapped persons may no longer be denied housing. In fact, the law goes much further. It says that handicapped tenants may make improvements in the dwelling at their own expense and do not have to restore the interior to its original condition when they move out.

— Construction of multi-family housing of four or more units intended for occupancy 30 months after the bill becomes law will have to meet expensive new standards for the handicapped. These include such things as lower light and thermostat switches, wider doors, kitchens wide enough for a wheelchair, and brace bars in the bathrooms.

Critics have called the bill a massive and unprecedented federal building code imposed on private sector housing. There is some truth in that. Does this mean the need for federal housing inspectors? In addition, enforcement of the housing law would seem to require thousands of investigators.

Under previous law, a person who has been discriminated against had to file suit as an individual. The new law says such a person may have the government investigate and prosecute. Cases could go either to a jury trial or before an administrative law judge. With an estimated two million cases of housing discrimination last year, investigations alone could require a major bureaucracy.

Fair treatment in renting or buying housing should be encouraged. But the federal government has a way of taking a principle and turning it into a huge and complex program that extends federal power into every little thing — like decreeing how far from the floor light switches must be.

Congress should keep a careful eye on the new law and take steps to curb some of its provisions if it appears the resulting red tape threatens to strangle the rental housing industry while trying to improve it.

The Miami Herald

Miami, FL, August 6, 1988

AT LAST the Federal Government is on the verge of putting enforcement teeth into the 1968 law that prohibits discrimination in housing based on race, religion, or national origin. Sex discrimination was added later, and the bill that passed the Senate on Tuesday adds the handicapped and children as categories gaining at least partial protection. The House already passed a similar measure, and the President says that he will sign it.

These expansions are welcome and important. Most significant, though, is the enforcement authority given the U.S. Department of Housing and Urban Development (HUD) and administrative-law judges, who can fine landlords $10,000 and up for a first offense. Without those teeth, it doesn't matter what kinds of discrimination are banned on paper.

Nowhere is open-housing enforcement more needed than in South Florida, where chronic school-desegregation problems stem directly from the failure to integrate housing. Too many neighborhoods are all-black, while blacks who seek housing elsewhere are frozen out. That must stop — and with the help of HUD and the new law, it can.

Builders and real-estate agencies that cater to whites, to childless adults, to Hispanics, or to some other particular group now will face serious punishment for their exclusionary ways. Race, religion, ethnicity, and sex are illegal grounds for screening potential buyers and tenants. And in areas not officially designated as retirement centers, the barring of young children will also be illegal.

The new Federal law thus is a massive cavalry charge over the hill of apathy to rescue local anti-discrimination efforts, which operate on good will and little more. Now those local activists will have a Big Brother to whom to turn — a Big Brother who has a stick.

It's about time. Work places are well integrated, and successfully so. Public schools, which have borne the heaviest burden of responsibility, are far more mixed than the neighborhoods from which their students come. But housing remains segregated far beyond the conscious wishes of the consumers who buy and rent houses and apartments. A blatant but unwritten system of value assessment has classified blacks as undesirable and blocked them from many new developments. The white and Hispanic character of western Broward and Dade counties attests to that.

Now, finally, the tools for social justice loom over South Florida's sprawling growth. Congress and the Administration will deserve the heartiest of congratulations when this overdue civil-rights initiative becomes law.

FORT WORTH STAR-TELEGRAM

Fort Worth, TX, August 4, 1988

Twenty years of vacillation in the federal government's commitment to eliminate discrimination in housing is about to come to an end, and it is about time.

The Senate, by a 94-3 vote, and the House, by 376-23, have approved an enforceable fair-housing bill, which President Reagan has promised to sign into law. When that occurs, all Americans will have access to much-needed remedies should they encounter discrimination in housing.

The nation has been dedicated, in theory, to such a policy since the passage in 1968 of a law aimed at preventing discrimination based on race, color, sex, religion or national origin. However, that law granted the government no enforcement authority, so its effectiveness was severely limited.

Currently, the Department of Housing and Urban Development can only act as mediator in disputes, and individuals who believe that they are victims of bias in the rental or sale of housing have to pursue any legal action on their own.

The newly approved legislation authorizes HUD, working with the Justice Department, to actually prosecute cases of housing discrimination and sets maximum fines for conviction at $10,000 for a first violation, $25,000 for a second and $50,000 for additional violations. It also broadens the law's scope to include the handicapped and, with certain restrictions, families with children.

Twenty years of "voluntary compliance" with the old law did not work. Discrimination is still widespread, as evidenced by HUD figures showing that 2 million cases of housing discrimination occur each year on racial grounds alone. A tougher law was needed to combat that kind of blatant bigotry.

This is such a law.

THE SPOKESMAN-REVIEW

Spokane, WA, August 3, 1988

That a fair-housing bill, barring discrimination against racial minorities in the sale or rental of housing, was even passed in 1968 was a major milestone. But, reflecting the sensibilities of the times, the bill, amended in 1974 to add sex discrimination, has been more policy statement than enforceable law.

Congress is finally on the verge of putting teeth in what has been called "a toothless tiger." It tried but failed in 1980 when a move to strengthen the fair-housing bill was killed by a Senate filibuster.

Under the existing bill, the U.S. Department of Housing and Urban Development is empowered to resolve housing discrimination complaints only through mediation. If that fails, the complainant's remedy is through the courts. The Justice Department can sue if it believes it can prove a pattern or practice of discrimination; otherwise the burden is on the aggrieved parties to pursue court action on their own.

The revised bill working its way through Congress would give HUD the long-needed ability to levy fines and issue injunctions to follow through on unsuccessful mediation efforts through the courts.

How to grant HUD additional authority in such cases is a question that prevented revision of the fair-housing bill in 1980. Realtors and the Reagan administration challenged the idea of taking the cases to HUD administrative-law judges, calling that approach unconstitutional because it would allow the levying of fines and damages without a jury trial. They said the Seventh Amendment to the U.S. Constitution specifically provides that a defendant has a right to a jury trial when more than $20 is at stake.

The involved parties — civil rights groups, the administration, Realtors' groups and congressmen from both sides of the aisle — deserve credit for hammering out a workable compromise that most everyone can live with. Under the proposed changes, cases could be pursued either before HUD administrative-law judges or, at the request of either party, in federal court, with HUD representing the plaintiff.

The administrative-law judges, subject to federal appellate court review, could set damages, injunctions, attorney fees and civil penalties of $10,000 for a first violation, $25,000 for a second within five years, and $50,000 for two or more within seven years. Federal court would have the additional power to levy punitive damages.

Individuals still could file private civil suits, but the new filing deadline of two years after the incident, compared with the current 180 days, allows more flexibility.

Both the Senate and the House have passed similar versions of a revised bill and are attempting to work out their differences. An endorsement of the Senate bill by the Reagan administration indicates smooth sailing when the measure reaches the White House.

The other major change in the revised bill, although perhaps not as widely discussed, is its extension of protection against housing discrimination to the handicapped and, except in housing developments specifically for the elderly, to families with children.

With those inclusions, the fair-housing bill becomes a well-rounded, strong tool that will do much to improve the availability of housing and give usable remedies to those unfairly denied it.

Chicago Tribune

Chicago, IL, August 15, 1988

Critics of the 1968 fair-housing law always decried its lack of "teeth." Now, after years of debate, Congress has approved overwhelmingly a new set that may bite some of the people it is intended to protect.

The good news is that the new legislation, after 11 years of disputes between civil rights groups and real estate associations, strengthens the original law enacted in 1968 by empowering Department of Housing and Urban Development officials to bring legal proceedings against parties they believe are guilty of housing discrimination. Under the original law, HUD could resolve such disputes only through mediation.

But Congress, unable to leave well enough alone, took the present law, which makes it illegal to discriminate on the basis of race, color, sex, religion or national origin, and added new protected groups that could raise the costs of dwellings and threaten legitimate rights of others who live in them.

The legislation, expected to be signed into law by President Reagan, imposes new restrictions on the ability of landlords, real estate agents and home sellers to discriminate against people who have disabilities and families who have children.

That sounds admirable. No one wants to discriminate against the physically handicapped or families with children. But when you consider the impact of a law that extends the principles of affirmative action to such groups, serious questions are raised.

For example, the new law establishes a national building code, passed without hearings, that requires all units in new apartment buildings of four units or more to be "reasonably accessible or adaptable to handicapped persons." Some senators said that would require only lowered light switches and widened doorways to accommodate wheelchairs.

But a stricter interpretation might find the law required ramps, elevators, special kitchen equipment and other features that could add thousands of dollars to the per-unit cost, even if no tenants needed them. An effort to soften that requirement by limiting it to a few units in such buildings was voted down.

While it makes sense for the government to require that public buildings be made accessible to the unassisted disabled, it makes much less sense for the government to impose similar burdens on private property owners. Those costs will be passed back to renters, further shrinking the affordable-housing market.

Bans on discrimination against families with children are already on the books in some states, including Illinois, but have been sporadically enforced for a number of practical reasons. Communities full of young singles have different needs from those of retirement communities or those whose residents want playmates for their children.

But fair housing, as defined by the new bill, sets up "familial status" as a protected group, presumably making it as illegal to "steer" a family to a neighborhood with schools and Little League as it would be to steer a black or Hispanic family toward a ghetto.

There is no reason beyond blatant bigotry for discriminating against racial, ethnic or religious minorities. But there are some practical reasons why night-shift workers or others might need the peace and quiet an "adults-only" environment affords. Lawmakers recognized this only to the extent of granting exemptions for some senior-citizen communities.

Other dangers lurk in the rules allowing the secretary of HUD to go to court to freeze a vacant house or apartment after its sale or rental has been challenged on fair-housing grounds. Less than a month is then allowed for those accused to ask for a jury trial. This may put undue pressure on landlords or sellers to buy off a claim, even if it has no merit.

Unfortunately, it's a bit late for objections. In this election year the flawed bill sailed through Congress on the merits of the rightful need to put some teeth in the old law. Both George Bush and Michael Dukakis have blessed it. Perhaps sober afterthought—after the election, that is—will lead to wise revisions later.

Part III:
Welfare, Social Security & Medicare

Western relief systems originated in the mass disturbances that erupted during the long transition from feudalism to capitalism beginning in the 16th century. Modern U.S. welfare commenced with the 1935 Social Security Act, which created the first permanent federally funded program in aid of destitute mothers and their children. Based on the assumption that work and welfare were mutually exclusive, the act was created in response to the prevailing massive unemployment wrought by the Great Depression and society's belief that mothers of small children should not be required to work.

Aid to Families with Dependent Children (AFDC), enacted by Congress in 1962, was an outgrowth of the 1935 Social Security Act. By 1967, increased interest in helping the poor help themselves for both altruistic reasons and in the interest of reducing welfare expeditures led Congress to enact the Work Incentive (WIN) program. WIN was intended to provide registrants with a variety of job-related services, including basic education, training, child care and other support services.

Most of the recent debate concerning the welfare system has focused on the able-bodied poor who do not work. The reality of families with able-bodied adults "living off the dole" has undermined support for all welfare programs as well as employment and training measures. Undoubtedly there are some impoverished adults who make little effort to help themselves, but spotlighting these cases obscures the problems of those unsuccessfully seeking employment and the working poor who do not earn sufficient wages to escape poverty. Current welfare policies aim at improving the prospects of the able-bodied but non-working poor in an effort to reduce the high cost to society that results in the antisocial behavior born of their often desperate circumstances and from welfare expenditures.

President Reagan has constantly introduced and supported proposals referred to as "workfare," which require welfare recipients to work off their welfare grants. Reagan administration efforts led to the passage of the 1981 legislation that gave states the option to establish mandatory or voluntary AFDC workfare programs. Although some of these welfare and work programs have shown promise, critics argue that it does not necessarily follow that mandatory workfare is a realistic option. Workfare opponents hold that experimental state programs differ radically from simple mandatory workfare because they more closely resemble employment and training programs that include temporary work in a public-service job.

Most of the current workfare programs are similar to the prior WIN programs. The preliminary experiments in workfare indicated that even temporary work experiences can give participants the opportunity to compete for jobs, enhance their dignity, and perform useful community services. In addition, workfare is supported by a vast majority of the public. Workfare supporters argue that if government assistance is targeted primarily to those who cannot help themselves, or who do work but cannot raise themselves out of poverty, or who work in return for benefits, public support for more generous antipoverty programs might increase. But there is a new increased emphasis on assessing the effectiveness of these programs. This interest has led to a growing consensus on the need to design programs that move welfare recipients into gainful employment. Unfortunately, most states have not been willing to contribute the up-front financial outlays neccessary for a comprehensive program.

Workfare provides, at best, a partial solution to welfare and poverty problems and many questions regarding its implementation need to be answered. To whom should work requirements apply? How can jobs be created without displacing public employees? How can sanctions be effectively applied without harming children of uncooperative parents? What pay level should recipients receive? Is it fair to pay them less than what permanent employees make on the same job?

In addition, policy makers and the public need to recognize that these programs can only moderately reduce welfare costs. Increasing the productivity of low-skilled individuals requires comprehensive programs with significant up-front investments.

Both opponents and critics of workfare agree that the scope of current efforts remains limited and that a number of important issues must first be resolved. Existing workfare models still neglect the needs of impoverished individuals who already have jobs as well as the employability problems of impoverished adult males who do not receive welfare. Females who lead households may be able to work, but it may be neither feasible not socially desirable for them to work full time. But in order to raise such women out of poverty, workfare advocates argue, work and welfare must go together. In addition, the effectiveness of programs designed to improve skills and those that ease the transition from welfare to private employment depends on the state of the economy and the availability of jobs.

Welfare Policies Under Fire, Debate

Aid to Families with Dependent Children (AFDC), enacted by Congress in 1962, was an outgrowth of the 1935 Social Security Act. For a family to qualify for AFDC cash assistance, there must be children who are deprived of financial support of one of their parents owing to death, disability, absence from the home, or unemployment. Also, the family's income must fall below a predetermined needs standard. The actual amount of the AFDC payment depends on the number of persons in the household and the amount of other income and assets. AFDC recipients may be eligible to receive medical services under the Medicaid program and other services, such as food stamps.

By 1967, increased interest in helping the poor help themselves for both altrusitic reasons and in the interest of reducing welfare expeditures led Congress to enact the Work Incentive (WIN) program. WIN was intended to provide registrants with a variety of job-related services, including basic education, training, child care and other support services. The law requires employable welfare parents with children over the age of six to register for work and training. Low funding levels have meant, however, that only a minority of AFDC recipients have been able to take advantage of WIN services. Moreover, the program has been criticized for focusing on employable recipients who might have found jobs on their own. But proponents of WIN point to a 1982 General Accounting Office study that found that half of WIN participants believed that program participation did help them find a job. The Reagan administration has repeatedly attempted to abolish WIN in favor of incorporating its structure into its workfare proposals. Although Congress has rejected these attempts, WIN expenditures dropped from $381 million in fiscal 1981 to an $110 million in 1987.

The current welfare policy debate centers on requiring welfare recipients to work off the assistance they receive. The most recent welfare legislation has been spurred by concern over welfare costs, anecdotes of welfare freeloaders and the Reagan administration's opposition to most income support for the able bodied poor. President Reagan has consistently introduced and supported proposals, referred to as workfare, which, in their simplest form, required welfare recipients to work off their welfare grants.

THE MILWAUKEE JOURNAL

Milwuakee, WI, April 19, 1984

American taxpayers are stuck with huge child-support payments — $8 billion a year to support 3.7 million families that receive federal aid for dependent children. It's an unwelcome burden for the payers and an indignity for recipients.

But Wisconsin is earning a reputation as a national pioneer in trying to do something about the problem. Some creative and ambitious people in this state recognize that there must be a better way to take care of the growing number of child-victims of divorce, desertion and poverty.

Congress can give that effort a boost by approving a pending waiver that would permit this state to serve as a laboratory for an entirely new approach to caring for impoverished children. The waiver would allow Wisconsin to use Aid to Families with Dependent Children (AFDC) money in a revolutionary experiment to subsidize inadequate child-support payments, thereby guaranteeing a minimum benefit for each child, whether on welfare or not.

The waiver is included in an omnibus child-support reform bill that unanimously passed the House and will soon be acted upon in the Senate. The bill also encourages other states to take many of the aggressive actions that Wisconsin has already taken to collect more court-ordered child-support payments from absent parents, including parents whose children are *not* on welfare. Those reforms are being tried in pilot programs in eight Wisconsin counties where, as a routine matter in divorces and paternity cases, child-support payments are deducted directly from wages of absent parents.

The commendable aim of this quiet revolution is to force parents to support their own children to the extent possible — and to assure that all children receive adequate support, avoiding the stigma of welfare wherever possible.

Seeds of these reforms were planted five years ago in an ambitious Wisconsin welfare reform study, and the germination process was assisted by many people — most notably by Assembly Speaker Thomas Loftus (D-Sun Prairie), and by Linda Reivitz and Donald Percy, respectively the current and immediate past secretaries of the State Department of Health and Social Services. The State Legislature set the stage for rapid progress by approving the following policy initiatives:

— Automatic payroll withholding. Recognizing the deplorable fact that more than half of the children eligible for child-support from absent parents received none, the Legislature decided to try collecting the money directly from the paychecks of non-custodial parents. This is one of the experiments currently under way.

— Payment as a percentage of income. Responding to concern about wide variations in child-support orders by judges, the Legislature allowed courts to use a percentage-of-income standard when calculating child-support levels. The suggested payments — ranging from 17% of the non-custodial parent's income for one child to 34% for five or more children — are based on estimates of the amounts that would have been spent for children had the family remained intact.

The reform-experiment is a logical third step. Where child-support withholding was less than the new minimum child-benefit, AFDC money would be added to bring the payment up to $3,500 for one child, $5,000 for two children and $6,000 for three or more. Presumably, that would eliminate the incentive that some families might feel to go onto welfare. If Wisconsin is authorized by Congress to conduct the experiment, and it succeeds, taxpayers should eventually see some deserved relief.

The Boston Herald

Boston, MA, April 16, 1984

THE WELFARE cutbacks of the past three years have done what they were supposed to do, according to a running study made by the General Accounting Office. But it has not been done without some pain.

The GAO said the Aid to Families with Dependent Children program now has nearly 500,000 fewer cases than there would have been under the old eligibility rules, and the total paid out in benefits is proportionately lower.

President Reagan's policy was to deny benefits to working parents who were using welfare to supplement their income, so as to adequately cover families who would be destitute without an AFDC check.

This did succeed in removing several hundred thousand clients from the welfare rolls. Those whose checks were cut off did seek to work more hours in an effort to make up the difference, and did increase their earnings.

But in being dropped from AFDC many families also lost their eligibilty for Medicaid, Food Stamps, and other non-cash benefits that came with being on welfare, and the net result was that they ended up with less even though they worked more.

Without wasting pity on cheats, this indicates that the system ought to be refined. Any time a welfare program offers a higher standard of living to those who don't work than a person can achieve by getting a job, it's seriously out of synch.

Yet neither the guaranteed annual income, the negative income tax, nor other proposed improvements in the system provide a satisfactory, fair answer to the question of how to make it more profitable to work than to stay on welfare.

That's a dilemma whose resolution could put a dent in the national deficit —which is one more reason by why the White House and Congress ought to work harder, and faster, to work out the right answer.

PORTLAND EVENING EXPRESS
Portland, ME, November 20, 1984

The public dollars which go as Aid to Families with Dependent Children are meant to help provide food, shelter and clothing for families unable to care for themselves.

The need is real, so is the public will to address it. But the Reagan administration, too, is acting to stem a real problem when it tries to assure that dollars meant to buy shelter for children do exactly that.

Maine tackled much the same issue last year after a Portland woman and her five children were evicted from a Riverton Park public housing apartment for non-payment of rent.

Nobody gained from the eviction. The family lost an apartment it had occupied at less than the market price and, instead, was crowded into a single motel room. Taxpayers found themselves out in the cold, paying roughly six times as much as they'd paid for the family's public housing.

The Maine Department of Human Services reacted. It successfully amended the rule book. When welfare dollars meant for housing fail to be spent that way, the department, whether by voluntary agreement with an AFDC recipient or by court order, can step in and divert a portion of a family's check to its landlord.

Now the federal government would go Maine one better. It would require that both landlords and tenants sign each welfare check, in effect giving first priority to payment of rent. That approach may be feasible, but it demands clear and competent safeguards. Not all landlords are honest; not all tenants have hurdled the language barrier; not every family can always, without exception, give rent its highest priority.

Allowing outsiders to direct the spending of a family's money is intrusive. Without adequate legal and practical safeguards, it can be exploitive as well.

But where parents fail to provide shelter for their families, government has no credible choice but to step in.

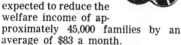

Los Angeles, CA, August 15, 1984

There are two points of controversy in the U.S. effort to crack down on working welfare recipients, and the more important point is being ignored.

First: In computing welfare eligibility, did the government unlawfully limit the amount recipients can deduct for work expenses? Supreme Court Justice William Rehnquist ruled last week that the federal action was legal. And in California, this decision is expected to reduce the welfare income of approximately 45,000 families by an average of $83 a month.

Second, and more important: Whether or not the action was legal, was it wise? We don't think so — not if the goal is to encourage recipients of Aid to Families with Dependent Children to break out of the welfare cycle.

The controversy is over a class-action suit brought by working AFDC recipients, who claimed that the specific $75 deduction limit set by the federal bureaucracy wasn't what Congress intended because the administration wrongly ordered that deductions be made from gross, not net, income. Before the law was changed in 1981, working AFDC recipients could deduct *all* reasonable work expenses before their income level was computed. This made it worth their while to take jobs, even low-paying ones.

A federal appeals court told the government to go back to the old, more lenient guidelines. Rehnquist disagreed. He may be on legally solid ground, but we don't agree that his action was needed to save the government from what he called "irreparable injury." The $2.6 million a month in AFDC payments at stake in California will be missed by the needy families far more than by Uncle Sam. Poverty lawyers say limiting deductions will make it unprofitable for some AFDC recipients to keep their jobs, and the arithmetic suggests they're right. If so, this seems a classic case of the federal government being penny wise and pound foolish.

The Supreme Court will decide this fall whether the deduction limits fairly reflect Congress' intent. The court may well rule against the AFDC families. But the issue here is larger than the letter of the law, and the White House and Congress should reconsider their actions. Giving welfare recipients an incentive to work increases the chances that they'll be able to get off the dole for good. ■

THE KANSAS CITY STAR
Kansas City, MO, July 8, 1984

The Child Support Enforcement Amendments of 1984 now pending in Congress put the emphasis of governmental collection efforts on the best interests of children. They have passed the House and Senate unanimously and await conference committee action.

The amendments are designed to build on present state systems. Provisions include increasing federal financial incentives for better performance and giving local jurisdictions stronger tools to help both homes getting Aid to Families with Dependent Children and non-welfare families. They will deal with the problem of sporadic support payments and those in arrears. Better interstate enforcement of support orders also will be possible.

Most affected will be men although the proposals are applicable to either absent parent and are expected to bring possible relief in situations where children are left with grandparents or other relatives. Protesting bitterly about misuse of support money, fathers have a legitimate complaint when they are denied access to their children and ex-wives suffer no court sanctions. That problem is not dealt with in this legislation. Perhaps it should be.

But the fact that in more than 50 percent of all cases where child support is due, nothing is forthcoming is a cruel deprivation to the child. It cries for immediate action. And the burden of easing that neglect falls to strangers, taxpayers who pay for the 87 percent of all AFDC recipients eligible due to continued absence from the home of a living parent. The Department of Health and Human Services is pressing aggressively for the stronger law.

The Child Support Enforcement Program works. In 1976, its first year, $500 million was recovered. Last year, the total was $2 billion. Looking just at the ratio of collections to administrative costs in welfare cases, last year Missouri took in $1.27 for each dollar spent, the national average; Kansas had $1.50. Both states were well below the national average on non-welfare collections.

Officials are convinced all states can do much better. These amendments will help.

The News and Courier

Charleston, SC, December 23, 1984

"Not since 1965, a year before full implementation of the Congressional poverty programs, have the 11 Southern states housed so many poor.... These increases have applied to people of every color. Not since the years before 1965 have there been as many poor whites or poor blacks in the South and the nation."

— Recently released conclusions found in a study of U.S. Census Bureau data by the Southern Regional Council (SRC).

It's been said that the greatest sins against social justice have been in its name. That's surely the case with the anti-poverty programs that have proved so counterproductive in this nation since the mid-1960s when Lyndon Johnson's Great Society declared its War on Poverty.

The SRC study showed that the national poverty rate was 12.1 percent in 1969 and had risen, by 1983, to 15.2 percent. The non-profit council estimates that the 1983 poverty rate among blacks in the South was 39 percent, with more than 60 percent of families headed by black women falling below the poverty level of $10,178 for a family of four. This despite federal spending on poverty programs that has more than doubled during these past two decades — some $500 billion on welfare benefits since 1966.

Ironically, the quality of life for the poor deteriorated during this time, despite these vast expenditures and the best of intentions, because these very programs have produced more poor, rather than more for the poor. A welfare state has been created, which, coupled with disintegrating families and chronic unemployment, has created a way of life that is welfare dependent; one that has undermined values, institutions and ambitions.

For example, Aid to Families with Dependent Children (AFDC) has discouraged young couples from marrying by making the mother's fertility the main source of income. It has also left little incentive to the father to take a minimum-wage job that, comparatively speaking, adds little to the total family income when taxes are subtracted. While that job could have led the family out of poverty, AFDC has, instead, encouraged a staggering rise in illegitimacy. In 1950, 17 percent of all births among blacks were illegitimate — today it is 55 percent nationwide; 85 percent in some ghettoes.

What's more distressing is that these very same programs have led the poor to believe that American society is to blame for their troubles so that they look on state and federal handouts as a birthright.

What should be done? To begin with, there should be a realization in Washington that those welfare programs that have discouraged honest employment have been an absolute failure. Federal and state financial assistance should provide incentives to work, not encourage dependency. Economic ladders should be put in place to teach self-sufficiency and the feeling of self-respect gained from an honest day's work. A step in that direction would be authorizing less-than-minimum wage summer employment for youths who are at their most impressionable age.

In these days of scary deficits, abandoning the habit of squandering hundreds of billions of federal dollars to salve some imagined national conscience could prove a real boon. The poor will always be with us, but they will be better off if government acts more pragmatically in dealing with their problems.

The Des Moines Register

Des Moines, November 28, 1984

The U.S. Department of Health and Human Services has proposed a change in welfare rules to ensure that welfare families pay their rent. Acting largely in response to requests from big-city welfare departments, HHS suggests that in certain cases checks for the rent require the signatures of both the client and the landlord before they can be cashed.

At present, an allowance for rent is figured into the Aid to Dependent Children grant given a welfare family. But landlords complain that families spend the grants and ignore the rent; clients complain that unless they can threaten to withhold rental payments, landlords won't make necessary repairs.

The two-signature requirement could satisfy both. Clients could not spend the rent money elsewhere, and landlords could not collect without the client's signature, which could be withheld if the landlord failed to maintain the housing unit properly.

Iowa welfare officials oppose the paternalistic approach inherent in restricting how grant money will be used; it implies that the client is incompetent to handle finances. But if a client repeatedly demonstrates an inability or unwillingness to budget the welfare grant, the Iowa Department of Human Services will name a third party to manage finances.

A similar provision is built into the federal proposal; two months of unpaid rent would result in a presumption that the client had mismanaged the money, and the two-signature requirement would go into effect. The client could appeal by showing that the landlord refused to maintain the property or that the client faced a life-threatening emergency that required use of the money.

The standoff between clients and landlords in some cities has resulted in the latter refusing to rent to welfare families, putting them in a serious bind where housing is in short supply. The disadvantages in issuing a separate welfare check requiring two signatures are offset by the potential decline in evictions and the possibility of a wider housing market for clients to choose from.

PORTLAND EVENING EXPRESS

Portland, ME, December 2, 1984

☐ An aura of optimism surrounds Maine's new "AFDC-U" program, expanding Aid to Families with Dependent Children to include two-parent families in which the main breadwinner is unemployed.

The upbeat attitude is fine as far as it goes. But AFDC-U should not go so far that it commits the public to permanent support of ever-growing, jobless families.

The purpose of the state's AFDC program, in a word, has always been: subsistence. As its name implies, AFDC exists to assure that children are not deprived of basic food, clothing and shelter.

For the kids involved in Maine's 18,500 AFDC cases, the monthly payments are a public substitute for private support. To receive it, however, the state has required them to live in families in which one parent, usually the father, has left or, alternatively, never been a part.

AFDC-U expands that subsistence support to intact, two-parent families. OK. But the thrust of the program applied to such families, too, must change. From long-term support of children throughout their dependent years, AFDC should concentrate on underpinning a family only until it can get back on its feet. And it must actively help the recovery along by strictly enforcing the requirement that breadwinners take the first reasonable jobs available.

Thirteen years ago, the state approved AFDC payments for intact families. The program lasted one year; 800 families qualified in only seven months; and lawmakers ran from the budget drain the expanding rolls—and expanding families—presented.

Yet this year, the Legislature approved AFDC-U as a "family unity" bill—and passed on the bill for financing 70 percent of it to the federal government. Federal deficit rumblings suggest that President Reagan may pass at least a portion of it back.

Before that happens, what we want from AFDC-U—and what we're getting—should be carefully evaluated. What we find in unity should not be weakness.

THE LINCOLN STAR
Lincoln, NE, November 16, 1984

There is a long-standing notion with many people that the poor in our society are the product of choice. But it is really inconceivable to think that such is the truth of the matter.

There may be a sense in which the skid row bums live the depraved lives they do as a kind of choice. Obviously, one could always choose to reform their bad habits and to pursue with determination a better and more productive level of living. In short, an individual can always reform themselves.

But that is speaking in a clinical, not a practical sense. By the time the person is sleeping in doorways, warming himself over exhaust vents, scavenging garbage for food and putting every cent he can beg or steal into booze, he has far more often reached a point of no return. No longer do these people have any mastery over their destiny.

There really is no true choice for these unfortunates. They lack the motivation, the ability, the reasoning, the opportunity and even any latent desire to make a change.

But those are the worst, the poorest of the poor. The others are those such as the welfare recipients discussed in a story in The Star Thursday morning.

THE NUMBER of clients receiving Aid to Families With Dependent Children (ADC) has grown from about 12,500 early in 1981 to a high of 15,578 last March. At this time, the number of ADC families is something under 15,000.

A state Department of Social Services official explained that those on ADC are characteristically young mothers with young children, lacking the skills to qualify for anything but low paying, part-time work. But the rules of welfare make it better to stay on that program than to enter the job market at such a lowly level.

A welfare mother with two children receives $350 monthly plus Medicaid health insurance coverage worth an estimated $177. You can't replace that with a low-paying, part-time job.

While welfare recipients generally remain on ADC no longer than two years, they are always replaced by someone else, it was explained.

Of course, $527 a month, plus food stamps, is still a relatively inexpensive way to provide for the care of two children. Institutionalization would be far more expensive and would be compounded by further sociological problems.

Still, it would be far better if a means could be found of integrating ADC recipients into the mainstream of the private economic system. But the department spokesman explained that it would take a major change in direction at the national level to substantially reduce the number of poor non-working people requiring assistance.

Job programs and money to fund them will be needed, he said, and he sees neither of them in the near future.

THUS, THE DILEMMA is that it could well cost us more to turn welfare recipients into productive wage earners than it is costing to maintain them at a subsistence level. It is not that the recipients favor such a life style, but that such is the hand fate has dealt them and society is not prepared to invest in anything but the least expensive remedy for the problem.

We do not absolve all the poor of any personal responsibility whatsoever, but we all share with them the burden of their destitution. Once down and out, we offer them no real way back but only enough to see them through one more day after another. It's not, of course, the least that could be done but it doesn't represent, either, a dawning of enlightenment.

St. Petersburg Times
St. Petersburg, FL, December 1, 1984

The Ramsey County Community Human Services Department ought to be able to recognize a family when it sees one. And if the state's regulations are too rigid to allow humane exceptions to aid a particular family, then the department should lobby vigorously to change those regulations.

A St. Paul woman has raised two children — a 5- and 6-year-old sister and brother — from infancy, since the woman who gave them birth traded them for beer in a bar. Now the kind soul who took them in is enmeshed in a ridiculous bureaucratic tangle that permits her to serve as their legal guardian, but denies her any financial aid for their upbringing. She is not their relative, you see, and the rules say she can't be their foster mother because she is already their guardian.

She may not be the foster mother of those children, but she is the only *mother* they know. And she is poor.

Generous offers from the community have cheered the family members since the Pioneer Press and Dispatch printed a story about them at Thanksgiving. But even those offers may be scuttled, many of them, because they could endanger food stamps and other aid that the woman receives for her teen-age grandson. She has been "mom" to him, too, for all of his life.

So for several years now the 60-year-old St. Paulite has managed to raise three youngsters on what the county allows her for one.

This woman — this *mother* — says that the welfare department told her that if she can't afford to support the little girl and boy, she should give them up. If that is what was said, with no options explored, then that is reason for outrage.

No one would deny the necessity for the network of regulations that governs Aid to Families of Dependent Children. But if this woman and her little ones are not a family, then the word has lost all meaning.

Human situations do not always slide tidily into slots molded by well-meant rules. An exception must be made. This woman — this *mother* — deserves both assistance and honor.

DAYTON DAILY NEWS
Dayton, OH, July 3, 1984

The Reagan administration claim that "poverty" spending has actually gone up during the 1980s deserves some consideration.

But not too much. The statistical arguments can become endless if you let them, so complex is the federal budget.

Most reasonably understood, "poverty" spending — that is, that part of the federal budget that is explicitly aimed at helping people in need — constitutes about 10 percent of the federal budget. The largest program in the category is Medicaid, followed by food stamps and aid to families with dependent children (AFDC).

Medicaid spending goes up constantly, of course, because of the price of health care; and Medicaid, AFDC and food stamps costs rise with unemployment. (In fact, during the recession, they did not nearly keep pace with new need.)

In other words, the government can raise "poverty" spending completely involuntarily.

Other programs in the category include unemployment compensation, child nutrition, housing assistance, low-income weatherization, and job training.

The entire category comes to about $80 billion, less than half the deficit.

The President supports most of these programs, especially the big ones, when they are taken one-by-one. Yet he often seems to imply that if we just become less generous with the undeserving among the poor, we can make major progress toward balancing the budget and reducing the size of government.

It just ain't so.

The Seattle Times
Seattle, WA, October 2, 1984

WHEN legislators are making a priority list for the 1985-87 state budget, the Department of Social and Health Services request for $40 million-plus for enhancement programs for children should be near the top.

State dollars are limited, but children's programs have limped along for too long — patched together with bandages and piecemeal approaches.

One of the most pressing needs is increasing the staff at Child Protective Services. Excessively large caseloads have reduced the effectiveness of the agency.

The present staff of 280 handles 2,300 reports a month of suspected child abuse and neglect. That's an increase of 600 cases a month since 1982. The DSHS budget proposes adding 200 people to the staff.

Other enhancement dollars would pay for support services for families, assistance to street children, aid for the Women, Infant and Children program, and support for the Division of Juvenile Rehabilitation programs for children leaving residential facilities.

The $40 million for children's programs is part of a $4 billion budget request from DSHS. Of course, legislators will have to make some hard decisions about which items are a must for funding.

Programs for children have received scant attention from budgetmakers in the past six years. Many activities, including group homes and mental-health treatment, cannot begin to meet the need.

The Idaho STATESMAN

Boise, ID, December 21, 1985

In 1981, Idaho's error rate in administering one of its major welfare programs was 9.1 percent, more than twice that allowed by the federal government.

Since then, the error rate in the Aid to Families With Dependent Children program has been dropping. The last available figures, for the federal fiscal year that ended in October 1983, put the error rate at 3 percent, lower than the allowable rate.

Although data are not available for fiscal 1984, the error rate is expected to be more than 5 percent, according to Jerry Quick of the state Department of Health and Welfare. He attributes that to changes in federal regulations and to the department's efforts to get a new computerized system in place by Jan. 1.

While the anticipated upswing is regrettable, the department's overall record is one of trying diligently to keep the error rate down. The new computer system, which replaces one installed in 1968, will be a key step in doing this.

Despite the state's obvious good-faith effort, however, the federal government has refused to waive a $691,000 penalty for the 1981 AFDC error rate.

The state has had more luck in controlling its Medicaid error rate. Assessed more than $200,000 for a 1981 error rate that was only slightly above the 3 percent allowed, Idaho since then has kept the error rate at less than 3 percent. A waiver for that fine also has been rejected.

What all this demonstrates is that Idaho is trying. Now, a bill in the U.S. Senate would help this state and others.

Originally proposed by Sen. Dan Evans, R-Wash., the bill imposes a two-year moratorium on AFDC and Medicaid fines until the government's across-the-board allowable-error rates are replaced by individualized, state-by-state rates.

States with large populations fare pretty well under the current methods for calculating error rates. They have large enough population samples to draw on to ensure that the rate calculated for them is representative.

But in small states such as Idaho, the statistical sample is small, and the ensuing results tend to be skewed.

In addition, conditions beyond a state's control – such as population and crime rate – affect a state's error rates but aren't taken into consideration under current law.

A precise statistical method, tailored to Idaho's individual features, is only fair. The cost of Mr. Evans' legislation – $3 million over two years – would be well worth it if it results in a quality-control system that is accurate and that works.

TULSA WORLD

Tulsa, OK, August 15, 1985

PUTTING a dent, even a small one, in the welfare load without hurting legitimate welfare recipients is desirable.

Oklahoma efforts aimed at putting able recipients of two major welfare categories, food stamps and Aid to Families With Dependent Children, to work appear to be doing just that.

State officials estimate that $4.5 million spent last year to help Oklahoma welfare recipients find jobs saved $17.2 million in grant payments, in addition to pumping millions more into the public coffers in the form of taxes paid.

Oklahoma was the first of 26 states to launch Work Incentive (WIN) programs, which offer job training and require able-bodied welfare recipients to look for jobs and accept them when they are available.

Welfare officials say one WIN program, involving AFDC recipients, has helped put 18,500 people to work, and more than 70 percent of those have not gone back on welfare rolls.

Obviously, these programs have not wiped out welfare chiseling in Oklahoma. And the amount of money saved pales in comparison to the hundreds of millions of dollars spent on welfare in the state.

But it is a dent in the total, and a step toward legitimizing the welfare system, and that's good news.

THE LINCOLN STAR

Lincoln, NE, August 15, 1985

Last week a woman wrote of her experiences with Lincoln's social services after reading a series on poverty in Nebraska by Star writer Don Walton.

A divorced mother of three, she receives food stamps and Aid to Dependent Children payments. Additionally, she takes advantage of programs such as the federal government's giveaway of surplus cheese and powdered milk.

We spoke with her by phone to verify the letter and she expressed her overwhelming gratefulness for the social safety net that held herself and her three daughters. Her letter also conveyed this gratitude as she listed the services provided her at no cost.

Several letters — one not signed — arrived in response. The more churlish of the comments struck a sour note with us and prompted these observations, none intended as portraying the original letter writer's circumstances, which are unknown to us. She chose to share some aspects of her life; beyond that her privacy should be respected.

THE MYTH of the welfare queen and the stigma of being on the dole persist. Certainly, there have been abuses in the programs. But the accusations they have created a permanent welfare class are unfounded. A 1979 Health and Human Services Department study reported that half of all welfare recipients were on the rolls for less than three consecutive years.

Many programs are like clipping coupons from the paper; they're available and they help improve the quality of life, even in small ways and certainly at small cost to the taxpaying public.

As an example, energy assistance, available from federal grants to local programs like the Lincoln Action Program, comes to mind. It's been highly successful in helping the poor weatherize their homes and in providing some aid with heating bills.

Medicaid, ADC and food stamps take the largest bite of the social services budget. Some three-quarters of the people receiving ADC do so because they receive little or no child support, which points up one of the big contributors to the poverty rolls — single-parent families, most of them headed by women.

DIVORCE CAN be the quickest route to poverty for some women. Traditionally, within a year after divorce her income has plummeted, while his rises. This gap is particularly acute for women whose sole occupation during marriage has been that of homemaker. Divorce leaves her unemployed without job skills or prospects. Nationally, 46 percent of divorcing mothers are awarded child support and about half of them will be able to collect it on a regular basis.

Because so many fathers were reneging on child support payments or providing inadequate support and therefore sending their families to welfare, the federal government got into the act in 1975 with a law it hoped would get back some of this money. It has, if Nebraska's experience is any indicator.

Divorced mothers relinquish child support payments to the state for ADC benefits. The state, in turn, attempts to collect child support from the father. The program is nearly self-sufficient, since the state and federal tax dollars paid into it are significantly reimbursed by the child support collection.

These programs mean the difference between hunger and a hot meal to many Nebraskans. Believing the general public does too much for the needy isn't a view we hold.

The Des Moines Register

Des Moines, IA, December 26, 1985

States and local communities decide whether and where to build roads and community improvements, and the federal treasury chips in. Federal aid depends on local enthusiasm for committing local money to the projects, and that enthusiasm is a measure of the degree to which such projects are perceived as contributing to the common good.

Welfare for the poor is another matter. Local government has little or no control over the factors that cause some to seek welfare, and the cost engenders resentment rather than enthusiasm, because the common good served by welfare is hard to define.

That resentment is often reflected in miserly grants. While the federal government will pay half or more of state welfare costs, the amount received by the poor is determined by the states — and the differences in state grants are far greater than any difference in living costs.

A California family of three on Aid to Dependent Children receives $555 per month; the same family in Alabama, $118; in Iowa, $381 (as of Jan. 1). Medicaid programs in some states deny health services provided in identical circumstances in other states.

Following an 18-month study, the Project on Federalism and National Purpose — produced by the efforts of 25 business executives, politicians and educators — has suggested that the federal government take over almost full financial responsibility for ADC and Medicaid, to even up the disparities in state welfare grants.

The $20 billion to $30 billion extra cost to the federal government would be offset by giving states and municipalities greater responsibility for financing community and road projects.

Similar disparities in state-federal grants to the needy aged, blind and disabled ended a dozen years ago, when Congress replaced state programs with the federal Supplemental Security Income program.

It is past time to extend federal control to the poor with children, with uniform grants (adjusted for local living costs) covering ADC and Medicaid.

Welfare is a federal problem. It begs a federal solution.

The Augusta Chronicle

Augusta, GA, October 18, 1985

The purpose of public welfare programs is to see to it that people who need help get it; and those who don't need it, or abuse it, don't get it.

A recent Sunday Perspective piece by staff writer Martha Anne Tudor revealed that Richmond County's Department of Family and Children's Services was denying aid to a number of needy people while socking away thousands of dollars in surpluses in investment certificates.

It was also revealed that the agency — funded mostly by the state, partly by the county — had not been audited since 1979. By default, the DFACS had evolved into a power unto itself, accountable to no one for the way it handled money.

DFACS officials complained their agency was choked by rules and regulations restricting the number of clients they could help. In response, the County Commission this week approved recommendations loosening eligibility requirements for aid recipients. Earlier, commissioners had arranged for closer oversight of the agency.

The latter reform is overdue and welcome; no government agency should be unaccountable. But the Commission may have acted precipitously in swiftly acceding to recommendations to loosen requirements.

Government bureaucrats, as a rule, make themselves slaves to regulations and red tape. If loosening eligibility requirements introduces some common sense and compassion into the system, so much the better. But if it encourages the agency to go overboard in the other direction — giving away benefits undeserved, instead of withholding those that are — then it is a bad idea.

We would have preferred to see a more compassionate and sensible application of the old requirements. There are many sources of welfare available, but people deserving of help often go to the wrong agency to get it. They ought to be sent to the right place instead of simply being told they don't qualify.

FORT WORTH STAR-TELEGRAM

Fort Worth, TX, May 28, 1985

Child poverty and child pornography are not too far removed on the spectrum of bad things that are happening to America's children.

There is something almost as obscene about reports of a marked increase in recent years of child poverty in this rich country as there is about the alarming degree of abuse and exploitation of children to cater to the sexual appetites of some depraved adults that also exists in the United States.

The child poverty reports issued by the Congressional Research Service and the Congressional Budget Office indicate that more than one in five children in the United States were poor in 1983, that children constitute 40 percent of the nation's impoverished, that child poverty rose 52 percent during the past decade, from 15 percent to 22.2 percent; that the child poverty rate for 1983 was the highest since the 1960s and that the number of children who are poor increased by 3 million, while the total number of children in the population declined by 9 million.

The reports indicate that the poverty rate among children, which had been cut in half between 1965 and 1979, increased by 35 percent between 1979 and 1983, when deep cuts in spending on social programs were pushed through Congress by the Reagan administration.

While it is true that reductions in spending on social programs has contributed to the rise in child poverty, the phenomenon cannot be explained entirely on that basis. Other causes include structural economic changes and demographic factors, such as declining employment in high-paying, heavy industry jobs; the rising number of female-headed, single-parent families, and the growing number of births to unwed mothers.

The government, however, cannot wait for those social and economic trends to take a different direction. It must do something to address the problem that presents itself, i.e., an obscene level of child poverty in this country that must not be allowed to continue to increase.

Legislation has been proposed in both the House and the Senate to deal with the child poverty obscenity. The bill, sponsored by Reps. Harold E. Ford, D-Tenn., and Charles B. Rangel, D-N.Y., and Sen. Daniel Patrick Moynihan, D-N.Y., would establish minimum benefit standards for Aid to Families with Dependent Children, require states to offer such aid to poor two-parent families and provide money for work programs aimed at reducing dependence on welfare.

That legislation should be supported by every member of Congress who cares about America's children, the embodiments of its future.

The Atlanta Journal
THE ATLANTA CONSTITUTION

Atlanta, GA, January 30, 1988

One of President Reagan's dearest assumptions, and one of Reaganism's, is sharply challenged by a new study of welfare recipients. The president likes to say, and said again in his recent State of the Union Address, that welfare programs make it harder for the poor to escape poverty, that, in practice, welfare causes poverty.

On the surface, the idea wouldn't seem to make sense. Surprise. It doesn't make sense.

A study by the University of Michigan's Institute for Social Research found that most welfare recipients spend only a short time on the rolls. Few fit the stereotype of welfare dependence passed down from generation to generation.

The study analyzed results from several research projects. It found that about 30 percent of families on Aid to Families with Dependent Children (AFDC) receive welfare for one or two years and a similar proportion had eight or more total years. The median length of benefits was less than four years. The amounts of AFDC payments were found to have no measurable impact on births to unmarried women and only slight effect on rates of divorce, separation or female head-of-household status.

"The majority of daughters who grew up in highly dependent (eight years or more on welfare) homes did not share the fate of their parents," the study reported. "Only one out of five of the daughters from highly dependent parental families were themselves highly dependent on AFDC in their early 20s." And 64 percent of the daughters with dependent backgrounds received no AFDC during a three year survey period.

None of this means that welfare reform isn't called for; it is. Or that there shouldn't be more job-training requirements for some recipients and even work requirements in certain circumstances; there should be.

But a politics that masks mere cheapness with unctous solicitude for the poor clearly has no support in reality. What does welfare really do? "Taken all together," the study found, "this evidence suggests that the welfare system does not foster reliance on welfare so much as it acts as insurance against temporary misfortune." It does just what it was supposed to do.

The Miami Herald

Miami, FL, June 8, 1985

EVERY WEEK another study alerts the American public to a travesty: a growing number of American children are poor, living at a pitifully meager level of subsistence in this country of unparalleled plenty. This horrible trend has persisted as Federal programs to help children have been cut or not adjusted to keep pace with real costs. As a result, in 1983, the last year for which data are available, the child-poverty rate was at "the highest level since the mid-1960s," a new Government study states.

Almost 13.8 million U.S. children, or more than one in five, lived in poverty in 1983, says the study by the Congressional Research Service and the Congressional Budget Office. That's a national disgrace. Extraordinary national policies must be enacted to end this plague.

In the 1970s, benefits for children under the Aid to Families with Dependent Children (AFDC) program declined by one-third while benefits for all other aid recipients were indexed, said Sen. Daniel Patrick Moynihan, Democrat from New York. Along with two other Democrats in Congress, he has introduced legislation to reduce child poverty.

Not surprisingly, a child's probability of being poor was linked to his parents' race, educational level, and age. Nearly 47 percent of all black children live in poverty; so do 38.2 percent of Hispanic children. More than half of poor children live in households headed by women, and women head 55 percent of all U.S. households. Three of four children born to unmarried women are poor, and about one-fifth of all births in this country were to unwed mothers.

The statistics for black children "essentially guarantee the poverty of black children for the foreseeable future," says another new study, by the Children's Defense Fund.

Central to the bill introduced by Senator Moynihan and Reps. Charles Rangel of New York and Harold Ford of Tennessee is the establishment of a minimum-benefit standard for AFDC and the requirement that states include impoverished two-parent families in this aid program. Florida is among the states that deny assistance to children who live with both parents, even if the family's income is zero.

The bill also calls for expansion of work programs, encouragement of state efforts to prevent teen-age pregnancy, and reducing the tax burden on working families and single-parent families. This bill deserves support. For a nation that condemns so many of its children to poverty thereby impoverishes not just them, but its own future.

The Washington Times

Washington, DC, May 18, 1988

While the public eye has focused on Capitol Hill's efforts to overhaul the nation's welfare system, Ways and Means Committee Democrats have been trying a little sleight-of-hand: a one-year extension of a moratorium barring the federal government from collecting over a billion dollars in penalties from states that made incorrect AFDC payments.

The issue involves a decade-long dispute over how to calculate error rates in the program. In 1979, Congress okayed an amendment by Rep. Robert Michel of Illinois requiring what was then the department of Health, Education and Welfare to force states to reduce AFDC waste, fraud and abuse, then running at close to 10 percent, to a level of no more than 4 percent by 1983. (The target was reduced to 3 percent in 1984.) By 1986, states that had accumulated $1.1 billion in uncollected penalties were complaining that HHS calculations exaggerated the error rates, so lawmakers approved an amendment mandating a two-year moratorium on sanctions and asked HHS and the National Academy of Sciences to study whether there was a better way to measure errors.

Both came back with their recommendations earlier this year, with the NAS calling for a dramatic overhaul of the current system, and HHS saying things are basically fine. But both reports missed the crux of the problem: There is massive fraud and waste in the program that goes undetected.

The point was made in a devastating report last November by HHS Inspector General Richard Kusserow. State fraud administrators, investigators and eligibility workers estimated that close to 30 percent of the AFDC population was involved in fraud, and some put the level as high as 50 percent. The study found that, pressed to process new welfare benefit claims as quickly as possible, eligibility workers (who complained of inadequate training) frequently had to follow a "get the check out and ask questions later" method of screening beneficiaries. They were reluctant to refer cases for fraud investigation because doing so "usually resulted in additional work."

Recipients with multiple fraud offenses adopted "very casual attitudes" toward state anti-fraud efforts because the perpetrators rarely go to jail and often are able to continue receiving benefits. The study reported that judges often are reluctant to throw mothers with multiple children off welfare and blame program managers for letting ineligible people onto the rolls in the first place. An offense treated as a crime in one area of a state wouldn't be handled as such in another, or, as one convicted AFDC offender in rural Michigan put it, "This (offense) isn't even a crime in Detroit."

"If you try to emphasize it," a state budget director told HHS, "you lose two ways. The liberals criticize you for squandering scarce resources on pseudo-issues and the conservatives point to convictions and tell you 'I told you so.' I just hold my nose and hope it goes away."

Despite this bleak situation, Rep. Thomas Downey's Ways and Means subcommittee on Public Assistance voted earlier this month to continue the current moratorium, which expires in July, for another year. This is understandable — Mr. Downey's state alone accounts for close to a fifth of the $1.1 billion owed HHS — but it's blatant special interest legislation that's a poor substitute for the inevitable: reforming a welfare system that cheats taxpayers and pushes recipients into a crippling dependency on Washington.

The Dallas Morning News
Dallas, TX, April 26, 1988

The first recommendation for the Moynihan welfare reform plan, recently approved by the Senate Finance Committee, is that it is based on reality rather than an out-of-date delusion.

The fact that the panel did not divide along party lines, but instead approved the plan by a 17-3 vote, indicates that this is not an old-fashioned, liberal-conservative issue. The fact is, as Sen. Pat Moynihan has pointed out, Aid to Families with Dependent Children was designed to provide temporary support for widows and their children. The idea was to help the family whose breadwinner had died until the children grew old enough to support their mother.

Anyone who thinks that such cases are typical of the recipients today has not been paying attention. This is the age of the third-and fourth-generation recipient, the welfare neighborhood, the epidemic of teen-age mothers bearing illegitimate children in the knowledge that the taxpayers will pick up the tab for their future living expense.

The Moynihan bill is an attempt to make the welfare system fit the realities of 1988 and to require the people who have heretofore made a cash cow of welfare take on the responsibility for their own lives and those of the children they bring into the world.

It would use a variety of tools, from a strong effort to collect child support payments from absent parents to beefed-up training and job-skills education. There are no guarantees that this package will be the solution, but at least it is a reform attempt that recognizes the real problem. No one can say that of the present system.

THE SACRAMENTO BEE
Sacramento, CA, February 5, 1988

The plight of poor young women and children has galvanized state legislatures and Congress to review social policy in hopes of breaking the cycle of welfare dependency. But what of "the forgotten half": the non-college youth who are the fathers of those children but, all too often, not the husbands of those young women.

Even though a higher proportion of America's youth are completing high school and delaying parenthood than ever before, they have less and less to show for their accomplishments, as statistics compiled by the William T. Grant Foundation Commission on Work, Family and Citizenship make plain. The real incomes of 20- to 24-year-old male high school graduates fell by 28 percent between 1973 and 1986. In 1986, fewer than half of high-school graduates not in college had full-time jobs two years after graduation. As a result, only 43.7 percent of non-college young men now earn enough to support a wife and child at or above the official poverty line. Lacking adequate incomes, they are less able to marry or hold families together. One American child in five is now born to an unmarried woman, a proportion that has tripled in a generation.

Part of this decline in the well-being of the young stems from causes that have afflicted the entire economy. The slump in U.S. manufacturing and the shift toward service jobs with higher educational requirements has decreased employment opportunities for non-college youth. Fifteen years of inflation and slow growth have squeezed incomes across the board.

But a larger part of the problems of non-college youth stems from sheer institutional neglect. While the United States lavishes more than $100 billion a year on education for college students, it invests a pittance in preparing non-college youth for the work world. Much of public vocational education is outdated, the federal Job Partnership Training Act serves only a small fraction of low-income youth, and the Job Corps has only 40,000 slots a year. "For the students not going on to college, school ends one day and the search for a job — any job, not a career — begins the next," the commission notes.

In the case of welfare mothers, policymakers now recognize the need to link recipients to the world of work through the training and educational services of workfare programs. But the larger need is to build reliable bridges between school and work for all non-college youth. In West Germany, half of all 15- to 18-year-olds participate in apprenticeships that combine schooling with on-the-job training and produce, at graduation, a young person with a skill, a job and an opportunity for adult responsibility.

Such institutions need a serious look in America, as does the whole range of programs the Grant Foundation report recommends: improved schooling for non-college-bound youth, more opportunities for national and community service and greater access to training and educational remediation for dropouts and high-school graduates needing to upgrade their job skills. Without a serious effort to improve the lives and opportunities of non-college young men, America's hopes of ending the welfare cycle, and the wasted lives it produces, are slim.

THE INDIANAPOLIS NEWS
Indianapolis, IN,
May 2, 1988

Congress and the Reagan administration are at odds once again with an expensive welfare revision legislation facing a veto from the president.

President Reagan is right to be threatening to veto this bill, which was originally proposed by Sen. Patrick Moynihan, D-N.Y.

Moynihan's analysis of the welfare problem is on target. He has traced the history of the Aid to Families with Dependent Children program in explaining how it has strayed so far from its original purpose of helping widows with small children. In recent years the AFDC program, combined with other government subsidies, has created financial incentives for the breakdown of the family.

But Moynihan's prescription for a cure has several flaws. In a time of $150 billion annual federal deficits, Congress should be looking for welfare reform with a lower price tag.

A version of Moynihan's legislation was approved by the Senate Finance Committee with a $2.8 billion price tag. Democrats in the House of Representatives are considering an even more expensive $7.1 billion plan over five years. In contrast, Republicans in Congress have offered a plan costing less than $1 billion, yet with the same emphasis on work and with more flexibility for states.

The legislation offered by Moynihan does have some commendable features, including an emphasis on work and steps to establish paternity and child support collection.

But the price tag does not need to be so high in a time of massive federal deficits. President Reagan's threat of a veto ought to prompt a more responsible approach to welfare reform.

Grace Commission Finds 2,478 Ways To Save $424 Billion in 'Waste'

A Reagan administration study panel released its final report on streamlining the federal government operation Jan. 12, 1984. The panel, the President's Private Sector Survey on Cost Control, was headed by J. Peter Grace, chairman of W.R. Grace & Co. Its report contained 2,478 recommendations that it said could save the government $424.4 billion over three years. A large chunk of the claimed savings—$58.1 billion—would come from a proposed revision of the federal pension system, which would require congressional action. In fact, most of the panel's suggested solutions would require congressional action; only about 27% of the alleged $424.4 billion cost cutting could be consumated through administrative action, according to the panel's estimate.

The panel proposed cutbacks in a number of well-established federal programs, such as food stamps, Medicare, housing subsidies and Farmers Home Administration loans. Its other proposals ranged from a suggestion to add soy extender to ground beef in the school lunch program to a plan to turn over the federally supported hydroelectric power system in the Pacific Northwest to private enterprise. The panel also recommended that the president be given a line-item veto power on appropriations bills, so "costly elements" could be deleted.

Critics of the panel claimed it strayed into public policy area, normally the domain of Congress, instead of sticking strictly to its intended purpose, which was to tighten federal operations by eliminating waste, inefficiency and unnecessary spending.

Grace stated at a news conference Jan. 12, "The government is run horribly," and warned that unless drastic action was taken the government would face deficits of "$1 trillion to $2 trillion" by the end of the century.

The Times-Picayune
The States-Item
New Orleans, LA, January 16, 1984

Because of political realities and bureaucratic resistance, it may be too much to expect that government can be run as efficiently as a well managed private business. Yet the cost-cutting recommendations of a special panel of business executives appointed by President Reagan deserve to be taken seriously by the Reagan administration and both Democratic and Republican members of Congress. The report demonstrates that despite the big cutbacks in federal spending to date, there remains tremendous waste in government programs and equally tremendous potential savings.

In fact, says the final report of the President's Private Sector Survey on Cost Control, federal spending could be cut by an additional $424.4 billion over three years. J. Peter Grace, the colorful chairman of W.R. Grace & Co., who headed the commission, predicted that the federal budget deficit, currrently projected to be in the $200 billion range for the next fiscal year, would reach almost $2 trillion by the year 2000 unless the panel's recommendations are adopted.

The report has obvious political ramifications in this presidential election year. The federal deficits could be a major domestic issue. There are growing signs that President Reagan will oppose tax increases to combat the deficits and will stress spending cuts instead.

Mr. Grace also opposes tax increases, and his panel's report provides Mr. Reagan with much campaign fodder. But, politics or not, the report makes 2,478 recommendations that the president, Congress or individual federal agencies could adopt to control government spending and establish management practices used in private business.

Some of the key recommendatins include:

—Reducing government pension plans to a level more competitive with those in private industry.

—Upgrading government computers, which are about twice as old as those in private businesses.

—Requiring the Pentagon to buy commonly used parts and equipment on a competitive basis.

—Increasing efforts to collect back taxes.

—Repealing the law that requires government to pay wages on construction projects that exceed those offered by smaller, more competitive local companies.

The commission also found many costly, bureaucratic "absurdities," including:

—Members of Congress will not let the Defense Department close some of its military bases.

—12,469 post offices provide service to 100 or fewer customers.

—The General Services Administration, the government's landlord and housekeeper, employs 17 times as many people and spends almost 14 times as much as a private company would on total management costs.

The list goes on, but taxpayers should get the idea.

To help get a better handle on spending, the commission recommended establishing a central Office of Federal Management.

In the eyes of top business executives, the federal government is run horribly, said Mr. Grace. The findings of the commission would appear to support that conclusion.

TULSA WORLD
Tulsa, OK, January 19, 1984

THE words of the philosopher, Pogo, are by now a cliche, but they are nevertheless true and summarize the findings of the Grace Commission, appointed to ferret out waste in government.

Pogo, the comic strip character, reported years ago that "We have met the enemy, and he is us."

Consider the Grace Commission's principal finding: Congress, not the bureaucracy so often criticized, is the real culprit in efforts to trim federal spending.

The commission outlined dozens of instances in which members of Congress interferred in efforts to close obsolete facilities, streamline operations or reduce manpower. The panel outlined cost-cutting steps involving Congress that would trim federal spending by more than $7.8 billion in thee years.

Included were the closings dozens of obsolete military bases, weather stations, forestry laboratories, food-inspection training centers and black-lung-program offices, as well as reductions of personnel in a wide variety of federal operations.

While Congress takes the brunt of the commission's findings in what's wrong with federal government, the fact behind the commission's view is this: Behind every member's interference in plans to close a facility or reduce operations, you can be sure there are an army of constituents pressuring their representative to keep that base open, keep that federal function going, because it is "our" installation and its payroll is important to "us."

Blame the bureaucracy? You bet. Blame the Congress. Ditto.

Blame "us?" Certainly. "We have met the enemy," said Pogo, "and he is us."

The Hartford Courant

Hartford, CT, January 21, 1984

Putting a business executive to work on waste in the federal government is like putting a rookie detective on the trail of a bookmaker. Both approach their tasks with gusto, and have little trouble finding what they're looking for. But they also find that detecting evil and eliminating it are two very different things.

The President's Private Sector Survey on Cost Control labored three years and produced a report bulging with 2,478 recommendations. Over three years, the panel said, its suggestions could save more than $424 billion; through the year 2000, a whopping cumulative savings total of $10.5 trillion is possible if all its remedies are applied. The federal deficit could be virtually eliminated.

The vision is dazzling. And atop that, the cost-cutting and "revenue-enhancing" steps could be taken "without raising taxes, without weakening America's needed defense buildup, and without in any way harming necessary social welfare programs," said Chairman J. Peter Grace in a letter to President Reagan.

The 161 executives and more than 2,000 others involved in the survey indeed identified a lot of improper government spending and lost income. But their report made a small splash, because little of what they found surprised federal employees, members of Congress or anyone else familiar with the way the government does business.

There's a reason why the Pentagon pays $91 for a 3-cent screw, why superfluous military bases and post offices soak up tax dollars and why federal pensions ooze generosity. The reason is that the government doesn't do business in a businesslike way.

Incompetence, laziness and corruption are part of the problem, though they probably don't infect the national government much more than they do some giant corporations. The primary source of waste is simply a result of this country's form of government: Those who make the decisions that produce waste tend to be acutely sensitive to political pressures, especially from organized interest groups.

The component of government most responsive to those pressures is Congress, and it is Congress that must act on about three-fourths of the waste panel's recommendations before they can go into effect.

Even if it were 1983 or 1985, most of the panel's recommendations would have an up-hill battle. In 1984, with political anxiety at its quadrennial peak, you can confidently wager that Congress will do with the report what it has done about government waste so far: precious little. That's unfortunate.

THE ARIZONA REPUBLIC

Phoenix, AZ, January 15, 1984

HEADLINES are sometimes misleading. This certainly was true in the case of the Grace commission's report.

Commission Chairman Peter J. Grace and his fellow businessmen on the president's Private Sector Survey of Cost Control did not, as the headlines suggested, show how the government could save $424.4 billion over three years by eliminating waste.

They had wandered beyond the mandate Reagan gave them 18 months ago into questions of domestic policy.

Most of the major recommendations they made would require acts of Congress.

To say this is not to denigrate the commission's recommendations, but to emphasize a fact many of those who rail against government spending do not seem to appreciate.

The mammoth budgets of recent years — and the $200 billion deficits that face the nation in the years to come — are not the result of waste, inefficiency or graft. And they could not be eliminated even if the government were as clean as a hound's tooth and as efficient as the solar system.

They are the result of policies that Congress has written into law. These policies have led to runaway spending that cannot be curbed unless the laws are repealed or drastically revised.

One of the commission's major recommendations, for example, is to bring civil service pensions closer into line with private sector pensions. This, the commission estimated, would save the government $30 billion over three years.

Bringing military pensions closer into line with private pensions would save another $28.1 billion.

This unquestionably is true. But federal pension systems are the brainchildren of Congress, and savings can be made only by act of Congress.

Similarly, the commission estimated that denationalization of the federal power marketing administrations could save $7.3 billion.

Again, that can be done only by Congress.

The commission did make some recommendations that could be carried out without congressional approval, and they do appear sound.

Improvement of the Defense Department's inventory management, it said, could save $6.1 billion over three years. Requiring the military to buy commonly-used parts and equipment competitively would save another $7.3 billion.

Where no congressional action is needed, the administration should put the commission's recommendations into effect at once.

Really substantial savings, however, will require drastic changes in the law. If the Grace commission's report does nothing else, it demonstrates that any politician who says he can balance the budget by eliminating inefficiency and waste is either a liar or a fool.

Regan Remarks Spark Fears of Reduced Benefits

A sensitive national issue was briefly rekindled May 6, 1984 when Treasury Secretary Donald Regan, appearing on NBC television's *Meet the Press*, said the government might have to "rethink" the Social Security system. The system, Regan said, had been designed "to help those who get destitute when they get older." But benefits also went to wealthy elderly people who do not need them, he said. "At some cutoff point, we may want to ask why a person such as that should receive Social Security," Regan suggested.

The White House acted quickly May 7 to quash the fear that benefits for some recipients might be eliminated, perhaps before the end of the decade. A presidential spokesman said: "We have no plans to change Social Security either now or in a second term." John A. Svahn, a former commissioner of Social Security and currently the President's assistant for policy development, asserted that the Social Security system was "in good shape well into the next century."

"There are no plans to change anything in the Social Security retirement system," he continued.

But Regan's remarks drew some political flak anyway. "These Republicans can't keep their hands off Social Security," Walter Mondale said May 7, campaigning in Ohio for the Democratic presidential nomination. Mondale added that Reagan was trying to convert Social Security from an insurance program to a welfare program.

St. Petersburg Times

St. Petersburg, FL, May 8, 1984

There it is again, the same old loaded question: Why pay Social Security benefits to retirees who don't need them? This time it's Treasury Secretary Donald Regan who's doing the asking. Only three years ago, it was President Reagan himself. You've got to believe they have something in mind, notwithstanding Monday's limp White House disclaimer that there are "no plans to change Social Security in the second term."

The President, it must be remembered, has had it in for Social Security ever since the early 1960s, when he first suggested that participation be made voluntary. He kept up the attack during his radio broadcasts of the 1970s. He relented long enough to get elected in 1980, whereupon he proposed long-term benefit cuts approximating 22 percent. In 1981, he decried the "sizeable percentage of recipients who are adequately provided for by pensions or other income and should not be adding to the burden of Social Security."

In 1983, Congress approved a program of slightly reduced benefits and slightly increased taxes intended to keep the trust fund solvent for 75 years. Only last month, the system's trustees formally reported that "benefits can be paid on time well into the next century." Yet here's the treasury secretary, managing trustee of the fund, suddenly turning up on on *Meet the Press* to say "we're going to have to revisit Social Security in the late 1980s, because it hasn't been permanently fixed." In fixing it, he implied, benefits might well be denied to people who also have substantial pensions or private savings.

INDEED, WHY should working people pay taxes to support wealthy retirees? The answer, simply, is that Social Security is *not* welfare. Neither is it an insurance program in the traditional sense. It is a government pension plan for *all* eligible citizens — and that's nine of every 10 of us — which assures them of benefits in retirement in return for the taxes they pay while they work. Personal savings or retirement incomes from other sources are not relevant to determining benefits. (They're not relevant to calculating private pension benefits either.) As the most universal federal program, Social Security has become a fundamental feature of the U.S. economy. In fact, many if not most private pension plans are calculated on the assumption that Social Security will also be paid.

But the surest way to destroy Social Security is to paint it as a welfare program, as Mr. Reagan has been trying to do for some two decades. It would become as politically vulnerable as food stamps or Aid to Families with Dependent Children. People who now pay willingly because they are assured of benefits in their own retirement would be left wondering where the cutoff line would be drawn. Social Security would be cheapened and degraded; to apply for benefits would become a symbol of shame instead of an honorable rite of passage.

WHY DOES THE Reagan administration persistently insinuate this? The answer is partly ideological, of course. But the apparent strategy also reeks of opportunism. If benefits can be cut — as by denying them to people who are supposedly well-to-do — there is a sudden, though artificial, reduction in the annual budget deficit. Never mind that Social Security pays its own way; use it to juggle the books. Nor mind that Social Security benefits are *decreasing* as a percentage of the gross national product while defense expenditures, by the same measure, go up.

Martin Feldstein, who is now the President's chief (in name only) economic adviser, wrote prophetically in 1977 that as "long as the voters support the Social Security system, it will be able to pay the benefits that it promises." The so-called "rescue plan" of 1983 proved that the voters still support Social Security. It seems only to be the Reagan administration that does not.

In light of all the complicated interweavings in the Social Security System, no one does either beneficiaries or policymakers a favor by tossing out rash notions like so much confetti. In the current case of Treasury Secretary Donald T. Regan's remarks about well-to-do retirees and benefits, the strong wind that catches it is the worry of 36 million beneficiaries.

Their confidence in the program has been toyed with enough in the last few years. They don't need Mr. Regan, who carries the prestige of administration insider and financial expert, to meditate aloud that maybe that unique insurance protection ought to be something else. Like a welfare program.

For that's exactly what Mr. Regan or anyone else who talks that way is embracing when they concentrate with horror on the fact that comfortable retirees, even wealthy widows and couples, also take Social Security checks. Powerful people who state such feelings are insensitive, at the least, and bypass established structures for change.

They act as if they are unaware the Congress would have to approve new legislation before such a thing came to pass. In actual fact, Mr. Regan for all his responsibilities has no direct influence on Social Security matters.

The issue here is a total change of philosophy of the Social Security System, from insurance to welfare, rather than some variety of tax or benefit adjustment. For many individuals, welfare might serve a comparable service and if the country wants to maintain security for its elderly and disabled purely through charity, that's not necessarily bad in itself. But rashness is.

There's the specter of unfairness, changing rules after some workers have paid into the trust fund for decades expecting their dollars will be returned to them. Tying benefits to wealth at certain income levels, particularly on the cutoff edge, would penalize nest-egg people and those who plan most carefully.

The entire discussion does nothing more than throw the fear of insecurity into the nation's elderly. And Democrats making a political tidbit out of Mr. Regan's remarks aren't helping at all. When elected senators and representatives are ready to delve into this issue, its facets can be adequately explored. Until then, it would be helpful if Washington's prestigious wouldn't play around with such dangerous trial balloons.

THE LOUISVILLE TIMES
Louisville, KY, May 11, 1984

Nothing could have been more predictable, not even a rainy Kentucky spring.

Appearing last Sunday on national television, Treasury Secretary Donald Regan suggested that Social Security benefits to wealthy recipients may have to be curtailed or even ended later this decade to keep the program solvent.

Then Monday, a fretful White House virtually declared it did not know who Mr. Regan was. No plans have been or will be hatched, said an aide to President Reagan, to cut back benefits.

Now, Mr. Regan did voice understandable frustration about rich people getting Social Security — especially if, as he and others predict, yet another expensive, politically divisive bailout may be necessary in the relatively near future. The shape and size of Social Security certainly bear addressing as payroll taxes consume increasingly larger proportions of income and the number of recipients increases as the general population ages. And the President's concern no doubt anticipated the opposition Democrats' inevitable accusations of bad faith in this election year.

Nonetheless, Mr. Regan's orientation betrayed a profound misunderstanding of what *The New York Times* terms the "political genius" of Social Security. This "genius" is, simply, that the 49-year-old New Deal program continues to work today because the overwhelming majority of employed people in America pay into it on the presumption that all who qualify may benefit. Limiting those direct benefits to lower income people would reduce public support for Social Security, while at the same time attaching the "welfare" stigma to the checks mailed out every month.

Back to Mr. Regan's complaint, however: Some spending restraints, beyond those Congress approved in 1983, may well be needed. A fifth of the federal budget now goes for Social Security, and some recent think-tank analyses suggest contributions will have to be increased considerably to meet the obligations to current workers.

But rather than *eliminate* payments above a certain cut-off, a potentially fairer, more acceptable approach is to extend the so-called reform of last year. That could mean raising taxes on the Social Security well-to-do recipients receive, as well as speeding up the raising of the retirement age and penalties on those who take early retirement.

As Mr. Regan's faux pas over the weekend demonstrated all too well, the chief trick to a constructive discussion of any Social Security problem is timing. An election year, unless there is truly a funding crisis, only invites demagoguery. The secretary shouldn't have to be reminded of this.

Herald News
Fall River, MA, May 8, 1984

Treasury Secretary Donald Regan has courageously raised the subject that Washington in general has been dodging.

Regan says the stop-gap changes in the Social Security System will not suffice to ensure the system's solvency in the future, and that as a result, sometime in the next few years the federal government will have to overhaul it again.

The Treasury Secretary raised the possibility that persons with considerable wealth would have to be ruled ineligible for Social Security, although he discounted the possibility of a means test to determine who would receive its benefits.

The point he was making was fair enough, that persons with real wealth do not need Social Security benefits. Nevertheless, they are eligible for them, and in many cases collect them.

Nevertheless, the Treasury Secretary's suggestion, although made in good faith and with the best of intentions, seems to involve a fundamental misconception about the nature of the Social Security System itself.

He says that when it was originated it was intended to help those who would have been destitute without it.

In a sense this is right. Social Security came into being during the Great Depression, and many of those helped by it would have been unable to survive without it.

But the system was always intended to pay for itself through the money contributed during their working lives by those who in time received its benefits.

Furthermore, for a long time, it did just that.

The beneficiaries were receiving back what they put into it. They were not, nor did they consider themselves, recipients of charity or a hand-out to keep them from being destitute.

It was precisely to avoid this notion that the Social Security System covered persons who would never literally need its benefits.

The half-century since Social Security's inception has, however, produced vast social and economic changes that have to some degree invalidated its premises.

For one thing the number of persons who live to become beneficiaries of the system has increased beyond the most optimistic notions of the persons who established and organized the system.

There are simply far more people covered by the system than was ever anticipated.

Leaving that major point aside, the astronomic increases in the cost of living have also placed an unforeseen strain upon Social Security's financial resources.

The two factors combined have threatened the system's solvency, and as Secretary Regan points out, the recent changes in the system will not solve the problem permanently. More changes will have to be made.

It is questionable, however, whether the vast majority of wage-earning Social Security investors will accept without a protest the imposition of income restrictions on those eligible to receive benefits.

Rather, they would prefer some other way of trying to make the system solvent.

The Treasury Secretary has done the nation a service by calling attention to the fact that more changes in the system will be needed.

He is to be congratulated for daring to raise this politically risky issue in an election year.

But it does not follow that his tentative suggestion of imposing an upper income limit on those eligible to receive benefits should be accepted.

The whole notion of Social Security was based on a pay-as-you-go arrangement and not on charity.

In that respect at least it should not be changed.

ST. LOUIS POST-DISPATCH
St. Louis, MO, May 10, 1984

The alarm bells were probably clanging off the wall before Treasury Secretary Donald Regan left NBC's studio following Sunday morning's interview on "Meet the Press." Setting them off was his impolitic remark that attempts to breach the deficit gap might prompt a re-examination of Social Security benefits.

Mr. Regan apparently thought to cut the political losses by limiting the review's scope. "At the lower end of the scale, we shouldn't do anything to Social Security," he said. At the upper end, though? "I think we better re-examine it."

The administration's attempt to distance itself from the very idea was quick and to the point. And rightly so. Scarcely a year ago, Congress approved legislation that was designed to put the Social Security system in good stead through the end of the century. Nothing yet indicates the plan isn't working. About the only thing that would call for a review — in fact, the very thing Mr. Regan cited in suggesting one — is the need to examine closely every federal program for ways to cut federal spending.

But Social Security is one federal program that is self-financing — that is, it depends entirely on payroll deductions and not on general revenues. Balancing the budget by reducing Social Security benefits would mean Social Security would actually be underwriting other government programs. Doubtless, many beneficiaries have enough other income from pensions or insurance or other sources to make Social Security payments little more than frosting on the cake — and it is this income, apparently, that has attracted Mr. Regan's green-eyed regard.

Perhaps one can question the equity of this arrangement. A means test or sliding scale of payments to retired and disabled people that looks to need might be desirable or even necessary at some future time. But as things now stand, the Social Security program ought to be off-limits to Mr. Regan and other scapegoat hunters.

THE BLADE

Toledo, OH, May 13, 1984

ONE would think by now that alarm bells would go off in the heads of Reagan administration officials whenever they feel inclined to sound off on Social Security.

Donald Regan, secretary of the treasury, wondered aloud last week whether a further examination of the Social Security system would not be necessary a few years from now to make sure it remains solvent.

There was nothing wrong with that, but it was coupled with another remark that any such reassessment should consider the question of whether upper-income retirees should continue to receive Social Security payments. He did not amplify his remarks, but what he said is enough to make many present and potential retirees nervous.

Many pensions in the private sector are computed on the basis of what a retiree's income would be when combined with Social Security payments. Newly hired federal workers now come under the umbrella of the system, a long overdue reform. President Reagan has had to fight to overcome the feeling among many older Americans that his heart really is not in the Social Security system and that he would just as soon let such matters be attended to by private insurance and pension plans.

Left unanswered is a major question: What would happen to the contributions made by upper-income Americans over the years if they were to be cut off from Social Security? Would the contributions be refunded, or would such persons simply receive no return for the money they involuntarily contributed?

To give some persons a pension and cut off the payments to others, even though all had contributed, could be construed as being in violation of the equal-protection clause of the 14th Amendment to the U.S. Constitution.

Moreover, once a ceiling was imposed, it would be easy for lawmakers to continue to tamper with the eligibility standards if the Social Security system got into a future financial bind. Eventually the federal insurance plan would become a matter of social and economic insecurity rather than security.

Mr. Regan does not seem to have thought through the implications of his remarks. He has in a rather off-handed style discussed discarding the cardinal principle of Social Security, which long has been universal coverage. That is a concept that helps keep the country's social fabric from unraveling, and it should not be discarded lightly. Mr. Regan's comments were, at the very least, unhelpful to his boss.

The Des Moines Register

Des Moines, IA, May 9, 1984

Just when it seemed that Social Security was finally secure, financially and politically, along comes Donald Regan with loose talk and dangerous ideas.

The treasury secretary went on television Sunday to suggest that maybe another Social Security crisis is in the works, and maybe the whole idea of Social Security ought to be changed.

When Regan was asked what President Reagan might do in a second term to reduce federal budget deficits, he replied that the government is going to have to "rethink" Social Security before the end of the decade.

Specifically, he raised the prospect of somehow linking eligibility to income. "At the lower end of the scale, we shouldn't do anything to Social Security," he said, but at the high-income end "I think we'd better examine it."

Though he denied that he was suggesting a means test, he added: "I do think that somewhere along the line, at some cutoff point, we may well want to say, well, why does such a person really have Social Security?"

His talk of a "cutoff point" clearly suggests a means test. In blunt terms, that points toward converting Social Security from a universal, guaranteed retirement-insurance system into another welfare program. Such a change would fundamentally alter its basic rationale, would undermine its broad political support and would practically guarantee a continuing crisis.

Beyond that, Regan's loose talk raises fresh questions about the system's financial outlook. Is it sound or isn't it?

Last year's amendments to the Social Security Act were intended to ensure the solvency of the program's trust funds for 75 years. The 1984 report issued last month by the system's trustees — of whom Regan is one — said the system is financially secure until "well into the next century" even under the most pessimistic of four sets of projections.

Regan now says that "we're going to have to revisit Social Security sometime in the late 1980s, because it hasn't been permanently fixed." Is he needlessly creating new worries or is he blurting out some horrible new truth?

The White House promptly denied any plans to tinker with Social Security, and Secretary Regan may have been talking off the top of his head. As the Reagan administration's chief economic spokesman, he owes the country a clarification of his views of Social Security's financial prospects and an explanation of why he said the president might propose such a drastic change.

The Washington Post

Washington, DC, May 9, 1984

IT SEEMS to be an ungovernable impulse. The people who speak for the administration know they shouldn't keep hinting at cuts in Social Security benefits. It always results in hasty retreats, denials and embarrassment. And yet, and yet . . . as the object of wishful thinking within the administration, Social Security is apparently irresistible. Last weekend, the Treasury secretary, Donald Regan, suggested on "Meet the Press" that it might be necessary to "rethink" the benefits for the well-to-do later in this decade.

To take Mr. Regan's comment seriously—more seriously, perhaps, than anyone outside the Treasury does—it raises two questions. First, is it possible as a matter of political reality to cut benefits? Next, even if it were possible, would it be a good idea? The answer to both questions is a flat no.

Regarding possibility, you need only note the speed with which the White House declared it has no plans, for present or future, to lay as much as a hand on Social Security. The whole structure of Social Security payments and financing has had a thorough and recent review culminating in important reforms last year.

Mr. Regan correctly points out that Social Security was originally designed only to provide a small stipend to protect the elderly from utter destitution. Why, Mr. Regan asks, pay benefits to those who are not poor? The answer is that just about all Americans regard Social Security as insurance, not welfare—insurance for which they have paid with heavy payroll taxes. The right way to handle benefits to the wealthy is to subject them to income taxation, as last year's legislation does. Any administration that tries to turn Social Security into a means-tested welfare program—one that cuts off benefits to people above a certain income—will run into more trouble than Mr. Regan has bargained for.

Above all other reasons, the middle class has embraced Social Security because of inflation. Only the federal government can run a pension system that is inflation-proof. Conservative theorists say that people ought to save individually for their retirement. But savers can't insure themselves, individually, against the kind of inflation that this country has experienced. What's wrong with people joining together, through their government, to protect themselves collectively?

Even people with rather high incomes now take Social Security into account in their planning as the only investment that can guarantee its real value. A Treasury secretary who presides over federal deficits on the present mindless scale is not in a strong position to argue that the risk of high inflation has been exorcised forever.

The Miami Herald

Miami, FL, May 9, 1984

NO other political question sets the hornets flying as quickly as does Social Security, and understandably so. Every American family is touched by the program, which is the cornerstone of the reforms of Franklin Roosevelt's New Deal.

Treasury Secretary Donald Regan stirred the nest again, perhaps unnecessarily, with his provocative comments on *Meet the Press* Sunday. Mr. Regan was asked whether the Reagan Administration planned to tamper with Social Security again during a second term.

Secretary Regan did little to allay the fears and resentments that the subject so easily generates. He suggested that in the future, Social Security benefits might be curtailed "at some cut-off point" of wealth. Those future recipients who are threatened, of course, are the working Americans of today who are forced each year to pay higher and higher percentages of their current income to support cost-of-living increases for today's retirees. Today's payment levels are politically determined by Congress and bear no actuarial relationship to the amount paid in by the recipient.

Today's workers thus rightly resent the notion that they should support today's retirees, who are not necessarily poor by any means, in the style to which they have become accustomed unless there is assurance that the same generous treatment will come to them in turn. Secretary Regan's remarks suggested that it will not.

To the contrary, Mr. Regan referred to the savings and pensions of future retirees — today's contributors — as potential considerations in reducing their Social Security benefits 20 years from now. The Treasury Secretary thus raised the spectre of a Federally imposed penalty on the thrifty to benefit the profligate. That is hardly an idea that one expects from an Administration that calls itself conservative. Nor is it defensible social policy.

If futher financial adjustments must be made to Social Security, they should aim to restore the balance of equity between the generations and to ensure that the unearned portion of any benefit is supported by the entire economy, not just by pay-check earning workers.

Certainly Mr. Regan is correct in his implication that wealthy recipients should not receive Social Security benefits that are out of proportion to what they paid in, and thus amount to welfare provided by workers. But today's young workers are entitled to a secure and comfortable retirement on the same level now enjoyed by the politically powerful generation of their grandparents. Any Administration that takes that security from them inevitably will succeed also in eroding the broad public support for Social Security on which the entire program rests.

The Boston Globe

Boston, MA, May 14, 1984

Although the White House moved quickly to try to disavow his statement, Treasury Secretary Donald Regan has reaffirmed the Reagan Administration's long-standing hostility to the Social Security system. In an election year, it is good to have such issues clearly before the public.

Regan, in a television interview, suggested that benefits may have to be cut or eliminated for retirees with excess income from savings or private pensions. He linked such moves to assertions that the retirement portion of the Social Security system is in danger of deficits, even allowing for changes made last year to improve the system's financial condition.

Proposals to cut or eliminate benefits would require application of a means test – inquiry into the personal finances of Social Security beneficiaries. Such tests have never been a part of the system, largely because Social Security is designed as a universal foundation for retirement income, patterned loosely and rather imperfectly after private annuity programs.

The system, to be sure, has never been totally blind to the incomes of beneficiaries. It has, for instance, provided minimum benefits even though payroll taxes for a given individual might not justify the total funds received. Furthermore, as part of the restructuring last year, benefits have become partially taxable for persons with higher incomes.

Nevertheless, Social Security was launched and has largely remained blind to income – sometimes perhaps too blind, as in the case of Medicare benefits, awarded solely upon the basis of medical need.

Were Regan's changes to be implemented, the Social Security system would be tranformed from its largely pension-oriented direction toward a welfare-like structure. Of the various flaws in such a system, the largest is having an utterly inappropriate tax structure – actually retrogressive – for an income-transfer project.

Lower-income taxpayers would pay higher rates than upper-income ones because of the ceiling on taxable income. A pure welfare system for retirees ought instead to be supported by general taxes, including the progressive income tax.

More insidiously, the changes would probably reduce political support for the system. Social Security has enjoyed widespread support because it has been perceived as an annuity insurance system – a perception that is only partly accurate, but that is widely regarded as vital to its long-standing support.

An attack of this nature on the political support for Social Security would be unfortunate, coming so soon after the enactment of Individual Retirement Accounts, which allow persons to reduce taxable income by as much as $2000 a year ($4000 for couples) to set aside retirement funds.

The timing of Regan's proposals is fortuitous. It opens the question of Social Security for the balance of the presidential campaign. The electorate should have a clearer understanding of the Administration's ultimate objectives for the system. Regan has made that more likely.

Legal Services Corp. Targeted in Reagan's Budget Proposals

President Reagan Dec. 5, 1984 gave his cabinet a fiscal 1986 budget draft that featured drastic spending cuts and even elimination of many politically popular programs. The President's preliminary plan would pare $34 billion from the 1986 budget. A further reduction of $8 billion would be sought, presumably from the defense budget, to reach a goal of reducing prospective massive federal deficits to about $100 billion by fiscal 1988. Among the popular programs the president proposed to eliminate was the Legal Services Corporation, the agency that provided legal assistance for poor people.

Goaded by President Reagan to put his fiscal 1986 budget to a vote, the Republican-controlled Senate Budget Committee did so March 13, 1985 and rejected the Reagan budget decisively, 17-4. The panel then struggled to round out its own budget plan, which would achieve savings of $55.1 billion in fiscal 1986—greater than those sought by the President—by slashing both military spending and a wide variety of domestic programs including the Legal Services Corp.

By 1988, president Reagan had abandoned his effort to abolish the Legal Services Corp. In the $1.09 trillion budget he submitted Feb. 18, 1988 to Congress for the fiscal 1989 fiscal year, the President accepted the continued existence of the agency he had repeatedly attempted to delete earlier. But he called for an 18% reduction in its budget, to $250 million.

The Boston Globe
Boston, MA, March 27, 1988

For three years President Reagan's Legal Services Corporation has sought with unceasing diligence to undermine local legal services programs across the country, to destroy the effort it is charged with maintaining.

Later this week the LSC board, at a meeting in Savannah, Ga., is scheduled to act on new regulations that would drastically limit the activities of Legal Services lawyers.

Perhaps the most instructive aspect of the proposed regulations is a provision that would prevent Legal Services lawyers from informing clients, agency officials, legislators, bar associations or the media about any LSC regulations proposed in the future.

Not only does the LSC want to limit the rights of the poor to counsel, it wants also to bar those most knowledgeable about any proposed limitations from spreading the bad news. It does not want debate.

That is only the most notable bit of malevolence embodied in the regulations that will be pondered in Savannah.

Also included is a provision that would bar Legal Services lawyers from participating in government agencies' rulemaking activities such as, say, proposals to change the way welfare eligibility is determined; a provision that would virtually prohibit Legal Services lawyers from giving testimony before legislative committees, even when that testimony was requested by legislators; a provision would prohibit Legal Services staff from helping clients draft letters or comments to public officials; a provision would prevent Legal Services lawyers from helping groups of the poor to form organizations designed to influence public policy and from representing groups of the poor.

When Congress established the LSC in 1974 – ironically with the intent of establishing a quasiprivate funding mechanism for legal services that was above the ebb and flow of ideological politics – it declared that "providing legal assistance to those who face an economic barrier to adequate legal counsel will serve the best ends of justice. . . ."

The point has been lost on the Reagan Administration. Not only has it moved to cut direct and indirect economic assistance to the poor, its campaign against Legal Services seeks to deny the poor the opportunity of full participation in the nation's legal and political system.

While the Reagan Administration does not seem to understand it, nothing could be more "conservative" in the truest sense than encouraging all Americans to participate in the system. Nothing could be more radicalizing than denying the possibility of such participation. If the LSC this week enacts its proposed regulations, Congress must once again step in and explicitly reiterate that participation in the political and legal systems of the land is not the special prerogative of people with means.

The Des Moines Register
Des Moines, IA, August 18, 1984

A serious inequity in the legal system is the growing number of Americans who cannot afford legal services, especially those faced with an opponent — a landlord, an ex-employer or the government — who is assured of competent legal representation.

The problem was exacerbated when in 1982 the Reagan administration cut about a quarter of the federal funding for the Legal Services Corp., a quasi-federal agency that provides free legal aid to low-income clients.

However, increasing numbers of attorneys — from country lawyers in Iowa to the legal staffs of giant corporations — are volunteering to help beleaguered Legal Services staff lawyers.

• In Iowa, some 700 private-practice lawyers are volunteering to handle one or more Legal Services cases a year through a the Iowa Bar Association's Volunteer Lawyer Program. In the first six months of the year, volunteers closed nearly 300 cases. Though a fraction of the 15,000 cases Legal Services has handled this year, Iowa Legal Services director Randi Youells said "These are people who would have been turned away."

• A growing number of corporate law departments across the country are freeing staff lawyers to take on cases for clients who normally could not afford a lawyer. The American Bar Association surveyed 1,000 corporate law departments and found 37.5 percent involved in public-service legal work.

• The Legal Services Corporation is testing the idea of giving direct grants to private-practice attorneys — instead of Legal Services staff lawyers — for such routine legal work as divorces and bankruptcies.

Youells fears the pilot project — which is being tested in Polk County in Iowa and eventually in about 25 other cities around the country — is a plot by the Reagan administration to abolish the Legal Services Corp.; but it's doubtful Congress would kill the service, and this seems a good way to relieve Legal Services lawyers of some tedious cases to focus their skills on poverty law.

The Legal Services Corp. should be considered an essential binding in President Reagan's so-called safety net; but Legal Services should enlarge the number of private-practice lawyers willing to lend their special expertise to the needs of the poor.

The Philadelphia Inquirer
Philadelphia, PA, April 7, 1984

The Reagan administration consistently has viewed the Legal Services Corp. as a troublesome thorn in its side. Legal-aid lawyers tend to challenge administration cuts and changes in programs for the poor.

Since taking office, President Reagan has been intent on ridding himself of this thorn, by refusing to fund the Legal Services Corp. and by packing its board with those who share his philosophical distaste for legal aid to the poor. On three occasions, Congress has blocked efforts to eliminate the corporation entirely by cutting off its funds.

Recently, the corporation board took another tack, deciding to adopt regulations that would restrict seriously the access of legal-aid lawyers to members of Congress, state and local lawmakers and the news media. The administration considers this lobbying and wants to forbid it. Others — including many in Congress, state capitols and city halls — characterize it differently. They view the lawyers who work daily with federal, state and local programs as experts on the strengths and weaknesses of those programs and knowledgeable about how to improve them.

The corporation's board was scheduled to vote on the new restrictive regulations March 30, just four days after the public-comment period had ended. By law, the board must study the public responses before taking any action. The unexpected deluge of criticisms from around the nation caused the board members to postpone any action, fearing a lawsuit if they did not review all the comment carefully. Some of the strongest criticisms came from Republicans and Democrats in Congress, who warned that the proposed regulations violated the intent of the Legal Services Corp. Act of 1974.

The reprieve may be short-lived, however. The board is free to take up the regulations at a future meeting, and probably will do so. The Reagan administration — which has made its insensitivity to the needs of the poor apparent time and time again — now intends to go one step further: to cut off those who might mount a protest to that insensitivity. That must not happen. The truly needy deserve a voice, even if the administration doesn't like what it says.

The Virginian-Pilot
Norfolk, VA, June 21, 1984

In all criminal prosecutions, the accused shall enjoy the right . . . to have the assistance of counsel for his defense.
Sixth Amendment,
U.S. Constitution

The U.S. Supreme Court, in *Gideon vs. Wainwright* (1963), held that the Sixth Amendment confers upon indigent defendants the right to counsel assigned by the state. "The noble ideal" of "fair trials before impartial tribunals in which every defendant stands equal before the law cannot be realized if the poor man charged with the crime has to face his accusers without a lawyer to assist him," the court wrote.

Virginia provides lawyers for "the poor man." But it provides them so cheaply that many poor men and women are apt to end up with poor lawyers. And "the noble ideal" may well be just an ideal, not a reality.

Virginia's record in paying court-appointed lawyers is a sorry one indeed. Because of low pay, many Virginia lawyers refuse to take court-appointed cases. The state's standard fees for these cases have not increased in more than a decade, and they actually decreased last year when across-the-board budget cuts were made by the General Assembly (the cuts will be rescinded July 1). Virginia ranks next to last in the South in compensating court-appointed lawyers. Imagine that: Virginia pays less than states such as Mississippi and Alabama, states just now struggling out of the social Dark Ages, states whose share of the poor is much higher than Virginia's.

The state's penny-pinching is bound to have a negative effect on the equitable application of justice. It is true that many able lawyers, spurred by social conscience, perform work that is in reality *pro bono* — accepting fees from the state that are far less than they would receive usually. It is also true that some inexperienced but competent lawyers "go to school" — gain courtroom experience — by taking indigent cases.

But lawyers, no less than anyone else, like to be paid for what they do. For most lawyers, accepting court-appointed cases is forfeiting income that could be made on other cases. Few will be so charitable as the two lawyers in the town of Warrenton who worked 700 hours on a capital murder case and had to be content with the state's maximum payment — $600 each.

Lawyers and judges throughout the commonwealth believe the quality of representation for indigents is diminished because of the state's low fees. Many of the legal profession's best won't take the cases at all; some who do admit that they cut corners in preparing the cases for court.

What can be done?

Tightening rules for indigent eligibility may eliminate some expenses. The state should make sure that people who receive help really need it. This year, the General Assembly approved a new set of guidelines to determine eligibility to obtain court-appointed lawyers.

Expanding the use of public defenders — lawyers who draw a salary for representing indigents full time — may also save costs. There are four public defenders' offices in the state, including one in Virginia Beach, and studies by the Virginia Public Defender Commission show that public defenders usually provide more efficient service less expensively.

But tightening eligibility will do only so much, and there doesn't seem much sentiment in the state to greatly expand the use of public defenders. So that means — guess what? — the General Assembly is going to have to put more money into fees for court-appointed attorneys. There's no way around it if the state intends to live up to the promise of the Sixth Amendment.

Newsday
New York, NY, May 8, 1984

In a nation dedicated to equal justice for all its citizens, poor people must be able to obtain a lawyer's services even if they can't afford to pay. Legal-aid organizations funded privately or by local governments provide such help, but their resources are limited. Federal legal-services programs could do more, but they've been crippled by severe cutbacks and targeted for elimination by the Reagan administration.

Drastic effects have been felt by the poor in civil cases involving landlord-tenant disputes, wrongful denial of government benefits, disability claims and consumer fraud. In New York City, it's estimated that only one out of seven eligible people seeking free legal services actually receives them.

While codes of professional responsibility oblige every lawyer to support the provision of legal services to the disadvantaged, relatively few fulfill that obligation to any significant extent. But finally something is being done about it. Some of the city's largest law firms and corporate legal departments — offices that employ more than 5,000 of the city's 35,000 lawyers — have agreed to contribute at least 30 hours per lawyer per year to public-service work.

The program's organizers in the City Bar Association describe it as the country's most ambitious private effort to provide legal services to the poor. The initial group will be joined by smaller law firms and individual lawyers recruited in the five boroughs. And working relationships are expected to be set up with the bar associations in Nassau and Suffolk, which have volunteer programs of their own.

The prominence of the project's participants insures wide attention, and it could serve as a model for bar associations across the country. But it shouldn't become a pretext to reduce federal legal services still further. That would be a calamitous misuse of a commendable professional commitment.

Minneapolis Star and Tribune

Minneapolis, MN, January 30, 1984

President Reagan persists in his efforts to dismantle the popular and effective Legal Services Corp., which funds a permanent staff of neighborhood lawyers to help the poor in civil disputes. Unable to persuade Congress to eliminate the agency, Reagan slashed its budget. Deterred from further cuts, Reagan tried to load up the corporation's board with directors who will subvert its work. Congress must continue to fight these acts of sabotage.

By law, the corporation is to be run by an 11-member board, nominated by the president and confirmed by the Senate. Reagan has proposed 26 people for the board — most of them openly hostile to the corporation's mission. The Republican-controlled Senate has declined to confirm even one of the nominees. So the president found a way around the law: He waited until last winter's congressional recess, when he could legally install several of those nominees without Senate approval. Last week, he circumvented the Senate again by making another recess appointment.

True to the president's wishes, the unconfirmed appointees — who now serve as the agency's only directors — keep hacking away at the programs they are supposed to oversee. One rule approved last month will make it unjustifiably harder for welfare recipients to qualify for legal assistance. Another prohibits housing cooperatives or other low-income neighborhood groups from getting free legal help. The most frightening change permits the board to cut off funds to any local legal-aid program if the agency finds another group it thinks can better serve clients. Congress responded to that rule by forbidding the board to take money away from current legal-aid programs.

Through its efforts, the Reagan-controlled board has ensured that increasing numbers of poor people will be turned away from legal-aid offices. Crippling the Legal Services Corp. with regulations and recess appointments is almost as bad as killing it outright. Having failed to persuade Congress to abolish the corporation, Reagan has a duty to administer it, not undermine it. The president can start by appointing directors who sympathize with the program's mission and submitting those nominations to the Senate.

The Register

Santa Ana, CA, August 31, 1984

It was buried amid the news of tenant evictions in Santa Ana and Garden Grove. It was buried amid the news of a federal grant to the Legal Services Corp. to pay lawyers to represent the poor of those cities in battles with their landlords.

Yet it was the genuinely good news of the week. The Women's Foundation Program has gathered more than $200,000 in donations for its homeless women's shelter. The money is in addition to a $200,000 loan guarantee from the Irvine Co.

Coming mostly from about 10 corporate sources, the funds are enough to allow the non-profit group to seriously pursue a county residence to house between 40 and 50 women who would have no other home.

The need for the shelter became critical after the Santa Ana Planning Department bowed to pressure from local businessmen and closed a shelter run by the local YWCA. For more than a year that organization had sheltered many of the county's homeless women; as many as 40 women a night slept inside cars and on carpet squares in the parking lot of the building at 1411 N. Broadway.

But the complaints became too much for politically-motivated bureaucrats to bear. That's usually the case with shelters. People who otherwise would proclaim themselves open-minded do not want to take direct responsibility — and certainly not in their own neighborhood.

In this case, they pounced on bureaucratic regulations, saying the YWCA facilities did not qualify it for an occupancy permit. And the homeless were once again out on the street.

In any society there are the people who fall through the cracks. People who, despite their best efforts, are unable to find a job or hold one; people who have no friends or relatives to turn to for help. These are not the people who could do better but don't want to make the effort; these are the people whose best efforts are not enough.

Social-service agencies estimate there are about 4,000 homeless persons in Orange County, about 600 of them women living within 10 miles of the Santa Ana YWCA.

The success of the Women's Foundation, however, proves that there are people willing to take the responsibility to help each other. There are people — corporations — who, recognizing a need, are willing to meet it.

The fund raising was the first step. Now the foundation must acquire a residence and convince the neighbors to be tolerant. That will be no easy task, but the groundwork has been laid.

Detroit Free Press

Detroit, MI, November 13, 1984

ONE OF the more justifiable budget proposals to come down the Potomac recently was the request last week of the Legal Services Corp. for a budget boost from its present $275 million to $325 million in the next fiscal year. The request should carry all the more weight with Congress because it comes from a board of directors appointed by a president who has not been entirely sympathetic to the agency's mission over the years.

Legal Services has undergone a long period of assaults for its activism on behalf of the poor, for its sweeping class action suits, for its lack of deference to local politicians and its willingness to sue when they default on some statutory obligation to provide justice or social services for their low-income constituents. The California Legal Services office once enraged a fellow named Ronald Reagan by opposing him and winning in a case involving the rights of farm workers.

When Mr. Reagan got to Washington, he tried various ways to leash the corporation, including replacing its directors with his own appointees. The president was not alone in his ire. Legal Services had also irritated some congressmen who also wanted to curtail the agency's ability to bring class action suits and "political" suits, and eventually succeeded in some degree.

But the meat and potatoes of Legal Services has not been the controversial cases, but the job of providing legal representation to low-income persons in the homely but critical areas of everyday life — custody and other family disputes, landlord-tenant disputes, employment and consumer disputes, representation for people arbitrarily cut off from public assistance programs. Before the inception of Legal Services, too many poor people had all the rights they could pay for, which were few indeed; the normal avenue of civil redress or enforcement that the courts provide was too often closed to them.

In hundreds of communities, Legal Services has changed that. For all the controversy stirred up by a handful of its cases, for all its irreverence toward local politicians, Legal Services may be the most deeply conservative program ever conceived in Washington. It rests on the assumption that the protection and power of the law should be available to everyone, regardless of their income. It recognizes that people have respect for the law and trust in government only as much as justice seems to them to be universally available and applied. As Mr. Reagan's appointees have affirmed, it is worth every dollar it costs, and more.

The Philadelphia Inquirer

Philadelphia, PA, June 16, 1984

The shrill resignation of Philadelphia regional director Marttie L. Thompson, after 16 years with the Legal Services Corp., increases concern about the future of legal protection for the poor.

Last month, amid public charges of harassment, Mr. Thompson left LSC after more than six years as regional director. His parting language included such inflammatory words aimed at Reagan administration officials who guide the corporation as *secrecy, raids* and *silencing of employees.*

Mr. Thompson, who was in charge of 41 programs in Pennsylvania, New Jersey, Delaware, Maryland and the District of Columbia, asserted that government officials continue to have a negative effect on legal protections for the poor.

He said he resigned because "there was no place to turn. I guess I just couldn't take the abuse anymore. My staff was reduced from 11 to three — two secretaries and a training coordinator. It was becoming impossible to get very much done."

The Reagan administration has made numerous attempts to gut the program and, according to some LSC staffers, drive out those with long-term legal-services experience. That effort, Mr. Thompson asserted, included attempts by Reagan appointees to demean and harass those from previous administrations.

An LSC spokesman in Washington, John Buckley, denied the allegations and countered that officials are merely trying to end "abuses" permitted in the past.

Nevertheless, the LSC continues to suffer from both political and ideological differences with the Reagan administration. Such an atmosphere is hardly conducive to providing the poor with the legal assistance they often need and to which they are entitled.

If there's any hope that LSC can survive, it lies with a well-informed, determined group of supporters in Congress. Public hearings have helped somewhat but alone are not enough to stem the determined drive to eliminate the agency.

Mr. Thompson's resignation underscores the need for a thorough examination of all charges and counter-charges between LSC staff and those at the top. The continuing controversy surrounding LSC undermines legitimate efforts to provide legal assistance to those who otherwise could not afford it. The poor should not continue to be victimized by battles between lawyers who have made poverty law their life's work and those in Washington who seek — largely for political reasons — control of the corporation.

Mr. Reagan has a long, turbulent and personal history of opposition to the LSC that dates back to his days as governor of California.

Senate and House members who support LSC must press their efforts to stop the administration's attempts to destroy it. If a strong LSC program is to be saved, it must be done through protective language in the appropriations bill. That language is needed to shield the program from arbitrary defunding and to safeguard quality representation. In addition, Congress must scrutinize the backgrounds of all interim LSC appointees to make certain they meet statutory requirements, especially that they support the agency's concept mandated to protect the legal rights and interests of poor Americans.

ST. LOUIS POST-DISPATCH

St. Louis, MO, March 11, 1984

Despite repeated rebuffs from Congress, the Reagan administration is still trying to cripple the federal agency that provides funds for legal aid to the poor in noncriminal cases. A federal judge in Washington has now blocked the latest effort by Reagan appointees on the Legal Services Corp. to undermine legal aid. U.S. District Judge Barrington Parker has ordered the corporation to continue supporting four regional legal services training centers that the LSC was trying to shut down.

In December the four regional centers, which help train lawyers in legal services organizations, applied for renewed financing and were told by the corporation that their grants, amounting to about $600,000 last year, would not be renewed. In response to a suit by the four centers — in Massachusetts, Indiana, Arkansas and Colorado — Judge Parker said it was clear that Congress intended to safeguard financing of the centers; and he ordered the LSC to provide them with about the same monthly allotments they had received since 1981, plus a 14 percent increase over last year's levels, as approved by Congress.

The LSC rationale that the centers were intended to have one-time grants only and not annual funding was only the most recent of many devices employed by the administration to undermine legal services. Because of the hostility to legal services from Reagan LSC appointees, the corporation during all of Mr. Reagan's term has never had a full slate of board members confirmed by the Senate. With a judge having staved off the latest attack on legal services — at least until new members are confirmed — the Senate should, among other things, make a point of asking the nominees about their attitude toward the training centers.

THE SACRAMENTO BEE

Sacramento, CA, October 4, 1984

Once again, the Reagan administration is trying to undermine the legal services program, which is intended to provide top caliber legal representation to the poor. Past efforts have aimed, first, at shutting down the entire enterprise, then at curtailing the services of local programs, which offer street-level legal help. Now it is the national centers, which have played a major role in shaping poverty law over the past two decades, that are feeling the heat.

The primary mission of these centers has been to provide effective national representation, both in Congress and the courts, for legal services clients. Over the years, they have pushed for better educational opportunities, a fairer welfare system and decent treatment of the indigent aged. The centers have been effective — and there's the rub.

Under a proposed new Legal Services Corp. regulation, these national centers would be devastated. Only 10 percent of their grant funds could go for advocacy, including all courtroom representation and legislative lobbying. The rest of their funds are to be spent on training, communications and library research, and while all of these are creditable enough activities, none is likely to have much direct impact on the lives of the poor.

This 10 percent rule flies in the face of advice proffered in the past by a Ford administration task force and by the American Bar Association. Just last January, a federal court halted the implementation of an almost identical regulation, describing it as seemingly capricious. Yet here is the LSC board, which is supposed to embody respect for the law, flouting the law one more time.

Reagan Presents Fiscal '87 Budget Seeking Drastic Domestic Cuts

President Reagan Feb. 5, 1986 submitted to Congress a $994 billion fiscal 1987 federal budget. The budget proposed a substantial increase in defense spending while meeting the $144 billion deficit requirement of the 1985 Gramm-Rudman balanced-budget law. The administration proposed reducing the deficit through cutbacks and elimination of a wide variety of domestic programs, sale of existing federal operations and assets to private business, and increases in charges for federal services.

Overall, the 1987 Reagan budget proposed major increases in military spending and foreign aid, while many nonmilitary programs would be frozen at the 1986 level, severely cut, or eliminated outright. The cuts in spending would entail ending or sharply reducing about 40 major programs, including passenger rail subsidies, block grants for community services, loans for rural housing and student loans, and child nutrition programs.

Net spending on the Medicare health care program would be $4.6 billion less than projected under current law because of increased payments by health care recipients. The Medicaid program of health care for the poor would be cut about $1 billion.

Funds for Aid to Families with Dependent Children (AFDC) would be $8.44 billion under the Reagan fiscal 1987 budget. That was a 6.9% decrease from spending in fiscal 1986. The money would be saved by several means. Work requirements would be stricter, unmarried mothers would receive payments only if they lived with their parents, and payments would be denied to families whose youngest child had reached 16 years of age. The current cutoff age is 18.

The budget proposal requested a 3.7% cost-of-living increase for Supplemental Security Income (SSI), a system of payments to the old, blind and disabled. Program funds would rise $10.54 billion, with increased maximum monthly benefits for individuals and couples. Both SSI and AFDC were exempt from cuts mandated by the Gramm-Rudman Act.

THE LINCOLN STAR

Lincoln, NE, February 6, 1986

In meeting the deficit reduction demands of the Gramm-Rudman-Hollings bill, President Reagan has submitted to Congress a budget with devastating impact upon domestic spending. At the same time, he proposes defense spending that translates into a 12 percent hike from the current year.

The president has proposed development of a new plan of assistance for those whose life savings would be wiped out by catastrophic illness. But his budget calls for cuts in both Medicare (for the elderly) and for Medicaid (for the poor).

He calls for study of the welfare program to devise a plan that will lead people to financial independence but his budget would drastically reduce or totally eliminate many programs of assistance to the poor. You have to wonder whether his plan for improvement is little more than grease upon the wheels of completely eliminating assistance to the needy.

INCLUDED IN his budget is termination of the Legal Services Corp., maritime loan guarantees, Amtrak subsidies, the work-incentive program for welfare recipients, new housing for the elderly and handicapped, the Small Business Administration and the Economic Development Administration, all mass transit aid, the Interstate Commerce Commission, the Urban Development Action Grant program, the Appalachian Regional Commission, the Economic Development Administration and the Soil Stabilization and Conservation Service.

Among other things, Reagan's 1987 budget would substantially reduce funds for college student loans, aid to education, the Department of Agriculture, highway construction, the Environmental Protection Agency and assistance to local public health programs. Additionally, he would dispose of a variety of national assets, including major public power generation and transmission facilities, as a fiscal 1987 funding expediency.

DISDAINED BY the president has been any increase in taxes to help meet the demands of deficit reduction, although some observers believe he would sign an increased tax on oil.

Reagan is not motivated by strictly economic matters, but also is advancing major sociological and political changes. If he prevails during this and the following two years, he will have greatly altered the role of the federal government and the lives of virtually all citizens.

Again, it is essential that the public understand what it is Reagan seeks to do. The budget issues in Congress during coming months should be the basis of a national debate, not settled by any personal popularity rating.

The Record

Hackensack, NJ, February 7, 1986

In his proposed 1987 budget, President Reagan provides a glimpse of the future as it will look if Congress allows him to get his way. He would cut job-training funds by 14 percent, enlarging the pool of untrained American workers. Pollution-control reductions would lead to dirtier air and water. Intercity rail transport — Amtrak — would become an endangered species, and local subway and commuter-train fares would approach prohibitive levels. An 18 percent cut in agricultural expenditures would probably mean more turmoil in the depressed Farm Belt. Cutting child nutrition by 11 percent and welfare by 8 percent would mean still more children growing up ragged and underfed.

The president would boost the Pentagon's budget by 3 percent — which works out, once you adjust for inflation and some fancy bookkeeping, to an actual 12 percent increase in spending. In Mr. Reagan's vision of the future, then, defense contractors and the military brass would stay fat and sleek. Navy Secretary John F. Lehman Jr. would get his 600 ships, and Secretary of Defense Caspar Weinberger would get his antisatellite weapons, his mobile Midgetman nuclear missile, his Star Wars space shield, and even his Bradley Fighting Vehicle, the armored troop carrier with the tendency to burst into flame at the drop of a match.

Not to worry, though. We'll be able to leave all these earthbound problems by stepping into hydrogen-powered planes that take off from conventional airports, accelerate to 25 times the speed of sound, and sail off into space. Australia will be only a hop away. We'll reach the Moon in the time it now takes to fly to Tokyo.

But "the race to the future," to use the president's phrase, will not necessarily be won by the country with the most ships, guns, and space planes, but by the society with the healthiest, best-educated, and hardest-working population on the ground. A modern, productive society does not get ahead by widening the gap between rich and poor. Nor does it scrimp on health care, mass transit, education, or AIDS research (down 22 percent in the Reagan budget). It recognizes that these are important areas of investment in its human capital, the only resource of any long-term value. Mr. Reagan has shown us the future, and it doesn't work. His budget is not a plan for victory but a recipe for defeat.

The Houston Post

Houston, TX, February 6, 1986

Like the hangover after a gala party, President Reagan's fiscal 1987 budget greeted Congress Wednesday morning, hard on the heels of his upbeat State of the Union speech Tuesday night.

The nearly $1 trillion package contains more than $38 billion in deficit-reducing cuts. But that may not be enough to satisfy the provisions of the Gramm-Rudman-Hollings balanced-budget law, which limits the deficit to $144 billion in the next fiscal year, beginning Oct. 1. The new law, passed by Congress last year, requires that budgetary red ink be reduced from the current level of more than $200 billion to zero by 1991.

The president, to no one's surprise, did not recommend a tax increase. Nor did he propose cuts in Social Security benefits, which are exempt from Gramm-Rudman. But his budget did call for numerous domestic spending reductions; killing such agencies as Amtrak, the Small Business Administration and the Interstate Commerce Commission; and reducing funding for various social services, including Medicare and Medicaid.

At the same time, however, the president asked for a 3 percent after-inflation increase in defense spending that would push the Pentagon's budget to more than $311 billion next year. It included a substantial boost in funds for space defense programs.

President Reagan should be applauded for admonishing Congress not to knuckle under to special interests when tough decisions on spending cuts have to be made. He should be given bipartisan support in his efforts to eliminate "ineffective, duplicative or unnecessary" federal agencies and programs.

Unfortunately, the White House Office of Management and Budget has based some of its savings estimates on questionable accounting and on assumptions about economic growth that many economists consider overly optimistic. These are old budget-writers' tricks, but in this case they could spell trouble if Gramm-Rudman survives court tests and its mandated deficit cuts retain the force of law.

What is needed more than anything else now is for both the executive and legislative branches to practice truth in budgeting. It is the only way they and the nation can escape the arbitrary cuts of the Gramm-Rudman guillotine.

DAYTON DAILY NEWS

Dayton, OH, February 12, 1986

Fun with Figures, 1986: Chapter I.

Last week when the Reagan administration released its proposed budget for fiscal 1987, it said it was asking for a 3 percent increase in real defense spending. Press reports, on the other hand, used the figures 6 percent, 8 percent and 12 percent. A casual news watcher might have wondered what was going on.

Well, it turns out that the administration was using a higher figure for 1986 than others were. It was dealing with authorizations — which are expenditures Congress has voted for but not necessarily put up the money for.

If you look at what the Pentagon actually will *spend* in 1986 and at what the administration is asking for in expenditures for 1987, the increase it is seeking is 12 percent before inflation, 8 percent after.

The administration seems to be proceeding on defense as if Gramm-Rudman doesn't exist.

In his budget message, the President said, "We can hardly back away from our defense buildup without creating confusion among friends and adversaries about our determination to maintain our commitments and without jeopardizing our prospects for meaningful arms-control talks."

The part about arms control is dubious. During the buildup, more time has passed without arms-control progress than ever before since the 1950s. Moreover, in 1979 — right in the grip of America's alleged unilateral disarmament — the two superpowers forged an agreement that Mr. Reagan has found meaningful enough to abide by all these years.

But the statement is not entirely wrong. Some confusion might well result from a change in U.S. policy. But there is a price to be paid for any way of dealing with the deficit problem. Yet it must be dealt with.

The confusion can be minimized by keeping the defense policy moderate, by avoiding major cuts.

In the future, the way to avoid such confusion is to avoid the major fluctuations in defense spending that have characterized the past decade. When it undertook its wartime-like buildup in 1981, the administration knew it was exacerbating the deficit. It should have known that the brakes would have to be applied eventually and possibly abruptly.

Newsday

Long Island, NY, February 7, 1986

President Ronald Reagan's budget for the 1987 fiscal year is no less an exercise in optimism than his State of the Union message. In fact, its economic assumptions are optimistic beyond any realistic expectations.

To reach the $144-billion deficit target next year and the subsequent reductions mandated by the Gramm-Rudman law, the administration forecasts a decline in interest rates to 6.5 percent next year and 4 percent by 1991. Inflation is projected to rise slightly next year but drop to 2.1 percent by 1991. And the economy is supposed to grow by about 4 percent annually through 1988, although the gross national product increased by only a modest 2.3 percent last year.

Even with these anticipated economic blessings, Reagan's 1987 budget calls for outright elimination of many federal programs and deep cuts in most domestic spending except Social Security and interest on the national debt. All this is necessary if the president is to avoid a tax increase and sustain his military buildup.

Far from declining or even leveling off, the Pentagon's spending authority would rise by nearly 12 percent next year, to $311.6 billion. If funds for the Energy Department's production of nuclear weapons are included, the budget authority for defense would reach $320.3 billion.

This is what the president described Tuesday night as "the bare minimum."

But what about poor youngsters trying to go to college? Reagan's budget would end federal help for a million college students and further restrict loans for those still eligible. Aid to vocational education would virtually disappear. All in all, federal spending for education would drop by $2.6 billion this year and next.

The president spoke eloquently about the need for people to escape welfare dependency. But his budget calls for eliminating the Work Incentive Program that for 19 years has helped welfare recipients find work. The budget would cut the summer youth employment program by a third and the Job Corps by half.

Medicaid would be capped at a time when more than 30 million Americans are without health insurance and ineligible for Medicaid and when hospitals are increasingly unwilling to accept charity cases. Aid to Families with Dependent Children would be further restricted, as would food stamps and other nutrition programs for the poor.

The budget calls for a $1.2-billion increase to help friendly nations acquire "modern military equipment necessary for their defense," while proposing a 16 percent cut in funds for the United Nations and its agencies.

Members of Congress, including those in Reagan's own party, have been saying for months that his budget would be dead on arrival at the Capitol. The president, in turn, has been warning that any bill increasing taxes would be DOA at the White House.

It would be unconscionable for Congress to accept Reagan's blueprint. National security isn't just guns and space lasers and nuclear missiles; it's food and job training and education and health care for all Americans. And it's a government that won't try to live forever on borrowed money and rosy economic predictions.

AKRON BEACON JOURNAL
Akron, OH, February 8, 1986

WHY IS THE federal deficit important? Some figures released along with President Reagan's budget proposal show the magnitude of the deficit and its potential impact.

Mr. Reagan's 1987 budget plan designates $147.9 billion, 15 percent of all government spending, to pay the interest — the *interest* alone — on the federal debt. If charged directly to the American people, that would mean interest payments that would amount to an annual surcharge of almost $2,000 on every U.S. family — $619 for every man, woman and child. And even if those payments were made, it still wouldn't include retirement of the debt's principal.

To add more perspective, the money that goes to pay the interest is more than four times the amount that will go for all education and training programs, five times that of veterans aid, 39 times that for space exploration; an incredible 38 percent of all income tax paid by individuals will go toward interest payments.

The interest, like the national debt, has more than doubled during Mr. Reagan's time in office. The debt now stands at $1.96 *trillion*, and will top the $2 trillion mark this summer. Also rising will be interest costs, adding awesome financial burdens to future generations and limiting America's ability to respond in times of financial crisis.

That is why the deficit issue is serious and has to be dealt with, even through drastic measures such as tax increases. Tax and spend may not be the best policy. But borrow and spend is much worse, and much more damaging to the economy.

The Seattle Times

Seattle, WA, February 6, 1986

THE Puget Sound region and the Pacific Northwest must absorb their part of deficit-reduction pain along with the rest of the country. That should be Point No. 1 in reaction to the Reagan administration's 1987 budget, which would indeed deal hard lumps to this corner of the nation.

The most counterproductive reaction would be regional paranoia, as expressed by Rep. Ron Wyden, D-Ore., who blurted: "Everything this administration does is designed with a single purpose in mind — to get more money out of the Northwest."

The fairest and potentially most effective regional response would be to separate the proposed budget cuts that fit the logic of national sacrifice from those that are simply asinine.

A much-prized Seattle project, the Metro bus tunnel, might fit the former category — even though it long has had top priority among Urban Mass Transit Administration projects, and even though no small amount of resources have been expended in planning for the project. In any case, the tunnel should not be considered dead, only perhaps — in the worst eventuality — postponed.

But being prepared to absorb deficit-reduction pain does not mean that this region and its federal lawmakers should fail to resist ill-conceived and nonsensical proposals such as those aimed at the Export-Import Bank and the Bonneville Power Administration.

David Stockman may be gone from the Office of Management and Budget. But one of his truly embarrassing legacies lives on in the form of yet another administration proposal to abolish the Ex-Im Bank's direct-loan program. The program was dangerously reduced, but not killed, in this year's budget.

The proposal would cripple the overseas sales of The Boeing Co. and other U.S. manufacturers. It would be directly counter to efforts to reduce the massive national trade deficit. Those who view America's future role in world trade as an exporter of soybeans and logs — and little else — will support the administration's efforts to kill Ex-Im loans.

The attack on Bonneville would take the form of two pieces of legislation. One would sell BPA for $8.85 billion by Oct. 1, 1987. The other would revise BPA's repayment schedule (on Federal Columbia River Power System projects) pending the sale, to destroy the region's traditional low-cost power base.

An eventual sale of BPA to some sort of regional agency may not be a bad idea. But so massive an undertaking should require years of preparation. Booth Gardner and other Northwest governers are only just beginning to take a look at the possibilities.

Meanwhile, the administration proposal as it stands represents, in the words of Rep. Al Swift, D-Wash., a triumph of right-wing ideology over common sense.

To send BPA rates skyrocketing from one year to the next would amount to a repudiation of a half-century-old compact between the federal government and the Northwest. The effects on employment and the regional economy in general would be devastating and probably counterproductive even in terms of federal revenues.

In dealing with the administration's budget proposals, it will be the task of the Northwest congressional delegation to separate that which represents hard but necessary sacrifice from half-baked, destructive theory — and to focus their bipartisan efforts on roadblocking the latter.

DESERET NEWS

Salt Lake City, UT, February 15, 1986

President Reagan had better brace himself for a tough fight over the proposed new $994 billion budget for fiscal 1987 that he submitted Wednesday.

And he had better be prepared to do plenty of compromising — not just with Congress but with economic realities. No Reagan budget has ever emerged from Congress without major changes; this one certainly seems no exception.

That's because many of his usual supporters in Congress don't share the same set of priorities that shaped this first budget to be formulated under the Gramm-Rudman deficit-reduction law. Many of them would prefer to hike taxes and cut Pentagon fat rather than make deep cuts in a long list of domestic programs while increasing defense spending sharply and auctioning off a variety of federal assets.

Nor do many economists think the future will be nearly as rosy as the White House does. No matter who occupies the Oval Office, the President traditionally makes budgets that turn out to be too optimistic. But such optimism seldom goes quite as far as Mr. Reagan carries it in his latest budget.

For openers, the new budget assumes that the Gross National Product will grow 4% in both 1986 and 1987, a rate far higher than forecast by most economists. Their more modest expectations are more in line with an economy that grew by just 2.3% in 1985.

The White House sees no downturn on the economic horizon. Many private forecasters, however, believe another recession is inevitable. A cautious forecast is usually safer. After all, the current recovery already has lasted longer than the post-war average.

The new budget also is based on the assumption that inflation will be held down to 2% in 1991, unemployment will gradually decline from 6.9% to 5.6%, and short-term interest rates will be as low as 4% in 1991. If that actually happens, the economy will, by the White House's own admission, have undergone the longest period of uninterrupted growth ever on record. Does the White House know something the rest of the country doesn't? Or is it just whistling in the dark?

Then there are the political assumptions underlying the new budget. In essence, the White House is assuming that Congress will change its spots.

Specifically, the President is asking the lawmakers to cut nearly every program serving the poor and eliminate 14. Among the programs to be terminated are housing assistance, emergency food and shelter programs, legal services for the poor, and the Work Incentive Program that provides job training for welfare recipients.

Also to be ended are the Interstate Commerce Commission, the Small Business Administration, Amtrak, the new GI Bill, and dozens of other programs.

Of the programs to continue with reductions, Medicaid would take the largest cut — $1.4 billion. Benefit levels also would be reduced for recipients of food stamps, Aid to Families with Dependent Children, and child nutrition programs.

Logically, many of these programs should indeed be slashed or eliminated. But this is virtually the same "hit list" that President Reagan presented to Congress a year ago — without any success.

Another major thrust of the new Reagan budget is something called "privatization." That term refers to the sale of a variety of federal assets and properties. Among them are the Bonneville, Alaska, Southeastern, Southwestern, and Western Area power marketing administrations, federally-owned oil fields in California and Wyoming, plus various outstanding government loans that would be sold to financial institutions at a discount.

Again, the President is right in wanting to make the government leaner by getting it out of competition with private business. But it would mean higher utility bills for many Americans instead of a tax increase. And it's hard to believe Congress can deal with such a complex and controversial new initiative by April 15 — the ostensible deadline for completing work on the budget — or even by next fall.

The new budget proposed Wednesday is only the opening round in the effort to balance the budget by 1991. With less and less fat to trim, each successive round is bound to become much more painful — particularly when the economy turns sour.

THE DAILY OKLAHOMAN
Oklahoma City, OK, February 14, 1986

WITH so much of the news focused on President Reagan's proposed cuts in various domestic programs while boosting outlays for defense, one obvious target for the budgetary ax is being overlooked.

It is the category of foreign aid, that hardy perennial that blooms in the budget every year despite repeated efforts to reduce it or eliminate it entirely.

At a time when both the administration and Congress are under the gun to start whacking the awesome federal deficit, foreign aid not only escaped pruning in the president's budget but is targeted for an increase into the $12-billion range. That will be hard if not impossible to sell in Congress, and deservedly so.

A certain amount of foreign aid, especially assistance to traditional allies and friends, is a budgetary fixture that will remain indefinitely. For example, our national interest is served by whatever help we can spare to those who are resisting communist aggression or subversion, such as the contras in Nicaragua and the Afghan freedom fighters.

But to suggest increasing the total foreign aid outlay when so many otherwise worthwhile domestic programs are slated for major reductions is inconceivable. We cannot continue to help others until we first help ourselves.

The Philadelphia Inquirer
Philadelphia, PA, February 7, 1986

President Reagan's speeches don't reveal his true vision of America. His budget does. Any chief executive's budget is a dollar-by-dollar blueprint of the society that he's trying to sculpt. Mr. Reagan's budgetary blueprint outlines a vision of America as a military state bristling with weapons — and little else. The overwhelming mission of the federal government, Mr. Reagan insists, is to invest the nation's treasure in machines of defense and destruction. He would sacrifice all other claims on the shared funds of citizens to the overbuilding of an enormous arsenal of weapons.

Do you think that vision is overstated? Look at his proposed budget for the next fiscal year. Military spending would rise — again — by 12 percent, and by 42 percent over the next five years. Federal spending on scientific research would leap 16 percent — but the increase would go only for military research; health research would decline. Spending on foreign aid would increase too, by $1.5 billion — $1.2 billion on military equipment.

But Mr. Reagan insists that this nation can't afford Amtrak. Or mass transit. Or student loans. Or any of several job-training programs. He would gut them all. He would slash money for pollution control, for aid to cities, to farmers, to the poor. Virtually every domestic service that has received financial support from the federal government would end or be greatly reduced if Mr. Reagan gets his way. America has no money for such things, he maintains, not in this era of a huge, mounting national debt — a debt that accumulated over 200 years, incidentally, before doubling during the first five years of Mr. Reagan's presidency.

•

The budget Mr. Reagan submitted to Congress on Wednesday is as flatly unacceptable as the vision of America that it portrays. Fortunately Congress seems to understand that. Congress has fought him to a draw on budget priorities in each of the past four years by running $200 billion deficits, but this year is different. This is the year of Gramm-Rudman-Hollings.

That law, enacted last year, limits next year's budget deficit to not more than $144 billion. Either the President and Congress agree on a budget meeting that limit, or in October Gramm-Rudman-Hollings imposes automatic across-the-board spending cuts on both military and domestic programs. Even the law's sponsors concede that such penny-wise-pound-foolish chopping at government programs is irresponsible, but it forces decision. Either Congress and the President compromise, or Gramm-Rudman-Hollings' ax will fall. Assuming the courts don't invalidate it, one way or the other the law will break the stalemate.

•

President Reagan is counting on the law's pressures and the fall elections to enable him to prevail in this struggle over budget priorities. Majorities of both parties and houses of Congress hope to draft an alternative budget that balances the nation's needs while meeting Gramm-Rudman-Hollings' limit. What's obviously needed, all agree, is a grand compromise, imposing balanced cuts on both military and domestic programs and, unavoidably, including a tax increase. Unfortunately it also requires President Reagan's approval before it can fly.

His vow to veto any tax increase freezes bargaining. Fear that Mr. Reagan would blast members of Congress as they seek re-election prevents most of them from taking the lead toward raising taxes. Fear of justified voter anger over lost federal services stops them from accepting Mr. Reagan's budget. A bipartisan coalition of senators threatens to freeze progress on income tax reform until Mr. Reagan compromises on the budget. That's a regrettably useful tactic worth pursuing. Meanwhile public opinion must be mobilized against Mr. Reagan's militarist vision of America.

As irresponsible as Gramm-Rudman-Hollings' blind budget cuts would be, at least they would force equal sacrifices on both military and civilian spending. The public and Congress must convince Mr. Reagan that his budget is simply not an option.

The Star-Ledger
Newark, NJ, February 7, 1986

Measured strictly on the basis of its bottom line, the President's new budget is right on target—a fiscal bull's-eye. But measured by another yardstick—the balance between spending for domestic and military programs—the Reagan Administration's budget of nearly a trillion dollars is way off the mark.

As he promised, Mr. Reagan has come up with a spending plan for the upcoming fiscal year that fully meets the demanding budget-balancing requirements of the Gramm-Rudman law. But, in meeting the initial test of the new constraints, the President has come down harshly on social programs, while asking for an increase in military outlays.

Although the Administration's deep cuts in the domestic sector are certain to arouse strong opposition in Congress, particularly in the Democratic House, they are consistent with White House budget policy, which is tilted toward a defense buildup.

Nevertheless, the sweeping cuts in health, housing and other domestic areas are much deeper and far more harmful than previous Reagan cutbacks and would have a devastating impact on state and local government.

And they no doubt will be even harder to accept on Capitol Hill in light of the President's request for a substantial increase in defense appropriations. That request could be a stalking horse, a budgetary ploy by the Administration. It is doubtful that Mr. Reagan is really counting on getting all of the money he has proposed for the defense sector. But if he gets half, or even less, of the increase he is seeking, he can count it a victory.

The President's spending proposals are the first round in the battle of the budget; the second round, in Congress, will be far more rigorous. The legislative branch may be deeply unhappy with the Reagan budget proposals, but it must meet the same challenge of producing a balanced budget.

Without question, the numbers will be greatly changed in the congressional version, but the bottom line will remain the same. Substantial savings must be found in this trying new era. Enormous record deficits have made budget-balancing efforts a necessity.

Large-scale cutbacks are painful, affecting disparate elements of our society. At this crucial stage, they can no longer be rationally deferred, as they have been too often in the past. But it is vital that fiscal sacrifices be imposed equitably, and that social concerns not be forgotten in dealing with the deficit burden.

Bowen Drops Plan to Cut Benefits

Dr. Otis R. Bowen, secretary of health and human services, Oct. 16, 1987 said he was issuing an administrative order to prevent the Social Security Administration from implementing a new policy, disclosed that day in the *New York Times*, that would have reduced welfare benefits under the Supplemental Security Income (SSI) Program. Some 4.3 million elderly, blind and disabled Americans with little or no income from other sources received funds under the program.

The new policy would have reduced benefits for SSI recipients who received free food, clothing and other non-cash assistance from churches and charitable organizations. Each SSI recipient would have been required to report all such aid to his case worker, who would have estimated its dollar value and reduced the client's monthly benefit by all but $20 of that amount.

According to the *Times*, the new policy had taken effect without public announcement Oct. 1 after having been declared in a confidential "emergency instruction" to Social Security field offices in September 1987. The policy had been adopted, Reagan administration officials said, because Congress had failed to extend a law exempting charitable aid from the computation of welfare benefits. The exemption had first been adopted, with bipartisan support, in 1983, and had been extended by Congress in 1984. It had expired Sept. 30, 1987.

Joseph R. Wright, deputy director of the Office of Management and Budget, Oct. 16 said Congress was to blame "for letting the law lapse. Members of Congress are the only ones who can pass a law. The President can't pass a law," Wright commented. He said that Bowen's administrative order effectively extended the exemption for six months. The order had been issued after the Reagan administration had come under a barrage of criticism for adopting the new policy, which Bowen himself was reported not to have known about until Oct. 16.

Members of Congress had not known of the new policy either at the time it went into effect, according to Sen. Daniel Patrick Moynihan (D, N.Y.), chairman of the Finance Committee panel on Social Security programs. Moynihan Oct. 16 said the new policy had been adopted "in the dark of the night" and termed it "sneaky, mean and contemptible."

Legislation that would permanently exempt charitable gifts from the computation of SSI benefits was pending in Congress but had become entangled with other issues. Moynihan Oct. 16 introduced a separate bill to protect SSI recipients.

The Washington Post

Washington, DC, July 5, 1987

EVERYONE WAS delighted when Congress and the president "solved" the Social Security problem in 1983, putting the system back on a supposedly sound financial footing. Now it turns out that the solution itself has problems. The Social Security system may not end up that much better off than before, and the government in general could end up worse off.

The plan made perfect sense at the time. The idea was to increase future taxes while moderating benefits to produce a giant surplus in the trust funds while the baby boomers were still in the work force. The surplus would then be drawn down in the next century to support the boomers when they retired.

That would be fine if Social Security were the great savings account in the sky that people think it is. But contrary to the mythology so assiduously built up over the years, it is much more a pay-as-you-go operation. The trust funds are merely accounting devices; there is no real accumulation of funds. Social Security dollars are not kept apart. They merge indistinguishably with all the others that flow into and out of the Treasury each year.

Social Security revenues are currently greater than costs. The extra dollars are simply being used to help finance other government programs. In that sense there is a form of double-counting going on. The same dollar is being counted on to support the future Social Security program and to reduce the current deficit. When the boomers do start to retire, the government will still have to 1) dig up more revenue to help pay their Social Security benefits; or 2) cut the non-Social Security programs the surplus Social Security revenues are now sustaining. There continues to be a crunch in the future. In the meantime, the regressive Social Security tax is also playing a larger role than before in federal finance. It is helping to pay for defense and the rest of general government as well as Social Security, and in that sense supplanting the progressive income tax.

The problem will become worse as the 1983 plan takes full effect. The "surplus" will grow to an estimated $12.7 trillion by the year 2030; that is $2.2 trillion in current dollars. But the government currently has no way to put such a sum in a genuine reserve—to "save" it, in the conventional, retrievable sense. Nor is it entirely clear that the political system could ever muster the will to do so; the temptation of that much candy in the candy jar would be too great. What to do?

Nothing while the deficit remains so large; the first goal of policy has to be to get it down. Then two possibilities occur. One would be to keep collecting the surplus Social Security taxes but create a serious savings mechanism through which the government could invest in items other than its own securities. The other would be to ease the tax rate until the boomers are much closer to retirement, stop using Social Security to mask so much of the deficit and force the rest of government back on the taxes on which it belongs. Either way would be better than what we are doing now, which is fooling ourselves.

FORT WORTH STAR-TELEGRAM

Fort Worth, TX, June 29, 1987

Nationally syndicated columnist Jack Anderson recently chastised James Roosevelt for invoking the name of his father, the late President Franklin D. Roosevelt, to beg for contributions from Social Security recipients in behalf of something called the National Committee to Preserve Social Security.

Roosevelt richly deserved the harsh words, and Anderson is not alone in his criticism of Roosevelt's activities. Dorcas R. Hardy, the commissioner of Social Security, has not only taken Roosevelt to task but has also issued a warning to the public about "misleading and deceptive mail solicitations directed at the elderly and disabled."

Roosevelt's mailings are made to look as if they are official government documents, and they warn of dire consequences for Social Security recipients unless they contribute money to enable the committee to lobby against so-called "destructive changes" in the Social Security law.

Actually, Roosevelt's committee has no government sanction. The same is true of similar organizations, such as the Social Security Protection Bureau, which guarantees a valuable "mystery gift" to people sending $7 for membership, and National Network Inc., which promises a "complete copy of your Social Security deposit record" for $9.50.

Actually, these groups are nothing but direct-mail peddlers, preying on the fears of the elderly. Their official-looking documents should be regarded as what they are — junk mail — and should be treated accordingly.

Richmond Times-Dispatch
Richmond, VA, September 28, 1987

Every so often, it seems, Congress faces a Social Security "crisis" that requires a payroll tax increase or two or three to stave off the program's looming insolvency. Such was the case in 1977 when Congress passed legislation to raise payroll taxes in 1978, 1979, 1981 and 1982. When 1982 arrived, however, Congress argued that the nation's workers and employers still weren't doing enough to save the system. So up went payroll taxes again in 1984, 1985 and 1986.

Additional increases are scheduled for next year and for 1990, by which time the total employee-employer payroll tax will have reached 15.3 percent compared with 11.7 percent in 1977. American workers and employers must be wondering where and when it will all end. The answer is that without some reform of Social Security, it may not.

In the short term, it's true, Social Security could well run a surplus resulting from two factors: continued economic growth in the 1990s and the movement of the enormous Baby Boom generation into its prime work years. Both are expected to push up Social Security tax revenues. Meanwhile a smaller group born during the Great Depression and World War II will begin entering retirement in the next decade, claiming far less of the Social Security funds than the Baby Boomers will be putting in.

But all that is expected to change after the turn of the century, when the Baby Boomers begin to leave the work force, the surplus dwindles and the smaller generation that follows is stuck with the bill for their retirement benefits. That bill, says Heritage Foundation analyst Peter Ferrara, could mean payroll tax rates of anywhere between 23 percent and 35 percent.

Ironically, the payroll tax increases in 1988 and 1990 may only speed up the day when the Social Security system runs out of money because of their depressing effect on U.S. economic growth. Estimated to cost workers and employers some $25 billion, the upcoming payroll tax hikes will discourage companies from hiring workers and workers from seeking jobs, says Mr. Ferrara. Moreover, both American workers and companies would be at a competitive disadvantage with foreigners unburdened by such costs. The lower U.S. economic growth that could result would also reduce payroll tax revenues and thus bring on the next Social Security shortfall sooner than expected.

Ultimately, says Mr. Ferrara, the United States ought to consider some private-sector alternatives to Social Security, income tax credits for contributions to private savings and insurance accounts, for example. But more and more payroll tax increases won't help in the meantime, he says. Recent history, we think, supports his claim.

THE PLAIN DEALER
Cleveland, OH, November 26, 1987

For political candidates, Social Security is a rug waiting to be pulled from under their feet. Those foolhardy enough to propose cutting or taxing benefits will run afoul of one of the country's most vociferous and best-organized lobbies. They can count on hearing from such spokesmen as James Roosevelt of the National Committee to Preserve Social Security and Medicare who declared recently: "We're serving notice that those who attempt to balance the budget on the backs of America's seniors do so at their own political peril."

In the context, Roosevelt was right to be indignant. He was commenting on a proposal by some budget-cutters to cut cost-of-living increases due Social Security beneficiaries. As Roosevelt said, in view of the fact that the Social Security trust fund is self-sustaining, such a step would be an "accounting illusion."

But in a broader sense, the fact that members of Congress, with an election year around the corner, had the temerity even to suggest a modest curtailment of Social Security benefits is significant. It means that, gradually, legislators are showing themselves willing to question the inviolability of Social Security payments and perhaps even the very existence of government-administered old-age insurance.

Such heresy even has been introduced into the presidential campaign by Republican candidates Pete du Pont and Pat Robertson. According to the New York Times, both favor phasing in a private pension scheme to replace Social Security. Du Pont and Robertson, as well as other critics of Social Security, believe that when the baby boom population retires,

the existing plan will be inadequately funded and massive tax increases will be required.

The Times report pointed out the evident foolhardiness of the two candidates' adopting revolutionary positions on the issue, thus inviting the fury of current and soon-to-be beneficiaries and their lobbyists. One issue guaranteed not to get intelligent, balanced, unemotional consideration is Social Security reform if the very concept of a government plan is called into question.

Four years ago, a bipartisan commission labored to remedy flaws in the system so that the Social Security fund will remain solvent into the early part of the next century. Critics, however, contend that a financial collapse was only delayed and that an opportunity was missed to revolutionize the whole concept of old-age insurance.

It is inevitable that younger persons will begin to question the fairness and soundness of Social Security. Already, sentiment is growing that well-off recipients should pay taxes on their Social Security benefits, an unthinkable idea not so long ago. It can't be long before young workers begin to ask if there isn't a better system.

What must be avoided is inter-generational warfare. Proposals for reform should be given mature consideration, not automatically rejected as cruel attacks on the elderly. Nobody is suggesting that retired Americans should be abandoned. But if politicians continue to shelter behind the conventional wisdom that Social Security reform is taboo, they might find that they have lost control of the issue—to their cost.

THE TENNESSEAN
Nashville, TN,
July 20, 1987

THE Social Security Administration has begun a process of medical re-evaluations which could partially right a great wrong which may have been done to some disabled Tennesseans.

The Reagan administration began a purge of Social Security disability rolls soon after it entered office in 1981. It believed that government payments were going to many people who just pretended a disability and did not deserve the money. So the government spent millions of dollars to hire consultants and physicians to find the deadbeats and get them off the rolls.

No doubt some undeserving people were receiving government payments. But it soon became clear that many genuinely disabled people were being cut off the rolls. People who obviously could not work were stripped of their benefits and left with no money to live on. Many well-publicized cases involved people with terminal diseases who were cut off and left to die without money to pay for their food and shelter.

The Social Security purge became a national disgrace until the federal courts began to step in. Federal District Judge Robert McRae Jr. of Memphis ruled last August that the government's disability evaluators in Tennessee did not give enough consideration to opinions of the personal physicians of those who were seeking Social Security payments. Too much reliance was being put on the diagnoses of doctors the Social Security Administration had asked to do the re-evaluations.

Last March Judge McRae ordered that all disability claimants in the state between 1982 and 1986 be asked to reapply and be given a new medical evaluation. This includes those who were denied benefits initially as well as those who were receiving benefits during the 1982-86 period and had them cut off. Letters have been sent to about 70,000 Tennesseans in that category by the Social Security regional office in Atlanta.

The court order for medical re-evaluations should make the public feel more confident that disabled people will get the assistance they are entitled to have.

A spokesman for the Social Security administration said each case would be evaluated individually. "In fairness to people who pay Social Security, we have to make sure all decisions are equitable," he said.

That is what the public expects. The people don't want deadbeats on the Social Security disability rolls. But neither do they want deserving people cut off because the Reagan administration wants the money for something else. ■

The Morning News

Wilmington, DE, December 3, 1987

IMAGINE you are 66 years old, a widow, living on $6,000 in Social Security benefits and some money you earn in a part-time job. Imagine further that you have the opportunity to convert your part-time job to full-time and you could be making $11,000 a year.

Sounds great, until you remember that under present Social Security rules a pensioner cannot earn more than $8,160 a year without having to give up part of the Social Security benefits. You would lose some $1,400 in Social Security benefits and would at the same time also have to pay Social Security and income taxes on your earnings. A quick calculation shows that a full-time job does not leave you with much extra income over the part-time one. So why work full time?

That kind of work disincentive in the present Social Security system makes little sense. It deprives society of skilled workers who can still make a significant contribution to our economy. It also means that the Social Security trust fund as well as state and federal treasuries lose out on taxes they might collect from these workers.

In short, nobody is helped by this Social Security regulation.

Nor is the regulation equitable. The same 66-year-old widow, or any other Social Security beneficiary, can be receiving thousands of dollars in interest on savings and investments and in pensions from a pre-retirement employer without being docked a single penny in Social Security benefits.

Fortunately, there is pressure within the Reagan administration to abolish this counterproductive Social Security regulation. Otis R. Bowen, secretary of Health and Human Services, is urging the change. There is strong sentiment in Congress, among liberals and conservatives, to abolish this outdated rule. And the nation's elderly — a potent political force — would like to see it thrown out too.

So where is the holdup?

When the change is first implemented, the Social Security Trust fund would have to pay out more to those folks who previously gave up some benefits in order to earn more money. But that shortfall would be for a brief time only. As more persons take on well-paying jobs in retirement, they would contribute more in Social Security taxes. Besides, the trust fund is currently in good enough shape to afford this short-term drain for the sake of long-range equity.

Furthermore, there is no need to change the rules abruptly. The limit on earnings can be removed gradually, say over five years. A phase-in would work well, especially since for those 70 years old and older, there is no earnings limit anyway.

Congress has too much on its plate already for the last few weeks of the current session. But this change in Social Security regulations should be done early in the next session. It is not only a desirable change, but it is also politically attractive. What more can one ask in an election year?

MILWAUKEE SENTINEL

Milwaukee, WI, November 30, 1987

Pending congressional legislation may, in fact, reduce the federal deficit by the promised $76 billion over the next two years but it is hardly a road map to legitimate fiscal reform.

That was swept under the rug when President Reagan swept "off the table" any movement to reduce the cost of Social Security and most other "entitlement" programs.

And, in Reagan's defense, had he proposed such an effort he probably only would have succeeded in making heroes of the lawmakers who righteously refused to go along with him.

The plain fact is that the growth in that segment of the population that is in or near retirement makes such reform nearly unlikely in the present climate.

As Milwaukee Sentinel columnist George F. Will has said, it seems that a democratically elected government simply cannot bring itself to address this problem.

But Peter Peterson, a former secretary of Commerce, recently repeated the truism that the deficit problem will not go away until this problem is solved.

"I do not know of a serious student of the budget ... who believes you can possibly solve the long-term budget problem without reforming entitlements," he said.

At the root of this problem is the fact that the number of employed people paying into the Social Security fund is dwindling while the elderly population grows. This is significant because, although it is widely believed that Social Security is financed by investments on accumulated payments into the system, the truth is that funding for retirement programs is essentially a matter of today's workers providing for today's retirees.

In any case, there are remedies that are palatable.

Foremost among them should be some sort of means test for Medicare, the most debt-ridden part of the Social Security system, coupled with a tax deductible individual retirement account that pays premiums for post-retirement health insurance supplements.

And a formula should be devised to shift revenues going to upper-income retirees in good health toward providing expanded care for those in nursing homes whether they are depleting their own resources for such needs or are being underwritten by federal programs.

Such reform would not only aid in the quest for a balanced budget but, in the process, address the major challenge involved in meeting responsibilities to the nation's elderly in the future.

The Houston Post

Houston, TX, December 7, 1987

Removing the outside earnings limit beyond which people 65 to 69 years old begin losing Social Security benefits is an idea that is overdue. The proposal, sent to President Reagan by Health and Human Services Secretary Otis Bowen and Social Security Commissioner Dorcas Hardy, makes good economic sense.

The earnings-limit law is unreasonable and unfair. This year, for example, a person 65 to 69 receiving a typical Social Security benefit of $6,000 loses $1 of it for every $2 earned in wages over $8,160. The prospect of such a loss can discourage retirees in this age bracket from doing outside work and deprive the economy of their experience, skills and productivity.

Social Security pensioners over 70 have no earnings limit beyond which they are, in effect, penalized by loss of benefits. Nor does the law apply to income from such sources as private pensions, capital gains, or interest and dividends. Voiding it would save the government $200 million a year it now spends giving earnings tests.

Bowen estimates that dropping the earnings limit would cost the Treasury $7.5 billion over the next five years. But he says that in the long run it would generate more federal revenue as affected pensioners paid taxes on a higher volume of earnings. Equity and common sense demand that this disincentive to work be scrapped.

TULSA WORLD

Tulsa, OK, December 7, 1987

AMERICA'S population is aging, and the cost of caring for the elderly will become an ever more onerous taxpayer burden. New strategies are needed.

Adult day care is a promising example. Adult day-care centers offer exercise, amusements and medical attention for elderly people who because of mental or physical problems cannot care for themselves. Everyone involved in adult day care wins: Seniors who might otherwise be shut-ins or hospitalized lead richer, more rewarding lives; so-called "primary care givers" — working children or spouses who might themselves be in ill health — get some respite, up to eight hours a day, from the task of caring for their loved ones.

Tulsa has two adult day-care centers; there are five others in Oklahoma. Except for some meager state funds — $150,000 last year — they are privately supported and thus not available to all who might benefit from them.

Now, according to the New York Times, the Veterans Administration has funded pilot adult day-care programs at 15 veterans' centers. The programs have demonstrated that they can provide day care for infirm veterans who otherwise would be in hospitals or nursing homes, men who suffer from Alzheimer's disease, cancer, blindness, heart failure and stroke. What's more, because they do not provide round-the-clock care, they cost a fraction of hospital or skilled nursing home care.

Talk of expanding entitlements now might seem foolish. Social Security, Medicare and other entitlements already are a huge burden on taxpayers. But it may be shown that spending money on adult day care will result in a marked savings from more expensive care. One way or the other, something must be done in coming years to deal with the growing problem of caring for the elderly.

The Register

Santa Ana, CA, November 22, 1987

It is still supposed to be part of the conventional wisdom that messing with Social Security is a surefire formula for political suicide. President Reagan, having been mildly burned a couple of times, has declared the system sacrosanct and off-limits in the current discussions of how to handle the federal budget deficit, although some Congressional Democrats are flirting with the idea of postponing benefit increases. Nonetheless, somebody should be willing to speak frankly.

The Social Security program is still what it has always been: a straightforward intergenerational transfer program. There is no "trust fund"; bookkeeping surpluses constitute an invitation to increase benefits and buy votes now. Social Security is the government's biggest transfer program, and a significant drain on U.S. competitiveness in the world marketplace. These facts will become increasingly important and apparent if two new increases in Social Security taxes, scheduled to kick in next year and in 1990, are not canceled. Frank discussion of the regressive nature of these tax increases may lead to a broader discussion of the system as a whole.

Every few years Congress has to "save" Social Security. In 1977 and 1983, Congress managed the enormously creative and innovative task of — raising taxes. Under those laws, payroll taxes are scheduled to increase automatically in 1988 and 1990, reaching a total of a 15.3 percent burden on workers and employers. Yet today's burden of 14.3 percent is already too high, destroying jobs, driving up labor costs, placing a disproportionate burden on workers with lower incomes, and undermining U.S. competitiveness.

The higher taxes are supposed to be building up a reserve to cover the time when the "baby boomer" generation begins to retire, about 2020. Because the boomers are working now, the system's solvency is not seriously threatened until then. But after the boomers start retiring, Social Security will face insolvency within a few years unless more thoroughgoing, privatization-oriented reforms are instituted soon. Meanwhile, higher taxes threaten the continued economic growth that is the best hope for retirement security.

Social Security is a tax on employment. It discourages employers from hiring and discourages workers from accepting jobs. The scheduled payroll-tax increases will increase the drag the system exerts on the economy by $25 billion per year. That's the last thing we need in an increasingly competitive global economy.

In the long run, the best hope for retirement security for today's baby boomers — aside from payroll-tax rates of 23 to 35 percent from about 2025 on — lies in the private sector. Proposals exist to grant income tax credits for worker and employee contributions to savings and medical insurance accounts, which would relieve the burden on the Social Security system and give today's young workers a better return on their money than they could ever get from Social Security.

Another way to relieve the Social Security spending burden would be to adjust benefits to the affluent. Although today's young workers will never get back all they're forced to pay in, current retirees (who paid low rates for many years) still get back all they've put in, plus compounded interest, within a couple of years of retirement. Why not stipulate that those above a certain income level will get back only their own contributions plus compounded interest — leaving more in the system for those for whom Social Security is their only or primary source of retirement income?

In the wake of the uncertainty engendered by the stock market crash, the U.S. economy can ill afford new blows. Letting the higher Social Security taxes kick in as scheduled will deter job creation and economic growth. They should be cancelled — as a first step in a more thorough overhaul of the entire system.

DESERET NEWS

Salt Lake City, UT,
December 14/15, 1987

One of the weaknesses of the U.S. economy is the failure of Americans to put away much in the way of savings. The U.S. ranks far behind most other nations in this regard. Yet the Internal Revenue Service seems to go out of its way to discourage thrift.

Under new IRS rules, any person who turns 70 plus six months must make a minimum withdrawal from his or her Individual Retirement Account. If such a withdrawal isn't made from an IRA, the penalty can be 50 percent of what should have been withdrawn. That's not a tax, it's wholesale confiscation.

In addition to the forced withdrawal, figuring what the minimum withdrawal will be a headache. A taxpayer has to calculate the minimum based on his or her life expectancy, or the life expectancy of the taxpayer and his or her spouse. Another way is to take a flat percentage. Either way, it has to be refigured every year.

The whole idea behind the IRA law was to encourage saving for one's old age. But once having reached those golden years, those prudent enough to have built up an IRA, find themselves threatened by their own government.

It's almost enough to give saving a bad name.

the Charleston Gazette

Charleston, WVA, December 11, 1987

WHEN asked, most Americans say they believe it's necessary to bring down the massive federal budget deficits. More to the point, they're willing to take on their share of the burden to reduce government spending — provided everybody else does, too.

But, when it comes to specifics, those attitudes change considerably. A recent New York Times/CBS News poll shows that, far from wanting to reduce the welfare state, Americans want more of it — while at the same time, they refuse to foot the bill.

By a margin of more than 3-to-1, respondents to the survey said the Social Security system should maintain the cost-of-living allowance, although everyone agrees that COLAs are among culprits responsible for boosting deficits through the ceiling.

The same ratio of Americans think it is a responsibility of government to "see to it that everyone who wants a job has a job." By an even higher proportion (4-to-1), the respondents said Washington has a responsibility to "guarantee medical care for all people." The ratio drops to 2-to-1 — still a majority, though — of those who support government-sponsored day care for children.

Yet, by exactly the same 2-to-1 scale, these supposedly thinking Americans also oppose increasing federal taxes to pay for these programs. Above all, support for a constitutional amendment requiring a balanced federal budget won favor by a margin of 5-to-1.

The hypocrisy manifest in this poll is as galling as it is unsurprising. When it comes to the programs and services provided by government, the watchword among Americans seems to be, "What's mine is mine; what's yours is cutable."

Governors Back Welfare Work Plan; Senate Moves Toward Welfare Reform

The National Governors Association Feb. 21-24, 1987 held its winter conference in Washington, D.C. The key issue taken up at the conference was welfare reform. With only one dissenting vote—that of freshman Gov. Tommy Thompson (R) of Wisconsin—the governors Feb. 24 endorsed an ambitious plan to overhaul the welfare system, emphasizing job training and work requirement for those receiving aid.

Three key parts of the plan ultimately endorsed by the governors were as follows:

■ A "flexible state-designed work program which accommodates remedial education, training and job placement and experience" for participants in Aid to Families with Dependent Children (AFDC), the country's largest welfare program, which was financed by the state and federal governments.

■ "A requirement that all recipients of cash assistance with children aged three or more participate in a work program."

■ "A binding contractual agreement between the recipient and the government which lays out mutual obligations—the client to strive for self-sufficiency and the government to provide adequate support services for a designated period of time as the client moves toward economic dependence."

President Ronald Reagan Feb. 23 told the nation's governors that he endorsed the three key provisions of their plan. The President, however, declined to endorse another provision that would have eventually established a national minimum standard of payments to the poor, adjusted for regional differences in the cost of living. Reagan reportedly also did not discuss the $1 billion or more in federal funding that the governors estimated would be needed for their first year of the plan.

The President's lack of support for a national minimum standard prompted the governors to modify that aspect of their plan to provide that any national standard intended to raise savings be made by reducing the welfare rolls under the work provision.

The U.S. Senate April 2, 1987 overwhelmingly approved legislation hailed by some as the first step toward a complete overhaul of the nation's welfare system.

By a 99-0 vote, the Senate passed a bill amending the Job Training Partnership Act. The bill would authorize bonus payments to states that developed and implemented programs to move long-term welfare recipients into private-sector jobs. The bonuses would average an estimated $3,700 per person over three years. They would be paid from savings to the U.S. government resulting from a reduced welfare caseload.

The bill would also amend the act to redirect funds earmarked for summer jobs for disadvantaged youth. States could use the funds instead to provide year-round training programs for recipients of AFDC, the main federal-state welfare program, and Supplemental Security Income (SSI), the federal welfare program for the aged, blind and disabled.

The Washington Post

Washington, DC, February 17, 1987

AT THE HEIGHT of his power in 1982, President Reagan made an ambitious "New Federalism" proposal to realign the responsibilities and programs of the federal government and the states. The proposal died, in part because it turned out to be a sham. Programs were not so much being shifted from one level of government to another as—in the guise of such a shift—they were being abolished.

Now the same sort of issue is arising with the president's pending welfare reform proposal. The idea is to turn over to volunteering states the money now going into about 100 different programs for the poor. A state would still have to spend the money on the poor, but, within limits still to be disclosed, could otherwise shape its spending as it chose.

The problem is that the programs on the list as last reported are wildly dissimilar. They range from the Aid to Families With Dependent Children that is the putative object of this exercise to compensatory aid for needy schoolchildren and college student grants and loans. There is no way that Congress either will or should permit the indiscriminate blurring of these programs into a lump sum. Among many other things, it is not clear what such an act would have to do with welfare or welfare reform. The contemptuous suggestion is that all dollars spent on the poor are the same; that is wrong.

A controlled program to allow greater welfare experimentation by the states is a good idea. It will—as to some extent on the issue of "workfare" it already has—tend to reduce the polarization that has followed this subject on the national level in the past. At the state level both liberals and conservatives seem able to take positions that on the national stage they cannot. But if the administration expects its proposal to be taken seriously, it must put sensible limits on it. Otherwise it will be no more than the diversion that the new federalism was.

Chicago Tribune

Chicago, IL, February 27, 1987

The nation's governors started at the right place in their campaign for welfare reform. What they want first of all is the freedom to experiment with different approaches—remedial education, job training, work requirements.

That request deserves bipartisan applause and a warm reception in both the White House and Congress. How to help dependent families become self-supporting is one of the toughest challenges this country faces. Proponents of one method or another can debate endlessly, but nearly all of them agree on this basic point: The federal government's 40 or so assistance programs, and the $130 billion they cost annually, are not breaking the chain of chronic dependency. If anything, they discourage people—young people, in particular—from working their way out of poverty and off the welfare rolls.

The plan approved Tuesday by the National Governors Association doesn't seek to replace the failed set of federal rules with new ones. Instead, it asks Washington to be more flexible, permitting states to design their own welfare programs without forfeiting federal subsidies. Small-scale pilot projects already are underway in several states, and they are promising enough to justify some major loosening of the federal clamp on welfare policy.

The governors want permission to demand something in return for welfare checks. They want adult recipients to participate in remedial education classes, job training or work programs. Only a parent responsible for the care of very young children would be exempt. That would change the whole concept of welfare assistance in this country. Now, it's a one-way contract: The government agrees to support people who are poor and jobless so long as they remain poor and jobless. That could be a lifetime or several lifetimes, as one dependent generation raises another. Under the governors' proposal, the contract would be two-way: The government agrees to support the poor and jobless if they strive to become self-supporting. To help in the transition, the government will assure that welfare recipients have training courses, child care, placement services and other back-up assistance.

Several congressional leaders are drafting proposals with a similar thrust. The concept is such a profound change, though, and could produce so many short-term problems that it's more prudent to let individual states develop their own versions. Flexibility should be the goal, and that's better achieved at the state level than in Washington.

Democrat Bill Clinton of Arkansas and Republican John Sununu of New Hampshire, chairman and vice chairman of the governors' group, say President Reagan endorsed their "state flexibility component" when they met with him early this week. Mr. Reagan was less enthused about providing the extra money needed for training programs, bonuses for finding jobs and other support services, but congressional leaders are correct when they argue that in the long run this can produce big savings in federal aid and even bigger returns in a healthier society.

As good as it is, the governors' plan has got to be labeled incomplete, perhaps even doomed to fail, unless it deals with one glaring omission. It puts all its emphasis on helping adults climb out of dependency. That must be done, but it's equally important to make sure their children don't get caught in the same trap.

Early learning programs can give children of dependent families the motivation and the skills they need to perform well in school and, later, on the job.

If enough public and private resources are funneled into preschool education today, tomorrow's bill for adult training classes, work programs and other projects to get people off welfare will dwindle. Young people will be making it on their own.

THE ARIZONA REPUBLIC

Phoenix, AZ, March 2, 1987

ALMOST as rare as lightning striking twice in the same spot, genuine legislative "miracles" have been few and far between up on America's grand knoll of intransigence called Capitol Hill.

After years of fruitless debate and multitudes of proposals on the subject, last year's approval of tax-reform legislation was just such a shocker. Disregarding the merits of the final law, that it was actually carried out in Congress was nothing short of miraculous.

That same electricity of action is coursing through the rarefied Washington air again over welfare reform, and it's hard not to be skeptical over the prospects. After all, we've already witnessed one "miracle" this decade.

But in view of the professed conversion of those who once fervently worshiped the Great Society dogma, there's more than a spark of hope that legislative lightning will strike again. Consider the astonishing list of converts:

● Sen. Edward Kennedy, D-Mass., the embodiment of big-spending liberaldom, now has proposed a program designed to break long-term welfare dependency by linking federal job-training programs with efforts to reduce welfare rolls. Even more remarkable, Kennedy says the states, not the federal government, should take the lead.

● Sen. Paul Simon, D-Ill., another big-spender and author of *Let's Put America Back to Work*,

wants to get poor people off welfare by requiring them to work on public-service projects — similar to activity undertaken decades ago by the Works Progress Administration — at a rate equal to or just higher than welfare or unemployment compensation payments. They would work a 32-hour week, and would be expected to spend the fifth day looking for jobs in the private sector.

● House Speaker Jim Wright, a Texan with a reputation for liberal leanings, now says Congress should give "high-priority" to so-called workfare programs that require those receiving federal assistance to work.

● The National Governors' Association, hardly recognized as a bastion of conservative thought, overwhelmingly endorses transforming the welfare system from income subsidies into job programs.

These and a multitude of similar proposals — including President Reagan's — touting what is essentially an end to the welfare state as we know it today, now are pending in the Democratic-controlled Congress.

While none of the new "converts" is yet ready to blame the welfare system for actually exacerbating the problem of the poor — the decline of the family unit, generations of dependency, lack of incentives and opportunity — they at least finally recognize that the current system of handouts is not working. That in itself is no small miracle.

The Atlanta Journal
THE ATLANTA CONSTITUTION

Atlanta, GA, March 30, 1987

It wasn't much of a honeymoon and now it's ending, with the administration and Congress going their separate ways on welfare reform. A plan unveiled by House leaders is "radically different" from the president's, a once-conciliatory White House spokeswoman now grumbles, putting an end to speculation that a consensus was near.

Actually, the House plan isn't all that different from one the president had praised a few weeks earlier as "consistent" with his goals. But problems arose in the fleshing-out of what virtually everyone now agrees will have to be some derivation of what used to be called "workfare."

Like the president's plan, the measure offered by Rep. Harold Ford (D-Tenn.) and House Speaker Jim Wright (D-Texas) provides incentives for people to take jobs. Similarly to a plan issued earlier this month by the National Governors' Association, it recognizes the importance of support services, such as day-care, transportation and health insurance. Both plans marked a real departure for liberals and moderates of both parties, who used to recoil from workfare.

But then, they had reason to expect concessions from the White House, which stressed the similarities rather than the differences to its own approach. Now, it seems, the differences are too vast to ignore.

Ford and Wright would provide up to $175 per month in federal child-care reim-

bursements for each preschool-age child and up to $125 a month in transportation for people who take jobs or enter job-training programs. The White House insists it is up to the states to provide such services. The House plan would extend coverage to needy two-parent families. It would require every state to pay benefits equal to at least 15 percent of its median family income, forcing Georgia and 17 other states to raise payments. The president is staunchly opposed to a minimum-support level.

The House plan would take effect immediately, whereas the administration plan would give states up to five years to experiment with alternatives, and grant them blanket waivers from existing regulations.

And it would cost up to $850 million in its first year, and add as much as $2 billion to welfare costs in subsequent years in contrast with the White House plan, which the president insists must be "revenue-neutral."

The Ford plan is by no means final, with fine points to be worked out and political compromises likely. But the governors and lawmakers have shown themselves far more disposed to reform than the president, who remains committed, as an aide now admits, to "an altogether different strategy."

Increasingly, it appears to be a strategy of cutting costs, and sloughing off responsibility to the states and localities. What was that about a consensus? Leadership?

The Miami Herald

Miami, Fl, February 21, 1987

SEN. DANIEL Patrick Moynihan, the thoughtful Democrat from New York, hopes for "syzygy" on welfare reform. If the major heavenly bodies can align themselves for a brief moment in history to produce rising tides, then perhaps an alignment of major political groups can produce true reforms. President Reagan is talking about it, Congress has a host of reform bills, and the nation's governors and mayors have made a major policy statement.

The rising tide of consensus is that the system is a nonsystem, that it does far more harm than good. Aid to Families with Dependent Children (AFDC) is the principal program, and it virtually guarantees that families will become female-headed households and permanently dependent. During their prime years for learning and earning, AFDC pays women to stay home with their children in a world where few women now do so. But that payment does not allow them to bring up those children with decent food and housing.

Worse, some states, Florida included, retain a "man in the house" rule, driving out fathers who may be unemployed or unable to provide adequate support. Should a welfare mother find work, she loses all or part of that meager benefit. She finds herself paying perhaps as much as half her take-home pay for child care or going without it.

A comprehensive plan must include several elements. Among them are jobs and training for the highest level of skill commensurate with ability, day care subsidized on a sliding scale, stiff child-support enforcement, housing and health assistance, and greater flexibility to design local programs.

The major contention is money and which pocket it should come from. The governors suspect that the President's statements about state and local initiatives mean a withdrawal of Federal dollars. That should not happen. Some states such Mississippi are so mired in poverty that they cannot help themselves entirely. Federal money provides the incentive to maintain some sort of floor for benefits. Florida, for all of its relative riches, ranks 50th in per-capita social-services spending.

What also should not happen is to permit the loss of the momentum for reform. Some 12 million children in the United States live in poverty, seven million of them on welfare. America has lifted most of its elderly from poverty. Now it must do the same for its children.

THE ANN ARBOR NEWS

Ann Arbor, MI, March 5, 1987

Work that is meaningful and that gives dignity to the individual is one of the basic building blocks of an orderly and productive society. Without work, either building a family, performing a service or putting one's hands to constructive use, a person is incomplete.

Failure to work and the feeling of dependence it brings rob many people of self-respect and the ability to manage their lives. Helplessness soon gives way to despair.

But what to do about a sub-class in society which is seemingly locked into a pattern of hostile economic conditions, lack of opportunity and joblessness? What can be done about an underclass which is characterized by poverty, failure to finish school and out-of-wedlock births?

Until recently, the emphasis on the welfare system has focused on income maintenance. "Welfare reform" as that battered concept has come to be known has made only halfhearted attempts at placing the emphasis where it belongs – on the value of work. Work for work's sake, even.

But now there seems to be a change in public attitudes. A report by a group of scholars – whose views range from liberal to conservative – at the American Enterprise Institute recommends that welfare recipients be compelled to finish school and participate in training and work programs.

Society, the report said, should emphasize showing the value it places on work, education and family life. Why family life? Because as Sen. Daniel Patrick Moynihan, D-N.Y., said recently, parental responsibility is "the oldest moral commitment we make."

The data, he said, are clear. "Too many single mothers are still not getting the help they need from the Child Support Program. Too many absent fathers are still behaving irresponsibly. As a result, too many children are still living impoverished lives."

The National Governors Association last month echoed the AEI report. "Work must be more attractive than welfare," said Gov. Michael N. Castle, R-Del., chairman of the NGA's task force on welfare prevention.

The governors overwhelmingly approved a far-reaching plan to overhaul welfare. In the simple form, it calls for a mandatory education and training program for able-bodied welfare recipients. The second part calls for government assistance for any family whose income falls below a set standard.

Although he endorsed the proposed education and training program, President Reagan did not agree to the governors' suggestion that the federal government pay most of the first-year costs.

The governors' plan is just one example of a change in thinking on the welfare issue. A consensus may be forming among both critics and supporters of the present system. According to Congressional Quarterly:

"Liberals are accepting the notion that able-bodied welfare recipients should be required to work. Conservatives are recognizing that government has a responsibility to help provide adequate education, training, and child care, and to see that recipients not be penalized for going to work by losing their health insurance."

Welfare has many and varied critics, but what have they proposed to remedy a system that most agree does not work? The AEI report noted a convergence of opinion on the importance of work for non-aged, non-disabled people in breaking the cycle of dependence that creates an underclass marked by a high drop-out rate from school, illegitimate births and widespread poverty.

Government needs to show that its heart is as noble as its intentions. Congress needs to fund programs which embrace the concepts on which more people seem to be agreeing. If one of the secrets of welfare reform – bona fide, results-oriented reform – is spending some money, then the people's representatives need to rob from a missile program here and a congressman's favorite pork barrel there to get the job done.

Shouldn't this be one of our highest national priorities?

DESERET NEWS

Salt Lake City, UT, March 9/10, 1987

The nation's governors are on the right track with their welfare reform proposal requiring most people to work or get training in return for the assistance they receive.

In a recent meeting with President Reagan, a group of governors urged that the federal welfare system join hands with the states in implementing such a welfare package.

Simply handing out aid doesn't do any good in the long run. It is destructive of personal esteem and ambition; it tends to foster dependence on the welfare system, and it sometimes makes it impossible to get off welfare, creating a cycle where parents, then children, then the children of children acquire a welfare lifestyle.

The best role of welfare is to support people in times of crisis, but with the main goal of getting them off welfare as soon as possible by making them contributing citizens and taxpayers. That's what most people on welfare desperately want, too.

Some states, including Utah, already have programs that seek to provide training, education, and jobs to welfare recipients — mostly single mothers — in order to move them off the welfare rolls. The plan in Utah has enjoyed success, but faces funding problems.

The welfare proposal adopted at the recent National Governors' Conference would require a "contract" to be signed between welfare recipients and the government. Any person on welfare with children over age 3 would agree to make every effort to get off public assistance.

In support of this goal, the states would provide education, job training, day care, and job placement programs.

Unfortunately, this is going to cost a staggering amount of money — an estimated $1 billion the first year. The governors would like the federal government to pick up three-quarters of that tab, but that won't be easy until the huge federal deficit is at least sharply reduced if not eliminated.

Most states aren't any better off. Utah, for example, already is unable to fund a similar program at the same level as previous years.

Any program that tends to move people off welfare rolls is certain to be less expensive in the long run, and ought to be viewed as an investment instead of simply a dole. If savings can be made elsewhere, fine. Meanwhile, it will be hard to make new investments until Washington gets further out of the red.

The Honolulu Advertiser

Honolulu, HI, Mar 8, 1987

Stop thinking welfare," New York Senator Daniel Patrick Moynihan likes to say, "Think children." Indeed, when it comes to welfare reform it's the future that must be considered foremost.

Two million more people are in poverty today than when President Reagan took office. The poverty rate is 14.4 percent but among children it's 20 percent and among black children 50 percent. That's a terrible indictment of our rich society.

Talk of basic agreement on welfare reform among the National Governors Association, Congress and the White House sounds impressive. But it comes up against an old, familiar obstacle — money.

Everyone now agrees welfare ought to be tied by contract to training or work for all "employable" recipients, those able-bodied with children past 3 years old. Despite the malicious stereotypes of recipients as bums or cheaters, most would rather not be on the dole if there were a better way.

Making "work more attractive than welfare" is a sound plan, but it's easier said than done. Training must be started; jobs found. For single parents, affordable child care is essential. But entry jobs do not pay enough for even a small family to live on. And most such jobs do not offer health insurance, as welfare does.

These obstacles can only be solved at considerable cost, much more than will come from good programs to make delinquent fathers pay more of their share.

The governors believe the federal government should pay the greater part of that cost, at least until theoretical savings begin from the drop in the welfare rolls.

Not surprisingly, the Reagan administration wants to leave the initiative — and expense — to the states. But a look at the wildly divergent welfare support rates from state to state shows that local authorities all cannot be "trusted" to offer equable support to welfare recipients.

States should have flexibility in how they run welfare programs, but there also must be a national minimum standard of support.

Poverty is a national problem felt more severely in some parts of the country, like big cities, than others. For that reason the basic cost of welfare programs must in fairness be borne by the federal government. That will be difficult in deficit-ridden times, but any other system just defers the cost, in both dollars and lost human potential, to later generations.

THE DAILY OKLAHOMAN

Oklahoma City, OK, February 25, 1987

THE nation's governors are flexing their collective muscle again, this time in support of basic changes in the welfare system.

At their winter meeting in Washington this week, the focus was on improved productivity, with an emphasis on welfare reform. Essentially the governors want to convert the welfare system from an income maintenance program with a minor jobs component into a jobs program supported by an income assistance component.

The concept was greeted warmly by President Reagan. A specific proposal that all cash assistance recipients with young children be required to take part in a work program is in line with policies he has long advocated. The administration did not embrace a suggestion that the federal government fund more than three-quarters of the estimated $1 billion first-year cost of the new program.

Reagan's own welfare plan derives from his philosophy — restated at a cordial meeting with the governors — that "the best thing the federal government can do for the states is get out of your pockets and out of your way." He proposes a strategy that encourages community-based, state-sponsored demonstration projects to find better ways of getting people off welfare and into jobs.

Ironically, Sen. Edward Kennedy, D-Mass., a champion of the federal dole, is sponsoring legislation to reward states with bonuses for developing job-targeted welfare programs. His bill is patterned after a successful plan that originated in the state of Massachusetts.

In recent years, the National Governors' Association has become increasingly active in efforts to influence national policy. Except for last year, when the organization concentrated on state and local initiatives to improve education, the governors have been raising their voices on fiscal and economic policies and other matters that have long been the exclusive preserve of the federal establishment.

Gov. Henry Bellmon, attending his first governors' conference in more than 20 years, noted that the state leaders are much more involved now in the national legislative process. Since the states are generally run much better than the federal government, that may not be so bad.

The Washington Times

Washington, DC, March 27, 1987

The prevailing wisdom has it that a consensus is evolving in favor of sweeping reform of the welfare system. Conservatives and liberals are said to be moving toward a "grand compromise" that would require welfare recipients to participate in work programs in exchange for government day care and transportation. Complete details have yet to surface, but to judge from the bare outlines, the plan is to perpetuate the status quo at higher cost.

Take, for example, the proposal unveiled last week by House Speaker Jim Wright and Rep. Harold Ford. It offers a few decent changes, such as requiring most welfare recipients with children over 6 to be employed or enrolled in schools or job training programs. From there, the proposal is all downhill.

In order to bloat benefits, the Wright-Ford plan — modeled after a scheme pushed by the National Governors' Association — would finesse federalism, forcing 18 states to increase welfare benefits to a new minimum level and requiring all states to pay benefits to families with fathers in residence (something only half now do). Additional outlays would be necessary to induce states to make further benefit hikes and to fund a costly array of remedial education, job training, and job placement schemes.

Cost? Rep. Ford says the plan could cost $2.5 billion a year more than existing programs, but he thinks spending would drop when welfare dependents started getting jobs. He neglects to say, unfortunately, how making benefits more generous helps pry people off the dole.

According to Sen. Paul Simon, the welfare reform movement "bodes well" for his pet boondoggle, a 1980s version of the New Deal's Works Progress Administration that would cost $13 billion in 1989-90 alone. This is the real liberal agenda: use incantations about "work" and "reform" as an excuse to concentrate control in Washington.

Welfare is a mess, to be sure. But the answer isn't higher benefits. The answer is to wrest it away from mountebanks who use it to buy votes.

Newsday

New York, NY, February 23, 1987

Could welfare reform become the great achievement of the 100th Congress, as federal tax revision was of the 99th?

Don't count on it. Rewriting the tax code was simple compared to untangling the welfare conundrum. But don't give up completely on reform either. So many people are fed up with the present welfare system — often for diametrically opposite reasons — that Congress might at least make a significant beginning.

The opening rhetorical salvos were fired weeks ago. Even President Ronald Reagan has been talking about turning the states loose to innovate better welfare programs — without, of course, giving them more money than they get now. But it was Sen. Daniel P. Moynihan (D-N.Y.) who really laid out the case against the present system.

The senator delivered a devastating attack on the program most people are thinking of when they talk about welfare: Aid to Families with Dependent Children. "A program that was designed for poor widows will not be supported in a world where mothers are poor because they are unsupported by their divorced husbands or because they are unwed," he said. "A program that was designed to pay mothers to stay at home with their children cannot succeed when we now observe most mothers going out to work."

Moynihan's plan for replacing AFDC rests on three foundations: more financial support from absent fathers, more paid work by welfare mothers and public jobs for those who fail to find private employment.

Gov. Mario Cuomo's Task Force on Poverty and Welfare laid some useful groundwork for the ongoing debate in a report last December. It too emphasized child support — to the point of suggesting withholding money from wages to prevent nonpayment. It called for education and training, if necessary, to make welfare parents employable.

The debate will undoubtedly go forward at the national governors' conference this week in Washington. The conference chairman, Arkansas Democrat Bill Clinton, predicted last week that it would back "a system that is first and foremost a jobs program, supported by an income assistance component." And he said this system might cost $2 billion a year more than the present welfare system.

That sounds more realistic than any suggestion that welfare reform can be done on the cheap. If it could, the politicians would have done it long ago. But Moynihan has put the emphasis where it belongs: on adequate financial support for children who are in no way responsible for their parents' economic condition. If the 100th Congress remembers that, maybe it *will* make a difference.

Houston Chronicle

*Houston, TX,
April 17, 1987*

In his State of the Union address in February 1986, President Reagan promised — but failed to deliver — a plan for "immediate action to meet the financial, educational, social and safety concerns of poor families."

The nation's governors have proposed and Congress is considering a welfare reform plan of their own. Its various versions, which all place heavy emphasis on work and training, deserve serious consideration — and a few words of caution.

The current welfare system suffers from three intolerable flaws: Its scores of programs constitute an inefficient maze that confuses honest recipients and aids cheaters. It rewards families that break up and punishes families that stay together. Finally, it discourages people from accepting low-paying jobs because work expenses and loss of welfare benefits would leave them worse off.

The administration has proposed a five-year period of state experimentation with welfare reform. That sounds promising, but the governors unanimously report that no more experimentation is needed: Workfare works, they say, and the federal government should pay for it.

Before the Democratic-controlled Congress rushes off along the golden brick road to welfare reform, however, it and the public should keep in mind a few salient points:

● Many recipients of various aid programs are disabled and cannot work. They must not be abandoned simply because they do not fit into the workfare mold.

● The vast majority of welfare recipients are single women and their young children. Workfare will mean expensive, government-subsidized child care, although savings should result in the long run.

● Welfare reform — if it does nothing else — should consolidate programs into a single entity where those in need can go for benefits, job applications, counseling, etc. The nation does not need yet another layer of welfare bureaucracy and higher costs.

Despite an administration with less than two more years in office and the chronic federal deficit, the emerging consensus on the need and proper path to welfare reform presents a historic opportunity. It must not be squandered.

Most welfare recipients say they want to work and deserve an opportunity to do so. At this point, partisan bickering and uninformed notions about welfare Cadillacs are the principal obstacles standing in the way of a system that would give them that opportunity.

The Washington Post

Washington, DC, April 17, 1987

THE WELFARE reform bill approved last week by a House subcommittee would not transform the system to the extent that the enveloping rhetoric on either side suggests. It is nevertheless an important bill. It would transfer resources to a part of the population desperately in need and, at a number of switching points inside the system, sweeten the incentives to induce both states and recipients to do the right thing.

The magic word for all welfare reformers now is work. Conservatives regard this as a major victory, but it is more rhetorical than real. A perfect example is the opposition speedily voiced by conservatives to this very bill. Everyone agrees that welfare mothers should work if they can. The question for government remains the same as always: What mix of stick and carrot?

This is a mildly carroty bill. It begins with a new program for both prodding and helping people to make the transition from welfare to work, in which services would range from providing the rest of high school all the way to underwriting or creating jobs. Each state would design its own array; the states would be encouraged to expand the programs they already have by a new federal matching formula. A state couldn't focus on just the easiest cases, those with people who are likely to move off welfare anyway; the bill defines target populations—teen-age mothers, families on welfare continuously for more than two years—that would have to be serviced first. There would also be limits on how far states could go in requiring recipients to work. The great rub is that this program is likely to be much smaller than it sounds. The estimate is that it might serve as few as 75,000 families a year, out of about 3.7 million on welfare at any one time. The limiting factor is that the program can only grow if the states increase their spending.

The bill would also reduce the costs to recipients of moving from welfare to work. It would subsidize day care for six months after a recipient found a job, continue Medicaid for nine months and reduce what amounts to the tax rate by which welfare checks are currently cut as earnings rise. There would be a greater effort to make absent fathers pay child support.

Only then would the bill also move to liberalize benefits proper. Beginning in 1990, it would require states to offer welfare to two-parent families where the main breadwinner is unemployed; only half the states do so now. Beginning in distant 1993 it would also require states to meet minimum benefit standards—no less than 15 percent of state median family income each year, adjusted for family size. Meanwhile, it would alter another matching formula to induce the states to raise benefits, by having the federal government pay more of the cost.

This bill won't wipe out the welfare system; it is not millennial legislation. But it is thoughtful legislation that would put the system on a better track at manageable cost. Conservatives will argue that it is counterproductive to have a bill start out emphasizing work and end up raising benefits. But the benefits have been allowed to lag too long. The committee and House should move this bill along.

THE SACRAMENTO BEE

Sacramento, CA, April 18, 1987

After a year of studying how to reform welfare, the Reagan administration last December could come up with no better answer than wait for the states. That doesn't satisfy either the nation's governors or members of Congress, who've found models worth acting on. Following the lead of states like California and Massachusetts, Democrats in both the House and Senate seem ready to move on some version of the governors' recent recommendation: a national reform to tie welfare benefits more closely to work requirements and create a national standard for benefits. That approach makes sense both as policy and politics.

Preliminary evaluations of "workfare" programs conducted by states suggest they can work for everybody. Making welfare benefits conditional on participation in organized job-search and work-experience programs results in higher rates of employment among welfare applicants, higher incomes and less dependence on welfare checks. That, of course, pleases conservatives.

But workfare also legitimizes funding an array of government services needed to move welfare recipients from the dole to the job market — child care, remedial education, job training, extended health coverage. And because, under workfare, many welfare recipients no longer would be "free riders" but underskilled parents working their way toward a job, Congress would find it easier to require that benefits be high enough everywhere around the nation to perform welfare's main task: protecting children from poverty. The workfare approach thus pleases liberals, too.

But even as Congress moves toward such welfare reforms, it needs to look hard at the broader picture. By itself, tinkering with the welfare system won't eliminate the sources of family poverty and dependency because workfare is directed mostly at mothers and aimed at picking up the pieces of the family instead of keeping them whole.

Among the main sources of female-headed, single-parent households and child poverty are the high rate of divorce among young couples and the high unemployment rate among young males, particularly black males. A thorough attack on dependency must thus include stricter measures to compel absent parents to fulfill their obligation for child support, as Sen. Daniel Patrick Moynihan is suggesting. More important, it must find ways to train and employ economically marginal young men so that they have the income and self-respect to be reliable fathers and husbands. No one is certain how that most difficult of social policy tasks can be quickly done, but better early education, job experience and public employment opportunities would certainly help.

As Moynihan urges, it's time to "stop thinking welfare. Think children." And, he might have added, think fathers and families.

LAS VEGAS REVIEW-JOURNAL

Las Vegas, NV, April 6, 1987

The full U.S. Senate has acted on a bill which may not overhaul the nation's welfare system, but which certainly is a step in the right direction.

On a 99-0 vote, the Senate last week approved the Jobs for Employable Dependent Individuals Act, the brainchild of Sen. Ted Kennedy, D-Mass.

What this measure would do is offer cash bonuses to states for successfully placing long-term welfare recipients in private or unsubsidized jobs.

The measure is designed to encourage states to train and find jobs for people who have become overly attached to welfare — those who are able-bodied and trainable but who have received welfare for two years or more and who are determined likely candidates to stay welfare-dependent for 10 years or longer.

If a state can manage to place such people in paying jobs, the federal government will kick in bonuses during the first, second and third year of a person's employment. To keep things equitable, no payments would be made until welfare savings are achieved.

Over the three years, a state would receive about $3,700 for having moved the person into a job.

Said Kennedy of the measure: "It does not pay for failure. It does not pay for headcounting. It does not pay for makework."

Well stated. It's high time that the concept of incentive be heavily infused into the welfare system.

THE SPOKESMAN-REVIEW

Spokane, WA, April 6, 1987

Ten years ago, Washington state began giving cash handouts to alcoholics and drug addicts whose dependency makes them unemployable. In a majority of states, such payments are not allowed. Washington's benefit, now at $314 a month, is the most generous in the country.

The result should have been predictable. In 1983, 1,400 people were enrolled in the program. Today, 6,000 are enrolled. Many of the beneficiaries are winos, recently arrived from other states. They slump in vacant doorways and stagger down alleys in Seattle, Spokane and other cities, guzzling or injecting their $314 check as soon as they can convert it into the desired commodity.

This program, known officially as the General Assistance Unemployable grant for alcoholics and drug addicts, has been a spectacular failure, a textbook example of good intentions gone awry.

The state Department of Social and Health Services, which administers the program, admits the need for a change and strongly supports a bill that would correct the situation.

The House has passed the bill, SHB 646, and now it awaits action in the Senate.

If enacted, SHB 646 would eliminate the cash grants. Instead, unemployable alcoholics or drug addicts would be eligible for limited periods of residential or outpatient treatment. They also would be eligible for state-funded shelter. The state would pay the service providers directly, on a per-client basis.

DSHS has estimated that if it continued the current benefit, the caseload would soar from 6,000 up to 8,000 by the end of the 1987-89 biennium, and the program would cost $55 million.

Under SHB 646, it estimates the caseload would decline and the program would cost $45.4 million for the upcoming biennium, a savings of $9.6 million.

The predicted caseload decline results from a reasonable assumption that some addicts will leave once the handout stops and that others will stop migrating here from out of state once the benefit change becomes known in wino circles. In addition, it is to be hoped that state funding for alcoholism and drug-dependency treatment might lead some to a better lifestyle.

The new program would, of course, deprive its beneficiaries of a cash source that may also have contributed to needs more legitimate than another bottle of fortified wine. To help meet those needs, DSHS intends to assist the addicts in applying for aid under the federal Supplemental Security Income program, which blends treatment with income incentives.

Obviously, many who seek this kind of assistance are so far gone that prospects for recovery are poor. There simply are no easy ways for the government to solve their problem.

But the state certainly should not be contributing to their problem, as it is doing now. Nor should the state tolerate a benefit that attracts bums from other states to our cities, worsening crime problems.

SHB 646 deserves speedy passage and the governor's signature.

The Boston Globe

Boston, MA, April 9, 1987

Although welfare reform continues to be an issue that engages the attention of presidential commissions and blue-ribbon task forces, the US Senate has taken speedy action on a bill that could provide the results needed.

With the 99-0 vote usually reserved for ceremonial matters, the Senate has approved legislation drafted by Sen. Edward M. Kennedy that would provide incentives for other states to adopt programs similar to Massachusetts' Employment and Training Program.

The Kennedy bill would reward states for moving people off the welfare rolls and into permanent jobs. It dodges, as neatly as does the Dukakis ET program, the old welfare-workfare argument by accepting the premise that people would rather work than collect benefits.

In the training programs which the states would have to establish, priority would be given to those who have been welfare recipients for two years or longer. This would focus the program on breaking the cycle of poverty.

Since the focus of the Kennedy bill is permanent employment, the House, which will now consider the bill, might want to change the schedule of bonuses to be paid to the states. In the Kennedy bill they would amount to 75 percent of the AFDC benefits that would have been paid in the first year the recipient is off welfare, dropping to 50 percent the next year and to 25 percent in the final year. Bonuses of 50 percent in the first year, 60 percent in the second, and 40 percent in the third would better reward training programs that lead to permanent jobs.

While the ET program has been successful in booming high-tech Massachusetts — moving some 30,000 AFDC recipients into jobs paying $12,000 a year or more — it is not certain that a similar program would work as well in states with high unemployment and sagging economies.

This question may never be answered until ET-type programs are established in other states. The Kennedy bill provides the necessary incentives to allow this experiment to be made. If it is unsuccessful, the states will be out the cost of establishing the training programs. But if it is successful, the goal of welfare reform could be reached before the next task force even gets its office furnished.

Moynihan Plan Reaches Senate; White House Cites Cost Concerns

After months of behind-the-scenes negotiations, Sen. Daniel Patrick Moynihan (D, N.Y.), chairman of the Senate Finance Committee's subcommittee on family policy, July 21, 1987 introduced a welfare-reform bill that would likely serve as the basis for Senate efforts to overhaul the welfare system. Moynihan was a longtime critic of the present welfare system, which he said fostered dependency on government handouts and led parents to abdicate responsibility for their children. His bill was based on proposals overwhelmingly endorsed in February 1987 by the National Governors" Association.

Some key provisions of the Moynihan bill were as follows:

■ The states, for the first time, would be required to set up comprehensive remedial education, job-training and work programs for welfare parents. There were currently about 3.8 million such parents, nearly all women, in the Aid to Families with Dependent Children (AFDC) program.

■ Enrollment in some such program would be mandatory for any welfare parent with a child age three or older, or, at state option, one or older, as long as appropriate day-care was available.

■ To discourage fathers from moving out, welfare support would be extended to needy two-parent families nationwide. About half the states currently denied aid to children in two-parent families.

■ Parents required to pay child support would have the designated amounts automatically withheld from their paychecks by employers. The employers would send the money to the state, which would forward it to the custodial parent. This provision would apply to nonwelfare recipients as well as those receiving benefits.

Sen. Moynihan unsuccessfully sought in the weeks previous to the introduction of his legislation to win White House support for his bill. However, two Republican members of the Senate Finance Committee, as well as six Democrats, did agree to cosponsor it. The two Republicans were David Durenberger (Minn.) and John C. Danforth (Mo.). The White House was said to be concerned with cost. The Congressional Budget Office had estimated that the bill would cost the federal government $2.72 billion over five years.

Legislation similar to Moynihan's but estimated to cost nearly twice as much had been moving through the House of Representatives. The House legislation had been reported June 17 by the Ways and Means Committee and had been approved with some amendments July 15 by the Education and Labor Committee. The major reason for the cost difference was the House bill included provisions encouraging states to raise benefits while Moynihan's bill did not. Benefits in many states, Moynihan said, had been outpaced by inflation, but he saw "no point" in introducing legislation to raise them because there was "no consensus" in the Senate for such a provision.

The Wichita Eagle-Beacon
Wichita, KS, July 24, 1987

CONGRESS appears to have reached a consensus that parental responsibility, not government programs, should be the foundation of the country's welfare system. Congress also seems to agree that job training and education are the best ways to get people off welfare rolls.

Legislation introduced this week by Sen. Daniel Patrick Moynihan, D-N.Y., a congressional expert on welfare, would make the most sweeping reform in public assistance programs since the Depression. The thrust of Mr. Moynihan's proposal is to force parents to support their children and to encourage states to set up employment programs for welfare recipients.

The Moynihan plan is similar to legislation drafted by the House Ways and Means Committee earlier this summer. Both bills would toughen child-support laws, with Mr. Moynihan's measure requiring employers to deduct court-ordered payments from an absent parent's wages. Mr. Moynihan also would make it easier to track down delinquent parents by requiring states to collect Social Security numbers from the mother and father when a baby is born.

Mr. Moynihan recognizes that divorce often leaves children in poverty. Many noncustodial parents, usually fathers, refuse to pay child support, often throwing the custodial parent and the children onto welfare. Ensuring child-support payments would help lift the welfare burden from the taxpayer.

Congress also is heading toward some form of "workfare," which requires able-bodied welfare recipients to perform public-service work or be in job training to get a benefit check. The goal is to end the cycle of government dependency that afflicts generations of some welfare families.

The welfare system needs an overhaul to reflect current social conditions. Mr. Moynihan and the House Ways and Means Committee have the right philosophy. The challenge is to build a welfare program that takes care of the needy, while encouraging people to take more responsibility for themselves and their families.

THE INDIANAPOLIS NEWS
*Indianapolis, IN,
July 28, 1987*

Sen. Daniel Moynihan is drawing much needed attention to weaknesses in the welfare system with his recent proposal for reform.

Moynihan's proposal to the Senate Finance Committee wisely would leave job training programs in the hands of the states, instead of the federal government, to help people move off welfare and into work.

He brings a historical perspective to the problem of Aid to Families with Dependent Children, which was designed as a pension program for widows during the Depression. But in recent years it has provided financial incentives for the development of single-parent families and dependency on welfare over several generations.

"We're trying to deal with the problem of dependency," Moynihan said in announcing his proposal. "It is a very large problem and it is not going to respond quickly to anything we do."

But his legislation does get at the problem of work, which needs to be at the center of any revisions in the welfare program. Moynihan's proposal would require states to up a Job Opportunities and Basic Skills program that would be mandatory for many welfare recipients, including mothers of children age 3 or over.

The Reagan administration has proposed a different version of welfare reform, but again with an emphasis on work and training. A number of states already have developed their own work and training programs, including Indiana during the past session of the General Assembly.

Reagan administration officials say they are open to compromise with Moynihan's proposal. What's needed in any final version from Congress is plenty of flexibility for the states to keep on developing their own work programs, with a minimum of interference from the federal government with rules and regulations.

The Atlanta Journal
THE ATLANTA CONSTITUTION
Atlanta, GA, July 30, 1987

The case for welfare reform is overwhelming. America spends a staggering $41 billion a year on public assistance aimed at lifting the homeless, the elderly and children out of poverty and dependency. Yet, virtually everyone agrees it's not working.

Yesterday's welfare children are today's pregnant teenagers and jobless adults. For every 100 children born today, 25 will depend on welfare for at least a portion of their lives. Increasingly, programs like Aid to Families with Dependent Children and the Job Training Partnership Act aren't even reaching the children most at risk, the hardcore unemployed, the people most in need.

But, as the nation's governors were reminded this week at their annual meeting, a consensus about what's wrong with the system may not be enough to fix it.

A broad-based bipartisan consensus has been building in Congress since at least February, when the National Governors' Association proposed a work-oriented program, buttressed by extensive support services. Two bills based on that proposal are currently before Congress. Each incorporates a work requirement with remedial education, job-training, day-care, health insurance and transportation for those who could not work or who would be discouraged from seeking work without them. And each bows to social realities by, for example, exempting mothers of preschoolers from the work requirement.

But as two White House officials made clear this week in separate meetings with the governors, President Reagan continues to oppose any increase in the welfare rolls and to demand broad waiver authority for states to be free to set up their own programs. These are major stumbling blocks — big enough to cripple the best shot at reform in almost 20 years.

There has been real movement among liberals and moderates to accommodate White House concerns. A stunning example is the Family Security Act, introduced last week by Sen. Patrick Moynihan (D-N.Y.), with 27 co-sponsors and half the $1 billion-a-year price tag of a House measure.

Deeply suspicious of waivers allowing state discretion but anticipating the administration's intractability on the point, Moynihan wrote them in — but with checks and balances aimed at keeping the damage to a minimum: No individual's benefits could be reduced under a waiver project. No unemployed parent could be denied child care. No "regular" worker could be displaced, or collective bargaining agreement impaired, by a welfare recipient. No "significantly different" federal expenditures could be allowed under a waiver agreement.

These assurances are critical if the purpose is to remove the barriers to self-sufficiency — the stated goal of all the key players, including the White House. It is time for Reagan to show some flexibility on that score. Without it, his waivers merely invite the states to cut corners. That is not reform but irresponsibility.

The Washington Post
Washington, DC, July 22, 1987

BACK IN JANUARY, Sen. Daniel Patrick Moynihan began a hearing on welfare reform, as only he can, by suggesting that the participants in the welfare debate might finally have achieved syzygy. Syzygy? You remember syzygy; it is, as Sen. Moynihan explained for anyone who may have forgotten, a term from astronomy, describing a particular alignment of earth, sun and moon. The various schools of thought on welfare also seemed miraculously aligned, in a way that after years of sharp dispute might "bring about genuine social change."

So much for astronomy. As with the sun and moon, the two main sides in the welfare debate have orbited on. The thin consensus of last winter has predictably broken down. A Democratic bill is taking shape in the House. It would require the states to make new efforts to move recipients from welfare to work, make such moves more attractive by providing various transition benefits (for example, women who went to work could keep their Medicaid for a while), then give the states incentives through an adjustment of the matching formula to increase their benefits. It would also require the states to offer welfare to families where the chief breadwinner is unemployed, not just where one parent is absent from the home.

The administration and House Republicans oppose the bill (never mind that the president started the process by calling for a study of welfare reform two winters ago), chiefly on grounds that it would be too costly and the sought-after benefit increases would make it more attractive to stay on welfare rather than leave. The Democrats, who have already trimmed the bill a little—an earlier version would have required benefit increases—have now begun to think about protecting it further by tucking it into this year's reconciliation bill, the omnibus measure by which Congress may seek to reduce the deficit.

In the Senate, meanwhile, Mr. Moynihan, chairman of the relevant subcommittee, has finally introduced his own bill. The price of syzygy turns out to be a certain tameness. Mr. Moynihan would change the name of welfare to reemphasize that it is a children's program and would turn it upside down, in that his bill begins with the responsibility of fathers to support their children, goes next to the responsibility of mothers to seek work and only then turns to benefits, which are thereby made to seem residual. But that is also how, with different emphases, the present system works. The senator would also provide transition benefits and extend the system to the unemployed. But to preserve bipartisanship he was forced to drop all thought of higher benefits, even though he is the first to remind us all, in every speech on this subject, that a fifth of U.S. children now live below the poverty line.

The Moynihan bill would improve the welfare system (the House bill, in our judgment, would improve it more). But it is not reform in the sense of any fundamental restructuring. They are tinkering with welfare up there, but not really reshaping it. There is no consensus how.

DESERET NEWS
Salt Lake City, UT, July 21, 1987

Even as Sen. Daniel Patrick Moynihan, D-N.Y., unveiled his $3 billion welfare reform package in the Senate this past weekend, seeking to put more emphasis on parents' obligation to get jobs and support their children, other members of Congress are working in the opposite direction.

Moynihan wants to toughen child support laws and force welfare recipients to enroll in job training. The purpose is to get rid of the dependency on welfare that seems to trap poor families in a dreary cycle of poverty and more welfare.

That's an admirable goal. Getting training and jobs and getting off the public dole ought to be the focus of all welfare programs.

Unfortunately, there are some in Congress who don't seem to have caught the idea. A measure currently in the House Education and Labor Committee would do just the opposite — put more people on welfare and keep them there longer.

Chairman of the committee, Rep. Augustus Hawkins, D-Calif., wants to force the government to give a job to anyone who claims he can't find one in the private sector, after training and job search services.

In addition, the committee wants to outlaw state rules requiring welfare recipients to work off their benefits at unpaid community jobs.

It's as if some congressmen think that requiring people to work for what they get is demeaning. Actually, it's the other way around. Work instills a sense of worth; a dole does not.

Still another provision in the committee's bill would permit a parent to remain on welfare rolls for four years while attending college, with no obligation to seek work or job training.

Help should be available for those in need. But that help should be a temporary measure, keyed to work, to getting off welfare. It should not become a permanent lifestyle. People need a hand up, not a handout.

Any program that does the opposite — putting people permanently on welfare and calling it a government "job" — would eventually bankrupt the nation, both financially and morally.

Perhaps many details need to be altered in the Senate bill, but Moynihan has the right idea. On the other hand, Hawkins' approach to welfare is a recipe for disaster. It is to be hoped that the House has enough sense to bury his proposals quickly and totally.

The Boston Globe

Boston, MA, August 9, 1987

President Reagan is not wrong in saying that a bill drawn up by a Republican task force to change the nation's welfare system is "on the right track." However, the train appears to be fueled by tightfistedness and meanness toward the poor. It should be overhauled or derailed.

Under the task force plan, parents of children over six months old would have to seek work, education or training. States would be required to subsidize day care and would also have flexibility in designing and implementing job-training programs. States would be held to performance standards and would lose federal funds if they did not measure up.

Most provisions of the bill seem reasonable enough, but an examination reveals that the Republican lawmakers on the task force do not understand the problems confronting poor Americans. Throwing money into a pot for day care, running job programs and telling people to go to work is a naive proposal for solving a decades-old problem.

The need for more day-care subsidies is indisputable, but the lawmakers failed to offer a plan for ensuring that enough day care will be available; there is now an acute nationwide shortage of adequate facilities. The Republican plan would allow states to run demonstration projects at the expense of other welfare programs. That would mean less for housing and other community-development projects that are also vital to the poor.

Rep. Bob Michel, the House Republican leader, proudly points out that the plan, with a $1.4 billion, five-year price tag, is cheaper than a Democratic House proposal with a price tag of $5.3 billion, as well as a $2.3 billion proposal by Sen. Daniel Patrick Moynihan (D-N.Y.). The Republicans could have done better if they had not been so preoccupied with spending as little money as possible to help the poor.

There are similarities between the Moynihan and Republican plans. Since Moynihan has bipartisan support, perhaps a good approach would be to combine the best provisions of the two.

The Republicans need to realize that although Moynihan's proposal costs more in the short run, it better meets the needs of poor people while they prepare to take their place on the tax rolls.

The Dispatch

Columbus, OH, July 22, 1987

A sweeping revision of the nation's basic welfare program, proposed by Sen. Daniel P. Moynihan, appears to be a sound starting point in replacing a system everyone agrees is not working.

Both conservatives and liberals generally agree that the current welfare system badly needs revision, mainly because it usually perpetuates a seemingly never-ending reliance on government aid.

Moynihan, a New York Democrat and an expert on welfare programs, is chairman of a Senate Finance subcommittee on family policy. Two Republicans joined him in sponsoring the measure, which he sees as compatible with a welfare bill approved last month by the House Ways and Means Committee.

A major feature of Moynihan's bill calls for automatic withholding of child support from parents' wages. Many welfare clients would be required to work, and states would be instructed to set up education, training and employment programs for those on welfare. Part of work-related expenses, such as child care and transportation, would be borne by the states.

His approach would turn the present welfare system "on its head," Moynihan said. "Rather than beginning with a public assistance payment that is supplemented by sporadic child support payments and occasional earned income, the bill places responsibility for supporting children where it has always belonged: with parents. Both parents."

This measure attempts to make the most significant changes in the nation's doddering welfare program since its enactment in 1935.

The present welfare system, Aid to Families with Dependent Children, pays cash benefits to 11 million people, in 3.8 million families. Including administrative expenses, the program costs nearly $18 billion a year, of which the federal government pays $10 billion.

Under Moynihan's proposal, states would have to strengthen their efforts to collect more child support from absent parents. And a person who got off welfare because of increased earnings would remain eligible for health insurance under Medicaid for up to nine months.

This measure deserves serious review. It could be the starting point for reforming a system that not only is bloated and costly, but makes too little effort to wean clients from dependence on government handouts. If ever there was a program that is broken, it is the welfare system; the time is ripe to fix it.

The Miami Herald

Miami, FL, March 28, 1987

WELFARE's old Depression-era name, "relief," reflects the American attitude that government financial aid to individuals is connected to a lack of jobs available to the recipients. When there's work, folks are supposed to support themselves.

That principle hasn't worked in America since the technological boom began in the 1950s. Men whose forebears proudly supported their families with a strong back and a willing attitude now are destitute. They've been pushed out of work by steam drills, power saws, hydraulic lifts, and digging machines.

Welfare-reform efforts got a boost from the recent U.S. General Accounting Office report that dispelled some myths about welfare. After analyzing more than 100 studies conducted since 1975, the GAO concluded that:

● Welfare has no significant impact on recipients' incentive to work.

● Welfare "has little impact" on the child-bearing rates of single women.

● Welfare does not encourage unemployed men to leave their families.

These data from the nonpartisan GAO should encourage congressional efforts to expand welfare and to link it more closely to education, job training, and work requirements. The House bill by Tennessee Democrat Harold Ford, which has Speaker Jim Wright's support, addresses these points.

It would require states to pay recipients of Aid to Families with Dependent Children at least 15 percent of the state's median family income. Florida and 17 other states would have to pay more than they do now. The bill also would include two-parent households in AFDC when the primary wage earner is unemployed. Florida now gives no help to intact families.

A key element of the bill would allow states to require that adult recipients go to school, take a job, or get job training. The inclusion of basic education and then technical training as a welfare requirement holds the seeds of true reform. Appropriately, the proposal would include child-care costs in the recipient's budget and would allow for continued Medicaid coverage after recipients work their way off the AFDC rolls.

Mr. Ford's proposal will get a thorough examination during its lengthy path through Congress. Its principles deserve serious consideration — both in Washington and in Tallahassee, where many could be implemented without waiting for the Federal overhaul.

The Register

Santa Ana, CA, July 27, 1987

For 20 years America's welfare system has bred crime and poverty. It has split families, made generations dependent on federal payouts, and devastated vast sections of our cities.

True welfare reform would shift federal responsibility and control back to states, counties, cities, and private groups. It's well known that decentralized welfare works better than centralized, and that best of all is self-reliance; the higher control extends, the more bureaucracy hampers true help to the poor.

Unfortunately, a plan offered by Sen. Daniel Moynihan only partly deals with these realities; it has some good points, but mostly would make matters worse.

The Moynihan plan's main tack is to shift responsibility back to the states, at least a sensible idea, while maintaining federal control, the worst idea possible. For example, it would make states require welfare recipients to take part in job programs, which usually means makework. A better tack would be to let states set up job-search programs, helping people find real jobs for the long haul.

There are tens of thousands of jobs available throughout America. But because many involve menial work, welfare looks better to a lot of people. Because industries differ greatly across America, states are more suited than the feds to finding programs that work in their areas.

The Moynihan plan would require states to give welfare not just to one-parent households, which encourages fathers to leave, but two-parent families as well. That's fine, but do states need to be told that? After all, it was Lyndon Johnson's ADC program that limited welfare to one-parent households, beginning the devastation of poor families.

A better idea for federal action would be for Congress to exempt poor families from Social Security payments, much as last year's tax reform exempted them from the income tax. Congress should also restrain itself from killing jobs by raising the minimum wage.

Moreover, Congress could establish full-blown enterprise zones, as proposed by economist Stuart Butler, in areas most stricken by poverty. This idea has worked in England.

In other ways the Moynihan plan uses wrong ends to achieve the right goal of ending the toll welfare takes on families. It would require employers to withhold paternity payments from employees' checks automatically, deputizing employers as federal collection officers. Because federal immigration laws have already turned employers into INS enforcement agents, it's a wonder employers find time to do their real work.

On the positive side, the Moynihan plan would extend Medicare payments until nine months after a person gets a job, allowing time for private health plans to kick in. This may cost money in the short run, but by encouraging welfare recipients to find jobs, it will easily pay for itself by reducing welfare rolls.

The main problem with the Moynihan plan, in brief, is that it does not encourage enough diversity in fighting poverty. It would keep state, local, and private efforts on a leash, discouraging them from developing localized programs that work. Far from reforming welfare, the Moynihan plan would give us another grandiose exercise in futility. Taxpayers would again foot the bill for programs that ultimately will hurt the poor.

Fort Worth Star-Telegram

Fort Worth, TX, July 23, 1987

Liberals and conservatives agree that the nation's primary welfare program — Aid to Families with Dependent Children — is less than an overwhelming success. It is abused. It is inefficient. It is self-perpetuating.

It is time to overhaul the system, and the best welfare reform ideas may belong to Sen. Daniel P. Moynihan, D-N.Y.

The program he proposes is designed to re-establish the parents' prime responsibility. Instead of beginning with government payments and supplementing them with parental contributions to child support, Moynihan would do it the other way around.

Like a pending House bill, Moynihan's would require training and employment programs to be financed largely by the federal government — the object being to enable parents to support their children. It also calls for help with child care and other work-related expenses.

The thrust of Moynihan's proposal is similar to that of the House bill, but Moynihan's has one important advantage: It would cost less than half as much as the House bill.

To require that parents assume the primary obligation of supporting their children, even with federal and state help, is an idea whose time has come.

To do it at minimum public expense, in a time of enormous federal deficits, is a bonus.

The Indianapolis Star

Indianapolis, IN, July 24, 1987

If the U.S. Congress has a resident expert on welfare it is Sen. Daniel P. Moynihan.

The New York Democrat was among the first to warn about the disintegration of the black family. He has catalogued many of the sins of federal poverty programs and written extensively on family policy.

His views and his formula for improvement are not universally supported but they contain a vital ingredient, personal responsibility.

This week Moynihan introduced a welfare reform bill in the Senate that has a very good chance of being adopted. For one thing, it is legislation whose day has come.

It was a long time developing, but there is a consensus in the land that the present welfare system is an unmitigated failure. It has not reduced poverty. To the contrary, it may well have expanded and solidified it as a part of the social and cultural fabric.

Moynihan's bill introduces responsibility early in the game by establishing parentage at birth. Fathers and mothers will be identified and followed through Social Security, thus enabling states, if necessary, to withhold child support from paychecks and tax refunds.

The underlying principle of establishing parentage, according to Moynihan, is to make parents — wed or unwed — assume the obligations of parenthood.

Within three years after passage of the proposal, states would be required to set up a job opportunities and skill training program. Participation would be mandatory for able-bodied welfare recipients, including the mothers of children over three years. In general, recipients under 22 who dropped out of school must get a high school diploma.

Moynihan's bill would add two-parent families to welfare rolls and exact from both parents the obligations of work or training.

Though many Republicans have agreed to co-sponsor the Moynihan bill, the White House opposes the automatic coverage of two-parent families as too much of a burden for many states. Also there is considerable support for requiring full participation by mothers of children over one year of age.

In general, however, the White House is more favorably disposed toward the Moynihan proposal than toward the more costly legislation now working its way through the House.

The present welfare system, Aid for Families of Dependent Children, serves 3.8 million families, not wisely and not well. In a host of ways it is a shameful disservice to both recipients and taxpayers. The conviction grows that systemic reform is both imperative and possible.

Moynihan's proposal is far from perfect. As in the case of immigration reform, truly solid, comprehensive legislation may well be impossible given the clash of interests and philosophies that are involved. But, again as with immigration, almost any change represents improvement.

The Moynihan bill deserves serious, objective consideration. It is probably the best achievable package at this time. Realistic reformers might be wise to settle for a victory in principle and leave the modifications and refinements for future sessions.

The Dallas Morning News

Dallas, TX, July 28, 1987

Welfare reform has stirred more congressional talk and less congressional action than any subject in the land during the past two decades. Now comes Sen. Daniel Patrick Moynihan, who has been in the thick of the fight throughout that time, with another try at making some sense of the welfare mess.

Even those who may not agree with the particulars of Moynihan's new reform plan must agree that its thrust is in the right direction: He would put the stress on the obligation of the two parents to support their own children.

The plan would require the withholding of child support from the paychecks of parents who do not voluntarily meet their obligations to the youngsters that they have brought into the world. There also would be new emphasis on job training programs, to get parents into the labor force so that they could earn their way instead of depending on the children's welfare, unemployment pay and other subsidies from the taxpayers.

As Moynihan and other experts on welfare have pointed out for many years, the present Aid to Families with Dependent Children never was intended for the purposes to which it is now put. It was originally a widows' and orphans' bill, designed to tide families over after they had lost male breadwinners. Today it is typically used to support mothers, many of them in their teens, who bear children out of wedlock. The irony is that a law once designed to keep families together has now become a factor in breaking up families or preventing families from forming.

The American family and the society itself have both changed from the days when the AFDC program was established. It is time to devise a family welfare approach that fits the reality, that improves the climate for this most basic of all human groups instead of making it worse. The eloquent Moynihan, who has worked in both Republican and Democratic administrations on this issue, is a natural leader in such important legislative work.

Fort Worth Star-Telegram

Fort Worth, TX, July 4, 1987

Congressional conservatives and liberals appear to have reached an impasse on welfare reform, which is not unusual, but the fact that the majority of both agree that the main goal should be to get as many people as possible off welfare and on the job provides reason to hope the obstacles can be quickly overcome.

The House Ways and Means Committee last week approved a plan that calls for the most sweeping overhaul of the nation's welfare program in a generation.

The bill would require states to establish programs involving mandatory job training, education and work in an effort to shift welfare recipients to private payrolls instead of relying on Aid to Families with Dependent Children.

Many conservatives say they approve of the purpose of the bill, but they are alarmed by the fact that it also calls for a substantial increase in benefits. The bill's cost during the next five years is estimated at $5.2 billion.

The bill is expected to be approved by the House. Because of the more conservative bent of the Senate, however, it could encounter trouble there. Even should it get through both houses, President Reagan is likely to veto it because of the cost.

This, then, is the time for serious compromise.

Both sides want people removed from the welfare rolls by being trained for jobs in the private sector. Surely responsible members of Congress of both conservative and liberal persuasion can develop a program that can accomplish that without bankrupting the treasury.

The Times-Picayune
The States-Item

New Orleans, LA, July 27, 1987

Sen. Daniel P. Moynihan of New York has strong bipartisan support for his proposed reform of the nation's welfare system. His proposed Family Security Act of 1987 would make a number of radical changes in the requirements for welfare benefits.

The essence of his plan, which is aimed at breaking the vicious cycle of dependency on government handouts by encouraging individual initiative and family bonds, has powerful appeal and support among liberals, moderates and conservatives.

The core of the Moynihan bill emphasizes family responsibilities. Among other things, it would require employers to withhold court-ordered child support from paychecks and forward the money to the state. The purpose is to force irresponsible fathers to help support their children.

Critics of the current system long have argued that it unwittingly contributes to fatherless families, childbirth out of wedlock and teen-age pregnancies. As matters stand, fathers are encouraged to leave so mothers and their children can qualify for Aid to Families With Dependent Children.

The Moynihan bill calls for states to hold fathers financially accountable for their children, including tracking them down and garnisheeing their wages, if necessary.

Another provision requires states to pay benefits to two-parent households in which both parents are unemployed. The object is to encourage families to remain together.

The bill also tightens AFDC requirements. Most recipients would be required to participate in education, training or work programs run by states. The provision is aimed at breaking the cycle of dependency on government support payments by encouraging work, self-esteem and self-reliance.

The bill also would discourage teen-agers from having children in order to receive welfare checks. AFDC would be denied to unmarried individuals 18 and under who live apart from their parents.

To encourage people to work their way off of welfare roles, Medicaid health benefits would be retained for up to nine months after increased earnings eliminate welfare eligibility.

Various features of the bill inevitably have their detractors. The White House has been cool to the entire effort despite strong support among congressional Republicans. President Reagan has threatened to veto the bill if it contains the requirement that two-parent households in which both parents are unemployed be paid benefits.

Meanwhile, the American Public Welfare Association complains that the bill does not set a minimum benefit or encourage states to increase benefits.

Sen. Moynihan himself has been quick to observe that the bill is not etched in stone and is subject to compromise and revision.

But the essential points are sound. Groups from across the political spectrum agree that the present system is self-defeating and drastically in need of change. The Moynihan bill holds out the first realistic promise in decades of achieving the basic changes required.

The Record

Hackensack, NJ, July 29, 1987

One American child in five lives below the poverty line, often with a single parent, on welfare benefits that sometimes leave the cupboard bare. The buying power of welfare allotments has dropped 35 percent in 15 years. The shameful destitution of children has finally prompted a coalition of conservative and liberal leaders to declare "Enough!"

The result is broad support — except in the White House — for a radical overhaul of the present federal-state welfare system. The principal bill, drafted by the National Governors Council and sponsored by Sen. Daniel Patrick Moynihan, D-N.Y., assumes that the present welfare system is part of the problem. It's a system that teaches generations of parents to rely on the government to support their children. It drives unemployed fathers from their families in the 25 states that won't aid children if they have two parents at home.

The system has led to pernicious dependency and despondence, says Mr. Moynihan, and "must be turned on its head." His bill is similar to a measure approved by the House Committee on Ways and Means, and to a Kean administration proposal now advancing through the New Jersey Legislature. All are premised on the expectation that welfare can become, instead of a habit, a temporary supplement in hard times.

It is a very large order to lift even some of the 3.8 million people now on welfare to financial independence. It is nothing less than a revolution and demands revolutionary ideas. Senator Moynihan's bill has them. The first is a provision that makes two-parent families eligible for Aid to Families with Dependent Children, the central federally subsidized welfare program. Half of the states cling to the old Depression concept of public welfare as help for widows with children, and refuse to aid families if the father is at home. The reversal of this policy is crucial to restoring a stable family environment for poor children.

For reasons the White House has not explained, Mr. Reagan objects to this provision. Mr. Moynihan won important support from other conservatives by saying that his program puts responsiblity for raising children where it

belongs — on their parents, rather than on the government.

To help families become self-supporting, the Moynihan bill would require every AFDC recipient with children over the age of 2 to go to work, school, or job training. In return, the government would compensate them for day care, transportation to work, and tuition. Medicaid coverage would continue through a one-year period of transition after they leave the welfare rolls. Job training and public-works jobs would be made available to fathers.

On the issue of parental responsiblity, working fathers and mothers who walk out and cross state lines to avoid court-ordered support payments would have those payments deducted from their wages. The Moynihan bill would require every state to set child-support payments at least at subsistence levels, for welfare and nonwelfare children alike.

Costs will be large. The hope is that they will eventually be canceled out by reductions in the welfare rolls. Governor Kean has estimated that New Jersey's pioneering work-for-welfare program will require an investment of $60 million before it begins to break even. New Jersey has two pilot programs underway. In Newark and Camden, welfare mothers are being required to go to school or get job training. For welfare recipients in four South Jersey counties, 1,500 casino jobs have been made available. The state has promised support for child care and the other needs. The program, called REACH (Realizing Economic Achievement) is to be extended to five North Jersey counties starting in October.

We believe that the public will support substantial investments of time and money to help families get off welfare, for the families' good and their own. Providing schooling and jobs and day care will be expensive in the short run, but good economics — and the only decent course — in the long run. We think people will agree that the welfare system should not be structured so that it drives families apart — even if that means subsidizing able-bodied men.

It's almost a given that the present system is a mess. It's time to fix it.

ST. LOUIS POST-DISPATCH

St. Louis, MO, August 3, 1987

Everyone agrees that the trouble with the welfare system is that it encourages dependency instead of self-sufficiency. Beyond that point, though, there is considerable difference of opinion on how to turn things around.

President Reagan, for example, favors mandatory workfare, and he opposes spending any more money on welfare than is being spent now. Sen. Daniel Patrick Moynihan of New York has introduced a bill requiring job training, education and job-search services for welfare recipients. The bill would cost $2.7 billion over the next five years. A similar but more generous version of the Moynihan proposal is making its way through various House committees. Its five-year cost was placed at $5.3 billion. The nation's governors have endorsed a comprehensive welfare reform measure with a first-year price tag of $1 billion. Whether differences can be resolved in a way that moves the welfare system in the direction intended is problematical.

There is little new about the job training and placement provisions in the Moynihan and House bills. The welfare law has contained an optional job training and placement component since the mid-1960s. About half the states have taken advantage of it on a limited scale. Since the advent of the Reagan administration, however, funding for the program — called WIN — has steadily declined, and will be formally terminated this year.

Though the WIN program was popular with welfare recipients, one of the principal reasons it was not put to greater use was its high cost. That does not bode well for the current drive to put welfare recipients to work. In the short run, letting people live on the dole is a good deal cheaper than training them for jobs and then placing them, especially when the cost of daycare is included. If job training is going to succeed, day-care is essential because the vast majority of welfare families are headed by single mothers.

But even if Congress and the states were willing to pay the extra expense, another obstacle looms: finding jobs for the welfare recipients once they have been trained. With 7 million people looking for work, and millions more who want full-time jobs able to find only part-time employment, placing them would be difficult.

Cost and other barriers notwithstanding, there is no doubt that job training and placement are the keys to ending welfare dependency, which is why they are superior alternatives to workfare. Workfare simply compels welfare recipients to accept public-sector jobs as a condition of receiving benefits. It forces them to work off their monthly payments, but does nothing to get them off welfare or to improve their lot. In short, it is punitive.

It is easy to deplore welfare dependency; it is quite another thing to do something meaningful about it. The test of the commitment of the president and Congress to welfare reform is whether they are willing to spend the money.

THE PLAIN DEALER

Cleveland, OH, July 29, 1987

Welfare reform is taking an overdue but well-deserved place on the nation's agenda. The growing consensus among liberals, conservatives, and even among some welfare recipients is that the current system encourages dependency and promulgates an unwieldy, ineffective method to address the needs of the poor.

Already suggested and, fortunately, abandoned, was a Reagan initiative to phase out the federal government's involvement in welfare by cashing out programs through block grants to the states. Allowing states more flexibility in determining programs is a good idea only when federal support is not severely reduced, and when federal guidelines establishing national minimum benefits and eligibility standards are maintained.

The most popular strategy to reduce welfare dependency is workfare, which would require able-bodied welfare recipients with children past infancy to work for part of their income. Other

ideas, including a bill introduced earlier this month by New York Sen. Daniel P. Moynihan, would require the automatic withholding of child support from absent parents' wages.

More controversial is a proposal requiring states to establish education, training and employment programs for welfare recipients. That is humane and responsible, liberals say; it would cost too much money, conservatives say. Still others say such special programs for those on welfare could create an unfair and undesirable discrepancy between them and low-income workers who would not be eligible.

None of the proposals on the table would end the welfare system or the need for it. But the growing consensus for change is giving Congress an incredibly important opportunity. Lawmakers have a chance to redirect the problems of illegitimacy and parental irresponsibility, and wean a growing number of Americans from a parasitic system that has rewarded them for becoming and remaining dependent and unproductive.

Chicago Tribune

Chicago, IL, July 24, 1987

The family welfare plan being pushed by Sen. Daniel Patrick Moynihan (D., N.Y.) is a sweeping mix of good ideas, good intentions and complicated, untested changes. It is designed to replace Aid to Families with Dependent Children, which often is blamed for breaking up families, trapping women and children in dependency for generations and encouraging teenagers to have babies out of wedlock by providing them independent support.

Laudably, the intent of the Moynihan proposal is to enforce the primary responsibility of both parents to support their children and to get as many as possible off the government dole. The plan may, however, increase bureaucratic red tape, require additional support services and at least in the short run cost taxpayers more—not less. The estimated price tag is $2.3 billion for five years, about half the tab for a package of somewhat similar legislation under consideration in the House.

Under the Moynihan bill, the child support payments a father or mother was ordered by a court to make would be deducted from his or her paycheck. The money would be sent to a state agency, which would pass it on to the parent taking care of the child, supplementing it if necessary to meet federal guidelines. States would be required to try harder to identify the fathers of youngsters born out of wedlock and to collect child support from them.

Both provisions would help boost the collection of court-ordered child support. Millions of fathers never pay their support obligations or do so only in part or for a short time. Federal legislation allowing income tax refunds to be tapped and wages to be garnisheed when a parent does not comply with court orders have helped considerably. But delinquent dads and men who don't legally acknowledge their offspring are still a major reason why so many women and children live in poverty and why welfare costs are so high.

The Moynihan plan also aims to put more welfare recipients to work, including mothers of children older than 3. States would have to provide job training and employment services and help pay for child care and work expenses. It would be expensive. The training and jobs would have to be real, not just teaching welfare mothers to work in day care centers to take care of the children of other welfare mothers. But the cost in tax dollars would be worth it, if the plan succeeded in getting parents out of the welfare trap and into the labor force.

One particularly good provision of the Moynihan plan would let welfare recipients keep Medicaid coverage for nine months after they take a job and are no longer eligible under current regulations. Many parents with young children are reluctant to take a low-paying, entry-level job if they cannot be assured of medical care for their offspring.

Also welcome—and long overdue—is the bill's provision that intact two-parent families should be eligible for help. Currently, 24 states do not include them, and sometimes desperate fathers decide they must leave home so that their wives and children can qualify for welfare. This is not only cruel for poor families but also counterproductive for taxpayers. Welfare reform legislation being considered in the House contains a similar change.

No legislation is going to solve all the problems of the current system, end the feminization of poverty or rescue the underclass from the welfare trap. But the Moynihan plan should help. It is worth doing. And it is particularly important to establish its underlying principle: Parents, not government, are responsible for their children.

The Clarion-Ledger
JACKSON DAILY NEWS

Jackson, MS, July 27, 1987

Welfare reform is inching along in Congress, but, while moving slowly, it seems to be on the right track.

As the House considers two similar plans to provide education and jobs to get welfare clients off public assistance, the Senate is preparing to take up the same type of program, with more emphasis — as is merited — on collecting child support payments.

Author Sen. Daniel Patrick Moynihan, D-N.Y., called the existing Aid to Families with Dependent Children program "a passive system . . . a widow's pension." He would replace it with a Child Support Supplement program that would require states to set up within three years a Job Opportunities and Basic Skills program. It would be mandatory for many welfare recipients.

The bill's child support provisions, many of them stiffer than those considered by the House, would require states to set and use guidelines on the amount of awards, collect the support payments directly from the employers of the parents, usually fathers, through withholding, and step up efforts to establish paternity or lose federal money.

While public welfare should be primarily a federal responsibility, the states have a role to play, and legislators must make clear the terms of the partnership.

In ironing out differences between House and Senate bills, once they've been approved by the full bodies, conferees should lean toward the least costly and the one that can be most uniformly applied to all the states.

BUFFALO EVENING NEWS

Buffalo, NY, July 21, 1987

TO PROVIDE compassionate help without fostering dependency — that should be the goal of welfare assistance for the needy. The federal bureaucracy has done a fairly efficient job on helping families in need through its Aid to Families with Dependent Children program. But the program has been poor at preventing dependency.

Sen. Daniel Patrick Moynihan is proposing a new approach that would do a better job of both.

With the country in the mood for welfare reform, Moynihan's proposed $2.3 billion program has a real chance for success despite some differences with the Reagan administration, which has its own ideas about changes. The White House plan, at $4.5 billion over five years (the same time span as the Moynihan program), would be more expensive and would put more emphasis on local demonstration projects.

The important underlying principle of reform should guide the discussions in Washington: Government should help when families are in need, but it should also insist on the responsibility of parents to support their own children when they are able to.

Moynihan's program has strong incentives and aid provisions to help make fundamental changes.

To see that court-mandated child support is always paid, the legislation would have the payments withheld from paychecks by employers. This system could take many children off the welfare rolls; a significant number of families now receiving public assistance are not getting court-ordered

child support. The legislation would also aid programs to establish paternity of children receiving public support.

Support for children should also be expected from able-bodied parents who do live with them — most often mothers. Moynihan's program would require even mothers of young children to seek work or job training.

As the senator has pointed out, with most American mothers of preschool children now employed outside the home, the public should no longer be expected to accept supporting mothers who want to stay at home after their children's earliest years.

But welfare-assisted parents also can't be expected to get work when many lack basic skills and have no access to child care, transportation or other services that would allow them to seek jobs. The proposed program would provide a stable source of funding to states to let them develop the needed services.

To help make all of this work, Moynihan's legislation would allow financial sanctions for welfare parents who did not cooperate with the work and job training requirements and, to help families stay together, would allow help to go to families with both parents living at home.

The aid program badly needs this overhaul. Compassionate help would still be provided — in many ways, much more compassionate help than is given now, because it would actively aid families in building a better future. And the public stands to benefit with big cost savings as families move toward self-support.

The Houston Post

Houston, TX, July 27, 1987

Sen. Daniel Moynihan, D-N.Y., has introduced a welfare overhaul plan he says will turn the present system "on its head." Our welfare system is in dire need of reform, and nothing short of upending it would seem likely to solve its multitude of problems.

Moynihan's plan, he says, places responsibility for supporting children on both parents. Establishment by the states of paternity would be encouraged, and employers would automatically deduct child support payments from paychecks of absent parents. The current Aid to Families With Dependent Children often allows absent fathers to evade all responsibility.

States would design remedial education and job-training programs, and most unemployed adults receiving welfare would be required to attend. Moynihan's measure would not, as AFDC sometimes does, force one parent to leave the home so benefits could be obtained. Welfare recipients who do find work could retain transitional Medicaid benefits and child support payments.

The bill approaches welfare reform sanely. It establishes responsibility and encourages welfare recipients to seek work without punishing them for having a job. It offers hope of breaking the demeaning progression from welfare generation to welfare generation.

Something like it should have become law long ago.

LEXINGTON HERALD-LEADER

Lexington, KY, July 26, 1987

Last year's second-ranked crisis, after the fury over drugs, was the American underclass. The underclass, popular wisdom decreed, was chock-full of Americans who had never made it and never would. The underclass would never have jobs; never attain an education; never raise bright, healthy children. It would remain a drag on the country; and we would keep right on supporting it, pouring money into an ever-deepening hole.

There seemed to be no way out.

But Sen. Daniel Patrick Moynihan, D-N.Y., has mapped out a revision of the welfare system that is a revolution in the way the United States looks at poverty. Called the Family Security Act of 1987, it would cost the federal government $2.3 billion over five years — a bargain when you consider that welfare benefits run the federal government $10 billion annually, with the states kicking in another $8 billion.

Moynihan, a noted scholar on the problems of America's poor, believes we have been going about it all wrong: The government started out with assumptions about America's responsibility to the poor. Now, Moynihan says, it's time to talk about the poor's responsibility to themselves.

The Moynihan plan includes these points:

• It would replace the basic assistance program, Aid to Families with Dependent Children, with a new federal-state program designed to supplement child support paid by parents. State officials would set the amount of the child-support supplements using federal guidelines.

• Parents who pay child support would have it automatically withheld from their paychecks. Employers withholding the money would send it to state agencies for distribution to families.

• States would intensify efforts to establish paternity so they could collect more child support from absent fathers. This means that states would have to keep records of both parents' Social Security numbers when a baby is born.

• Welfare recipients would be required, where available, to participate in job programs.

• The federal government would help pay child-care costs up to $160 a month.

• A person who leaves the welfare rolls because of increased earnings would remain eligible for health insurance under Medicaid for up to nine months. There is no transition period at present.

Moynihan has worked hard to assure that Senate Republicans agreed with the bill's contents. He's confident that the House will come around to agreement. The only missing element in the Moynihan equation is the White House, which is odd. You'd think that this variety of up-by-your-own-bootstraps welfare reform would be precisely the Reagan administration's cup of tea.

Moynihan argues that his bill places responsibility for supporting children "where it has always belonged: with parents. Both parents."

It's hard to quibble with Moynihan there. It's equally hard to dismiss a plan that treats America's disadvantaged as a resource rather than an eternal, expensive liability.

The Evening Gazette

Worcester, MA, July 27, 1987

Welfare conditions in the United States have deteriorated to the point where a major reform seems inevitable this year. The sooner it comes, the better.

Aid to Families with Dependent Children, the principal federal-state welfare program, currently provides monthly cash payments to about 11 million persons at a total cost of almost $18 billion. The program is badly outdated and flawed. Its worst aspect is that it helps perpetuate what the experts call a "permanent underclass" — people who are dependent on government support for generations.

Some states, most notably Massachusetts and California, have made some strides toward combining welfare benefits with job training and placement. A key element in these programs is child care, which frees mothers to enter job training and the employment market.

The jury is still out on these experiments, which themselves require a substantial public investment. The Bay State's ET program claimed some successes in getting people trained, off welfare and into jobs. Any progress in this area translates into savings for taxpayers and happier and more productive lives for welfare recipients.

More is needed. A top-to-bottom overhaul of the welfare structure nationally is in order. Most everybody in government, from President Reagan to congressmen and governors, agree that a reform is overdue. What is missing is a consensus on a specific model.

Sen. Daniel Patrick Moynihan, D-N.Y., has heated up the issue by introducing his own sweeping proposals. At first blush, his package seems to have a number of positive aspects. It would not be surprising if his ideas became catalysts for major welfare revision this year.

The strength of the Moynihan plan lies in its emphasis on parental responsiblity for child care. The bill would require withholding child support payments from parents' wages. The states, with federal help, would then supplement the amounts paid by the parents.

The proposal also requires welfare recipients to participate in job training to the extent it is available. The federal government would help pay child care costs up to $160 a month per child. A person who managed to get off welfare would remain eligible for Medicaid for up to nine months.

Ensuring that both parents shoulder child support is a measure long overdue. The current system allows, actually encourages, fathers to leave home and forget they have responsibility for their offspring. It creates an intolerable situation.

The notion of withholding money from payroll checks and then having the state distribute the money is neither new nor simple. It would take some doing to track down and establish paternity for absent fathers. What kind of burden all this may place on employers is yet to be determined. Still, whatever shape national welfare reform takes, it is not going to gain public support if it fails to emphasize child support by both parents.

Ours is a compassionate society. It has no desire to see the truly needy suffer. What society can no longer tolerate, however, is a continuation of the bankrupt policies that help create generations of people depending not on productive work but on handouts.

The Moynihan plan needs careful scrutiny and fine-tuning. Some of its aspects may be integregated with other proposals that are in the works. Together they should provide the basis for a much-needed welfare reform.

Congress Approves Major Welfare Overhaul

The House Sept. 30, 1988 and the Senate Sept 29 approved the welfare reform plan. Sen. Daniel Patrick Moynihan (D, N.Y.), chief architect and mover of the legislation, received the accolades of his colleagues when more than a dozen senators took the floor to praise his efforts.

"We have redefined the whole question of dependency," Moynihan said Sept. 26 in describing the revised welfare system as it was being forged in a Senate-House conference committee. "This is no longer to be a permanent or even extended circumstance. It is to be a transition to employment, and it is to be accompanied by child support from the absent parent." The conferees gave final approval to the compromises Sept. 27.

The Senate June 16, 1988 had adopted a comprehensive revision of the nation's welfare program with a major emphasis on work requirments. The legislation was sent to conference with the House, which had passed a differing measure in December 1987. The House bill did not contain a work requirement. The Reagan administration considered the House version unacceptable and the Senate measure, even, not stern enough on the work program.

The legislation represented the first major revision of the welfare program since its enactment in 1935. Currently, the program, known as Aid to Families with Dependent Children (AFDC), paid monthly benefits to 3.3 million mothers, 400,000 fathers and 7.3 million children. The federal government financed about 55% of the cost, the states the rest.

The Senate bill, adopted by a 93-3 vote, projected a $2.8 billion program over five years, compared with a House program estimated at $7 billion. The Senate measure called for the states to set up basic education, job training and related work programs. Welfare parents who were able would be required to participate in the programs, except those whose children were less than three years old, or, at state option, one year old.

The training would be directed especially at those who were not high school graduates or who had been on welfare for long periods. To promote the movement from welfare to the work force, the bill called continuing child care for up to nine months and Medicaid for up to a year after a parent left welfare. Child-support laws would be strengthened under the welfare bill, to the point that employers would be required to automatically deduct any legally due child-support payments from the paycheck of an absent parent even if the individual were not in arrears.

In a last-minute amendment offered by Senate Republican leader Robert J. Dole (Kan.) and Sen. William L. Armstrong (R, Colo.), the Senate decided to mandate certain "workfare" requirements. It called for at least one parent in two-parent welfare families to work a minimum of 16 hours a week in unpaid community work projects, "workfare," or other jobs, while on the welfare rolls. The amendment was offered with a view to make the legislation more palatable to the Reagan administration, which considered the original bill's requirements—where workfare was an option for the states—too weak.

Still another strengthening provision, to allay White House opposition, was added by the Senate to require the states to enroll by 1994 at least 22% of those eligible on a training, education or other work-related program. State programs on training and education were required to include job search, subsidized employment and workfare as possible options.

The legislation would also require states to provide welfare benefits to families in which both parents were present but the principal wage earner, presumably the father, was unemployed. This provision, which was expected to affect some 65,000 families, was intended to keep families together, instead of forcing the father out of the home to ensure benefit eligibility.

The Courier-Journal & Times
Louisville, KY,
June 19, 1988

MORE than two decades have passed since Daniel Patrick Moynihan started alerting the nation to the plight of the poor and the disadvantaged. His family was on welfare when he was a child, so he spoke from first-hand knowledge of the dangers of the cycle of poverty in which so many welfare recipients are trapped.

His quest for a more humane welfare system — one that encourages self-sufficiency — is now nearing its goal. Only agreement by a Senate-House conference committee and the signature of President Reagan are needed.

But obstacles remain. Differences between the House measure, passed last December, and the Senate version, approved by a 93-3 vote Thursday, are substantial. And President Reagan, despite calls to turn the welfare system into a "ladder of opportunity," really wants to throw the responsibility back to the states.

One late amendment to Senator Moynihan's bill addressed a major White House demand by adding a requirement that at least one parent in two-parent welfare families work a minimum of 16 hours a week in "workfare," or community work projects, while on welfare rolls. This requirement would be phased in by the mid-1990s. The administration had argued that the Moynihan bill, which made workfare an option for the states, was too weak.

In broad outline, the House and Senate bills would encourage individual initiative in breaking the poverty cycle. As Senator Moynihan has argued, Americans are not going to support higher welfare benefits if the system continues to encourage long-term dependency.

Both the Senate and House measures promise to break the cycle. Conferees should waste no time in blending a reform measure that is less costly than the House's $5.7 billion, five-year proposal but that retains the most humane features of both measures.

The Register

Santa Ana, CA, June 20, 1988

When a business makes a mistake in making a product, it tries to correct itself by building a better one. The bottom line is that it has to build a better one, or risk bankruptcy. When government makes a mistake, it shuffles a few papers and spends more money. The bottom line is that the taxpayers pay for mistakes, so blunders need not be corrected.

A case in point is the country's welfare mess. It's obvious now that the $130 billion now spent at all levels of government on anti-poverty programs only gets people addicted to government doles, while fattening bureaucrats and professional poverty workers. As Kevin P. Holsclaw wrote in the *Register* in January, "Despite the best of intentions, the empirical evidence seems to suggest that increased levels of benefits have been associated with increased rather than decreased levels of poverty."

Last week the Senate voted to make the problem even worse. By a 93-2 vote it approved the euphemistically named Family Security Act, a five-year, $2.8 billion measure sure to grow into another huge program — especially since the House has already passed a $7 billion version of the same bill. The Senate bill is more likely to survive reconciliation meetings, inasmuch as the Reagan administration supports it, but the tendency is obvious.

The White House supported the Senate version only after more stringent work requirements were included, by which some recipients will have to work 16 hours a week, either for private companies or on government projects. Such "workfare" schemes are already at work in many state welfare programs, and may seem a good deal. People should work for the money they get.

Yet "workfare" only encourages people to look to the government for work. Especially with America's economy booming so strongly, people don't need the government to help them find jobs. This should never have become a role of government, and the Family Security Act — billed by its sponsor, Sen. Daniel Moynihan of New York, who terms it a "reform" of our 53-year-old welfare system — will in fact further entrench the government in this role.

This new program, ironically, will make jobs more scarce, making worse the "problem" it is supposed to solve. It will take more money from the economy — $2.8 billion to start — which means either higher taxes or more public debt. This burden will be paid by businesses through higher taxes or higher interest rates paid on company loans, which reduces business expansion, and so reduces the number of private jobs offered by these businesses.

Finally, even with the "workfare" sections added, the Moynihan bill includes many loopholes that will simply increase the size of the existing federal welfare behemoth. This is the opposite of what is needed. In their study "Paying People to Be Poor," Lowell Gallaway and Richard Vedder of Ohio State University write: "The US welfare system is creating poverty, not destroying it .... At least 5.7 million people — about one-sixth of the poverty population — are living in poverty by choice as a result of the generosity of public welfare. Each additional $1 billion in welfare spending increases the poverty population by 250,000."

Let's see. The new welfare "reform" will cost at least $2.8 billion. That comes to 700,000 more people in poverty.

ST. LOUIS POST-DISPATCH

St. Louis, MO, June 21, 1988

Both houses of Congress have now approved bills seeking to make jobs the new cornerstone of the nation's welfare system. Beyond that general goal, however, only the House's proposal represents a compassionate and realistic approach to getting the most recipients off the dole and into private employment. That is why House negotiators ought to insist at the coming conference with Senate representatives that the final welfare bill include most of the House's language, programs and benefits.

The House bill would cost roughly $5.2 billion over five years and would do much to encourage recipients to find work. It would offer states more funds to cover education, training and employment activities under the federal Work Incentive (WIN) program; it would permit recipients to use $100 a month of their incomes for transportation and other job-related expenses; it would offer day-care allotments of up to $200 for children under the age of 2 and $175 for those over 2; and it would offer higher federal matching rates to states that raise welfare benefits to more livable levels.

The Senate bill, which would cost roughly $2.8 billion, excludes or reduces many of the House provisions. The Senate, moreover, has included an amendment requiring recipients to take part in a workfare program. The administration had urged the Senate to require that 70 percent of all recipients enroll in workfare in order to remain eligible for welfare. The Senate caved in halfway to this nonsense by limiting the workfare requirement to 22 percent of recipients.

Most governors, who are conservative about welfare spending, say the workfare provision is counterproductive. Proof is in the fact that only nine states have set up such programs. The governors know that recipients must receive real job training — not make-work assignments — if they are to become employable in the private sector.

What tasks would these recipients perform? Restack library books? Cut weeds? Just the kind of work experience that private industry isn't looking for.

Demanding the right kind of work from welfare recipients should, of course, be encouraged. Congress has, in fact, included work provisions in many welfare programs as far back as 1962. One of the more notable has been WIN, the job training and placement program that seeks to make recipients economically self-sufficient by training them for private industry jobs. If the administration were serious about putting recipients to work, it would have expanded WIN — as the House welfare proposal seeks to do — instead of wasting time with mandatory workfare.

What's most troubling about the Senate's bill is that it aims more to please an unenlightened president than to provide maximum opportunities to help many of this nation's 3.7 million public aid families break out of the welfare cycle. Because the House bill offers these families a better chance of succeeding, it deserves to become the law.

Chicago Tribune

Chicago, IL, June 21, 1988

The Reagan administration, objecting to what it regards as serious defects in the welfare reform bill passed last week by the Senate, has said the President may veto it. There are flaws in this measure, the first overhaul of the welfare system since it was created a century ago. But it also makes overdue improvements and enshrines important principles that may prepare the way for still greater improvements.

Equally important, with a price tag of $2.8 billion over five years, it shies away from large new spending plans. It deserves President Reagan's approval.

The most welcome part of the package is a stiff work requirement on fathers in two-parent families that get payments. In 23 states, Aid to Families with Dependent Children excludes households in which both parents are present, which encourages family disintegration. The new welfare system would require all states to drop this self-defeating exclusion, with a catch: The father would have to work 16 hours a week in community service. That should act as a deterrent to staying on welfare, while providing society something valuable in exchange for its spending.

The bill suffers, though, from not applying that logic consistently. Single parents on welfare get more lenient treatment. Recipients may participate in education and training programs, which are often more attractive and less effective than actual work. By 1994, at least 22 percent of a state's recipients must do something in exchange for benefits—work, attend remedial classes or train for a job. That figure is far too modest and the timetable is too leisurely to really alter the culture of the urban underclass.

But any measure that ties welfare to work, however loosely, is a step forward. The bill has other merits in addition to removing the discrimination against fathers who stay with their families. One is that it calls for withholding child support payments from the paychecks of absent fathers, reducing the burden on taxpayers. Another is that it allows recipients moving into jobs to keep their Medicaid benefits for a year after they leave the welfare rolls and provides child care for the first nine months, removing major obstacles to efforts at self-reliance.

In this new program, mothers will be expected to accept work or training supplied by the state when their youngest child reaches the age of 3 instead of the current 6—and states have the choice of lowering that to age 1. In an era when most mothers work at least part-time, it's not too much to expect that those on welfare do likewise.

Work requirements offend some welfare-rights organizations, and the bill passed by the House avoids them. Properly handled, mandatory work programs offer those with little job experience a chance to learn how to function as employees, which improves their chances of earning their own way. And they prove to demoralized welfare recipients that they can contribute to society, a lesson badly needed in the inner city.

Contrary to popular stereotype, those forced to work generally say they approve of the requirement. No doubt they gain a great deal of self-respect from the sense of earning their benefits, not simply receiving them. The purpose of a work requirement is to help the poor, not to punish them. As New York University scholar Lawrence Mead puts it, "If lower-income men and welfare mothers worked regularly, the underclass would be well on its way to dissolution."

Dissolving the underclass ought to be a central point of welfare policy. This measure isn't perfect, but it's a start in the right direction. Next, the work-study requirements should be tightened, and welfare recipients who do well in classes should be rewarded as Jesse Jackson suggests: a small bonus for a high school diploma, a bigger one for a community college degree. With those incentives, a mandatory work requirement will be more realistic and easier to enforce.

Pittsburgh Post-Gazette

Pittsburgh, PA,
June 20, 1988

During the Great Depression, President Franklin D. Roosevelt initiated a welfare system that enabled impoverished people to recover from the worst economic nightmare of our time. That system may have been effective for meeting the needs of American society then, but times and people have changed. So must the welfare system.

Last week the U.S. Senate took a giant step in that direction. By a 93-3 vote, it passed a bill that could result in a historic overhaul of the welfare system. The tireless sponsor of the legislation, Sen. Daniel Patrick Moynihan of New York, said it was designed to "turn the welfare program upside down."

That is not an exaggeration. Like somewhat less stringent legislation already passed by the House of Representatives, the Senate bill would transform the Aid to Families with Dependent Children program from a system of payments, with little emphasis on jobs, to a jobs program in which welfare payments would be assumed to be temporary.

But the bill doesn't stop at requiring able-bodied welfare recipients with children over the age of 3 to find work. It also would require states to establish flexible work programs that would include remedial education as well as job training and placement. If those programs were to reduce the number of recipients, the $1 billion they would cost the states would be small in comparison to $15 billion the federal government pays each year in benefits.

Serious education and placement programs are essential if the legislation's "work requirement" is going to be more than another bankrupt phrase. Few of the mothers getting AFDC are capable of entering the work force immediately, and the federal government realizes this. Instead of telling people to "pick themselves up by their own bootstraps," Washington would provide the bootstraps.

Furthermore, the bill would ease a woman's transition into the work force by requiring that a state provide child care for nine months to families who become ineligible for AFDC. And it ties its work requirement to the larger good by requiring fathers in two-parent families to spend at least 16 hours a week in community service in exchange for welfare benefits.

Society also benefits from strong and intact families. The Senate bill encourages family responsibility by requiring states to withhold child-support payments from absent fathers' wages and by allowing two-parent families to receive welfare benefits when the principal wage earner is unemployed. Currently only 27 states provide welfare payments to such families. In other states, the able-bodied father must leave the family so that it can be eligible for AFDC benefits, regardless of how small the family's income may be.

Supporters of the Senate bill insist that it essentially will pay for itself. Even if they are being optimistic, the long-term advantages if the policy works are immeasurable. Past debates on welfare have pitted those who emphasized the government's duty to help the poor against those who stressed the importance of letting the poor help themselves. The policy embodied in the Senate bill seems to combine the best of both worlds.

The Washington Post

Washington, DC, June 22, 1988

AN UNSUSPECTING Senate fell through a trap door in the tax code the other day and found that what it had thought was rational policy could be construed as sex discrimination. The issue has still not been resolved.

The question was how to finance the welfare bill the Senate later passed. The Finance Committee had proposed to raise the necessary money the same way the House agreed to do it: by phasing out for higher-income families the child care credit now available to all. That seemed to make good tax policy and good family policy all at once; an existing subsidy would be redirected from rich families to poor. Indeed, it was such a good idea that advocates of a new federal child care program had also thought of it, but the welfare people got there first.

Then Sen. Bill Bradley popped the balloon. He rose to tell his colleagues that, on the contrary, a limit on the child care credit would be a very bad idea, and discriminatory besides. For women, he argued, the cost of child care is a cost of producing income, and such costs are supposed to be deductible. "No other cost of earning income is subjected to a means test, not the cost of a salesman's car, not the cost of a secretary, not even the three-martini lunch. Yet this bill takes, of all things, child care, and says if you are a successful mother who works, you cannot deduct your child care. To me, Mr. President, it is as if the Senate had a big blind spot on this issue."

The Senate, Sen. Bradley said, was "robbing Jill to pay Jane," and he proposed instead that another cost of earning income be means-tested—the deduction for business meals and entertainment. Among other advantages, this tends to be thought of as a man's deduction.

Mr. Bradley's proposal was not all that well drafted. Other members of the Finance Committee pointed out that it would disallow some legitimate deductions as well as some that are excessive. But in the end the cowed Senate gulped and went along, at least until conference with the House.

Our own thought is that Mr. Bradley and Sen. Barbara Mikulski, who supported him, are only half right. The cost of child care is *not* quite the same as the cost of the salesman's car. The tax code shouldn't favor women over men, and should favor lower-income families over high. The government has only so much money to spend on child care, and it should spend that money on the families in greatest need. What the welfare conferees should do is adopt *both* revenue-raising proposals, the committee's and Mr. Bradley's. Then it could finance not only the rather parsimonious Senate bill but some of the proposals on the House side to increase benefits, which in recent years have lagged behind inflation. Congress wouldn't be giving women the back of its hand, but wouldn't be giving well-off women a free ride, either.

Arkansas Gazette.

Little Rock, AR, June 20, 1988

Like most everything else, poverty has not been untouched the past 50 years by racing change in American society. Once unchoosing between the sexes and a phenomenon mainly of the elderly, it now clutches mostly mothers and children.

It has left Americans with a terrible ambivalence toward public welfare — a conflict between a revulsion for dependence on government and protective impulses for children and mothers. Public assistance programs serve one in six children — more than 7 million of them, an overwhelming majority of them in the households of divorced or unwed mothers.

The same conflict has afflicted Congress and presidents — yes, even Ronald Reagan. The Senate finally overcame its ambivalence last week and passed, by an astonishing vote of 93 to 3, the first dramatic overhaul of welfare since the enactment of survivors' insurance and aid to families of dependent children during the Great Depression. The House of Representatives had approved a similar but costlier bill in December. Each is aimed at pushing parents and families off public assistance into work. The two houses will work out a compromise bill by fall.

President Reagan promised a veto of either bill, though the Senate inserted a few harsh provisions in its version at the last minute to try to avert a veto. Senate Republicans were mystified about what the president really wanted. Indeed, Mr. Reagan's ambivalence seems to be deeper than anyone's. He thinks mothers should be at home, but he has wanted mandates for them to work. Though professing deep concern about keeping families intact, the president has fought to preserve laws that penalize unemployed couples and give them incentives to separate.

At the end, the Senate, which already had harsher provisions than the House for households where both parents were at home but unemployed, partially capitulated to the president. It required states like Arkansas to extend public assistance to two-parent households where they are otherwise eligible but only for six months of a year, and in at least half the cases in the state one parent would have to find at least 16 hours of work a week.

Both bills would require states to provide incentives for parents to support their families. There will be tougher laws to force fathers to support their families, including mandatory wage-withholding after child-support orders. With federal assistance, the states will insure child-care for mothers who take work, continue their education or train for jobs, continue Medicaid health insurance for their children for a period after they find private employment, arrange job training and help in the search for jobs. Those are the central pieces of welfare reform. The House bill would go further and put a national floor under benefits. If the change really helps reduce poverty and dependence, it will not be owing to punitive laws but to positive reinforcement of the instincts for self-reliance. The present welfare system isn't working, not because it rewards indolence but because it offers no way out of deep poverty. The conference committee ought to keep its focus on that goal and not punitive measures that might ease the president's dilemma.

The Washington Times

Washington, DC, June 17, 1988

The Reagan administration may be about to capitulate on one of the important domestic issues of the 1980s: welfare reform. At issue is Sen. Daniel Moynihan's "Family Security Act of 1988" (S. 1511), which has more than 60 cosponsors and is now being debated in the Senate. Many welfare reformers are unhappy about a "Statement of Administration Policy" released Monday, which said the administration would support the bill if it included tougher work requirements and allowed states to experiment with pilot welfare reform programs of their own.

The bill contains far graver flaws than those mentioned by the White House. The most important is the fact that it would, in the name of ending AFDC's anti-family bias, extend the program to two-parent families at least six months per year. The only studies available on such programs indicate that they actually increase marital separation rates and hence the number of single-parent families on welfare. George Gilder argues this is because welfare programs "destroy the key role and authority of the father" by making the welfare office the family's chief breadwinner and, through program regulations, disciplinarian as well.

Nor will AFDC for unemployed parents cure the problem of out-of-wedlock births. Some of the highest rates of illegitimacy occur in states with two-parent welfare. In the two-parent welfare states of Maryland and New York, three of four births to women under the age of 20 occur out of wedlock; 91 percent of such births occur out of wedlock in the District, which also offers AFDC for two-parent families. The Department of Health and Human Services estimates that the extension of AFDC to two-parent households would lure 82,000 additional families onto the rolls, including 1,000 in Virginia.

The bill also creates a new job training program in which welfare recipients must participate in order to receive benefits. Sen. Bill Armstrong of Colorado notes that some states may allow participants to meet this requirement by attending high school or college, something that is certain to encourage greater federal intervention and control of education.

Other provisions would require all states to implement entitlement programs that provide child care for nine months after people leave the rolls, and continue Medicaid for a full year after people stop receiving AFDC. Under what is essentially a guaranteed annual income provision, states would also be prohibited from forcing people to accept a job that would pay less than recipients were receiving from government assistance programs. In states such as New York and California, the welfare recipient in effect would have to be "guaranteed" a job that pays more than $12,700 annually. This provision would cost state governments more than $5 billion over the next five years, and probably would cost much more since it would tell marginally skilled poor people that they can earn a pretty comfortable living by relying on Uncle Sam, rather than fighting their way up through the job market.

In short, the White House's "compromise" would leave intact a host of provisions that actually worsen the present welfare system — a situation that could only deteriorate as the Senate tried to reconcile its bill with an even more expensive and objectionable version passed by the House. What's particularly tragic is that Mr. Moynihan, who played such a critical role in calling attention to the problems of the underclass more than two decades ago, has lent his name to legislation that will invite tens of thousands of Americans to join that underclass by becoming dependent on government.

The Atlanta Journal
AND
THE ATLANTA CONSTITUTION

Atlanta, GA, June 4, 1988

Sometime this month — as early as the end of next week, perhaps — the Senate will take up the knotty issue of welfare reform; knotty, because a bill that has angered conservatives and liberals alike looks to be the only one with a chance of clearing Congress this year.

The question is not whether New York Democrat Daniel P. Moynihan's $2.6 billion welfare reform plan is the best way to go about overhauling the nation's cumbersome welfare machinery (it isn't), but, rather, whether the nation would be better off without it.

It would not. The costs of dependency are too great to withhold any longer the child-care, insurance and other support services it would provide, in a limited way, to Americans trying to get off the dole and into paying jobs.

It is tempting to hold out, until President Reagan leaves office, for a more comprehensive House bill. But there is no guarantee the House measure, with a $7.1 billion price tag, would fare better next year; the climate could be even worse if the recession economists have been predicting hits early in the next administration.

And the moment could be lost forever if no consensus is reached this summer.

The White House may have acted rashly in threatening to veto what is in fact a very modest proposal, but the Senate is in no mood to pass a bill it can't pay for. The "revenue-neutral" Moynihan bill's chief virtue is that it would put welfare recipients to work and extend benefits to two-parent families, without increasing the deficit. It might even save a bit by flagging some applications for Aid to Families with Dependent Children for extra scrutiny at the front end, as a hedge against cheating.

Its chief failing is that it is sometimes harsher on individuals (requiring welfare mothers of children over 3 to work or attend school) than on state and local governments (permitting them to opt out and run "demonstration projects" of their own). Despite opposition by conservatives, it is so bare-bones frugal it's under attack by church groups as offering the poor "the boot, rather than a hand."

But it's a place to start if America is serious about giving welfare recipients a shot at self-sufficiency. If the climate does improve under Reagan's successor, it will be easier to enhance and expand it in a year or two than to start from scratch.

DESERET NEWS

Salt Lake City, UT, June 19, 1988

Now that the Senate has passed a welfare reform bill aimed at putting welfare families to work, the measure must still be reconciled with a similar House version — a task that may not be too easy.

Both pieces of legislation call for comprehensive education, training, and employment programs for people on welfare — very similar to a pilot project started this month in Davis County.

The emphasis would be on helping welfare recipients become self-sufficient, instead of simply providing necessities of life. Included in the program would be child daycare, help in finding a job, and incentives to keep working.

Those goals are admirable. The only question is the cost. Some sacrifices would be worth making now if they succeed in getting people off welfare later. Whether the savings justify the expense is what the reform is supposed to show in the next five years.

Chief difference between the House and Senate bills is the price tag. The Senate bill would run to $2.8 billion over five years, while the House measure would cost an estimated $7 billion.

The Senate version would be preferable. First, it would allow the reform to be tried out on a slightly smaller scale to see how well it works. If the results show real promise, some adjustments upward could then be justified. Second, if the price tag is too high, President Reagan may veto the package.

The country badly needs welfare reform and a national policy aimed at getting people off the dole, not keeping them on. The existing welfare system simply isn't doing the job.

Let's start making changes, but carefully. And let's make sure the reform is achieving what it should before throwing $7 billion into the pot.

THE INDIANAPOLIS STAR
Indianapolis, IN, June 23, 1988

The biggest potential overhaul of the nation's welfare system in 53 years could go a long way toward reducing the cycle of dependency that has produced a permanent undercaste of Americans unable or unwilling to support themselves.

When it was created in 1935, during the Depression, the national welfare program was intended to provide emergency relief. Over the years it has been transformed into a perpetual handout system that has kept families on relief for as many as five generations.

Its regulations have been blamed for the multiplication, on an immense scale, of single-parent families unable to break out of the dependency cycle..

The Senate last Thursday passed, by a 93-3 vote, legislation calling for an education, training and job program and including a provision that would require some welfare recipients to do 16 hours of community work a week. It would emphasize parental responsibility through automatic deductions of child support payments from wages and provide participation standards for welfare recipients.

The Senate version would cost $2.8 billion, while a House version, passed by a 230-194 vote in December, would provide more generous benefits and cost $7.1 billion.

President Reagan threatened to veto the original bill because of its high cost, its expansion of the present system and what he called its failure to make recipients "actually work if they're able to do so."

The bill now goes to a House-Senate conference committee where attempts will be made to work out a compromise.

White House spokesman Marlin Fitzwater said that many of the House provisions will have to be stripped from the final version in order to win administration support.

He said, "We'll try to get changes in conference, but it's going to be very tough to reconcile with the House bill that is so far out of line in our judgment. . . . I would say that it's a case of . . . pushing a rock up a hill at this point."

The most important thing about the bill is that it is intended to encourage people to break the bonds of dependency and advance along the course of self-sufficiency.

If legislators can iron out their differences and produce a final version that is fair and sensible, that is what will happen.

Reaching that goal is worth the efforts it will take to push the rock up the hill.

DAILY NEWS
New York, NY, June 19, 1988

THE U.S. SENATE FINALLY DID IT. Sen. Daniel Patrick Moynihan's welfare reform package was approved Thursday, 93 to 3. No law, or sausage, is perfect—there's a lot that even the wise can't instantly recognize. But overall, the bill is splendid. It hews good sense from the existing overgrown thickets of programs. It encourages work and personal ambition where dependency has reigned. It is lean but not mean. In short, it is the most responsible, thoughtful, realistic federal undertaking in the area of welfare in a generation.

Moynihan deserves great credit for the conception, for putting it together and for managing passage. History will recognize and reward him. But today the most vital concern must be for the work of the Senate-House Conference Committee, which still could snatch from the Senate victory defeat for both the taxpayers and the most needful of America. An earlier House-passed measure is packed with excesses that would guarantee a presidential veto.

It is absolutely vital that the conferees fashion a compromise that will be passed and signed with all deliberate speed, lest a historic accomplishment be lost to pettiness.

Portland, ME, June 24, 1988

The best thing thing government can do for people who need economic assistance — welfare — is to help them to work their way out of that need.

That is the basic philosophy behind a bill approved 93-3 last week by the U.S. Senate — a proposal aimed at getting people off the welfare rolls and into jobs.

That was the philosophy behind a state "welfare-to-work" program in Maine which has provided subsidized on-the-job training in private sector jobs for welfare recipients.

And, if the Maine experience is any guide, it is a philosophy that works.

A national study of experimental state programs similar to those proposed by the Senate bill showed welfare recipients making sizable gains in job earnings as a result of work training. In Maine, for example, enrollees earned, on the average, $952 more than those who did not take part in the voluntary program.

It is a statistic which provides a glimmer of hope. And it supports the notion that the best way to rescue a generation of poor Americans from an empty life on the dole is to help them to find the road to self-sufficiency and productivity.

WORCESTER TELEGRAM.
Worcester, MA, June 27, 1988

The landmark welfare-reform plan passed recently by the U.S. Senate offers the country a golden opportunity to break out of a long-standing cycle of failure.

The measure, proposed by Sen. Daniel Patrick Moynihan and refined with contributions from governors and the Reagan administration, is a historic effort that seeks to reshape the very philosophy of public assistance. It would make education and training the cornerstones of the welfare system and provide the kind of services that are truly needed by the poor. It would offer the means for millions of people to make a gradual transition from welfare rolls to payrolls.

Neither Congress nor the White House can afford to let this chance slip away. President Reagan should indicate his willingness to back a compromise in which the Senate proposals dominate those contained in a more expensive measure passed by the House.

Every set of statistics indicates that reform is crucial. The current system dates from the New Deal years of Franklin D. Roosevelt and no longer reflects the needs of the country or the shape of its population.

In 1985, the last year for which complete figures are available, welfare payments cost the taxpayers $15 billion. The sums that will be expended in the future — with or without an overhaul — are staggering.

Despite all the spending, studies show that half of all welfare recipients are mired in dependency, with no hope of getting out. Yet get out they must if the nation is to live up to its potential — or even fill all the jobs that will be available in the next decade.

That is where the Senate proposal comes in.

It links jobs and benefits. Its programs are modeled on experiments that have shown success in individual states, including Massachusetts. And the bill provides a "safety net" of health care, day care and other support services for those in dire straits.

While the plan would not force all recipients to work, it would offer an incentive for able-bodied people to get jobs — and give them the means to make it through a period of transition. It would give states a role in ensuring that absentee fathers helped pay to raise their abandoned children. And it would remove any incentive for married couples to split up in order to obtain benefits.

As it stands, our welfare system helps no one, least of all those in poverty. Children on welfare become adults on welfare, and the nation spends and suffers.

The Senate plan may need some fine-tuning. But it reflects elements of both liberal and conservative philosophies, seeks to ease a major national malady and offers a way out of the dismal pattern of welfare dependency.

Enacting this reform would be a credit to Congress. Signing it into law would be a worthy accomplishment for President Reagan as his term draws to a close.

The Houston Post

Houston, TX, June 26, 1988

America's welfare system is a costly, outdated, misdirected failure. It keeps millions of people on the dole from generation to generation. It saps adult recipients' incentive to lead independent, productive lives. And it condemns their children to a bleak future.

After 20 years of debate and half-measures, the House and the Senate have each passed comprehensive welfare reform bills. The measure the Senate passed by an overwhelming 93-3 vote last week is easily the better and less expensive of the two.

Both bills have the same goal — to break the cycle of dependence on welfare services by giving able-bodied recipients the skills to work. When the program to aid mothers with dependent children was created in 1935, most of its beneficiaries were widows. Now a majority are divorced or never-married mothers.

A major focus of the bills is on getting these women into the job market, where they will be increasingly needed as the U.S. workforce shrinks in future years. At the same time, the measures would toughen regulations to collect child support from absent fathers.

The states would provide the education, training and job-search programs, as well as interim child-care facilities for mothers with children older than 3 years. States, which share welfare financing with the federal government, badly want reform of the system.

The Senate bill incorporates ideas from states that led the way in devising workfare and other programs to trim their welfare rolls in the face of declining federal funding. The bill would cost an estimated $2.8 billion over five years, less than half that of the House bill. But the Senate version reflects the acknowledged welfare expertise of its author, Sen. Daniel Patrick Moynihan, D-N.Y.

A House-Senate conference committee will now attempt to reconcile differences between the bills. The final legislation should correct a system that hands out a total of $15 billion a year to 3.7 million families, but keeps too many of them in subsistence dependency.

The Philadelphia Inquirer

Philadelphia, PA, June 21, 1988

The Senate showed leadership last week when it gave up waiting for President Reagan's support and passed legislation to shake up the current welfare system. The overwhelming vote of 93 to 3 suggests that lawmakers have fashioned a reform package with the kind of solid support that would enable the legislation to be passed over a veto, if necessary.

Apparently, lawmakers have shucked old stereotypes about welfare and become intolerant of a system that victimizes children — more than 7 million of them — most of all. As the House did last year, the Senate has voted to replace Aid to Families with Dependent Children (AFDC) with a program that links financial support to training and employment and also cushions the loss of Medicaid and child-care assistance when an AFDC recipient takes a job.

Despite substantial differences between the House and Senate legislation, either would be such a welcome step away from welfare's current cycle of dependency that it would be irresponsible for Mr. Reagan to veto any conceivable hybrid of the two.

The bill must go through a Senate-House conference to reconcile the differences between the two versions before it is sent to the President. The Senate version, for example, is sterner about requiring beneficiaries (except for mothers of children up to age 3) to work or train for work. Yet it would be dunderheaded if the bill were to founder on how best to push AFDC parents into the job market. The administration's zealotry on this point ignores a reality that under the current system, as Sen. Daniel Patrick Moynihan (D., N.Y.) has put it, "... welfare mothers are for all practical purposes prevented from working."

One fundamental purpose of the administration's veto threat is to keep the House and Senate from reaching an "expensive" compromise. Yet in light of what can be accomplished by revamping welfare, even the House's bill with a cost of $1.4 billion annually (twice as much as the Senate's) would be a bargain. One of the major differences in cost, for example, comes from the House plan's financial incentives for states with inhumanely low welfare benefits to raise them. The only good argument against doing that involves practical politics: It probably would turn enough lawmakers against the legislation to prevent the Congress from overriding a veto.

With Mr. Moynihan as the indefatigable prime mover, Congress finally has moved close to a goal that got lip-service in the President's 1986 State of the Union address: recasting a welfare system that everyone knows to be a failure. In doing so, lawmakers have balanced responsibilities: the responsibility of parents (including fathers whose lone participation in parenting now occurs in the conception phase); and the responsibility of government to give young women from deprived backgrounds a real opportunity to become self-supporting. As Mr. Moynihan says, welfare reform can "bring a generation of young American women back into the mainstream of American life." That opportunity should not be lost in bickering over petty details.

The Grand Rapids Press

Grand Rapids, MI, June 19, 1988

The true sin of the nation's welfare system is not that it rewards the "undeserving" poor — that's more folklore than fact. Rather, its greatest weakness is the failure to help put welfare recipients in the work force. Measures before the Congress and Michigan Legislature would help repair that flaw.

The federal legislation promises the most fundamental changes. The Senate last week passed a reform plan sponsored by Sen. Daniel Patrick Moynihan, D-N.Y., which makes a fundamental policy change. Instead of regarding welfare as primarily an income source, Sen. Moynihan's bill would make job training and placement its top priority.

This approach recognizes that the Aid to Families with Dependent Children program can become a welfare trap, offering recipients a regular check but little help in breaking away from those payments. The $2.8 billion Senate bill and, to a lesser extent, a similar, more expensive plan passed by the House, aim to break that dependency.

The Senate bill requires states to set up education, job training and work programs for welfare recipients. These programs would emphasize training for people without high school diplomas or who have been on welfare for the longest time. Parents whose children are at least 3 years old or, at state option, 1 year old, would be required to participate, with child care provided. For Michigan, however, that's a step backward: The state considers mothers ready for job training when their babies are 6 months old.

The package also requires that at least 22 percent of a state's welfare recipients be enrolled in work programs, and that one parent in two-parent welfare families spend at least 16 hours a week in a work project. It also looks after people who are moving off welfare by requiring states to extend child care for up to nine months and Medicaid for a year after a parent leaves welfare. Why train a person for a job when the cost of child care and medical insurance makes work less lucrative than welfare?

This bill still has to be reconciled with the House version. The Senate proposal should prevail. It addresses the issues more clearly at less expense and is less likely to draw a veto from President Reagan. The president's objections, primarily to allowing two-parent families on the welfare rolls at all, don't outweigh the bill's merits.

In Michigan, the Senate Appropriations Committee is considering a trial of a plan by Gov. James Blanchard to give jobs to all 18- to 20-year-olds who are on general assistance jobs. The work would be in renovating urban neighborhoods. Anyone refusing the $3.35-an-hour jobs would lose his welfare benefits. The panel is looking at a test program in Genesee County.

Ironically, this worthwhile idea faces the heaviest opposition from Gov. Blanchard's fellow Democrats in the House. In a wild flight of logic last winter, they knocked out the provision making the work program mandatory. If it were forced, argued Rep. David Hollister of Lansing, many youths would refuse the jobs, lose their benefits and turn to crime.

Welfare is supposed to help disadvantaged people through hard times; but by Rep. Hollister's logic, it's a giant protection racket in which young people too lazy to work are given regular payoffs to keep them from dealing drugs or robbing old ladies. That's an insult to the people on welfare and the taxpayers who pay for it. The Legislature should support at least the trial run in Flint.

The good in tying job training to welfare benefits can be found in Kent County, which has been a nationally recognized leader in such efforts. When Kent's mandatory job-training rules were overturned by state law making such efforts voluntary, participation plunged. The Legislature soon reversed itself and let Kent put people to work. Happily, our ideas are starting to trickle toward the top.

The Grand Rapids Press

Gary, IN, June 19, 1988

There is a consensus on one aspect of the big welfare reform packages passed by the Senate and House: Reform is long overdue. This is the first major effort to change the system since it was created in 1935.

Some high hopes and great expectations are justified, but this maze of patchwork regulations will not surrender easily because the practices are embedded deeply in America life.

A Republican senator said, "People ought to work because it's unfair to ask other people to support them indefinitely." Hardly anybody would disagree, but statements of principle often become snagged on the sharp points of reality.

Work is a major emphasis in the Senate bill that passed 93-3 after some tougher restrictions demanded by the administration were added. Another version was passed by the House in December. The two bills must now be blended into one.

The present system creates a dependency cycle that for some people becomes permanent. The fault is not entirely with the people.

States would have some big responsibilities under the Senate bill. They would have to find ways to withhold wages from absentee fathers, for example. They would have to create training and education programs and attempt to put able-bodied adults into jobs, except those who are caring for children under 3.

What about people whose wages increase and wipe out their eligibility? The penalty would be eased by the states through child care programs that last for several months and through temporary Medicare aid.

The Reagan administration insisted on fewer benefits and more stringent rules than are in the House bill, and unless some of those requests stay in the bill, the president might veto it.

Putting people to work makes sense. Where are the jobs? Only work that has meaning and promise will turn the welfare program around.

The administration wants people to do community service work and participate in workfare programs to help pay off aid grants. Not a bad idea, especially if there is important work to be done. But as a long-term solution to anything, such jobs have no muscle.

What the lawmakers face — what the whole country faces — is a severe course correction in the application of welfare. Making the system work will take years and it will require attitude reforms. What was a noble idea at its inception has been perverted.

Wisconsin ▲ State Journal

Madison, WI, June 28, 1988

When the Senate voted, 93-3, in favor of a bill aimed at getting people off the welfare rolls and into jobs, many supporters started to celebrate. They assumed differences between the Senate bill and a House version would be quickly resolved, and that a swift signature by President Reagan would bring about the most sweeping welfare reforms in a generation.

Hold the applause. This bipartisan effort to break the cycle of dependency among the nation's underclass could fail to win approval this year — or ever, depending on the mood of the next Congress. For millions of poor people looking for a way up and out, that would be a crime.

The Senate bill would cost $2.8 billion over five years (compared with $7 billion for the House version) and would for the first time give states authority to operate education, training and work programs for welfare recipients. It would make participation in such programs mandatory for most able-bodied recipients with children over age 3, and provide transitional child care and Medicaid health coverage for those who take jobs. The bill also strengthens federal rules aimed at forcing absent fathers to pay child support.

The bill reflects a broad consensus, cutting across party, ideological and geographic lines, that the current welfare system is beyond repair. It also proves that "bottom-up" changes in federal programs are possible, because virtually everything in the bill was pioneered in the states.

The bill draws heavily on a program instituted by New Jersey Gov. Thomas Kean as well as welfare reforms in Delaware, Arkansas, Maine, Maryland and Virginia. Wisconsin's Learnfare program is too new to have been much of an influence, but Kean and others in the National Governors' Association say the Wisconsin law is consistent with what they have tried to do.

New Jersey's program, for example, is built around a contractual link to "rights" (getting public assistance) and "responsibility" (finding a job or getting training). Welfare recipients in New Jersey sign contracts with the state, promising to get a job or train for a job or go to school. The state promises to provide day care for children, health benefits and transportation.

Sadly, too many members of the House are living in the past. They cling to the failed notion that welfare is an entitlement — a right — and they are loathe to require work or training in return for public assistance.

That philosophy doesn't wash in today's world. In an era when most mothers work at least part-time, is it too much to expect that those on welfare do likewise? The Labor Department reported the week of June 13 that for the first time, more than half of the nation's new mothers are returning to work before their babies reach age 1. Those mothers with toddlers are paying taxes so that other mothers can stay home. It isn't fair.

Welfare dependency has long been regarded as a drain on tax resources, but one of the driving forces behind the Senate bill is the knowledge that this country cannot afford to waste human resources. We will need all the skilled workers we can get in the years to come. That cannot be accomplished when the welfare status quo mires half of all children it touches in permanent dependency.

This bill is an example of federalism at its best, and it comes not a moment too soon. Don't botch it, Congress.

Newsday

Long Island, NY, June 15, 1988

By the end of this week, the U.S. Senate will probably pass Sen. Daniel Patrick Moynihan's (D-NY) welfare reform bill — and with less hassle than a similar but more contentious bill passed by the House last year.

So the questions now are: What will Congress wind up with after the House and Senate meet to combine their bills? And, will the White House accept it?

Moynihan's bill does not have all the features of the House version (in large part the handiwork of Long Island Democrat, Rep. Thomas Downey), and would be a great deal less expensive — $2.8 billion over five years compared with the Downey bill's $7 billion.

But what's more important, both have essentially the same underlying purpose — to break the growing dependency on welfare that has evolved among some poor households over the past three decades. Both would do that by establishing new education and job training programs for welfare parents, spurring the provision of day care for their children and liberalizing welfare rules to make the transition to work more viable.

You'd think the Reagan administration couldn't carp about a program attacking welfare dependence. But it has, claiming the House version would "dramatically *increase* dependency . . ." How is unclear.

That's a clear veto signal — and a reason for hewing to the Senate's less ambitious design.

The plan is an investment that should pay off in the long run, in salvaged lives and lower costs. Ultimately, the revised welfare program may prove worthy of a bigger commitment of federal dollars than the Senate bill anticipates. But what's important now is to make the turn from the present dead-end welfare system to one that opens doors to increased independence and self-respect. This week, the Senate holds the keys.

Herald News
Fall River, MA, June 21, 1988

The welfare reform bill, which has been discussed for so long, now seems on the verge of passage.

The Senate passed its version of the bill by an overwhelming majority last week. The House has already passed its version.

The House and Senate measures must now be reconciled, and a joint committee will be appointed for this purpose.

Senator Daniel Patrick Moynihan of New York, one of the measure's sponsors, says the differences between the House and Senate versions are mainly technical, and that in its final form the bill will be passed and sent to the White House for signature by Labor Day.

The President's attitude toward the measure is unclear, although he is known to prefer the Senate's version to the House's. There is no present indication whether he is likely to veto it, but the margin by which the Senate passed its version would provide an ample number of votes for an override.

The main provision of the welfare reform bill is that makes it mandatory for the states to develop job training programs and for welfare recipients to undergo some form of training and then actively to seek work.

The principal exception to this requirement would be those persons caring for children who are under three years of age.

Massachusetts has had a job training program for the past few years, and is therefore in the vanguard of the states seeking to shift the welfare emphasis from relief to education and employment.

The reform reflects the vast change in the nation's social climate since the federal government initiated the welfare program.

The welfare program was founded in depression times when it was only too true that many people were unable to find work and, without help, would have been destitute.

There are doubtless still many who cannot find the kind of work they would normally seek, but there are relatively few who, after retraining in necessary skills, cannot find a job if they want one.

This is the premise on which the welfare reform bill is based, and its premise is sound.

Two or three decades ago it might have been criticized as inhumane, but the change in industrial and social patterns is so marked that it is by no means unreasonable to expect people in need of work to acquire new techniques in order to arrive at economic indepdendence.

Whatever the differences of opinion about details of the measure, the basic notion of welfare reform is valid. The measure deserves passage by Congress and signature by the President.

THE SUN
Baltimore, MD, June 21, 1988

House and Senate negotiators who must hammer out a compromise on welfare reform legislation have a major job ahead if Congress is to pass a bill this year. The Senate overwhelmingly approved a welfare measure last week after it had been weakened sufficiently to gain the backing of conservative Republicans. But the measure differs vastly from a version passed earlier this year by the House and from proposals supported by welfare reform advocacy groups.

The Senate bill was sponsored by Sen. Daniel Moynihan, D-N.Y., a longtime proponent of government policies to strengthen families. It would require states to set up large-scale education and job training programs for welfare recipients, and require them to provide child care for up to nine months and Medicaid benefits for a up to a year after a parent leaves the welfare rolls for a job. The measure also would strengthen enforcement of child-support laws by requiring employers to automatically deduct legally due child-support payments from a parent's check.

Senator Moynihan said his bill would rescue women from a life of welfare dependency, but some critics say the bill, with a price tag of $2.8 billion over five years, is insufficiently funded to have a serious impact on many recipients. The House measure is estimated at $7 billion, and welfare reform groups say any serious effort to educate, train and provide support services to make welfare mothers self-sufficient is bound to cost that much. There are 11 million people on the welfare rolls, 3.7 million mothers, 7 million children and 400,000 fathers.

Cost is not the only issue that divides liberals and conservatives on this issue. President Reagan wanted a stronger work requirement than the one finally included in the bill, which would require that at least 22 percent of those eligible enroll in a work-related program. He also wanted to give states the power to set aside normal welfare rules in putting together welfare programs, but senators rejected that as a move that would allow states to ignore federal rules protecting the poor.

With so much dividing the House from the Senate and liberals from conservatives on this issue, the question is whether any bill can emerge this year. The Senate's passage of a welfare measure means the idea of reform has advanced another step, but the real test now is whether the House and Senate negotiators can find enough common ground to make the next step.

THE SPOKESMAN-REVIEW
Spokane, WA, June 20, 1988

After half a century of experience, America's leaders have reached the bipartisan conclusion that our welfare system is a failure — at least for the needy whom it was intended to serve.

Rather than supporting the helpless and lending a temporary hand to those who are trying to get back on their feet, the system has become a monster that devours ambition and blocks the path away from poverty.

Generations are now being reared with the assumption, gained literally at their parents' knee, that public assistance is not a last resort but a career choice.

Finally, lawmakers at both the federal and state levels are coming to the conclusion that it's time for a few refinements.

Agreeing on the problem is easier than agreeing on the solution, naturally, but some progress is being made. The most encouraging development probably is the emerging consensus that for welfare to work as intended, namely as a temporary measure, there must be clear advantages associated with escaping it.

The U.S. Senate last week passed a comprehensive reform bill by a 93-3 vote. The House earlier had approved another, costlier version. The president, who may or may not sign whatever compromise package is produced by a conference committee, has advanced his own alternative.

Meanwhile, such states as California, Massachusetts and Washington have come up with their own welfare-reform measures.

While the various approaches differ in their details, sometimes significantly, there is a welcome common thread. No longer will it be regarded as insensitive to expect welfare recipients who can work to do so in exchange for their grants; at the same time, no longer will it be assumed that reducing the welfare rolls can be accomplished without investing public resources in job-training and day-care services.

In Washington state, a five-year experiment known as the Family Independance Program gets under way July 1 in eight locations including Spokane. At least at first it will be mostly voluntary but the underlying theme is that welfare recipients who want to can work their way out of poverty without first having to make things worse for themselves.

Voluntary or not, a better standard of living and a renewed sense of personal dignity could be powerful incentives to attract more participants. Certainly that approach stands to be more effective than the present system in which going to work often means giving up public assistance checks and medical benefits in return for a meager, entry-level paycheck out of which child-care expenses take so much that the old welfare income looks good by comparison.

It has taken 50 years for a compassionate and well-intentioned policy to deteriorate as badly as this one has. It will not be rehabilitated overnight.

As first steps go, the fact there is general agreement on the need for correction should not be understated.

ST. LOUIS POST-DISPATCH

St. Louis, MO,
September 29, 1988

Though the welfare bill that Senate and House leaders have agreed on represents a major revision in the nation's cash assistance system for poor families, it is a disappointment even so. The measure does not go nearly far enough to help families move from welfare to work, which means that if it does not live up to its promise the poor will be blamed.

Moreover, it contains a mean-spirited workfare provision that was the condition President Ronald Reagan set for signing it. What a telling commentary that is on the president's attitude toward the poor. He was willing to offer poor families a helping hand only if he could also punish them for being on welfare.

The measure agreed to by leaders of the conference is closer to the Senate version than the House version, which held a better prospect of being able to get the heads of welfare families into the work force. The compromise bill contains a five-year price tag of $3.3 billion, less than half what the House measure would have cost.

The bill calls on the states to provide child care, transportation assistance and job training for welfare recipients. However, the states will be required to enroll only 7 percent of their welfare recipients in educational and training programs in 1990. That figure is to rise to 20 percent over a five-year period.

This is not the first federal attempt to move welfare recipients into the work force. During the Johnson administration, Congress approved a job training and placement program dubbed WIN. It was popular with welfare recipients, but both the states and Washington discovered that it was far cheaper to keep a family on welfare than to pay for day care, transportation, job training and placement. Accordingly, the program — never operated on a large scale — slowly faded away. A similar fate may await the new welfare measure.

The workfare provision is not likely to be abandoned, however. At Mr. Reagan's insistence, the bill is to require that either the father or the mother in two-parent welfare families works at least 16 hours a week without pay, doing something called community service. Only 5 percent of welfare families have two parents, so few people will be affected. But the provision is precedent-setting, nevertheless, in its punitive treatment of welfare recipients.

If a welfare recipient must work, then he or she should be paid. If the person is not paid, there is no way he or she can get off welfare. The scheme is counterproductive as well as mean.

THE ARIZONA REPUBLIC

Phoenix, AZ, September 29, 1988

AFTER 20 years of fits and starts, Congress finally has taken a step toward revising the massive federal welfare system, agreeing to a package of reform legislation that promises real relief not only for needy Americans, but for taxpayers as well.

Agreement on the compromise bill, worked out by House and Senate negotiators, marks the first time that Congress has admitted — and done something about — what everyone has known for years: that the welfare system is a national disgrace.

A look at the poverty statistics shows that. While the vast majority of Americans have gained economically in recent years, many of those at the lower end of the income scale actually have lost ground. Despite billions of dollars spent each year with the best of intentions, the results have been deplorable.

Although conceived in the spirit of compassion amid the liberal fervor of the Great Society, the great welfare expansion accomplished the cruelest of results. Instead of freeing people from poverty, the welfare system has trapped millions of poor Americans in a cycle of dependency and hopelessness through counterproductive incentives that discourage work and encourage the breakup of families.

Imperfect as it is, the reform package shifts the emphasis from merely giving handouts to actually lending a helping hand. By requiring able-bodied recipients to enroll in state job-training and employment programs, the reform should ease people off the dole and onto payrolls. To help cushion the transition, the legislation provides for day-care assistance and health-care services for a year after recipients initially begin working or attending school.

It might have been better to make the so-called "workfare" requirement begin immediately (it is to be phased in over a five-year period), but at least it represents a positive step for those recipients deprived by the present system of both initiative and opportunity.

Just as important, the new legislation would require states to pay benefits to two-parent welfare families, provided that one parent perform at least 16 hours of community service or other work in return. This provision, along with a strengthening of child-support collections from absentee parents, should help remedy a major cause of poverty — single-parent households.

The cost of the legislation — $3.3 billion over the next five years — is substantial. But the payout at least offers something the current system does not — a pay back. Both recipients, who might get off the dole, and taxpayers, who fund the programs, will be enriched by every success.

THE SACRAMENTO BEE

Sacramento, CA, September 30, 1988

The welfare bill finally approved this week by a House-Senate conference committee began as an effort not just to reform welfare but to replace a system born a half-century ago in vastly different economic and social times. In its final form, it begins to move welfare policy in the direction of work instead of the dole, but falls short of what America must do to start reducing the cycle of poverty and welfare dependency.

The bill would, for the first time, require all states to set up training, education and job-search programs for able-bodied parents receiving welfare checks. In return for their grants, welfare recipients with children over 3 would be required to prepare themselves to work. To further underline parental responsibility, the bill would also require states to stiffen efforts to collect child support from absent fathers.

This change of direction is overdue. Launched in the 1930s as a safety net for widows and abandoned families, welfare support to allow poor single women to stay home to raise children has increasingly lost its legitimacy in an era when the majority of mothers work outside the home to support their families. While Americans remain ready to help the poor achieve dignity and security, they want to do so in ways that reinforce society's core values of work, parental responsibility and self-reliance. To that end, states such as California and Massachusetts have already redirected welfare toward work.

But if this bill underlines the value the nation places on work, it does not do credit to its compassion. Because of the stinginess of President Reagan and Senate conservatives, the bill includes no provision to raise the inadequate levels of aid families who participate in the program will receive in many states. And though it finally requires all states to provide benefits to poor two-parent families with an unemployed breadwinner, the bill mandates, at Reagan's demand, that recipients of such aid work off their grants at minimum wage in community work programs. Since such families typically do not remain long on welfare, such a workfare requirement is mostly a symbolic show of toughness, which will force states like California to waste millions on workfare that could be better spent training the young, unwed mothers who are most likely to linger on the welfare rolls.

That poor targeting of resources is doubly damaging because the bill does not provide nearly enough money to do the job right. At $3.4 billion over five years, less than half the amount the House approved, the new federal money in the bill will not adequately fund the training, education and child care needed to make the bill work. Thus, while this reform represents a good start toward a modern welfare policy, it will remain to the next president and Congress to honor this new social contract and guarantee that parents who fulfill their obligation will receive the training, jobs and income they need to give their children a decent start in life.

BUFFALO EVENING NEWS

Buffalo, NY, September 21, 1988

MAJOR AND PRODUCTIVE changes in the nation's welfare system seemed on the brink of becoming law earlier this year when both the House and Senate passed bills aimed at replacing the grim cycle of dependency with jobs.

But now strong differences over details of the legislation threaten to block a compromise and prevent this reform from winning final adoption this year — an impasse Congress should do everything possible to avoid.

The principal stumbling block concerns a feature called "workfare" specified in the Senate bill but not the House version. It mandates that when two unemployed parents on welfare are in the home with children, one must work in community projects or receive job training for at least 16 hours a week.

House liberals strenuously object to this provision. On the other hand, President Reagan recently said he supported the broad welfare-reform measure — but only if the workfare requirement was retained. Hence the stalemate.

"We don't think that workfare works," said Rep. August F. Hawkins, D-Calif. "I see no reason to mandate workfare for people who would be very glad to get jobs. It's the undesirability of the jobs that they don't like."

Certainly, the workfare program must not interfere with the education and training of persons on welfare in preparing them for gainful employment. That they receive appropriate job training is a key goal of the entire bill. Given that, however, we see no reason to object to the Senate plan.

The House liberals also object to a Senate provision forbidding former welfare recipients from getting Medicaid, child care or other benefits for more than 18 months in any three-year period. On this, the dissenters have a point. Such a flat ban could override special circumstances, particularly during a recession.

But the critical need here is for the House and Senate conferees, striving to negotiate a compromise, to reach an accommodation that while not completely satisfying everyone, provides a bill generally acceptable to the president and the vast majority of members of Congress.

Times and social conditions change, and the welfare system has not kept pace. It requires significant changes to modernize it. This legislation, of which Sen. Daniel P. Moynihan, D-N.Y., is a leading architect, offers real promise of achieving that.

Both House and Senate bills, for example, would require states to offer comprehensive education, training and employment programs for welfare recipients. In turn, the measures would require welfare parents to become involved in those programs — and would provide child care to help make it possible.

Population trends indicate that in the years just ahead, proportionately fewer workers will be available to fill available jobs. Thus, realistic new federal programs to enrich education, training and job opportunities for welfare recipients — particularly those who have languished in dependency for many years — are well timed.

Clearly, what the House, Senate and White House agree upon is more important than what they disagree over. That fact — and the urgency of replacing the cycle of poverty with productive work for millions of Americans who now lack only the skills to work — should energize Capitol Hill's search for a prompt and fair compromise.

The Duluth News-Tribune

Duluth, MN, September 28, 1988

You call that major welfare reform?

U.S. Senate and House conferees on Monday came to terms on what is being billed as the first major reform of our nation's welfare system in the past half century. After months — indeed, years — of partisan wrangling and political posturing, the congressional negotiators endorsed a federally mandated work program for welfare recipients.

Workfare is a prudent and praiseworthy public policy initiative. It is a social services concept that has met with success in varying forms in various states and regions. It is a concept that merits general application and thus makes this week's legislative concurrence noteworthy.

But to call this particular legislation major reform carries all the exaggerated rhetoric of election year campaigning, an activity in which many of its backers are now fully engaged.

The federal mandate would not begin to take effect until 1994. And at that time the work requirement would be imposed on only 7 percent of welfare recipients from two-parent families. And such families account for only 5 percent of the nation's welfare caseloads. Thus the reform will affect less than one-half of 1 percent of welfare recipients, and it won't affect them for another half dozen years.

There will be two more federal elections before then, not to mention untold missed opportunities for providing welfare recipients with an avenue for breaking out of the cycle of welfare dependency.

THE PLAIN DEALER

Cleveland, OH, September 28, 1988

Welfare. The term evokes images of dependency and despair—of a bureaucracy so complex that the needy cannot understand it, and so inefficient that the taxpayers resent it. As the welfare trap has caught millions of people in its downward spiral of hopelessness, Washington for 20 years has shrunk from the task of overhauling its confused machinery.

But congressional negotiators this week rescued a promising welfare, job-training and child-support initiative from end-of-session oblivion. If the House and Senate follow through on the final steps of the process, there at last will be a more coherent framework to promote help and self-help for people in poverty.

The architect of the initiative, New York Sen. Daniel Patrick Moynihan, detailed the failures of the welfare system in his book "Family and Nation." He argues that the present system's centerpiece—the Aid to Families With Dependent Children (AFDC) program—gives its 3.7 million families little incentive to seek private-sector jobs while making them dependent on handouts that keep them near the poverty level. Since most welfare recipients are women with children but without a husband, dependency sometimes discourages families from staying together; perverse regulations have encouraged some men to abandon their families to help them become eligibile for AFDC.

By combining cash payments, child-support enforcement and education and training incentives, the overhaul will refocus welfare as a transition to employment. To encourage recipients to seek a job, the bill will continue Medicaid and child-care eligibility for one year for anyone leaving the welfare rolls. To reduce the breakup of families, the states will be required to provide welfare for at least six months each year to two-parent households with an unemployed breadwinner. A requirement for states to expand education and training programs will be phased in, requiring states to enroll 7% of welfare recipients by 1990 and 20% by 1995 in a JOBS (Job Opportunities and Basic Skills) plan.

One central aim of the bill, in keeping with its theme of individual responsibility, is to require absent parents to support their children; in 1985, more than half of absent parents (in most cases, the father) failed to meet their child-support obligations. Court-ordered child support now will be withheld from absent parents' paychecks so they cannot neglect their families. Shifting the child-support burden from the government back to parents will save Washington more than $400 million and the states $635 million over five years.

The entire package nearly fell apart because of House objections to a "workfare" provision. But denunciations of "slave-fare" were overdrawn. Under a compromise that would begin in 1993, one adult in a two-family household receiving welfare must go to school, take a government job or perform unpaid community service at least 16 hours per week. Although criticized as not cost-effective by governors and state welfare commissioners, "workfare" was the price the liberals had to pay for conservative support.

The package's cost will be about $3.34 billion over five years—more than the $2.8 billion that the Senate wanted, but far less than the $7 billion that the House sought. The president is expected to approve it.

Congress tackled this complex problem because a bipartisan combination of forces refused to let past outrages continue. Governors and social workers complained of the system's confusion; conservatives deplored its uncontrolled costs; liberals condemned its toll of human despair; and a handful of pragmatists —led by Moynihan—prodded Congress' conscience. If it is remembered for nothing else, the 100th Congress deserves praise for advancing a welfare-reform plan that balances discipline with compassion.

Catastrophic Care Clears Congress

The U.S. Senate June 8, 1988, by a vote of 86-11, gave final approval to a bill that would expand the Medicare program to protect the elderly and disabled against "catastrophic" medical costs. The House had passed the legislation June 2, by a vote of 328-72. House and Senate negotiators May 20 had cleared the way for the expansion of Medicare by reaching agreement on a formula to cover prescription drugs under the program. The issue had been the last of the legislation, preliminary versions of which had passed both houses easily in 1987. The measure, which was first proposed by Secretary of Health and Human Services Dr. Otis R. Bowen, was the largest expansion of benefits in the 23-year history of Medicare.

The cost of the new benefits, estimated at more than $32 billion over the next five years, would be borne entirely by the beneficiaries themselves. All beneficiaries would pay a higher monthly premium. Also, the 40% with enough income to pay federal taxes would pay an income tax surcharge of up to $800 per beneficiary in 1989, rising to a limit of $1,050 per beneficiary in 1993.

The legislation would guarantee a Medicare beneficiary unlimited free hospitalization after payment of an annual deductible estimated at $564 in 1989 and rising with inflation thereafter. Medicare currently paid full hospital charges for no more than 59 days a year. Beneficiaries paid a separate deductible for each hospitalization.

The bill would also limit a Medicare recipient's out-of-pocket expenses for doctor services to $1,370 a year. At present there was no limit. Beyond the $1,370 deductible, Medicare would pay 100% of doctor bills that met its specifications.

Another new benefit created by the bill would be one that provided "respite" for those caring for an elderly relative at home: Medicare would pay for up to 80 hours a year of outside assistance.

The bill would include Medicaid provisions to prevent the impoverishment of spouses of individuals admitted to nursing homes and would ensure that Medicaid paid for all Medicare premiums and copayments of Medicare-eligible individuals below the poverty line.

Arkansas Gazette.

Little Rock, AR, June 5, 1988

Though it is only treating the least of the health insurance problems of the nation's elderly, Congress has taken an important step with the Medicare catastrophic costs bill. It can only make the next ones more compelling.

The House of Representatives, by a vote of 328 to 72, passed a bill hammered out in conference with the Senate after the two houses approved different bills last year. The Senate this week will pass the legislation and send it to President Reagan, who surely will sign it in spite of his strenuous objections to much of it.

The bill is even restrictive in covering the costs of acute illness, which is about all it tries to do. It doesn't address, at all, the problems of long-term nursing home care or of long-term home care. Still, who would have thought two years ago that the first major expansion of Medicare since its creation in 1965 was possible in the term of Ronald Reagan, whose administration had been dedicated to scaling back the medical benefits of the aged?

But let us give credit to Mr. Reagan and to his Health and Human Services secretary, Otis R. Bowen, who persuaded the president to raise the issue in his State of the Union address in 1987. Bowen helped craft the compromise even while the administration fought parts of it — the progressive financing, the inclusion of prescription drugs and of payments for respite care for families who tend to the severely disabled, the scope of benefits for hospital and doctor care and a little more protection for spouses who are impoverished by nursing home costs.

Bowen endorsed the final bill though he could not promise that he would deliver the president's signature. No one, however, expects Mr. Reagan to veto a bill wanted by the nation's elderly and that will add nothing to the government's budget deficit. All the costs will be met by premiums from Medicare beneficiaries.

Over time, the bill will protect the 32 million Medicare beneficiaries from the ruin that acute illnesses often bring. It will cap the out-of-pocket costs of beneficiaries — at about $580 a year for hospital stays and $1,370 a year for doctors' bills. Now, hospital coverage diminishes after 60 days and stops after 150, and Medicare doesn't pay more than 80 per cent of doctors' bills. Coverage of part of the costs of outpatient prescription drugs will be phased in over four years. The bill increases from 100 to 150 days the coverage of nursing home stays for acute illnesses and ends the requirement that the patients spend three days in a hospital first.

Not terribly many of the nation's elderly actually will benefit from the insurance against catastrophic costs. Millions of the elderly and their families will still experience the ruin that usually follows chronic, long-term nursing home care and the poor care that the present system often means. Congress is moving hesitantly on these problems, too. The House this year may approve a bill that would provide help for the infirm elderly at home by lifting the income cap on the Medicare payroll tax, though it has no chance of navigating both the Senate and the White House this year.

Having turned back one small column of the advancing health care crisis, Congress cannot ignore the rest. The government is moving glacially toward universal health insurance and someday will leave South Africa as the only industrialized nation without it.

FORT WORTH STAR-TELEGRAM

Fort Worth, TX, March 26, 1988

No matter how well-intentioned a law may be, if it creates so much fear that it harms the people it was intended to help, lawmakers are obligated to scuttle it and start all over.

That is what must be done with a law authorizing the state to obtain liens on the homes of certain Medicaid recipients after their deaths. It was enacted by the Legislature in 1987, apparently without the knowledge of a great many legislators, and was scheduled to be implemented on April 1.

It was put on hold this week, however, because of panic that ensued when the general public (and most of the Legislature) became aware of its existence.

The law was not designed to let the state run amok and seize the property of the elderly poor or their families. It *was* designed to allow the state to recoup some of the money it spends on Medicaid recipients and to help hundreds of others.

Texas distributes about $530 million a year through the program, financed jointly by state and federal funds, to pay for nursing-home care and other medical needs of low-income residents. Of nursing-home patients on Medicaid who die each year, about 2,000 own houses. The controversial law authorized the state to obtain liens on those houses only when there was no surviving spouse, dependent or disabled child. Money thus gained would be used to extend the program's coverage to some 1,250 low-income Texans not currently eligible.

Unfortunately, when many older citizens learned of the law, they misunderstood its intentions and panicked. Some have even refused needed Medicaid assistance for fear of losing their homes, and that has been detrimental to their health.

The next Legislature, mindful of what has happened, should conduct well-publicized hearings on this matter to eliminate the fear and confusion that currently exists. Once citizens understand that the proposed change could actually benefit more people, opposition should diminish considerably.

FORT WORTH STAR-TELEGRAM

Fort Worth, TX, April 6, 1988

On Friday, unless Congress intervenes, the Reagan administration will implement a change in Medicaid regulations that could have a harmful effect on some of the poorest of the nation's elderly citizens.

The new rules would increase the costs of nursing-home care for hundreds of thousands of low-income people, but to understand the effects of the proposed change, it is necessary to understand how the overall program works.

Medicaid is financed jointly by federal and state funds but is administered by the states, which enjoy a limited amount of freedom in drawing up their individual programs.

To qualify for Medicaid assistance in Texas, for example, a person must have an income of less than $354 per month and resources, which could include a savings account or similar items but not a homestead, of less than $1,900. To be eligible for Medicaid-assisted nursing home care, the income level must be less than $687.15 monthly. Other states operate with different figures.

Medicaid officials decide how much a particular nursing home should receive for the care of each patient. Patients with an income — from Social Security, pension, insurance, etc. — are required to pay a portion of the nursing home bill, and the balance is paid by Medicaid. A regulation applicable to all state programs enables an individual to keep $25 a month for clothing and other personal needs, such as soap, toothpaste, etc.

Under many state programs, the government has allowed Medicaid recipients to exempt certain medical expenses before determining their share of the nursing-home costs. Exemptions are allowed for such items as eyeglasses, hearing aids, dentures and a limited number of prescription drugs.

Here is how the current rule works:

Assume the government decides that a particular nursing home should get $1,000 per month per Medicaid patient, and a patient has a monthly income of $400. That patient would be assured of keeping $25 per month plus any other amount spent for allowable exempted items. For the purpose of this example, let us say that, in a given month, that comes to $100. The patient, then, could deduct $125 from the $400 and would owe the nursing home $275. Medicaid would pay the balance of $725.

Under the proposed change, the patient would still be entitled to $25 for personal needs, but states could reduce or eliminate the exemptions for medical purposes. In the case above, the patient could be responsible for paying $375, reducing the government's share to $625.

Nursing home residents under Medicaid care in Texas will not be affected by the new regulation unless the state changes its system because the program pays for most of those incidental medical expenses here. But hundreds of thousands of elderly poor in other states *will* be affected.

Obviously, the purpose of the new regulation is to permit the states and the federal government to save money, which is a very popular goal these days. But there is a not-so-obvious agenda at work here also.

A government official familiar with the proposed changes said that they are a product of the Reagan administration's obsession with "welfare cheats." Key administration figures apparently believe that people with "discretionary income" are hiding that fact in order to qualify for Medicaid and are letting taxpayers absorb expenses that the recipients themselves should pay.

That may be so, but the guilty would be hurt much less by the new rule than the poorest among recipients, who have no discretionary income and could be forced to forgo purchasing needed medical items in order to avoid eviction for failure to pay their nursing home costs.

It would be much fairer to devise a system to ensure that ineligible people are prohibited from entering the Medicaid program than to punish the innocent elderly, which is what the new regulation will do.

The Register-Guard

Eugene, OR, February 3, 1988

The Reagan administration has found another way to ingratiate itself with avid anti-abortionists at the expense of the poor. The tactic is predictable, but nonetheless shameful.

The administration has given mainly lip service to the anti-abortionists' main goal — adoption of an amendment that would nullify current Supreme Court interpretation of the Constitution and allow the government to make abortion illegal again. But to assuage the crusaders and quiet their complaints about doing too little, the administration has come up with an easy "victory" on another front.

The Department of Health and Human Services is issuing new rules that forbid any family planning program that receives federal funds from providing abortion counseling or making any referrals to abortion providers.

Current federal guidelines say that clinics receiving federal funds must, on request, offer counseling about abortion and make referrals to doctors who provide abortions. Under the new rules, if a young woman comes in and asks for advice about abortion in any way, the advisers will have to play dumb.

For some time now, federal law has prohibited any use of federal medical aid for the poor for abortions. Medicaid pays for almost all other kinds of medical service. But the law says that if you're a woman poor enough to have to rely on this form of help, you can't get an abortion — something that is legally available to all middle- and upper-income women. Some states, including Oregon, have come to the rescue by providing state money for this purpose to substitute for the missing federal dollars.

Unable to impose their wishes on anyone else, the militant anti-abortionists thus wreak vengeance on the poor. The new rules prohibiting abortion counseling or referral represent one more way — petty but at the same time significant — of doing that.

Federal assistance for family planning dates back to the Public Health Service Act of 1970. Under Title X of that act, $143 million was spent on family planning and related services benefiting an estimated 4.3 million people last fiscal year. More than 85 percent of the recipients were low-income women.

While 4,000 clinics around the country depend on the federal government for an average of about 30 percent of their funding, some receive as much as 90 percent of their money from the government. This gives the government a powerful policy lever.

The new rules are to take effect in early March, but the states of New York and Massachusetts, the City of New York, the American Civil Liberties Union, the Planned Parenthood Federation of America and the national organization representing federally funded family planning clinics are expected to file a lawsuit to block their implementation.

We hope the suit is successful. But it would be better and simpler if Congress would step in and overrule the administrative agency. Congress should just say: Enough. Leave the rules the way they are. Let the battle over public policy on abortion proceed, as it will regardless, but do not visit any more inequities on the poor.

EVENING EXPRESS
Portland, ME, June 1, 1988

Millions of elderly Americans live in dread of a lengthy illness that would wipe out their savings and leave them bankrupt. Who can blame them? Although they may be covered by Medicare, they aren't insulated from the threat of massive hospital, doctor and drug bills.

Fortunately, help's on the way. Congress has responded to President Reagan's urging and is passing a national insurance plan to protect about 32 million Medicare recipients who face the possibility of a catastrophic illness.

In brief, the bill's major provisions call for unlimited free hospital care after the patient pays the first $564 each year and unlimited free physician care after the first $1,400 is paid annually by the patient. Partial prescription drug payment will be authorized in three years.

Equally important, the legislation prevents the spouses of long-term nursing home patients from being drained of all their assets. A spouse would be entitled to keep $750 in monthly income as well as half the couple's assets up to a total of $60,000.

So who foots the bill? Every Medicare recipient will pay an additional $4 a month insurance premium, plus a 15 percent federal income tax payment surtax, up to a maximum of $800 a year.

The bill is geared to be self-financing; Congress should make sure it stays that way. Too often, Congress has undertaken similar programs and then raided the Treasury — rather than taxing recipients — as costs rise or new benefits are added.

In short, there's a clear need for the catastrophic insurance program. But there's an equal need for Congress to have the courage to assure that it operates as a federal *insurance* program rather than turning it into a taxpayer-subsidized *welfare* program.

LANDING GEAR FOR THE STEALTH BOMBER

NURSING AND HOME

HEALTH

CARE

LAS VEGAS SUN

Las Vegas, NV, June 5, 1988

The House took a firm first step to protect the elderly and disabled against massive medical bills from catastrophic illness by expanding health care benefits.

The House this past week voted overwhelmingly — 328-72 — to give 32 million Medicare beneficiaries unlimited hospital care days, a ceiling for personal expenses for doctors' bills and partial prescription payments under the Catastrophic Illness Protection Act.

The news gets better. The Senate is expected to approve the bill and President Reagan is expected to sign it, phasing in benefits over the next three years.

Both Nevada Reps. Jim Bilbray and Barbara Vucanovich voted for the measure, displaying the strong bipartisan support the catastrophic benefits received.

The bill will benefit thousands of seniors who live in Nevada, a state with the fastest-growing elderly population in the country.

The $31 billion the bill will cost will be paid by the elderly and disabled themselves through higher monthly premiums.

But Bilbray called it an "important first step" for an obvious reason: the bill does not cover the most devastating financial threat for seniors, the high cost of nursing home care.

The average cost for a year's stay in a nursing home is $22,000 per patient.

However, the current bill does provide some form of protection to the spouse of an elderly person in an institution. The spouse gets $786 a month in family income to live on and keep more assets than presently allowed.

Senior advocate groups vow to continue pressing for better coverage for those in long-term care, a burden that sends many senior spouses into bankruptcy.

Those receiving greatest benefits under the bill will be 2 million indigent elderly who live below the poverty level, but earn too much to qualify for Medicaid benefits.

After the phase-in period, the program will pay all of these beneficiaries' premiums and deductibles, so they will receive totally free care.

A group not included in current Medicare coverage also will benefit from the bill. Poor pregnant women and infants under the age of 1 will receive new protection. Those living below the poverty line, but unable to qualify for Medicaid, will automatically be enrolled in Medicaid.

The bill also offers home health-care coverage for seven days per week for at least 38 days — providing a brief respite for family caregivers — and eliminates the 210-day limit for hospice care.

The House deserves praise for what it has accomplished, but the needs of seniors who need long-term skilled care are waiting in the congressional wings, still falling under the financial burdens.

FORT WORTH STAR-TELEGRAM

Fort Worth, TX, June 6, 1988

The U.S. House of Representatives acted with commendable compassion — not to mention political astuteness — in giving overwhelming approval to a catastrophic-illness insurance bill last week. The Senate should follow the House's lead, and President Reagan should sign the measure into law at the earliest opportunity.

Americans of both genders and all ethnic backgrounds are living longer these days. That, of course, is good news. But for many people, increased longevity is accompanied by serious illness, which saps not only their physical strength but also their financial resources. The House-approved bill, which ties the insurance program to Medicare, is designed to help older citizens cope with the economic burdens by limiting the out-of-pocket expenses they would have to pay in any one year.

If the bill becomes law, as expected, it would represent the largest expansion of the Medicare program since its inception in 1965. Coverage for the plan would be available through the optional portion of Medicare, to which 98 percent of Americans over 65 subscribe.

Here are the bill's key features:

■ Beginning next Jan. 1, the full cost of a hospital stay would be covered after payment of an annual $564 deductible.

■ Out-of-pocket costs for doctors' bills and outpatient care would be capped at $1,370 a year starting in 1990, with the cap indexed so that no more than 7 percent of Medicare beneficiaries exceed it in future years.

■ Fifty percent of outpatient prescription drugs would be paid for after a patient has met a $600 deductible in 1991. After the deductible, 60 percent would be covered in 1992 and 80 percent in 1993.

The package differs from other federal entitlement programs in that the benefits would be paid for by Medicare beneficiaries themselves. The flat premium for Medicare Part B services would rise gradually from $24.80 to $35 a month by 1993.

There also would be a sliding-scale supplemental premium, paid only by the 40 percent of Medicare beneficiaries who pay $150 or more in federal income tax. Some Medicare enrollees have protested that feature, but it is only fair to require those who can best afford it to shoulder a larger portion of the burden.

The bill does not cover long-term home care or extended nursing home care, which are the two potentially highest costs that elderly Americans face, but help appears to be on the way on those items. The House has agreed to consider a home care bill this week.

Until those issues can be properly addressed, however, the catastrophic insurance bill is a perfect example of an idea whose time has come. That it was pushed along by the force of election-year politics in no way diminishes its importance.

Detroit Free Press

Dertiot, MI, June 10, 1988

THE U.S. HOUSE showed commendable — if unusual — election-year restraint this week when it defeated a bill that would have mandated at least $30 billion in new federal spending on long-term home care for the chronically ill. Certainly Congress must address the special expenses of elderly people and disabled children who do not need to live in institutions, but do need help to move around, go to the bathroom, and feed, bathe and dress themselves. Yet the measure properly rejected by the House was an irresponsible, underfunded mess, less a genuine response to the problem than an attempt to cater to Washington's powerful senior citizens lobby.

At the same time, Congress has taken a more useful approach to easing the medical burdens of households with elderly or disabled members. It has adopted a compromise plan offering greater federal health insurance coverage — and capping out-of-pocket costs for doctors, hospitals and prescription drugs — for Medicare patients who suffer from catastrophic illnesses. The measure is the largest expansion of benefits in Medicare's 23-year history. Unlike the home care bill, though, the plan is carefully defined and solidly funded; Medicare recipients would pay for it themselves. The bipartisan measure is before President Ronald Reagan, who should sign it.

The home health care bill failed to distribute scarce medical resources properly, or restrict its proposed federal aid to households in genuine need; potentially, the program could have used payroll tax revenues to pay for a wealthy family's maid or cook. Its eligibility rules were vague and cumbersome, its costs understated. Moreover, its sponsors rushed the bill to the House floor without hearings or committee examination. Rep. John Dingell, D-Trenton, deserves special credit for leading the opposition to the deeply flawed measure.

The catastrophic-illness bill approved by Congress, by contrast, is pegged to ability to pay. It places a relatively heavier, but reasonable, tax burden on better-off Medicare recipients; it offers new benefits to poor households under Medicaid. Most important, it removes the dilemma now facing many spouses of nursing home patients: They virtually must deplete their life savings before qualifying for federal aid.

Millions of Americans need and deserve help with their medical bills: those who lack health insurance, those whose extraordinary hospital or nursing-home expenses have propelled them into poverty. *Ad hoc* approaches such as the home care bill, which are politically motivated and fail to set proper priorities, contribute to the problem of — not the solution to — rising health care costs.

The Idaho STATESMAN

Boise, ID, June 6, 1988

Older Americans, for whom serious illness often is the "worst fear of old age," have reason to smile.

Congress is set to give final approval to a landmark catastrophic health insurance bill that will ease that "worst fear" cited by President Reagan when he asked for legislation last year.

The bill is broader than what the president had in mind, and for good reason. Financial disaster can strike through sky-high prescription bills – not included in the president's plan – as well as doctor bills and long-term hospital care.

There's plenty of compromise built into the version passed 328-72 by the House last week and sent back to the Senate for final approval. Many of the dollar amounts have been changed from the original bill, and several provisions become more generous over time.

The catastrophic plan is the first major expansion of the Medicare program for the elderly since it was established in 1965. It is designed to protect the nation's 32 million Medicare recipients by capping their out-of-pocket expenses.

For example, the bill provides for full hospital coverage after an annual deductible estimated at $564 in 1989 and indexed to hospital inflation. Medicare payments now are limited to 59 days a year, and each hospitalization is subject to a deductible.

Recipients would have to pay no more than $1,370 in doctor bills after a $75 deductible before Medicare coverage kicks in, paying 80 percent of approved costs. Starting in 1989, the $75 deductible and the 20 percent share paid by beneficiaries counts toward the $1,370 cap. After that is reached, Medicare pays 100 percent of approved doctor bills.

The new prescription drug benefit – hotly contested by pharmaceutical companies during congressional debate – pays half of outpatient drug costs in 1991 after a $600 deductible is met. The government share rises to 60 percent in 1992 and 80 percent in 1993. The deductible, too, will go up with rising drug costs.

The beauty of these added benefits is that the recipients will pay the cost through a combination of flat monthly premium increases deducted from Social Security checks and an additional, sliding-scale supplemental premium charged to the 40 percent of the elderly with enough income to make them subject to federal income taxes.

Catastrophic health insurance, badly needed now, will become even more urgent as more Americans live longer and face health problems.

Setting up a system that allows the elderly to help themselves and relieves them of the nightmare of finanical disaster is a humane and decent task, the kind of work for which government was created.

Part IV:
Education & Poverty

Lack of education has long been pointed to as one of the many obstacles that impede the poor's ability to raise themselves out of their situation. Though the general level of education has risen in the U.S., there are a large number of individuals who lack basic skills. As a result, these individuals have great difficulty competing in today's job market and their difficulties are often passed on to their children. The children of the poor and unskilled are more likely than the children of the affluent to be poorly prepared when they enter the work force.

The skill levels of American workers are largely determined by the quality of the basic education system. But some individuals fall through the cracks even when proper educational facilities are available. Federal programs have played an important role in opening opportunities to the unskilled or handicapped adults, and the need for such assistance has not diminished.

The level of workers' education or skills and their earnings are highly correlative. In 1984 college-educated householders aged twenty-five or older employed full time year-round earned twice as much as individuals who had completed only eight years of schooling and who worked full time. Though this general relationship between educational attainment and earnings does not hold for all groups, there is, nevertheless, a connection between the educational attainment of the work force and productivity. Raising the education level of workers is likely to raise their incomes. Increasingly, a strong back alone is an insufficient employment skill as the job distribution in the economy continues to shift from the manufacturing to the service sector.

As a result the crucial need for many of the poor is competency in the three Rs (reading, writing and mathematics). While private-sector training is generally geared to the specific needs of the business, the task of providing basic-skill training is left to the government. It is in the government's interest, but not necessarily a particular firm's interest, to provide general-skill training that can be used in almost all jobs. For example, a firm that provides general training will not benefit if the trained employees change companies.

Today's work force has attained a high level of education that is unprecedented. Since 1950 the number of adults aged twenty-five or older who have from graduated high school has jumped from only a third to nearly three-quarters. But there is widespread debate and justifiable concern as to whether these increased years of education have led to equivalent increases in skill levels. It is argued that the good news about rising years of average educational attainment should not obscure the problems confronting specific categories of individuals. The children of the poor and uneducated continue to be more likely to lack basic competency, often because of their unstimulating home environments and health problems. In addition, the poor often live in geographic areas where education and funding are inadequate. Millions of Americans who dropped out of high school are illiterate or suffer learning disabilities. All these groups are likely to experience difficulties in finding employment that will provide them with sufficient earnings to escape poverty's vicious cycle.

Census Pegs Adult Illiteracy at 13%

Studies over the years have indicated that the number of years of education positively correlates with skill levels and with earnings but only indirectly measures occupational skills. Some high school dropouts may have the same reading and math skills as high school graduates. The illiteracy rate is a reasonable measure of skill levels: individuals who fail to meet minimal competency levels generally lack skills. Because most jobs require workers with basic reading, writing and math proficiency, basic competency is essential to function effectively in today's labor market, even in most entry-level jobs. Low competency usually correlates with low earnings and low educational attainment.

A U.S. Census Bureau study had found 13% of adults living in the U.S. to be illiterate in English, the *New York Times* reported April 21, 1986. The bureau said the study provided the most accurate measurement yet of U.S. illiteracy. The Census Bureau's last estimate of adult illiteracy, in 1979, had placed the rate at just 0.5% for those over age 14. That figure was based simply on how many of those surveyed reported fewer than six years of education. The new estimate derived from a 26-question multiple-choice test given 3,400 adults in 1982. The sample did not include prisoners or hospital patients. A score of fewer than 20 correct answers was taken to show illiteracy.

Critics contended that many of the questions were framed in bureaucratic language difficult even for literate citizens to understand. But they disagreed on whether the survey's estimate of the illiteracy rate was too high or too low.

The project had been supervised by Robert E. Burns, acting director of the Education Department's planning and technical analysis division. The department had not yet released the findings officially. According to the Census Bureau, the test results showed an illiteracy rate of 9% among U.S. adults whose native language was English. But that figure rose to 48% among adults for whom English was a second language.

Of all adult illiterates, 51% were found to live in small towns and suburbs, 41% in metropolitan areas. Forty-one percent were found to be English-speaking whites, 22% black and 22% Spanish- speaking. A plurality, 40%, were aged 20 to 39. These results were reported in the May 5, 1986 issue of *Time* magazine. About 60% of native English speakers who had graduated from high school answered every question correctly; 70% of those who failed had not finished high school; and 42% had been without work for a year before taking the test.

Most U.S. students were "unable to write adequately except in response to the simplest of tasks," according to a report released Dec. 3, 1986 by the National Assessment of Education Progress. The study, entitled "Writing Report Card," found among other things, that fewer than 25% of the high school students surveyed had performed adequately on tests of the writing skills needed for success in business, the professions or academic study. Fewer than 33% of all the students surveyed had been able to adequately back up a point with evidence, and students at all levels were found "deficient in higher-order thinking skills." The study drew on writing samples from 55,000 public and private school students in the fourth, eighth and 11th grades.

The Boston Herald

*Boston, MA,
December 5, 1988*

CHALK up another big failure for public education. According to a recent study, public school students lack basic writing skills, the absence of which will be a serious handicap in years to come.

Lately, a number of surveys disclosed that America's school children have reading problems, do poorly at math and are deficient in historical knowledge. Now the National Assessment of Educational Progress reports that public school students lack the ability to communicate in writing.

The survey of 55,000 students in the 4th, 8th and 11th grades disclosed that the overwhelming majority failed dismally at the simplest analytical task — comparing and contrasting in writing. In an understatement, Archie La-pointe, NAEP executive director, comments, "performance in writing in our schools is, quite simply, bad."

The study was highly critical of both educators and instruction, noting the average student was assigned written home work only once every two weeks. Moreover, teachers rarely request that students revise an assignment, once it's handed in.

According to a congressional study, 60 percent of the nation's 110 million salaried workers are required to do some writing as part of their employment. In our increasingly information-oriented society, good communication skills — written and verbal — are essential. Without them, graduates are doomed to menial positions.

The answer to this problem, along with so many other educational shortcomings, is to promote diversity. Only the competition offered by a strong system of private education will force public schools to shape up. This is another excellent reason to support the Reagan administration's proposal for tuition tax credits, to foster that competition.

The Dispatch

Columbus, OH, December 1, 1988

The problem of illiteracy in Asian countries is getting increased attention and Asian and U.N. officials hope that the attention may go a long way to sharply reducing the problem. The goal of eliminating illiteracy is a worthy one deserving of universal support.

Some countries, such as Japan, Australia and South Korea, have achieved virtually total literacy. But others are still coping with bringing the very basics of education to remote villages, poverty-stricken tribes and downtrodden, poorly motivated rural women, who make up about 60 percent of Asia's illiterates.

All Asian nations gave the go-ahead for the campaign against illiteracy at the 23rd session of the U.N. Educational, Scientific and Cultural Organization General Conference last year. It will officially be launched before the end of this year under the acronym APPEAL — Asia-Pacific Program of Education for All.

In addition, Chinese leader Deng Xiaoping and Indian Prime Minister Rajiv Gandhi have voiced their support for efforts to increase the educational levels of the citizens of their countries. Although China has achieved a literacy rate of more than 70 percent, 229 million Chinese still could not read in 1985. India had more than 263 million illiterates last year.

Literacy has been used as a political weapon in some countries where leaders have withheld educational resources for fear that increased understanding among the populace would threaten the government's standing.

But those attitudes appear to be changing, and the international pressure to eliminate illiteracy is doing much to bring needed resources to bear on the problem.

Whatever the United States can do to assist these efforts should be done. The goal is worthy and should be attained.

ST. LOUIS POST-DISPATCH

St. Louis, MO, December 2, 1986

As the nation addresses the reform of the educational system, one subject of rising concern is the limitations of standardized tests, particularly I.Q. tests, in accurately measuring intelligence.

While such tests have long proved to be reasonably useful indicators of how well students perform academic tasks requiring primarily verbal and mathematical skills, many educators and psychologists question whether they are useful guides to other kinds of intelligence.

This might not matter if the only task schools faced was to promote academic ability, some of whose skills are important tools in later life. But since so many real-life situations hardly require them, but are instead mastered by other kinds of intelligence, there is legitimate doubt as to whether the schools are pitching their focus broadly enough.

Two psychologists in particular, Dr. Howard Gardner of Harvard University and Dr. David Feldman, professor of developmental psychology at Tufts University, are doing extensive work with preschool children to identify these other forms of intelligence.

They argue for a definition that includes many talents they consider to be as important as verbal and mathematical ability. Insight, a capacity to work with spatial relationships or to solve problems from context rather than from explicit instructions are just a few. Hardest to measure, but no less important, are social skills — not charm, but the ability to lead, mediate or give care.

Today's special programs for gifted children — entry to which is usually based on achievement on standardized tests — tend to discriminate against children possessing these other kinds of gifts.

To underline the point, researchers have long since demonstrated that the majority of adults who have made outstanding contributions in a variety of fields typically scored below the 95th percentile on I.Q. tests.

But the ruling prejudice that mathematical and verbal skills — as well as speed in employing them — are the only real forms of intelligence won't be easily overcome. After all, those in charge of education usually excel in just these traits.

Intelligence has never been easy to measure, and there has never been a consensus on just what it is or how it works. But we must try to reach a more inclusive, sophisticated definition of the term. Unfortunately, until fairly precise ways are found to measure ability other than primarily by standardized tests, new definitions aren't likely to be accepted widely enough to be employed in the system.

Unhappily, this means children will continue to grow up in ignorance of or misunderstanding their abilities, a handicap almost as serious as not having enough of them. As adults, they will often wind up in jobs that don't employ their true gifts because neither they nor their employers know what they are.

This is a social and psychological failure by society of major dimensions, and harmful as well to our economy's productivity, which at the root depends on talent properly developed and intelligently employed.

The Star-Ledger

Newark, NJ, December 27, 1986

There is a growing movement to have English declared the official language of the United States. Of all the problems that Americans can find with their language these days, this seems to be the least important. Reading and writing should be given a much higher learning status.

Advocates of the "English First" coalition are fearful that our common language is not getting its deserved pre-eminent standing from newly-arrived immigrants who are inclined to speak in the foreign tongue of their native countries.

The concern of the English First movement appears to be misplaced. There is a need for diversity of languages, for this is a nation that prides itself on the ethnic diversity of its citizens, and the varied cultures and languages they bring to our shores.

There is no threat to the English language from immigrants; many of them are in bilingual programs that will enable them to speak two or more languages, a facility that large numbers of native-born Americans do not possess.

On a practical basis, English is the basic, working language—a reality widely recognized and accepted by most Americans, including newly arrived immigrants. Whether it is official or not, there are formidable economic and social problems.

A more serious problem concerning usage of language in the United States is illiteracy. It cannot be solved merely by making a declaration of an official language, but will require a major effort. There are 27 million adult Americans who are functionally illiterate—they cannot read or write. Forty million Americans are marginally illiterate.

The problem has been long acknowledged by the academic community. There have been national efforts in the past by the federal government to combat illiteracy, but they have been largely ineffectual. Nor have public schools been able to remediate illiteracy in a significant manner.

The English First movement would have been better directed if it had channeled its efforts in trying to begin reversing the deplorable, negative effects of illiteracy. Its mission would have more contemporary relevancy if it was concentrated on a common purpose—drawing on the nation's broad spectrum of educational resources to help the millions of unlettered Americans learn how to read and write their common language.

ILLiTeRACy

THE RICHMOND NEWS LEADER

Richmond, VA,
May 22, 1988

Literacy experts disagree on whether a recent Census Bureau report putting the national rate of illiteracy at 13 per cent overstates or understates the problem. The experts agree, however, that the criteria by which the Bureau reached its conclusion may have been rigged.

The Bureau says it wanted to find out how well the 3,400 adults tested in the 1982 literacy test could follow instructions. So one of its questions was composed of this gem derived — you guessed it — from an official government document:

"You may request a review of the decision made on the application or recertification for assistance and may request a fair hearing concerning any action affecting receipt or termination of assistance."

On the basis of the large number of flunkees who expressed bafflement at the meaning of that gibberish, the Bureau says millions of Americans are functionally illiterate.

You bet. And if the Bureau devised a test based on the instructions in the IRS booklet accompanying the 1040 form, it might conclude that the only functional literates in the land are lawyers and accountants.

Chicago Tribune

Chicago, IL, May 10, 1988

Illiteracy is a quiet tragedy. Its victims rarely churn up a public protest or ask legislators for help or sue a school for failing to perform its duty. Instead, they live behind walls of embarrassment, pretending and failing, seriously handicapped in the job market and in almost every other phase of American life.

No one is even sure how many adults are illiterate or how they should be defined. Should the number include those who cannot cope with IRS Form 1040? Manage a driver's license test? Fill out an employment application? Understand a newspaper? Read what's necessary to hold a job? Or decipher anything in print?

Most recently, the U.S. Census Bureau estimated that 13 percent of American adults are illiterate—approximately 23 million people—based on a 26-question literacy test taken by a sampling of 3,400 people. Those rated as illiterate include 48 percent of those whose native language is not English and 9 percent of those who grew up speaking English.

The current Census Bureau count is considerably higher than a cheerful estimate the agency made in 1979, when it guessed that only one-half of one percent of adult Americans over age 14 couldn't read, based on the number who had finished 5th grade. Other surveys put the number of illiterates much higher, especially if those who are defined as "functionally" and "marginally" illiterate are included. In his 1985 book on the problem, Jonathan Kozol concludes that at a minimum, 25 million adults read at less than 5th grade level and 35 million more have less than 9th grade reading skill.

But counting illiterates, however it's done, isn't the major point. What's essential now is to develop a range of public and private outreach programs to locate these millions of socially and vocationally handicapped people and help them learn to read. It's also urgently important to strengthen school programs so that no more children slip through the system without learning to read well.

Many school reading programs still do not incorporate the best of current knowledge about how reading can be taught most effectively. Studies show clearly that children do best when they are first taught simple phonetic rules for decoding printed words and when they have a wealth of good books and stories to read for pleasure. A relaxed, low-key opportunity to learn to read starting during the preschool years is enormously successful for most youngsters. Ways to make such an experience available to more young children should be explored. Teachers should also be sensitized to diagnosing reading problems and learning disabilities as early as possible and should be able to arrange for special help.

Increasing the variety, accessibility, outreach and public acceptance of literacy programs for adults also should help. Churches, community organizations, service clubs, community colleges, vocational training programs, welfare agencies and branch libraries all should be offering reading classes and private tutoring options. Adults who need help learning to read should be made to feel as welcome and intelligent as any other adults who are getting more education and training for personal or professional reasons.

The San Diego Union

San Diego, CA, April 27, 1986

Xlmyhpwkq oznlve

No, the garbled headline is not a typographical error. That jumble of letters is no more indecipherable than are these words for millions of illiterate Americans, who are restricted to a nether world of ignorance, humiliation, and hopelessness.

A recent study by the U.S. Census Bureau disclosed that 13 percent of American adults are illiterate in English. Nearly half of the adults whose native language in not English are classified illiterate. Approximately 25 million adults cannot read a simple menu or understand a bus schedule. They cannot comprehend a letter from their child's teacher or the front page of a daily newspaper. An additional 35 million are semi-literate, which means they can read just well enough to barely get by in society. All told, these 60 million persons represent more than one-third of this nation's adult population.

And more of them are on the way. Approximately 50 percent of all black 17-year-olds are functionally illiterate. Some 15 percent of recent graduates from urban high schools read at less than sixth-grade level and 1 million teen-agers cannot read above the third-grade level.

The economic costs of illiteracy are staggering. An estimated $10 billion is forfeited in lost income annually by persons unable to read and write. Each year, more than $8 billion in welfare is earmarked for adults who cannot find and hold jobs. Several billion dollars are spent annually for workers' compensation, damaged equipment, and industrial insurance costs directly caused by on-site accidents because workers are unable to read safety warnings and instructions for the operation of complex machines.

The U.S. military pays a high price as well. Nearly 30 percent of naval recruits were recently described as "a danger to themselves and costly naval equipment because of their inability to read and understand instructions." Little wonder training manuals that resemble comic books are commonplace throughout the armed services.

How can the U.S. public-education system produce so many functional illiterates? That question was asked three years ago by a Presidential Commission, which correctly concluded that this is "a nation at risk."

Stung by recent criticism, many public schools have returned to the basics. Numerous districts have also scrapped their social-promotion policy that passed students along to the next grade, despite the youngsters' inability to read at grade level. The recent trend of educational reforms notwithstanding, thousands of illiterate and semi-literate students still slip through the cracks each year in our public schools.

What can be done?

Obviously, the schools must do a better job. In fairness, however, many school districts are overextended by mandated programs that strain their already limited resources. Granted, the good teachers still give individual attention to those students who need extra help. But there is a limit to such conscientiousness when class sizes exceed 35 youngsters and classes are constantly interrupted.

Thus, it is too often left to other programs to pick up the slack. The federal government's Adult Basic Education program purportedly serves 2 million persons. In truth, nearly half of the students fail to complete the program and only 8 percent of those who do so have been able to get jobs or better jobs. The military operates a remediation program for about a million recruits but seldom accepts a person reading at below fifth-grade level.

Private programs such as Laubach Literacy and the Literacy Volunteers of America do an excellent job with the limited numbers of those persons they reach. The same is true for the California Literacy Campaign, an impressive statewide program that allocates $2.5 million for an estimated 5 million non-readers.

San Diego County efforts of note include Project READ, a volunteer tutoring program run by National City's library system, that has challenged other cities throughout the county to a literacy race. Lemon Grove, Poway, Ramona, and Santee are served by Project SURE, sponsored by the county library system. And North County residents have access to the Tri-City Literacy Coalition.

San Diego's Reading is Fundamental (RIF) program provides free books to needy youngsters. The driving force behind Southeast San Diego's successful RIF program is Roosevelt Brown, who has distributed books from his home to hundreds of children. This worthy program does more than encourage youngsters to read. It often prompts some of their parents to follow suit, become examples, and enroll in a literacy program.

Illiteracy is not irreversible. In fact, studies show that adults are able to improve their reading skills by more than one grade level with 35 hours of individualized instruction. Unfortunately, all federal, state, municipal, and private literacy programs in this nation reach only about 4 percent of the illiterate population.

A comprehensive effort is needed to help most of the 60 million American adults who live in the shadows. Failing that, they and many of their children are condemned to a life of failure, frustration, and futility.

WORCESTER TELEGRAM.

Worcester, MA, June 12, 1986

The illiteracy problem among adults in the United States is a lot worse than most people think. A government study looking at whether Americans can read uncomplicated English found that between 17 million and 21 million adults can't read simple instructions. That's 13 percent of the population.

The figures include 48 percent of the adults whose native language is not English; many of them can read their own language. For Americans whose basic language is English, 9 percent of them cannot read it, according to the English Language Proficiency Test conducted by the Census Bureau. The study was based on multiple-choice tests, designed to see whether people could read and understand government notices and applications.

Even more deplorable are some basic underlying facts. For example, more than 35 percent of English-speaking adults classified as illiterate are in their 20s or 30s. More than 42 percent of the English-speaking illiterates had no earnings in the year before the 1982 study and more than 70 percent had not finished high school. That leaves 30 percent who did finish high school and still cannot read.

Of all U.S. adults considered illiterate, regardless of primary language, more than half — 56 percent — are younger than 50 years old, and 41 percent live in cities. Only 8 percent live in strictly rural areas, a factor that indicates "internal migration" from the country to the city compounds illiteracy. It also shatters the myth that the problem is greater "on the farm."

The figures shook government officials because 1979 study estimates showed only about one-half of a percent of the population over 14 years old was functionally illiterate. The estimate was thought too low; it led to the later survey.

The important message in the results is that formal education is necessary. But the youngster who hasn't learned to read is often frustrated in school and becomes a dropout. The drop-out rate of native English-speaking students is more than 20 percent nationwide, much higher in the cities, and even worse when students whose native language is not English are added in.

It is next to impossible to get and hold onto a meaningful job when an adult can't read English. Much has to be done — to teach young children to read, to stem the drop-out flood, to encourage young adults to continue learning. The United States can't write off 20 million people.

Los Angeles Times

Los Angeles, CA, July 27, 1987

It has been more than 20 years since we were told why Johnny can't read. Despite the ensuing years of classroom emphasis on reading skills, the U.S. Department of Education now estimates that national illiteracy increases by 1.5 million people each year. For these Americans, the reason why they cannot read no longer matters.

The ability to read and write—sometimes as little as one's own name—has traditionally determined whether or not a person is literate. But the world has changed. Warning labels, sales contracts and even the occasional traffic ticket demand an ability not only to read but also to understand and appropriately respond. For millions of Americans this task is impossible. Unable to function independently in today's complex society, they are considered to be "functionally" illiterate.

The number of functionally illiterate adults in the United States is not really known. Estimates vary from 17 million to 75 million, depending on the breadth of the definition. What is known is that more than 50% of the nation's prison inmates are not able to read newspaper headlines or understand written instructions. And last year 40% of the armed services' enlistees were found to read below the ninth-grade level.

The cost of illiteracy is as impossible to estimate as the problem itself, but it is enormous. While some people succeed despite a lifetime struggle with reading disabilities, most do not. Experts say that illiteracy is responsible for many industrial accidents, higher welfare and unemployment benefits, increased poverty, crime and drug use and losses in international trade.

Sen. Edward M. Kennedy (D-Mass.) has introduced legislation that would be a promising and inexpensive solution to the illiteracy problem. He calls it the Literacy Corps. The program would utilize one of the nation's best resources, the university student. For a one-time cost of $20 million, about 800 universities and colleges across the nation would be able to start programs in which their students, under professional supervision, would each provide 60 hours of reading instruction at local schools, adult-education programs, community groups and prisons. In return for their work, the students would receive college credit for the elective program.

This is an innovative and cost-effective project that deserves congressional support. The Literacy Corps, along with other literacy programs, makes up the Senate's Education for Competitive America Act (S 406). Unfortunately, this measure has now been attached to the Senate's controversial trade bill. As currently written, this protectionist trade bill has little chance of surviving a presidential veto.

The Senate should reconsider the Education for Competitive America Act on its own. This is an appropriate vehicle for congressional action on the nation's escalating illiteracy problem. The Literacy Corps would offer to thousands, perhaps millions, of non-readers an opportunity to participate in today's world at today's standard. The rewards would be great, the cost so low.

LOS ANGELES HERALD

Los Angeles, CA, July 30, 1987

If Congress agrees, as it should, to establish Sen. Ted Kennedy's national "Literacy Corps" to teach millions of illiterate Americans to read, Norman Manasa deserves the credit. Everything but the name is his idea.

When Manasa was a junior at the University of Miami in 1968, he saw two converging needs. In inner-city schools, migrant camps, orphanages, prisons there were people needing individual attention to improve their academic skills. At the university were students that Manasa figured could use a dose of the real world to flesh out the abstractions they were learning in the classroom.

So he he put together a unique program that gave college students in sociology, economics and educational psychology credit for tutoring. The project was an immediate and stunning success. Ultimately, more than 1,000 students participated.

Manasa's approach is even more important now than then. Basic educational skills, particularly reading, are essential to get a job in an increasingly technological society.

For the past 10 years, at the helm of the non-profit Washington Education Project, he has worked to expand his innovative tutoring concept to every college campus in the nation. Progress has been slow, but more colleges are coming on board.

Corporate donations provide two-year, $25,000 grants for administrative costs to each college involved in the program. Tutors, who receive course credit but no pay, spend 60 hours a semester teaching children and illiterate adults how to read.

If even 5 percent of the nation's 10 million college students were to join in a literacy program, they would provide 30 million hours of free tutoring each semester.

Although Manasa is having somewhat better luck these days in attracting corporate support, Kennedy's legislation would provide $20 million for grants, enough to get the Literacy Corps started at 800 colleges. Unfortunately, his proposal is attached to an untenable Senate trade bill. It ought to be reintroduced so it can be passed on its own merits.

THE SACRAMENTO BEE

Sacramento, CA, May 6, 1987

The most revealing thing coming from the state's survey of welfare recipients is not that some are incapable of getting a job because they can't read, write or add, but how many of them there are.

The survey, covering some 6,000 cases in nine counties, indicated that at least 57 percent of those interviewed, most of them new applicants, required remedial education in basic skills. (For chronic welfare recipients, the number is almost certainly even higher). Nearly two-thirds of that group scored so low that they were given at least six months of remedial classroom work before they received any job training or work assignments. As a result, the state's recently enacted workfare program, designed to train welfare recipients and get them employed, is off to a slower start than expected and could cost considerably more than what the state budgeted.

Although the number of the illiterate is larger than expected, that ought not to be surprising. The connection between basic skills — the ability to read signs, fill out forms, perform elementary calculations — and the ability to get and keep a job has been articulated so often that it's become banal. The problem is how to provide those skills before children turn 18 so that remedial education in basic skills becomes unnecessary. The schools obviously have a major responsibility, as does the state in providing the resources, but merely to demand improvement is hardly enough.

In an economy that accepts a chronic 7 percent unemployment rate — and with unemployment running much higher in some parts of the country — better schooling alone is hardly a guarantee against the need for welfare. Indeed, as long as unemployment continues to run at 30 percent or 40 percent among young men and women in the inner cities, it's probably as much an invitation to fail and drop out of school as it is a result. Combine that with the cluster of other problems that plague not only the inner cities but the rural poor — teenage pregnancy, drugs, despair — and it would be myopic to point to any single thing as the source. Illiteracy is one element in welfare; but disease, poverty and alienation are themselves contributors to illiteracy.

None of that ought to be used as a rationale for doing nothing. On the contrary, unless every segment of the social system acts as if it can make a difference, nothing will ever change. Certainly every dollar that's intelligently invested in education and decent medical care for children will pay for itself in subsequent savings. And certainly, it's useful to acknowledge that it isn't laziness that drives people onto the rolls. But to suggest that one thing alone will solve the problem is to invite further failure and frustration.

THE ASHEVILLE CITIZEN
Ashville, NC, March 7, 1987

Adult illiteracy has long been one of the negative factors in efforts to improve the economic climate in any state and North Carolina is no exception.

There have been, over the years, numerous calls to get busy and overcome this drawback.

Another call was issued this week by former North Carolina Gov. Robert W. Scott, now president of the state's Community College System.

Adult illiteracy is not a new theme for Scott. He has been preaching the need for adult education for a long time. In 1984, in a talk at the 25th anniversary celebration of Asheville-Buncombe Technical College, he referred to adult illiteracy as the "soft underbelly" of the economic growth of North Carolina.

Others have joined in the effort to push a tough program of adult education, including the present governor, Jim Martin, who proclaimed 1987 as the "Year of the Reader" in his State of the State address last month.

Simultaneously, the governor announced the creation of the Governor's Literacy Council to coordinate the state's literacy programs.

With more than 835,000 adults over age 25 who haven't completed the 8th grade, North Carolina can ill afford to let the situation deteriorate any further. The problem is further complicated by the knowledge that an additional 700,000 people have not finished high school and the dropout rate exceeds 27,000 per year.

Although the state's community colleges, given Scott's enthusiasm, are prepared to play a major role in helping illiterate adults learn basic skills, it will take more than just this system to sustain the momentum.

It is with this in mind that Scott has urged all state agencies to become involved in the illiteracy fight.

Add to this an effort by the private sector and we just may begin to reverse the trend.

The economy is just one of the areas where the effect of adult illiteracy is felt; it is perhaps the one most often mentioned in references to the need to overcome illiteracy.

But there are other consequences that have a far more personal meaning. In Scott's words, "the dimensions of human and economic misery spawned by adult illiteracy defy description..."

Yes, it is time to step up the fight against adult illiteracy. There is much at stake, and it isn't all economics.

AKRON BEACON JOURNAL
Akron, OH, September 10, 1987

THE LATEST report on school reform shouldn't be left collecting dust. This one is worth more than several others combined, namely for its clear focus on a problem and its proposals for substantive change.

The report, titled "Children in Need: Investment Strategies for the Educationally Disadvantaged," says it straight: That nearly 30 percent of the public school students are disadvantaged in some way — because of poverty, for example, or because of no good guidance at home — and that these students face the risk of "educational failure and lifelong dependency."

In essence, they could become a permanent underclass of people not qualified to hold jobs, and they could put America at a disadvantage in competing in a global economy.

Solutions are possible, and the report lists some good ones: quality preschools for all disadvantaged 3- and 4-year-olds; quality child care for working-poor parents; heath care for pregnant teens, and health care for their babies.

Of course, the costs would be staggering. But what study group would be more aware of that than the Committee for Economic Development, which issued the report.

Actually, the committee's recommendations are aimed at saving money by preventing problems. In truth, the public has only two choices: pay now or pay more later.

Plenty of evidence affirms this. One government study, for example, shows that for every $1 invested in quality preschool education, the public saves nearly $5 in costs of special education, public assistance and crime.

Early intervention does work. Head Start and programs in remedial reading and math have proved that. It would be only sensible to expand these programs and create new ones to begin intervention even earlier.

Federal officials would do well to heed the powerful messages of this report. As those who wrote the report know, quick fixes and fast results won't work. The challenge is for an overhaul of the system.

Anyone who doubts one is needed, or questions the scope of the problem, need only consider that one of every four ninth-graders today won't even graduate from high school.

THE ARIZONA REPUBLIC
Phoenix, AZ, September 11, 1987

HIGH SCHOOL students in the towns of Paris in Illinois, Kentucky, Tennessee and Texas, to name only four of the U.S. communities bearing that name, have a pretty good idea of the geographical location of their state in relation to the others.

But as for the location of that other Paris, the one in France, there seems to be some confusion. One third of the American students can't even locate France on a map.

That's one of the findings by the authors of *What Our 17-Year-Olds Know,* who reported that U.S. high school students flunked the first national history and literature test. Some of the other findings are no less discouraging.

"We are deeply uneasy about what it portends for these boys and girls" and "for the society they will inhabit ...," said the report's co-authors, Chester Finn Jr., assistant secretary of education, and Diane Ravitch, a Columbia University professor.

The authors' test of 8,000 high school juniors last year provided correct answers to an average of 54.5 percent of 141 questions on history and 51.8 percent of 121 on literature.

It is worth noting, as the authors did, that in terms traditionally used by teachers, "a score of less than 60 is failing".

Consider, for example, these results from the history test: Two out of three don't know the Civil War occurred between 1850 and 1900; 35 percent aren't aware that Watergate took place after 1950; and 70 percent don't know about the Magna Carta.

As for the students' knowledge of literature, only 20 percent could identify James Joyce, Feodor Dostoevski, Joseph Conrad, Henrik Ibsen, Thomas Hardy or Geoffrey Chaucer. This, the authors noted, amounted to "a rate of success that random guessing would produce."

So what's the answer to the overall problem of students lost in a fog of non-literacy?

Maybe the test questions should be easier, confining them to the current culture, whatever that is. Most students, it was reported, could identify stories and legends that are found in comic books, movies or television.

Or maybe, just maybe, classroom instruction and demands made on the students should be harder.

The Providence Journal

Providence, RI, May 19, 1987

An organization called the Commission on Global Education recently urged that American schools infuse their students, and a range of basic courses, with "a global perspective."

Said the commission: "We, quite literally, are potentially defenseless on this earth unless global, as well as domestic, problems are handled in a way that fuses aspirations for peace and security with the inevitability of change."

Of course, education is one important key to resolving this problem. And the commission, funded by the Rockefeller, Ford and Exxon foundations, and containing such luminaries as Clark Kerr, Ernest Boyer, Michael Novak and Albert Shanker, suggests that elementary school children examine "a variety of cultures, past and present, at home and abroad."

It also urges that secondary school students be required to study "at least two other cultures" in detail, one of which should be non-Western.

These suggestions make sense, but efforts to implement them should not be taken at the expense of other subjects where American students have demonstrated weakness. Too many young Americans cannot read, write or figure well enough, and they are ignorant of the history and geography of their own country.

Secretary of Education William Bennett recently declined to meet with a delegation from the commission. "When I hear 'geography' and 'history,' I'm pleased," he said. "When I hear 'global perspectives,' I'm usually a little nervous."

Americans who know something of themselves — of their origins, their country, of the way this nation has grown and changed — are the best equipped to benefit from "global perspectives."

Mr. Bennett's point is well taken. Americans are better citizens when they know something about the world. But the primary key to understanding lies in first teaching students how to read, write and think about their own society.

Newsday

New York, NY, July 4, 1987

Adult illiteracy is costing this nation dearly. It's now estimated that as many as 23 million Americans can't read beyond fourth grade level. In fact, the United States has the poorest literacy record of all the industrial nations.

That's a debilitating problem for someone who can't read a newspaper or the warning on a can of pesticide. But it also hurts this country's ability to compete with other industrial nations, such as Japan and Korea, in a world that is increasingly dependent on technology. The cost in economic terms comes to an estimated $225 billion in unrealized productivity; in tax revenues that aren't generated; in welfare, poverty, crime and related social ills. And the problem is getting worse: About 400,000 Americans join the illiterate population each year; more than 800,000 a year drop out of high school.

There is a measure before the Congress that could significantly help to reduce illiteracy: It would create a Literacy Corps, in which college students could work part-time as tutors in schools and community agencies as part of a special college course. St. John's University established such a program in 1986 with extremely good results.

The legislation would provide $20 million for Literacy Corps projects at colleges throughout the country. Each participating school would receive $25,000 to cover initial costs, mainly faculty salaries. Students would be trained in class and then assigned as tutors.

This seems to be a very small investment in a program that could have a very large payoff. It deserves Congress' support.

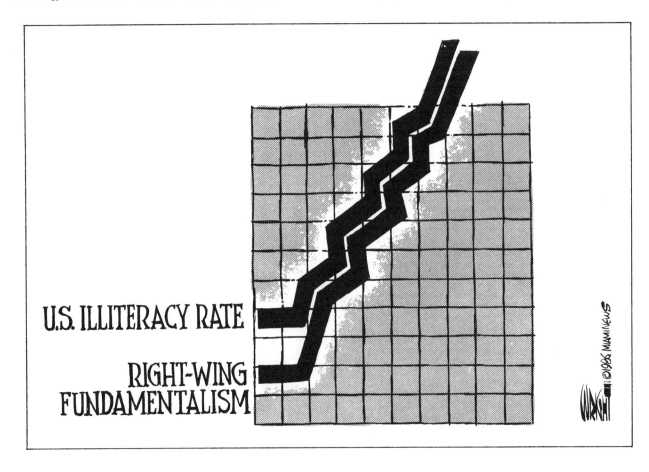

the Charleston Gazette

Charleston, SC, March 20, 1988

LITERACY horror stories abound:
▲ Last year, New York Telephone Co. recruited new workers to expand operations. Astonishingly, 84 percent of the applicants failed the company's entry exam, a simple test of elementary questions on vocabulary and mathematics.

▲ A pen full of cattle was killed when a feedlot operator gave the animals poison instead of grain. Why? He misread the labels.

▲ An insurance claimant was paid $2,200 instead of the $22 he should have received, because a clerk handling the claim couldn't understand the decimal system.

Too many Americans can't read or write well enough to work at most basic jobs or accomplish everyday tasks. The Department of Education figures that more than 27 million Americans above age 17 fall into this category. Another 45 million are barely competent at these skills.

These statistics are frightening — and not just for the unfit group. All of America suffers when young people flunk out of school or otherwise fail to become prepared for employment.

The cost to the United States can be summed up by its slide as the world's leading economy. While Asian and European nations provide schooling that put this country's to shame, an estimated 2 million Americans join the ranks of the illiterate each year.

Some businesses have responded by simplifying tasks so employees will have to read little or nothing. "Dumbing down," as this process is called, may have advantages in the short-term. Ultimately, however, it is not the answer to America's literacy crisis.

If current trends are not altered, it is evident the U.S. work force will be polarized between the educated, trained — and well-paid — elite, and others relegated to simple, repetitive, low-paying jobs — or none at all. This development will hit blacks and Hispanics especially hard, for historically they have composed a high percentage of the illiterate.

At the same time, America's overall competitive edge with the rest of the world will erode.

Although basic manufacturing drove industrialization in the past, it is clear the 21st century belongs to those able to function in high-tech fields already propelling the world economy. In other words, it will be a battle of brains over brawn, and the latter has little chance on its own.

Rather than dumbing down America, government and industry must combine to raise this country's literacy rate. Programs such as the federally funded Adult Basic Education Service already assist millions. In 1984, 2.5 million men and women were enrolled in the program. In 1986, that number had jumped to 3.1 million.

Meanwhile, corporations such as Standard Oil, Ford, Polaroid and Liberty Mutual Insurance offer remedial classes to employees. Between the two of them, General Motors and IBM spend $70 million a year providing adult

DESERET NEWS

Salt Lake City, UT, June 4, 1988

Twenty-nine million American adults — one in every six — cannot read even a newspaper headline.

Another 35-million read below the level considered necessary to function successfully in our increasingly sophisticated, technological society.

In Utah, more than 200,000 adults lack a high school diploma, most of them because they don't read very well.

We mention this because illiteracy exerts such a heavy drain on the economy in the form of lost opportunities and needlessly high welfare rolls. And because Congress needs to make sure that a promising new program for reducing illiteracy does not get lost in the fight over the vetoed trade bill.

Among the many provisions of that long, complicated bill is one that would set up a national Literacy Corps, which would enlist college students in semester-long stints as tutors for students with reading problems.

If the Senate sustains the veto of the trade bill as expected, Congress should find another way to set up and fund the Literacy Corps.

But even if it is created, such a corps is still no substitute for getting parents more deeply involved in making sure their children learn how to read. A recent Roper poll found that even though parents across the educational and economic spectrum place a high value on reading, less than half say their children read for pleasure every day.

With the ranks of the illiterate growing by 2.3 million American adults every year, the U.S. needs to apply new impetus to efforts to combat illiteracy. A person who can't read can't fill out an employment application. No wonder one study found that 42% of the illiterate earned no money in the year before they were tested.

As long as America remains saddled with so much illiteracy, there are sharp limits to how well its citizens can function in an increasingly technological society and how much they can contribute to its progress.

The Atlanta Journal AND THE ATLANTA CONSTITUTION

Atlanta, GA, March 10, 1988

For millions of Georgians, the Super Tuesday primary was the biggest political wingding in many a year. But for thousands of others, it was a party they'd just as soon forget. They did not participate, but not because they were displeased with the field of candidates.

They didn't vote because they, like one in every four adults in this country, are functionally illiterate. They didn't vote for the same reason many of them do not drive a car, go shopping alone or order a meal in a restaurant: Their handicap makes them feel inadequate, ashamed or embarrassed. It isolates them and reduces them to being half-citizens who are unable to participate fully in American life, but who are afraid to reveal their deficiency to others.

They don't want others to know they do not read well enough to understand the instructions on a voting machine or be able to pick the candidate they prefer from the names printed on a ballot. It is shameful in a nation with as many financial and technical resources as ours that more than a quarter of all adults suffer from a debility that is correctable.

Cooperative efforts between civic and government groups have helped many (programs like Literacy Action, for example, and Reading Is Fundamental.) But the job is too large to be left mainly to volunteerism. Illiteracy is an acid that eats at the fabric of our society. Its damage can be seen in long unemployment lines, deepening poverty and worsening crime.

Federal, state and local governments must redouble their efforts and invest more time and money in tackling the problem. More must be done to fight it on the front end, too. That means dealing with the school drop-out problem and catching as many potential illiterates as possible before they give up on school.

Private employers can help, too. They can sponsor in-house training programs that teach workers how to improve their reading and writing skills or underwrite such programs at nearby colleges or vocational schools. The solution won't come cheaply, but if it means salvaging the futures of millions whose contributions would otherwise be lost, there couldn't be a better way to spend the money.

Survey Shows Graduation Rates

It is well established that individuals without high school degrees tend to lack skills and to experience economic and labor market hardship. They experience higher unemployment rates than high school graduates, are less likely to seek work, and, if employed, earn lower wages in low-skilled jobs with poor work conditions. Further, the income gap between dropouts and graduates has increased sharply since the 1960s and high school dropouts have had a relatively more difficult time in the labor market than they had had previously. This trend may be the result of rising educational requirements for jobs and the larger pool of high school graduates available to employers even for those jobs that require limited skills. In such cases, the high school diploma serves as a screening device and indicates that the prospective employee has basic skills and can adjust to the discipline of the workplace.

The Census Bureau Dec. 1, 1987 released a report comparing high school and college graduation rates in 1985 with those from 1940. The report, titled "Educational Attainment in the United States," was based on the bureau's annual survey of 58,000 households.

The proportion of adults age 25 and older who had graduated from high school rose to 74% in 1985 from 24% in 1940. The percentage who had completed four or more years of college rose to 19% from 5% over the same period.

The census report found little difference between the sexes in high school and college completion rates. The report also noted that racial differences in completion rates had "narrowed considerably" between 1940 and 1985. The report stated that, in 1985, 76% of white adults (age 25 and older) and 60% of black adults had been high school graduates. The respective proportions in 1940 had been 26% and 7%. In 1985, 20% of white adults and 11% of black adults had completed four or more years of college; in 1940, only 5% of white adults and 1% of black adults had been college graduates.

The Record

Hackensack, NJ, August 28, 1986

Millions of American teen-agers will be going back to school next week. But one in four will never graduate. Some will drop out because they are bored or cannot make the grade academically; others say their families need the money they'd make by working; some are pregnant, some are getting married. Whatever the reason, these lost kids represent a brain drain of monumental proportions.

Not everybody needs a high-school diploma. But for too many youngsters, dropping out is a ticket to oblivion — a life of dead-end jobs, poverty, unemployment, and crime. As a group, dropouts finish billions of dollars behind high-school graduates in lifetime income and cost the government billions in welfare payments and lost income taxes.

What's the government doing to stem the tide of dropouts? Education Secretary William Bennett says it spends more than $3 billion a year on grants to the states for various educational-improvement programs. But something isn't working. In some states, the dropout rate is more than 40 percent. Even states with relatively few dropouts (New Jersey, at 17 percent, ranks 11th lowest) have inner-city pockets where the rates are far too high.

Unwilling to accept the administration's do-nothing-more posture, the House of Representatives passed a bill this month calling for $50 million in grants to school districts — seed money to encourage them to devise ways of dealing with dropouts. The full Senate is considering several companion measures.

Measured against the scale of the problem, $50 million isn't much. But these grants can go a long way if they focus on what works. A three-year program based on tutoring, counseling, and crisis intervention reduced the dropout rate in a suburban Massachusetts high school by 10 points. In New York City, 10 high schools hired dropout-prone students to work at in-house jobs that allowed them to earn money as they built their self-esteem through tutoring and counseling. It cost $5 million, but reduced the schools' dropout rate from 42 percent to 35 percent.

Anti-dropout programs won't do the whole job. Dropouts aren't made in high school; many children start elementary school with huge socioeconomic disadvantages, and the schools fail to teach them to read and write and get along. But the experiences in Massachusetts and New York teach us that we don't need to solve all society's problems in order to keep large numbers of kids in school. The dropout-prevention act is a beginning, and Congress should pass it.

The Des Moines Register

Des Moines, IA, Sept. 7, 1986

What's the usual question you ask when you first meet a child? Chances are that it's, "What grade are you in?" Being identified by grade is the universal American childhood experience.

Virtually all schools have grades. It's astonishing, when you reflect upon it, that with all the diversity in America virtually every school in every region has the same structure, from the most poverty-stricken inner-city public school to the wealthiest private school.

They all have grades. They all have 12 grades. Children of approximately the same chronological age are marched in lockstep through school, no matter if some get trampled in the process.

Often there is an agonizing dilemma: Which is worse, inflicting on a child the stimga of being "held back" or advancing the child who isn't ready for the next grade?

Many education reformers over the years have pointed out that the system makes no sense. Different children mature at different rates. They are ready to master various skills at different times. Yet school is organized on the assumption that all children of a given age should be taught the same things at the same time.

An interesting suggestion by Secretary of Education William Bennett is that the "chronological lockstep" in schools be loosened.

There have been experiments with various arrangements to loosen the lockstep, but they generally were abandoned. The more recent trend has been to reaffirm the "traditional" school, Americans want children to experience schools more or less as they themselves experienced them. The concept of grades in school is perhaps indelibly ingrained in American culture.

In a new era of school reform, Bennett is right to raise the question of the schoolhouse lockstep anew, but it would take a tremendous effort to do anything more than talk about it.

Chicago Defender

Chicago, IL, Sept. 9, 1986

Education is a powerful thing. It is so potent that, before the Civil War, a slave could be put to death for attempting to learn how to read Whites or free Blacks who were caught teaching slaves how to read could be severely reprimanded, fined or imprisoned. Why? Because education is enlightenment and no truly enlightened person will stay enslaved long.

Books, schools, writing materials and other similar things are symbols of education. They are doors to enlightenment. They are emancipators of the human spirit from intolerable human conditions.

School dropouts today are, for the most part, among the new slaves of society According to the National Center for Education Statistics, a variety of reasons were given by a sample group of sophomores who did not graduate in 1980.

Some were expelled or suspended, had poor grades, felt that school was not for them, believed that the school ground was too dangerous, admitted they couldn't get along with teachers, felt they didn't get into a desired program, dropped out for pregnancy and/or marriage, had to support a family, left because their friends were dropping out, couldn't get along with other students, left because of illness or a disability, were offered a chance to work, wanted to enter the military, moved too far from school or wanted to travel.

The reason dropouts are like modern slaves is because, as a group, the former students are financially poorer than others of society. They are locked in chains and shackles of poverty and this bondage is nearly as effective as the metal chains and anklets which held slaves of the past.

Dropouts also form a great portion of the illiterates of our country. These are people who can't: read or fill out job applications; decipher bus or street signs; sign their names to checks; understand their children's report cards, insurance policies, medical brochures or a wide variety of other necessities of life.

Since dropouts are so economically and educationally burdened, they find it very difficult to get and keep jobs, even the low-paying ones.

As a result, their financial movement in society is very small compared to other groups. They are economically imprisoned by their lack of education. It is difficult for them to get credit or properly purchase a home because they have trouble reading deeds and related documents.

They usually don't have checking accounts since many of them can't write.

But there is a way that dropouts can escape the awesome slavery of poverty and illiteracy -- by going back to school. It doesn't have to be a daytime high school. Nor does it have to be for seven or eight hours a day. One course at a time after work or on weekends, with guidance from a qualified educational counselor, can begin to free dropouts from modern bondage. Strengthening reading habits and abilities through going over the various sections of a newspaper (comics and sports sections are good beginnings) can eventually enable the person's learning ability to grow.

Since minorities comprise a disproportionate percentage of dropouts, we strongly encourage them to seek help in completing their high school education. It's tough enough to make it through life with a diploma but it can be the equivalent of a living nightmare to attempt to do it without one.

The Atlanta Journal
and
THE ATLANTA CONSTITUTION

Atlanta, GA, December 17, 1986

Distressingly high drop-out rates in the Southeast and other areas of the country deserve the national attention they have finally begun to receive. Society pays a dear price because of the problem. The National Education Association estimates that dropouts cost the public $75 billion a year in unemployment and welfare benefits.

But concern must be tempered by a sense of proportion, flexibility and sensitivity. Getting tough with those who have opted to leave school by encouraging local employers not to hire them, as some communities are doing, is a quick fix that misses the point. If enough employers take that advice, the number of dropouts will not decline appreciably, but there would be an additional problem: more unemployment and more dependence on public assistance.

A less punitive approach is suggested by work being done in the Dalton-Whitfield County vicinity of north Georgia, where a steady demand for low-skilled workers in the area's carpet industry may be a contributing factor in the school system's abominable drop-out rates, which have ranged from 37 to 57 percent over the last five years.

Whitfield officials and business leaders have reduced the drop-out rate 16 percent since 1983 by using, among other techniques, high school equivalency programs *on-site* at some of the carpet mills and personal testimony from dropouts who wish they had stayed in school. The program also unfortunately leans on education requirements for hiring, but it recognizes, as some other approaches do not, that the lure of jobs, especially low-paying ones, is not the sole reason students quit school. Poor classroom performance, pregnancy, low self-esteem and difficulties at home contribute to drop-out rates.

The need for sensitivity should not be lost on education reformers intent on improving student performance by raising academic standards. While reforms must be firm, they must also be flexible, so that marginal students aren't kicked aside or frustrated to point of giving up. "Improvements" like "no-pass, no-play" requirements for extracurricular activities, more testing and exit exams for high-school seniors must be monitored closely to make sure they do not add to drop-out rates as they seek to bolster academic performance.

THE DALLAS TIMES HERALD

Dallas, TX, January 18, 1986

One of the most disturbing problems in education is that nearly half of all Hispanic students drop out before completing high school.

Why so many? Documentation is difficult, but local experience shows that Hispanics have difficulties with language differences, cultural-economic barriers and, in some schools, inhalant abuse. Dropping out adds to their later economic burdens and perpetuates an unfortunate cycle of undereducation.

Dallas school administrators have recommended that a San Antonio-based research firm be awarded the $250,000 contract for a 30-month study of the problem.

That's a lot of money for a problem the district should already be studying in depth. But if the school board decides the situation can best be studied by outside observers, the study may be cheap at the price. The cost of undereducating half of the Hispanic students who become tomorrow's workers and citizens is incalculably greater.

The consultants' first report would be due on June 13; a final report on longer dropout trends would come in September 1988.

That shouldn't mean that the district should wait 30 months before increasing efforts to reduce the Hispanic dropout rate, however. Hispanic and business leaders should start now to create the kind of tutoring, drug counseling and job assistance that could provide diplomas and greater expectations for Hispanic youth.

The San Diego Union

San Diego, CA, December 13, 1986

Two recent studies underscore a public-education problem that threatens dire economic consequences for the United States in general and California in particular.

The Washington, D.C.-based Population Reference Bureau discloses that minority students, particularly Hispanics, are dropping out of school in record numbers. And a study by the Education Research Service of Arlington, Va., shows a "precipitous decline" in the number of high-school graduates at a time when new jobs require even more education.

Nationally, the number of high-school graduates has declined 18 percent during the last decade. This slippage is alarming if for no other reason than it bodes ill for America's chances of becoming more competitive at home and abroad.

California's problem is especially acute because Hispanic students account for more than half of the state's estimated 37-percent dropout rate. The state's Hispanic public-school enrollment, in fact, is expected to increase 250 percent during the next two generations.

What can San Diego do to help slow this dropout rate and make its high-school graduates more employable? A good place to begin would be for local businesses and the public schools to work together in motivating minority students.

The framework for such cooperation is already in place. Earlier this year, the National Alliance of Business selected San Diego and five other U.S. cities as a testing ground to replicate the successful Boston Compact, which draws on corporate contributions to bring the public and private sectors together. Unfortunately, the San Diego Compact has been slow in getting organized.

Under the Boston Compact, which was begun in 1982, participating businesses give preference to qualified high-school graduates for entry-level jobs. In return, the partner schools consciously prepare students for such work.

Career specialists work with recent and prospective graduates and seek to match them with available jobs. Meantime, counselors target high-risk students and encourage them to stay in school so they can get on the first rung of the employment ladder.

Bill Nelson, chairman of the Greater San Diego Chamber of Commerce, is willing to head the countywide effort through the auspices of the Private Industry Council. He and others in the business community understand that San Diego's greatest resource lies with its younger generation, trained as part of a high-

ly productive work force. A broad-based community effort will be required for this goal.

San Diego's most visible link between industry and education is the Partnerships in Education program that encourages companies and several Navy groups to "adopt" individual schools. Clearly, more businesses are needed to expand these partnerships.

The county compact also should support other efforts such as Project Success. This worthwhile, albeit modest, program currently provides direct services to minority students at Memorial Junior High School and

Keeler Middle School, both of which have high dropout rates. The students are counseled, tutored, and, most important, encouraged to complete their education. Such positive reinforcement is essential, given the dropout rate of 47 percent among San Diego's Hispanics and 41 percent among blacks.

Mr. Nelson is correct, of course, when he says that such statistics are a time bomb that threatens the very future of this community. The San Diego Compact should be organized now. We can't wait.

The Dallas Morning News

Dallas, TX, February 21, 1987

The dropout rate reported by the Dallas Independent School District this week is shocking: More than half of the seventh-graders tracked through the system did not finish high school.

Another study prepared by the Texas Education Agency showed that the dropout rate for Dallas freshmen who began school in 1982 is 43 percent, the second highest in the state.

The fact that nearly half of the students in public school are dropping out is outrageous and unacceptable.

Several programs already are being implemented by the Dallas district to address the dropout rate, including a $125,000 study to track reasons for the high Hispanic dropout rate. But the top leadership should feel morally and professionally challenged by the new figures to redouble their efforts to stop the hemmorhage of students.

■ The district must do a better job of bilingual education, to help the students struggling unsuccessfully to master courses in English. These students are the leading candidates for failure. The proposed $4.3 million "newcomer school" to provide concentrated attention for foreign-born students who are English-limited would be a step in the right direction. But the district will need more qualified language teachers and may have to pay premiums to get teachers with linguistic ability, or may have to recruit bilingual individuals without teaching certificates to serve as teacher's aides. Here's a place where the Hispanic and Asian professional community could do more to help reinforce district efforts.

■ Drug education and prevention need stronger support. Because of financial pressures, the district has cut the staff of its drug education and prevention staff from eight to

three in the last year. although the loss of the five positions is assuaged somewhat by the addition of five Dallas Challenge counselors who are working as part of a special grant from the Crystal Charity Ball, the district needs to be looking at ways to bolster its in-house programs.

■ The district must do a better job with counseling, to help students struggling with the extra burdens placed on today's adolescents — drugs, teen-age pregnancy, the pressures of single-family homes. The recent proposal to hire extra counselors should get prime consideration when budget levels are set. Currently, the district has one counselor for every 500 students. Lowering that to one counselor for every 250 students would cost the district $3.3 million over the next three years.

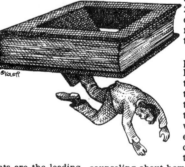

■ Middle school principals have been highly pleased with the intervention teams started last year to target youths in distress and help provide whatever is needed to encourage them to continue their education, such as tutoring, counseling about home problems. A similar "intervention" approach is being tried in the district's Pupil Assistance and Support System (PASS) and the Communities in Schools program, which is funded partly by corporations such as IBM and Southwestern Bell. All are the kind of programs that are needed to remind potential drop-outs that somebody cares.

In truth, the best dropout programs are those that provide person-to-person teaching, tutoring or counseling. The dropout figures reported this week are intolerable and demand better, more personal approaches. That may be more expensive in the short run. But Dallas can't afford *not* to improve efforts to keep students in school rather than in maternity wards, in juvenile detention or on the streets.

DAILY ◼ NEWS

New York, NY, May 21, 1988

According to a study by the U.S. Census Bureau, substantially fewer black students across the country between the ages of 18 and 21 dropped out of high school in 1985—17%, contrasted to 1975's 27%. In the same period, their graduation rate increased from 61% to 71%. This is good news.

The reasons given? Plain, hard work by parents to keep their kids in school; growing awareness by parents *and* kids of the importance of that diploma; effectiveness of remedial education in elementary schools; success of programs such as Operation Headstart, and the high unemployment rate among blacks 16 to 19—31.4% nationally—which makes it far less attractive to drop out of school in search of a job.

According to the National Foundation for the Improvement of Education, the major causes of school dropouts are low achievement, alienation, economic reasons, peer pressure, pregnancy and drug and alcohol abuse. All of which are at work here in New York, where the Board of Education says the overall high school dropout rate exceeds 30%—with that of blacks even higher.

Along with a reported increase in college applications by black students, the Census Bureau figures offer real hope. They indicate it is possible—even in New York—to stem and reverse the tide. But it takes drive, determination and commitment on every level. If black students can stay in high school and out of trouble in Cincinnati and San Diego, they ought to be able to do so in New York.

THE INDIANAPOLIS NEWS

Indianapolis, IN, July 9, 1988

Teachers, administrators and parents — especially parents — should take a lesson from what is going on in a special high school in New York City.

International High School is called an "alternative" school for disadvantaged students, but what is happening there should evoke deep thought — and some shame — among parents and students who treat their eduational opportunities with neglect and contempt.

Writing in The New York Times, Herbert Sturz describes a high school with a remarkable record of success. Its facilities aren't much — a windowless basement. And all of its students are deprived persons who, according to conventional educational norms, are doomed to failure.

Only students who have been in the United States less than four years and who score below the 20th percentile on an English language proficiency test are eligible for admission.

Of course all teaching is done in the students' native language — that's what the educationists prescribe. Wrong. All teaching is in English. Thirty-seven nations and 32 languages are represented in the 310-member student body.

Classes are small — that's one educational plus the professionals would approve. There are 24 or fewer students per class.

In a city where the daily student attendance rate is 80 percent, International's rate is 90. New York City's citywide dropout rate is 30 percent. At International it is 3.9 percent.

The "spirit, imagination and dedication of its faculty" ranks high in the list of reasons for success, according to Sturz. Faculty join this school because they are eager to work with students motivated to attend and to do their work.

The most obvious reason for success in this so-called "disadvantaged" school is the traditional drive of new Americans. Not all immigrants are motivated to this degree, but many of them are.

Sturz tells the story of a typical International student — an 18-year-old Asian youth named Chan. Chan was born in Hong Kong, emigrated to the Dominican Republic and entered the United States with his mother on a tourist visa in 1986. She returned to the Dominican Republic, but he stayed.

Chan works a 10 p.m. to 5 a.m. shift in Chinatown washing dishes and cooking. He arrived recently at high school to start a typical day with only an hour's sleep, and that was on the subway. If he doesn't work, he doesn't eat, and he wants to complete high school and go to college.

If American young people expect to compete with the thousands of industrious and educated Chans around the world — not just the ones here in the United States — they should begin now to demonstrate the same kind of work and commitment to education that is evident in International High.

Los Angeles Times

Los Angeles, CA, June 10, 1988

Dropouts and gang activity in the state's high schools are such formidable problems that when someone offers a solution that addresses both, the temptation is to embrace it wholeheartedly—even unthinkingly. We think that is what happened last week, when the California Senate approved a bill that would require every high-school student applying for a driver's license to prove that he was passing all his courses, meeting the requirements for graduation and staying out of trouble. If a student flunked a course, became a truant or carried a gun or drugs to school, no license.

There's no question that the bill, the brainchild of Sen. Gary Hart (D-Santa Barbara), is well-intentioned; Hart, a former high-school teacher, says he wants to "get students to focus on what is most important in their lives—getting a diploma and an education." The bill was approved and sent to the Assembly despite objections that it would impose white, middle-class standards on the state's blacks and Latinos. That point seems to us almost racist; nearly half the state's minority students do drop out before graduation, but not because they lack what it takes to finish high school. Our objections to the bill are more fundamental: We doubt that it could achieve its purposes, however noble, and, if strictly enforced, could make the plight of high-school dropouts even more hopeless.

Linking passing grades to a driver's license might provide some incentive to stay in school, but only up to a point—that moment, usually soon after a 16th birthday, when a student passes the road test and secures the coveted license. What's to prevent a student from dropping out of school the very next day? Nothing in this bill. Nor is it likely that the prospect of forgoing a driver's license would persuade many teen-agers to leave drugs and weapons at home; the same youths who blithely violate criminal statutes aren't likely to worry about driving without a license.

Students drop out of school for all kinds of reasons—because they're bored, because they're attracted to gangs and the street scene, because they lack the basic skills to handle high-school academics, because they become pregnant, because they are so poor that they must work to help support their families. If the Legislature is genuinely concerned about stemming the dropout rate, it ought to grapple with these underlying problems, which defy easy answers.

But denying a driver's license to a dropout would simply add to the burdens of a youngster who might already have more than his share. Particularly in Southern California, a dropout without a driver's license is virtually unemployable. The bill contains a hardship provision that would allow a teen-ager to get a license if he dropped out of school for financial or medical reasons, but he would need permission from a Superior or Municipal Court—a step so formidable that we doubt few would take it. Surely the Legislature cannot want to consign dropouts to the unemployment rolls permanently; the Assembly should avoid the Senate's mistake and reject this legislation.

Black Education Evaluated, Debated

Urban education is one segment of the larger educational structure in the U.S. To consider the state of urban education is to focus on public schools in cities, and some schools just outside those cities in the standard metropolitan statistical areas surrounding them. Even though increasing numbers of black children are enrolled in private and parochial elementary and secondary schools, the primary source of the education of black children is the public school.

In the 1980s an air of pessimism began to pervade individuals and communities supportive of big-city schools and the children who attended them. Critics of the Reagan administration's educational policies have asserted that "passing the buck" for the ills of urban education became the norm rather than the exception. Negativism has been both the cause and the effect of doubts about the ability of urban public schools to succeed in educating black youth. In recent years, however, there are some signs of change that might signal new beginnings in school success.

The current alarm concerning the state of education for blacks is indeed ironic. Black parents and community leaders have been pace setters in the forefront of calling for educational improvement. Since the 1950s, these black Americans have agitated for better schools for their children. In many communities theirs were voices crying out as they demonstrated, boycotted, picketed, sat in, and sought community control of public schools in their neighborhoods as they pursued educational betterment. Black parents permitted their children to be bussed and to be involved with progressive educational policies in an effort to gain equal educational opportunity for them. They elected school board members and selected superintendents in an effort to change and shape educational policy decisions. Despite many problems in the quality and quantity of education for blacks in the inner city there is reason for hope in educational improvement since the issue of high educational standards has entered the mainstream political arena with solid middle-class and intellectual backing behind it.

The Times-Picayune
The States-Item

New Orleans, LA, May 26, 1987

Secretary of Education William Bennett is well known for his pointed criticism of the American educational system, but the latest report from his department is pointed praise. The report praises and profiles schools that, while facing difficult educational challenges, perform to high standards.

The new booklet is "Schools That Work: Educating Disadvantaged Children," and it describes almost two dozen schools and programs nationwide that have achieved high student grades and low dropout rates in environments that are usually known only for failure. In the book can be found, Mr. Bennett declares, "the best strategy for breaking the cycle of poverty."

Speaking to reporters on the effectiveness of these schools and programs, Mr. Bennett said, "What happens to these children in many cases is nothing less than transforming." And the successful schools, he pointed out, often have no more resources than unsuccessful ones, but they deploy them better.

"These schools," he said, "hold to the traditional American view that no immutable law dooms a child to failure simply because he or she is born into poverty." They "do not trade fundamentals for novelty, and they tend to avoid what is not tried and true."

In today's urban society, poverty tends to be almost synonymous with minorities and ghetto-like neighborhoods, which can put children at many kinds of disadvantages. Such disadvantages need not be absolute, but children need many kinds of help to overcome them.

In education, it is encouraging to have proof that they can be overcome not merely by exceptional individual students but by the generality when helped by an effective school system.

This is society's obligation on several counts. Mr. Bennett repeats the obvious public safety and economic aspect: "High school boys with poor grades are more than six times as likely as boys earning above-average grades to be in trouble with the law. Low achievers are five times more likely than other students to become dependent on welfare."

President Reagan, who wrote the introduction to the booklet, put the social responsibility in broader perspective: "Generations of Americans who began life in the humblest of circumstances counted on our schools to help them and their children enjoy the personal and material blessings this nation offers. . . . We have an obligation to see to it that this ladder to success works as well for young people today as it did for those in our past.

The State

Columbia, SC, May 31, 1987

THE OTHER day we ran a piece by Washington columnist James J. Kilpatrick reporting that, after 33 years, the historic *Brown v. Board of Education* case had finally ended with an order by a court in Topeka, Kan., which has had the case on remand ever since.

This, of course, was the U.S. Supreme Court decision that wiped out the old "separate but equal" standard for public schools and started the process that ended segregation. Few if any cases have inspired more litigation. Few have so shaken the foundations of Southern life by striking down a practice now viewed by all right-minded people as an evil.

But, as the *Harvard Law Review* detailed recently, this great decision was sullied by an unholy alliance between the late Justice Felix Frankfurter, who took part in the unanimous opinion, and Justice Department lawyer Philip Elman.

It seems that Justice Frankfurter met frequently with Mr. Elman his former law clerk, and tipped him to the innermost secrets of the court as it approached its landmark decision. Mr. Elman used the inside information to alter briefs he filed on behalf of black plaintiffs in the cases, including one from South Carolina, that were consolidated in the opinion. It is said that he advanced an argument that helped produce a unanimous opinion, which was important in making the decision stick.

They opened this back channel to the court out of a strong belief in the correctness of the cause, but, as *The New York Times* rightly stated, they "crossed a clear ethical line." The deliberations of the court are closely guarded, and collaboration between judge and advocate tramples on the rules of proper conduct and tips the scales of justice.

Brown v. Board of Education, of course, is a part of history now. We just hate to see such a bright page darkened by a such a footnote.

The Honolulu Advertiser

Honolulu, HI, June 21, 1987

Who will be able to lay claim to the future jobs with the greatest income, status and security? The ideal in an egalitarian society is that all children, irrespective of background, will have relatively equal chances of "making it." We have rarely approached this ideal in the past, but if we were doing so now, it would be reflected in two measures:

First, we would expect increasing movement among occupations, reducing the close association between parents' status and their childrens' achievements. Second, we would expect to find evidence that an increasing number of children were moving "above" the status level of their parents' occupations ("upward mobility"); and correspondingly that fewer were moving "below" ("downward mobility").

Yet what limited data are available on the subject run counter to these expectations. Recent research by sociologist Michael Hout of the University of California at Berkeley indicates that occupations of employees are now more his trend is most striking in managerial and professional ranks, in which the index of the similarity between current occupation and parental attainment increased by roughly one-third from the early '70s to the early '80s. In short, established parents are passing their mantles to their children.

Another fairly dramatic development involves a reduction in the ratio of employees experiencing upward and downward mobility. In the early 1960s, the number of male employees experiencing upward mobility was 238 percent higher than those experiencing downward mobility — where mobility is defined in terms of an index reflecting both income and the perceived status of occupation. By the early 1980s, that ratio had dropped by two-thirds, falling to 78 percent. (The earlier studies did not provide comparable data for women.)

Although there remains slightly more upward mobility than downward mobility, the recent trends point fairly decisively toward an increasingly frozen class structure.

Finally, it appears that the gates of access to more advantaged occupations are closing. Historically, as professional and managerial employment has supplanted self-employment as the goal of the American Dream, the relative importance of higher education has risen dramatically. Achieving more equitable opportunity requires increasingly open and equal access to college and postgraduate degrees. That is what we had in the first three postwar decades.

And that is what we are no longer getting. College enrollments rose steadily through the late 1970s but have leveled off. The portion of the population between 18 and 24 currently enrolled in college has also hit a plateau at approximately one-third.

Despite the drop in inflation over the past five years, the rate of increase in college tuition (and other required fees) has nearly doubled over the preceding decade. And whereas the real value of federal outlays for higher education rose more than 200 percent during the 1970s, it declined by almost 20 percent between 1981 and 1985.

Detroit Free Press

Detroit, MI, January 7, 1987

THE BLOATED $1.024-trillion budget proposal President Reagan has just sent to Congress wouldn't do much to help the country's poorest students stay afloat. Though Mr. Reagan likes to talk about building a productive America, his proposed budget makes it tougher for many of America's most disadvantaged young people to become competitive.

The Reagan proposal would cut Pell grants for needy college students by almost a third and reduce federal subsidies of student loans to save the government almost $2 billion next year. The sharp reduction in college student aid is part of $12 billion in cuts Mr. Reagan is proposing in social programs, including vocational education, housing, welfare, job training and food and nutrition programs.

Work-study and Supplemental Educational Opportunity Grants would be eliminated under this proposal. Money for Pell grants would drop from $3.8 billion to $2.7 billion. The total number of Pell awards would decrease from 2.9 million to 1.9 million.

A case can be made for making it more difficult for students to establish their eligibility for Pell grants. It makes little sense, though, to reduce drastically a program that is the last resort for many lower-income students who have trouble finding jobs paying enough to see them through college. These students' economic problems would be compounded if work-study programs are eliminated, too.

Already, more and more young people, particularly minorities, find themselves ill-prepared for the technological revolution. In 1985, the average unemployment rate for black teens aged 16 to 19 was 61.6 percent. Between 1980 and 1984, black undergraduate enrollment in colleges and universities fell from 932,000 to 897,000, while on the graduate level the number of blacks enrolled declined from 60,000 to fewer than 53,000. In the country's continuing battle against black youth unemployment and despair, the availability of Pell grants is a lifeline that should not be cut.

The Virginian-Pilot

Norfolk, VA, July 17, 1987

A disturbing trend in American education is the decline in the percentage of black teachers in public schools. A new National Education Association study shows that the percentage dropped almost a full point in five years — from 7.8 percent in 1981 to 6.9 percent in 1986.

If the trend continues, only 5 percent of the teachers will be black by the turn of the century. This projection is doubly alarming because the study also indicates that minority pupils will account for 30 percent of enrollment in the year 2000.

Hence the need for black role models will grow at a time when the availability of such models for the classroom will be shrinking. Samuel Husk, executive director of the Council of the Great City Schools, which represents urban school districts, said: "More youngsters in our urban schools are poorer and more disenfranchised than they were 20 years ago, so we need more minority teachers to serve as role models. Without them, we could have two societies — separate and unequal."

There is of course ample evidence of a widening gap in U.S. society between haves and have-nots. And because a larger percentage of the black population than the white is poor, that gap exacerbates the plight of millions of anonymous blacks even as other blacks climb the high-profile success ladders.

Most disturbing is the reason for the decline: Fewer black high-school graduates are entering college. This in turn increases the competition for black college graduates, and teaching school doesn't compete well with the higher-paying jobs in business. (The NEA study shows that a third of all teachers hold part-time jobs to supplement their incomes.)

This evidence of a nationwide drop in college enrollment among blacks comes only months after Virginia statistics revealed a disturbing downward trend in percentages of blacks enrolling in this state's colleges. In 1979, 33 percent of Virginia's black high-school graduates went on to state institutions of higher learning; in 1986, 30.86 percent.

These totals become even more discouraging when compared with the sharp growth of white high-school graduates entering Virginia colleges. This percentage rose from 41 in 1979 to 50.62 in 1986.

Also, the contradictory trends have developed even as the State Council of Higher Education and the school systems jointly established a variety of special programs designed to channel more black high-school pupils into college-preparation courses and to acquaint both pupils and parents with college opportunities.

Quite clearly, the percentages in Virginia challenge the state to improve its college-orientation efforts. Just as clearly, the unhappy results of the NEA study extend this challenge to the nation as a whole.

St. Petersburg Times

St. Petersburg, FL, April 6, 1987

For most American families, sending children to college always has meant sacrifice. The struggle was hardest for the relatively few black families who dared aspire to a college diploma for a son or daughter. Education was their surest passport out of the poverty cycle, their best chance of gaining economic equality and opportunity.

Spiraling college costs in the last 15 years made that dream more difficult for everyone. Then came the Reagan administration's slashes in student aid programs — federally insured loans and Pell Grants for disadvantaged students. While that increased the hardship for whites, it made college plans impossible for many young blacks.

A study of students at the nation's 57 historically black private colleges shows how black students have been hit the hardest by the cutback in federal grants. It is believed to be responsible for a 4 percent drop in black college enrollment from 1980 to 1984, a time when the number of black high school graduates was increasing.

The study was conducted by the United Negro College Fund and the National Institute of Independent Colleges and Universities.

For many young blacks trying to stay in college, despite the new financial obstacles, the cuts have meant trying to obtain loans bigger than their families' total income. Among the black students, the median family income was $10,733, one-third the median income of all families with a child in college. Forty-two percent of the blacks are from families below the poverty line.

Young people in those circumstances cannot attend college without help. At the historically black colleges, more than 80 percent of the fulltime students have depended on federal aid.

And that is where the Reagan cuts were deepest. In 1979-80, before Americans had heard of the mythical "safety net" for the "truly needy," federal grants accounted for 53 percent of all student financial aid in the United Negro College Fund's 43 member colleges. By 1984-85, the grants dropped to 37 percent. On top of that, the purchasing power of Pell Grants has fallen 37 percent in the 1980s, according to the study.

The Reagan administration's reaction to the plight of black colleges and students was typical. A functionary at the Reagan Education Department called the study false and malicious and said, no matter how much grant money was available, the black institutions would not be satisfied. An administration that has spent six years dismantling or damaging every government program to help minorities and the poor is not mellowing now. Mr. Reagan does not view education as an investment in the nation's future, or as a chance for the poor to avoid welfare dependency, gain economic independence and become contributing citizens. The nation will pay later for his mistakes.

The News and Observer

Raleigh, NC, March 25, 1987

The U.S. Supreme Court opinion in Brown v. Board of Education runs a mere 13 paragraphs, but it is impossible to imagine the second half of the 20th century in the United States without it. While the ruling stands as a monument to the nation's fundamental concept of justice under law, the case also illustrates that fallible humans can succumb to unethical methods even as they seek to do great good.

The U.S. Supreme Court's decision in Brown v. Board of Education not only was a landmark in a strict legal sense but also a decisive turning point in history. "We conclude that in the field of public education the doctrine of 'separate but equal' has no place," wrote the high court, "Separate educational facilities are inherently unequal."

In the context of the mid-1980s, those words appear almost quaint. At the time they were written in 1954, they were powerful words, and they led to the crumbling of the whole structure of legalized segregation of the races. To re-read them is to understand anew how far the United States has advanced in race relations in three decades.

Now, a historical footnote has been written, and it shows how far the nation has come in another aspect of public policy — the scrupulous imposition of standards of ethics in government. The Harvard Law Review contains the recollections of Philip Elman, who as a Justice Department lawyer wrote a crucial brief in the case. It was Elman's brief that helped fashion the concept of dismantling desegregation with "all deliberate speed" that was written into the follow-up ruling of 1955. Justice Felix Frankfurter gave Elman, his former law clerk, confidential information that helped shape the Justice Department position.

"It did grow out of my many conversations with him over a period of many months," said Elman. "He told me what he thought, what the other justices were telling him they thought."

Such discussions between a justice and a lawyer in a pending case are highly improper. Regulations codified since then declare as unethical anything like the Frankfurter-Elman conversations.

History abounds with ironies. And in this footnote to history, ironies are manifest: Enormous reform flows out of a decision made at least in part through flawed means; two great legal minds help set more humane rules for American society, even as they break rules themselves.

If it is crucial that the United States adhere to the standards set forth in the Brown case, it is also important that public officials adhere to ethical standards that Frankfurter clearly violated.

The Miami Herald

Miami, FL, May 14, 1987

PRESIDENT Reagan was right in saying that to succeed socially and economically, blacks should enlist in the country's scientific and technological revolution. It's interesting that he made those remarks at the historically black Tuskeegee Institute in Alabama. Tuskegee was founded more than a century ago by Booker T. Washington, who believed that blacks could help themselves best by getting a practical vocational education.

Mr. Washington also felt that blacks shouldn't agitate for equal rights. That put him into sharp conflict with W.E.B DuBois, who urged blacks to demand their rights. Mr. DuBois also believed that college-educated blacks should lead the way. Vocational training had its place, but the jobs and security that it could provide weren't worth trading for human dignity, he argued.

As it happens, both men's views have currency for today's black Americans. Not everyone needs a college education. Witness the proliferation of service and skilled jobs. But those who want a degree should get help in pursuing one. America's strength and future depend on an educated and skilled populace. The aerospace and science center that the President dedicated in Tuskegee was named for Gen. Daniel "Chappie" James, the first black four-star Air Force general, a Tuskegee graduate, and the youngest of 17 children.

Unfortunately, Mr. Reagan's policies have made it harder for students from poor families, as General James was, to pursue college and vocational educations. This Administration has slashed job-training programs and proposed deep cuts in student financial aid. Florida's Sen. Lawton Chiles, chairman of the Senate Budget Committee, says that the cuts would force students to incur massive debts to pay for a college education. Some will forgo that dream, contributing to the already-pronounced reduction in black college enrollment.

President Reagan ought to make more aid available to minority students, who are more likely to be needy, and make it available on good terms. Colleges and universities ought to redouble recruitment efforts and give more scholarships. And black parents must stress the importance of learning. Education *is* the great equalizer.

THE INDIANAPOLIS NEWS
Indianapolis, IN, April 11, 1987

A turbulent chapter in American history may have ended this week, right where it began more than three decades ago.

The location is Topeka, Kan.

In 1954, the U.S. Supreme Court issued its landmark ruling in the case of Brown vs. the Topeka Board of Education. That ruling was important not merely because it outlawed dual school systems in the United States. It overturned a doctrine of separate-but-equal schools, which fostered a morally corrupt society resulting in the unequal treatment of blacks.

Brown vs. Topeka did not achieve the overnight dismantling of dual school systems.

A succession of court decisions — Brown II, Charlotte-Mecklenburg, Keyes and others — were required to forge a policy of integrating the nation's schools. As September traumas from Little Rock, Ark., to Boston, Mass., would reveal, school desegregation did not take place without incident or without cost.

Nor did desegregation always succeed in all respects.

In school system after school system, resegregation would occur as whites fled to the suburbs or established private academies.

School desegregation was no educational panacea for blacks. Often, particularly in urban cities, school desegregation was a matter of mingling poor white children with poor black children — upgrading the quality of education of neither.

And, school desegregation was implemented at a time of rising black self-determination when many questioned the assumption that blacks could succeed only if integrated with whites. Many blacks came to regard that as a racist assumption.

But, through all the turmoil and shortcomings left by the legacy of Brown vs. Topeka, it is a ruling that has pretty thoroughly abolished the acceptability of *de jure* (by official law or policy) segregation. That has been no minor feat.

Educational opportunities for black youngsters have improved.

And, despite headlines about racial hostilities from time to time, surveys of racial attitudes overwhelmingly show that there is far greater racial understanding and harmony now than in the past. Although racism has not been abolished, there are few who would turn back the clock to the shameful era of deliberately segregated schools.

U.S. District Judge Richard D. Rogers ruled this week that Topeka's public schools have eliminated the dual school system that gave rise to the lawsuit filed in 1951 by Oliver Brown on behalf of his daughter. Although racial imbalance exists in the Topeka schools as a consequence of racial residential patterns, Rogers properly held that exact racial balance is not required — only that the school system not deliberately discriminate.

Topeka school officials, however, indicated they would probably take voluntary steps in connection to draw neighborhood school boundaries or create magnet schools, to improve racial balance in the school system — a far cry from the school board that battled to maintain a segregated school system by law.

Thus, this chapter may have come to an end where it began. But much has changed in the interim.

The Boston Globe
Boston, MA, May 17, 1986

President Reagan correctly notes that blacks will experience social and economic progress through increased participation in science and technology. Reagan's encouraging words to graduates at Tuskegee University were appreciated; but a commitment to education and equal opportunity would be praiseworthy.

The president, in his speech last week, did what he does best – looked at the world through rose-colored glasses, assuring the audience that opportunities are there for all who want to take advantage of them, while ignoring the existence of bigotry, burdened urban school systems, and other social and economic ills.

Reagan said the black unemployment is "far too high" and "totally unacceptable." He said nothing about solutions he is considering. In fact, the Reagan administration remains strongly opposed to affirmative action programs; and the president has yet to authorize extension of the executive order that requires minority employment on jobs where federal funding is involved. Reagan sidestepped the fact that the black unemployment rate (13 percent) is still more than double that of whites, saying that "black employment has increased 1.8 million since 1980."

The speech was upbeat, typically Reagan. He said he wants to make certain that children see stories of black success and triumphs. Maybe the president should be given the benefit of the doubt. Maybe he is not aware of the impact that his cuts in funding for education and social programs have had on black progress, as well as the harm done by the administration's unconcern for civil rights.

Maybe Reagan is sincere. But it is easy to talk of opportunity and upward mobility at Tuskegee, whose graduates have historically pursued careers in science, medicine, technology and engineering. Here Reagan was addressing blacks who have the credentials to participate in the technological revolution.

It will take more than eloquent words, however, to provide opportunity for inner-city children of the unemployed and undereducated. They will not become upwardly mobile unless they are first helped onto the ladder.

ST. LOUIS POST-DISPATCH
St. Louis, MO, June 13, 1987

When he was elected president, Ronald Reagan pledged to dismantle the Department of Education. But when the "Nation At Risk" report caught the public's imagination, the president, always eager to take advantage of a good issue, began emphasizing the benefits of educational excellence — though never backing up his speeches with the budget requests needed to help pay for meaningful reform.

Then came William Bennett, the inflammatory education secretary who earned headlines and the anger of many educators with his talk of students who cared too much for their vacations at the beach and of colleges trying to gouge the public.

Through all of this tough talk — and maybe because of it — Congress has never given in to the administration's demands to cut spending for schools. Now, in an apparent request for a cease-fire, if not necessarily an admission of defeat, Secretary Bennett is backing down from his earlier rhetoric. Mr. Bennett says he is switching strategy because his adversarial relationship with Congress has overshadowed both his educational philosophy, which he claims much of the country shares, and the administration's educational accomplishments, which he says are substantial.

No doubt Mr. Bennett's new approach will win him a friendlier reception on Capitol Hill. But some wary education leaders view his change of heart as little more than a public relations ploy. If the administration wants to make a real impact, it should propose real increases in education funding. Until it does, members of Congress and the public should be skeptical that Mr. Bennett has really learned his lesson.

Bennett Charges Parochial Schools With Responsibility for Needy

Education Secretary William J. Bennett April 7, 1988 said in a speech in New York City before the National Catholic Education Association that parochial schools should take in the worst students in their communities, educate them and "then ask society for fair recompense for your efforts."

The Honolulu Advertiser
Honolulu, HI, April 10, 1988

Education Secretary William Bennett has turned heads with another radical-sounding idea: Let Catholic schools educate the "at-risk" students, and pay the schools for every one that graduates.

Like his annual "wall chart" that purports to compare public schools across the nation, this is a glib answer that is no real help to the schools.

Non-public schools don't have the public schools' mandate to be all things to all people. This basic difference is sometimes forgotten when schools are compared. But it influences how they spend their money, who enrolls, who stays, and the climate on campus.

In his speech to the National Catholic Education Association, Bennett extolled the Catholic schools for often achieving better education on smaller budgets. He flattered his audience, but he wasn't fair to the schools.

Assistant Secretary of Education Chester E. Finn Jr. told the National Association of Independent Schools several weeks ago there may be "a very small differential" between the average performance on standardized tests of non-public-school students and public-school students.

He pointed to two 1986 surveys by the National Assessment of Educational Progress, the Education Department's research arm. Finn said what little difference there is may be due largely to non-school factors. Students at independent schools (including Catholic schools) were more likely to have parents with college educations, to have attended preschool, to watch less television, and to attend school more regularly

To answer Bennett's challenge, the Catholic schools would have to vary and beef up their programs to meet the needs of a different mix of students, just as the public schools have done, perhaps with no assurance of better results. Bennett's proposal to reimburse them with taxpayer money raises serious constitutional questions.

Why not just give the public schools more of a helping hand?

The Hartford Courant
Hartford, CT, April 13, 1988

If the top education official in the federal government isn't trying to weaken the nation's public schools, he's misleading his listeners. Time and again U.S. Secretary of Education William J. Bennett has proposed ideas that would strike directly at the financial underpinnings of public-school systems across the country.

Mr. Bennett, who attended parochial school, seems intent upon encouraging the transfer of students from public to private schools. He has suggested giving tuition tax credits to parents of private-school students, and issuing tuition vouchers that could be used at private schools. Either way, the government would subsidize private — and in most cases religious — schools.

His latest idea along this line is to recommend that Catholic schools accept the least promising public-school students ("the poor, the disadvantaged, the disruptive, the dropout") and then ask local or state governments for "fair recompense." That, too, would channel public dollars to private institutions, in this case all of them religious.

There's a constitutional dimension to these proposals that Mr. Bennett seems to overlook, or at least not to fully appreciate. The First Amendment forbids government financial support of religion. Under the policies he advocates, public money would go to religious schools in the form of tax credits, vouchers or direct grants.

But that's no less disturbing than Mr. Bennett's almost palpable contempt for public schools. The secretary of education should be leading the way in building a stronger national public-school system, not suggesting schemes that would hurt it. He may believe that aiding private schools would create healthful competition, but he ought to realize that such a diversion of resources would far more likely harm public schools.

Public schools, after all, aren't selective, nor can they be. Unlike private schools, they have a legal responsibility to work with whatever children show up in their classrooms. Public-school educators struggle, sometimes desperately and unsuccessfully, just to cope with the awesome task before them. Competition wouldn't make the coping perceptibly easier. It could make it harder, in fact, by taking money away.

We suspect, though, that competition isn't Mr. Bennett's primary goal. Those who share his view tend to simply want the government to help finance private education, perhaps because many of them have children in private schools and resent having to pay private-school tuition in addition to taxes for public schools. They're in that situation by choice, however.

If American private education needs more support, it's up to private benefactors, not the government, to provide it. If private schools want to accept difficult students from public schools, they deserve praise, but not government money.

There's no question that public schools need more support, moral as well as financial. In both categories, Mr. Bennett proposes to give them less.

TULSA WORLD

Tulsa, OK, April 11, 1988

U.S. EDUCATION Secretary William Bennett ought to be the chief advocate for the nation's public school system. Instead, he promotes private schools.

The secretary was at it again last week, calling on Roman Catholic school administrators to seek out the "worst 10 or 15 percent" of public school students and show the public schools how they ought to be handled.

A parochial school product himself, Bennett can be forgiven for having fond memories of private schools, but he ought to realize that turning troubled students over to Catholic educators isn't a practical solution.

Perhaps Catholic educators have done a better job with difficult students than the public schools but they have a clear advantage in being able to expel troublemakers and make it stick. Let a public school administrator try that and he will find himself in deep trouble.

Bennett's suggestion that Catholics take the worst and show "educators around this country what works" simply tells everyone remotely familiar with public schools that Bennett has no idea of their problems.

Does he really think Americans are going to agree to shift public school money into parochial schools?

The suspicion here is that if Bennett had bothered to check with Catholic officials about his plan that he would have been instantly discouraged.

One small matter: If his suggestion were followed, how would Catholics manage to build the millions of dollars in new buildings and facilities needed? Who would pay the additional teachers needed until a grateful public volunteered compensation?

With a friend like Bennett, public education in America doesn't need any enemies.

The Evening Gazette

Worcester, MA, April 15, 1988

Education Secretary William J. Bennett's proposal that Roman Catholic parochial schools take and shape the worst students in public education seems little more than a trial balloon. Still, it is Bennett's habit to make provocative suggestions, and this idea is thought-provoking indeed.

He seemed to be putting the onus on parochial schools to find and serve those students that the public school system is failing — dropouts, underachievers, troublemakers. Part of the program cost would have to be collected from the communities.

The idea is apt to stir up a hornets' nest, even though it's not without logic. Parochial schools have long had a reputation for discipline and high academic standards — the two going hand in hand. So why not ask them to tackle the hard-core problems?

The reasons are numerous. Because enrollment in a private parochial school is voluntary, it's hard to see how the same values could be embraced by a largely unmotivated, non-religious and academically disadvantaged student population transferred to Catholic schools.

Then there's the question of constitutionality, based on the principle of separation of church and state. It is all but certain to prevent reimbursement for educating public school children in a church-affiliated school.

Bennett says public school systems save $14 billion annually because the Catholic schools educate 2.5 million students — thus arguing that it should entitle parochial schools to a share of the tax dollar. Yet the Supreme Court has drawn the line between supporting public and private education time and again.

And what if the parochial schools simply do not want to take on the worst students public education can offer? What would happen to parochial schools if they became semi-remedial, semi-reform institutions? More than 4,000 Catholic schools have been closed in the last 20 years, and many parishes and dioceses struggle to keep the remaining ones open. Catholic school enrollments are 22 percent minority, many non-Catholic, already. Adding the troublesome and disadvantaged cases to the system could destroy its already fragile existence.

It's unlikely that Bennett's idea will fly. But, as always, the secretary has managed to call attention to the shortcomings and inadequacies of American education and start a dialogue. And that in itself is valuable service.

Post-Tribune

Gary, IN, April 25, 1988

William Bennett is the country's secretary of education. That's his title, anyway. At times he seems to be genuinely interested in making the country's schools do a better job. Often, he is more like a sailor who puts out to sea with no compass or destination.

He is quick with provocative recommendations, addicted to exaggerations and eager to criticize.

But where is the country's education policy? Maybe Bennett will write one after he leaves office.

Last week he complained to education writers about

Bennett

"a rising tide" of intolerance on campuses of conservative speakers and issues. There is no tide, but of course anybody who is blocked from a speaker's platform because of his views is a victim of boorish behavior. It happens, but rarely. It is a convenient issue for Bennett to complain about, but hardly an educational crisis.

It is not his off-the-cuff remarks that hurt the debate on education, though. It is his recommendations — his suggested cures — like the one on the dropout problem, for example.

He urges Catholic schools to accept and educate the toughest students and then send the bill to society. Catholic schools, he said, should ask the state or local governments to pay half the cost of teaching the public school students. A leader who is serious about reversing the dropout rate couldn't be serious about that recommendation.

If Bennett was only trying to draw attention to the issue, he left out some of the script.

He needs to take some remedial work, maybe during the summer.

He's right. The dropout rate in Catholic schools is much lower than in public schools — he says the estimates are 3 percent vs. 14 percent. Is the difference entirely because of superior methods in the private schools, or partly the result of parental attitudes? Parents paying tuitions probably will be more involved in what their children do in school. Bennett makes a simplistic use of statistics — he should first find out what they mean.

The Catholic schools deserve support, but it should come from private sources. Bennett urges such private support, and he should have stopped there. Suggesting that public funds should be used for such purposes is a waste of time because it would not pass a legal test. Because of that obstacle, Bennett's proposal is a diversion from reality.

Later, he gave gratuitous advice to the faculty at Stanford University, where a new, broader program of Western civilization has been approved. The program will give more attention to gender, race and class issues. Bennett said the change was a capitulation to political intimidation. The Stanford faculty hardly needs help from Bennett.

He is adept at skipping from one issue to another and getting headlines. As the head of a department that is supposed to enrich educational opportunities and provide national leadership, he does not score a passing grade.

In the beginning, the Reagan administration wanted to fold up the Department of Education. It's hard to tell what Bennett is trying to do.

AKRON BEACON JOURNAL

Akron, OH, April 11, 1988

WILLIAM J. Bennett, the U.S. Secretary of Education, put Catholic educators on the spot. At their national convention, Bennett challenged them to "seek out the poor, the disadvantaged, the disruptive, the dropout and take them in, educate them."

Bennett then suggested that the Catholic schools "ask society for fair recompense." The Catholic Church, with its commitment to serve the poor, could hardly say no.

In truth, donations to the Catholic church already subsidize the schools, so that tuition can be affordable to low-income families. Many Catholic schools have scholarship programs for families unable to pay anything.

Also to keep costs down, teachers in the Catholic schools are low paid; many of them work out of commitment to the church.

Even so, Catholic schools have trouble enough meeting expenses. Bennett surely knows that.

But Bennett didn't get specific on how the Catholic schools should pay for educating the poor. Possibly, he's thinking of government vouchers or some other form of tuition assistance. President Reagan has supported such dangerous ideas since he's been in office, without regard for how they would infringe on the constitutional separation of church and state.

On the other hand, Bennett might be wondering how Catholic schools would handle the most troubled students. Public schools are failing to educate these students; maybe the Catholic schools would do better.

Indeed, it would be well if Catholic educators could raise enough private money to give it a good try.

But realistically, Catholic schools can't be expected to relieve inner-city schools of their troubled students. The crisis facing large-city schools won't be that easy to solve.

Ultimately, public schools will have to solve their problems from within. And if there's any extra public money to go around, they deserve it. The goal should be to provide quality education to all, and do it through the public schools.

The Register

Santa Ana, CA, April 11, 1988

Secretary of Education William Bennett has grandly filled an office that rightly shouldn't exist. He has used his post as a bully pulpit to encourage educational excellence and attack pedagogical incompetence. The teacher unions despise him, a sure sign that he's doing a good job.

But Bennett sometimes stretches himself too far. When this happens he usually works from premises that are sound enough, but from which he derives an erroneous conclusion. An example came last week. Speaking before a group of Catholic schoolmen, he called on Catholic schools to enroll the "worst 5 or 10 percent" of public-school students. To pay for the new burden, he said the schools should ask state or local governments for money.

His sound premises are these. Catholic schools generally provide a better education with stronger discipline than do public schools. They also enrolled 21.8 percent minority students in 1986; and of black students, 64 percent were non-Catholic. In some inner-city areas Catholic schools provide the only real education, since the public schools have become gang combat zones.

Yet Bennett ignores several other important premises. Catholic schools today enroll only 56 percent of private-school students. And from 1970 to 1986 the number of Catholic school students dropped by 37 percent, a loss of 1.6 million. Catholic schools are clearly in a period of transition, are already doing much to teach minority and inner-city children, and they don't need another burden placed on them. To be consistent, Bennett should have called on other private schools — both religous and non-religious — to enroll more minority and inner-city students.

And Bennett called for government funding. But surely he knows about the recent Grove City College controversy, in which Congress last month passed a law saying that any school that receives even $1 in tax money must comply with a host of federal regulations, guidelines, and decrees. Giving Catholic schools state and local money could make them essentially extensions of the state and local governments. They could, in essence, cease to be private.

Finally, Bennett ignores the hard fact that some students are simply not educable. While some delinquent students might shape up being sent to strict private schools, most others wouldn't learn discipline even in Marine boot camp. As Albert J. Nock wrote, "Our system is based upon the assumption, popularly regarded as implicit in the doctrine of equality, that everybody is educable."

But on the contrary, "The philosophical doctrine of equality gives no more ground for the assumption that all men are educable than it does for the assumption that all men are six feet tall. We see at once, then, that it is not the philosophical doctrine of equality, but an utterly untenable popular perversion of it, that we find at the basis of our educational system."

So the true conclusions from Bennett's premises should be these: that some children are not educable; and that any school, public or private, that accepts such students will of necessity debase the education it gives other students able to learn.

The Atlanta Journal
THE ATLANTA CONSTITUTION

Atlanta, GA, February 27, 1988

Give the federal appellate courts their due. They are emphatically saying "no" to overwrought fundamentalists who would pull the nation from its traditional moorings of official neutrality in religious matters. The latest affirmation came Monday, when the Supreme Court let stand a decision that public-school textbooks needn't satisfy the religious imperatives of students.

The case originated in Tennessee, after parents objected to things like references to magic in the Wizard of Oz. They were upset because they found traces of "occultism," "secular humanism" and other beliefs in the texts without an accompanying statement that their own religious beliefs were the right ones. A District Court judge decided that their children could be excused from reading class and taught at home.

Fortunately, the 6th U.S. Circuit Court of Appeals would have none of this garbled logic. And now the good conservatives on the Reagan Supreme Court have allowed the appellate court to have its way

The action rescues local school boards from an impossible responsibility. By the original decision, a school system might have been forced to bend its practices to meet the scrutiny of every religious sect represented in its classrooms. Imagine the hopelessness of that task in a place like New York City, or even Atlanta.

If the idea was educational madness, just as bad was its erosion of government's religious neutrality. The original decision would have destroyed the wall of separation between church and state. It would have given school boards a new client: religious zealots acting as textbook police.

The courts have admirably saved the public schools from other nonsense in the last year. In June, the high court declared that creationism was a religious doctrine — not a science. A Louisiana law requiring that it be taught in tandem with evolution was religiously motivated, the court said, and hence unconstitutional.

And in August, the 11th U.S. Circuit Court of Appeals in Atlanta delivered the students of Mobile, Ala., from parents who found traces of "secular humanism" lurking on the pages of 44 textbooks. A District Court judge, in a bizarre decision, banned the books. Actually, said the 11th Circuit, the texts promulgated nothing worse than "independent thought, tolerance of diverse views, self-respect, maturity . . ." and so on.

In each case, a religious group wanted public schools to accommodate its beliefs, jeopardizing tolerance *and* neutrality. In each case, thanks to the appellate courts, they lost. When fundamentalist parents are offended by mainstream curricula, they can always enroll their kids in private schools. They should not try to impose their narrow views on public systems, and the courts are making that crucial point increasingly clear.

The Seattle Times

Seattle, WA, April 13, 1988

IN Seattle to accept the Evergreen Safety Council's Statesman of the Year award, U.S. Secretary of Education William Bennett limply defended his unstatesmanlike and simplistic suggestion that Catholic schools might be a better place for the worst of public-school students.

No, Mr. Bennett, that's not where the solution lies. It lies in solid federal support for public schools — not a problem-student bypass into the parochial classroom.

It was only a few days ago that Bennett told Catholic educators they should take on the "worst 5 or 10 percent" of public-school students and show other educators what can be done . . . and then ask society for fair recompense." Recompense? Federal money?

While in Seattle Monday, he defended that statement by saying he was referring to dropouts — not present public-school students, and no drain on public-school resources was intended. He cited a national public-school dropout rate of 12 percent for sophomores compared with 3 percent in Catholic schools — an unfair comparison in that public schools are expected to serve every student.

When told by Seattle School Supt. William Kendrick that urban school systems need help because they have special problems, Bennett said he spends most of his time talking about and supporting urban schools.

Bennett heaped well-deserved praise on Meany Middle School as he presented the inner-city school with the National Award for Excellence it won last May.

Meany is only one of many urban success stories. They all hold a lesson:

Bennett's rosy rhetoric will be more meaningful when he matches it with stronger advocacy of sound federal financial support for public schools.

Detroit Free Press

Detroit, MI, April 23, 1988

IN HIS CHOSEN role as the hair shirt of higher education, the secretary of education, William Bennett, often performs a useful service in making life uncomfortable for those who preach openness and practice something else. He unfortunately often goes on to cloud the truth he speaks by stretching the point — or by attempting to superimpose an orthodoxy of his own on the dogmatism that he challenges.

The last few days have provided an excellent sampler of both the good and bad side of Secretary Bennett's dealings with high education. His indictment of the intolerance of some university communities for conservative thought is much more on target than many university presidents would like to admit. The occasional outbursts against the appearance on campus of some conservative speaker are outrageous; most university presidents would agree that discourtesy and intolerance have no place in a university that purports to be a place of academic freedom. Moreover, Mr. Bennett's claim that the charge of racism is sometimes used to silence legitimate disagreement or concerns is undoubtedly also at least partially true.

Where Secretary Bennett sometimes distorts the debate is in underestimating the capacity of traditional liberal education to accommodate the kind of challenges it has been getting from, for example, black students who demand that universities pay more attention to the contributions of African culture or black figures in the United States. There is a perfectly legitimate way, consistent with the emphasis on basics that Secretary Bennett espouses, to broaden the vision of what goes into the making of an education. An inclusive approach to higher education — an approach that reaches out beyond the Eurocentric framework in which most American college graduates were trained — need not be the kind of watered-down, trivialized process Secretary Bennett fears we are producing. His criticism of the changes in Stanford's Western culture course, for instance, seems to ignore what is being retained in criticizing what is being eliminated.

Bennett: Good and bad sides

Many universities and colleges in the '60s did go too far in weakening their definitions of what a liberal education should include. Some of them made their approach so eclectic, so open-ended, that they did serious injury to their students. Many of them have sought in the '70s and '80s to strengthen the core curriculum, including some of the classical elements emphasized by Secretary Bennett. The process probably hasn't gone far enough to assure that graduates have a broad and deep schooling in the values and ideas of American culture. It certainly has not yet found the right formula for accommodating the challenges of those who have felt excluded by the Eurocentric focus.

What gives us more hope than Secretary Bennett's broadsides are the quiet efforts of university people to find a sensible approach to making education both more inclusive and more clearly grounded in some of the splendidly liberating thought of the classics of Western civilization. Education can be liberating. In America's universities, it often still is. Secretary Bennett's polemics against the transgressions of higher education might well be more credible if he recognized, a bit more often, the subtleties of the challenges he tries to reduce to such simplistic equations.

THE SACRAMENTO BEE

Sacramento, CA, April 21, 1988

For better or worse, Education Secretary Bill Bennett's most consistent attribute is that he's so rarely for real. A salvo at the universities for overcharging for their shoddy educational product; some banal curriculum proposals; a blast at educators for abandoning Western Civilization as we know it. Plenty of tour-de-force rhetoric, high ratings on the applause meter, but not much follow-through at the office.

Now comes Bennett to tell Catholic school officials they should seek out the failures, dropouts and misfits of the public schools, "take them in and educate them," then charge the public schools for their services. A beau geste, indeed, but, as usual, so lacking in substance that it's questionable whether it was meant as anything other than rhetoric.

Is Bennett proposing another voucher plan, something his administration flirted with for years but never managed to develop? Has he thought about the constitutional questions? Probably not. More likely it's just a cheap shot at the public schools, which, though they have little to brag about in the inner cities, hardly deserve this kind of invidious comment. It's the private schools, secular and parochial, that can chuck out the trouble-makers, the failures, the misfits. It's the public schools that have to take them in. If the public schools had the luxury of choosing their clients, or at least tossing out the worst of them, they could no doubt do a lot better with what remains. But, of course, by the time you reach such questions, Bill Bennett is long gone, off to another platform.

Bennett School Critique States That Nation Is 'Still at Risk'

Secretary of Education William J. Bennett declared in a report released to the press April 24, 1988 that the U.S. education system was "still at risk" despite five years of improvement. The report, officially presented to President Reagan April 26, was intended as an evaluation of the nation's schools on the fifth anniversary of the release of "A Nation At Risk," a landmark 1983 report published by the government's National Commission on Excellence in Education. That report had painted a bleak picture of the state of the American educational system and had spurned a national reform movement.

Bennett's report, titled "American Education: Making it Work," asserted that "undeniable progress" had been made over the previous five years to boost academic standards and student achievement. "We are doing better than we were in 1983," the report said. "But we are certainly not doing well enough, and we are not doing well enough fast enough. We are still at risk."

The first part of the report identified a number of key problems afflicting U.S. schools, including low graduation rates, a lack of basic skills among those students who did graduate, the widely varying quality of school curricula, a lack of good schools for disadvantaged and minority children, a high dropout rate among urban black and Hispanic students, and ineffective procedures for hiring and promoting good teachers and principles. "The entire project of American education remains insufficiently accountable for the result that matters most: student learning," the report declared.

In the second part of his report, the education secretary outlined "the five fundamental avenues of reform necessary for better schools: strengthening content, ensuring intellectual opportunity, establishing an ethos of achievement, recruiting and rewarding good teachers and principals, and instituting accountability throughout our educational system."

The report was met with criticism by a number of educational groups.

The Record

Hackensack, NJ, May 2, 1988

Secretary of Education William Bennett has angered teachers and school administrators by saying that they haven't worked hard enough at improving schools. This verdict was delivered on the fifth anniversary of a scathing assessment of American public education by the former education secretary, Terrell Bell. Mr. Bell's report, "A Nation at Risk," warned of a "tide of mediocrity" from slack teaching and flimsy course content.

The Bell report spurred action in schools, legislatures, and governors' offices across the country. Proposals for higher teacher salaries, merit pay, curriculum reform, standardized tests, and improvement of teacher training were part of the response. Change is on the way, but this big job will take years to finish.

Secretary Bennett conceded that high-school students were taking more challenging courses and had improved their scores on college-entrance exams. But in the next breath, he said teachers were "cavalier" about homework assignments, and schools were still giving too many lightweight courses. He continued to pound on a familiar Bennett theme: Americans should imitate foreign teachers and students, who perform better because they work harder. That's oversimplifying a complicated difference. Many European school systems are centralized and state-run. Their students are less diverse than American youngsters.

Mr. Bennett accused school officials of "defeatism" in their belief that "some children can't learn because their color, class, or family background gets in the way." That's unfair. It twists the view of educators who argue that inner-city and poor rural students need special help in overcoming educational deficits. Mr. Bennett seems to imply that teachers are prejudiced against minority youngsters.

The differences are largely economic, not racial. The children helped by programs like Headstart are kids who don't have books at home or visit libraries or museums. They don't have experiences that are common for middle-class youngsters. Headstart can overcome those deficits — as the creditable high-school performance of Headstart kids has consistently proved.

But Mr. Bennett seemed to ignore that. He insisted that it's what students study in *high school* that counts in future success. That begins to sound like an alibi for cutting federal aid to remedial and elementary programs. Teacher organizations were quick to point out that the federal contribution to elementary and secondary education has dropped from 9.2 percent in 1983 to 6.2 percent in 1988.

Mr. Bennett's judgment of the teaching revolution is harsh and premature. This is a time when public schools need all the support the secretary of education can bring to them. Undeserved sniping at teachers and principals accomplishes nothing.

Buffalo Evening News

Buffalo, NY, May 12, 1988

FIVE YEARS AGO this spring, a national report entitled "A Nation at Risk" spared nothing in its criticism of American education. The educational foundations of American society, it warned, "are presently being eroded by a rising tide of mediocrity that threatens our very future."

The report called for greater attention to the process of educating the nation's young. It urged tougher school curriculums, with greater focus on core subjects such as math and science, and a return to more rigorous standards.

The report shocked many Americans concerned with education, and it triggered a series of changes in state laws across the country.

Now Education Secretary William J. Bennett, reviewing the results since that landmark report, concludes that the "precipitous downward slide" has been arrested and the nation's schools have "begun the long climb back to reasonable standards," but he is far from satisfied.

"We are certainly not doing well enough," he said, "and we are not doing well enough fast enough."

Unquestionably there have been heartening gains, including here in Buffalo where student scores on standardized state tests show marked improvement.

Moreover, average teacher salaries for the nation, just reported at $28,031 ($33,600 in New York State) for last year, are up 62 percent from the beginning of the decade. And the number of freshmen entering college with plans to teach in elementary and secondary schools, which dropped to a low point six years ago, is also on the rise.

Similarly, there has been a wholesome general movement back-to-basics — to the more rigorous curriculums — in many schools.

Despite those impressive gains, however, Bennett is correct to scorn complacency. Educational problems remain both conspicuously clear and persistently troublesome.

Who, for example, can remain sanguine in light of high dropout rates? Or the studies cited by Bennett showing foreign students, who spend more time in class, outperforming their American counterparts?

And what of the inequality of educational opportunities for students, depending all too often on the accident of where their parents live? Good schools for disadvantaged students, Bennett said, "are much too rare."

These are the kinds of problems, difficult to solve but amenable to serious and determined effort, that U.S. education must surmount, for the benefit of both individual students and America as a whole.

The 1983 report stung the nation into action. It helped trigger reforms, some of which have produced impressive results. But it also outlined goals not yet reached. Much remains to be done.

As Bennett concluded: "We are still at risk."

The Hartford Courant

Hartford, CT, May 3, 1988

Education Secretary William J. Bennett, who has earned a reputation for shooting from the hip, has again taken aim at America's schools, whose performance, he said, is "unacceptably low."

Mr. Bennett's assessment came on the fifth anniversary of the release of "A Nation at Risk," a national commission's report that warned of a "rising tide of mediocrity" in public schools. No other document in recent decades triggered as much debate — and inspired educators and government officials to raise standards and take other steps to improve student achievement.

Mr. Bennett didn't disclose surprising information: Most people already know that the quality of elementary and secondary education is not what it should be for an advanced industrial society.

Still, teacher unions and their academic and political allies blasted Mr. Bennett's report card as another of his hypocritical broadsides. He again failed to address the federal government's anemic role in improving education, they complained.

Although Mr. Bennett's crusade against poor and mediocre public education is wearing thin with the rank and file, few would dispute the key content of his five-year progress report.

Mr. Bennett is wrong in not spreading the blame from bottom to top, and he needs a lesson or two in diplomacy about getting the message across without turning the messenger into an issue. But give him credit for increasing federal spending for schools and for directing much of it at disadvantaged schoolchildren.

One can argue endlessly about reforming education. In reality the reform movement, only 3 or 4 years old, is too young to judge accurately. Its fruits must be allowed to ripen. There is still little consensus on how to achieve the goals of reform.

We won't know what works until we have dependable and uniform measurements for assessing schools. What's available today is garbled statistics on test results, dropout rates, college-entrance-exam scores and such.

Ways have yet to be devised to compare results. Most school boards don't ask the staff to compare individual schools' performances in their district. Failure and mediocrity are tolerated. Conversely, where there's progress, the news about it travels slowly from one school to another, one state to the next.

Another linchpin of reform — holding teachers and administrators accountable — also depends on having reliable and comparable information.

Public education could use an occasional prod from a credible secretary of education, but what it desperately needs are methods of knowing what works in the classroom and what doesn't, and which teachers and administrators deserve their jobs.

Los Angeles Times

Los Angeles, CA, May 1, 1988

Education Secretary William J. Bennett argues that U.S. public schools have barely improved. California Superintendent of Public Instruction Bill Honig insists that they are much better than they were. Both agree that the quality of education remains too low.

Both are right if they are talking about education for college-bound students. But their evaluations certainly do not apply to potential dropouts, who have scarcely been touched by reforms.

Too many students still cannot fill out job applications, let alone unravel the mysteries of science or savor Shakespeare. Too many teachers quit prematurely in frustration over discipline problems or depressing working conditions.

Bennett reassessed schools on the fifth anniversary of a landmark report, "A Nation at Risk," a report that helped launch education reform. Bennett's assessment is right when he said that reforms still must be made in course content, textbooks, minority access to a sound education, teacher preparation, and recruitment of good principals. He is wrong to keep saying that reforms are possible without more spending on schools by communities and state and federal governments.

Bennett reports that fewer than 5% of the nation's 17-year-olds read at advanced levels, that few students write well or even adequately, and that fewer still are familiar enough with books. American students still rate near the bottom in international math comparisons.

California has been trying to reform classrooms longer than most states, and the effort is starting to show results. Students are taking more rigorous courses to prepare themselves for college, Honig says, and they are doing better on the Scholastic Aptitude Test than they did five years ago.

Albert Shanker, president of the American Federation of Teachers, says, the reforms to date largely benefit students "who are able to listen to lectures and read books," a group that he thinks represents 25% of the student population. Assuming that he is right, schools must change dramatically for the other 75%. That will mean better prepared—and better paid—teachers, strong principals, and school boards that concentrate as hard on making school work as well in poor neighborhoods as they do in affluent areas.

Bennett's approach to school improvement is the old ruler-on-the-knuckles approach, never less useful than when he said recently that appeals for more money for schools are a form of "extortion, the false claim that to fix our schools will first require a fortune in new funding." Congress recently voted for an education bill that would strengthen remedial reading and math programs for poor youngsters and create programs to help local schools where academic failure seems permanent. Bennett should work to persuade the White House to support the program instead of spending so much time trying to improve his grade of "A" for Abrasive.

The first wave of reforms may be over. Compared to what lies ahead, they may have been the easy ones. The next wave involves changing credential requirements for teachers, recruiting more minorities into teaching and finding ways to keep students in school where they can learn. The nation's children indeed remain at risk until that job is done, too.

The Honolulu Advertiser

Honolulu, HI, May 14, 1988

Education Secretary William Bennett's controversial statements have seemed to widen, and keep lively, the debate on education issues. He's argued forcefully for tougher standards for schools. So he'll be missed by some when he leaves office early this fall to go on the lecture circuit full-time.

But Bennett has also been controversial because he's often been half wrong. And perspective may show that his rhetoric was a cover for Reagan administration inattention to today's most critical problem: the schools' failure to educate more than 30 percent of those in their care.

Bennett's latest report said schools have improved somewhat since "A Nation at Risk" was published five years ago, but they still have a long way to go. He again needled teachers' unions and the education bureaucracy — with some justification — for being slow to change. But the report is silent on the federal government's role.

Money isn't everything, but Bennett has been an articulate defender of presidential efforts to cut funding for public education, just when it seemed more support was called for.

Terrel Bell, President Reagan's first-term education secretary and the man behind "A Nation at Risk," says education reform has done nothing for the poor, minorities and dropouts.

"We missed the opportunity to fully take advantage of 'A Nation at Risk' and all the attention on it by not giving it a high priority and a high profile in the second term," Bell says.

"In my mind, nothing could have assured Ronald Reagan's place in history more than his enduring commitment to the school reform movement that he supported so effectively for 18 months, only to abandon it after the election."

Bennett will issue at least two more reports before he leaves — one on a model elementary education curriculum and one on colleges and their cost. These too will no doubt provoke discussion that will help clarify the issues.

It's just too bad Bennett, the nation's top education official, hasn't done more.

THE SACRAMENTO BEE
Sacramento, CA, May 2, 1988

There's undoubtedly been progress in upgrading the educational standards of the nation's schools in the past five years, as Education Secretary William Bennett noted the other day, particularly in the elementary grades, but little thanks to Bennett or the administration he serves.

The essence of that progress is a new appreciation, after the indifference and cultural relativism of the '70s, that there is an irreducible core of academic material and effort without which schooling is more charade than substance. A great many states, including California, have acted on that understanding, in many cases long before the publication in 1983 of the government's scathing educational critique, "A Nation At Risk," whose fifth anniversary Bennett's report is supposed to mark. They've done so with no real help — financial, technical or legal — from Bennett; on the contrary, they've often taxed themselves to make those efforts even while Bennett was running around the country proclaiming that more money wasn't necessary or perhaps even desirable.

Bennett's right, of course, that the entrenched schoolhouse interest groups – administrators organizations, teachers unions — have been among the major stumbling blocks to educational reform. Bennett's speeches may even help draw attention to the issue. But still, one should also expect something more from the man who is supposed to be the nation's leader on educational matters. If Bennett knows a way to reduce that inertia without money, let him tell the nation how. No doubt the Japanese can run classes with 49 children; if he can find a way to import Japanese cultural standards wholesale into the inner-city schools of New York and Los Angeles, it could be done here too. Perhaps something could even be done if the community could just get the rats out of the tenements and the crack off the streets. Does the secretary have a suggestion?

Bennett keeps forgetting the salient fact that this country is trying to do what no nation anywhere has ever tried, much less succeeded in doing: to educate children from an almost indescribable variety of cultural and language backgrounds, many of them dreadfully poor and disadvantaged, and educate all of them through the 12th grade and beyond for a world of unprecedented social and technical complexity.

There's no argument that it's often done badly. Too many times those who are charged with the task have contempt for the very things they are supposed to be fostering: people who hate reading trying to teach children literature; teachers who think history dry and boring trying to drill tired clichés and old slogans into the heads of passive children; politicians who see schooling principally as an economic weapon against the Far East. But the only way to change that is to retrain them; to get better materials; to change attitudes, inside and outside school; and to get better people. If Bennett has any suggestions or resources to bring to those tasks, they'd no doubt be most welcome.

THE CHRISTIAN SCIENCE MONITOR
Boston, MA, May 2, 1988

EDUCATION Secretary William J. Bennett has again cracked the whip for school reform with his new report, "American Education: Making It Work." He surveys educational progress since publication of the stirring 1983 paper, "A Nation at Risk," and says, in essence, we've got a long way to go.

His reminder is well taken. Education reform was a big story a few years ago as politicians, school administrators, teachers, and parents sought ways to respond to the dire picture painted by the National Commission on Excellence in Education, which produced "Nation at Risk." It has since tended to recede from view.

Reform of the 100,000 or so public schools in the United States is, after all, a massive, slow process – not the stuff of daily headlines. It is, however, very much the stuff of equal opportunity, civic spirit, self-sufficiency, and other values most Americans hold dear.

And thanks to Mr. Bennett, the headlines have returned for a time. His point, and it's a good one, is to reaffirm the direction of reform. In doing this, the secretary doesn't note shortfalls alone. He acknowledges improvement in test scores, more time spent on math and English, and a 40 percent increase in state spending on education over the past five years. But the emphasis is unmistakably on public education's shortcomings.

Again, he sounds the drum for a rigorous core curriculum – stripped of frivolous electives. No one can argue, surely, with the need for a strong grounding in English, math, science, and history. Such basic subject matter serves both students' potential to make a living and their ability to function as citizens – to make informed decisions and express themselves clearly.

"Back to basics," however, should never become a straitjacket. Biology can be taught through field trips and experiments, or through textbook drudgery. History can mean reenactment of key debates, or memorization of dates.

Good teachers find ways to engage imagination and intellect. They should never have the feeling that someone else is specifying the details of their teaching – only an outline of what needs to be taught. As a concept, core curriculum sets a direction; it doesn't, or shouldn't, imply classroom rigidity.

What about the reach of reform? Secretary Bennett underscores the continued poor showing of many inner-city schools. Again, the need here is for maximum room to explore ways of reaching kids, combined with the toughness required to overhaul schools, if necessary. New Jersey has a new law allowing deficient school districts to be declared "bankrupt," clearing the way for major restructuring and, hopefully, improvement. That's an extreme approach, but in many cities the problem is extreme.

If efforts to improve education are to succeed, teachers must be collaborators in reform, not the scapegoats of reformers. Secretary Bennett's typically blunt emphasis on the need to work even harder should not obscure the good job already being done by thousands of committed teachers. Their numbers have to grow.

ST. LOUIS POST-DISPATCH
St. Louis, MO, April 26, 1988

"If an unfriendly foreign power had attempted to impose on America the mediocre educational performance that exists today, we might well have viewed it as an act of war. As it stands, we have allowed this to happen to ourselves."

Those words helped shake up the nation five years ago. Part of "A Nation at Risk," the report of the National Commission on Excellence in Education, they cautioned Americans that "the educational foundations of our society are presently being eroded by a rising tide of mediocrity that threatens our very future as a nation and a people." Today, Education Secretary William Bennett will present an update: While American schools have reversed a longstanding slide, "we are still at risk" because of mediocre education.

Are American schools deficient? If so, are they doing poorly because of a lack of effort, a lack of money or a lack of commitment by educators and the public? Is Secretary Bennett, who more frequently has been a critic of the nation's schools than a supporter, correct when he says the "false claim that to fix our schools will first require a fortune in new funding" amounts to "opposition by extortion"?

There is no single test to show how well education is doing, and the many measures that different educators use lead to almost as many different conclusions. Secretary Bennett's five-year update compares the transcripts of 15,000 high school graduates in 1987 with those of 1982 to show a "movement back into a more rigorous academic curriculum." Teacher salaries have improved, and many states have encouraged tougher graduation standards and provided incentives to improve the performance of both students and teachers.

Perhaps the most lasting effect of "A Nation at Risk" is the prolonged spotlight it has shone on education. Few issues remain prominent in the nation's consciousness for as long as five years, and improving schools promises to play a highly visible role in this fall's election campaign as well.

Yet clearly, much more needs to be done. Teachers may earn more money, but their profession has not always earned the respect that should come with it. Students could definitely benefit from a longer school year, but more days in class will require more money to pay for them, and many states are barely making do with the budgets they have now. In education, as in most of life, money isn't everything, but it makes accomplishing what needs to be done a lot easier.

Also crucial is effective leadership. When the "Nation at Risk" report came out, President Reagan greeted it with a push for his pet education issues such as tuition tax credits — issues that not only were not in the report but detracted from its serious discussion. Secretary Bennett has concentrated more on education itself, but his combative style often has turned the education debate into a tug of war. His agenda for the schools — merit pay, more rigorous courses and more accountability — can work, but the most crucial ingredient missing from his tenure has been positive leadership. With such direction, on all levels, schools can change for the better, and in another five years, perhaps "A Nation at Risk" will be viewed as the turning point in American education.

WORCESTER TELEGRAM
Worcester, MA, April 29, 1988

Five years after the watershed report, "A Nation at Risk," Education Secretary William J. Bennett says the overall performance of the nation's schools has improved somewhat, but not nearly enough.

His predecessor, T.H. Bell, reveals that he was never able to persuade President Reagan and his top aides that reforming American education had to be a national priority.

All of that is disturbing. If policy-makers in charge are unwilling, or unable, to tackle the problem, what hope is there?

Bennett made his remarks five years after release of the famous report commissioned by Bell. "A Nation at Risk" — which hit educators like a bombshell — issued a stern warning: "The educational foundations of our society are presently being eroded by a rising tide of mediocrity that threatens our very future as a nation and a people."

Now, five years later, there is still no national consensus on what should be done. To be sure, there was a flurry of activity in state legislatures for a while. Prestigious think tanks issued their own studies. Vested interests were quick to offer their predictable positions. But then the flames of enthusiasm died down.

Evidently, today's society has difficulty sustaining interest in any cause. Easily bored by difficult topics, we soon tend to flit on to the next sexy issue.

True, there has been limited commitment to spending more money to bring about reforms. But then money by itself is no guarantee of excellence in education. Far more important than expensive new programs and gadgets is a consensus among schools, students and their parents that places top priority on learning.

Quality education has three basic ingredients: good teachers who are dedicated to their work; students who are willing to learn, and supportive parents who pay close attention to their children's progress in school. If any one is missing, success is threatened.

If Bennett, Bell and the others are correct — and there is no reason to believe otherwise — our survival as a nation depends on how well we educate our children to compete in a world marketplace. Graduates of private academies and affluent suburban schools will continue to do well. The majority of ordinary public high school graduates is apt to fall further behind. And the emergence of an underclass of disadvantaged and minority pupils, destined to failure in school and in life, represents a monumental challenge.

Education deserves to be the most hotly debated topic of this year's presidential election, but don't hold your breath. Politicians are apt to wait for a national consensus to emerge — if it ever does — before spending their precious 30-second nightly allotment of national television on something as abstruse as education.

Yet the dramatic words — "A Nation at Risk" — will continue to haunt us. The fact that we have managed only marginal progress during the last five years is scary indeed.

The Miami Herald
Miami, FL, May 2, 1988

MOST FEDERAL studies gather dust. Not the 1983 report of the National Commission on Excellence in Education. Entitled *A Nation at Risk*, the strongly worded report served as a catalyst for school reform.

Now, in a wave of introspection on the report's fifth anniversary, observers are asking, "Are America's schools any better?" Some say it's too soon to tell. But Education Secretary William Bennett has a ready answer: "Yes, but . . ."

Although conceding that reforms have "stopped the slide," Mr. Bennett contends that the quality of American public education is still "unacceptably low," especially in inner-city areas.

About this he may be right. Few would dispute Mr. Bennett's conclusion that more needs to be done. Even so, many educators vigorously disagree with his recipe for reform.

Perhaps, as Mr. Bennett suggests, more academic rigor is still needed. For although progress has been noted, the United States still lags other nations.

And yet, as several thoughtful educators were quick to note, the nation's many disadvantaged pupils will need additional help to reach the higher standards. Providing extra help may entail smaller classes, more counseling, and so on. That costs money — a topic that Mr. Bennett generally shuns.

And no wonder: As critics of the Reagan Administration have pointed out, Federal aid this year will defray about 6.2 percent of the cost of public education compared with 9.2 percent just prior to *A Nation at Risk*.

Granted, the states rather than Washington ought to be the wellsprings for school reform. Indeed, some states — notably those in the South — had begun overhauling their schools even before being goaded by *A Nation at Risk*.

Those state-initiated reforms must continue, too, lest there be serious erosion of recent gains. For Florida, this presents tough budgetary challenges in a year when the governor wants to divert millions of potential school dollars to road building. If that were allowed to happen, it would sabotage Florida's school reforms of recent years and make Florida "a state at risk."

THE SPOKESMAN-REVIEW
Spokane, WA, April 26, 1988

Nobody is going to accuse Education Secretary William J. Bennett of sugarcoating the condition of American schools.

After a yearlong assessment of the state of education in this nation, Bennett has acknowledged that, yes, some improvements have been made in the past five years. But it was the negative findings that he emphasized.

A report of the findings was being submitted to the White House today, the fifth anniversary of a harsh critique of the U.S. school system, "A Nation at Risk," prepared by Bennett's predecessor, Terrel H. Bell.

"Curricular foolishness has not been eliminated from American high schools," reported Bennett, an ardent believer in a more traditional and demanding course selection than is found in many schools today. Science, mathematics, foreign languages and literature including the classics — these are offerings Bennett believes are being sadly neglected.

Interestingly, the statistics included in Bennett's report suggest impressive progress has been made in that direction in the five years since Bell's startling findings catapulted educators and legislators around the nation into motion.

Of last year's high-school graduates, for instance, 12.7 percent completed four years of English; three years each of math, science and social studies; a half-year of computer science; and two years of foreign language if they were headed for college. Those courses are key elements of a curriculum recommended in "A Nation at Risk." Among 1982 graduates, the corresponding percentage had been less than 2 percent.

Bennett ought to be pleased, and no doubt he is. But that doesn't mean he's satisfied, and he's not about to let up pressure on American educators, many of whom are unhappy with his approach.

For one thing, they think the federal government ought to back up its high expectations with a higher level of funding for education. Bennett, on the other hand, thinks the idea that education can be improved through large infusions of money is a discredited one.

Actually, the money question is, to some degree, moot. No level of government — federal, state or local — is awash in cash these days, so even if money were the sole answer, government's ability to respond would be limited.

The fact that exemplary teachers continue to toil in the classrooms, despite higher pay levels in other fields, suggests that the challenge is more complex than a simple matter of money. And the National Education Association's rigid opposition to the concept of merit pay for outstanding teachers undercuts the NEA's contention that higher salaries and improved performance should be linked.

No matter how long and loudly he thumps the tub for school reform, William Bennett never will have the dramatic impact on American education that Terrel Bell had when he released "A Nation at Risk." In the long run, though, Bennett can make just as vital a contribution by refusing to let the matter of educational excellence die.

Part V:
Families & Poverty

Federal social service programs are aimed at helping poor families achieve self-support, preventing the neglect of children and helping to secure institutional care. These efforts can assist a poor family in providing care for its children, in dealing with emotional problems and in securing employment.

The Family Nutrition Program, widely called the food stamp program, was begun in 1961 under the U.S. Department of Agriculture (USDA). It is now in effect in all 50 states, usually administered by the state's department of welfare or social services. Under the Food Stamp Act of 1964, food stamp eligibility was tagged to the USDA poverty level, with semi-annual adjustments for inflation and allowable deductions for household living expenses. Once eligibility was proved, a family could purchase stamps from a local office, up to a maximum amount based on family size. The cost of the stamps to the family was variable, depending on the family's net income. The Food Stamp Act of 1977 mandated that free food stamps be made available to low-income households lacking the cash to buy stamps. To determine the amount of stamps available to a family, 30% of its net monthly income was subtracted from the Thrifty Food Plan cost for a family of its size, and the balance was allotted in free coupons. Coupons were issued directly to eligible households, eliminating the purchase step. The USDA pays the full value of food stamps and provides states with half of the costs of administering the program.

But, according to scholarly and government reports, just over half the households in poverty in the U.S. receive food stamp assistance. This, of course, means that literally millions of impoverished Americans are not being helped by the food stamp program. But for those fortunate enough to receive assistance, benefits are not necessarily based on human need. The evidence is that neither food stamps nor Aid to Families with Dependent Children (AFDC), nor both together, provide American families with the level of support required to eat nutritiously and to maintain health.

A group of recent studies has demonstrated the positive impact of nutritional supplementation for pregnant women. In 1972 the United States established the Women, Infants, and Children Special Supplemental Feeding Program (WIC) in response to evidence of poor birth outcomes related to maternal nutritional deprivation. Although these studies look at the program in different ways, their findings are encouraging. In 1983, a prominent researcher, Milton Kotelchuk, explained results of one of the studies to a congressional committee when he said: "WIC participation is associated with improved pregnancy outcomes; in particular, a 21% decrease in low-birth-weight infants, a major decrease in neonatal mortality, and a 45% reduction in the number of women with inadequate or no prenatal care. The benefits of WIC participation are strongest in women who participate in WIC for more than six months or two trimesters of their pregnancy."

Any young child, regardless of initial birth weight and maternal nutrition, is at risk from postnatal nutritional deprivation. The human brain grows most rapidly during the earliest years of life. After the preschool years, brain growth slows until maturity when it stops. Children deprived of adequate nutrition during the critical years of brain growth are at risk of cognitive and other developmental disabilities.

Family disintegration among the poor has provoked anger and debate for a generation. In 1960, 8.1% of white households and 20.9% of black households were headed by a woman. In 1981, the white percentage had risen to 11.9, the black to 41.7. Since 1950, the number of children born out of wedlock in the U.S. has more than quadrupled for both blacks and whites. In 1987, more that half of the black births in the U.S. were out of wedlock. Among black women, teenagers accounted for 44% of those pregnancies out of wedlock.

Though this is not simply a poverty phenomenon but a general national trend, the poor have participated in ways that hurt them more than anyone else. Unlike a middle-class woman who when divorced or separated does not usually apply for welfare, a poor woman has no alternative. And research has revealed that divorce, separation and childbearing out of wedlock are major causes of welfare dependence. In the vast majority of these cases, women are left with unsupported children and are pushed over the poverty line if they weren't already there.

Only 30 percent of all families headed by woman are poor. However, the decline in intact families, the epidemic of unmarried teenagers in poverty, the growing number of families headed by a poor woman have significantly changed the structure of poverty in the U.S.

PRESIDENT REAGAN HAS THE COUNTRY MOVING AGAIN

Infant Death Rate Studies Debated

A study by the U.S. Public Health Service (PHS) had expressed concern about a slowdown in the decline of the nation's infant mortality rate, particularly in nine states, it was reported May 4, 1985. The study, based on provisional data, reported that the 1984 rate dropped to 10.6 infant deaths per 1,000 live births, down from 10.9 in 1983 and 11.2 in 1982. Although the mortality rate continued to drop, its decline was less than in previous years and appeared to be leveling off.

The new report, which came in response to a congressional request, was the Reagan administration's first state-by-state analysis of infant death rates. It identified nine states—Florida, Georgia, Illinois, Kentucky, Michigan, Missouri, Ohio, South Carolina and Wisconsin—as having "adverse trends" in infant mortality that could not be explained by "random fluctuations."

The report found that, while the 1984 death rate for babies younger than 28 days had declined, the rate for infants from 28 days to one year old had actually increased. That was considered significant, because the deaths of older infants were deemed more susceptible to preventive efforts. In addition, the study noted that if the current trends continued, the U.S. would not achieve a number of the goals it hoped to reach by 1990. Although the overall goal of nine infant deaths per 1,000 live births would probably be met, it was estimated that the 1990 rate for blacks would be 14 rather than the goal of 12. The black infant mortality rate was 19.6 in 1982, the last year for which data by race were available. On March 23, 1985 Secretary of Health and Human Services Margaret Heckler had became the first federal official to acknowledge that the goal for cutting black infant deaths would probably not be met.

The PHS study said that the overall goals for increasing prenatal care and reducing the number of low-birth-weight babies (the leading factor in infant deaths) would also probably not be met by 1990.

The PHS in April 1984 had proposed a study of the "relationship between federal programs and changes in the infant mortality rate," but the Office of Management and Budget had rejected the proposal as unneccessary, the New York Times reported May 4, 1985. Child advocacy groups and some Democrats in Congress charged that the Reagan administration's budget cuts in health and welfare programs—particulalrly those that served pregnant women and young children—had caused, or at least contributed to, negative changes in the infant mortality statistics. Administration officials continued to reject the hypothesis as unproven.

The Children's Defense Fund, a nonprofit child advocacy group based in Washington, D.C., released a report Feb. 2, 1987 that said the U.S. infant mortality rate as one of the highest in the industrialized world. The report said that in 1984, the last year for which government figures were available, there were 10.8 infant deaths for every 1,000 live births in the U.S. According to the report, black American babies were nearly twice as likely as white babies to die in their first year of life.

The U.S. was found to be tied for last place with Belgium, East Germany and West Germany among the 20 industrialized nations surveyed. Three countries, Finland, Iceland and Japan, tied for the lowest rate, six deaths per 1,000 live births. Thirty years earlier, the U.S. had ranked sixth, ahead of both Finland and Japan.

At a news conference held the day the report was released, Marion Wright Edelman, president of the Children's Defense Fund, blamed the U.S. government for what she said was an inadequate effort to meet the health needs of poor women. She charged that cuts in federal programs, including Medicaid and Aid to Families with Dependent Children, had left many poor families without access to adequate prenatal and postnatal care. The main medical reason for high infant mortality rates in the U.S. was said to be the relatively large number of babies who were underweight (under 5.5 pounds) at birth.

In 1980 the U.S. surgeon general had set a national goal to reduce infant mortality rates of minorities and poor women by almost half by the end of the decade. The Children's Defense Fund report concluded that that goal would not be met. According to some experts, there was no assurance that the goal could be met before the 21st century.

FORT WORTH STAR-TELEGRAM

Fort Worth, TX, July 28, 1984

Not long ago, there was a report that life expectancy in the United States has increased.

So people can expect to live longer in this nation.

Now, there is another report the death rate for American infants has declined.

So more people will survive to expect that longer lifetime.

The federal government's Center for Disease Control in Atlanta has concluded the infant death rate has declined dramatically since the early 1960s. One major reason is because there is more success in preventing childhood deaths from infections.

Unfortunately, however, the study also showed black babies still have a death rate twice as high as white children, that the death rate for babies living in rural areas is higher than those for metropolitan areas and that there has been an unusual increase in the proportion of infants who die without warning. This is usually referred to as sudden infant death syndrome, or crib death.

Sometimes there is the tendency to think maybe all the frontiers have been crossed in this nation, that there is not much remaining of major import to be accomplished.

But then along comes something like the report on what is yet to be done to further reduce the infant mortality rate in this nation and we are reminded there still is plenty of challenge to go around.

AKRON BEACON JOURNAL
Akron, OH, December 17, 1984

THERE IS little reason, at least in Summit County, for any pregnant woman not to be getting prenatal care.

Certainly, money should be no obstacle. Prenatal programs are available at area health departments. No one will be turned away for lack of ability to pay for these services.

Yet the infant mortality rate in Summit County is higher than both the state and national averages. And the 1983 infant death rate in Akron was 16.8 per 1,000 births, a substantial increase over the previous year.

Undoubtedly, the region's economic problems contributed to the increased deaths.

Yet the real tragedy of these statistics is that many of the deaths would not have occurred had women sought medical care early in their pregnancies.

Both Ohio and Summit County are making a commendable effort to improve prenatal care for mothers and their babies.

The state increased financial support for maternal health services and targeted extra money for health departments in counties in which death rates are rising. By 1986, all of Ohio's 88 counties will have prenatal programs.

An important part of the state's effort is aimed at increasing awareness — particularly among pregnant teen-agers — of the crucial connection between early prenatal care and the birth of a healthy infant.

When that connection isn't made, a tragedy sometimes results. Women who ignore their need for medical care, particularly during the first three months of pregnancy, run a greater risk of giving birth to premature or low-weight babies.

Those infants, in turn, are more likely to suffer medical problems and mental and physical handicaps. A lifetime of suffering and staggering medical expenses might easily have been avoided had some simple steps been taken before birth.

The higher-than-average infant mortality rate in Summit County is surely worrisome. But it also is preventable, as health officials readily recognize. Women must realize it, too.

A pregnant woman should want to do everything possible to give her unborn baby a good start in life. Good prenatal care is the first and best gift that a mother can bestow on her child.

ST. LOUIS POST-DISPATCH
St. Louis, MO, January 9, 1984

Like most other statistics, infant mortality rates aren't likely to move many people to tears. Cold, tabulated accounts resist translation into the small, warm human bodies whose comings and goings give us joy and rend our hearts. But recently, two different agencies have issued reports on just this issue. And their conclusions are enough to force a tear from all but the driest eye.

In the last five years, a city of more than 20,000, roughly the size of Bridgeton, could be populated with the infants who died for no reason but that they were not favored to be born into white families in the 36 states and 16 cities studied by the Food Research and Action Center. The good news — that overall infant mortality rates are on the decline — is itself perverse in that it masks the shame that the improvement is so lopsided, with white babies' survival rates increasing at a pace seven times that for blacks. Nationwide, black mothers are more than twice as likely as whites to bury their children before their first birthday. Low birth weights, linked to congenital defects and retardation, also afflict blacks at a rate twice that of whites.

Nor is the chasm likely to be bridged soon. If anything, the Children's Defense Fund suggests it may be widening. While the number of children living in poverty has grown at an alarming pace, more than 700,000 poor children have been taken off Medicaid and welfare rolls in the last two years. In 1982, Medicaid served about 74 children for every 100 living in poverty; in 1979, the ratio was 90 in 100. The proportion of children who benefited from Aid to Families with Dependent Children plummeted even more sharply — from 72 per 100 in 1979 to 53 per 100 in 1982.

Authors of both studies minced no words in assigning blame: Federal and state programs to serve the poor are being slashed to the bone at the very time when the number of those needing such services is growing.

Comes now a third report from Washington — that still further cuts are being sought in programs that bear directly on the health and well-being of our country's smallest, most helpless citizens. A reduction of 11 percent in Aid to Families with Dependent Children has been proposed, with substantial cuts as well in Medicaid and the Women, Infants and Children program, designed to make sure nursing mothers and their babies get the nutrition they need.

In simplest terms, money spent on Medicaid, welfare, and other programs for the needy buys lives. Such thrift as that planned by President Reagan squanders them. A heedless president surrounded by advisers blind to the hunger and despair of the dispossessed can little be expected to shed a tear for the children sent to early graves as a result of his policies. Dare we hope Congress will be sensitive enough to recognize the outrage and bold enough to put an end to this national disgrace?

The Miami Herald
Miami, FL, January 6, 1984

RISING U.S. infant-mortality rates pose an embarrassing paradox: America is among the world's most advanced nations, yet it inches backward in protecting its most vital resource — its children.

The cruel fact of increasing infant mortality was documented for the second consecutive year by the Children's Defense Fund, a research group based in Washington, D.C. The data are supported by studies from the Congressional Research Service, a nonpartisan arm of Congress.

Both studies show that the rate of infant mortality has increased in 11 states: Alabama, Delaware, Iowa, New Jersey, North Carolina, New Hampshire, Nebraska, Oklahoma, Virginia, Utah, and Washington.

The reports show precipitous increases in the death rate of black babies, which now is twice that of white infants. In some urban areas, that mortality rate may rival that of Third World countries.

A principal cause of increased infant deaths has been a gradual shift from early prenatal care among pregnant women. The data invariably are linked directly to poverty.

The reports, in sum, describe the fatal consequences of poverty in America. Since 1979, the number of children who live in poverty has increased 31 per cent.

At fault are recession, the highest unemployment since the Depression, and Reagan Administration policies that significantly have trimmed Federal spending on health, nutrition, and child-care programs.

Though rising infant-mortality rates are the demonstrable result of inadequate prenatal care, they are symptomatic of larger problems. Logic suggests that if increasing numbers of children die within a year of birth, rising numbers who survive are burdened with health deficiencies. The consequences of declining health among children are far-reaching — from diminished educational achievement to increased dependency on health and social-service institutions.

If the Administration desires authoritative information on the extent of health and nutrition problems in America, it seriously should review the data of these reports. They describe the fatal, and unacceptable, results of the Administration's withdrawal of support from America's children.

THE ANN ARBOR NEWS
Ann Arbor, MI, August 19, 1985

A report in the New England Journal of Medicine has helped to bring into sharper focus the issue of child mortality rates and the quality of health care.

Child mortality rates for lower-, middle- and upper-income families in the U.S. have dropped dramatically since the 1960s, but differences in child mortality among the groups have remained the same.

Poor children, the report said, are one-third more likely to die prematurely than are members of economically better-off classes even when all have equal access to quality health care.

A study of child mortality rates in Boston found that equal access to high quality health care does not by itself reduce the disparity in child mortality rates between rich and poor families. To eliminate that disparity requires greater emphasis on preventative care, improved environmental influences, education and better nutrition.

The great strides this country has made in prenatal and neonatal care may make for fine reading in pediatrics journals, but child mortality rates are still a darker side of the picture.

The World Health Organization, using 1980-1981 figures, ranks the U.S. 20th in infant mortality rates behind such countries as Great Britain, Spain, Japan and Canada. Among major industrial countries America ranks 12th.

In 1982, 42,400 newborn infants died in the U.S. The national infant mortality rate was 11.5 per thousand, with a 10.1 rate for whites and 19.6 for blacks.

Another report just issued by the U.S. Public Health Service says the current American infant mortality rate is 10.6 deaths per 1,000 live births, down from 10.9 in 1983. The steady, 20-year decline in the number of American babies who die before their first birthday is slowing.

Columnist Julian Bond writes that when infant mortality rates for 1985 are released, "population experts expect that the rate for blacks will have actually *increased*." Bond criticized Reagan administration cutbacks in social welfare and public health programs "that clearly mean the difference between life and death for Americans at the bottom of the economic scale."

Denise Holmes is deputy chief, bureau of community services for the Michigan Department of Public Health. Speaking at a Law Day conference in Lansing last May, Holmes presented statistical background information on infant mortality.

Michigan's rate, she said, is 11.8/1,000, slightly higher than the national average. But in urban areas and for special population groups, the problem is much more severe. Detroit, for example, leads the nation's 22 largest cities with an infant mortality rate of 19.8/1,000 in 1983.

That sad statistic for Detroit climbed to 26.8 per thousand in 1984, which approaches the rate in some Third World countries. The problem is acute among minorities and teen-agers, especially those living in poverty.

To that end, Department of Social Services director Agnes Mary Mansour earlier this year announced an educational campaign against teen-age pregnancies. Called "Do Yourself a Favor, Save It For Later," the campaign aimed to educate teens about the hazards of early sex and pregnancy.

Again, the statistics are depressing. Teen-agers account for 32 percent of abortions in Michigan each year. Teen-agers account for 10 percent of U.S. pregnancies; half of the mothers who receive AFDC had their first child when they were teenagers. These child-mothers, whose own bodies aren't yet fully developed, produce offspring whose chances for a normal, healthy first year of life are greatly diminished.

More education on birth control would cut infant mortality rates in places such as Detroit. More information on nutrition and better care for pregnant women would successfully combat low infant-birth weight, a big factor in infant deaths. Teen-age promiscuity needs to be countered with programs which offer hope and jobs which promote responsibility.

THE TENNESSEAN
Nashville, TN, January 3, 1985

TWO Nashville babies, one four months old and the other three months old, were found dead in their cribs New Year's morning of what the medical profession terms Sudden Infant Death Syndrome (SIDS).

SIDS, also called "crib death," simply means that apparently healthy infants die suddenly in their beds for unexplainable reasons. There are numerous theories about the cause of crib deaths, but so far no definite cause of the deaths can be given in about 80% of the cases.

One thing is certain about crib death: It is a growing cause of concern to the parents of small babies. It is estimated that about 25 deaths a year in Nashville involve SIDS. Nationally, the death toll is considerable.

There was no connection between the two deaths here on New Year's. It was just a coincidence that the two babies, whose families live only about a mile apart, died on the same night. But it is a coincidence that has turned a spotlight on the sad reality of crib death and one that, it is hoped, will help to spur further research into the cause of this frightening phenomenon.

Nashville, TN, March 27, 1985

THE Reagan administration has given up on reducing the death rate among black infants enough to meet the national goal for the year 1990, but some administration health officials seem to be concerned with finding the causes of black infant mortality which is helping keep the rate high.

Several years ago health officials set a goal for 1990 of having no racial or ethnic group in the population showing a death rate of more than 12 for each 1,000 live births. But in 1982, the last year for which figures are available, the rate infant mortality rate for blacks was 19.6 per 1,000.

The health officials still hope to achieve the 1990 goal for the overall infant mortality rate of nine deaths for each 1,000 live births; the overall rate was 10.6 last year. But Secretary of Health and Human Services Margaret M. Heckler says the goal for black infants will be "more difficult to achieve."

At a news conference, Ms. Heckler said "a large portion of the difference in infant mortality by race can be attributed to a higher incidence of low birth weight among black infants." But the health secretary seemed at a loss to explain the prevalence of low birth weight among blacks.

"Statistics show that regardless of known factors like income, age of the mother, and access to prenatal care, low birth weight occurs more often among black Americans than among whites. This is a puzzling fact."

However, this doesn't seem to rule out the possibility that underweight babies among blacks without adequate nutrition and medical care make up the larger part of the infant mortality rates.

Underweight babies born to poor black mothers who have not had good nutrition and prenatal care seem less likely to survive than those born to parents who are able to provide their children with wholesome food and medical necessities.

Whatever the explanation may be, medical care and balanced diets for pregnant women seem likely to help reduce the black infant mortality rate. But this cannot be achieved when needed government spending for these purposes is always being cut back.

The United States has one of the highest infant mortality rates of any of the industrialized nations. Sweden, Japan and France already have rates less than 10 deaths for each 1,000 live births. Those are statistics which should be improved upon before 1990.

ST. LOUIS POST-DISPATCH
St. Louis, MO, May 11, 1985

Why is the risk of death for young babies on the rise? And why is the decline in the death rate for newborn infants slowing? The answers to those questions cannot be found in a study by the Public Health Service reporting the distressing trend in mortality rates.

A search for an explanation ought to be the next step, even though the administration has rejected proposals to review the effects, if any, of federal cutbacks on infant mortality. Until a disinterested analysis is undertaken, the assumption is bound to be that the culprit is the cuts in domestic assistance programs or in block grant consolidations. While federal action would be most beneficial, the states can and should act on their own. Missouri and Illinois were among nine states singled out for special concern by the Public Health Service. Statistics indicate that the slowdown in the reduction of infant mortality rates is more severe here than in the majority of states. Why?

Under the previous governor, Christopher Bond, Missouri began a program of targeting high-risk pregnant women and emphasizing well-baby care. Is this program reaching the people in need? Is it being properly funded? Or are any positive results simply too recent to be seen in the available statistics?

The new federal study, which, incidentally, reinforces the findings contained in a report made to the National Governors Association earlier, ought to raise concerns in Jefferson City and Springfield that will translate into reviews of the programs for poor pregnant women and their babies.

The Miami Herald

Miami, FL, July 9, 1985

IF YOU CAN, forget the human anguish of losing a baby or of rearing a child who has birth defects. Concentrate instead on money. In the absence of a national policy, efforts aimed at curbing the United States's unconscionable infant-mortality rate have focused on saving babies born with a low birth weight, not on preventing that low birth weight. Developing that policy is the goal of a national commission proposed by U.S. Sen. Lawton Chiles, Democrat of Lakeland.

Although the U.S. infant-mortality rate is higher than those of 16 other nations, including Japan and most of Western Europe, it has fallen by more than half in the last two decades. While that improvement might be heartening, it has come mostly through improved care for low-weight babies in neonatal units, not through improving their or their mothers' health.

Treating the effect but not the cause rings up a $1.5-billion-a-year bill nationwide for intensive neonatal care. In Florida, taxpayers and insurers pay $82.5 million of that. The bills don't stop there, however. Often these tiny survivors grow up to have multiple health problems, learning disabilities, and cerebral palsy.

The tragedy is that the causes of low birth weight are well known and largely preventable. They include smoking, drug and alcohol abuse, poor nutrition, and a lack of medical care. Poor black mothers and teen-agers are the most likely to have low-weight babies. In a one-year experiment in California to provide proper prenatal care, premature births dropped by two-thirds.

It is cheaper by far to prevent low birth weight than to treat its effects. Yet there is no effort to coordinate medical services and nutrition programs for low-income women, and the Reagan Administration has cut back some of those programs. Senator Chiles's proposed commission would be charged with pulling together and strengthening those programs. Healthy babies must be a national priority. His bill deserves swift passage.

The Hartford Courant

Hartford, CT, January 13, 1985

Of every 1,000 babies born in Connecticut, 11 will die before they are a year old Of every 1,000 babies born in Hartford, 19 will die. Of every 1,000 babies born in Hartford's Asylum Hill or Clay Arsenal neighborhoods, 30 will die.

Ninety percent of the infant deaths in Hartford occur in only half its neighborhoods.

These neighborhoods are among Hartford's poorest, where between 10.5 percent and 56 percent of the people live below the poverty level. The death of three times as many babies in some neighborhoods of Hartford as is typical in Connecticut as a whole should be unacceptable to society.

Poor mothers, especially those who are teenaged, are less likely than others to receive proper prenatal care or nutrition and are consequently more likely to give birth to sickly, underweight or premature infants, who are at highest risk of dying. Seeing to it that every poor expectant woman receives prenatal care should be of the utmost importance to every elected public official, social policy planner, medical worker and citizen in Hartford.

Poverty deprives human beings of many things, material and spiritual, but in an area as affluent as Greater Hartford, it should not be permitted to deprive babies of life.

Washington, DC, July 25, 1985

A baby is born, and a mother holds it in her arms. She gazes at the tiny creature, so new, and in that moment knows utter joy and soaring hope.

Then tragedy: The baby dies before its first birthday. And a void is left in the parents' hearts forever.

A rare calamity? No. In the USA it happens 110 times each day. It happens 40,000 times each year.

It is much more likely to happen to a poor family and twice as likely to happen among blacks as whites. Last year, there were 10.6 deaths for every 1,000 live births.

Despite medical advances that have caused the USA's infant mortality rate to improve for 20 years, the gap between the black and white rates has remained 2-to-1.

Recently, in tandem with federal spending cuts, the progress in infant mortality rates began to slow. Only one-fourth of the women and children who need the government's food program for Women, Infants, and Children are served by it. Many women have been squeezed off Medicaid rolls.

Health advocates are especially worried because some key indicators hint that baby death rates may even start going up: For example, the national death rate for infants between one month and one year rose 6 percent last year.

Making the tragedy of lost babies more tragic is the fact that we know how to prevent many infant deaths — but we often fail to act. Scientists say there is overwhelming evidence that early prenatal care and proper maternal nutrition save babies' lives.

Most of the lost babies are born too small. A newborn weighing less than five-and-a-half pounds is 20 times more likely than a larger child to die before its birthday.

Many mothers-to-be — especially young, unwed, black women — receive little or no medical care before their babies are born. Many of them are poorly educated and don't seek help until well into their pregnancies.

There are those who say government should not spend more on the problem because baby deaths have shrunk to an irreducible minimum. That makes no sense when you realize the USA has an infant mortality rate worse than 16 other industrialized nations. If only 6 Finnish infants die for each 1,000 born, how can we be satisfied with 10.6?

Responsibility for saving babies rests on many shoulders.

The federal government must spend the modest sums needed to give prenatal care and nutrition to every needy pregnant woman. States must supplement federal maternal care programs or offer their own. Schools, churches, and charities must reach out to young people, counseling against unwed parenthood and advising those girls who do become pregnant to stay healthy and stay in school.

And the media must deliver the message that timely prenatal care is essential.

It is tragic that 40,000 U.S. babies die each year. It's more tragic that we don't save them.

THE MILWAUKEE JOURNAL

Milwaukee, WI, February 28, 1985

The image of America-the-bountiful pales in light of a new report revealing that a two-decade decline in the rate of infant mortality in the United States is slowing sharply. It's disgraceful that a nation as wealthy as this one sees a higher proportion of its infants die than do 11 other developed countries.

The infant mortality rate is a key yardstick used to measure the health of a nation. It is generally believed that the lower the death rate per 1,000 babies under age 1 — as a group, the weakest members of a population — the better a nation's health care.

By that standard, health care in America got dramatically better from the mid-1960s through 1982, with infant mortality declining an average of 4.6% a year, from 24.7 deaths per 1,000 to 11.2.

But that rosy picture may be changing. According to an unpublished report prepared by the US Public Health Service, the decline slowed in 1983 to 2.7% and in the first nine months of '84 to less than 2%. The overall rate now stands at just under 11 infant deaths per 1,000 births. (For black infants alone the rate is far worse: 19.6.)

Why the slowdown? Public health experts speculate on three causes: (1) no recent growth in the proportion of pregnant women who get prenatal care; (2) limits on what medical technology can accomplish; and (3) Reagan administration restraints — in some cases cutbacks — in spending for government medical and nutrition programs.

Given the present political climate, it is probably naive to hope that the medical and nutrition programs will be bolstered, although that is precisely what needs to be done. Failing that, health agencies and schools need to reach out even more to educate women about what they can do to minimize risks to their babies, and step up efforts to make prenatal care universally available.

On the latter point, Wisconsin would seem to have a jump on the feds. The state's health chief is seeking budget approval to begin paying the state's portion of AFDC grants upon confirmation of pregnancy for first-time mothers trying to finish school. It's a sound idea, because teen births account for 17% of all infant deaths in the state. Perhaps Wisconsin's initiative can become a model for a nation whose infant death rate is shameful.

Lincoln Journal

Louisville, KY, January 22, 1986

KENTUCKY MEDICINE, which has had much favorable publicity in the past 18 months, is now in the news for unflattering reasons. The Children's Defense Fund in Washington, D. C., reports that of the 50 states, Kentucky ranks second in the percentage of white babies who die in their first year of life. And though the Kentucky infant mortality rate is slightly below the national rate for non-whites, it still greatly exceeds the rate for whites.

This high infant mortality rate is traced to two main causes: the large number of teen-age pregnancies in Kentucky, and the inadequate number of people covered by Medicaid. No state has a higher percentage of its white babies born to teen-agers. Only South Carolina requires its residents to be poorer before they qualify for medical assistance.

Teen-agers aren't likely to receive prenatal care and counseling, at least in the early stages of pregnancy. Neither are poor women. Yet medical supervision can make a big difference in whether a baby is born healthy, or tiny and premature. And a baby who has an abnormally low birth weight is 20 times more likely to die than a baby who weighs more.

So the way for Kentucky to get off the list of the worst states for infant survival is clear. But cutting the number of teen-age pregnancies, and making medical care available to more pregnant women, means spending more money.

The Cabinet for Human Resources says that only 53 percent of the women in the state who are eligible for family planning counseling are getting it. Prenatal care services are meeting only 47 percent of the need. Therefore, the cabinet asked Governor Collins to triple the amount of money in the budget for prenatal care — to $12 million — and increase the amount available for family planning services from $4.5 million to $6 million.

Certainly money is tight and the General Assembly is being assaulted with requests to increase spending on many worthwhile programs and services. But this is an area in which an increase in funding makes not just moral but fiscal sense.

If all mothers received comprehensive medical care, at least 25 percent of the children who end up in neonatal care units would be born healthy. The average cost of keeping a baby in a neonatal care unit is $1,000 a day. The average length of stay is 23 days.

Most low birth-weight babies do survive. But that doesn't mean they necessarily become healthy, contributing members of society. The problems of low birth-weight affect a child's mental as well as physical development. Too often they become adults forever dependent on the government.

There are, of course, many other contributing factors to the high infant mortality rate in Kentucky. They include the high rate of poverty (infants can die because an apartment is cold), the low number of families that receive payments from Aid to Families With Dependent Children, and the scarcity of doctors in parts of eastern and central Kentucky.

But studies have found that if the number of teen-age pregnancies can be decreased, and the number of women receiving prenatal care increased, then the infant mortality rate goes down.

Steps must be taken to achieve these goals. Otherwise Kentucky won't be remembered for medical achievements such as the artificial heart experiment and its high-tech medical centers. Instead, it will be remembered for its shocking infant mortality statistics.

The Atlanta Journal
THE ATLANTA CONSTITUTION

Atlanta, GA, May 7, 1986

Black infants are dying at twice the rate of white infants, as they were a generation ago. America's infant mortality rate still exceeds that of most European countries, Canada and Japan. And, the national Centers for Disease Control suggest in their first nationwide study of infant mortality in two decades, many of those deaths are preventable.

That shameful report is not meant to suggest that there hasn't been progress over the years. Babies were dying at even greater rates in 1960. But America's continued poor showing in several categories suggests it hasn't moved as vigorously as it could have, or as determinedly as other nations, to avail itself of solutions at hand.

The reasons for high infant mortality are clear. For all races and in every nation, experts agree that infant mortality is best prevented by prenatal care, beginning in the first three months of pregnancy. Mothers-to-be who fail to obtain it or receive it later than that are *three times* more likely to have stillborn, sickly or severely underweight babies than those who receive medical care, counseling and nutrition supplements throughout their pregnancies. And despite impressive advances by U.S. doctors in the technology of neonatal intensive care and high-risk pregnancy, women who are poor, black and American are, on average, less likely to have adequate prenatal care than women in other western nations.

Tragically, though this isn't a problem of the administration's making, it is worsening because of cuts engineered by Reagan appointees — in Medicaid, nutrition, education and birth-control programs serving poor families. There are now parts of America where, the CDC reports, a baby doesn't have as much chance of living to be a year old as in Panama, Guyana or Cuba.

States are taking up the slack where possible. Georgia, with one of the worst mortality rates in the nation at 13.7 deaths per 1,000 births, has set itself a goal of "9 (per 1,000) by 1990," through a multimillion-dollar statewide program of insurance supplements, hospital reimbursements and increased support of midwife services in rural areas; more than a third of Georgia's 159 counties have no obstetrician at all.

But skyrocketing insurance rates for obstetricians and the inability of many midwives to obtain insurance work against such efforts, threatening to create greater health care gaps in the future.

There simply is no substitute for prenatal care, as even the administration has acknowledged while cutting back on programs that provided it and railing against the loss of life through abortion. With the evidence mounting that tens of thousands of young lives can be saved, it's time the administration became part of the solution.

THE PLAIN DEALER

Cleveland, OH, January 27, 1986

The most troubling aspect about the lead story in this newspaper the other day—the one about the high rate of infant mortality—is that we have read it before. Not the same details, but the same problem. Black infants—from birth to a year old—are twice as likely to die as white babies. The gap is now the widest it has been in 40 years.

Cleveland's record is one of the worst in the nation, and some neighborhoods have rates that are worse than Third World countries. Despite major gains, this community, resurgent in other ways, has not been able to overcome the burdens of poverty, teen-age pregnancy and poor prenatal care—all of which contribute to low birth weights, the greatest killer of infants.

Not that people haven't tried to make improvements. There is the Cleveland Regional Perinatal Network based at University Hospitals, and a mothers-and-infants care program based at Cleveland Metropolitan General Hospital. There have been advertising campaigns, surveys of new mothers to find the causes of low birth weights, and efforts to have clergy promote prenatal care among their parishioners. The Celeste administration has expanded a state program for pregnant women; the total will reach 77 counties in July, up from 28 four years ago.

The decline in infant mortality, starting in the 1960s, bottomed out in 1982 and the rate began to go back up. The Children's Defense Fund blames deep cuts in federal programs for the poor. In the last full year for which state-by-state statistics were available—1983—the fund reported a rate of 9.7 deaths per 1,000 live births, but a rate of 16.8 deaths among blacks. The United States' rate is far higher than the rate of Scandanavian countries—a little more than 6%—as well as that of Japan and several other industrialized nations.

The fund's report is comparable to those of the Public Health Service, the Institute of Medicine of the National Academy of Sciences and other studies. The pattern of causes is the same: poor nutrition, continued use of alcohol, cigarettes and drugs, and inadequate, sometimes total, lack of medical care. The conditions are most prevalent among teen-agers and women below the poverty line, but also are common with the medically indigent—women who are uninsured but are just above the poverty level.

Prevention of problems is the logical answer, both in humane terms and in monetary savings. The cost of prenatal care, to assure a healthy full-weight baby, is a fraction of the cost of medical bills for premature and sick babies, and children with learning disabilities or physical handicaps.

These arguments underscore the importance of such programs as the East High School health clinic and the health maintenance program for Medicaid patients being set up by a consortium of Cleveland-area hospitals, clinics and doctors. The future of this community and this country rest in part on the health of Americans born each day. It is morally and financially imperative that we make sure those babies are as healthy as possible.

Birmingham Post-Herald

Birmingham, AL, January 18, 1986

The statistics are new, but the story, unfortunately, is an old one. Alabama remains among the leaders in infant mortality. More than 13 out of every 1,000 babies born in Alabama in 1983 died before they were one year old. Worse, we are not keeping pace with the rest of the nation in reducing this death rate.

The Children's Defense Fund concludes that Alabama will not meet federal goals for reducing infant deaths if it continues at the pace reflected in the 1983 figures upon which the Fund's nationwide study is based.

It should be noted that the Children's Defense Fund is a lobbying group, one of whose goals is to increase public assistance or welfare spending. So it is not surprising that the study seeks to refute the "common belief that more generous levels of public assistance encourage teenage pregnancy." The report says, "...an examination of 1983 teen births and state welfare payment does not show this to be true."

We are not prepared to accept that statement without qualifications because of the many other social factors that affect teenage pregnancy.

But the Alabama statistics do indicate some of the reasons we have the seventh highest infant death rate in the country.

Our welfare payments do not come close to the state's own assessment of the amount of money a family needs to subsist. The 1984 standard of need was about half the federal poverty level — reflecting our economic level — but welfare payments were only 31 percent of that lower standard. If a family doesn't have the money, nei-ther an expectant mother nor a child is likely to have an adequate diet.

One important factor in determining infant mortality is birth weight. Babies who weigh 5.5 pounds or less at birth are much more likely to die. About 8 percent of babies born in Alabama in 1983 had low birth weights compared to the national average of 6.9 percent.

The percentage of low birth weights is even higher for those infants born to teenage mothers, 10.6 percent in Alabama, 9.5 nationwide. And only two states have a higher percentage of babies born to teenage mothers than Alabama's 19.1 percent.

These figures are an indictment. They say we are not doing enough to prevent teenage pregnancy. They say we are not doing enough to help expectant mothers during pregnancy so that babies will be born healthy and large enough to survive. They say we are not doing enough after a baby is born to ensure that child's well-being.

Many of these problems are directly related to poverty. Cure that and the infant mortality rate is sure to drop. But short of such a miracle, there is much more we can do to provide birth control information, especially to teenagers, and to provide health care during and after pregnancy for all mothers and their babies.

What has to be done is known. And we are doing some of it through various government and private programs.

But not nearly enough, as is seen by the number of infants who die in Alabama each year.

The Morning News

Wilmington, DE, May 5, 1986

ONE WAY to evaluate a nation's health status is to look at its infant mortality rate — the lower the rate, the better a country's medical care and living conditions.

The United States has regularly reported higher infant mortality rates than other industrialized nations. The high mortality rate for black infants has consistently raised the average infant mortality rate in the United States. Unfortunately, that pattern is continuing.

According to the latest figures from the Centers for Disease Control, the mortality rate for black infants under age one is 18.4 deaths per 1,000 live births; for white infants, the rate is 9.3 deaths per 1,000 live births.

Insufficient prenatal care, teen-age pregnancy and the resultant low-birthweight babies as well as socio-economic problems account for more deaths for black infants. These same factors are also often involved in giving a white baby a slim chance at life.

The importance of prenatal care shows up startlingly in the CDC study. When prenatal care was begun in the first trimester, the infant mortality rate was 9.7 per 1,000 babies, regardless of race. When mothers waited until the last three months of pregnancy to seek care, the mortality rate for their infants was 12.7 per 1,000. And for those who received no care, the mortality rate was a stunning 48.7 percent per 1,000 live births.

Socio-economic factors, such as the level of the mother's education, also give clues about the likely outcome of a pregnancy. The CDC study found that for women with four years of college education, the infant mortality rate was 7.3 per 1,000 births, while the rate for babies of women who had not finished high school was 16.3 per 1,000.

These figures reinforce what medical professionals have been telling us for a long time — good care and a sensible life style during pregnancy can go a long way in ensuring the delivery of a healthy infant with good life expectancy. But what neither doctors, nor nurses, nor anyone else has yet figured out is how to persuade expectant mothers to follow that wholesome course.

• • •

It has been known for some time that the life expectancy of adult males is lower than that for females. The CDC study shows that in infancy too, baby boys are more at risk than baby girls. The mortality rate for baby boys is 12.1 for every 1,000 live births; for baby girls, it is 9.7 per 1,000 live births.

The Evening Gazette

Worcester, MA, May 5, 1986

College break time is nearly done for another year. The annual rites of spring are concluding in Fort Lauderdale and other points south. Each year, thousands of students flock to Florida resorts for a week of fun. For most it's been a chance to unwind after a hard winter of hitting the books, and to rest up for the final-exam push that is just around the corner.

For some, though, final exams will never come. Last year, three students on spring break died in accidental plunges from hotel balconies alone. At least five students have died this year in balcony falls; seven have been seriously hurt.

Officials say most of the deaths are alcohol-related. Pumped up with beer and bravado, students make a game of climbing from balcony to balcony. Inevitably, some don't make it. Police and hotel security people say they are doing everything they can to ensure the safety of students. "Outside of tying a cowbell around some of these people's necks, I just don't know what can be done," said one police spokesman.

Spring break has become big business in the Sunshine State. Hotel and bar owners, chambers of commerce and others discovered long ago that catering to the annual influx of students is a great way to stretch the season. If the drinking gets out of hand, go easy: The customer's always right.

Worst of all is the way the rest of us all seem to accept the carnage. We shake our heads and ponder for a moment the waste of young lives. The next spring, our children go south again.

Americans are inured to death. Husbands kill wives. Diplomats are assassinated. Astronauts die. The annual slaughter on the highway goes on. And saddest of all, on spring break in the Florida sun, rendered insensate by booze, children are dying.

ST. LOUIS POST-DISPATCH

St. Louis, MO,
January 26, 1988

About 40,000 infants die before their first birthday, giving the United States an infant-death rate of roughly 10.8 per 1,000 live births. The rate is much higher in inner cities across the nation. Part of the cause of infant mortality is that many children come into the world without having had access to early and continuing prenatal care. They have a low birth weight (5.5 pounds or below), which not only increases an infant's chance of dying before its first birthday but also increases the risk of serious illnesses or permanent handicaps.

Because infant mortality in St. Louis is about twice the U.S. rate, it is understandable that many health-care professionals have taken the city to task for doing too little to address the problem. City officials have finally responded by appointing a health officer to tackle the problem.

The appointee is Eme Udofia-Ekpo, a Regional Medical Center administrator. She will serve as the chief of maternal and child health services. Without question, the city could have acted much earlier in making this appointment. It might even be argued that more babies have died needlessly because of the city's failure to hire someone earlier to coordinate these services. The head of the St. Louis Medical Society, Dr. William C. Banton II, has repeatedly assailed the city's failure to fill this post. More criticism came last week in the form of an aldermanic resolution urging that the position be filled quickly.

While city officials argue that it took its time in filling the position because it wanted to find a qualified person, there is no question that the criticism helped to speed the process. The next step is for city officials to give Ms. Udofia-Ekpo adequate resources to allow her to devise an effective plan to reduce the shamefully high rate of infant deaths in St. Louis.

Los Angeles Times

Los Angeles, CA, July 22, 1988

A child born in any of 16 other industrial nations has a better chance of living to its first birthday than a child born in the United States. In addition, infant-mortality statistics have not improved in this country since 1980. Why that is true and how to change the situation are the focus of a chilling report from the Congressional Office of Technology Assessment.

No one should have to talk dollars and cents when it comes to trying to save the lives of the 40,000 babies who die before their first birthday each year. That's about 1% of all babies born in the United States annually. But OTA did just that to make the point that preventive medicine pays off for people who may look only at the bottom line instead of at the need to reduce suffering.

Most often babies die because they don't weigh enough at birth to thrive—that is, they weigh less than 5 pounds, 8 ounces. That often happens because they are born prematurely; their mothers don't know how to take care of themselves during pregnancy or don't realize that they have health problems that affect an unborn child. If women visit a doctor regularly during pregnancy, some of these problems can be prevented so that they have a better chance of having a baby that can survive.

The congressional researchers found that $14,000 to $30,000 is saved each time a newborn infant can survive without intensive hospital treatment and long-term care. But many women can't afford good prenatal care. Many don't have health insurance or aren't covered by the Medicaid program. If Medicaid coverage were expanded to all pregnant poor women, about 194,000 more women would be eligible for good care. That would cost $4 million a year.

Here's where the saving comes in. If $14,000 to $30,000 is saved each time an infant doesn't require intensive care at birth, then only 133 to 286 low-weight births have to be prevented to break even. And the evidence is convincing that earlier prenatal care makes that kind of reduction "quite feasible," the study said.

Babies can also be helped to better lives through screening early in their lives for disorders like phenylketonuria (PKU), which leads to mental retardation, as well as for congenital hypothyroidism, sickle-cell anemia and cystic fibrosis. Even a modest PKU and hypothyroidism screening program involving the testing of only one blood specimen saves almost 1,300 infants from lifetimes of severe disability. It also saves the U.S. health-care system about $120 million a year.

A complete program of shots for children provides what the researchers called "the starkest example of the power of prevention to save or prolong lives [and] prevent significant disability." It, too, saves money, yet federal investment in immunization programs lags seriously.

Why, with these programs and techniques available, aren't infant-mortality figures improving? Attempts are made to save more of the tiniest babies today than ever before, the researchers said, so that may skew the figures. But in addition the federal government simply has not undertaken a real effort to make sure that poor women and their children get decent health care. Cutting funds at the very time poverty is increasing raises the risks that babies will die, the report said.

Of course people want babies to live. But neither Washington nor Sacramento is trying to make a public case for the importance of the mission or for advancing the money needed to start reducing the infant-mortality rate. Now the Office of Technology Assessment has pointed to areas in which what's good for babies is good for the budget. That is a true investment in the future, and one that any humane and prudent government should make.

The Washington Post

Washington, DC, July 25, 1985

THE LATEST statistics on infant mortality in the District are shocking. Deaths of children under a year old rose by 16.5 percent last year after three years of steady decline. For every thousand live births in this city, there were 21.2 infant deaths. This is one of the worst records of any city in the country, and government officials are properly concerned.

A year ago, the Greater Washington Research Center, in cooperation with the National Institutes of Health and the D.C. Department of Human Services, embarked upon a project directed at reducing the rate of infant mortality. The primary purpose of the Better Babies Project was to reduce the incidence of low birth weight, which is a known cause of early death and occurs twice as frequently in Washington as in the nation as a whole. The project was set up in nine census tracts in Ward 5 and Ward 6, and individual counselors were hired from the community to work on a one-to-one basis with pregnant women. The staff arranges medical care, helps the women to obtain social services and educates them about the dangers of tobacco, alcohol, drugs and stress during pregnancy.

Data are not yet available about the success of the project in reducing low birth weight, but project workers already know that their task is even more complicated than they had anticipated. Most of the pregnant women in the targeted area are unmarried and have been abandoned by the father of the child they are carrying. Some have been rejected by their families; a few have not a single friend. A number are homeless, living on the street or in abandoned buildings, and others have severe alcohol and drug problems. Very few have any education or any prospects for employment. The project provides personal and comprehensive advice and assistance to these women, but it is extremely difficult to convince a prospective mother that it's important to quit smoking and control her weight for the baby's sake when the general conditions of her own life are so dismal.

The Better Babies Project is operating against strong odds. If the program is successful it will be because workers were able to change basic attitudes in these young women. Self esteem and hope must be generated; the essentials of life—food, clothing, shelter—must be ensured if we really want to do something about high infant mortality. The community must pitch in.

The Clarion-Ledger
JACKSON
DAILY NEWS

Jackson, MS, March 23, 1988

During the last seven years, Mississippi's infant mortality rate has dropped consistently from a high of 17.6 deaths per 1,000 live births to 12.3 in 1986.

The improvements in the survival rate reflect this state's emphasis on providing care for all infants. For example, the State Department of Health, with the cooperation of the University of Mississippi Medical Center and physicians, have put together a unique system that regionalizes health care for normal, high-risk and critical-care newborns.

Last year the Legislature took a giant leap toward preventive medicine when it passed the Mississippi Health Improvement Plan for Mothers and Children that, among other things, extends Medicaid services to all pregnant women with incomes below the poverty level, instead of the previous limit of 50 percent.

Yet, Mississippi and other states are facing critical shortages of family medicine physicians who will care for expectant mothers and deliver their babies. In addition, some part-time workers and employees of small businesses can't afford quality care because they don't have insurance benefits and cannot qualify for assistance.

Gov. Ray Mabus is testifying today before the U.S. Senate Finance Committee on the efforts being made to reduce the nation's infant mortality rate.

But federal assistance is required. Congress must move on bills currently being considered to make prenatal and perinatal care available to more people.

LOS ANGELES HERALD

Los Angeles, CA, March 25, 1988

If the U.S. rate of 10.6 infant deaths per 1,000 live births had matched the Japanese rate of 5.5 in 1985, 19,000 fewer U.S. babies would have died that year. Compassion alone ought to dictate a change in the government policies that permit this appalling disparity. But the economics of the situation make it doubly hard to understand why it's taking so long to get action.

Inadequate perinatal care is much of the reason the U.S. ranks below 16 other nations in infant mortality. Many poor pregnant women don't visit a doctor until they're in labor. Because poverty often means poor nutrition and poor health habits, their babies are more likely to be premature and weigh less at birth than other women's, or to have other problems contributing to early death. Early diagnoses and therapy as well as counseling can ensure that they bear healthier babies.

Such measures are also highly cost-effective. Including a hospital birth, full perinatal care for a woman from the onset of her pregnancy until 60 days after delivery runs about $1,200. The cost of trying to save a newborn in an intensive care unit can easily hit $30,000 or more.

All pregnant women can't obtain the needed care, however, until some obstacles are cleared. As a recent report by the Southern California Child Health Network points out, clinics are turning away pregnant Medi-Cal patients in droves. Reimbursement rates are so low that many doctors refuse to care for poor women. As a result, California's infant mortality rate has slipped to 17th among the states.

State Assemblyman Burt Margolin, D-Los Angeles, has introduced legislation — AB3646 — that would raise reimbursement rates for deliveries, provide cash incentives to doctors to offer prenatal care, reduce reimbursement red tape and expand an outreach program in counties with high rates of low birthweight babies.

At the federal level, Rep. Henry Waxman, D-Los Angeles, has proposed to revise eligibility and reimbursement rules and force every state to provide at least a minimum level of Medicaid benefits for poor pregnant women and infants.

The long-term results of enacting these proposals are indisputable: Tens of thousands of young lives and hundreds of millions of taxpayer dollars would be saved.

St. Paul Pioneer Press & Dispatch

St. Paul, July 12, 1988

In the Carter presidency, the surgeon general set some sturdy health goals for this nation, to be met in 10 years — by 1990. Of 226 objectives, 13 that were awarded top priority had to do with the well-being of mothers and babies.

How many of those 13 are likely to be met? Three. That disturbing news surfaced last week in a report from the Centers for Disease Control.

What about infant and maternal health in Minnesota? It's somewhat more robust than is the case nationwide. Much of the credit for that belongs to an enlightened Legislature and to vigorous lobbying by organizations like the Children's Defense Fund. But even here, it is not what it could and should be.

What's needed here is wider public awareness of maternal and infant services already available to low-income families. Services like these:

■ Pregnant women and nursing mothers go to the top of the eligibility list in this state's Women and Infant Care nutrition program.

■ Poor families get prenatal care free.

■ The 1988 Legislature passed a law designed to encourage prompt medical attention in every income bracket: No deductibles or co-payments for prenatal care or infant checkups will be allowed on any medical insurance policy issued or renewed in Minnesota after Aug. 1.

Early prenatal care is one key to maternal and infant health. In fact, one national goal says that no more than 10 percent of pregnant women in any racial or ethnic group, no matter how poor the county where they live, should go without prenatal care in the first three months of pregnancy. The Centers for Disease Control predict the percentage for all women will be more than twice that in 1990, with the figure for black women nearly four times as high.

That indicator is not much rosier closer to home. In 1985, the latest year for which statistics are available, 20 percent of expectant moms in Minnesota got no early care; for black moms, it was 39 percent. Those figures are stagnant for whites and worsening for blacks.

Luanne Nyberg, Children's Defense Fund director in this state, described it to us like this: "With as many medical resources as we have, there is no excuse for a state or a country not to meet every single one of the goals for every single mother and child."

Even goals America will meet, or nearly meet, suffer in comparison with other developed countries. For instance, consider the infant mortality rate, or number of babies dying before their first birthday. The U.S. goal is no more than nine per 1,000 live births by 1990. That's already achieved in Minnesota; nationally, a slow but heartening decline will probably brush up close to, but not quite meet, the goal.

Good news? Well, yes. But the rate of infant deaths in Sweden stands at 3.3 per 1,000 right now.

So it can be done. The health goals for American mothers and babies can be met — if not by 1990, then by another date set anew. This nation needs fresh resolve to summon the necessary resources. There is no excuse for babies and mothers who are not as healthy as they might be — or who die — for lack of nourishing food and early medical attention.

Day-Care Needs of the Poor Recognized

Goals of federal social service programs include helping poor families achieve economic self-support, preventing the neglect of children and helping to secure day care. These efforts can, among other things, assist a poor family in providing care for its children. But between 1981 and 1986 government funds available through the 1981 Omnibus Budget Reconciliation Act decreased by 25%. The legislation consolidated federal funding of social services (Title XX of the Social Security Act) into block grants, distributed to states based on population. The service most commonly provided by the legislation was day care.

More than half of all women heads of household with a child under six years old worked in 1987. Affordable, adequate day care is essential for the working poor as it enables a poor mother to work without endangering the health and well-being of her children. Before the 1981 amendments to the Social Security Act, more than one-fifth of total social services funding was allocated to child care. There were also federal standards regulating the operation of social service day-care centers. Currently, the states determine how much of their block grant is allocated to day care and they establish their own standards for these facilities. According to the Children's Defense Fund, in 1981 Title XX served 472,000 of the 3.4 million impoverished children under six years old. By 1988, there were more than five million children in the same age bracket, but there was less money available under Title XX.

Perhaps the most effective child-care and development program for impoverished children is Head Start. The program provides a comprehensive range of services to 452,000 preschool children, and had a price tag of $1.1 billion in fiscal 1986. This approach has been successful in helping children of the poor overcome their background deficiencies. Longitudinal studies have found that Head Start participants are more likely to graduate from high school, enroll in college, and obtain a self-supporting job than nonparticipants with similar backgrounds. For many, the program's success highlights the importance of a nurturing environment for the young and of the federal efforts to assist poor children. As an answer to the day-care problems of the working poor, however, it is limited because its funding is low relative to the potential number of participants. In most cases, Head Start provides care for only four to six hours a day, and thus the children of full-time workers are excluded. The cost per participant would be sharply increased if Head Start served as a provider of child care for impoverished families with full-time working mothers.

The child-care tax credit provides substantial indirect federal funding for child care. In 1986, it amounted to a revenue loss for the U.S. Tresury of an estimated $3.2 billion. Even though the program provides the largest tax credit, 30%, to low-income individuals, the program primarily benefits middle- and upper-income families. This is because the tax credit is of little help to poor parents with limited federal income tax liability who are not able to afford the up-front costs of day care. Day-care experts say that the tax credit would be of greater benefit to the working poor if it were refundable.

Other federal programs, including Aid to Families with Dependent Children and the Work Incentive Program (WIN), also promote and provide child-care funding. Together, however, the wide range of federal programs providing child-care assistance fails to reach many low-wage parents. A woman who works at the minimum wage and earns $7,000 a year can scarcely afford even low-cost day-care. Consequently, poor working mothers are often forced to cope with inadequate care for their young children and many older children return from school to empty homes.

The Des Moines Register

Des Moines, IA, April 13, 1984

Protection of children cared for outside their own homes is an emotional issue, and in the wake of reports of abuse, it is only natural to want to do something to prevent a reoccurrence. No one wants a child to be at risk; but finding the best way to enforce security is difficult.

A bill to do this by tightening registration requirements on family-day-care centers has been on an odyssey through the Legislature this session, and although it has been knocked down several times, it may not yet be out. Despite its recent failure in the Senate, House support may be strong enough to send it to conference committee.

As sincerely well-intentioned as this effort is, it would be best if it were not revived yet again. The reason is that not everything that is worthy is workable.

This bill would require centers caring for six or fewer children to register annually with the state, and therefore be subject to periodic inspections to ascertain whether they meet state standards. Such facilities now have the option of registering, but need not do so.

The intent is to subject them to closer scrutiny; but in effect the bill does little more than add another layer of work to an already overburdened bureaucracy. This would, as one legislator put it, do nothing more than "create a false sense of security."

The well-being of children is important, but this piece of legislation offers little to improve their care. It should be left to fade away.

St. Petersburg Times

St. Petersburg, FL, May 9, 1984

In proper concern over child abuse, which seems to have become epidemic in the United States, the Florida House of Representatives acted this week to stiffen penalties, require criminal background checks on teachers, make child abuse a custody factor in divorce cases and permit victimized children to testify on videotape instead of in open court. But one important bill was missing from the package. The law that provides for state licensing of children's homes expires Oct. 1. If that is allowed to happen, there will be a very serious potential for substandard treatment and outright abuse.

Legislation (HB 1220) to re-enact and improve the law is caught up in a church-state controversy. Some of the 70 group homes to which it would apply operate under the sponsorship of religious denominations that not only accept licensing but are encouraging the Legislature to pass the bill. But the religiously affiliated operators of seven other homes have held out for a weak form of registration that, by some interpretations, could qualify even the most questionable cults to get into the group-home business free of state supervision. For some time, the bill has been pigeonholed in the House Appropriations Committee, whose chairman, Rep. Herb Morgan, D-Tallahassee, sides with the religious resistance.

THE BILL'S sponsors and supporters (including the Florida Group Child Care Association, which represents the homes that want to be licensed), proposed an amendment to insure that the state would have no authority over the religious component of any church-sponsored program. In all other respects, however, the Department of Health and Rehabilitative Services (HRS) would have the same authority to inspect and approve health and safety conditions, budgets, the qualifications of staff and the treatment of the children. But the objectors would not accept this.

Morgan has since drafted an alternative under which the church-sponsored homes, "registered" rather than "licensed," would have to observe all HRS health and safety standards and be subject to inspection at any time. But they would still be exempt from other HRS programmatic and budget reviews. It is not clear, for example, whether the state could say anything about the qualifications and training of their staffs, or prohibit corporal punishment, which would be forbidden at all other group homes. The exemptions would apply to all homes with their own pre-existing statewide accreditation organization and which accept no direct referrals or money from the state.

THAT'S NOT good enough. The appropriate issue is not state support but the protection the state owes all children, wherever they are. Many of the children go to live in group homes because they already are victims of child abuse or neglect. Some are retarded, emotionally disturbed or delinquent. All are vulnerable. They are no less vulnerable because the home happens to be under religious sponsorship.

As America's eyes open to the prevalence of child abuse, one of the facts that becomes clear is that it can be committed by anyone regardless of age, intelligence, reputation or religion. Whether religious or secular, group homes for children must be held to the same rules and regulations, with exceptions allowed only for that to which the First Amendment actually applies — religious instruction and practices. Hospitals that operate under religious auspices do not seek or receive special treatment. Children's homes shouldn't either.

Fort Worth Star-Telegram

Fort Worth, TX, May 15, 1984

We stated last week our reluctant opposition to inclusion on the agenda of the forthcoming special session of the Legislature the request for additional funding by the Department of Human Resources. There is no question that more money is needed for the department's programs, but we feel the special session should concentrate on finding funds for shoring up the state's schools and highways.

In all, the DHR wants four items added to the agenda. The first three, dealing with welfare matters, should be considered together when the time is more propitious. But the fourth item, by itself, deserves far more study than lawmakers would be able to devote to it in the brief time allotted to them this summer.

That is a request for $2.2 million to permit the department to increase its staff for the licensing of day care facilities and the inspection of family day care homes. There can be no doubt as to the importance of this matter. Both members of more and more families are being required, or in many cases prefer, to work outside the home, meaning that more and more children must be cared for elsewhere.

Few jobs will have more impact on the future psychological health of this country's citizens than those carried out by day care center employees. Recent revelations of widespread instances of physical and sexual abuse of children entrusted to such centers emphasize how vital careful regulation of the industry is.

One vital question the Legislature needs to study is this: Is the Department of Human Resources the proper agency to operate the regulatory machinery? The DHR does a good job in fulfilling its primary function, which is providing assistance to needy families with dependent children and overseeing the Medicaid program for low-income groups. But should the department's limited physical and financial resources continue to be devoted to performing a clearly regulatory function?

The protection of children who are cared for outside the home is a matter of utmost importance. Stringent controls must be exercised over facilities in which such children are cared for. While large day care facilities are inspected as a prelude to the granting of a license, private homes that provide care aren't. They must register with the DHR, but there are no provisions for state inspection.

The major reason for that, of course, is a lack of money and personnel to do the job. As day care needs continue to expand, so, too, will grow the problems inherent in non-regulated facilities.

Perhaps the time has come to form a separate agency to deal specifically with day care centers of all sizes and descriptions. The Legislature, in its next regular session, should explore that possibility thoroughly.

The Oregonian

Portland, OR, March 3, 1984

The relationship between reliable child care and employment opportunities is a bit like the weather. Everybody, it seems, from Congress on down to local community groups has been talking about it for years. Now Portland may be on the verge of doing something about it as a matter of good business.

Executives of many Portland-area corporations are reviewing the results of a study conducted by the Child Care Coordinating Council and the Regional Research Institute for Human Services of Portland State University. The goal is a communitywide referral system accommodating parents needing the service, child care providers wanting clients and employers seeking a stable work force. It is the type of arrangment that the City Club of Portland concluded a year ago was needed here.

Should the companies decide to fund the central referral service as a legitimate cost of doing business, they will create a national model that other cities may copy.

The study found a direct connection between suitable child care and worker productivity. About one-third of Portland's work force needs a place to leave children while parents are on the job. Change is so frequent that about two-thirds of this number will be shopping for care in the course of a year.

While there are many care centers, at least 1,400 inventoried so far, child care is largely a disorganized industry, with about 80 percent of the listings in private homes.

The lack of dependable means of putting parent and provider together, according to the study, is a major cause of absenteeism from the job and a principal factor in employee stress. That is why business executives are contemplating financing the referral service.

The service would have nothing to do with paying for the costs of child care, which would remain a parental expense and certainly a separate problem, for the study also found that affordable care ranked with reliable care among employee concerns.

But establishing a central place where providers can list their services and parents can seek care for their youngsters has merit, especially if it comes with professional screening of facilities and counseling for the workers. It may indeed be a standard service in future employee benefits package in a society of working parents. And it may be closer to happening right here than anywhere else across the country.

The Boston Herald

Boston, MA, October 7, 1984

WE READ shocking tales of child abuse in day care centers, of baby sitters clearly ill equipped to care for the children in their charge and the often tragic results, and of the so-called latchkey kids coming home to empty houses and too often to trouble.

We read about them. We are often shocked and disturbed, but we feel so helpless. Clearly as a society we have not been able to accommodate the needs of the rising number of mothers who through choice or economic necessity work outside the home. A recent study showed that 45 percent of mothers with children under the age of one year are in that category now. And the result has been a hodge-podge of caretakers — ranging from the superb to the dismal — for the children left behind.

Last week the Select Committee on Children, Youth and Families issued its report, the most comprehensive such study by Congress in more than a decade. And with it came a blueprint for addressing the pressing needs of working families and their children.

U.S. Rep. Dan Mariott, R-Utah, who described himself as "about as conservative as you can get," said, "We ought not to sit around scrutinizing why women work and recognize that they do. Good day care in our society is absolutely necessary."

He pointed out that the $500 personal tax exemption to child care passed in 1952 and since increased to $1,000, should be $5,600 now just to keep up with inflation.

That's the kind of concrete proposal that can help make a dent in the child care problem. If parents can afford to spend more on child care, they have at least a shot at finding decent care.

With that carrot also comes the stick of stricter regulation and licensing standards for all out-of-home child care.

The report also recommends tax incentives for employers who help provide day care for their employees, including on or off-site facilities or referral services.

And the committee wants to see schools providing more supervised after-school activities for latchkey kids.

The recommendations are barely the start of a process aimed at addressing a problem too long neglected.

But what, after all, is more important than the welfare of this nation's children?

The Virginian-Pilot

Norfolk, VA, September 13, 1984

Day care for children has become a hot public-policy issue. More young mothers are working, and demand for day-care services has risen considerably. Unfortunately, the supply of day-care facilities cannot meet the demand, and quality is uneven among the day-care centers that exist. In a few sad cases, child molesters have been hired by marginal mom-and-pop day-care centers, and nasty scandals have resulted.

Naturally, there is a bias in Congress and among advocacy groups toward government-centered solutions. Bills are circulating on Capitol Hill to beef up spending on day care for low-income families and to impose tough, national day-care standards.

But the answer to day care's problems isn't likely to be found in more government. The federal goverment already spends around a half-billion dollars through Title XX to subsidize day care for around 600,000 low- and moderate-income families. It also provides food assistance to day-care centers and family day-care homes serving nearly a million children. Obviously, the deficit-ridden federal budget can't easily accommodate the scope of service that has been envisioned by the most ardent day-care advocates.

Back in the early 1970s, Congressional Democrats unsuccessfully pushed day-care bills priced at $2 billion. There was talk of building a $10 billion program of centers by 1980. Conservatives managed to prevent this from happening, but the debate has been renewed by today's demographic picture — Baby Boomers are having children.

The federal government can expand its role modestly, perhaps creating child-care information centers so parents will know what is available in their communities. Also, tax policies can be modified to encourage more employers to furnish day-care assistance — either on site or through payments to workers — and tax credits can be increased for family day-care costs.

But the real responsibility lies not with the federal government. State and local governments, the private business sector, and parents should play the greatest roles.

● Although funds are scarce, state and local regulators — in health, welfare and law enforcement — must determine that day-care centers and home child-care operators are complying with health, fire safety and hiring standards. Unfortunately, recent press accounts suggest that although many of the nation's estimated 30,750 day-care centers and child-care homes comply with state and local regulations, thousands do not. If state and local health and welfare officials pay little attention to the quality of day care, federal regulators will eventually gain the political backing of Congress to move in.

● Parents should not leave it up to government to certify the quality or safety of a care provider. Parents must investigate beforehand, then ask the child about what he or she does at the center after enrolling the youngsters.

● American business has a vested interest in a stable work force with low absenteeism and low turnover. And the provision of day-care assistance is proving to be a boon to employee satisfaction. For example, one Texas corporation — Intermedics — is subsidizing a low-fee day-care center for its employees serving nearly 300 children. Intermedics says it has saved $2 million in reduced turnover costs since opening the center in 1979.

In some cases, small firms have pooled together to form day-care centers. Other firms have offered to help with outside day-care costs as one option in fringe-benefit plans. Ideally, companies could contract with providers to furnish day care for employees' children. This would build in pressure on these day-care operators to maintain quality service or risk losing a lucrative deal. Eventually, more and more businesses will come to view day care as a recruiting tool to attract motivated, bright, productive and loyal workers and not as a drain on company earnings.

Let's give the private sector, parents and local governments a chance to respond before we make federal government an expensive nanny of the first resort.

The News American

Baltimore, MD, February 16, 1984

The decision to slam the doors of state-subsidized day-care centers to any more working parents looking for a safe place for their kids is particularly disturbing. The Department of Human Resources has ordered the freeze, and calls it "indefinite." The decision is especially hard on Baltimore, where the demand for day care is high, and going up.

Why the freeze? Without it, says the state, the day-care programs in the city and six of the counties will be in the red by June 30, the end of the current fiscal year. With more than four months left, some jurisdictions have all but exhausted their funds.

Of course it is in the interest of the state to try to avoid ending the fiscal year over budget. But that does not make the situation any less unfortunate and the solution any less unsatisfactory.

The city and those counties are running out of day-care money because the demand is going up, and the reason is ironic: Most of the parents who depend upon day-care are just getting back into the work force because of the turnaround in the economy.

The effect of the freeze is to shut the door to needed day care in the face of Marylanders who a little more than a year ago were shut out of the work place. Surely there is a solution, and we urge state Department of Human Resource officials to search harder for it. Balancing the budget on the backs of small children and their already put-upon parents hardly makes sense.

The Atlanta Journal
THE ATLANTA CONSTITUTION
Atlanta, GA, October 10, 1984

It has been more than 30 years since a startled Congress, responding to findings that all working moms had *not* quit their jobs in droves when hubby came marching home from World War II, set up a $500 personal tax exemption to help them pay for child care. Twenty percent of the mothers of preschool children held jobs outside their homes; the need was obvious.

Since then, the work force and the "typical" family have changed beyond recognition — to the point that 60 percent of the mothers work; fully 45 percent return to work before their children are even a year old.

Congress has been slow to grapple with those changes, as a House committee observed last week in a report urging major increases in federal tax breaks for child care, incentives for schools and employers that provide it, and matching funds for child-care research and referral.

Just to keep up with inflation, the $500 tax exemption established by Congress in 1952 would have to be $5,600 now. It's currently $1,000.

The demand for low-cost child care has never been greater; there are 6 million child-care slots, most of them in friends' or relatives' homes rather than day-care centers, to accommodate an estimated 13 million eligible kids — leaving some 7 million to fend for themselves for several hours each day.

And, officials say, the lack of affordable child care has become the major factor in the joblessness of welfare mothers; they frequently come out better by staying home and collecting public assistance than by paying someone else to look after their kids while they work.

Whether the government ought to be involved in child care is moot, and has been since 1952. It *is* involved, as a matter of necessity and public policy, at no-longer-adequate levels.

It will cost more at the outset to provide tax credits for employers and federal incentives to schools that set up on-site day-care facilities, and increased tax breaks to parents to help defray the cost, as the committee proposes. But those outlays would certainly be offset by decreases in government subsidies, such as welfare.

It's high time the tax laws were revised to ensure that families raising children aren't penalized for choosing day-care over welfare. The House committee's report sets out a necessary agenda. It would be a costly program, at a time when few such can be funded, but decency and common sense require that a strong beginning be made on it.

FORT WORTH STAR-TELEGRAM
Fort Worth, TX, September 2, 1984

Shocking incidents occurring at child-care centers in various parts of the country, including the Fort Worth-Dallas area, have awakened public concern and spurred calls for stricter government regulation of such centers.

People throughout the nation were stunned by accusations of long-term sexual abuse of children enrolled in a California day-care center. Closer to home, of course, an infant was kidnapped from a Grand Prairie care center by a woman claiming to be the child's aunt. The child was found abandoned but unharmed four days later, which provided a happy ending for the story. But it was something that never should have been allowed to happen.

The Grand Prairie case provided the impetus for the move toward dramatic changes in child-care regulations in Texas. First, Grand Prairie, itself, approved strict regulations. Currently, the Department of Human Resources is conducting meetings throughout the state to solicit public comment on proposed changes that would make the state code far stricter than it is now.

No one can argue with the sentiment that stricter controls are necessary to ensure that children enrolled in day-care facilities are safe from harm and abuse. But in implementing new controls, great care must be exercised to prevent creating problems that could be as serious as those already in existence.

Some of the proposed changes could increase the cost of child care considerably. For example, the new regulations would lower the permissible staff-child ratio, meaning that more staff members would have to be hired by many centers. New safety standards also would require:

● Smoke detectors in all centers and licensed homes in which children are cared for.

● Presence "at all times" of a staff member trained in cardiopulmonary resuscitation.

● Installation of resilient surfaces such as sand or rubber beneath swings and other playground equipment.

● Greatly increased record-keeping, designed to prevent unauthorized people from taking children from care centers.

All of the proposed changes are commendable, but caution must be taken that their implementation doesn't drive the cost of child care past the level young parents can afford. If that happens, many couples will be faced with an unpleasant choice — one of them would have to quit work, which would further complicate their budgetary problems, or they would have to entrust their children to an unlicensed caretaker.

Strict regulation of child-care centers is a must, but common sense must be brought into play, also. And parents are going to have to be extremely selective in choosing a center. For the safety of their children is the most important responsibility with which they have been entrusted.

THE KANSAS CITY STAR
Kansas City, September 4, 1984

Statistics are always behind the facts, perhaps that's one reason children with working parents are increasingly getting attention.

They're in the spotlight now in Kansas City and around the country. Children alone, before and after school and at other times while parents are on the job, naturally draw a community's sympathy. So should parents, caught between the high cost of child care, the often impossible task of finding reliable caretakers and the demands of a career.

An estimated 6.5 million U.S. children are left alone or with slightly older brothers or sisters. With the number of working women with school-age children growing steadily, the number can only increase in the future.

Now as schools open, concentrated efforts to aid families are being made here. The Living Center, a division of Family and Children Services of Kansas City, offers several programs through its School Age Child Care Project. A major thrust has been its development of model after-school day care programs. Ten are located in non-profit agencies throughout the metropolitan area, including several at YWCA facilities and others in suburban schools.

The project is acting as a central information source about these and other alternatives parents might try. It is the administrator for PhoneFriend, a telephone reassurance line for children alone at home in Kansas City, which joins at least 200 other cities with such a service.

As long ago as 1980, the Working Parents Project put the number of latchkey children here at 80,000. Their needs are not being ignored. But as the number increases, it is evident that resources are inadequate. It is to be hoped the focus on this problem, now as the schools open, will generate concern that endures the rest of the year and into the next.

The Record

Hackensack, NJ,

August 5, 1985

Getting a job is hard enough for many women, but working mothers have an extra burden. They must find day care that is safe, accessible, and affordable. The number of women entering the work force has risen steadily in the past two decades; but child-care facilities are scarcer than ever in relation to the demand for them. As The Record's Elli Light reported last week, Bergen and Passaic counties suffer from an acute shortage of centers and day-care workers, and the cost of care is prohibitive for poor and middle-income families.

The day-care dilemma demonstrates that, at least where families are concerned, public policy has not caught up with changing reality. In the typical family of two or three decades ago, dad was the breadwinner and mom stayed home to mind the kids. Today the picture is very different. One in two marriages ends in divorce; the percentage of families headed by one parent has tripled. Increased educational opportunities have encouraged women to take jobs and careers previously left to men.

One thing that hasn't changed, of course, is that people continue to have children. Some 7 million children are in formal day care, including after-school programs and nursery schools. But many others pay a heavy price for parental employment. Five million youngsters — 10 percent of them preschoolers — have no one watching them once school is out. These "latchkey" children are often lonely and prone to mischief, or become candidates for kidnapping and abuse. Millions more, particularly children from poor families, are cared for in unlicensed, often substandard facilities.

The scarcity of day-care centers and people to run them has driven up the cost of care. It isn't uncommon for a single mother to spend nearly half her income on day care. Small wonder many find that it's cheaper to stay home and collect unemployment or welfare benefits.

A society that values both initiative and children cannot sacrifice one for the other. But the United States, unlike most other industrialized democracies, has no comprehensive national commitment to child care. (Sweden, to cite one example, provides free supervision for every child beginning at 6 months.) Federal day-care subsidies have been paltry, and efforts to encourage more private centers have been half-hearted.

The Reagan administration has steadily made a bad situation worse. Day-care subsidies have declined 21 percent annually since 1981. This year the president proposed to cut nearly the entire budget. It is a penny-wise, pound-foolish policy. Mr. Reagan says that our nation's strength lies in strong and stable families. He won't help build them by making working parents choose between unemployment and unsupervised children.

The Louisville Times

Louisville, KY, April 2, 1985

"We fear for our children, for we find ourselves fixed upon a course that is leading Kentucky to an inevitable rendezvous with disaster. The gradual decay in the services provided our troubled children is eroding the social fabric of this state. No community of people can hope to prosper that so flagrantly neglects the needs of its youth."

That is the chilling preface to the thoughtful report — released last week — of the Governor's Protective Services Advisory Committee, a panel appointed to seek ways to improve services for that group least able to protect itself.

As so graphically pointed out last year by the case of Eugene D., the 17-pound nine-year-old who had been neglected by his foster parent, and by the disclosure of sexual abuse of children in Henry and Bullitt County foster homes, the current system hasn't been working, with sometimes shocking results.

The committee, whose chairman was Lt. Gov. Steve Beshear, noted that since 1980 Kentucky's Department for Social Services has lost more than $18 million as a result of state and federal budget cuts. One hundred forty-one social work positions and 152 paraprofessional jobs have been abolished during a time when reports of child neglect and abuse more than doubled.

The report emphasizes the need for more, better-trained social workers. Not only are they needed properly to monitor foster homes but also to intervene with counseling and other support services in order to prevent abuse and to keep families intact where possible. Most experts, the report notes, think it is usually best for all involved if foster care is considered only as a last resort. Not only is it more expensive in dollars and cents, but it rarely provides the stability needed if a child is to become a fully functioning contributor to society.

The committee concluded that an average caseload of 47 per social worker is too high if quality service is to be provided. Therefore, all of its other recommendations for improvements in services center on the hiring of staff — first to meet "the short-term critical need" and, second, to lower caseloads to a more manageable 25. Other recommendations include requiring that new social workers be licensed, improved department-run training programs, implementation of a "career ladder" for social workers and certain management improvements.

The committee's report is not a pie-in-the-sky dream list, but a careful analysis of how the state can meet its obligation to protect and serve children. Mr. Beshear noted a close connection between his committee's work and the push for educational reform. He's right; both are vital to the state's future and deserve the support of the public, as well as of elected officials.

Implementing the proposals would cost the state a relatively modest $20 million a year. It's up to Governor Collins to follow through by seeing that the necessary bureaucratic changes are made and prodding legislators to come up with the funding.

LOS ANGELES HERALD

Los Angeles, CA, March 24, 1985

Women are now an established part of the work force. There's also a small baby boom under way. The result: Daytime child care is no longer necessarily provided by the mother, in the home.

But finding good alternatives is tremendously difficult for too many parents. With the current child-abuse epidemic, parents are thinking twice about entrusting children to private day care. When they do, they often find it too expensive or too far away

Help is on the way. Corporate leaders have been aware and concerned that workers are less productive when child-care problems preoccupy them. United Way and the White House's Office on Private Sector Initiative have been urging executives to join the public sector in finding new ways to provide good, accessible day care. Now, the first, wonderful flowers of these efforts are blooming in California.

Union Bank will build a child-care center on the first floor of its new building in Monterey Park. Several other corporations are joining with the state to provide $400,000 to six agencies that refer parents to child-care centers and train new child-care providers for certification. Meanwhile, a Burbank hospital, the city of Burbank and six local firms are jointly financing a day-care center in an old school building.

Businesses need not build their own centers, however. They might help finance existing centers, in return for which places would be reserved for the employees' children. Or they might provide information and referral services to help employees locate suitable facilities. Or various kinds of joint efforts, like the one in Burbank, might be tried.

A United Way survey last year indicated that L.A. parents, unlike those in other major cities, are willing to bring their small children downtown for day care. Good. We think downtown *should* be a place where forward-looking corporations provide day-care facilities that could be models for the rest of the nation. And we are pleased to note that many firms already recognize and are doing something about the need of both men and women to be able to work *and* raise happy, healthy children.

Pittsburgh Post-Gazette

Pittsburgh, PA, March 19, 1985

The importance of child day-care services in the 1980s is demonstrated by state Auditor General Don Bailey's proposal that state agencies be allowed to offer on-site day-care services to their employees.

Mr. Bailey's request for legislation to accomplish that objective follows Lt. Gov. William Scranton's plea in January that employers become more active in providing and promoting "quality day care." Like Mr. Bailey, the lieutenant governor argued that quality day-care services promote both productivity and family values. And on April 9 the Human Resources Committee of the National Governors' Association is sponsoring a conference to highlight ways government and business can work together to provide day care for children. New Jersey Gov. Thomas H. Kean is chairman.

In announcing the conference, Gov. Kean noted that today 52 percent of the nation's children under 6 have working mothers, and 44.5 million children under 14 have mothers in the workforce. The demand for day care, he said, is becoming comparable to the demand for education and medical care.

Gov. Kean said the states are working to meet four goals: to make day care more available at a cost affordable to businesses, non-profit organizations and government, as well as families; to determine how properly to license and regulate day care; to relate day care with educational systems; and to recognize that any opportunity to break the welfare cycle depends on day care.

His own state of New Jersey has been sponsoring experimental day-care projects, such as a voucher program to reduce child-care costs and to enable clients to place children in facilities near their homes. Another program provides technical assistance to businesses wanting to offer day care for employees. Since 1982, the number of firms participating in the New Jersey program has increased fourfold.

Working mothers always have had difficulty squaring their work roles with providing care for their children. In the past, there often were grandmothers or aunts or non-employed neighbors with whom a child could be left. But in today's mobile society, in which so many more women are working in paying jobs, the situation has changed. And the cutback in federal subsidies for day-care facilities has made the service less affordable for many women.

That seems to be the situation in Pittsburgh, according to Nancy Brown, director of the Child Care Hotline Project. With 400 day-care homes (smaller, state-licensed but self-certified facilities) and 180 day-care centers (larger, state-licensed and inspected operations), there are enough facilities. The problem is that many people can't afford the fees, which range from $35-$90 a week. There is a state-subsidy program for certain categories of low-income people, but far from enough slots, so that by the time some mothers work their way up on the waiting list, their children have outgrown the need.

Only Mercy Hospital and the campuses of Community College of Allegheny County have day-care centers exclusively for their own employees. The University of Pittsburgh, Carnegie-Mellon University, Chatham College and Magee and Presbyterian hospitals have free-standing child-care facilities available for the general public as well as employees.

Mellon Bank has a "cafeteria plan" under which employees can take some of their pre-tax benefits in the form of subsidies for child-care services at whatever location they choose. Bell of Pennsylvania and IBM offer information and referral services to help their employees obtain day-care services, either near home or near the office, and a number of other local firms are investigating various options.

Ms. Brown said this particular development — employer support — is vital. Obviously, there will have to be a considerable sorting-out of exactly how day-care services are to be provided for working mothers and who will pay for them. Hence the significance of the initiatives by Messrs. Bailey and Scranton, the National Governors' Association and numerous Pittsburgh businesses and institutions.

THE SAGINAW NEWS

Saginaw, MI, Sept 22, 1985

When Saginaw Board of Education members argued the merits of extended day programs for "latchkey kids," the discussion was identical to debates that have raged across the country.

Ruth A. Braun, board vice president, said school systems should not "babysit" youngsters whose parents work before or after regular school hours.

The board majority, led by Ruben Daniels, said the district should get involved and do something about the problem. The result is a pair of pilot programs at Handley Elementary (before school) and Morley Elementary (after school).

Parents pay $1.25 an hour for the service. School officials say the fees cover the entire program cost.

"I don't see how the program could cost the taxpayers anything," said Donald R. Scott, assistant superintendent and organizer of the program.

If that's the situation, who could object? Braun does, noting that taxpayers funded the salaries of administrators who planned the program. That criticism seems petty, considering that Scott's assignment is an addition to his other duties, but Braun obviously has strong feelings.

We support the concept of fee-supported latchkey services, and we hope the school board moves quickly to expand the program to other elementary schools.

But we anticipate more local debates, and similar discussions are occurring elsewhere, according to a recent New York Times article. Some selected quotes:

• "I think it is a marvelous investment, being applied in a way which will allow us to reconsider schools and how they are used," said Nathan Quinones, chancellor of New York public schools, after the Board of Education approved $5.6 million to cover the maintenance cost of keeping schools open after regular hours.

• "Somebody has to assume this responsibility, but it shouldn't be the local taxpayer. This is an auxiliary service required by a small group of parents," said Mary e Fitzgerald, superintendent of schools in Montclair, N.J.

• "Latchkey programs won't go very far unless the state and federal governments give them some operating money," said Alfred J. Kahn, a Columbia University professor of social policy.

• "What happened to the poor kids? They're gone. The poor are getting killed," said Paul Boranian, a Minneapolis school administrator, after the district lost government subsidies for latchkey programs.

• "The non-profit organizations have to sit down with school districts and local governments to work out innovative solutions. There is no institution, organization or government unit that is going to solve the problems of latchkey kids by itself," said Stephen M. Delfin, a national United Way vice president.

The article shows that latchkey programs in most larger cities, unlike Saginaw, are not supported solely by parents' fees.

That's a point in Saginaw's favor, and that's why Braun should soften her criticism.

We oppose taxpayer funding of extended day services. Working parents, even those earning the minimum wage, should be able to afford a small fee. Saginaw's program, so far, is operating properly under that philosophy.

AKRON BEACON JOURNAL
Akron, OH, July 11, 1988

IN CONGRESS, the debate over whether the federal government should spend money on child-care programs seems virtually over. Enough conservatives and liberals agree the answer is yes. Now, the question is how much to spend and what to spend it on. As it appears, even that issue may be resolved soon.

In both the House and Senate, the Act for Better Child Care Services is on a fast track. It could become law by the end of this year.

For the most part, the bill is well-conceived. Most of the proposed $2.5 billion in funding would be for free or reduced-priced day care for low-income families. Single mothers have the most to gain. Often, they are forced to choose welfare over a job, because they cannot afford day care. This bill would make employment more feasible.

Further, the bill would require minimum health and safety standards to be met over five years by all day-care providers receiving federal reimbursements. The hope is that children would not just have a place to stay; rather, that they would be given adequate care, also.

Unfortunately, the Act for Better Child Care also has a salient flaw. It is that day-care subsidies would not be limited strictly to the poor. Middle-income families, making as much as $33,900 a year, could be eligible for subsidies, too. The bill specifies that the first priority be lower-income families. But that is not enough. There should be a cap on the family income allowed for eligibility.

Why should a taxpayer making $20,000 a year be asked to subsidize day care for someone else making $30,000 a year? Congress should amend the bill before passing it.

To be sure, there are other ways government can and should help all families using day-care programs. For example, minimum standards should be set for all day-care providers. And at the state level, there should be rigid licensing requirements.

It also should be remembered that day care is not only an issue for government. Employers have a stake as well, since workers are likely to be more productive when they are at ease about their child care.

Some employers already provide on-site day-care centers, or flexible benefits packages, allowing employees to forgo certain fringes and apply the savings to day care. Unfortunately, many more employers are far behind Congress, and are not even debating whether to do anything at all.

Herald American SYRACUSE

Syracuse, NY, February 14, 1988

"Who will take care of the children." 1988 is the year, obviously, in which we will earnestly seek to answer that question.

By now, most people — parents, child care workers, politicians — realize that caring for children no longer can be a low priority on the national agenda, and that the realities of American society indicate the issue is here to stay.

Those realities say that most women either do not want to or cannot afford to stay at home full-time to care for their children, that there are more female-headed households than at any other time in our history.

Since the majority of women in America work, their children must be cared for by someone else. But there are far more children than child care providers or slots in child care centers. There are less than 135,000 spaces in certified care centers in New York state — nowhere near the number necessary for the estimated 1 million children in need of care. Many parents are forced to leave their children in "underground" care areas, which have not been licensed by the government and may not meet safety requirements.

Child care advocates predict a further decline in the number of spots for children because child care centers cannot afford to pay their employees competitive salaries. And, even the least expensive child care program may be too costly for the low-income worker. Consequently, some of them may end up or remain on welfare, particularly teen-age parents, because they can't find or pay for child care services.

Government officials and lawmakers at every level agree something must be done.

The House Subcommittee on Elementary, Secondary and Vocational Education has introduced a bill to provide states with day care money that would be given to parents in the form of grants.

In his proposed 1988-89 budget, the governor is asking that $50 million be committed to day care projects. Low-income families and teen-age parents are the target groups for state assistance, in addition to child care providers who begin new centers with services geared toward low income families.

Last week, Mayor Young, in his state of the city address, named day care among his top priorities for the year, and said the city would create space for 100 children, many of them disadvantaged. And, two weeks ago, 1,500 child care advocates from around the state went to Albany for a rally to solicit state aid for child care programs, particularly money to increase the salaries of day care teachers.

Certainly, the time has come for parents, child care groups, state and federal government and private industry to join forces. Yet, it is essential the potential for conflicts that thwart these positive efforts be minimized.

For example, state Sen. Tarky Lombardi, R-Syracuse, and Gov. Cuomo are proponents of state aid for child care programs. Yet, they are already divided on a major issue involving state funds. The governor wants to spend $25 million for existing and new pre-K programs. Lombardi wants to take $12 million of that money and use it to improve day care salaries.

There are basic questions that must be answered as the state moves toward more subsidies of child care programs.

Is the state moving toward operating its own child care facilities?

Must all child care programs and child care providers meet certain education requirements? For example, should only certified teachers be allowed to work at day care centers?

Are early childhood educational programs being substituted for regular day care programs in the theory that every child needs pre-K to avoid problems in later life?

Should welfare mothers be utilized to care for other welfare mothers' children, something the governor endorses?

Will the state require licenses for every child care provider? Will the state subsidize only non-profit day care centers?

Why are day care centers so costly to operate that many can only afford to pay teachers little more than minimum wage?

Something must be done about child care. But, before the crowd goes off in every direction to address the needs, they should make sure they know exactly where they're going, or at the very least, have a plan on how to get there.

Richmond Times-Dispatch

Richmond, VA, March 7, 1988

Del. C. Richard Cranwell, among other of the all-lawyer, all-male members of the House Courts of Justice Committee, opposes the proposed legislation that would permit immediate payroll deduction of child support payments. He dislikes proponents' wrapping themselves in "holy cloth" by suggesting it would help take care of children. But an argument the Roanoke County Democrat made against the legislation in a hearing Thursday is, instead, one of the best arguments for it.

"The truth of the matter is," he asserted, that immediate withholding "would improve statistics" cn child support collection.

Well, let's hope so.

Because if the statistics improve, that will mean the incidence of child support payments *by*

parents who are least meeting their obligations now must have improved.

Because if the statistics improve, that will mean it is taking months fewer than the 160 days it can now take to get a non-paying parent paying; and that will mean fewer families doing without, or moving on and off welfare, for lack of dependable child support.

Because unless the statistics improve, Virginia will lose millions in federal welfare aid.

Because until enforcement improves, Virginia will continue to send a message that maddens the commonwealth's majority of responsible parents and misleads those hundreds of thousands for whom child support isn't a priority: that problems created by their erratic or non-payment are somebody else's to solve.

Detroit Free Press

Detroit, MI, April 16, 1988

AN EXPANDED federal role in providing affordable, quality day care is an idea whose time has finally come. The surge of interest on Capitol Hill would appear to be roughly in proportion to the increase in the number of working mothers (and fathers with sole child-care responsibility) — and that is as it should be.

Judging from the sponsorship of bills now pending in Congress, day care — like welfare reform — has become an issue for lawmakers who span the political spectrum. Sen. Edward Kennedy, D-Mass., for example, is advocating a plan to encourage the states to make pre-school education and day care available to all four-year-olds. Meanwhile, even conservative Sen. Orrin Hatch, R-Utah, has gotten in on the act with his sponsorship of legislation to provide $300 million a year to expand day-care programs, give tax breaks to companies that provide child care for employes, and set up insurance pools to lower liability costs for day-care centers.

There is no question of the need for expanded services: In 1979 there were 7.2 million children younger than six with mothers in the labor force; in 1985 there were 9.6 million. By 1995, the number is expected to rise to 15 million. Moreover, the typical cost of full-time child care is $3,000 for one child, or one-third of the poverty level for a family of three. And research has shown that lack of child care is a key barrier to employment for many welfare mothers.

Several dozen day-care bills have been introduced in this session of Congress. Attracting much attention is the bill co-sponsored by Sen. Christopher Dodd, D-Conn., and Rep. Dale Kildee, D-Mich. Called the ABC bill (the Act for Better Child Care Services), it earmarks $2.5 billion for grants to states for expanded child-care services to families earning up to 115 percent of median income. It would also provide funds for training of day-care workers and for referral services, and would establish federal standards for child care.

The act would represent the first major child-care initiative since 1971 when President Nixon vetoed then Sen. Walter Mondale's bill to create a national day-care system. At the time, the president said it would be a mistake "to commit the vast moral authority of the national government to the side of communal approaches to child rearing," rather than to the family-centered approach.

We've come a long way since then. Proponents express optimism that with more than 150 co-sponsors, the ABC bill's chances for passage in some form are good. That, too, is as it should be.

ST. LOUIS POST-DISPATCH

St. Louis, MO, May 4, 1988

Phyllis Schlafly, the ultra-conservative activist from Alton, has warned that the Dodd day-care bill would "Sovietize the American family." Shrill language, indeed, and way off the mark.

Neither the measure sponsored by Sen. Christopher Dodd, a Democrat from Connecticut, nor its many variants also before Congress, aim to put government in the business of running child care, as Mrs. Schlafly asserts when comparing the proposals to day-care as run by the Soviet state. Their principal purpose is to provide financial assistance for facilities and personnel training in centers licensed by the states.

The licensing provisions are to protect the health and safety of the children, a necessity where large numbers are cared for in a group. There is nothing in the Dodd bill that would impose controls on the nature of the care offered.

To be sure, parents who elect other forms of day care — through a family member, friend, neighbor or through other informal arrangement involving only a few other children — wouldn't be helped by government assistance.

But many mothers who must work don't have these options, particularly those heading low-income and single-parent families. It is unreasonable to deny them the benefit of safe and healthy institutional settings for their children because a much smaller number, who can make arrangements of their own, won't be beneficiaries under a government aid program.

Mrs. Schlafly's argument that licensing requirements for day-care facilities and the principle of separation of church and state will discriminate against church-run day-care centers is as false as her claims of Sovietization of the American family. There is no reason church-run centers couldn't meet minimum health and safety standards and no case for excusing them from doing so. The community's responsibility for its children's physical safety is paramount. And providing money to train day-care providers hardly discriminates against religious institutions, which would be as free to hire them as secular day-care centers would be.

Mrs. Schlafly's greatest complaint is that assisting those in need of day care at a price the majority can afford "discriminates against mothers who take care of their own children ... and favors those who don't." This is the speciously egalitarian argument that either everyone should be helped or no one should be. This is the old chestnut used by those who simply seek to stop aid in the first place.

Besides, most women with small children work because they must. Staying home, thereby relieving themselves of the need to pay for day care, doesn't put them ahead, but leaves them less well off. Government, in aiding the development and staffing of day-care establishments, isn't encouraging women to park their children outside the home. It is simply making it safer to do what they must to make ends meet.

The Wichita Eagle-Beacon

Wichita, KS, June 20, 1988

SEN. Bob Dole is responding to a problem that affects the country's most important asset — its children. The Census Bureau reported that in 1987, 50.8 percent of mothers, within a year of giving birth, were continuing in the job market. In 1976, 31 percent of the new mothers remained in their jobs. Mr. Dole has been receptive to these changing figures, and has introduced the Federal Child Care and Child Development Act of 1988. Child care is a sensitive issue for many mothers, and especially for mothers from low and moderate income families.

Mr. Dole's bill should help these mothers with their child care problems. Grants would be provided to states that could allow for seed money. The child care initiative would fund "neighborhood child-centers and after-school child-care programs." It would provide responsible care for children of families that are struggling with the question of insufficient nurturing and unaffordable child care. The investment in available child-care is an investment in creating a strong family.

Within the Dole initiative, day-care services could be provided in small businesses with the aid of seed money. Grants also could be used to recruit and train day care employees. The bill is designed to look toward employment needs of senior citizens and disabled citizens as employees in the day care industry. These children in need of child care one day will decide this nation's future. Their care should be the concern of all citizens.

The Dole child-care initiative would be funded by phasing out "the dependent care tax credit for upper-income families." The bill wouldn't add to the budget deficit. It is an opportunity to help many mothers improve the lives of their children. Its passage should have a high priority. Our children deserve a more secure future.

Sunday News Journal

Wilmington, DE, March 27, 1988

UNTIL RECENTLY day care was a bleeding-heart type issue, promoted by women's organizations and social workers. But in the last year or two, it has become respectable for business leaders and conservative politicians to call for more and better day-care programs for children.

A few months ago, William C. Wyer, president of the Delaware State Chamber of Commerce, cited day care as one of the necessary components for continued economic growth. Day-care centers are no longer being relegated to church basements; some major new office buildings now include space to rent out to day-care operators. And now Sen. William V. Roth Jr., a Republican best known for his concern over waste in government, has picked up the gauntlet on the need for funding day-care programs.

In mid-March, the senator introduced his Child Care Development Act of 1988. Under this proposal, the federal government would in the next three years spend a little over $1 billion to help with the establishment and operation of day-care programs.

To ensure flexibility and innovation, the money would be distributed as grants and loans through the states. Only a few criteria would have to be met to qualify for the federal dollars: accreditation standards for the centers; at least 25 percent of the clientele would have to be from low-income families; coordination with other day-care programs to avoid duplication.

Those are good rules, not difficult to meet.

An innovative feature in the Roth legislation is its mechanism for attracting day-care workers. For persons over age 62 and on Social Security, their child-care income would be exempt from the normal earnings test and these folks would not lose any of their Social Security benefits. This feature could draw well-qualified retired people into the day-care centers.

Since staffing day-care centers is not easy, that would be a welcome boost. Having older people interact with today's youth would also be good; it could help the old stay young in spirit, and the young can benefit from interaction with a different generation.

One obvious question to ask about the Roth legislation is where do the $340 million a year ($1 billion over three years) come from. Sen. Roth, who is a determined deficit-reducer, has an answer for this.

The necessary money would come from repeal of two federal programs — Urban Development Action Grants and Public Works Construction — that played an important role in revitalizing communities but are no longer urgently needed. Sen. Roth concedes that it is never easy to terminate a program. But, he argues persuasively, "that a program aimed at confronting the shortage of child care throughout the nation must take priority."

Furthermore, he adds, "availability of child care is itself a stimulus to economic development." And that in turn promotes community revitalization.

The Child Care Development Act of 1988 is a constructive piece of legislation. It merits prompt, positive consideration by Congress.

Portland Press Herald

Portland, ME, March 2, 1988

"Big and growing." That's how Barbara Collier, child care coordinator for the state Department of Human Services, last year described the need for day care in Maine.

There's still no end in sight. As Collier predicted, "With the thrust on economic development in Maine through the next decade, it's clear that for Maine to grow, people will need quality places to put their kids while they work."

Indeed they do. And they form a large and varied constituency.

There are, for instance, thousands of mothers on welfare and other low-income workers. For them, state-subsidized slots in existing day care facilities mean the difference between staying home and becoming self-sufficient by working. More than $600,000 is being spent over a two-year period to increase the number of subsidized day care placements available for them. And that won't be enough.

There are middle-income families for whom dependable quality day care also is crucial.

In all, nearly 60 percent of all children under age 6 have mothers in the work force. To help them, the state last year authorized $250,000 worth of regional offices to work with business, labor and non-profit institutions to develop more day care.

Yet another group consists of those who work for Maine's largest employer: the state. Rep. Harlan Baker, D-Portland, proposes the state establish a model day-care program in Augusta, both to serve state workers and to provide a how-to lesson for the rest of Maine. Preference would be based on economic need. However, details, including cost, have to be developed. Gov. McKernan, for his part, is supporting day care programs for state workers in Bangor and Augusta.

OK. But just as the need for quality day care exists across-the-board, so must state leadership move in more than one direction. Mothers trying to work their way off welfare deserve as high a priority as anyone who works for the state.

The Cincinnati Post

Cincinnati, OH, March 13, 1988

From time to time the Washington establishment anoints something "an idea whose time has come" and pushes it through Congress with the power of a locomotive. The tab comes in later, and usually is enormous. It's about to happen again with the issue of government subsidized child care.

Now, a person has to be hard-hearted and shortsighted to oppose federal aid to poor mothers — single or married — who want to get ahead by working and need a helping hand with child-care costs.

Unfortunately, though, Congress has a rotten record in targeting aid to the poor. It sells programs by pointing to the plight of low-income people, then giving most of the benefits to the middle- and upper-income groups.

Farm subsidies, for example, were meant "to keep poor farmers on the land," but rich and corporate farmers make off with billions annually. Millionaires get unneeded Medicare and Social Security benefits just because they hit 65. And so on.

Two major child-care bills are moving in Congress, one introduced by Sen. Christopher Dodd, D-Conn., the other by Sen. Orrin Hatch, R-Utah. Both would send most subsidies to day care centers. But many poor working mothers leave their children with a relative or pay a neighbor to watch them.

Douglas Besharov, a scholar at the American Enterprise Institute, points out that the best way to evaluate any federal child-care program "is whether its benefits are directed to those in greatest need.

"Both major bills ... fail this test. Their subsidies will go to middle-class rather than low-income families, while driving up the price of child care for all families."

Unfairly, the family in which the mother stays home to rear the children would be taxed to assist the two-earner family's child care. Worse yet, the two-earner family has, on average, 50 percent more income than the one-worker family.

Congress can do much better than either bill — by aiming child-care aid to the poor. The question in this election year is: Will it?

The New York Times

New York, NY, April 25, 1988

Governor Cuomo, in his State of the State address this year, argued that New York's economic survival may depend upon guaranteeing its poor children a fair chance. He declared the next 10 years "The Decade of the Child." If the fiscal 1989 budget is any guide, the decade is off to a modest start.

Mr. Cuomo's most dramatic proposal called for "universal" pre-kindergarten for 4-year-olds by 1993. The plan was to set up half-day programs in every school district. But half-day preschool doesn't meet working parents' needs. A better plan would provide valuable early childhood education in a full day-care setting. No funds were allocated to universal preschool, but the Legislature added $6 million to an existing program for low-income children.

Day care programs will benefit from a $12 million increase to augment the salaries of day care workers, the first time that state funds have been earmarked for wage increases. Training funds for day care were also provided, as were funds to encourage employers to set up pilot day-care programs. A promising child-care resource and referral network will get an additional $1 million.

The Legislature voted a $9 million increase in nutrition assistance for women, infants and children. But it turned down the Governor's more ambitious plans to extend Medicaid eligibility to 55,000 children now without any health insurance, and to establish a new category of health care coverage for 65,000 children of the working poor. Nor will the state be able to benefit from $45 million in Federal funds for prenatal care. Approval bogged down in disputes over matching cost obligations and use of the money for abortions.

Liberty Scholarships, an ambitious anti-dropout effort, formed the centerpiece of the Governor's education program. Combined with existing assistance, the scholarships would guarantee poor high school graduates four years of higher education at a New York college or university. But the Legislature has not yet gone along with this idea, which would eventually cost about $60 million a year.

Governor Cuomo also promised to come to the aid of the New York City school system. But his legislation authorizing a subsidiary of the State Dormitory Authority to build city schools appears uncertain of passage. So does a bill to eliminate the Board of Examiners, whose requirements now unnecessarily impede recruiting of teachers. The legislators, however, are considering a compromise that should ease teacher recruitment.

The first months of the Decade of the Child, therefore, remain notable more for what has not happened than for what has. That is no doubt inevitable given the steep fiscal implications of some of the Governor's initiatives. But the results so far remain disappointing.

Some in Albany might assume that a campaign intended to last a decade can afford modest results at the outset. Mr. Cuomo at least deserves credit for getting important ideas on the agenda. But while legislators debate, New York's children grow a little older every day.

copyright © The New York Times 1988

Los Angeles Times

Los Angeles, CA, March 2, 1988

Politicians do not seem to kiss as many babies as they used to. But they are beginning to pay attention to children when they discuss issues. It is a trend that we hope continues.

It also is a trend that the Children's Defense Fund—which lobbies for health, education and other welfare programs for those who are too young to lobby for themselves—is trying to encourage. The most recent move by the organization in that direction is a report on "what every American should be asking political leaders in 1988."

"The first high-school graduating class of the 21st Century will enter first grade in September, 1988," the fund's president, Marian Wright Edelman, often points out. The class faces a future of risks. One in four of its members is poor. One in five may become a teen-age parent. One in six is being raised with no health insurance. One in seven may drop out of school.

"And one out of every two has a mother in the work force, but only a minority have safe, affordable, quality day care," Edelman adds.

To try to reverse the adverse statistics on health care, Edelman and her group recommend that political candidates be asked what policies they propose in order to reduce infant mortality, like having the government help provide better prenatal care; how the candidates would halt the decline in childhood immunization rates, and how they would vote on the measure by Sen. Edward M. Kennedy (D-Mass.) and Rep. Henry A. Waxman (D-Calif.) that would require employers to provide health insurance to all employees and their families.

With half the mothers of preschool children now in the work force, the Children's Defense Fund recommends asking candidates whether they think that the federal government should have a role in helping low-income families pay for day care and in developing good care for children from all economic backgrounds. Specifically, how would candidates vote on S 1885 and HR 3660, the Act for Better Child Care Services, which would offer these subsidies and establish procedures for setting standards for care?

Does the federal government have a role in overcoming mental-health problems that lead parents to abuse children? Should federal fair-housing laws be expanded to prohibit discrimination against families with children? How can the federal government expand the successful Head Start program so that it will serve more than the 18% of those eligible that it now serves? And do the candidates support expansion of the popular program of nutritional supplements for pregnant women, infants and children that now serves only 40% of those eligible?

It's a long list, longer than this sample of questions indicates, and an expensive one if implemented. But for a country that ranks 19th in the developed world in keeping children alive through their first year of life, it's an agenda to which attention must be paid before more and more children die or are forced to go through life handicapped by poor health and poor education.

Los Angeles, CA, May 2, 1988

I t used to be that only the very poor, or single parents, had to worry about caring for kids *and* earning a living. Today most households are either two-earner or single-parent, and, as Herald Examiner staff writers Betsy Bates, Alina Tugend and Deborah Anderluh reported last week in a series on child care, more than 500,000 children in L.A. County need child-care services, but only 124,000 spaces are available. And many families cannot meet the costs.

The need has stirred up a broad political response. Many leaders think the answer is getting women out of the workforce and back home. Even if that goal were reasonable and just, which it isn't, it ignores economic reality.

During the past 20 years, as women entered the job market, average family income in inflation-adjusted dollars has remained level. Women's earnings don't go to luxuries or "little extras," but for essentials. The two-income family has been key in keeping the economy healthy and growing. Coming up with the economic incentive to make families return to single-earner status would not only devastate business, but would be far more expensive than providing child care.

On the state level, a sudden explosion of proposals includes some good ideas, like the five-bill package of Sen. Art Torres, D-Los Angeles. He would require better school-related programs, reorganize the system of services and offer support for latch-key children.

Assembly Republicans like Gil Ferguson of Newport Beach, Phil Wyman of Bakersfield and Paul Zeltner of Lakewood, are among those who don't seem willing or able to acknowlege the scope of the need. They recommend increasing the state dependent tax credit from $52 to $100 and seek to deregulate child care — a business not unduly saddled with restrictions. Their naive approach won't help and could hurt.

Children aren't a luxury, and society should help the people who are raising tomorrow's generation to do the best job possible. This means that business and government must step into what was once just a family affair. But families themselves have changed dramatically. We can't afford to ignore this change by failing to provide adequate child care.

U.S. Teen Pregnancy Rate Called Highest

A private foundation report issued March 12, 1985 said that U.S. teenagers 15 to 19 years old had a pregnancy rate more than twice that of their counterparts in other industrialized nations. The report, prepared by the Alan Guttmacher Institute, said much of the difference was accounted for by the other countries' nationwide programs of classroom sex education, and by government and private efforts in those countries to supply teenagers with low-cost contraceptives.

The study had taken two years to complete and compared the pregnancy rate and sexual habits of U.S. teenagers with those of teenagers in 36 other industrialized countries. It gave special attention to Canada, France, Sweden, as well as the U.S. According to the report, U.S. teenagers had a pregnancy rate of 96 per 1,000.

U.S. blacks, according to the report, had a teenage pregnancy rate of 163 per 1,000, while white U.S. teenagers had one of 83. The study found that 60 of every 1,000 U.S. women had had an abortion by the age of 18.

The report questioned arguments that liberal sexual views or high welfare benefits increased pregnancy rates. It found that the average age for first sexual intercourse—just under 18 years—was roughly the same as in the five other countries examined in depth. The study also claimed that in most of the countries examined, "the overall level of support" given welfare recipients "appears to be more generous" than that received in the U.S.

Adolescents should not be forced to seek parental consent for abortion and should have easy access to contraceptives, according to a report released Dec. 9, 1985 by a panel of the National Academy of Sciences. The U.S. had "no coherent policy" to control adolescent pregnancy, the committee said, and its adolescents suffered far higher pregnancy, childbearing and abortion rates than did teenagers of most other developed nations. This was despite the fact that U.S. teenagers did not have notably more active sex lives than their foreign counterparts did, the committee claimed. The report said there was no solid case to be made that access to contraceptives encouraged teenagers to have sex.

Los Angeles Times
Los Angeles, CA, October 4, 1985

One out of five American babies is born to an unwed mother, according to federal health statistics, and that new mother is often a teen-ager. More than 1 million American teen-agers got pregnant last year, most of them by mistake.

The United States has the highest adolescent pregnancy rate of five similarly developed nations, according to the research division of Planned Parenthood. The causes are complex. The solutions are numerous, controversial and in some cases as unreliable as some methods of birth control.

This public health emergency needs urgent attention. The Reagan Administration would prefer to leave these matters to parents, an ideal solution for ideal families. Congress has provided funding for family planning, but it is inadequate.

Private foundations, organizations and individuals should also respond. On that score, five foundations have funded a clinic that provides general medical attention, including birth control methods, at DuSable High School in Chicago.

Making such information easily available for teen-agers with the hope that they will practice what they learn is one practical approach to the problem. However, there are fewer than 30 clinics dispensing birth control methods in U.S. high schools and none in Los Angeles.

The Chicago clinic opened in June, so it is too early to determine if the accessibility will reduce the high rate of teen-age pregnancy at the high school—about 200 of the 900 female students have babies annually. The Chicago parents, for the most part, welcome the clinic, which is run by a local hospital, but critics who equate birth control with abortion want it closed.

The objectors should approve of approaches that reduce the need for abortion, which they find most abhorrent. They should also sanction the private support that does not involve their tax dollars. More effective solutions would convince teen-agers, young men and young women, that they are independent, have choices and can control their futures.

Teen-age pregnancies cripple futures. Few young mothers develop into independent, productive women. In California, 80% drop out of school. Their children often grow up poor, supported by taxpayers. More than half of the state's welfare budget is spent on mothers who first gave birth as teen-agers, according to the University of California at San Francisco.

This epidemic is burdening families, communities and taxpayers. The extent of the crisis demands public and private attention. The coalition that funded the Chicago clinic includes the Robert Wood Johnson Foundation of Princeton, N.J.; the Community Wealth Fund of New York and the Joyce Foundation, the Pittway Corp. and the Charitable Foundation of Chicago. Their efforts inspire hope.

A clinic at a high school is not the only solution to the tragedy of teen-age pregnancies. But it is an approach worth duplicating in an atmosphere without hysteria.

THE KANSAS CITY STAR
Kansas City, KS, July 29, 1985

Although the family planning debate in Washington recently has centered on U.S. assistance to developing countries, the need for federal dollars at home must not be forgotten. Title X, which funds clinics providing family planning services mainly for adolescents and low-income persons, is going to expire at the end of September. Now is the time the Congress should be renewing this funding for another three years, rather than waiting until the last minute as was done a year ago. Even then, Title X was renewed for only another year.

The reauthorization for Title X gets stalled in the abortion debate, which is illogical. These federal dollars go to help people with birth control, not for abortions. They prevent unwanted pregnancies which lead to abortions. In approving them, Congress is voting to cut down the number of abortions.

Unfortunately, that is not what the abortion opponents are telling the public. The defeat of a motion to pass Title X in the House came about because anti-abortion forces circulated word that they would publicize House members' votes for it as pro-abortion. Some legislators don't have the backbone to stand up to that type of advertising onslaught, however inaccurate it is.

Furthermore, those who oppose the renewal as it is are back with an old fight—requiring clinics which receive the federal dollars to notify parents whenever their children seek contraceptive help. Again, this flies in the face of logic. Many teen-agers won't seek birth control services if they know their parents will be told. The result is more unwanted pregnancies and abortions.

Title X pumped about $6 million into Missouri during 1983-85. Not enough money, but a lot better than not having it. In fact, not having family planning is more expensive to the federal budget and to society than having it—both in terms of tax dollars spent for public assistance for these children and their mothers and in terms of abortions. Congress must get off dead center on this issue and renew Title X for three more years.

The Evening Gazette

Worcester, MA, November 11, 1985

According to the American College of Obstetricians and Gynecologists, in 1980 in this country there were 2,694,000 intended pregnancies and 3,349,000 unintended pregnancies.

Of the latter number, 1,553,000 were terminated by abortion.

Most people, whether right-to-life or freedom-of-choice, think that abortions are to be avoided if possible. Sex education is one possible way to reduce unwanted pregnancies. According to a poll, 81 percent of Americans believe that children should get sex education in junior high school. But politics at all levels seems to stand in the way of effective sex education.

Some fear that telling children anything about sex will somehow encourage sexual activity. But it is doubtful that anything taught in class would have a fraction of the effect that comes from the constant sexual stimulus of television, movies and rock concerts. Hundreds of thousands of teen-age girls are having babies every year. Some of these mothers are as young as 14. The need is for more information, not less. These teen-age pregnancies pose a national dilemma.

Family planning information has for years been provided by the federal Family Planning Program through local clinics and hospitals. No one knows how many unwanted pregnancies these programs have averted, but the number must be in the tens of thousands. Young persons, who are sometimes astonishingly ignorant about the facts of life, get counseling on health, nutrition, emotional problems and contraception.

But when the American College of Obstetricians and Gynecologists proposed a public service ad on avoiding unwanted pregnancies, all three major networks refused to run the ad. They finally agreed, after the word "contraception" was removed.

In Washington, things are not much better. Funding for the Family Planning Program is being held up while Congress debates abortion. Although no FPP funds can be used for abortion, the law specifies that pregnant women must be told of their legal rights to have an abortion and where. Rep. Jack Kemp and Sen. Orrin Hatch are trying to change the law so that women could be given that information only in cases where their lives would be threatened by continuing the pregnancy.

That would mean that some major FPP programs would no longer get federal funding. Planned Parenthood, for example, gets FPP funds to do family counseling. It also uses private funds to do abortions in special clinics. The proposed law probably would end FPP funding for Planned Parenthood. That would mean that some of the most experienced and effective family planning clinics might have to close down or at least sharply curtail their counseling programs.

The results would be harsh on many women, particularly those at the poverty level, and it probably would not reduce the number of abortions by one iota. It might mean that some abortions would be done under unsanitary or risky conditions.

In dealing with this delicate and controversial issue, lawmakers should consider the whole problem, not just a part of it. The teen-age pregnancy problem in this country is appalling. Tens of thousands of babies are being born to girls who are little more than children themselves. Tens of thousands of other young girls need counseling and information so that the same thing will not happen to them.

The challenge is to make things better, not worse.

Portland Press Herald

Portland, ME, September 17, 1985

The controversy over sex education in public schools has flared up again, this time in Gray where some parents are objecting to a state-mandated "family life" course. But Gray-New Gloucester High School officials apprear to be dealing with the course and the complaints in a reasonable, responsible way.

The school board has appointed a panel to study the complaints and review course material, and a state Department of Education representative has been asked to address a gathering of concerned parents this week. Meanwhile, teacher Susan Rivard defends the program as essential to "clear up a lot of myths" teenagers have about sex.

She's right. Kids today are bombarded with music, movies, television shows, magazines, advertisements and products that present sex as glamorous, exciting and very tempting. It's essential that factual, complete and candid information be made available to counter the hype.

Obviously, the best place for youngsters to get sex education is at home, from parents. But far too many kids simply aren't getting the information they need. That's apparent from the increasing problem of teen-age pregnancy in Maine.

Some 3,000 teens become pregnant in this state each year. Many have abortions; many others give birth and wind up on welfare.

Teen pregnancy rates are higher in the United States than in other developed nations. A study by the Alan Guttmacher Institute and Princeton University suggests that's because sex education is more regularly taught and birth control information more readily available in Sweden, France, Canada, the Netherlands and other countries than in the United States.

Teaching kids about sex includes teaching them about pregnancy—and how to avoid it. The best way for teens, of course, is abstinence. But those who become sexually active despite the advice of parents should have access to straightforward, factual information.

The Des Moines Register

Des Moines, IA, October 31, 1985

The federal Family Planning Program, begun in 1970, expires on Nov. 15. Opponents of abortion are trying, with the blessing of the Reagan administration, to limit its renewal in such a way that family-planning agencies must make a choice between doing without federal funds or not even mentioning the word "abortion" (except in cases where the pregnancy is life-threatening).

Such agencies as Planned Parenthood, which received $30 million from Washington last year, have not been allowed by law — and have not sought — to use federal money for encouraging or performing abortions. But they do tell women of their legal right to abortion and provide names of abortion clinics.

This has been done in the context of a complete range of advice. Federal program guidelines in effect for a decade say that women with "unintended pregnancies" shall be "given non-directive counseling on ... prenatal care and delivery; infant care; foster care or adoption; pregnancy termination."

Senator Orrin Hatch of Utah and Congressman Jack Kemp of New York accept the complaint of anti-abortion groups that the family-planning agencies encourage abortions, although the General Accounting Office has found "no evidence" of this.

Family-planning agencies say that no "medically ethical" program can be run without including advice on abortion. To do otherwise would be to conceal a legitimate medical option.

Under the Hatch-Kemp amendment, agencies would face the dilemma of having to operate an "unethical" program with federal aid or, without the aid, cut back their services overall, with the unhappy result of many additional unwanted pregnancies.

Of course, the federal government is under no obligation to finance any kind of family planning. But it does have an obligation not to base its decisions on the religious belief of many people that abortion is a sin.

The U.S. Supreme Court has ruled it legal, and the Supreme Court is what Congress and the administration should be heeding if they propose to do any kind of financing of family planning.

THE BLADE

Toledo, OH,
November 4, 1985

THE New Right is renewing its efforts to make it impossible for millions of women to have an abortion. This time its convoluted campaign is aimed at a group who declares its primary function is to *prevent* abortions.

A favorite whipping boy for some conservatives has been Planned Parenthood. Rep. Jack Kemp and Sen. Orrin Hatch say they are going to try to cut off federal funds for that group and others that provide abortion referral and counseling. The specific target is Title X of the Public Health Service Act, which would provide $142.5 million for 4,000 clinics that offer family planning and counseling.

The legislators say the money should not be used in programs where abortion can be proposed as a method of family planning. But Planned Parenthood has no particular interest in advocating abortions; it informs individuals that abortion is a legal option.

What the anti-abortionists choose to ignore is the work that Planned Parenthood and other agencies do to try to discourage unwanted pregnancies. Providing counseling for young women, many of them poor, helps reduce the number of abortions that take place. If the conservatives succeed in blocking Title X funds, they would be inviting more illegitimate births among poor women and a subsequent increase in abortions, many of them in undesirable circumstances.

Another battle is being fought in the seemingly never-ending war against not only abortion but also birth control and sex education. As undesirable as these programs may be to some persons, as a whole they promote sensible family planning. Most important, they are legal and should be preserved and strengthened, despite reactionary cries to the contrary.

SYRACUSE
HERALD·JOURNAL
Syracuse, NY, October 24, 1985

No industrialized nation has the rate of teen-age, out-of-wedlock pregnancy that the United States has.

No Western country is even close. Every year, hundreds of thousands of American girls, most of them unmarried and still in high school, get pregnant. The results: hundreds of thousands of abortions and a like number of births. The births, far more often than not, are to child-parents who have no ability to care for themselves, much less infants.

Teen pregnancy is an epidemic in this country, especially in some urban areas.

Part of the problem is a continuing lack of comprehensive sex education and conservative attitudes toward contraception.

"There is — and I'm not sure this is confined to teen-agers — a certain mind-set. If you're taught that sex outside marriage is bad, then if you use contraception, it looks like you meant to, which makes it badder," she said. "Whereas, if you don't (use contraception), you can act surprised, as if you were overcome by sudden impulse," says Angela Holder, a clinical professor of pediatrics and law at Yale University's School of Medicine. "If you get overcome by sudden impulse every time you go out on Saturday night with your boyfriend, the inevitable will occur."

But the causes of the teen pregnancy epidemic go deeper, she believes.

For many girls, even as young as 12 or 13, having a baby is one way they seek to appear "adult." Moreover, the changing face of America's workforce has an impact: Holder believes girls are sexually active because "as more and more mothers go back to work, more and more teen-age girls and their boyfriends are coming home to an empty house than there were 25 years ago."

Meanwhile, the numbers keep piling up, as do the economic and social consequences, including poverty and child abuse.

Too much of the teen pregnancy discussion has centered on abortion, not enough on prevention. Sex among teen-agers is a fact-of-life that isn't going to change, no matter how adults feel. Yet information about contraception and the consequences of teen pregnancy remain, too often, hidden from the young people who need it most.

We're not providing enough sex education in schools and at home. Until we do, the numbers of teen pregancies, the numbers of ruined teen lives, the numbers of disadvantaged children can only increase.

The Wichita
Eagle-Beacon
Wichita, KS, August 15, 1985

EVERY year, more than a million U.S. teen-agers become pregnant. Nearly half have abortions, nearly 150,000 miscarry. In Kansas, in 1980, one teen-age girl in 20 had a baby or a miscarriage or an abortion. These figures ought to be shocking, a subject for active concern.

Unwanted pregnancy and miscarriages and abortion can be traumatic for women of any age, but the emotional problems are greatest for the young. Pregnancy can threaten relationships with family and friends. For many, there are scars.

Babies born to teen-agers are more likely to be underweight. In Wyandotte County, teen-agers account for a fifth of all births — and a third of all underweight babies. In Kansas, in 1983, 8.3 percent of babies born to teen-agers were underweight; for mothers more than 20, the figure was just 5.8 percent. Low birthweight often hinders the growth of the child. It's also a burden for society, because the cost of caring for an underweight child is more than $10,000 — 20 times the cost of caring for a normal baby.

Pregnancy is for many teen-agers like a prison, a terrible sentence of dependency. Fewer than half of teen-age mothers finish high school. In fact, teen-age mothers are twice as likely to drop out of school than girls who wait until the age of 20 to have children. Teen-age mothers are much more likely to suffer poverty. Half of all federal Aid for Families with Dependent Children payments are necessitated by teen-age pregnancies. Many teen-age mothers end up on welfare.

The poverty of teen-age mothers is just the beginning, though. Poor children are more likely to be burdened by ill health, to be physically or sexually abused, to suffer the death or absence of a parent, to be ill-educated, to be unemployed as teens, to be institutionalized. According to a Maine study, poor children are three times more likely than their peers to die before the age of 18.

Despite the gravity of the problem, teen-age pregnancy still is a subject too many prefer to ignore. This month, the national television networks refused an American College of Obstetricians and Gynecologists public-service announcement about sexual responsibility. Too controversial, they said. But it shouldn't be. Teen-age sex is more and more a fact of life, and teen-age pregnancy is going to be more and more of a problem — unless there's more honest public discussion of contraception.

That's not a comforting thought, of course. But it's better to be frank.

The Miami Herald

Miami, FL, July 29, 1985

SOCIAL and economic dynamite hide in the recent task-force report that one of every five babies born in Dade has a teen-age mother. Those young women rarely possess the personal maturity or the earning potential to provide the child a stable, secure home. Half these children are illegitimate; the other half are born into marriages whose risk of divorce is three times the norm.

Thus such infants are behind from the day they are born. In fact, many are behind even before birth. Ninety percent of the teen-agers giving birth at Jackson Memorial Hospital, where most go, received no prenatal medical care. Their infants suffer low birth weights, higher rates of retardation and other deficiencies, and double the risk of early death. And one-third of the teen mothers will become pregnant again before age 20.

This situation threatens social disaster. A community that continues to produce so many children doomed to deprivation can expect to see its quality of life decline and its tax base erode. These are the demographics of the Third World, where half the population is under 15, poorly educated, and jobless.

That dismal future won't do for Dade County. A steering committee of social-service representatives is seeking $1.6 million for a pilot project to work with 100 young mothers. Sparked by the Urban League, the group includes the Public Health Trust, the school board, the health department, the state welfare agency, the YWCA, and the Perinatal Network. They want to improve upon Federal projects elsewhere that met only limited success in helping young mothers to become self-sufficient and in preventing them from becoming pregnant again too soon.

Certainly the community ought to provide that $1.6 million. But that is a pittance in the face of a problem so pervasive. No agency or individual who comes in contact with adolescents ought to wait for a three-year pilot project. Every adult shares the responsibility for imparting to young people — boys as well as girls — the critical importance of avoiding early pregnancy. Abstinence, birth control, and abortion all are techniques available to teen-agers. Each has its advantages and drawbacks, which may be different for the 13-year-old than for the 18-year-old.

It is irresponsible for adolescents to blunder into parenthood, and it constitutes near-criminal negligence for the adults of the community to allow such blundering to continue *en masse*. There is no higher priority for securing the community's future than to reduce the incidence of teen-age childbirth.

THE ARIZONA REPUBLIC

Phoenix, AZ, May 5, 1985

THE U.S. birthrate, which has been climbing steadily for the past decade, is now in the midst of a marketing boom.

Some 3.6 million births occurred last year. A major reason for the surge is that the number of women in childbearing years has constantly increased over the past 10 years.

The total is far below the record number of 4.3 million births which occurred in 1957 at the peak of the postwar baby boom.

However, current births are setting new spending records in children's markets — nearly $14 billion in annual sales today.

These are expected to hit $20 billion by 1990.

For nearly 20 years, some demographers and sociologists have been systematically underlining the decline of the American family.

From increasing divorce to live-in relationships, they have stressed the approach and dangers of zero population growth in the United States and other highly developed nations.

Now, with the birthrate continuously moving upward, they are proven wrong once again.

The simple fact is, although couples are now marrying two years later than their parents and wait longer to have children, their increasing numbers have reached a childbearing threshold.

The number of first births is more than 42 percent, which equals the record pace of the baby boom years.

Also, since more families have incomes from both spouses, parents are willing to spend more money on their children.

This is a strong rebuke of critics who saw this as a selfish, self-indulgent generation whose primary goal was its own luxury and comfort.

However, they are lavishing expensive goods and services on their children — from the best clothes to better and more costly day-care centers. They are buying educational toys in record numbers as well as new health and informational magazines on child upbringing.

The list is topped by $50 designer jeans for tots.

This is not to say divorce and live-in relationships are declining.

Rather, delayed parenthood is causing an explosion in economic endearment.

Most mothers return to work. That is because the cost to bring one bundle of joy to kindergarten now averages more than $21,000.

The American family, bless it, is once again overcoming its detractors and pessimists.

Motherhood, however changed by centuries and culture shocks, is still the world's oldest and noblest profession.

The Boston Globe

Boston, MA, October 2, 1985

Since its creation in 1970, Title X of the Public Health Service Act — as the national family-planning program is known — has served American families by offering affordable contraceptive services in clinics across the country. Congress has consistently supported funding the program as sound and cost-effective public policy. Now that policy is under attack.

Some members of the House and Senate are attempting to sabotage the reauthorization of Title X because they oppose abortion. They refuse to acknowledge that providing birth control is the best way to prevent unwanted pregnancies and reduce the need for abortions.

In recent months, Title X's opponents, led by Sen. Orrin Hatch (R-Utah) and Rep. Henry Hyde (R-Ill.), have held the legislation in committee or blocked it on the floor. Now they are drafting amendments designed to cripple Title X, which has been funded by a continuing budget resolution through November.

Congress should resist any effort to eliminate or weaken the family-planning program, which is depended on by millions of Americans.

During the past year, government assistance to international agencies providing birth-control information and contraceptive services to developing countries has been withheld, withdrawn or redirected. Again and again, it has been argued that no American dollars should be spent to promote abortion — even though no funding earmarked for family planning was being used for abortion by those agencies.

The same arguments are now being used against Title X. The opposition has repeatedly charged that family-planning money supports abortion in this country.

To do so would be against the law. Moreover, General Accounting Office audits show that the restriction has been scrupulously observed by American hospitals and clinics.

Tampering with Title X can only lead to an increase in abortions. If the program's critics were as opposed to abortion as they profess to be, they would support additional funding, expanded family-planning assistance and improved sex education — in this country or in any other country where there is need.

Food Stamps' Reach Found Short

A report by a private panel issued Jan. 14, 1986 said that in 1984 the federal food stamp program had served just 55% of those eligible. In 1980, that figure had been 65%, the report said.

"Not only is hunger increasing as a problem, but federal food programs designed to feed the hungry have been weakened," the report charged. The study had been conducted by the Harvard University School of Public Health's Physician Task Force on Hunger in America.

The panel identified 150 "hunger counties," ones where more than 20% of residents were poor and only 33% of that group received food stamps. These were in the Midwest as well as in the South, where hunger had once been concentrated. The findings were based on statistics rather than field work. The task force matched the number of poverty-level families counted in 1984 against the average number of food stamps issued over the months of that year. Federal officials argued that this figure concealed the number of seasonal workers who used the program only during months of unemployment. In all, the government claimed, food stamps reached 80% of those eligible—35 million people.

According to the panel, real spending for food stamps and WIC (Women, Children and Infants) programs had increased dramatically since the mid-1960s, but in 1984 only one in three poor households in which the head worked for part or all of the year received food stamps. As of 1988 half of all nonworking poor households received food stamps.

The food stamp program is funded almost entirely by the federal government. The food stamp allotment is designed to enable a family to maintain what the Department of Agriculture calls a "nutritionally adequate" diet, but this regimen requires sophisticated nutritional planning skills, refrigerated storage spaces, equipment, and low-cost markets—all resources frequently unavailable to the poor. In addition, according to the Physician Task Force report, roughly 10 million individuals who are eligible for food stamps do not receive them. Many do not apply because they would qualify for limited assistance, lack information about the program or because of the stigma involved in receiving food stamps.

THE SUN

Baltimore, MD, June 24, 1984

The Hughes administration has decided that poor women and children with medical problems will not be made to suffer for the bureaucratic snafus that led to a $2 million deficit in a federally financed program to prevent malnutrition. Instead of its original plan to lop 28,000 recipients of this special food allowance off the rolls to save money, the administration will come up with enough extra money to keep 15,000 of the low-income recipients eligible for the $27 a month in iron-fortified foods. Only those with no medical difficulties will be dropped after their present eligibility expires.

That should have been the initial decision. Instead, it took protests from citizens groups and Mayor Schaefer and six county executives to persuade the state that it would be more costly to reduce the rolls of the Special Supplemental Food Program for Women, Infants and Children (WIC) than to spend the additional $1.7 million.

Adele Wilzack, state health secretary, got a late start on WIC's funding difficulties. Since then, she has acted decisively, firing the assistant secretary in charge of WIC, instituting a strict weekly accounting system and hiring more data processors to handle the big caseload. Now Governor Hughes has approved shifting health department funds so that women and children in the highest-risk categories remain in the program.

This marks the first time the state has contributed its own money to help malnourished women and children. Other jurisdictions might want to follow suit. Montgomery county has set an example by allocating $175,000 to help 3,700 local residents. WIC is one of the best health-prevention programs offered by government today. Everyone benefits if malnutrition is reduced.

THE SUN

Baltimore, MD, June 6, 1984

First it was feast, now it is famine. The state's Special Supplemental Food Program for Women, Infants and Children, known as WIC, is discovering that too little is even more troubling than too much. It faces a $2 million deficit that means painful cuts in nutrition aid for pregnant women and children below the poverty level. More than half its 58,000 recipients will have to be dropped when their initial six-month certification period is up. Additionally, no new recipients will be added. This is a blow to poor women who depend upon WIC to prevent malnutrition in their children.

Health Secretary Adele Wilzak is trying to discover how the state got itself in this jam. That question is being asked too late, though. This problem has been building for months, and health officials should have been sounding the alarms sooner.

Last spring, Maryland received an extra $1.5 million for WIC under the federal jobs bill. However, the money had to be spent before October or it reverted to Washington. This persuaded state bureaucrats — unwisely as it turned out — to start recruiting new WIC recipients. The state expanded its rolls, but not fast enough to avoid losing $500,000 that was unspent.

Once the recruitment drive had been launched by the state, it did not stop. That was the crucial mistake. The roster is twice the size it should be, given WIC's depleted budget. Compounding the problem, Congress has yet to decide on WIC's funding level in the fiscal quarter starting next month. So Maryland officials have no idea if they will be getting more, less or the same amount of money for WIC.

Asking bureaucrats to spent money in a hurry or risk losing it is unwise policy. Yet that is what Congress decreed with the extra WIC money. Maryland's bureaucrats fell into the spend-now trap. Unfortunately, it is the undernourished women and children dropped from the WIC rolls who will pay the price for this whole tangle.

Mrs. Wilzak has asked her aides to devise a plan for eliminating peaks and valleys in the WIC rolls, so the state does not keep swinging between deficit and surplus. Meanwhile, the health secretary is requesting (along with several other states) extra money from the U.S. Department of Agriculture to avert the drastic cutoff of nutrition aid that may occur. Women and children in the three lowest-risk categories already have been removed from the roster and put on a waiting list. Poverty always presents painful choices. The food supplements provided in WIC reduce government-paid medical expenses later and help children grow up without the handicaps — physical and mental — that can come from malnutrition.

The TENNESSEAN
Nashville, TN, February 13, 1986

HOUSE and Senate Democrats think they have found the reason why the Reagan administration finds it so easy to cut food and health care funds for indigent women and children: simply claim the programs do no good and delay releasing evidence of the good they do.

The Democrats accuse the administration of deleting favorable summaries from a report on the Women and Infant Children's food program (WIC) and charge that the Agriculture Department has delayed releasing the document.

The Agriculture Department commissioned a $5 million study of the WIC program five years ago. But now that the study has shown the program to be reducing premature births and infant mortality, increasing birth weights and improving the nutritional habits of pregnant women and their children, the administration has been slow to let these facts come before the public.

"This study has been plagued by repeated delays, culminating in nearly a year's hiatus between USDA's receipt of the final report, and printing and delivery," said Rep. George Miller, D-Calif. He said executive summaries were deleted by the department when it released the report Jan. 10.

"These actions are consistent with the administration's efforts to cut WIC by 30% in 1981...and to undermine the program through impoundment and other administrative maneuvers," the congressman said.

Sen. Tom Harkin, D-Iowa, said the report showed that "we can all feel assured that our tax dollars" used for WIC are being well spent.

The Agriculture Department ridiculed the charges from the Democrats. But the principal investigator of the study said he could see no reason why administration officials took nine months to study the report before releasing it.

Maybe the administration had legitimate reasons for holding up the report. But it still hasn't greatly emphasized the favorable contents of the report. And the President apparently thinks that programs that feed and improve the health of poor children are contributing to the breakup of the American family. ■

THE SACRAMENTO BEE
Sacramento, CA, February 13, 1986

When your message is that government programs don't work, a little bit of good news can be a bad thing. Presented recently with the results of its five-year, $5 million national evaluation of the Women-Infants-Children (WIC) supplemental feeding program, the U.S. Department of Agriculture had an embarrassing public relations problem: For the first time, here was scientific evidence that WIC, which provides nutrition supplements to poor pregnant women, their infants and preschool children, works to improve their health.

The evaluation found that WIC increased early prenatal care, raised the birthweight of newborns by lengthening pregnancies, and reduced fetal death. Among preschoolers, long-term enrollment in WIC was associated with higher vocabulary scores. In general, the evaluation indicated that WIC's effects were greatest on less-educated and minority-group women, who are at greatest risk for premature delivery and infant mortality.

The Reagan administration's answer to this good news? Chop from the evaluation the executive summary that lists, in non-technical language, the positive findings of the study; bury the study's good news about WIC in the fifth paragraph of a six-paragraph press release tinged with disappointment that the results weren't better, and then hope no one will notice the altered emphasis.

It was a vain hope. The way USDA released the evaluation was "incomplete and potentially misleading" and obscured its meaning, complained Dr. David Rush, professor of pediatrics at Albert Einstein College of Medicine in New York and principal investigator for the study. Members of Congress accused the Reagan administration of suppressing the study. Not so, replies John Bode, assistant secretary of agriculture for food and consumer services. He didn't try to suppress the study, only to keep USDA's imprimatur from going on an "unbalanced" executive summary that overstates the results of a study that is not "clear cut."

It's an unconvincing explanation. In fact, the "unbalanced" summary of findings in the excised introduction is identical to one that appears in the body of the report. And if it is clear-cut results USDA wants, the way to get them would be to continue the study to track the intellectual and psychological development of WIC children, as Rush has proposed. Such research might show even more strongly that WIC works to give poor babies a better start in life. So far, USDA has turned him down. Apparently that's something the Reagan administration doesn't want to know, and doesn't want anybody else to, either.

Newsday
New York, NY, June 22, 1986

How many times do you get something wrong before you take action to get it right? The question would have been an appropriate one for members of the Senate Oversight Committee to ask state Department of Health officials responsible for the Women, Infants and Children (WIC) program.

In 1983, again in 1984 and yet again last year, the program failed to spend federal funds available to it, despite a lengthy waiting list of eligible women who were callously turned away.

Not only did the eligible women get no benefits, the state had to return the unspent money to the federal government in each of the three years. The funds are appropriated by Congress and allocated to the Health Department. The state then distributes the money to local WIC agencies. Eligible WIC mothers receive monthly checks with which they purchase food packages at any of 300 stores. A package averages a modest $33 per person monthly.

Because state officials feared the cost of the program would outstrip the federal allocation, they imposed freezes on the local agencies. As a result, children who needed the additional food came up empty-handed, while a total of $4.8 million went back to Washington during the three-year period. And State Sen. Christopher Jackman, a Hudson Democrat, conceded that there were problems during some of the earlier years of the 11-year-old program.

Certainly this is no way to run a program designed to fortify the nutrition of needy youngsters. The Oversight Committee, happily, was told that some states had solved the problem of unused federal funds by creating a state buffer fund, which would be able to make up any deficit in the program resulting from uncertainties in federal funding. And Assemblyman David Schwartz, a Middlesex County Democrat, said he would sponsor legislation to give New Jersey a $1.5 million buffer fund.

Quick passage of a buffer fund bill would put the WIC program back on track.

No longer would officials have to fear a budget shortfall. No longer would needed money be sent back to Washington because of misjudgment. Most important, no longer would children be deprived of foods that could benefit their health, growth and development.

The Atlanta Journal
THE ATLANTA CONSTITUTION
Atlanta, GA, December 15, 1987

The food stamp rolls have been shrinking, though the number eligible for assistance grows and grows. Why? Because of the Reagan administration's relentless imposition of unreasonable burdens on those applying for assistance. And unless Congress moves quickly, it's about to get worse.

Just listen to what the folks who brought you ketchup as a vegetable are up to now. The administration would:

• Allow states to deny benefits immediately to applicants missing a single interview (junking a requirement that they reschedule and keep providing benefits until two interviews and 30 days have passed).

• Immediately deny benefits to applicants who don't turn in all documentation by an assigned date (i.e., no extensions).

• Eliminate information on written notices that includes telephone numbers to call for information or free legal advice.

• Permit states to do away with local appeals hearings and require applicants to make their cases in writing.

What purpose can these inflexible regulations have but to make it easier to deny benefits to eligible people?

Federal studies show that 23 percent of those eligible for food stamps are currently denied assistance. The proposed regulations callously ignore the possibility that people who are poor, in crisis and without day care or transportation may have difficulty meeting deadlines or keeping appointments with caseworkers. And they discriminate against the illiterate, retarded or foreign-born.

These regulations, a perversion of what Congress intended when it created the program, will take effect in the New Year unless Congress takes action to block them. There's no time to lose.

THE PLAIN DEALER
Cleveland, OH, March 18, 1985

One of the more cumbersome social service programs in the country provides food stamps to needy persons. Despite the noble purpose, the program has been fraught with theft, fraud and costly paper work. To combat those ills, the Cuyahoga County commissioners and the county human services department are turning to technology.

The 191,000 households that receive food stamps each month are being sent two computerized cards —one stating the amount of stamps someone is eligible to receive and the other serving as an identification card. They will be permanent—as long as a "client" remains eligible—and will replace the monthly mailings that often are lost, stolen or misused. Starting April 1, recipients will take the two cards to food stamp issuance centers on specified days each month, eliminating the wait for authorization to arrive in the mail.

In another change, the stamp issuance will be staggered over 10 days, eliminating the one-day jam-ups at supermarkets and at welfare offices by people who did not get their mailed authorizations.

Both changes appear eminently sensible and beneficial to food stamp recipients. County officials also expect an advantage for taxpayers generally. The startup cost of $1.3 million is estimated to be offset by a net savings of $598,000 in annual operating expenses. Thus, the new system would pay for itself in a little more than two years and produce a $500,000 annual savings thereafter.

Given the size and complexity of the food stamp operation, it may take a few months for the Fastamp system to become the "faster, safer and more efficient" program that the commissioners envision. Nonetheless, the present system begs for improvement. Fastamp sounds like a better deal.

The Chattanooga Times
Chattanooga, TN, April 21, 1985

Politicians love to talk about being "pro-family," but sometimes their actions don't live up to their words. There is a move in Tennessee, however, to change a law that is distinctly anti-family in its effect.

The law in question denies benefits under the Aid to Families with Dependent Children (AFDC) program to any household where both parents are present, regardless of the family's financial distress. That means unemployed fathers who cannot provide the necessities of life for their families often have no alternative but to leave — so their wives and children can become eligible for the welfare assistance they desperately need.

It is a sad situation when the law forces a man to make such a cruel choice. And it is no wonder that the veiled woman who testified last week before the black caucus of the General Assembly broke down in tears. "In order to get the benefits," she told the legislators, "we had to separate."

Obviously, as UTC social work professor, Dr. Tommie Brown, has said, the one-parent-only restriction on AFDC is a disincentive to family unity. As such, it can be seen as a contributor to the breakdown of the family so often cited as an underlying cause for social problems, particularly among the poor. In that sense, it works against the best interests not only of the families involved, but of the state as a whole.

Legislation pending before the General Assembly would remove this counterproductive restriction. It would expand Tennessee's AFDC program to allow benefits to two-parent families under certain conditions.

The AFDC-Unemployed Father Program has been an option available through the federal government since 1961. Half the states already take advantage of it. Tennessee should as well. That is so not only because public policy should always seek to strengthen families rather than tear them apart, but also because, in the words of a Memphis minister at last week's hearing, "Any law that prevents a man from living with his wife ... because he is unemployed is unjust."

The Burlington Free Press
Burlington, VT, August 29, 1985

Tightening the rules for distribution of food stamps in Vermont is a reflection of the conservative tide that has been running in the country since the accession of President Reagan to the White House.

Editorials

Cutting money for social programs not only carries the Reagan stamp but also draws appreciative nods from millions of Americans who are convinced that poor people are lazy loafers and parasites on the body economic. It is ironic that many people in the country who are willing to give generously to programs for aiding people in other nations cannot perceive the needs of the poor in their own land. They have perhaps been misled by the number of horror stories about welfare recipients who drive luxury cars and live an otherwise fast life on the money they receive from the government. The blunt fact is that few people choose to be poor; most want something better for themselves and their families. Circumstances — illness, lack of education, scant job opportunities — doom them to poverty. Food stamps certainly will not put them on the road to riches.

What is troublesome about a proposal to change food stamp eligibility rules in Vermont is the fact that the stamps are given to the working poor. Were they not receiving the stamps, many would not be able to feed their families. But for that help, some probably would be forced to give up their jobs and go on welfare. That a legislative committee rejected the state welfare commissioner's proposal to tighten the standards is an encouraging sign that some lawmakers recognize the problems of the working poor.

Commissioner Veronica Celani then decided to postpone plans to put the new rules into effect by Sept. 1. She told lawmakers that the state is under pressure to reduce its food stamp error rate from 8.9 percent to 5 percent and could lose $705,000 if it did not do so. The new rules would require Vermonters to prove their income by providing a pay stub or letter from their employers on a monthly basis.

Cheryl Rivers of the Vermont Low Income Advocacy Council contended that many low-wage earners would be ashamed or reluctant to tell their employers they were getting food stamps. She predicted some might leave their jobs and go on welfare.

Indeed the regulations seem to be designed to further humiliate people who are willing to work to better themselves and need some help in supporting their families.

Either Gov. Madeleine M. Kunin or lawmakers should request that the commissioner explore other measures which will satisfy the federal standards while at the same time demonstrating greater compassion for the working poor.

Even the most hidebound conservative should agree that low-income people should not be subjected to such shoddy treatment.

Detroit Free Press

Detroit, MI, April 18, 1986

A NATIONAL drive to increase funding for the special supplemental food program for women, infants and children (WIC) deserves support not only from a budget-conscious Congress but from ordinary citizens as well. WIC is quite literally a lifeline for the country's growing army of poor children, but thousands who need help don't get it.

Joint resolutions were introduced recently in both the U.S. House (JR 192) and the Senate (JR 99) to increase the funding for WIC by $150 million in fiscal 1988. Supporters know that won't be easy. President Reagan has proposed slicing $27 million from WIC, a reduction that would remove 50,000 people from the program. But congressional sponsors of these resolutions believe the American people would rather pay the price now of feeding poor children rather than dealing later with those children and their problems.

WIC is a 15-year-old feeding program for low-income pregnant women, infants and children under five who are at risk of being malnourished. WIC helps prevent malnutrition by providing a medically prescribed package of iron-fortified infant formula, cheese, milk, fruit juice, cereal and other foods based on the individual's need. The medical attention and foods are supplemented with nutrition education for parents.

A Harvard School of Public Health study found that for every dollar spent on WIC for pre-natal care and nutritious foods, up to $3 in hospital costs is saved. This doesn't begin to calculate the program's long-term benefits, which include higher birth weights and lower infant mortality rates. In addition, according to a U.S. Department of Agriculture evaluation, even children who did not receive their first food supplements until after their first birthdays had significantly better numerical memories than comparable children who did not receive WIC foods.

Despite the evidence that WIC is a fiscally responsible program that helps children reach their potential, the program still serves only about 42 percent of those eligible for it. Congressional supporters would like to boost these numbers incrementally until 65 percent of the eligible are being served by 1991. They believe that people concerned about the fact that one of every five American children now lives in poverty will flood their congressional representatives with letters urging them to support the resolutions introduced by Rep. George Miller, D-Calif., and Sen. Dennis DeConcini, D-Ariz. We hope they are right.

THE SPOKESMAN-REVIEW

Spokane, WA, March 28, 1988

U.S. Supreme Court Justice Thurgood Marshall has some curious ideas about neutrality.

Dissenting from a decision handed down last week, Marshall wrote that a 1981 law limiting food stamp eligibility for striking workers "amounts to a penalty on strikers, not neutrality."

If refraining from using taxpayers' money to subsidize strikes isn't neutrality, pray tell what is?

Fortunately, Marshall was on the losing side on this decision. By a 5-3 majority, the court upheld the 1981 provision which disallows food stamps to a family whose income level dips below the eligibility threshold because a worker goes on strike.

The ruling, and the law it affirms, make sense. The federal food stamp program was implemented in 1964 to make sure children in needy families don't go hungry, not to remove a burden from unions' strike funds. The federal government has no more business tiding striking workers over during a work stoppage than it would paying the rent and utility bills of the affected business.

The labor movement was a response to the exploitation and abuses of the Industrial Revolution. The right to form unions and bargain collectively — gained after a lengthy, arduous and frequently violent struggle — enabled workers to pool their strength and deal with businesses and factory owners on a more even footing.

The decision to strike is a last-ditch tactic which unions use when negotiations break down and the long-term gains for workers are deemed worth the short-term financial sacrifice of walking off the job. To remove the financial-sacrifice consideration, which giving food stamp benefits to strikers tends to do, makes the federal government more a participant and less a referee.

As Justice Byron R. White wrote in the majority opinion, "Exercising the right to strike inevitably risks economic hardship, but we are not inclined to hold that the right to association requires the government to minimize that result by qualifying the strikers for food stamps."

Union officials, by arguing that the 1981 law punishes the children of strikers, are trying to make those children pawns in their strategy.

In 1981, Congress launched a major effort to tighten up eligibility requirements for food stamps. The final package was designed to trim the rolls by about 1 million people and reduce the taxpayers' burden by $1.5 billion.

Whether that was a proper direction to take was a subject of sharp dispute at the time and remains so seven years later. There should be no disagreement, however, that when difficult economic conditions force a reduction in the amount of assistance the government can provide for those in need, the ones to be protected are those least able to fare for themselves.

It would have been a scandal if, under those circumstances, able-bodied workers who choose to forgo income in hopes of achieving personal financial gain, should have been among those protected.

The Gazette

Cedar Rapids, IA, March 14, 1987

IF CONGRESS has lacked motivation for overhauling the nation's welfare system, that no longer is the case. The non-partisan Congressional Budget Office reports a deeply disturbing historical "first": Children have become the poorest segment of the population. Census-based data indicate that a child in the United States is more than twice as likely to be poor as an adult. As long as nearly 25 percent of the nation's children live with only one parent — usually the mother — the trend surely will continue. It is no secret that such families tend to have low incomes.

Congress is virtually certain to act. Just as the plight of the elderly poor triggered profound changes in the 1960s and '70s, the compelling needs of poor children will force changes the next few years.

Which program to adopt?

As indicated here before, the most promising and economical plan is one fashioned by Sen. Daniel Patrick Moynihan, the New York Democrat who has spent a quarter century trying to pump sense into the welfare program. The Family Security Act would attack poverty by emphasizing the collection of child support payments and the education and training of adults in programs geared to getting them off welfare. Estimated at $2.7 billion over five years — as compared with the $5.7 billion House bill — the Senate measure would put a lot of responsibility on the states. One of its attractions is elimination of the stigma surrounding youngsters from poor households.

While the impoverishment of children is traceable to the so-called feminization of poverty — not to the dictates of politicians — there is no denying that Congress has aggravated some of the problems. Consider, for example, lawmakers' treatment of two major child-care provisions growing out of Social Security legislation of 50 years ago — Aid to Families with Dependent Children and Survivors Insurance. As Sen. Moynihan is quick to point out, AFDC goes mainly to blacks, SI generally to white households. Since 1970 Congress has increased the real benefits received by children under SI by 53 percent. It has cut AFDC benefits by 13 percent. As a result, government now provides a child receiving SI benefits almost three times what it provides a child on AFDC.

"Those who say we don't care about children in our country should note that since the 1970s, the average provision for children under SI has been rising five times as fast as average family income," said Moynihan in a Los Angeles Times guest column. "We do care about some children. Majority children. It is minority children who are left behind."

Despite bipartisan support for the Family Security Act, Senate Finance chairman Lloyd Bentsen continues bumping it in favor of deliberation on trade and Medicare. The public won't tolerate that for long. Demand is high for extensive welfare reform — with a deserved emphasis on child welfare.

Detroit Free Press

Detroit, MI, May 6, 1985

IS THE FEDERAL government refusing to spend some of the money allocated for the Women, Infants and Children (WIC) nutrition program? Five congressmen and five states think so, and they have filed a suit to force the government to spend the money. It is a suit with broad implications for hungry Americans and those who care about them.

The federal government is accused of refusing to spend $76 million out of $1.5 billion Congress allocated for WIC for fiscal year 1985. The complainants charge that this refusal by the Office of Management and Budget is not only illegal but potentially harmful to the health of 250,000 poor pregnant women, infants and children up to age five who will have to be dropped from the program if the withheld money is not spent.

The suit comes against this backdrop: Nine states are already reducing their WIC caseloads or the amount of food they provide to eligible people. Virtually all the states are preparing to trim their programs by limiting eligibility or taking other actions.

But no one denies the need for WIC. Along with food stamps, school breakfasts and lunches and feeding programs for the elderly, the WIC program has enabled America to make significant progress toward eliminating hunger. Yet millions of Americans continue to live right on the edge, with supplementary feeding programs their only cushion against hunger. Alarming numbers of black babies still die at birth in Detroit and Michigan because young, often malnourished mothers give birth to fragile, low-weight babies. This is no time to be finding devious ways to tighten the screws on WIC.

In his last budget message, President Reagan listed WIC as one of several programs that he would not touch. In the 1986 budget compromise tentatively approved by the Senate, WIC is allocated $1.5 billion, the same as this year. But according to the complainants, WIC money has been distributed so as to avoid using the full appropriation for the final two months. If true, this would leave states uncertain about program funding and undercut the effectiveness of the country's best defense against infant mortality.

The dispute seems to be between those bent on stabilizing the WIC caseload at a certain number and those who want to see available money used for pressing needs. On what is truly a life-or-death issue, the parties involved ought to be able to find a compromise that feeds the hungry without taking anybody to court.

THE SUN

Baltimore, MD, March 22, 1985

Since its inception in 1972, the WIC feeding program has stood out as exemplary among federal social efforts. Through WIC, low-income pregnant women and their babies receive vouchers that can be exchanged at the supermarket for vital foods. As a result of nutritionally sound diets, WIC infants' mortality rates are lower than their non-participating counterparts; WIC children are healthier and do better in school.

WIC provides free food by distributing vouchers for everything from bread, cereal and eggs to infant formula. The latter benefit is important, since formula prices are high. Without help, poor women sometimes substitute sugar water in the bottles of hungry babies. Today, one-third of WIC's $1.8 billion budget is reserved for buying infant formula, but the system under which it is purchased may be serving big business far better than the poor.

In most states, WIC participants get a voucher that allows them to buy any brand of infant formula. Being the single largest customer of infant formulas in the world, WIC should be getting a price break. But the states pay retail cost. With no incentive to compete for lower prices, infant formula makers doubled their prices from 1980 to 1987 — a rate of increase three times that of groceries, and WIC was forced to foot the bill.

In response, Oregon and Tennessee ventured into a freer market arrangement; Texas will do so May 1. These states provide WIC vouchers for only one brand of formula, based on competitive bidding. The company that offers the state the highest rebate per can gets the contract. In Texas, the maker of SMA formula, seeking to expand its meager market share, offered to return 71.5 cents per can, which sells for $1.40 to $1.50. Enfamil, trying to retain its share, countered with a startling 99.6-cent-per-can rebate, which will save Texas $14.6 million a year. Officials estimate that if every state were to institute similar cost-cutting measures, WIC — which currently can serve fewer than half of the eligible poor — could feed as many as half a million more citizens.

In Maryland, WIC participants in five jurisdictions get home delivery of formula, a service provided by private companies that bid for the contract. But 40 percent of Maryland's WIC recipients use the voucher system. Certainly a competitive bidding plan that would give all the state's WIC business to one formula maker in return for a rebate would save money and allow more eligible Marylanders to join the program. The escalating price of infant formula already has stretched WIC dollars too thin; making the limited funds go as far as possible should be a priority.

The Washington Post

Washington, DC, August 19, 1985

IN A CAPITAL where it has become conventional wisdom that government programs don't work and that efforts to help the poor inevitably lose ground, it is something of an event to see a group of Republicans and Democrats agreeing that certain programs do work. That's the conclusion of a bipartisan staff report released last week by the House Select Committee on Children, Youth, and Families. It is subscribed to not only by chairman George Miller, a Democrat who comes from the wing of his party that has never given up on government programs, but also by ranking Republican Dan Coats, who comes from the wing of his party that has for 50 years been skeptical of government initiatives.

Singled out for praise are eight specific programs. Studies are cited, data presented, costs noted. The programs for infants include the WIC supplemental food program for pregnant women and babies, prenatal care programs and Medicaid neonatal and infant mortality programs. For young children, there are immunization subsidies, preschool programs such as Head Start, and compensatory education programs. For older children, there are education for the handicapped and the Job Corps. The report talks in cost-benefits language and argues a little tendentiously that spending money now on these programs saves certain specific larger sums later. That stretches it a bit. The case for these programs doesn't depend on their making some kind of profit. What is critical is that they do useful things, useful for the immediate beneficiaries and for society—and do them well.

The willingness of the Republicans to subscribe to this report is not an isolated occurrence. Many Republicans, on Capitol Hill and elsewhere, have wondered as they nurture family values whether families are really nurtured by laissez faire economic policies. They have been stung by the taunt that opponents of abortion care about the quality of the child's life only from conception to birth, and they have been thinking hard about what can be done to improve the quality of life in early and middle childhood. They have been reflecting also, more hardheadedly, on the consequences of raising a generation an increasing proportion of which is affected by poor health and nutrition, and poor education.

Some of the programs praised in this report have come in for rather different treatment in Reagan administration budgets. The Job Corps, for example, was to be zeroed out, child nutrition deeply cut, child welfare benefits cut back. The Republicans who find themselves agreeing that these programs also help are quick to add in the same breath that there's just not any more money for them and not likely to be much in any out years either. A lot of Democrats are inclined to agree. For the short term, they may be right. As a matter of sensible and humane public policy, for the long term, they are surely beginning to wonder whether they may be wrong. In the meantime, let politicians of both parties take note. Some programs do work. Some people do need help.

St. Petersburg Times

St. Petersburg, FL, March 23, 1985

Put aside, for a moment, the humane considerations of caring for children. Forget compassion and concentrate on the raw economics of providing adequate nutrition and health care for the babies of poverty — to prevent deformity, disease and death.

Is it more cost-effective to build healthy babies with a relatively minor investment in prenatal care for their mothers — or to spend billions of dollars trying to heal sick children and adolescents?

Research has demonstrated that the risk of infant death increases as birthweight decreases. Low-birthweight babies also are far more likely to suffer cerebral palsy, retardation, seizures, respiratory tract and vision problems — and to require public funds for treatment. Many of these problems can stay with them throughout life.

A FEDERAL advisory panel recently estimated that each dollar spent on prenatal care for women at risk of bearing low-birthweight babies will save as much as $3.38 in specialized care later.

Other studies project even higher cost-benefit ratios from adequate prenatal care to prevent at-risk babies — those weighing less than 5½ pounds at birth.

Research in Ohio in 1983 indicated that the savings would be $4 for each $1 invested in prenatal care.

Southern governors last year formed a Task Force on Infant Mortality. Their report, which cited the work of many researchers, concluded that "Preventive prenatal and infant health care more than pays for itself." By reducing the number of unhealthy babies, the task force said, "prenatal and infant care can save $2 to $10 for every preventive dollar invested."

"Paying for high-tech medical rescues, as opposed to prevention, is a poor method of investing our health dollars," said South Carolina Gov. Richard W. Riley, who headed the task force.

THIS MODERN proof of the proverb — "An ounce of prevention is worth a pound of cure" — does not dissuade President Reagan from the relentless cutbacks in basic health services for the women and children among the 35.3-million Americans living below the poverty line.

In 1982, the Reagan administration put maternal and child health programs into a block grant and cut spending 18 percent. Federal support for community health centers was cut 13 percent. The WIC (Women, Infants, Children) program, which provides diet supplements and checkups for poor pregnant and nursing women and their children, only reaches one-third of those eligible.

But those callous, and false, economies are not enough for Mr. Reagan. Despite the increasing numbers of the poor, the administration now proposes a limit on federal Medicaid grants to the states and would cut WIC to eliminate another 1-million participants by 1986.

THE TRAGIC effects of Reaganomics and vengeful policies toward the poor are showing. The world's richest, most advanced nation ranks 12th among developed countries in infant mortality. It also leads the industrialized world in teen-age, high-risk pregnancies, births and abortions.

From 1965 to 1980, the U.S. infant mortality rate declined 47 percent. Two years after Mr. Reagan took office, the decline slowed in 1983-84 and appears to be stabilizing at slightly less than 11 deaths for each 1,000 live births.

The federal-state Medicaid program for the poor, created in 1965, and costly new improvements in medical technology combined to produce the major decline in infant deaths. Many health officials believe the leveling off in the 1980s is due to another combination — modern technology is reaching its limits in saving smaller and smaller babies and the Reagan administration's cutbacks have reduced the states' abilities to provide health care for the poor.

THE INCIDENCE of low birthweight is higher in the United States (more than 248,000 babies under 5½ pounds each year) than in at least 12 other developed countries. The plight of those infants is unconscionable because their low birthweights and health problems could be prevented in a nation of bountiful resources. Quality prenatal care, maternal and child nutrition programs and the prevention of unwanted pregancy, especially among teen-agers, could prevent untold human suffering, save taxpayer dollars and build a stronger, healthier nation.

But Mr. Reagan would rather build the MX.

The Atlanta Journal and THE ATLANTA CONSTITUTION

Atlanta, GA, May 10, 1985

How pro-life is the White House?

Georgians may be forgiven if they find a stunning hypocrisy in official policy. At the same time that improvements in the state's infant mortality rate have begun to erode, the White House has set about to pare money that nourishes impoverished mothers and their babies. It is a course of callous folly.

Georgia's infant mortality rate long has ranked among the nation's highest. Part of the problem involves access to prenatal care and hospitals; all of the problem is enmeshed with racial disparities and poverty Yet thanks to programs like WIC — for Women, Infants, Children — progress has been made.

WIC provides pregnant women and breast-feeding mothers with nutritional counseling, fortified cereals, blood tests and other help. It also supplies infant formula and other nutrition for children up to 5 years old. The results are increased birth weights and fewer infant deaths. Moreover, the program has cumulative effects. Because education is emphasized, mothers can apply their knowledge to the care of subsequent children.

In short, WIC is a program that works. It is (happily) humanitarian and (carefully) pragmatic. After all, healthy children make better students, better students make better workers, and better workers mean a sounder society. WIC is an investment in self-sufficiency.

So what more could the administration want? The answer is strange indeed. The White House wants *less* of this program than Congress has appropriated. It has decided to save $70 million by using 10 months' funding over 12 months.

For Georgia, this means a reduction of $897,954. No, that is not a major bite from a $50 million program (the nation's eighth largest). But it will hurt. The current WIC program serves only one-third of Georgia's need, health officials estimate. Other reductions (for things like school lunches) could further threaten the health of children.

The cuts will leave some states worse off than Georgia. New Mexico can only cover children up to 18 months now (instead of 5 years). Maine is dropping 1,300 people from its program, and Arkansas will drop 3,600.

But in Georgia, meanwhile, the infant mortality problem worsens. The federal cuts are not in keeping with Congress' wishes. Nor will they save much money. Nor do they fit into some grand ideology for a brighter future. They are mean and small and myopic and nothing more.

Arkansas Gazette.

Little Rock, AR, July 20, 1985

The federal Office of Management and Budget has released much of the appropriation for the Supplemental Food Program for Women, Infant and Children (WIC) that it had impounded early this year, which means that the Arkansas Health Department will not have to end health screening and nutrition this summer to another 3,600 poor pregnant mothers and children with high health risks.

Even with the restoration of the funds, the state is serving about 2,000 fewer women and children who have health-impairing nutritional deficiencies than it was at the beginning of the year. Before the cuts, the health office was reaching only a fraction of those in need and those, in the case of pregnant women, frequently were delayed past the point where health screening and nutritional help could be the most beneficial in insuring the health of newborns. In the almost 20 years since the program was begun, evidence has shown that the program has sharply reduced the number of babies with low birthweights and permanent handicaps and the number of infant deaths. Even one with a flinty eye for economic costs can calculate the future savings in health and welfare spending.

The WIC program provides health education and vouchers that pregnant women and mothers can use to buy infant formula and high-protein foods. It is not an entitlement, and the money has been sufficient to reach only about 30 per cent of the eligible women, 45 per cent of the infants and 20 per cent of the children who have medical risks. The state has been ending help for children and concentrating the money on pregnant women and infants. Owing to the rising cost of food and formula, the assistance has been declining in the '80s.

It would be refreshing if OMB had found a soft spot for this program that provably reduces the social and economic costs of poverty.

Study Finds Rising Child Poverty

The rate of poverty among U.S. children had climbed by 54% from 1973 to 1983, according to a federal report issued May 22, 1985. The report found that 13.8 million children, or 22.2% of Americans under 18 years old, were poor in 1983. The Congressional Research Service and the Congressional Budget Office had prepared the study. It was presented to the House Ways and Means subcommittee on public assistance and unemployment compensation.

According to the report, the U.S. had three million more poor children in 1983 than in 1968, even though there were nine million fewer children in the entire population. The U.S. had 62.1 million children altogether in 1983. The report said the number of poor children in households without fathers had increased dramatically. Some 19.6% of poor children lived in homes headed by a single woman in 1983, compared with 9% in 1959. The report said that three-quarters of all children born outside of marriage were poor, and that in 1980 unmarried women had almost 20% of all births. The study found that 48% of black children born in 1980 did not have married parents. Eleven percent of white births were also out of wedlock.

The study also found that:

■ The real value of cash welfare payments, Social Security and unemployment payments targeting children in 1983 had declined by 6% from the amount allocated in 1973, after adjusting for inflation. Total federal spending for social welfare programs, including money that targeted adults, rose 83% after inflation during that period.

■ There had been more poor children than poor old people since 1974. The rate of poverty among people 65 years old or older had dropped by about half since 1966, reaching 14.1% in 1983. The report said this was because Social Security benefits rose with inflation.

■ Among Hispanic children, 38.2% were poor in 1983, as were 17% of white children. The proportion of black children who were poor was 46.7%.

■ Black children were the most likely to stay poor for long periods. During a 15-year period, 66% of all poor children stayed poor no longer than four years, while one out of seven would stay poor for 10 years or longer. About 90% of the second group was black.

the Charleston Gazette

Charleston, WVA, March 25, 1988

ABC DESERVES great praise for its Monday night presentation of "God Bless the Child." The film was a moving depiction of America's shame, and the president's disgrace — the plight of the homeless.

Following a fictional character and her daughter, the movie showed how families can fall into the hellish cycle of poverty and how current governmental policies make the situation even worse.

"People look at us like we're trash," said the mother in this story. "They don't wanna stand next to us. They don't wanna talk to us. They don't wanna know we're there."

She might as well have been speaking about one man — and he sits in the White House.

According to Jonathan Kozol, spending for low-income housing has been cut three-fourths by the Reagan administration. Kozol's new book, "Rachel and Her Children," is an all-too-real account of homelessness in America. He points out that in 1980 the federal government spent nearly $32 billion on low-income housing. Today, less than $8 billion is spent on these programs.

Reagan can say all he wants about presiding over the longest peacetime economic expansion in this nation's history. He can claim credit, too, for the creation of millions of new jobs.

What he cannot admit is that many of these jobs are minimum-wage replacements for traditional high-paying employment that kept Americans above the poverty line. The brutal truth is that more of this nation's citizens live in poverty today than in 1969.

Far too many of them are children. Over the last decade, the number of children living in poor families climbed by 2.5 million. Of that number, half a million are homeless. Because they constantly are on the move, these children are 50 percent less likely than other children to attend school.

Congress, finally, has accepted that children shouldn't be punished because they are poor. With support from both parties, legislation has been introduced to provide for an ambitious preschool program. "After eight years of institutionalized meanness," said Kozol, "a bipartisan revulsion has set in."

The reaction is long overdue. Yet, these children will have no real chance until their families are properly housed. In a nation as rich as this, the plight of the homeless is a thundering disgrace.

It's said that in his Hollywood career, Reagan played the villain in only one movie. As president, he has chosen that role many times. But none is more despicable than his attitude toward the poor.

If, when this president leaves office, his supporters want to erect a statue in his honor, they needn't waste the effort. Reagan's monument is the unwashed faces and empty lives of the homeless who haunt this land.

The Charlotte Observer

Charlotte, NC, March 23, 1988

ABC's made-for-TV movie, "God Bless the Child," which aired Monday night, offers an unflinching look at the cruelty of contemporary poverty. Though it is fiction, the film is a composite of bitter truths.

Anyone who has read of the increase among street people or watched TV news clips about the spread of urban poverty would recognize the film's heroine, Theresa Johnson, played movingly by Mare Winningham. A pale, red-haired woman who works as a hotel maid, she has been abandoned by her husband and clings desperately to a 7-year-old daughter, her only source of joy. But she encounters more defeats than her impoverished upbringing, meager education and gritty determination can bear.

When her tiny apartment is demolished to make room for a new building, she cannot find another in her price range. She stores her few furnishings with a friend and resorts to a community shelter, where there's a limit on how long she can stay. She loses her job when she sneaks away from work to look for an apartment and seek beds at a different shelter.

She discovers that without an apartment she can't get a job. Without a job she can't rent an apartment. She applies for government assistance, only to learn the application takes four weeks to process. With less than $100 in her purse, she and her daughter, now a truant from school, sleep in doorways and eat out of garbage bins.

Through a church worker, they find a low-rent apartment — replete with rats and a leaking roof — and are given food. But when the rats attack the child, the mother complains to health inspectors — and is evicted by the offended landlord, who sneers, "You people are never satisfied."

The real crisis comes when the daughter is hospitalized with lead poisoning. Her hopes ebbing, the mother agonizingly concludes that she cannot provide for the girl's future. Without a family to lean on, she faces an agonizing choice. The ending, like the rest of the movie, is uncompromising.

"God Bless the Child" should be rebroadcast often. It has the eloquence to persuade comfortable, secure Americans that poverty is not the fate of deadbeats, but often engulfs people who are caring and courageous but trapped by forces beyond their control. Like something Lincoln Steffens might have written in the age of the muckrakers, the film has the power to inspire social reform.

THE KANSAS CITY STAR

Kansas City, MO, May 29, 1988

In its annual report on the state of the nation's youth, the Children's Defense Fund quickly makes its point that for them the American standard of living is nothing to brag about. In this decade, children lost ground.

"The federal budgets of the 1980s placed little value on America's children and sacrificed their future and the nation's future, creating both budget deficits and human deficits of crisis proportions," the private organization says in *A Children's Defense Budget*. "Congress now must exert the leadership and courage to chart a new budgetary course."

Periodically blasts are heard about cuts to one or another public program geared toward children. Note is taken of a drop in an internationally accepted standard for educational achievement or health. Isolated statistics are alarming enough. But it is only when a comprehensive list of items integral to a good quality of life is examined that the full impact hits. What the United States has allowed to happen is disgraceful. Even worse, the final consequence has not yet been reaped.

Just a few numbers illustrate:

● One in four of all pre-school children is poor.

● In 1985, one out of every three non-white, inner-city children between the ages of 1 and 4 received no immunization against measles, mumps or rubella.

● In 1986, Medicaid served 200,000 fewer children than it reached in 1978 when there were nearly a third fewer poor children.

● Half of the nation's food stamp recipients are children. The number of recipients dropped from 68 to 60 for every 100 poor people between 1980 and 1986.

● Homicide is the 15th leading cause of infant death.

● One child in seven is at risk of dropping out of school.

● The proportion of young men earning enough to lift a family of three above the federal poverty line fell by nearly a third from 1973 to 1984. Poverty in young families ensures poor children.

Perhaps no indice underlines the racially discriminatory aspect of this self-perpetuating society better than a survey of its children. Time and again, CDF data show the condition of white children to be inadequate but that of minority children on a par with those in unindustrialized countries. The 1985 U.S. black infant mortality rate ranked 28, behind Bulgaria and Cuba, for example, while the white rate was 15.

It is such facts that lawmakers and leaders must understand as they make the federal budget. Citizens who care about them will yell and scream and vote.

DAYTON DAILY NEWS

Dayton, OH, June 1, 1988

Secretary of Education William Bennett has called Chicago's schools the nation's worst.

Recently, the *Chicago Tribune* disagreed only marginally. It said its seven-month investigation found "that whether the system is the worst or not, it is a disgrace."

The *Tribune* series is compelling. It's frightening how kids are being left to rot — intellectually, emotionally and physically — because too many people don't know how to reach, help and control them. This problem is not just confined to Chicago, though. Poor kids across the country are being denied or seriously shortchanged on the very thing they definitely need to escape poverty — an education.

If Chicago is one of the more horrifying examples, it's only because of the numbers. It's one of the country's bigger school systems. It is, however, no less significant when smaller communities — cities and suburbs alike — fail the disadvantaged. You lose one kid, and you've lost something valuable.

The strength of the *Tribune* series was that it didn't stop with a description of a system that's given up on kids; it spotlighted the people who have stopped caring. Its profile of a fourth-grade teacher who four principals have tried to fire and who refused for a year to bring in lesson plans received national attention.

Fewer people will hear of or remember another teacher the series focused on. Fani Cahill, a 16-year veteran of the system, is hanging in tight, sometimes against the odds. She tells, for instance, of once going to a student's home to retrieve a book only to find that it had been placed in the bathroom, with the pages to be torn out for toilet paper.

Ms. Cahill also tells of giving a lesson on why flowers should be left for all to enjoy after someone picked all the buds on her plants in the classroom; and of another lecture on the value of dictionaries after students started ripping out the pages of their books when they had come upon a word they had been told to look up.

Schools aren't the only institutions that are failing kids. Society is, and so are their parents. Without help from others, schools can't reasonably be expected to succeed. This conclusion isn't a new one, and not very many persons disagree with it. The disappointing thing is how few people are willing to respond with a sense of urgency.

A former Chicago school board president recalled that when financial problems resulted in school employees going without paychecks, everybody jumped in to settle the crisis; a new authority was established to make sure that nobody ever again would work without their pay. "Do we see that reaction," he asked, "when we hear that 40 percent of the students are dropping out?"

The question is a good one. Not unlike other communities, Chicago can't be proud of how the city has answered it.

The Washington Post

Washington, DC, March 3, 1988

THE LINE is already forming to spend the money the next administration will not have. Children's advocates are at the head of it. There are two great dependent groups in this as any society—children and the elderly. The elderly, who vote, have been well attended to. Children have not. Their poverty rate is 20 percent (as against only 12 percent for the elderly and about 14 percent for the population as a whole). The infant mortality rate, after years of decline, has leveled off and in some states turned up again.

The Children's Defense Fund, the leading advocacy group, wants to require states to give prenatal care to all low-income pregnant women under Medicaid and health care to all young children in low-income families. Only some states do so now; the states and the federal government split the cost of Medicaid. CDF would also expand the WIC program that supplements the diets of these groups. CDF and others are pressing Congress, in addition, to begin giving federal day-care subsidies to lower income women and to increase federal funding of compensatory education programs. Normally conservative business groups have joined in calling for a broad children's program of this kind. The businessmen particularly fear for the quality of the future work force if no such steps are taken.

There is little opposition to these various proposals on the merits. The resistance has to do mainly with cost. CDF's agenda might, if fully funded, take $10 billion a year. The advocates say the country can't afford *not* to take the steps they propose, some of which they argue will have the net effect of reducing spending—preventive health care costs much less than the alternative. Some of the advocates are also disposed to shrug the cost problem off as someone else's worry, much as Ronald Reagan did with the cost of the defense buildup. (Indeed, some would like to recapture for domestic programs some of the money he shifted to defense.) But unfortunately the country can't afford to be so blithe about costs again because Mr. Reagan has already spent a lot of his successor's money; the next administration and the children's groups will have to choose among their goals.

The health proposals are the most compelling. America has slipped to 19th in the world in infant deaths. More black children in large U.S. cities die before their first birthday than babies born in Jamaica or Costa Rica. Black babies are twice as likely to die as white babies, but white infant mortality has also risen lately in 19 states. The number of low-birth-weight babies in the United States is increasing for the first time since 1960. Such babies are more likely to die or be impaired. Prenatal and postnatal care has been shown elsewhere to make a difference. Medicaid is already in place and, in fact, has been quietly extended in the past several years in precisely the direction the children's advocates want to go. The WIC program is also established. These programs can be affordably expanded. So perhaps can federal aid to education, though this remains essentially a state and local responsibility.

The day-care proposal is a different matter. Conservatives as well as liberals have lined up behind day-care bills in Congress, which loves to enact brave new programs in election years. But here the government would be taking on a major new obligation when it can't fulfill the heavy fiscal and social obligations it already has. Day care is a serious problem, but so are a lot of things. Congress shouldn't promise what it can't afford.

Index